INTELLECTUAL PROPERTY RIGHTS
AND CLIMATE CHANGE

As the world confronts global warming, there is a growing consensus that the TRIPS Agreement could be a more effective instrument for mitigating climate change. In this innovative work, Wei Zhuang systematically examines the contextual elements that can be used in the interpretation of the TRIPS Agreement with a view to enhancing innovation and transfer of environmentally sound technologies. Zhuang proposes a balanced and pro-competitive interpretation that could be pursued by policy makers and negotiators. This comprehensive multidisciplinary study will help academics and policy-makers improve their understanding of the contemporary international legal regimes governing intellectual property rights and innovation and transfer of environmentally sound technologies. It also offers practical guidance for further developing a legal system capable of responding to the challenges posed by climate change.

WEI ZHUANG is an Associate Lawyer in the Geneva Office of Van Bael & Bellis. She assists governments in WTO dispute settlement proceedings and advises companies and governments in trade remedy investigations. Previously, she worked at the United Nations and the WTO. She was also a Marie Curie Fellow with the DISSETTLE (Dispute Settlement in Trade: Training in Law and Economics) Programme, a Visiting Fellow at the University of Cambridge (Lauterpacht Centre for International Law) and a Research Fellow at the Max Planck Institute for IP and Competition Law.

Intellectual Property Rights and Climate Change

INTERPRETING THE TRIPS AGREEMENT FOR ENVIRONMENTALLY SOUND TECHNOLOGIES

WEI ZHUANG

University of Geneva

CAMBRIDGE
UNIVERSITY PRESS

CAMBRIDGE
UNIVERSITY PRESS

University Printing House, Cambridge CB2 8BS, United Kingdom

One Liberty Plaza, 20th Floor, New York, NY 10006, USA

477 Williamstown Road, Port Melbourne, VIC 3207, Australia

314-321, 3rd Floor, Plot 3, Splendor Forum, Jasola District Centre, New Delhi - 110025, India

79 Anson Road, #06-04/06, Singapore 079906

Cambridge University Press is part of the University of Cambridge.

It furthers the University's mission by disseminating knowledge in the pursuit of education, learning and research at the highest international levels of excellence.

www.cambridge.org
Information on this title: www.cambridge.org/9781108726214

First published 2017
First paperback edition 2019

A catalogue record for this publication is available from the British Library

Library of Congress Cataloging in Publication data
NAMES: Zhuang, Wei, 1983– author.
TITLE: Intellectual property rights and climate change : interpreting the TRIPS Agreement for environmentally sound technologies / Wei Zhuang, University of Geneva.
DESCRIPTION: Cambridge, United Kingdom ; New York, NY : University Printing House, Cambridge University Press is part of the University of Cambridge, [2016] | Includes bibliographical references and index.
IDENTIFIERS: LCCN 2016040378 | ISBN 9781107158085 (Hardback : alk. paper)
SUBJECTS: LCSH: Intellectual property (International law) | Agreement on Trade-Related Aspects of Intellectual Property Rights (1994 April 15) | Technology–Environmental aspects. | Climatic changes–Law and legislation.
CLASSIFICATION: LCC K1401 .Z489 2016 | DDC 346.04/8–dc23 LC record available at https://lccn.loc.gov/2016040378

ISBN 978-1-107-15808-5 Hardback
ISBN 978-1-108-72621-4 Paperback

Contents

Figures

Foreword

The implications of intellectual property have been extensively studied in some areas, such as those relating to public health and, to a lesser extent, food security. A large number of books, journal articles and other documents have been published on issues relating to access to medicines, and on modalities of intellectual property protection for seeds. There is also a growing number of scholarly contributions and other studies on such protection as applied in the field of environmental technologies, including on the role that patents may play as incentives for innovation or as potential obstacles for the dissemination of those technologies.

Despite the global consensus about the need to address the effects of climate change, the North-South divergences that have characterized the debates on intellectual property, public health and food security have also emerged in relation to environmental technologies. There is great disagreement on the best ways in which the development and diffusion of the required technologies will be encouraged. Thus, in the negotiations conducted in the context of the United Nations Framework Convention on Climate Change (UNFCCC), some developing countries submitted proposals aiming at the exclusion from patent protection of environmentally sound technologies (ESTs) or subjecting them to compulsory licenses. One developing country submitted to the Council for TRIPS in WTO a proposal to carve out an exception under the TRIPS Agreement for such technologies. Not surprisingly, these proposals have encountered a strong opposition from developed countries, which account for an overwhelming share of the granted patents relating to ESTs worldwide.

The impact of intellectual property in relation to ESTs also became an important issue in the debates leading to the adoption of the Sustainable Development Goals (SDGs). In its Synthesis report on the Sustainable Development Goals, UN Secretary General called upon governments to "make substantial progress in the development, transfer and dissemination of such technologies and knowledge to developing countries on favourable, concessional and preferential terms", and to "ensure that our global intellectual property regimes and the application of the flexibilities of the Agreement on Trade-Related Aspects of Intellectual Property Rights (TRIPS) are fully consistent with and contribute to the goals of sustainable development".

The subject of development and diffusion of ESTs is particularly complex, because – unlike the case of medicines and seeds – ESTs comprise a wide range of technologies including, inter alia, solar photovoltaic, geothermal, wind, and carbon capture technologies. The modes of production and exploitation of ESTs vary significantly, as well as the extent to which patents and other forms of intellectual property rights may prevent competition and, in particular, the transfer of technology to developing countries to deal with the effects of climate change. Despite the progress made in some fields in countries such as China and India, the North-South technological asymmetry is, overall, deep and limitations to the access to protected technologies may not only undermine national and regional but also global efforts regarding adaptation to and mitigation of climate change.

This book contains what is perhaps the first comprehensive study on the characteristics and possible implications of the international intellectual property and technology transfer regime as applied to ESTs. To this end, the author delves into the foundations of intellectual property and reviews the historical developments that have led to the current international system, including the failed initiative to adopt an International Code on Transfer of Technology. As a starting point for characterizing the problem existing in this field, the book presents an exhaustive literature review and explores which countries are major ESTs creators, which countries derive income from intellectual property rights associated to those technologies, and how the TRIPS Agreement influences the trends of technology transfer. Valuable insights on the available empirical information are provided in this respect. Importantly, this book is the outcome of an interdisciplinary research combining economics and various disciplines of national and international law, including law of the treaties, WTO law and competition law.

Although the study of international intellectual property rules is the core of the book, it also examines the EST transfer obligations under the UNFCCC Agreement, and the extent to which they have been complied with. The author explores who the obligation-bearers are, whether EST transfer commitments are binding on Parties, what kinds of mechanisms exist for the implementation of EST transfer and whether they are adequate. This analysis is of particular importance to understand the failure of the current system to ensure a wide dissemination of climate change mitigation and adaptation technologies.

As noted, the author undertakes a thorough analysis of the minimum standards incorporated into the TRIPS Agreement and the room they leave for innovation through imitation and technology transfer to developing countries. This study is particularly relevant for ESTs. But the discussion of the main interpretive issues presented by the TRIPS Agreement and the positions taken by WTO panels and the Appellate Body provide useful elements to consider the extent of obligations under that Agreement in any field of technology. The same comment applies to the detailed analysis of the patent- and competition-related provisions of said Agreement. Without losing its focus on ESTs, the careful interpretation (based on the principles of the Vienna Convention on the Law of Treaties) offered by the author is relevant and useful beyond the field of ESTs.

Based on the analysis carried out, the author confirms a number of "TRIPS flexibilities" allowed by the TRIPS Agreement. Although there is a vast literature on the subject, she specifically explores how to make the TRIPS Agreement a more efficient and effective instrument for facilitating innovation and transfer of ESTs through legal interpretations.

Among other important contributions made by this book, it is worth mentioning the empirical study on the global distribution of innovation and international transfer of ESTs based on the latest available data; a comprehensive study of the effects of the minimum standards contained in the TRIPS Agreement on innovation and transfer of ESTs to developing countries; a thorough exploration of the contextual elements for interpreting the TRIPS Agreement for facilitating innovation and transfer of ESTs; and concrete recommendations on how relevant TRIPS provisions could be interpreted to that end. The author proposes in this respect a Declaration on intellectual property and climate change (similar to the Doha Declaration on the TRIPS Agreement and public health) with a view to confirming a balanced and pro-competitive interpretation of the TRIPS Agreement. Given the limited guidance provided by competition-related provisions in the Agreement, the author also briefly recommends international guidelines for licensing of intellectual property protected ESTs.

Carlos Correa
Buenos Aires

Acknowledgements

This book would not have been possible without the support of many people and institutions. I take this opportunity to extend my sincere gratitude and appreciation to them.

First and foremost, I am grateful for the research guidance by my PhD supervisors, Prof. Marceau and Prof. De Werra. I would also like to extend my sincerest thanks and appreciation to Prof. Carlos Correa, Prof. Alexandre Flückiger and Ms. Jayashree Watal for having agreed to sit on my thesis defence jury.

Second, very special thanks go to the Max Planck Institute for Intellectual Property and Competition Law and the German Association for Industrial Property and Copyright Law for having provided me with a two-year fellowship which enabled me to develop and deepen this work in a pleasurable work environment. I thank Prof. Drexl, Prof. Hilty, Dr. Lamping and Dr. Grosse Ruse-Khan for the fruitful discussions concerning my PhD research and for allowing me to participate in some high-level Institute meetings that gathered leading IP law experts from all over the world.

Third, I wish to sincerely thank my former colleagues Christoph Spennemann, Kiyoshi Adachi and Charles Gore from United Nations Conference on Trade and Development. The tasks they assigned to me inspired me to choose intellectual property and climate change as my PhD topic. Through monitoring international negotiations at the WIPO and the WTO, I gained a lot of first-hand information for my PhD research.

Fourth, I have also been fortunate to participate in the Doctoral Support Programme in the Economic Research and Statistic Division of the WTO. I am very grateful to my mentor, Ms. Watal, for her eight-month supervision as well as for insightful discussions and suggestions. My deep sense of appreciation also goes to the librarians and staff of the WTO Library for their kind help.

Fifth, the one-year research stint at Cambridge University strengthened the international law elements of my book. Their seminars and conferences were highly motivating and I also had the opportunity to design and roll out a workshop with the kind support of Dr. Michael Waibel and Dr. Markus Gehring from Lauterpacht Centre for International Law.

Sixth, I wish to express my sincere gratitude and appreciation to Prof. Giorgio Sacerdoti from Bocconi University for his supervision during my Marie Curie Fellowship, which allowed me to sew the final threads of my thesis. I am further indebted to many other people who contributed to this book by giving me valuable comments, references and/or other advice, including Prof. Carlos Correa (Buenos Aires), Prof. Graeme Dinwoodie (Oxford), Prof. Liyu Han (Renmin), Dr. Reto Malacrida (WTO), Prof. Joost Pauwelyn (the Graduate Institute), Prof. Jerome H. Reichman (Duke), Pedro Roffe (ICTSD), Antony Taubman (WTO), Prof. Jorge Vinuales (Cambridge), Dr. Michael Waibel (Cambridge), Prof. Ke Wang (Renmin), Prof. Mark Wu (Harvard), Xiaoping Wu (WTO), Prof. Peter Yu (Texas) and Judge Abdulqawi Ahmed Yusuf (ICJ).

Last but not least, I would like to thank my family for all their love and encouragement. Special thanks and appreciation go to my friend Peter for his unconditional support. I would also like to take this opportunity to express my thanks to my friends including Nicole, Linda, Christian, Greta, Meg, Marios, Silvana, Joseph, Katerina, Eric, Margeretha, Jingjing and many others. Because of you, my life has become more colourful.

Abbreviations

ALBA	Bolivarian Alliance for the Peoples of Our America
AWGLCA	Ad Hoc Working Group on Long-Term Co-operative Action
BASIC	Brazil, South Africa, India and China
BRIC	Brazil, India, China and Russia
CBD	Convention on Biological Diversity
CBDR	Common but differentiated responsibilities
CCS	Carbon capture and storage
CDIP	Committee on Development and Intellectual Property
CDM	Clean Development Mechanism
CETs	Clean energy technologies
CFI	Court of First Instance
CIEL	Centre for International Environmental Law
CISDL	Centre for International Sustainable Development Law
CJEU	Court of Justice of the European Union
CO_2	Carbon dioxide
COP	Conference of the Parties
CSP	Concentrated solar power
DOC	Document
DSU	Dispute Settlement Understanding
EC	European Community
EGTT	Expert Group on Technology Transfer
EPO	European Patent Office
ESTs	Environmentally sound technologies
EU	European Union

FDI	Foreign direct investment
FRAND	Fair, reasonable and non-discriminatory
FTA(s)	Free Trade Agreement(s)
G77	The Group of 77
GATS	General Agreement on Trade in Services
GATT	General Agreement on Tariffs and Trade
GEF	Global Environment Facility
GHGs	Greenhouse gases
GPRS	General packet radio service
GSP	Generalised System of Preferences
HFC-134a	Tetrafluoroethane
ICC	International Chamber of Commerce
ICTSD	International Centre for Trade and Sustainable Development
IDEA	Innovation, Development and Employment Alliance
IGCC	Integrated Gasification Combined Cycle
ILC	International Law Commission
ILO	International Labour Organisation
IP	Intellectual Property
IPC	International Patent Classification
IPCC	Intergovernmental Panel on Climate Change
IPRs	Intellectual property rights
IUCN	International Union for Conservation of Nature
LED	Light-emitting diode
MEAs	Multilateral Environmental Agreements
MFN	Most favoured nation
MNCs	Multinational companies
NGOs	Non-governmental organisations
NIEO	New International Economic Order
OECD	Organisation for Economic Co-operation and Development
OPEC	Organisation of the Petroleum Exporting Countries
PATSTAT	Patent Statistical Database
PCT	Patent Cooperation Treaty
PV	Photovoltaic
R&D	Research and development
SAIC	State Administration for Industry and Commerce
SBI	Subsidiary Body for Implementation
SBSTA	Subsidiary Body for Scientific and Technological Advice

SIDCs	Small island developing countries
SMEs	Small and medium enterprises
SPS Agreement	Agreement on the Application of Sanitary and Phytosanitary Measures
TBT Agreement	Technical Barriers to Trade Agreement
TEC	Technology Executive Committee
TOT Code	International Code of Conduct for the Transfer of Technology
TRIPS Agreement	Agreement on Trade-Related Aspects of Intellectual Property Rights
UK	United Kingdom
UN	United Nations
UNCED	United Nations Conference on Environment and Development
UNCLOS	United Nations Convention on the Law of the Sea
UNCSD	United Nations Conference on Sustainable Development
UNCTAD	United Nations Conference on Trade and Development
UNDP	United Nations Development Programme
UNEP	United Nations Environment Programme
UNFCCC	United Nations Framework Convention on Climate Change
UNGA	United Nations General Assembly
UNIDO	United Nations Industrial Development Organisation
UNU-MERIT	United Nations University-Maastricht Economic and Social Research Institute on Innovation and Technology
US	United States
USC	United States Code
USD	United States dollars
USPTO	United States Patent and Trademark Office
VCLT	Vienna Convention on the Law of Treaties
WCED	World Commission on Environment and Development
WHO	World Health Organization
WIPO	World Intellectual Property Organization
WTO	World Trade Organization

Table of Cases

NATIONAL COURTS

OTHERS

Table of Treaties, Declarations, Resolutions and Others

DECLARATIONS

RESOLUTIONS

Draft Ministerial Declaration on the Uruguay Round, 20 September 1986, GATT Doc. MIN (86)/W/19

Draft Text, Non-Paper No. 36, Contact Group on Enhanced Action on Development and Transfer of Technology, Ad Hoc Working Group on Long-Term Cooperative Action under the Convention, Barcelona, 2–6 November 2009, 6 November 2009

Draft Text, Proposed by Co-chairs, Non-Paper No. 36, Contact Group on Enhanced Action on Development and Transfer of Technology, Ad Hoc Working Group on Long-Term Cooperative Action under the Convention, Barcelona, 2–6 November 2009, 03.11.2009, available at http://unfccc.int/files/kyoto_protocol/application/pdf/technology29091009v03.pdf

Elements for a Draft Negotiating Text, Annex, Decisions adopted by the Conference of the Parties, 1/CP.20: Lima Call for Climate Action, FCCC/CP/2014/10/Add.1, 2 February 2015

Enabling Environments for Technology Transfer, Technical Paper, UN Doc. FCCC/TP/2003/2, 4 June 2003

EU Position for the Copenhagen Climate Conference (7–18 December 2009)-Council Conclusions, Doc. No. 14790/09, General Secretariat of the Council of the European Union, Brussels, 21 October 2009, available at http://register.consilium.europa.eu/pdf/en/09/st14/st14790.en09.pdf

Government of India (2013), Submission to the UNFCCC on the Work of the Ad Hoc Working Group on the Durban Platform for Enhanced Action: Workstream I, New Delhi, available at https://unfccc.int/files/documentation/submissions_from_parties/adp/application/pdf/adp_india_workstream_1_20130913.pdf

Guidelines and Objectives Proposed by the European Community for the Negotiations on Trade-Related Aspects of Substantive Standards of Intellectual Property Rights, Negotiating Group on Trade-Related Aspects of Intellectual Property Rights, including Trade in Counterfeit Goods, 7 July 1988, GATT Doc. MTN.GNG/NG11/W/264

Guidelines for Negotiations that Strike a Balance between Intellectual Property Rights and Development Objectives: Communication from Peru, 27 October 1989, GATT Doc. MTN.GNG/NG11/W/45

India (2009), Submission to UNFCCC on Technology Transfer Mechanism, available at http://unfccc.int/files/kyoto_protocol/application/pdf/indiatechtransfer171008.pdf

International Law Association (2002), Declaration of Principles of International Law Related to Sustainable Development, Resolution 3/2002 adopted at the Seventieth Conference of the International Law Association, held in New Delhi, India, 2–6 April 2002, UN Doc. A/CONF.199/8, 9 August 2002

International Law Commission (2014), Second Report on Subsequent Agreements and Subsequent Practice in Relation to the Interpretation of Treaties, UN Doc. A/CN.4/671

Joint Communication from the African Group in the WTO, Proposal on Paragraph 6 of the Doha Declaration on the TRIPS Agreement and Public Health, WTO Doc. IP/C/W/351, 24 June 2002

FREE TRADE AGREEMENTS OR REGIONAL TRADE AGREEMENTS

US–Bahrain Free Trade Agreement, 2006
US–Chile FTA, 2004
US–Jordan FTA, 2010
US–Morocco FTA, 2004
US–Singapore FTA, 2004

NATIONAL LEGISLATIONS OR FREE TRADE AGREEMENTS

Andean Community, Decision 486: Common Intellectual Property Regime, 2000
American Clean Energy and Security Act of 2009, H.R. 2454, 26 June 2009, 111th Congress, available at www.opencongress.org/bill/111-h2454/text
Brazil, Law No. 9.279 of 14 May 1996 (Industrial Property Law), reproduced by WIPO, available at www.wipo.int/edocs/lexdocs/laws/en/br/br003en.pdf
Constitution of the United States
Foreign Relations Authorization Act, Fiscal Years 2010 and 2011, H.R.2410, 22 June 2009, 111th Congress, Section 329, available at www.govtrack.us/congress/bills/111/hr2410/text
Indian Patents Act 1970
Patent Law of the People's Republic of China (2008 Amendment), adopted at the Sixth Meeting of the Standing Committee of the Eleventh National People's Congress on 27 December 2008
Patent Law of the People's Republic of China (2000 Amendment), Standing Committee of the National People's Congress, 25 August 2000
Restatement (Third) of Unfair Competition § 43 [Improper Acquisition of Trade Secrets], 1994
35 United States Code
42 USC § 7608 (Clean Air Act)
US Patent Law
The Basic Law of Hong Kong Special Administrative Region of the People's Republic of China, Adopted at the Third Session of the Seventh National People's Congress on 4 April 1990 and effective as of 1 July 1997
The Basic Law of Macao Special Administrative Region of the People's Republic of China, Adopted at the First Session of the Eighth National People's Congress on 31 March 1993, and effective as of 20 December 1999
Provisions on Prohibition of Abuse of Intellectual Property Rights to Eliminate or Restrict Competition, promulgated by Decree No. 74 of the State Administration for Industry and Commerce on 7 April 2015, effective as of 1 August 2015

1

Introduction

1.1 THE IMPORTANCE AND PURPOSE OF THIS STUDY

Climate change is "the defining challenge of our era".[1] The UN General Assembly, by its resolution of 43/53 of 1988, recognised that climate change is "a common concern of mankind" and should be dealt with effectively within a comprehensive global governance system.[2] Innovation and transfer of technologies play an essential role in creating an effective and meaningful global response to climate change.

Provisions for the development and transfer of technologies are at the centre of "any significant international agreement" to limit developing countries' greenhouse gas (GHG) emissions.[3] According to the Intergovernmental Panel on Climate Change (IPCC),[4] despite widely different perceptions and interests, all parties to the United Nations Framework Convention on Climate Change (UNFCCC) have agreed that the use of energy-efficient and cleaner technologies will benefit all and that "transfer and cooperation to advance the availability and use" of such technologies is one of the most effective ways to

---

[1] Ban Ki-moon (2008), Statement by United Nations Secretary-General Ban Ki-moon at the opening of the High-Level Segment of COP 14 in Poznan, p. 4, available at http://unfccc.int/2860.php
[2] Protection of Global Climate for Present and Future Generations of Mankind, United Nations General Assembly Resolution, A/RES/43/53, 6 December 1988.
[3] John H. Barton (2008), *Mitigating Climate Change through Technology Transfer: Addressing the Needs of Developing Countries, Energy, Environment and Development Programme*, Programme Paper 08/02, Chatham House, p. 2.
[4] IPCC was jointly established by the World Meteorological Organization and the United Nations Environment Programme to provide scientific assessments of human induced-climate change. See Protection of Global Climate for Present and Future Generations of Mankind, UN General Assembly, A/RES/43/53, 6 December 1988, para. 5.

reduce global GHG emissions.[5] Article 4.1(c) of the UNFCCC obliges all Parties to promote and cooperate in the development and transfer of environmentally sound technologies (ESTs). Developed countries have committed themselves under Article 4.5 to "take all practicable steps to promote, facilitate and finance" the transfer of ESTs and associated know-how to other Parties, particularly developing country Parties, to "enable them to implement the provisions of the Convention".[6] Moreover, facilitating the innovation and transfer of ESTs to developing countries was high on the agenda in the negotiations over a post-Kyoto agreement. The recent adoption of the Paris Agreement signalled participating countries' determination to speed up low-carbon growth, including via development and wide dissemination and adoption of ESTs.

The innovation and transfer of technology has also been a central theme of several multilateral negotiations and agreements, most notably the Uruguay Round of multilateral trade negotiations resulting in the Agreement on Trade-Related Aspects of Intellectual Property Rights (TRIPS).[7] The TRIPS Agreement includes a number of provisions that govern or facilitate innovation and transfer of technology because some World Trade Organization (WTO) members see technology transfer as part of the bargain in which they have agreed to provide a fairly high protection of intellectual property rights (IPRs), which was deemed to be essential to incentivise innovation by some other countries.[8] Notably, the objectives of TRIPS (Article 7) affirm that the protection and enforcement of intellectual property (IP) rights should contribute to technological innovation and to the transfer and dissemination of technology.[9] Article 66.2 of the Agreement obliges developed countries to provide incentives to their companies to promote and encourage technology transfer to least developed countries (LDCs).

Yet, some commentators claim there has been very little actual and effective implementation of technology transfer provisions in international law.[10]

---

[5] IPCC (2000), *IPCC Special Report: Methodological and Technological Issues in Technology Transfer*, Cambridge University Press, p. 87.
[6] United Nations Framework Convention on Climate Change (UNFCCC), Article 4.5, 1992, FCCC/INFORMAL/84, GE.05–62220 (E) 200705.
[7] UNEP, EPO and ICTSD (2010), *Patents and Clean Energy: Bridging the Gap between Evidence and Policy*, Munich: Mediengruppe Universal, p. 14.
[8] World Trade Organization (2008), *Understanding the WTO*, p. 43.
[9] Agreement on Trade-Related Aspects of Intellectual Property Rights (TRIPS), Article 7, 15 April 1994, Marrakesh Agreement Establishing the World Trade Organisation, Annex 1C, 33 I.L.M. 1197.
[10] See, e.g., Moon Suerie (2011), Meaningful Technology Transfer to the LDCs: A Proposal for a Monitoring Mechanism for TRIPS Article 66.2, UNCTAD-ICTSD Project on IPRs and

In reality, the transfer of technology has not taken place at a scale large enough to effectively mitigate climate change. Empirical studies indicate that the innovation of ESTs is highly concentrated in a few industrialised countries and these technologies are rarely transferred to developing countries; when transferred, they primarily go to a handful of emerging economies (see Section 2.4).[11] Developing countries, which are in the greatest need of ESTs, generally have insufficient access to, or possession of, such technologies.

Different explanations have been given to account for the slow and inadequate transfer of ESTs to developing countries.[12] To the extent that ESTs are protected by IPRs, the role played by global IPR regimes (in particular, the TRIPS Agreement) in the process of technology transfer to developing countries has become one particularly contentious issue. Due to the existing asymmetries in the ownership and transfer of EST IP assets and the urgent need for a transition to a low-carbon economy the post-Kyoto negotiations have witnessed a North-South divide over IPRs and the innovation and transfer of ESTs. Briefly speaking, policy-makers in some developing countries argued on numerous occasions that the global IPR regime imposed by the WTO constitutes a (potential) barrier to the transfer of ESTs.[13] Thus, they advocate the use and expansion of the TRIPS flexibilities and push for

Sustainable Development, Policy Brief No. 9; International Council on Human Rights Policy (2011), *Beyond Technology Transfer: Protecting Human Rights in a Climate-Constrained World*, International Council on Human Rights Policy, Geneva, Switzerland, p. 36.

[11] See, e.g., UNEP, EPO and ICTSD (2010), *Patents and Clean Energy: Bridging the Gap between Evidence and Policy*, Munich: Mediengruppe Universal, p. 9 (further noting that "The leading six countries – Japan, the USA, Germany, Republic of Korea, France and the UK – are the source of almost 80 per cent of all innovations developed worldwide in the field of CETs"); B. Lee, L. Iliev and F. Preston (2009), *"Who Owns Our Low Carbon Future?"*, Intellectual Property and Energy Technologies, A Chatham House Report, p. 25.

[12] Padmashree Gehl Sampath and Pedro Roffe (2012), *Unpacking the International Technology Transfer Debate: Fifty Years and Beyond*, ICTSD Programme on Innovation, Technology and Intellectual Property, working paper, ICTSD, Geneva, Switzerland, p. 29 (noting that other conditions are required for technology transfer include "infrastructure, human capital, financial investment, and a favourable technological regime that is geared towards creating greater opportunities for access to and absorption of technologies"), yet, developing countries generally lack of such enabling environments. Meanwhile, multinational companies who are often profit-oriented and want to maintain their competitiveness lack sufficient incentive to transfer their technologies to firms in developing countries.

[13] See, e.g., UNDP (2011), *Technological Cooperation and Climate Change: Issues and Perspectives*, working papers presented at the Ministry of Environment and Forests, Government of India-UNDP Consultation on Technology Cooperation for Addressing Climate Change, UNDP, New Delhi, India; UNCTAD and ICTSD (2003), Intellectual Property Rights: Implications for Development, UNCTAD-ICTSD Project on IPRs and Sustainable Development, Policy Discussion Paper, UNCTAD and ICTSD, Geneva, Switzerland.

stronger language on compulsory licensing or even the exclusion of ESTs from patentability.[14] In contrast, multinational companies (MNCs), with advanced ESTs, often cite insufficient IPR protection in developing countries as a barrier to innovation and transfer of technology and suggest stronger IP protection, for instance, by a full implementation of the TRIPS Agreement or TRIPS-plus provisions in free trade agreements (FTAs).[15] Most developed nations believe that only strong IP regimes will facilitate the necessary innovation, diffusion and transfer of such technologies,[16] thereby ignoring developing countries' positions. Notably, the US House of Representatives, on the road to Copenhagen, voted unanimously (432–0) to pass the legislative amendment to:

> prevent any weakening of, and ensure robust compliance with and enforcement of, existing international legal requirements as of the date of the enactment of this Act for the protection of intellectual property rights related to energy or environmental technology.[17]

However, neither side has fully proved its case and the evidence remains inconclusive. Nevertheless, this divergence over the IPR issue in innovation and transfer of technology threatens the long-term prospects for a comprehensive international solution to mitigate climate change. There is an urgent need to conduct an in-depth study on the interface between the TRIPS Agreement and innovation and transfer of ESTs.

This book attempts to fill this gap with a view to making the TRIPS Agreement a more efficient and effective instrument for facilitating innovation and transfer of ESTs, mainly through legal interpretative devices. Two main research questions will be addressed: First, whether and, if so, to what extent do the minimum IPR standards established by the TRIPS Agreement facilitate or inhibit innovation and transfer of ESTs? Second, whether and, if so, to what extent the TRIPS flexibilities can be interpreted to facilitate innovation

---

[14] See, e.g., Keith E. Maskus (2010), Differentiated Intellectual Property Regimes for Environmental and Climate Technologies, *OECD Environment Working Papers*, No. 17, OECD Publishing, doi: 10.1787/5kmfwjvc83vk-en, p. 7; Sangeeta Shashikant (2009), No Patents on Climate-friendly Technologies, Says South, 12 June 2009, *TWN Info Service on Intellectual Property Issues*, available at www.twnside.org.sg/title2/intellectual_property/info .service/2009/twn.ipr.info.090609.htm

[15] Nicholas Stern (2007), *The Economics of Climate Change – The Stern Review*, Cambridge University Press, p. 566.

[16] UNEP, EPO and ICTSD (2010), *Patents and Clean Energy: Bridging the Gap between Evidence and Policy*, Munich: Mediengruppe Universal, p. 14.

[17] Foreign Relations Authorization Act, Fiscal Years 2010 and 2011, H.R. 2410, 22 June 2009, 111th Congress, Section 329, available at www.govtrack.us/congress/bills/111/hr2410/text

and transfer of ESTs so as to address global climate change. Taking into account, inter alia, the WTO's sustainable development objective, the object and purpose of the TRIPS Agreement and relevant rules of international law, this book seeks to propose a balanced and pro-competitive interpretation of the relevant TRIPS provisions. With a view to making such interpretation more authoritative, this book additionally proposes a Doha-type Declaration on Intellectual Property Rights and Climate Change. In order to further remedy the insufficiency of the treaty interpretation, this book also briefly recommends international guidelines for licensing of IP-protected ESTs as possible pathways to improve the current international IP regime for facilitating innovation and transfer of ESTs.

1.2 THE SCOPE AND STRUCTURE OF THIS STUDY

To the extent that ESTs are protected by IPRs, as found in Section 2.4, strict IPRs protection may help emerging economies access ESTs through market-based channels, though this may not be the case for other developing countries, in particular LDCs. Therefore, the findings in this book may not apply to LDCs. To the extent that innovation is the source of technologies, this book addresses not only the transfer of ESTs but also the innovation of ESTs.

This book includes two parts: Part I, entitled "Intellectual Property Rights, Innovation and Transfer of ESTs", introduces the basic concepts of ESTs, technology transfer and IPRs, examines the legal framework governing innovation and transfer of ESTs, and studies the role of minimum IPRs established by TRIPS in innovation and transfer of ESTs. Part II is dedicated to investigating whether, and to what extent, the limits to patent protection and the competition-related provisions in the TRIPS Agreement, when properly interpreted, could be applied to facilitate innovation and transfer of ESTs, thus contributing to reconciling the public interest in tackling climate change with the private sector's interest in IP protection. Part I contains the first three chapters (Chapters 2 to 4), and Part II includes the remaining four chapters (Chapters 5 to 8).

Chapter 2, entitled "Concepts and Context: IPRs, Innovation and Transfer of ESTs", first studies innovation and transfer of technology as part of the solution to climate change, followed by a description of transfer of ESTs including defining the concepts of ESTs and technology transfer. It then explores the fundamental issues in innovation and transfer of ESTs, including (1) ESTs as global public goods; (2) failures in the market for technologies and IPRs as a policy response to correct the market failures and (3) the concept of IP rights and their justifications. Subsequently, this chapter examines through literature review and empirical studies the global distribution of innovation and international transfer of ESTs.

Chapter 3, entitled "International Legal Framework Governing IPRs, Innovation and Transfer of Technologies, Including ESTs", introduces three approaches to regulate IP rights, innovation and transfer of technologies: the New International Economic Order (NIEO) approach, the market-based development approach, namely the TRIPS Agreement, and the sustainable development approach, with a focus on the UNFCCC. It first discusses the NIEO model, which was dominated by the revision of the Paris Convention and the creation of an UNCTAD Code of Conduct for Transfer of Technology during the 1970s and 1980s. It then provides a more detailed legal analysis of IP and technology transfer under the TRIPS Agreement. Finally, this chapter first examines EST transfer commitments in multilateral environmental agreements, in particular, the UNFCCC, and then discusses the interface between IPRs and innovation and transfer of ESTs in international climate negotiations.

Chapter 4, entitled "The Effects of Minimum IPR Standards Shaped by TRIPS on Innovation and Transfer of ESTs", seeks to examine the implications of minimum IPR standards for innovation and transfer of ESTs, in particular, whether strong IPRs protection is a prerequisite for innovation and transfer of ESTs and whether strong IPRs protection presents a barrier to EST transfer to developing countries. This chapter studies in turn (1) mandatory minimum IPR standards under TRIPS; (2) the positive role of minimum IPRs protection in facilitating innovation and transfer of ESTs and (3) the potentially negative effects of strong IPR protection on innovation and transfer of ESTs.

Chapter 5, entitled: "Rules Governing Treaty Interpretation and the Elements against Which the TRIPS Agreement Should Be Interpreted", identifies the methodology and relevant elements for interpreting the TRIPS Agreement. Under Articles 31 and 32 of the Vienna Convention on the Law of Treaties (VCLT), the terms of a treaty including the TRIPS Agreement shall be interpreted in good faith in accordance with their ordinary meaning in their context and in light of its object and purpose. This chapter first studies the customary rules governing treaty interpretation and then examines the elements in light of which the TRIPS Agreement should be interpreted, including the object and purpose of the treaty, subsequent development, as well as relevant rules of public international law.

Chapter 6, entitled: "Interpreting Patent-Related Flexibilities in the TRIPS Agreement for Facilitating Innovation and Transfer of ESTs", examines to what extent patent-related flexibilities can be interpreted to facilitate innovation and transfer of ESTs so as to address global climate change concerns. It first addresses the interpretative issues regarding the patentable subject matter under Article 27 and then examines the limits to patent rights in the TRIPS Agreement, followed by a study of compulsory licensing under Article 31. Their relevance to innovation and transfer of ESTs is addressed respectively.

Chapter 7, entitled: "Interpreting Competition-Related Flexibilities in the TRIPS Agreement for Facilitating Innovation and Transfer of ESTs", examines to what extent competition-related TRIPS flexibilities can be interpreted to facilitate innovation and transfer of ESTs so as to address global climate change concerns. This chapter addresses, in turn, the interpretative issues of the basic principle established under Article 8.2, control of anti-competitive practices in contractual licences under Article 40, and compulsory licensing as a remedy to anti-competitive practices under Article 31(k). Their relevance to the innovation and transfer of ESTs is addressed respectively.

Chapter 8 serves as the conclusion to this study. It also identifies potential challenges and provides recommendations. This chapter summarizes the main findings contained in Chapters 1 to 7. With a view to making the balanced and pro-competitive interpretation of the TRIPS Agreement contained in Chapters 6 and 7 more authoritative, this chapter additionally proposes a Doha-type Declaration on Intellectual Property Rights and Climate Change. In order to further remedy the insufficiency of the treaty interpretation, this chapter briefly recommends international guidelines for licensing of IP-protected ESTs as possible pathways to improve the current international IP regime for facilitating innovation and transfer of ESTs.

PART I

Intellectual Property Rights, Innovation and Transfer of ESTs

2

Concepts and Context: IPRs, Innovation
and Transfer of ESTs

Chapter 2 of this book introduces the concepts and context of this research topic. It includes the following sections: (1) innovation and transfer of technology as part of the solution to climate change; (2) describing innovation and transfer of ESTs; (3) fundamental issues in innovation and transfer of ESTs and (4) the global distribution of innovation and international transfer of ESTs: evidence to date.

2.1 INNOVATION AND TRANSFER OF TECHNOLOGY AS PART
OF THE SOLUTION TO CLIMATE CHANGE

The IPCC's Special Report on Technology Transfer (2000) states that "achieving the ultimate objective of the UNFCCC, as formulated in Article 2, will require technological innovation and the rapid widespread transfer and implementation of technologies, including know-how for mitigation of greenhouse gas emissions".[1] IPCC (2014) reaffirms that innovation and investments in environmentally sound technologies can reduce GHG emissions and strengthen resilience to climate change.[2] IPCC (2007) warns that without the effective transfer of technology, it may be "difficult to achieve emission reduction at a significant scale".[3] It is, thus, well-established that innovation and transfer of ESTs are part of the solution to climate change.

---

[1]   IPCC (2000), *IPCC Special Report: Methodological and Technological Issues in Technology Transfer*, Cambridge University Press, p. 3.
[2]   IPCC (2014), *Climate Change 2014 Synthesis Report: Summary for Policymakers*, p. 26, available at www.ipcc.ch/pdf/assessment-report/ar5/syr/SYR_AR5_SPM_Final.pdf
[3]   IPCC (2007) (a), *Synthesis Report, Contribution of Working Groups I, II and III to the Fourth Assessment Report of the IPCC*, Core Writing Team, Pachauri and Reisinger (eds.), IPCC, Geneva, Switzerland, p. 58.

Chapter 34 of Agenda 21 makes it clear that the availability of scientific and technological information and access to and transfer of ESTs are "essential requirements for sustainable development".[4] Transfer of ESTs benefits both technology recipients and providers. The former can acquire advanced ESTs to enhance their abilities to combat climate change whereas the latter can obtain a return from their past investment in R&D. Technology transfer would also avoid the wasting of resources and human effort spent reinventing technologies which already exist, thereby significantly reducing the costs of achieving the climate stabilisation goal.[5]

Development and effective transfer of ESTs are urgently needed to help developing countries make the transition to a low-carbon and sustainable development path. The contracting Parties to the UNFCCC have acknowledged that "the share of global emissions originating in developing countries will grow to meet their social and development needs".[6] As their economic growth is largely driven by carbon-intensive energy, developing countries' share of global emissions has risen significantly during the past decade.[7] For instance, China (share 29 per cent) is now estimated to be the largest emitter of GHGs, and its emission has increased by 171 per cent since 2009, while India (share 6 per cent) has emerged as the world's third largest emitter of CO_2.[8] Without a rapid transition to a low-carbon economy, emissions of GHGs from developing countries are expected to soar in the coming decade. IPCC (2000) has thus warned that "it will not be sustainable if developing countries simply follow the historic greenhouse gas emission trends of developed countries".[9] Development, wide dissemination and transfer of ESTs to

---

[4]   Agenda 21, chap. 34, para. 7, Transfer of Environmentally Sound Technology, Cooperation and Capacity-building, UN Documents Cooperation Circles, available at www.un-documents.net/a21-34.htm

[5]   ICTSD (2008), Climate Change, Technology Transfer and Intellectual Property Rights, paper prepared for Trade and Climate Change Seminar, 18–20 June 2008, Copenhagen, p. 1.

[6]   The Preamble of the UNFCCC.

[7]   World Economic Forum (2013), *The Global Energy Architecture Performance Index Report 2014*, published by The World Economic Forum and Accenture, December 2013, p. 53 (noting that "[F]or South Africa, India, China and Brazil, growth has come from expansion in heavy industries, manufacturing, mining and construction, while Russia has pursued the expansion of production and export of oil and gas. In recent years, BRICS economies have increasingly come under the spotlight for the contribution to climate change of their energy- and carbon-intensive economies").

[8]   See, e.g., Rogers Simon and Evans Lisa, World Carbon Dioxide Emissions Data by Country: China Speeds Ahead of the Rest, *Theguardian*, 31 January 2011, available at www.guardian.co.uk/news/datablog/2011/jan/31/world-carbon-dioxide-emissions-country-data-co2; Olivier et al. (2012), *Trends in Global CO2 Emissions: 2012 Report – Background Studies*, PBL Netherlands Environmental Assessment Agency, p. 11.

[9]   IPCC (2000), *IPCC Special Report: Methodological and Technological Issues in Technology Transfer*, Cambridge University Press, p. 15.

developing countries must, therefore, operate on a broad front to enable them to reach the same level of carbon efficiency as developed countries.

2.2 DESCRIBING INNOVATION AND TRANSFER OF ENVIRONMENTALLY SOUND TECHNOLOGIES

2.2.1 *Defining Environmentally Sound Technologies*

There is no agreed-upon definition for what constitutes "environmentally sound technologies". Literally, the concept refers to technologies that are environmentally sound. This section addresses first what the term "technology" means and then explores what environmentally sound technologies are.

The dictionary meaning of "technology" is "the branch of knowledge that deals with the mechanical arts or applied sciences".[10] The UNCTAD Draft International Code of Conduct on the Transfer of Technology, to be further discussed in Section 3.2.2, describes technology as "systematic knowledge for the manufacture of a product, for the application of a process or for the rendering of a service and does not extend to the transactions involving the mere sale or lease of goods".[11] Some studies define technology as encompassing capital goods such as equipment and machinery,[12] and this is largely based on the belief that "when a technological product is transferred or diffused, the knowledge upon which its composition is based is also diffused".[13] Some commentators contest that "it is the knowledge that goes into the creation and provision of the product or service constitutes 'technology', not the finished product or service as such".[14] It is, however, generally recognised that technology is closely linked with industrial

---

[10] *Shorter Oxford English Dictionary*, 6th edn, vol. II, Oxford University Press, 2007, p. 3194.
[11] Draft International Code of Conduct on the Transfer of Technology, as at the close of the sixth session of Conference on 5 June 1985, Geneva, Switzerland, United Nations document No. TD/CODE TOT/47, 20 June 1985, chap. 1, para. 1.2.
[12] See, e.g., UNCTC (1987), *Transnational Corporations and Technology Transfer: Effects and Policy Issues*, ST/CTC/86, New York: United Nations, p. 1 (defined technology as encompassing technical knowledge or know-how, the human skills required for the application of these techniques as well as capital goods such as tools, machinery, equipment and entire production systems); OECD (1995), *Technologies for Clearer Production and Products: Towards Technological Transformation for Sustainable Development*, Paris: OECD, p. 13 (supporting the UNCTC definition and contending that the word "technology" should be understood as "encompassing techniques, management approaches and information as well as hardware").
[13] See, e.g., Barry Bozeman (2000), Technology Transfer and Public Policy: A Review of Research and Theory, *Research Policy*, vol. 29, pp. 627–55, at p. 629.
[14] See, e.g., Peter Muchlinski (2007), *Multinational Enterprises and the Law*, 2nd edn, New York: Oxford University Press, p. 430; UNCTAD (2001), *Transfer of Technology, UNCTAD Series on Issues in International Investment Agreements*, New York and Geneva: United Nations, p. 6; Steven Anderman (2007), *The Interface between Intellectual Property Rights and Competition Policy*, Cambridge University Press, p. 468.

hardware. Though the hardware or technological product is not technology in itself, it is a carrier of "technology".[15]

The most widely used definition of ESTs is the UN Agenda 21 definition developed by the United Nations Conference on Environment and Development (UNCED), following the Rio Conference in 1992, which states that:

> Environmentally sound technologies protect the environment, are less polluting, use all resources in a more sustainable manner, recycle more of their wastes and products, and handle residual wastes in a more acceptable manner than the technologies for which they were substitutes.

> Environmentally sound technologies in the context of pollution are "process and product technologies" that generate low or no waste, for the prevention of pollution. They also cover "end of the pipe" technologies for treatment of pollution after it has been generated.[16]

Agenda 21 reveals several key features of ESTs. First, ESTs are "not just individual technologies, but total systems which include know-how, procedures, goods and services, and equipment as well as organizational and managerial procedures."[17] Agenda 21 emphasises the importance of endogenous capacity-building and shares the popular view that "technology transfer is by definition in vain, unless adequate measures are taken with regard to human resource development."[18]

Second, when defining ESTs, Agenda 21 uses "less" and "more", suggesting that the "environmental soundness" of technology is relative, varying temporally and geographically. Because of the evolving nature of environmental problems and science, a technology that is considered environmentally sound today may not necessarily be seen in the same way in a few years' time. Similarly, what is environmentally sound in one country may not be in

---

[15] See, e.g., Yuwen Li (1994), *Transfer of Technology for Deep Sea-bed Mining: The 1982 Law of the Sea Convention and Beyond*, Berlin: Kluwer Academic Publishers, pp. 120–1 (arguing that "the importation of hardware systems has an indirect effect on transferring technical knowledge" as it not only helps to improve production capacity but also facilitates training and acquisition of foreign technology).

[16] Agenda 21 of the Rio Declaration on Environment and Development adopted at United Nations Conference on Environment and Development, Rio de Janeiro, 3–14 June 1992, chap. 34: Transfer of Environmentally Sound Technology, Cooperation and Capacity-building, UN Documents Cooperation Circles, paras. 1 and 2, available at www.un-documents .net/a21-34.htm

[17] Agenda 21, chap. 34, para. 3.

[18] Gaetan Verhoosel (1998), Beyond the Unsustainable Rhetoric of Sustainable Development: Transferring Environmentally Sound Technologies, *The Georgetown International Environmental Law Review*, vol. XI, pp. 49–76, at p. 63.

another, "unless it is redesigned or adapted to make it appropriate for addressing local needs".[19] It is thus clear that environmental soundness is "not an attribute of technology by itself but of technology in the particular socio-ecological context in which it is intended to be applied".[20] In other words, the environmental soundness of certain technology should be assessed on a case-by-case basis, taking into account the level of economic and technological development and the state of the environment in the country concerned and the world as a whole.[21] Therefore, as suggested by Agenda 21, ESTs should be compatible with nationally determined socio-economic and environmental priorities.[22]

In the context of climate change, Article 4.1(c) of the UNFCCC identified ESTs as those that "control, reduce or prevent anthropogenic emissions of greenhouse gases in all relevant sectors, including the energy, transport, industry, agriculture, forestry and waste management sectors".[23] Examples include energy-efficient technologies, renewable energy (such as hydropower, solar, wind, geothermal and biofuel) technologies, and carbon capture and storage (CCS) technologies.[24] Whereas some technologies, such as irrigation systems, are already well established, major investments in research and development (R&D) may be required in other sectors, such as wind, solar, CCS, and biofuels.[25]

The fact that "the burning of fossil fuels is the major contributor to climate change, being responsible for over 75 per cent of human-caused CO_2 emissions"[26] requires the wide deployment and transfer of ESTs. The next section examines the definition and channels of technology transfer.

---

[19] UNEP (2003), Phytotechnologies: A Technical Approach in Environmental Management, IETC Freshwater Management Series 7, available at www.unep.or.jp/Ietc/Publications/Freshwater/FMS7/2.asp#Ia

[20] Kotelnikov Vadim, Environmentally Sound Technologies (ESTs), *Ten3*, available at http://it4b.icsti.su/1000ventures_e/environment/est_main.html

[21] Gaetan Verhoosel (1998), Beyond the Unsustainable Rhetoric of Sustainable Development: Transferring Environmentally Sound Technologies, *The Georgetown International Environmental Law Review*, vol. XI, pp. 49–76, at p. 64.

[22] Agenda 21, chap. 34, para. 3.   [23] UNFCCC, Article 4.1.

[24] IPCC (2007a), *Synthesis Report, Contribution of Working Groups I, II and III to the Fourth Assessment Report of the IPCC*, Core Writing Team, Pachauri and Reisinger (eds.), Geneva: IPCC, p. 60.

[25] Latif Ahmed Abdel et al. (2011), Overcoming the Impasse on Intellectual Property and Climate Change at the UNFCCC: A Way Forward, *Policy Brief* No.11, at p. 4.

[26] IPCC (2007b), *Climate Change 2007: The Physical Science Basis*, Contribution of Working Group I to the Fourth Assessment Report of the IPCC, Solomon et al. (eds.), Cambridge University Press, p. 115; International Energy Agency, Prospect of Limiting the Global Increase in Temperature to 2°C is Getting Bleaker, 30 May 2011, available at www.iea.org/journalists/latestinformation.asp. They estimate that "energy-related CO_2 emissions in 2010 were at their highest level in history and 80 per cent of all projected 2020 GHG emissions from the power sector are already locked in".

2.2.2 *Describing Technology Transfer*

2.2.2.1 Definition of Technology Transfer

There is no consensus on how the term "technology transfer" is defined. The literature concerning technology transfer has grown exponentially over the past 40 years and has confirmed the difficulty of defining technology transfer because its precise meaning critically depends on the importing nation's stage of development and the complexity of its process.[27] Simply speaking, it is a series of processes covering the flow of technology among different stakeholders. In 2010, the Members of the World Intellectual Property Organization (WIPO), a specialised UN agency, agreed upon a definition of technology transfer in the context of a project on Intellectual Property and Technology Transfer: Common Challenges-Building Solutions (CDIP/4/7).[28] Transfer of technology was broadly defined as "a series of processes enabling and facilitating flows of skills, knowledge, ideas, know-how and technology among different stakeholders such as university and research institutions, international organizations, NGOs, private sector entities and individuals, as well as international technology transfer among countries".[29] The Members explicitly emphasised that the transfer of technology is often considered to "include the absorption of new technologies".[30]

Similarly, the IPCC in its special report on technology transfer describes technology transfer in the context of climate change as being composed of:

> the broad set of processes covering the flows of knowledge, experience and equipment amongst different stakeholders such as governments, private sector entities, financial institutions, NGOs and research/educational

---

[27] Rachel McCulloch (1981), Technology Transfer to Developing Countries: Implications of International Regulation, *Annals of the American Academy of Political and Social Science* 458, pp. 110–22, at p. 115; UNCTAD (2001), Transfer of Technology, *UNCTAD Series on Issues in International Investment Agreements*, New York and Geneva: United Nations; K. Ramanathan (2011), An Overview of Technology Transfer and Technology Transfer Models, available at www.businessasia.net/Pdf_Pages/Guidebook per cent20on per cent20Technology per cent20Transfer per cent20Mechanisms/An per cent20overview per cent20of per cent20TT per cent20and per cent20TT per cent20Models.pdf

[28] This project was adopted in the sixth session of the WIPO Committee on Development and Intellectual Property (CDIP) in Geneva, Switzerland, on 22–26 November 2010; see Project on Intellectual Property and Technology Transfer: Common Challenges – Building Solutions (Recommendations 19, 25, 26 and 28), WIPO Doc. CDIP/6/4 REV., 26 November 2010.

[29] Project on Intellectual Property and Technology Transfer: Common Challenges – Building Solutions (Recommendations 19, 25, 26 and 28), WIPO doc., CDIP/6/4/ Rev., 26 November 2010, Geneva, Switzerland, p. 3.

[30] Ibid., at p. 3.

institutions ... It comprises the process of learning to understand, utilise and replicate the technology, including the capacity to choose it and adapt it to local conditions.[31]

Both definitions suggest that one critical characteristic of technology transfer is the absorption of and mastering the received knowledge. Indeed, it is widely accepted that the transfer of technology assumes that the recipients will absorb the technology in a manner that enables them to reproduce it.[32] As Foray (2009) notes, a successful technology transfer "goes through the perilous phases of the assimilation and absorption of technological knowledge: adaptation to local conditions, absorption of subsequent improvements and generalisation of the transferred knowledge".[33] Accordingly, the effectiveness of technology transfer has to be assessed jointly with the absorptive capacity, local conditions and development status of the recipient countries. To some extent, this verifies that transfer of technology requires facilitating access to related technical knowledge and the human skills needed to effectively use it.[34]

It may be useful to explain the difference between technology transfer and technology dissemination (diffusion). To "disseminate" means to "scatter in different directions, as in sowing seed; spread, disperse; diffuse, promulgate".[35] Dissemination of technology generally takes place through non-market-based spillovers and reaches an undetermined number of potential users.[36] As Muchlinski (2007) observed, such dissemination may be "a benefit of technology transfer in that once technology is transferred it will create a 'demonstration effect' by raising awareness of its existence, and the possibility of a

---

[31] IPCC (2000), *IPCC Special Report: Methodological and Technological Issues in Technology Transfer*, Cambridge University Press, p. 55.

[32] Nuno Pires De Carvalho (2010), *The TRIPS Regime of Patent Rights*, 3rd edn, Alphen aan den Rijn, Netherlands: Kluwer Law International, p. 208; Kavasseri Ramanathan, Keith Jacobs and Madhusudan Bandyopadhyay (2011), *Technology Transfer and Small and Medium Enterprises in Developing Countries*, New Delhi, India: Daya Publishing House; Seaton Associates (2002), Knowledge Transfer, discussion paper prepared for the AQUADAPT workshop, Montpellier, France, p. 9; Keith E. Maskus (2004), *Encouraging International Technology Transfer*, ICTSD and UNCTAD Issue Paper No. 7, Geneva, Switzerland, p. 9.

[33] Dominique Foray (2009), *Technology Transfer in the TRIPS Age: The Need for New Types of Partnerships between the Least Developed and Most Advanced Economies*, ICTSD programme on IPRs and Sustainable Development, Issue Paper No. 23, Geneva, Switzerland, p. 4.

[34] ICTSD (2008), *Climate Change, Technology Transfer and Intellectual Property Rights*, paper prepared for the Trade and Climate Change Seminar, Copenhagen, Denmark, p. 3.

[35] *Shorter Oxford English Dictionary* (2007), 6th edn, vol. II, Oxford University Press, p. 715.

[36] Carlos M. Correa (2007), *Trade Related Aspects of Intellectual Property Rights: A Commentary on the TRIPS Agreement*, Oxford University Press, p. 99.

'spill-over' to local firms in the course of time".[37] It may be "unintentional or as a result of deliberate government policies, including training requirements or compulsory licensing of technology for local firms".[38] In contrast, technology is often transferred from one person or entity to another, mostly in a bilateral context. It is generally "intentional and goal-oriented but not a free process".[39] Accordingly, the transfer of technology usually involves agreements, for example, a licensing or joint-venture agreement, and is, in general, much more complex and costly for technology recipients than technology dissemination.

Technology transfer takes place within and between all countries. At the international level, technology is exchanged mostly between developed countries. Increasingly, technology is transferred from developed nations to developing countries – "North to South"; or between developing countries – "South to South".

2.2.2.2 Channels of Technology Transfer

Technology transfer, embodied in the actions taken by individuals, governments or organisations, can be government driven or private sector driven. According to IPCC (2000), government-driven pathways are technology transfers initiated by governments to achieve specific policy objectives whereas private-sector-driven pathways primarily involve business transactions between enterprises or/and private institutions.[40] Undoubtedly, private-sector-driven pathways have become the prevailing mode of technology transfer,[41] largely occurring through market-based channels that involve consensual legal arrangements, such as foreign direct investment (FDI), licensing and trade. Technologies are also transferred through informal channels, such as imitation and reverse engineering, which are not based on legal arrangements, require no consent from technology owners and confer no compensation to technology transferors.[42]

---

[37] Peter Muchlinski (2007), *Multinational Enterprises and the Law*, 2nd edn, New York: Oxford University Press, p. 431.

[38] Ibid.

[39] Erkko Aution, Ari-Pekka Hameri and Olli Vuola (2004), A Framework of Industrial Knowledge Spillovers in Big-Science Centres, *Research Policy*, vol. 33, pp. 107–26, at p. 108.

[40] IPCC (2000), *IPCC Special Report: Methodological and Technological Issues in Technology Transfer*, Cambridge University Press, p. 57.

[41] Ibid.

[42] UNCTAD and ICTSD (2003), Intellectual Property Rights: Implications for Development, UNCTAD-ICTSD Project on IPRs and Sustainable Development, Policy Discussion Paper, ICTSD and UNCTAD, Geneva, p. 85.

2.2.2.2.1 FDI. FDI can be described as "the act of establishing or acquiring a foreign subsidiary (or foreign affiliate) over which the investing firm has substantial management control".[43] It is an important vehicle for host countries to gain access to new technologies and skills.[44] Foreign investors, sharing control and profits with local partners, are motivated to provide their affiliates with more efficient production technologies and expand technical training for the labourers in host countries.[45]

Whereas FDI may be efficient in respect to the transfer of operational technology, some commentators regard its contribution to the development of local innovative capacities as limited.[46] In particular, it is observed that foreign investors tend to do most of their R&D in their home countries, limiting the development of core technologies in host countries.[47] The extent to which FDI could speed up technological progress in host countries may not only depend on the types of technologies but also the economic and technological development levels of the host countries. As observed by Athreye and Cantwell (2007), on average, FDI is not a key development tool in the initial stages of technological development across countries, but it plays an increasingly important role in more advanced stages.[48]

2.2.2.2.2 LICENSING. To "license" or "grant a licence" is to give permission.[49] In the context of technology transfer, licensing covers a broad spectrum of

---

[43] Maskus Keith E. (1998), The Role of Intellectual Property Rights in Encouraging Foreign Direct Investment and Technology Transfer, *Duke Journal of Comparative and International Law*, vol. IX, pp. 109–61, at p. 119.

[44] See, e.g., UNCTAD (2014), *Transfer of Technology and Knowledge Sharing for Development: Science, Technology and Innovation Issues for Developing Countries*, UNCTAD/DTL/STICT/2013/8, Geneva: United Nations, p. 16; Chantal Dupasquier and Patrick N. Osakwe (2005), Foreign Direct Investment in Africa: Performance, Challenges and Responsibilities, African Trade Policy Centre, Work in Progress No. 21, p. 5.

[45] P. S. Ho Samuel (1997), Technology Transfer to China during the 1980s – How Effective? Some Evidence from Jiangsu, *Pacific Affairs*, vol. 70, no. 1, pp. 85–106, at p. 105.

[46] See, e.g., Steven Anderman (2007), *The Interface between Intellectual Property Rights and Competition Policy*, New York: Cambridge University Press, p. 474; John Ecos, Sanjaya Lall and Mikyung Yun (1997), Transfer of Technology: An Update, *Asian-Pacific Economic Literature*, vol. 11, no. 1, pp. 56–66, at p. 56.

[47] See, e.g., UNCTAD (2001), *Transfer of Technology*, UNCTAD Series on Issues in International Investment Agreements, New York and Geneva: United Nations, p. 11; John Ecos, Sanjaya Lall and Mikyung Yun (1997), Transfer of Technology: An Update, *Asian-Pacific Economic Literature*, vol. 11, no. 1, pp. 56–66, at p. 56.

[48] Suma Athreye and John Cantwell (2007), Creating Competition? Globalisation and the Emergence of New Technology Producers, *Research Policy*, vol. 36, pp. 209–26, at p. 224.

[49] "License". Dictionary.com. *Collins English Dictionary – Complete and Unabridged*, 10th edn, HarperCollins.

permissions that are granted to make use of another's technology under carefully laid out conditions and terms. According to Foray (2009), licensing involves the purchase of IP-protected production rights, and in numerous cases, the provision of technical information and know-how necessary for the adoption and adaptation of the technology.[50] The licensing of existing technologies has several advantages. For licensees, or the technology recipients, acquiring existing technologies through licensing might be cheaper and faster than developing technologies themselves.[51] For licensors, or technology suppliers, licensing provides entry into new markets and more liquidity, which can be used to grow their core business.[52] In other words, licensing is often a mutually beneficial business proposition.

Licensing is a major channel of international technology transfer. According to World Bank (2008), some countries such as Japan and South Korea had limited FDI in the earlier stages of their industrial development and pursued a licensing-based strategy of technology acquisition in the belief that "domestic firms will be able to upgrade their own technological capacities by working with licensed technology".[53] However, this approach is likely to work only if the technology-receiving enterprises or countries have sufficient bargaining power. In principle, licensing may provide an economical way of transfer of standardised, mature and relatively simple technologies to recipients that have absorptive capabilities.[54] The quality of the licensed technologies may depend on whether the product manufactured is for a global market or a local market. According to Barton (2007), if the agreement is to produce goods for a global market, the licensor may be motivated to provide the best possible and most advanced technologies, whereas if the purpose of the licence is to produce for a local market, which is likely for service industries or for a very large market such as China, the foreign firm tends to supply less advanced technologies.[55]

---

[50] Dominique Foray (2009), *Technology Transfer in the TRIPS Age: The Need for New Types of Partnerships between the Least Developed and Most Advanced Economies*, ICTSD programme on IPRs and Sustainable Development, Issue Paper No. 23, ICTSD, Geneva, Switzerland, p. 24.

[51] John H. Barton (2007), *New Trends in Technology Transfer: Implications for National and International Policy*, ICTSD, Issue Paper No. 18, at p. 22.

[52] David Popp (2008), *International Technology Transfer for Climate Policy*, Centre for Policy Research, Paper No. 4, p. 11.

[53] World Bank (2008), *Global Economic Prospects: Technology Diffusion in the Developing World*, Washington, D.C.: World Bank, pp. 121–2.

[54] OECD (2002), *Foreign Direct Investment for Development: Maximising Benefits, Minimising Costs*, OECD, Paris, p. 96.

[55] John H. Barton (2007), *New Trends in Technology Transfer: Implications for National and International Policy*, ICTSD, Issue Paper No. 18, p. 22.

2.2.2.2.3 TRADE. Trade in goods and services, especially high-tech products, is an important mechanism through which technologies can be spread internationally.[56] Imports of technologically sophisticated goods carry some potential for developing countries to improve their domestic technology as they boost local firms' productivity. Several studies have found that the greater the imports of technological goods or equipment are, the higher the benefit of the stock of foreign knowledge is.[57] The empirical research produced by Coe, Helpman and Hoffmaister (1997) suggests that foreign R&D influences domestic productivity and that "a country that is more open to machinery and equipment imports derives a larger marginal benefit from foreign R&D".[58] Blalock and Veloso (2006), using detailed firm-level data from Indonesia, show that imports, in particular, downstream imports, "play a role in the creation of technological capabilities, as measured by productivity".[59] Exports have also been identified as forming an indirect channel through which technology is transferred to developing countries. The literature suggests that developing countries' exporting enterprises can improve their technological capabilities through their interactions with competitors or customers abroad.[60]

---

[56] The 1985 Draft International Code of Conduct on the Transfer of Technology listed services involving technical advisory and managerial personnel, and personnel training as one type of technology transactions. In other words, trade in services can be important channel for the transfer of knowledge when it involves technical advisory and managerial personnel and labourer training.

[57] See, e.g., David T. Coe, Elhanan Helpman and Alexander W. Hoffmaister (1997), North-South R&D Spillovers, *The Economic Journal*, vol. 107, no. 440, pp. 134–49, at p. 134 and p. 135; Kamil Yilmaz and Ashoka Mody (2002), Imported Machinery for Export Competitiveness, *World Bank Economic Review*, vol. 16, no. 1, pp. 23–48, at p. 24.

[58] The study, based on data for 77 developing countries, also suggests that R&D spillovers from 22 industrialized countries over 1971–1990 are substantial; see David T. Coe, Elhanan Helpman and Alexander W. Hoffmaister (1997), North-South R&D Spillovers, *The Economic Journal*, vol. 107, no. 440, pp. 134–49, at p. 134 and p. 135.

[59] Garrick Blalock and Francisco Veloso (2006), *Imports, Productivity Growth, and Supply Chain Learning*, Department of Engineering and Public Policy, Paper No. 127, at p. 30.

[60] See, e.g., Marc Laperrouza (2010), Trade, Technology Transfer and Institutional Catch-up, in Lehmann and Lehmann (eds.), *Peace and Prosperity through World Trade*, Cambridge University Press, pp. 222–26, at p. 222 (noting that exporting enterprises can "learn by observing their competitors on international markets and aim to reach the same efficiency as their competitors by adopting their technologies"); World Bank (2008), *Global Economic Prospects: Technology Diffusion in the Developing World*, Washington, D.C.: World Bank, p. 110 (finding that foreign customers may have higher quality standards than domestic buyers and "implicitly or explicitly provide guidance in meeting the specifications required for access to global markets").

Trade has become an increasingly important source of new technologies. Hoekman et al. (2004) gathered data on the flow of the technology trade and found that total trade in technology-intensive goods had grown rapidly since 1970s.[61] According to World Bank (2008), developing countries' high technology imports had increased over the past decades.[62] Yet, the extent to which these imports boost local technological capacity depends heavily on the country's absorptive abilities and the role that the imported high technology played in modernising domestic production capacities.[63]

2.2.2.2.4 IMITATION. Imitation is one of the most significant informal channels of technology transfer through which societies can develop their technological capacities. Imitation is defined as "a process in which a rival firm learns the technological or design secrets of another firm's formula or products".[64] Though it does not provide any financial compensation to the technology owners, "imitation" itself may be a costly investment both in terms of time and money. According to Foray (2009), this makes imitation tolerable from a competition point of view, as the initial inventor can use the "lead time", that is the gap between invention and the entry of imitators, to capture a larger portion of the benefits and thereby cover the fixed costs of R&D.[65] However, the legality of imitation may depend on "the scope of intellectual property protection and the security of trade secrets from unfair competition".[66]

---

[61] Bernard M. Hoekman, Keith E. Maskus and Kamal Saggi (2004), Transfer of Technology to Developing Countries: Unilateral and Multilateral Policy Options, *World Bank Policy Research Working Paper No. 3332*, p. 6.

[62] World Bank (2008), *Global Economic Prospects: Technology Diffusion in the Developing World*, Washington, D.C.: World Bank, p. 112.

[63] In 1990s, the degrees of industrial specialisation of China and Turkey were similar, but they have diverged since. China has become an assembly country because most of China's high-tech imports are parts and components and they are predominately incorporated into the production of exports while Turkey's high-tech imports consist mainly of capital goods and primarily aimed at upgrading indigenous industrial capacities. See Francoise Lemoine and Deniz Unal-kesenci (2003), Trade and Technology Transfers: A Comparative Study of Turkey, India and China, *CEPII*, Working Paper No. 2003–16, p. 4.

[64] Keith E. Maskus (2004), *Encouraging International Technology Transfer*, UNCTAD-ICTSD Project on IPRs and Sustainable Development, Issue Paper No. 7, ICTSD and UNCTAD, Geneva, Switzerland, p. 12.

[65] Dominique Foray (2009), *Technology Transfer in the TRIPS Age: The Need for New Types of Partnerships between the Least Developed and Most Advanced Economies*, ICTSD Programme on IPRs and Sustainable Development, Issue Paper No. 23, ICTSD, Geneva, Switzerland, p. 26.

[66] Keith E. Maskus (2005), Using the International Trading System to Foster Technology Transfer for Economic Development, *Michigan State Law Review*, vol. 2005, pp. 219–41, at p. 232.

Imitation ranges from simply copying existing goods, that is, duplicative imitation, to generating similar products but with new features, that is, creative imitation/imitative innovation. Duplicative imitation, including counterfeits and knockoffs, "conveys no sustainable competitive advantage to the imitator in a technological sense, but it sustains [a] competitive edge in price if the imitator's wage cost is significantly lower than the originator's".[67] To catch up with advanced countries, simple copying is not enough. Developing countries need to actively adapt and improve their existing technologies. According to Van Ark et al. (2008), the imitation and adaptation of foreign technology allowed European countries to speed up growth and productivity quite rapidly following the devastation of Europe's economies during World War II.[68] Furthermore, various studies indicate that technology development in many countries, for instance, Korea, Japan, Singapore and the US, passed through three stages: duplicative imitation, creative imitation and innovation.[69] It can be seen that countries generally adopt an imitation-based catch-up and development approach at earlier stages of their technological develop-ment and switch to an innovation-based strategy when their economies become more advanced. This ample historical evidence also shows that, traditionally, "freedom to imitate was an essential step towards learning how to innovate".[70]

2.2.2.2.5 REVERSE ENGINEERING. Reverse engineering is broadly defined as "the process of working backward to determine the nature of a product or service, or the method used to produce it, by examining, dissecting, or analysing the product or service itself".[71] Reverse engineering can be used as

---

[67] Linsu Kim and Richard R. Nelson (2000), *Technology, Learning, and Innovation: Experiences of Newly Industrializing Economies*, Cambridge University Press, p. 4.

[68] Bart Van Ark, Mary O'Mahony and Marcel P. Timmer (2008), The Productivity Gap between Europe and the United States: Trends and Causes, *Journal of Economic Perspectives*, vol. 22, no. 1, pp. 25–44, at p. 28.

[69] See, e.g., Kichan Park, Murad Ali and Francoise Chevalier (2011), A Spiral Process Model of Technological Innovation in a Developing Country: The Case of Samsung, *African Journal of Business Management*, vol. 5, no. 13, pp. 5162–78; Linsu Kim (1997), *Imitation to Innovation: The Dynamics of Korea's Technological Learning*, Cambridge, MA: Harvard Business Press; Michele K. Bolton (1993), Imitation versus Innovation: Lessons to Be Learned from the Japanese, *Organisational Dynamics*, vol. 21, no. 3, pp. 30–45.

[70] Graham Dutfield and Uma Suthersanen (2004), Harmonization or Differentiation in Intellectual Property Protection? Lessons from History, *Occasional Paper*, 15, QUNO, Geneva, Switzerland, p. 15.

[71] Jay Dratler (1991), *Intellectual Property Law: Commercial, Creative, and Industrial Property*, New York: Law Journal Press, para. 4–84; *Kewanee Oil Co. v. Bicro Corp.*, 416 US 470, 476 (1974) (defining reverse engineering as "starting with the known product and working backward

a learning tool to develop a more competitive product or an interoperable product. Yet, not all technologies can be easily reverse engineered and a substantial investment in terms of skills and R&D is generally required.

Reverse engineering could benefit the public through encouraging investors to develop similar products and facilitating healthy competition in the marketplace. As Samuelson and Scotchmer (2002) observed, "[r]everse engineering may be a slower and more expensive means for information to percolate through a technical community than patenting or publication, but it is nonetheless an effective source of information".[72] Reverse engineering often leads to dependent creations; however, this does not taint it, "for in truth, all innovators stand on the shoulders of both giants and [little persons]".[73] The US Supreme Court explicitly recognised that "reverse engineering often leads to significant advances in technology".[74] Thus, reverse engineering plays a vital role in fostering innovation and the transfer of knowledge.

The TRIPS Agreement is silent on the issue of reverse engineering, neither expressly prohibiting nor permitting it as such. Yet, the right to reverse engineer is, however, restricted in some cases, such as shrink wrap licenses that seek to prohibit reverse engineering through private contracts. According to Mahajan (1999), if such contractual prohibitions were enforceable, the delicate balance between the public and private spheres would be shattered as the public's right to access the ideas in protected items would be wholly circumscribed by private legislation.[75] Nations should protect the public's right to reverse engineer while respecting the IPRs embodied in the studied items.

In sum, technologies can be transferred through different means depending on the types or nature of technologies and the specific circumstances, for example, the development status of technology-receiving countries or the market power of the technology provider. Almost all the channels are interdependent processes. The policy environment influences the choice of the channel which is often "made jointly by firms seeking to maximize returns

---

to divine the process which aided in its development or manufacture"); the dictionary meaning of reverse engineering is "to study or analyze (a device, as a microchip for computers) in order to learn details of design, construction, and operation, perhaps to produce a copy or an improved version" (see reverse engineer. Dictionary.com. *Dictionary.com Unabridged*, Random House, http://dictionary.reference.com/browse/reverse engineer)

[72] Pamela Samuelson and Suzanne Scotchmer (2002), The Law and Economics of Reverse Engineering, *The Yale Law Journal*, vol. CXI, pp. 1575–1663, at p. 1662.

[73] Ibid.   [74] *Bonito Boats Inc. v. Thunder Craft Boats Inc.*, 489 US 141, 160 (1989).

[75] Anthony J. Mahajan (1999), Intellectual Property, Contracts, and Reverse Engineering After ProCD: A Proposed Compromise for Computer Software, *Fordham Law Review*, vol. 67, no. 6, pp. 3297–335, at p. 3318.

on their technological assets".[76] No matter how technologies are transferred, the absorptive capacities of the technology receiving countries, that is, the abilities of the recipient to properly understand and effectively use the technology, which are generally measured by the level of local education and R&D investment, matter greatly to the success of technology transfer.

2.3 FUNDAMENTAL ISSUES IN INNOVATION AND TRANSFER OF ESTS

2.3.1 *ESTs as "Global Public Goods"*

Global public goods are defined as those goods "that are systematically under-provided by private market forces and for which such under-provision has important international externality effects".[77] According to Bodansky (2012), global public goods create incentives for free-riding, and, "in many cases, they require international governance to provide" them.[78] ESTs capable of mitigating climate change are global public goods. For instance, clean energy technologies provide a global public benefit by replacing fossil fuels with renewable energy, which would mitigate the emission of GHGs.

It is well recognised that technology bears the characteristics of a "public good", including "non-rivalry" in consumption and "non-excludability" in use.[79] This means that technology can be understood and used by everyone simultaneously ("non-rival") and no one could be excluded from enjoying its value without compensation or authorisation ("non-excludable").[80] Consequently, people may "free ride" (not pay) once technology has been provided and a technological external benefit cannot be priced. In other words, a

---

[76] Keith E. Maskus (2005), Using the International Trading System to Foster Technology Transfer for Economic Development, *Michigan State Law Review*, vol. MMV, pp. 219–41, at p. 231.

[77] Keith E. Maskus and Jerome Reichman (2005), The Globalization of Private Knowledge Goods and the Privatization of Global Public Goods, in Maskus and Reichman (eds.), *International Public Goods and Transfer of Technology under a Globalized Intellectual Property Regime*, Cambridge University Press, pp. 3–45, at p. 8.

[78] Daniel Bodansky (2012), What's in a Concept? Global Public Goods, International Law and Legitimacy, *The European Journal of International Law*, vol. 23, no. 3, pp. 651–68, at p. 668.

[79] See, e.g., Jaime Ros (2013), *Rethinking Economic Development, Growth, and Institutions*, Oxford University Press, p. 51; Robert J. Barro and Xavier Sala-i-Martin (2004), *Economic Growth*, 2nd edn, Massachusetts Institute of Technology, p. 24; Hendrik den Berg and Joshua J. Lewer (2007), *International Trade and Economic Growth*, Armonk, NY: M. E. Sharpe, p. 124.

[80] UNIDO (2008), *Public Goods for Economic Development*, United Nations Industrial Development Organisation, Vienna, Austria, p. 7.

company that invests in innovation develops new technology while other companies can use it without paying for it, thus creating an appropriability problem. The social value of technology may be greater than its private values, but this does not provide sufficient incentive for firms to develop and transfer new technologies, resulting in underinvestment in innovation and commercialisation of technologies. In the long run, technological products will be undersupplied in the markets, making citizens worse off, which is socially inefficient.

In comparison with other technologies, the number of persons that might benefit from the wide application of ESTs is much larger, as "the whole world is expected to be the beneficiary".[81] ESTs are thus recognised as global public goods. Accordingly, the international community generally agrees to promote and finance "the access to and the transfer of environmentally sound technologies and corresponding know-how, in particular to developing countries, on favourable terms, including concessional and preferential terms, as mutually agreed".[82]

2.3.2 *Failures in the Markets for Technology and IPRs as a Policy Response*

The bulk of technology transfer occurs through business transactions in private markets, as noted in Section 2.2.2.2. These markets for technology are inherently subject to failures that affect the decisions regarding whether, what, where and how to transfer, leading to price distortion and inefficient allocations of resources. Often, market failure is associated with information asymmetries, externalities, or non-competitive markets. Their presence means that the market system does not result in a social optimum, and thus provides a prima facie reason for public intervention. At the international level, the problems of market failure become more acute. As a result of failures in private markets for technology, the flows of international technology transfer to developing countries are inadequate for their competitive and social needs, suggesting that "the volume (and quality) of technology transfers is well below optimal".[83]

---

[81] IPCC (2000), *IPCC Special Report: Methodological and Technological Issues in Technology Transfer*, Cambridge University Press, p. 58.

[82] Agenda 21, chap. 34, Transfer of Environmentally Sound Technology, Cooperation and Capacity-building, UN Documents Cooperation Circles, para. 14 (b), available at www.un-documents.net/a21-34.htm

[83] Keith E. Maskus (2004), *Encouraging International Technology Transfer*, ICTSD and UNCTAD Issue Paper No. 7, Geneva, Switzerland, p. 15.

Information asymmetry occurs when one party to a transaction has more or superior information about markets and values than the other. Both innovation and the transfer of new technologies are subject to asymmetric information problems. The large uncertainty associated with the returns on innovation investment often results in too little R&D. Technology transfer involves the flow of information between those who know its true value and those who do not know before buying it. At the global level, technology transfer "faces additional hurdles: information problems are more severe and the enforcement of contracts is more difficult to achieve".[84] To reduce information asymmetry, public intervention is needed to "increase the certainty with which technology owners can signal the true value and characteristics of their inventions to buyers without excessive concerns about losing that value without compensation".[85] On the other hand, the policy should "increase access of local buyers to the international stock of knowledge about available technologies".[86] The international IP, in particular patent, system can to some extent remedy this market failure as it allows the innovator to disclose the technological information without losing the power to exclude others from using it. This will be further elaborated in Section 4.3.1.2 on patent-induced information disclosure.

In the context of technology transfer, externalities occur if "market priced transactions do not fully incorporate all the benefits and costs associated with transactions among economic agents".[87] As Hoekman et al. (2004) observed, a major share of benefits to technology recipient countries is likely to arise from "uncompensated spillovers, wherein technological information is diffused into the wider economy and the technology provider cannot extract the associated economic value".[88] Such positive externalities stem from the "public goods" nature of technology itself.[89] Incentives for technological advancement should be in place when externalities in new technologies create a high marginal

---

[84] Kamal Saggi (2004), *International Technology Transfer to Developing Countries*, Commonwealth Secretariat, p.58.

[85] Keith E. Maskus (2004), *Encouraging International Technology Transfer*, ICTSD and UNCTAD Issue Paper No. 7, Geneva, Switzerland, p. 16.

[86] Ibid.

[87] Frances Stewart and Ejaz Ghani (1991), How Significant Are Externalities for Development? *World Development*, vol. 19, no. 6, pp. 569–94, at p. 569.

[88] Bernard M. Hoekman, Keith E. Maskus and Kamal Saggi (2005), Transfer of Technology to Developing Countries: Unilateral and Multilateral Policy Options, *World Development*, vol. 33, no. 10, pp. 1587–1602, at p. 1590.

[89] A positive externality occurs when a transaction benefits a party external to the transaction. An important example is the positive spillovers associated with R&D. The cost of an externality is a negative externality, for instance, unpriced pollution.

social benefit. Besides a subsidy policy to encourage positive externalities, (temporary) legal monopolies, that is, IP protection, are designed to counterbalance this perceived market failure.

Market power is the ability to increase prices of a good or service "above competitive levels and profitably keep them there".[90] Because of economies of scale in R&D and production and strong IPR protection, the high technology market is generally characterised by imperfect competition. Owners of new (high) technologies "typically have substantial market power, resulting from lead time and fixed (sunk) costs, or from the granting of IPRs".[91] To prevent the abuse of market power, many developing countries passed technology transfer laws during the 1970s to control the undesirable terms and conditions in technology transfer agreements.[92] Specialised technology transfer regulations have not delivered the hoped for improvements in access to technologies while the negotiations of the code of conduct ultimately failed[93] (see also Section 3.2.2). With the adoption of the TRIPS Agreement, many developing countries have introduced the same sort of competition rules that developed countries had put in place before 1990s to curb the abuse of market power.[94]

Overall, the markets for technology are inherently subject to failures such as information asymmetries, externalities, or non-competitive markets. Intellectual property rules are primary policy interventions to correct these failures in the markets for technology.[95]

2.3.3 *The Concept of IP Rights and Their Justification*

Intellectual property rights are defined as "the rights given to persons over the creations of their minds. They usually give the creator an exclusive right over

---

[90] Jeffrey L. Harrison (2003), *Law and Economics in a Nutshell*, 3rd edn, Eagan, MN: West Publishing, p. 261.

[91] Bernard Hoekman and Beata Smarzynska Javorcik (2006), *Global Integration and Technology Transfer*, World Bank and Palgrave Macmillan, p. 12.

[92] UNCTAD (2001), *Transfer of Technology*, UNCTAD Series on Issues in International Investment Agreements, New York and Geneva: United Nations, p. 94.

[93] Peter Muchlinski (2007), *Multinational Enterprises and the Law*, 2nd edn, New York: Oxford University Press, p. 451.

[94] As observed by Papadopoulos (2010), by 2008, 111 countries had competition rules in place while 81 of them adopted their competition law after 1991; see Anestis S. Papadopoulos (2010), *The International Dimension of EU Competition Law and Policy*, Cambridge University Press, p. 15.

[95] Keith E. Maskus and Ruth L. Okediji (2010), *Intellectual Property Rights and International Technology Transfer to Address Climate Change: Risks, Opportunities and Policy Options*, ICTSD's Programme on IPRs and Sustainable Development, Issue Paper No. 32, International Centre for Trade and Sustainable Development, Geneva, Switzerland, p. 12.

the use of his/her creation for a certain period of time".[96] This definition implies that IPRs are exclusive rights, often of a temporary nature, and granted by the State according to national or domestic law. Exploitation of IPRs without the permission of rights holders may constitute infringement. IPRs, however, may have the potential to limit local imitation of the new technology and raise its price, thereby restricting its availability, at least temporarily.[97]

There has been a lot of debate over the implicit rationale for IPRs.[98] Traditionally, the debate has been principally between two philosophical foundations: utilitarian theories and rights-based property theories. These two approaches are, however, neither contradictory nor mutually exclusive. The rights-based property theorists believe that creators have a natural property right to control their work.[99] In their view, "property in intellectual works is primarily a matter of justice rather than of public policy" and enjoying a property right over one's creative work is a natural right and, arguably, also a human right.[100] In contrast, utilitarian theorists consider that IPRs create incentives for innovation and creativity.[101] This incentive theory "focuses on promoting the general public good, not on placing the individual creator as an

---

[96] WTO, What Are Intellectual Property Rights?, available at www.wto.org/english/tratop_e/trips_e/intel1_e.htm

[97] See, e.g., R. Radhakrishnan and S. Balasubramanian (2008), *Intellectual Property Rights: Text and Cases*, New Delhi, India: Anurag Jain for Excel Books, at p. 249; Simon Walker (2001), The TRIPS Agreement, Sustainable Development and the Public Interest, Discussion Paper, IUCN, Gland, p. x.

[98] As Pugatch (2006) observed, there are "four dimensions in which the patent debates took place: (1) the natural property right in ideas; (2) the just reward to the inventor; (3) the best incentive to invent and (4) the best incentive to disclose secrets" whereas Prof. Fisher William argues that IP rights can be viewed through four political lenses: labour theory; utility theory, personality theory and social planning theory. See Meir Perez Pugatch (2006), *The Intellectual Property Debate: Perspectives from Law, Economics and Political Economy*, Cheltenham, UK: Edward Elgar Publishing, p. 2; William Fisher (2001), Theories of Intellectual Property, in Munzer (ed.), *New Essays in the Legal and Political Theory of Property*, Cambridge University Press, pp. 168–200.

[99] See, e.g., Peter S. Menell (2000) argues that the non-utilitarian theorists emphasise creator's moral rights to control their work (see Peter S. Menell (2000), Intellectual Property: General Theories, in Bouckaert and De Geest (eds.), *Encyclopaedia of Law and Economics*, Cheltenham, UK: Edward Elgar Publishing, pp. 129–88); Singer and Schroeder (2009) notices that creators and inventors have a natural right to IPR protection (see Peter Singer and Doris Schroeder (2009), *Ethical Reasons for Intellectual Property Rights Reform*, A Report (D 1.3) for INNOVA P2, CAPPE, University of Melbourne, p. 4).

[100] UNCTAD and ICTSD (2003), Intellectual Property Rights: Implications for Development, UNCTAD-ICTSD Project on IPRs and Sustainable Development, Policy Discussion Paper, ICTSD and UNCTAD, Geneva, Switzerland, p. 30.

[101] See, e.g., Graham Dutfield (2000), *Intellectual Property Rights, Trade, and Biodiversity: Seeds and Plant Varieties*, Oxford, UK: Earthscan Publications, p. 18; Marianne Levin (2011), The Pendulum Keeps Swinging – Present Discussions on and around the TRIPS Agreement, in

independent object entitled to a right".[102] Accordingly, the utilitarianism proponents advocate that public interest should come before the recognition of the natural right to property in intellectual production.[103]

Most continental European countries, "notably France and those countries whose legal systems are also based on the Napoleonic Code" have long favoured the notion of natural property rights in intellectual creations.[104] This is particularly true regarding "the protection of literary and artistic expression and publicity".[105] There is, however, substantial doubt on the natural rights-based justifications.[106] A basic argument against this justification is that intellectual creations are "mostly a social creation of collective, cumulative and interrelated work to which we all contribute and therefore no one person or firm should be able to claim the property".[107]

Natural property rights notwithstanding, "the strongest and most widely appealed to justification for intellectual property is a utilitarian argument

Kur (ed.), *Intellectual Property Rights in a Fair World Trade System: Proposals for Reform of TRIPS*, Cheltenham, UK: Edward Elgar Publishing, pp. 3–60, at p. 8.

[102] Lior Zemer (2007), *The Idea of Authorship in Copyright*, Farnham, UK: Ashgate Publishing, p. 12.

[103] Carla Hesse (2002), The Rise of Intellectual Property, 700 B.C.–A.D. 2000: An Idea in the Balance, *Daedalus*, pp. 26–45, at p. 43.

[104] John Howkins (2002), *The Creative Economy: How People Make Money from Ideas*, London: Penguin Press.

[105] Peter S. Menell (2000), Intellectual Property: General Theories, in Bouckaert and De Geest (eds.), *Encyclopaedia of Law and Economics*, Cheltenham, UK: Edward Elgar Publishing, pp. 129–88, at p. 156.

[106] See, e.g., Singer and Schroeder (2009), who elaborates three arguments against the natural rights based justifications: first, "IPRs can be shaped in myriad ways, each specifying differently their mode of acquisition, scope or duration"; second, "like ordinary property rights, IPRs often clash with other important natural rights, such as the right to life"; and third, "IPRs are not compatible with the very natural-law understanding of property rights adduced to support them" (see Singer and Schroeder (2009), *Ethical Reasons for Intellectual Property Rights Reform*, A Report (D 1.3) for INNOVA P2, CAPPE, University of Melbourne, pp. 4–5); Peter Drahos (1999) argues that unlike other natural rights, such as the right to life and liberty, "intellectual property rights exist for a limited period of time, or their continued existence is subject to requirements of registration", see Peter Drahos (1999), Intellectual Property and Human Rights, *Intellectual Property* , 3rd series, pp. 349–71.

[107] Birgitte Andersen (2006), *Intellectual Property Rights: Innovation, Governance and the Institutional Environment*, Cheltenham, UK: Edward Elgar Publishing, p. 114; Meir Perez Pugatch (2006) quoted *The Economist*, issued in 1850, stating that "before the inventors can establish the right of property in their inventions, they ought to give up all the knowledge and assistance they have derived from the knowledge and inventions of others. That is impossible, and the impossibility shows that their minds and their inventions are in fact, parts of the greater mental whole of society". See Meir Perez Pugatch (2006), *The Intellectual Property Debate: Perspectives from Law, Economics and Political Economy*, Cheltenham, UK: Edward Elgar Publishing, at p. 3.

based on providing incentives".[108] The incentive-based utilitarian theory is perceived to be the dominant foundation of the IP system in the Anglo-American legal tradition.[109] For instance, the US Constitution grants Congress the power to enact patent and copyright laws with the explicit aim to "promote the Progress of Science and useful Arts".[110] This utilitarian purpose is supposed to be achieved through "securing for limited times to authors and inventors the exclusive right to their respective writings and discoveries".[111]

From the utilitarian standpoint, granting inventors, authors or artists a temporary exclusive right to prevent others from reproducing and selling their works is an appropriate means to foster innovation and creativity, leading to a correspondingly optimal amount of social utility.[112] According to UNCTAD and ICTSD (2003), this contention is based on two assumptions: first, it assumes that "the greater the quantity of inventions and creative works eventually released to the public domain, the more the public benefits"; and second, it presupposes that IP rights incentivise people to create more intellectual products.[113] As discussed in Section 2.3.1, the "free-rider" problem associated with intellectual products, which are public goods by nature, may lead to underinvestment in innovation and creation. Therefore, without IP protection, the amount of such wealth would be below its optimal level, that is, lower than the level we would achieve if there was IP protection.[114] In other words, "wealth is optimized or at least increased", by granting temporary monopolies that allow IP holders to recover their initial R&D investments

---

[108] Edwin C. Hettinger (1989), Justifying Intellectual Property, *Philosophy & Public Affairs*, vol. 18, no. 1, pp. 13–52, at p. 47.

[109] See, e.g., Adam D. Moore (2003), Intellectual Property, Innovation, and Social Progress: The Case against Incentive Based Arguments, *Hamline Law Review*, vol. 26, no. 3, pp. 602–28, at p. 606.

[110] US CONST., Art. I, Sect. 8, cl. 8. This clause is sometimes referred to as the IP Clause, the Copyright and Patent Clause, the "Science and Useful Arts Clause" and the Authors and Inventors Clause.

[111] US CONST., Art. I, Sect. 8, cl. 8.

[112] See, e.g., Peter S. Menell (2000), Intellectual Property: General Theories, in Bouckaert and De Geest (eds.), *Encyclopaedia of Law and Economics*, Cheltenham, UK: Edward Elgar Publishing, pp. 129–88, at p. 129; UNCTAD and ICTSD (2003), Intellectual Property Rights: Implications for Development, UNCTAD-ICTSD Project on IPRs and Sustainable Development, Policy Discussion Paper, ICTSD and UNCTAD, Geneva, p. 30; Adam D. Moore (2003), Intellectual Property, Innovation, and Social Progress: The Case against Incentive-Based Arguments, *Hamline Law Review*, vol. 26, no. 3, pp. 602–28, at p. 611.

[113] UNCTAD and ICTSD (2003), Intellectual Property Rights: Implications for Development, UNCTAD-ICTSD Project on IPRs and Sustainable Development, Policy Discussion Paper, ICTSD and UNCTAD, Geneva, Switzerland, p. 30.

[114] Stephan N. Kinsella (2008), *Against Intellectual Property*, Ludwig von Mises Institute, p. 18.

or make a profit large enough to induce such investment."[115] The advocates of the utilitarian justification thus perceive granting limited rights to creators and inventors as a necessary condition for promoting the creation of intellectual works.[116]

Pursuant to this view, patents, copyrights, trade secrets and trademarks, although with different flavours, can be essentially viewed as "incentives to create".[117] Yet, the ongoing expansion of IPRs has caused much debate over the incentive effects of IPRs on innovation and technology transfer. Nevertheless, the precise role of IPR protection in innovation and transfer of technologies is context specific, depending on characteristics of different technology sectors and circumstances of countries, in particular, their level of technological development. Sections 4.3 and 4.4 address how and to what extent protection of IPRs, especially that of patents, influences development and transfer of ESTs. The following section uses literature review and empirical studies to examine the global distribution of innovation and international transfer of ESTs.

2.4 THE GLOBAL DISTRIBUTION OF INNOVATION AND INTERNATIONAL TRANSFER OF ESTS: EVIDENCE TO DATE

To better appreciate the impact of the global IPR regime on innovation and transfer of ESTs, it is necessary to know who creates and owns ESTs and who the major technology recipients are. This section, drawing on a growing body of literature and corroborated by original empirical analysis, examines the global distribution of the innovation of ESTs in particular, and the direction of international transfer of ESTs between countries.

2.4.1 *Literature Review: Who Owns ESTs and Who Are the Major EST Transferees?*

The general view arising out of the literature appears to be that the innovation of ESTs is highly concentrated in developed countries and that such

---

[115] Ibid.
[116] See, e.g., Adam D. Moore (2003), Intellectual Property, Innovation, and Social Progress: The Case against Incentive-Based Arguments, *Hamline Law Review*, vol. 26, no. 3, pp. 602–28, at p. 611; Intellectual Property, *Stanford Encyclopedia of Philosophy*, available at http://plato .stanford.edu/entries/intellectual-property/
[117] Giovanni B. Ramello (2010), Intellectual Property, Social Justice and Economic Efficiency: Insights from Law and Economics, in Flanagan and Montagnani (eds.), *Intellectual Property Law: Economic and Social Justice Perspectives*, Cheltenham, UK: Edward Elgar Publishing, pp. 1–23, at p. 3.

technologies are rarely transferred to developing countries, and when transferred, they primarily go to a handful of emerging countries.[118] A number of empirical studies have provided evidence substantiating this view.

A study conducted by Dechezlepretre et al. (2011), titled *Invention and Transfer of Climate Change – Mitigation Technologies: A Global Analysis*, used data from the EPO Worldwide Patent Statistical Database (PATSTAT)[119] to examine the dynamics, distribution and international transfer of patented inventions between 1978 and 2005 in thirteen climate-mitigation technology classes. The targeted technologies included seven renewable energy technologies (wind, solar, geothermal, marine energy, hydropower, biomass, and waste to energy), methane destruction, climate-friendly cement, thermal insulation in buildings, heating, electric and hybrid vehicles, and energy-efficient lighting.

Dechezlepretre et al. (2011) found that nearly 90 per cent of all inventions in climate-mitigation technology between 2000 and 2005 were concentrated in the top twelve countries: nine Organisation for Economic Co-operation and Development (OECD) countries (Japan, United States, Germany, South Korea, Australia, France, UK, Canada, the Netherlands) and three emerging countries (China, Russia, Brazil). The top three countries – Japan, Germany and the United States – together accounted for 60 per cent of the total technological innovation for climate change mitigation, but the innovation performance of certain emerging economies, particularly China and Russia, is far from being negligible.[120] Yet, taking into account the value of inventions, the innovation performance of emerging countries – in particular China and Russia – becomes much less impressive.[121] As Dechezlepretre et al. (2011) observed, emerging economies such as China and Russia innovate, but their

---

[118] See, e.g., Daniel K. N. Johnson and Kristina M. Lybecker (2009), Challenges to Technology Transfer: A Literature Review of the Constraints on Environmental Technology Dissemination, *Colorado College Working Paper* 2009–07, p. 6; Wei Zhuang (2011), Intellectual Property Rights and Transfer of Clean Energy Technologies, *International Journal of Public Law and Policy*, vol. 1, no. 4, pp. 384–401, at p. 397; Antoine Dechezlepretre, Matthieu Glachant, Ivan Hascic, Nick Johnstone and Yann Meniere (2011), Invention and Transfer of Climate Change-Mitigation Technologies: A Global Analysis, *Review of Environmental Economics and Policy*, vol. 5, no. 1, pp. 109–30, at p. 124.

[119] According to Dechezlepretre et al. (2011), "PATSTAT is unique in that it covers more than eighty patent offices and contains over [60] million patent documents. It is updated biannually". Patent documents are categorised using the international patent classification codes, developed by the WIPO, and some national classification systems. See Dechezlepretre et al. (2011), p. 113.

[120] Dechezlepretre et al. (2011), pp. 115–16.

[121] Dechezlepretre et al. (2011) referred to those inventions with patents filed in several countries as high-value inventions. See Dechezlepretre et al. (2011), p. 116.

inventions tend to be "of relatively minor economic value".[122] This is consistent with Zhuang's (2013) findings, which underline that the patent inventions owned by Chinese entities generally embody lower levels of innovation and economic value than those possessed by developed countries' entities.[123]

This study uses international patenting, that is, an inventor residing in one country seeks patent protection in another country, to measure technology transfer, on the grounds that "patenting provides the exclusive right to commercially exploit the technology in the country where the patent is filed".[124] In the view of Dechezlepretre et al. (2011), maintaining a patent is costly; inventors seek patent protection in a country because they plan to use the technology locally.[125] This approach (i.e. using international patenting to measure technology transfer) was also used by other scholars such as Eaton and Kortum (1999)[126] and Lanjouw and Mody (1996).[127] To the extent that international patenting protects the commercialisation of the patented technologies and the patents are worked locally, international patenting can be used to measure the transfer of technologies.

Through examining the distribution of climate-mitigation technology flows between OECD and non-OECD countries from 2000 to 2005, Dechezlepretre et al. (2011) found that climate-mitigation technology was exchanged mostly between developed countries (about 73 per cent), while transfer between developing countries was almost non-existent (around 1 per cent). Despite an increase, technology flows from OECD to non-OECD economies accounted for only 22 per cent of all transfers of climate-mitigation technology. Yet, climate mitigation technology flows to non-OECD countries mostly

[122] Dechezlepretre et al. (2011), p. 117.
[123] Wei Zhuang (2013), Evolution of the Patent System in China, in Abbott et al. (eds.), *Emerging Markets and the World Patent Order*, Cheltenham, UK: Edward Elgar Publishing, pp. 155–80, at p. 157.
[124] Dechezlepretre et al. (2011), p. 121.   [125] Ibid.
[126] Jonathan Eaton and Samuel Kortum (1999), International Technology Diffusion: Theory and Measurement, *International Economic Review*, vol. 40, no. 3, pp. 537–70, at p. 539 (through relating the decision to patent an invention internationally to the cost of patenting in a country and to the expected value of patent protection in that country, thus inferring "the direction and magnitude of the international diffusion of technology from data on international patenting, productivity, and research" and further noting that "international patenting reflects the link between the sources and uses of innovations").
[127] Jean Olson Lanjouw and Ashoka Mody (1996), Innovation and the International Diffusion of Environmentally Responsive Technology, *Research Policy*, vol. 25, pp. 549–71, at p. 569 (finding that "The correspondence between sources of equipment and sources of foreign patents in developing countries suggests (although it does not prove) that most of the patents in such countries are intended to protect export markets").

concerned fast-growing economies, in particular China, which accounts for about three-quarters of such transfers.[128]

A report by the UK think tank Chatham House (2009), entitled: *Who Owns Our Low Carbon Future? Intellectual Property and Energy Technologies*, relying on the International Patent Classification (IPC) system, presented data on the global patent ownership and deployment rate for six clean energy technologies – wind, solar PV, concentrated solar power (CSP), biomass, cleaner coal and carbon capture – for the period 1976 to 2006.[129]

The Chatham House study pointed out that across the six technologies, the top ten reported locations of patents assignees or owners were primarily OECD countries, with the United States in the lead, followed by Germany, Japan, Denmark and South Korea.[130] China was an exception as it placed fourth across the six sectors by this measure and had a significant share in all except carbon capture technology.[131] Yet, as the report suggested, the ultimate ownership of the local technological and innovation capacities may have a quite different geographical distribution, as some patents are registered by the local subsidiaries of parent companies based in another country. For instance, most patents "originating" from China are in most cases filed by foreign subsidiaries, as evidenced by China's low share of "parent companies of patent owners that have more than four patents at the time of filing".[132]

In the view of Lee et al. (2009), companies also seek patent protection in potential markets, where they intend to invest, license or sell, so as to reduce future competition. The composition of patent-filing destinations thereby pro- vides an indication of commercially attractive markets for foreign inventors.[133] Through analysing the composition of patent-filing destinations, the Chatham House Report found that most FDI, licensing and sales were likely to be concentrated in a few developed country markets, with China on the rise as a patent-filing destination.[134] Despite the difference in the scope of the technologies targeted, the Chatham House Report reached similar conclu- sions to Dechezlepretre et al. (2011) by concluding that technological devel- opment and transfer in the six selected technologies primarily took place within the OECD countries and companies whereas much had been made of the fast growth in innovation capacities and market destinations in emerging countries such as Brazil, China and India.[135] This conclusion is

---

[128] Dechezlepretre et al. (2011), p. 122.
[129] Bernice Lee, Ilian Iliev and Felix Preston (2009), *Who Owns Our Low Carbon Future? Intellectual Property and Energy Technologies*, A Chatham House Report, Royal Institute of International Affairs.
[130] Ibid., p. 14.   [131] Ibid.   [132] Ibid., p. 15.   [133] Ibid.   [134] Ibid., p. 16.
[135] Ibid., p. viii.

further confirmed by the findings of the UNEP, EPO and ICTSD Report (2010) entitled *Patents and Clean Energy: Bridging the Gap between Evidence and Policy.*[136]

Based on a technology mapping study, a new taxonomy for clean energy technologies (CETs) is being established in order to derive patent data. UNEP, EPO and ICTSD (2010) found that patenting in selected CETs fields was dominated by OECD countries whereas a number of emerging economies showed specialisation in individual sectors. The leading six countries – Japan, the United States, Germany, Korea, the UK and France – accounted for almost 80 per cent of all patent applications in the clean energy technologies reviewed (i.e. solar, wind, ocean, geothermal, hydropower, biomass technologies), each showing leadership in different sectors for the period 1978 to 2007.[137] UNEP, EPO and ICTSD (2010) explained that this data reflected "similar trends when compared with the total patent filings for all technologies by country".[138]

The study also discussed trends in patenting by inventors from some selected countries in other jurisdictions. It found that most patent-filing activity took place among the leading patenting countries such as Japan, the United States, Germany, Korea, France and the UK. Within this group, inventors from Japan and the United States, followed by the UK, France and Korea, own the highest numbers of claimed priority patents filed in China, suggesting that China is considered an important market or a strong competitor. However, Chinese inventors did not have a large number of patents filed first in China and then in any of the top patenting countries.[139] This finding is consistent with the conclusion of Dechezlepretre et al. (2011) and Lee et al. (2009), showing that patent filing in emerging countries (particularly China) was significant but such priority patents were mainly owned by foreign companies.

UNEP, EPO and ICTSD (2010) questioned the reasonableness of using patent filing in at least two countries as an indicator of technology transfer in Dechezlepretre et al. (2011) and Lee et al. (2009), by arguing that: first, patent disclosure or even the sale of a patented technology does not equate to technology transfer in the traditional sense; second, patent filings are often made in another country "for defensive purposes, such as to preserve competitive advantage in a particular market or to be able to license the technology"; moreover, patents may not fully disclose a technology in such a manner that "it can be practised, developed or improved locally".[140]

---

[136] UNEP, EPO and ICTSD (2010), *Patents and Clean Energy: Bridging the Gap between Evidence and Policy*, Munich, Germany: Mediengruppe Universal, p. 9.
[137] Ibid.   [138] Ibid., p. 33.   [139] Ibid., p. 49.   [140] Ibid.

Based on this argumentation and given the relatively weak innovation and technological capacities and the lack of a sound competition regime in developing countries, the ratio of technology flows to developing countries calculated by Dechezlepretre et al. (2011) and Lee et al. (2009) can be exaggerated. Through conducting the licensing survey, UNEP, EPO and ICTSD (2010) revealed that there was overall little CET out-licensing activity towards developing countries; and when the licensing agreements had been entered into, the main beneficiaries were companies in China, India, Brazil and Russia.[141] However, given the difficulties of obtaining relevant data on licensing activities when the licensing agreements are confidential,[142] the survey outcome has its limits.

The survey carried out by UNEP, EPO and ICTSD (2010) found that only 5 per cent of interviewed technology owners had frequently licensed their technologies to entities based in developing countries, and 12 per cent had done so occasionally. In the vast majority of cases (83 per cent), technology owners had either not (58 per cent) or rarely (25 per cent) entered into licensing agreements with users in developing countries during the past three years.[143] Notably, engagement in licensing or other IP-based activities in developing countries was concentrated in emerging countries such as China (25 per cent), India (17 per cent), Brazil (12 per cent) and Russia (10 per cent) which all constitute vibrant markets and/or potential competitors.[144]

All empirical studies have some limitations: first, all the studies discussed in this section focus on a subset of ESTs *inter alia* those in the areas of wind, solar, ocean, biomass and carbon storage, thereby only partially reflecting the current patent trends in emerging ESTs; second, some methodologies can have drawbacks, for instance, the licensing surveys are quite subjective and the patent-counting methods based on the IPC alone can be problematic, as it may be difficult to categorise new technologies within existing schemes due to "their overlapping nature" or as a consequence of "disagreements on terminology";[145] and third, the patent data used in the studies is relatively outdated with the data from 2007 being the most recent. Moreover, indicators of "technology transfer" such as the filing of a patent in at least two countries can be challenged at a conceptual level. This is because filing a patent in a country does not necessarily lead to a transfer of technology to that country. For instance, companies may file patents in a country without working the patent locally.

---

[141] Ibid., p. 64.
[142] This is the rule applicable to almost all licensing agreements in a business setting.
[143] UNEP, EPO and ICTSD (2010), p. 58.   [144] Ibid.   [145] Ibid., p. 65.

Despite the above-mentioned limitations, a similar conclusion arises out of the literature: innovation and development of selected ESTs are highly concentrated in developed countries (around 80 per cent); emerging countries such as China, Brazil, Russia and India have owned a significant amount of patents in selected ESTs yet the economic value of their invention is generally relatively low. International transfer of ESTs primarily occurs between developed countries whereas ESTs are seldom transferred to developing countries, in particular LDCs. Among developing countries, emerging countries (China in particular) are the main beneficiaries in terms of patent filing and out-licensing destinations.

2.4.2 *Empirical Study: Global Distribution of Innovation and International Transfer of ESTs*

This section seeks to add value to the current literature in at least three ways. First, in contrast to previous work, the present study covers more recent data and also takes advantage of time series to inquire into a possible relationship with the introduction of the TRIPS Agreement; second, the involved ESTs covered by this study extend beyond select clean energy technologies, covering almost all climate-related ESTs;[146] and third, the indicator used for international technology transfer is the charges for the use of IPRs. This section attempts to answer the following questions: which countries are major EST creators? Which countries derive income from IPRs? How does the TRIPS Agreement influence the trend of technology transfer?

2.4.2.1 High Concentration of EST innovations as Indicated by Patent Filing under PCT

This book finds that innovation of ESTs, as measured by patent filing under the Patent Cooperation Treaty (PCT) by inventors residing in the same

---

[146] OECD REGPAT Database has established a new classification of climate-related ESTs, including technologies relating to energy generation from renewable and non-fossil sources, combustion technologies with mitigation potential (e.g. using fossil fuels, biomass, waste, etc.), technologies specific to climate change mitigation, technologies with potential or indirect contribution to emissions mitigation, emissions abatement and fuel efficiency in transportation, energy efficiency in buildings and lighting. Note: the group of selected environmental-related technologies identified by OECD also includes general environmental management technologies but they are not directly climate change related; therefore, the following data analysis will not consider this category of environmental technologies. See Patents by Technology: Patents in Environment-related Technologies, OECD. Stat Extracts, available at http://stats.oecd.org/index.aspx?queryid=29068

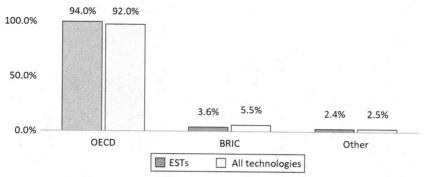

FIGURE 2.1: Share of claimed priority patents of ESTs vs. all technologies under PCT (1999–2011)
Source: OECD REGPAT Database, author's calculations.

country, is concentrated in developed countries whereas developing countries hold a marginal share of world EST patents. Based on OECD data,[147] EST patent applications under the PCT by inventors residing in OECD countries constitute 94 per cent of all EST patents filed under the PCT during the period 1999 to 2011 (see Figure 2.1). The six leading countries – the United States, Japan, Germany, France, UK and Korea – account for 78 per cent of world total of EST patents. Those of non-OECD countries comprise only 6 per cent, out of which Brazil, India, China and Russia (BRIC) account for 3.6 per cent. The ratio of China's ESTs as a share of the world total ESTs for the period of 1999 to 2011 is 2.5 per cent. As shown in Figure 2.2, BRIC patenting activity in the field of ESTs slightly increased from 1999 to 2011. These figures confirm earlier findings of the literature.

The concentration of EST patenting activities mirrors overall global patenting trends in all fields of technologies, as found by UNEP, EPO and ICTSD (2010).[148] Indeed, this study (see Figure 2.1) finds that the total patent application filed by OECD countries under the PCT (1999–2011) is 92 per cent of the world total. BRIC countries account for only 5.5 per cent with China constituting 3.9 per cent. These figures reflect the fact that technology innovation is highly concentrated in OECD countries. Moreover, OECD countries appear to be more specialised in developing ESTs compared to non-OECD countries, because OECD's total share in patents is 92 per cent and 94 per cent in EST patenting whereas BRIC's total share amounts to 5.5 per cent compared to 3.6 per cent in EST patenting (see Figure 2.1).

---

[147] OECD Patent Databases, Innovation in Science, Technology and Industry, OECD website, available at www.oecd.org/sti/inno/oecdpatentdatabases.htm.
[148] UNEP, EPO and ICTSD (2010), p. 9.

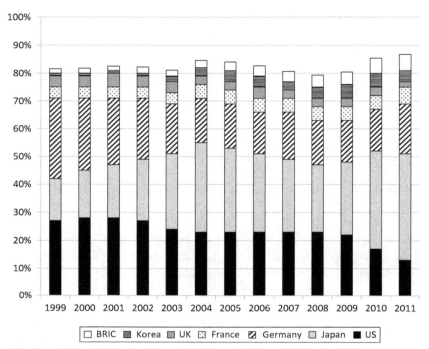

FIGURE 2.2: The patenting trend as measured by annual share of claimed priority patents filed under the PCT in the EST fields from 1999 to 2011
Source: OECD REGPAT Database, author's calculations.

The unbalanced global pattern of innovation of ESTs partially derives from the asymmetries in global R&D investment. As pointed out by Gaillard (2010), in 2005, the OECD countries accounted for 78 per cent of global R&D expenditure whereas developing countries accounted for a growing but minor proportion of global R&D.[149] Asia (without Japan) accounts for 19 per cent, 11.8 per cent corresponds to China alone, while Latin America accounts for 2.4 per cent, the near and Middle East 1.2 per cent and Africa 0.7 per cent.[150]

[149] Jacques Gaillard (2010), Measuring Research and Development in Developing Countries: Main Characteristics and Implications for the Frascati Manual, *Science, Technology & Society*, vol. 15, no. 1, pp. 77–111, at p. 95; see also Carlos M. Correa (2012), *Mechanisms for International Cooperation in Research and Development: Lessons for the Context of Climate Change*, Research Paper No. 43, Geneva: South Centre, p. 5.

[150] Jacques Gaillard (2010), Measuring Research and Development in Developing Countries: Main Characteristics and Implications for the Frascati Manual, *Science, Technology & Society*, vol. 15, no. 1, pp. 77–111, at p. 96.

Therefore, the concentration of innovation in OECD countries is not in itself surprising, as it mirrors the global distribution of R&D investment.

2.4.2.2 The Direction of International Technology Transfer – Which Countries Are Deriving Income from IPRs?

Unsurprisingly, the concentration of technologies has led to a significant volume of international technology transfer, as indicated by the large flows of licence fees and royalties at the international level. This study uses World Bank data on charges for the use of IPRs, which are payments and receipts between residents and non-residents, for the period of 1986 to 2012.[151] IPRs include patents, trademarks, copyrights, trade secrets, industrial processes and designs. Licensing of some IPRs, such as trademarks, generates revenue but does not necessarily lead to technology transfer. Yet, various studies show that patents and trade secrets account for the bulk of royalty receipts and payments.[152] Therefore, the flows of licence fees and royalties can roughly reflect the transfer of technologies.

As shown by Figures 2.3 and 2.4, in the period 2005 to 2011, around 80 per cent of payments are made by OECD countries, whereas around 98 per cent is paid to OECD countries. The United States is the largest recipient of IPR income, accounting for 50 per cent of world receipts, whereas its payments only account for around 15 per cent of world payments. Developing countries are net IPR importers, with payments accounting for around 20 per cent and revenue around 2 per cent.

Important conclusions that can be drawn are that developing countries are net technology importers, with BRIC countries being the main

---

[151] Charges for the use of intellectual property, payments (BoP, current US dollars), World development indicators, the World Bank, available at http://data.worldbank.org/indicator/ BM.GSR.ROYL.CD

[152] Marshall Reinsdorf and Matthew J. Slaughter (2009), *International Trade in Services and Intangibles in the Era of Globalization*, University of Chicago Press, p. 16; Carlo A. Robbins (2009), Measuring Payments for the Supply and Use of Intellectual Property, in Reinsdorf and Slaughter (eds.), *International Trade in Services and Intangibles in the Era of Globalization*, University of Chicago Press, pp. 139–71, at p. 162 (showing that IP-licensing receipts for the use of industrial processes protected by patents and trade secrets account for 55.1 per cent of world royalty receipts); Athreye Suma and Yang Yong (2011), Disembodied Knowledge Flows in the World Economy, *WIPO Economic Research Working Papers*, no. 3, p. 10 (noting that "Although many types of activities can earn royalties, the authors' calculations based on US data from the Bureau of Economic Analysis (which have the finest breakdown on the different categories of royalty revenue) suggest that industrial processes [protected by patents and trade secrets] and computer software account for over 70 per cent of all royalty receipts and payments").

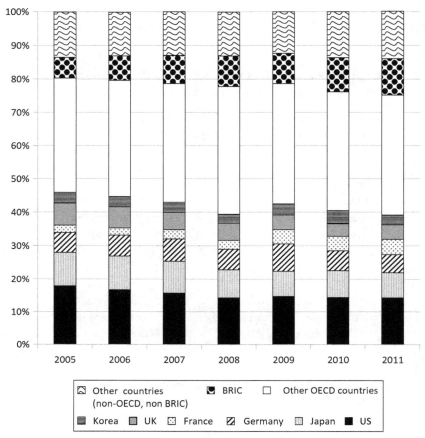

FIGURE 2.3: Share of charges for the use of intellectual property, payments (BoP, current US$) (2005–2011)
Source: World development indicators, the World Bank, calculated by author.

recipients among them and international technology transfer is mainly occurring among OECD countries. This data is not EST-specific. However, given that ESTs involve most fields of technologies and the lack of technology transfer to developing countries in general, it can be inferred that the transfer of ESTs to developing countries is far from being adequate to respond to the need for mitigating climate change.[153] This conclusion is consistent with the findings of the literature dealt with in Section 2.4.1.

---

[153] Different factors such as tax minimisation strategies used by firms may affect the accuracy of the findings.

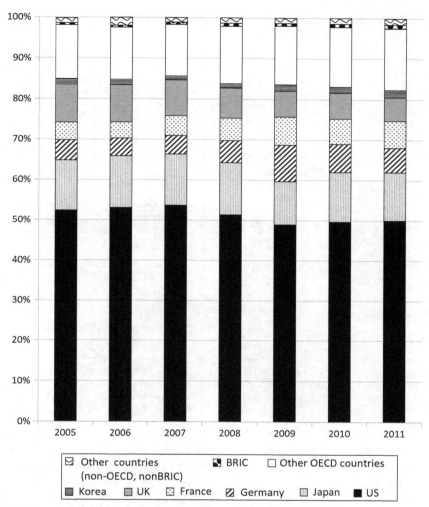

FIGURE 2.4: Share of charges for the use of IP, receipts (BoP, current US$) (2005–2011)
Source: World development indicators, the World Bank, calculated by author.

2.4.2.3 The Strengthening of IPRs and the Rise of Revenue Transfer

As shown in Figure 2.5, which displays the trend of annual net incomes arising from licence fees and royalties for all technologies between 1986 and 2012, the surge of annual net income flows to OECD countries largely coincided with the strengthening of IPRs.[154] The impact of the financial crisis can be

---

[154] The TRIPS Agreement entered into force on 1 January 1995. Developed country members have had to comply with all of the provisions of the TRIPS Agreement since 1 January 1996.

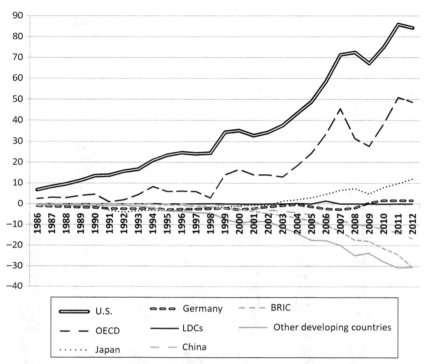

FIGURE 2.5: The trend of annual net incomes from licensing fees and royalties of all technologies (1986–2012, in current billion US dollars)
Source: World Development Indicators, (World Bank), author's calculations.

discerned: in 2008 and 2009, OECD countries' net income from IPRs went down while developing countries' net payments stagnated for one year in 2008. Nonetheless, revenue transfer trends continued unabated after 2009.

The United States in particular comes out as the largest gainer in terms of net income from IPRs, around USD 85 billion in 2012. In other words, the US is the largest exporter of IPRs. This can explain why the United States has been adamantly pushing strong IPR protection in different fora for negotiation. Germany, commonly known for its innovation prowess, does not gain on a net basis, according to the balance of payment accounting techniques of

Developing countries and economies in transition from central planning did not have to apply most provisions of the TRIPS Agreement until 1 January 2000. Some developing countries delayed patent protection for pharmaceutical products (and agricultural chemicals) until 1 January 2005. Most new members who joined after the WTO was created in 1995 have agreed to apply the TRIPS Agreement as soon as they joined. See Articles 65 and 66 of the TRIPS Agreement.

the World Bank/IMF, which implies that German companies' payments for other countries' intellectual property rights is similar to the income gained from the international commercialisation of German IPRs. These figures would suggest that countries such as Germany could be more inclined to adopt a more balanced approach to IPR protection.

Developing countries' payments for the use of IPRs increased significantly, especially since 2000 when their transition period for TRIPS implementation expired.[155] Similar trends can be discerned for BRIC and developing countries other than LDCs. It can be seen that the strengthening of IPRs has led to an increase in revenue transfer from developing countries to developed countries. It is noted that LDCs' net incomes from licensing fees and royalties are almost zero (see Figure 2.5). One reason is that LDCs are still in the transition period to becoming TRIPS compliant. Most importantly, the poorest countries attract few technologies, largely due to their weak technological base and poor market conditions. In contrast, the payments made by the BRIC countries account for almost 50 per cent of the payment by all developing countries (see Figures 2.3 and 2.5). Therefore, strict IPR protection for emerging economies may, to a certain extent, help them access more advanced technologies through market-based channels while this may not be the case for poorer developing countries.

The implications of increased revenue transfers are twofold: on the one hand, to a certain extent, it indicates that the technological catching-up process for developing countries has become more costly since the adoption of the TRIPS Agreement as strong IPR protection prevents them from free-riding technologies developed by industrialised countries.[156] This finding has been well-documented in previous research done by scholars such as Kim (2003) and Zaman (2013).[157] On the other hand, it suggests that with the

---

[155] The transition period for LDC provided for in paragraph 1 of Article 66 of TRIPS has been extended until 1 July 2021 (see Decision of the Council for TRIPS of 11 June 2013: Extension of the Transition Period under Article 66.1 for Least Developed Country Members, WTO Doc. IP/C/64, 12 June 2013, at p. 1).

[156] This finding is based on the presumption that technologies are patented in the country at issue.

[157] Zaman Khorsed (2013), The TRIPS Patent Protection Provisions and Their Effects on Transferring Climate Change Technologies to LDCs and Poor Developing Countries: A Critical Appraisal, *Asian Journal of International Law*, 3, pp. 137–61, at p. 145 (stating that "TRIPS ... does not allow developing countries to have unfettered freedom to use non-market channels [imitation and reverse engineering] that the developed countries had previously used"); Kim Linsu (2003), *Technology Transfer and Intellectual Property Rights: The Korean Experience*, UNCTAD-ICTSD Project on IPRs and Sustainable Development, Issue Paper No. 2, ICTSD and UNCTAD, Geneva, Switzerland, p. 8 (finding that "the economic consequences of strong IPR protection for products ... are devastatingly costly for aggressive large and small local firms in developing countries that depend on imitative learning and find that their growth stifled").

strengthening of IPRs, international technology transfer (as indicated by the flows of licence fees and royalties) has increased. This means that strong IP protection expands the market-based international technology transfer. This is consistent with the findings of various scholars such as Maskus (2005) and Falvey and Foster (2006).[158] Indeed, without high standards of IP protection to ensure that MNCs can extract rents from their creations, up-to-date high technologies may not be transferred to developing countries. Nevertheless, whether the transfer of technology to developing countries rises or falls as a result of TRIPS depends on several factors such as the level of their techno-logical development and market conditions.

[158] See, e.g., Keith E. Maskus (2005), Using the International Trading System to Foster Technology Transfer for Economic Development, *Michigan State Law Review*, vol. MMV, pp. 219–41, at p. 240; Falvey Rod and Foster Neil (2006), The Role of Intellectual Property Rights in Technology Transfer and Economic Growth: Theory and Evidence, *UNIDO Working Papers*, Vienna, Austria, p. 51.

3

International Legal Framework Governing IPRs, Innovation and Transfer of Technologies, Including ESTs

3.1 INTRODUCTION

IPR regimes have long been seen as "the classical policy instrument" to influence the generation, diffusion and transfer of technology.[1] The initial IP rules governing innovation and transfer of technology were perceived in the 1960s and 1970s to serve the interests of industrialised countries and IP rights holders.[2] As net technology-importing countries, the then developing countries claimed that they had suffered from many cases of patent abuse, especially by MNCs, such as "the non-working of patents by foreigners, the restrictive practices in licensing agreements, [and] the payment of high royalties".[3] Thus they considered that the granting of IP rights in their markets "favoured the commercial strategies of foreign enterprises over national interests".[4]

Thus, as observed by Deere (2009), in the 1970s, when the global oil crisis shifted the power dynamics in their favour, developing countries seized the opportunity to incorporate their reformist agenda into a broader call for fairer international economic regulations at the UN.[5] They demanded the New International Economic Order (NIEO) approach to regulate innovation and

---

[1] UNCTAD (2001), *Transfer of Technology, UNCTAD Series on Issues in International Investment Agreements*, New York and Geneva: United Nations, p. 18.

[2] See, e.g., UNCTAD (1974), *The Role of the Patent System in the Transfer of Technology to Developing Countries*, UN Doc. TD/B/AC.11/19, p. 139.

[3] See, e.g., Andrea Koury Menescal (2005), Changing WIPO's Ways? The 2004 Development Agenda in Historical Perspective, *The Journal of World Intellectual Property*, vol. 8, no. 6, pp. 761–96, at p. 764.

[4] Carolyn Deere (2009), *The Implementation Game: The TRIPS Agreement and the Global Politics of Intellectual Property Reform in Developing Countries*, Oxford University Press, p. 43.

[5] Ibid., p. 44.

transfer of technology with a view to promoting their interests and acquiring the technologies on more favourable terms. The best-known efforts to introduce such regulations included: (1) the revision of the Paris Convention for the Protection of Industrial Property and (2) the creation of an international code of conduct for the transfer of technology (TOT Code) that was responsive to the needs of developing countries.[6] The TOT Code was designed to encourage technology transfer to developing countries under more favourable conditions whereas the revision of the Paris Convention aimed to improve developing countries' access to patented technologies, in particular.

Beginning in the 1970s and lasting until the mid-1980s, these initiatives ultimately failed due to the firm opposition of the technologically advanced countries who sought to remove many of the restrictions on technology transfer and to strengthen the protection of IPRs worldwide. In the meantime, many developing countries lost their interest in NIEO. The increased globalisation, and the continuous liberalisation of trade and FDI regimes shifted the widespread suspicion that existed in 1970s towards the operation of MNCs to "a more welcoming attitude".[7] Controversies of the past regarding the role of IP in the transfer of technology to developing countries were thus superseded by the new focus on "how to make such systems efficient and useful instruments for encouraging innovation and diffusion of technical knowledge".[8]

Led by the United States and heavily influenced by MNCs, a new regime aiming to loosen technology transfer restrictions and set minimum standards of IPR protection was put in place in the multilateral trading system in the 1980s. Through incorporating minimum standards of IP protection and the

---

[6] The Programme of Action on the Establishment of a NIEO provided that "all efforts should be made: to formulate an international code of conduct for the transfer of technology corresponding to needs and conditions prevalent in developing countries"; see Programme of Action on the Establishment of a New International Economic Order, UN General Assembly Resolution, A/RES/S-6/3203, 1 May 1974, Article IV. Other efforts include a code of conduct for transnational corporations, a set of rules and principles on restrictive business practices.

[7] Surendra J. Patel, Pedro Roffe and Abdulqawi A. Yusuf (2001), *International Technology Transfer: The Origins and Aftermath of the United Nations Negotiations on a Draft Code of Conduct*, Kluwer Law International, p. xxiii.

[8] Pedro Roffe (1998), Control of Anti-Competitive Practices in Contractual Licences under the TRIPS Agreement, in Correa and Yusuf (eds.), *Intellectual Property and International Trade: The TRIPS Agreement*, Kluwer Law International, pp. 261–96, at p. 262; the author noticed the 1975 UN report on "the Role of the Patent System in the Transfer of Technology to Developing Countries" (TD/B/AC.11/19/Rev.1), jointly prepared by the UN Department of Economic and Social Affairs, UNCTAD Secretariat and the WIPO; he also noticed that at the UNCTAD IX Conference governments from developed and developing countries acknowledged that "Intellectual property is an essential component of an environment conducive to the creation and international transfer of technology".

technology innovation and transfer objectives, TRIPS has become the "centre-piece of the global system of rules" and institutions governing the generation and transfer of technology.[9] The extent to which TRIPS may contribute to technology innovation and transfer depends on how it is structured in order to address the inherent tension that exists between strong IP protection and access to technology.

With the culmination of the Uruguay Round of negotiations, the countries realised that major global environmental challenges such as climate change and ozone depletion cannot be tackled by action within national boundaries alone. Instead, developed countries needed the developing countries to cooperate, and thus "EST transfer became the proverbial carrot that would have to assure this cooperation".[10] Meanwhile, the Rio Earth Summit – one of the most important global environmental initiatives – held in 1992 viewed the transfer of ESTs to developing countries as a significant instrument for sustainable development. Under the impetus of the Rio Summit as well as the results of the UNCED, the term "technology transfer" became a core element of international environmental treaties introduced since the 1990s, such as the UNFCCC and the Convention on Biological Diversity (CBD).

This chapter examines the international legal framework governing innovation and transfer of technology, starting with a brief introduction of the revision of the Paris Convention and the creation of an UNCTAD Code of Conduct, and carries out a more detailed analysis of IP rights and technology transfer under TRIPS. It ultimately considers the EST transfer provisions of the UNFCCC and briefly discusses the interface between IPRs and innovation and transfer of ESTs in the climate change context.

3.2 THE NIEO APPROACH TO REGULATE INNOVATION AND TRANSFER OF TECHNOLOGY

At the request of developing countries in the 1970s, the United Nations General Assembly (UNGA), in a number of its resolutions, proclaimed the right of every country to benefit from advances and developments in science and technology.[11] The 1974 Declaration on the Establishment of a New

---

[9] Carolyn Deere (2009), *The Implementation Game: The TRIPS Agreement and the Global Politics of Intellectual Property Reform in Developing Countries*, Oxford University Press, p. 1.

[10] Gaetan Verhoosel (1998), Beyond the Unsustainable Rhetoric of Sustainable Development: Transferring Environmentally Sound Technologies, *The Georgetown International Environmental Law Review*, vol. 11, pp. 49–76, at p. 53.

[11] For instance, Charter of Economic Rights and Duties of States, UN General Assembly document, A/RES/29/3281, 12 December 1974, Article 13; Declaration on the Establishment of a

International Economic Order provides that one of the governing principles of a new economic order should be "promoting the transfer of technology and the creation of indigenous technology for the benefit of the developing countries".[12] Transfer of technology to developing countries was integrated as one of the fundamental tenets of the NIEO.[13] The revision of the Paris Convention and the creation of an international TOT Code are the best-known efforts to achieve the objective of technology transfer.

3.2.1 *The Revision of the Paris Convention*

3.2.1.1 Introduction to the Paris Convention

Rights arising out of patent and trademarks are governed by the principle of territoriality.[14] With the rise of free trade and globalisation, "the prevalent system of bilateral treaties based on the principle of material reciprocity soon became rather impractical".[15] International protection of IPRs became necessary when foreign inventors refused to attend the International Exhibition of Inventions in Vienna in 1873. Many inventions remained secret because their inventors were afraid that "their ideas would be stolen and exploited commercially in other countries".[16] As a response to this increasing unrest, the Paris

---

New International Economic Order, UN General Assembly document, A/RES/S-6/3201, 1 May 1974, Article 4.

[12] Declaration on the Establishment of a New International Economic Order, UN General Assembly document, A/RES/S-6/3201, 1 May 1974, Article 4.

[13] The main tenets of NIEO include: (1) Developing countries must be entitled to regulate and control the activities of multinational corporations operating within their territory. (2) They must be free to nationalize or expropriate foreign property on conditions favourable to them. (3) They must be free to set up associations of primary commodities producers similar to the OPEC; all other States must recognize this right and refrain from taking economic, military or political measures calculated to restrict it. (4) International trade should be based on the needs to ensure stable, equitable, and remunerative prices for raw materials, generalized non-reciprocal and non-discriminatory tariff preferences as well as transfer of technology to developing countries; and should provide economic and technical assistance without any strings attached.

[14] Each country having its own law independent of each other made it difficult for companies to obtain protection for their industrial property beyond national boundaries. Moreover, patent applications had to be filed almost at the same time in all countries to prevent loss of an invention's novelty. See WIPO (1997), *Introduction to Intellectual Property: Theory and Practice*, Kluwer Law International, p. 359.

[15] Martin Pflüger (2008), Paris Convention for the Protection of Industrial Property, in Cottier and Véron (eds.), *Concise International and European IP Law: TRIPS, Paris Convention, European Enforcement and Transfer of Technology*, Kluwer Law International, pp. 175–269, at p. 175.

[16] WIPO, *WIPO Treaties – General Information*, available at www.wipo.int/treaties/en/general/

Convention for the Protection of Industrial Property was adopted in 1883. It sought to "provide the stimulus for individuals to develop new technology and inventions and to share the innovations with others".[17]

The Paris Convention protects industrial property, that is, patents, utility models, industrial designs, trademarks, service marks, trade names, and appellations of origin, and it addresses unfair competition at the multilateral level.[18] It requires each contracting State to guarantee the same rights to the nationals of the other members as it provides to its own nationals in respect to their industrial property.[19] The Convention further establishes guidelines for national industrial property legislation and practices. For example, it allows the contracting State to grant compulsory licences on the ground of failure to work or insufficient working, subject to certain limitations.[20]

When the adoption of the Paris Convention was discussed, only twenty-two countries had their own national patent laws.[21] The Paris Convention entered into force in 1884 with just fourteen of them as signatories. They were: Belgium, Brazil, El Salvador, France, Guatemala, Italy, the Netherlands, Portugal, Serbia, Spain, Switzerland, Great Britain, Tunisia and Ecuador.[22] The United States joined in 1887. By the end of the nineteenth century, the Convention had nineteen members but only three of them were developing countries.[23] Almost all the then technology-rich countries were parties to the Paris Convention. It was only after World War II, when many developing countries gained independence and joined the Convention, that it significantly increased its membership. As of the present,[24] the Convention boasts 176 Contracting Parties.

3.2.1.2   The Demand for the Revision of the Paris Convention

The Paris Convention was developed at a time when most developing countries were politically dependent on the developed nations; hence, as UNCTAD (1974) observed, the Convention might not reflect the then

---

[17] Susan K. Sell (1989), Intellectual Property as a Trade Issue: From the Paris Convention to GATT, *Legal Studies Forum*, vol. 13, no. 4, pp. 407–22, at p. 408.

[18] Paris Convention for the Protection of Industrial Property, Article 1(2), 1883, WO020EN.

[19] Ibid., Articles 2 and 3.   [20] Ibid., Article 5.

[21] UNCTAD (1974), *The Possibility and Feasibility of an International Code of Conduct on Transfer of Technology*, UN Doc. TD/B/AC.11/22, at p. 26.

[22] El Salvador, Guatemala and Ecuador later denounced the Paris Convention to join again in 1990s.

[23] WIPO (1997), *Introduction to Intellectual Property: Theory and Practice*, Kluwer Law International, p. 360.

[24] 18 November 2016.

developing countries' interests.[25] It's noted that significant revisions of basic provisions further extended the rights of patent holders including by relaxing the requirements to work the patent.[26] When MNCs emerged as the major patent holders, they started to exploit patents to maximise their profits rather than worked the patent in the country concerned. According to the UNCTAD Report (1974), by the mid-1970s, about 84 per cent of the patents granted by developing countries were owned by foreigners or foreign entities; an overwhelming majority (about 90–95 per cent) of these patents had been used as import monopolies while only a small portion were actually used in production processes in these countries.[27] The study further found that as to the small number of foreign patents used in manufacturing processes in developing countries, the agreements concerning the use of patents through foreign investment or licensing arrangements frequently contained high royalty payments or restrictive practices.[28]

Frustrated by these documented patent abuses, some developing countries promulgated national remedial legislation to ensure a greater use of patents for manufacture and to arm the state with various measures to deal with patent abuses.[29] They no longer perceived patents as "an aid to their development by promoting technology transfer"[30] but as a barrier for them to access technology. As observed by UNCTAD (1974), the then developing countries criticised

---

[25] UNCTAD (1974), *The Possibility and Feasibility of an International Code of Conduct on Transfer of Technology*, UN Doc. TD/B/AC.11/22, p. 26.

[26] Regina A. Loughran (1981), The United States Position on Revising the Paris Convention: Quid Pro Quo or Denunciation, *Fordham International Law Journal*, vol. 5, no. 2, Article 7, pp. 411–439, at p. 418; as Loughran noticed, "when the Paris Union was founded, almost every member required the patentee to work his invention. Non-compliance resulted in forfeiture. However, it became evident that the patentee's right would be impeded by the obligation to work in all Union countries and as the ultimate motive of the Union is strengthening the patentee's position, the goal of revision became complete abolition of any requirement to work the patent".

[27] UNCTAD (1974), *The Role of the Patent System in the Transfer of Technology to Developing Countries*, UN Doc. TD/B/AC. 11/19, at pp. 123 and 139.

[28] Ibid.; with regard to restrictive practices, see 3.2.2.2.

[29] A typical example is Article 3 of the Mexican Law on Inventions and Trademarks (1976), providing that "the use of patent rights is expressly subject to the limits imposed by public interests"; see Paul S. Haar (1982), Revision of the Paris Convention: A Realignment of Private and Public Interests in the International Patent System, *Brooklyn Journal of International Law*, vol. 8, no. 1, pp. 77–108, at p. 84.

[30] Most countries that replied to the UN questionnaire on which the 1964 UNCTAD report, entitled *"The Role of Patents in the Transfer of Technology"*, was based said that patents were an aid to their development by promoting technology transfer. Only India, Lebanon and Cuba offered the opposite opinion; see Peter Muchlinski (2007), *Multinational Enterprises and the Law*, 2nd edn, New York: Oxford University Press, p. 444.

the international patent system as embodied in the Paris Convention for acting as "a reverse system of preferences granted to foreign patent holders" in their markets.[31] Thus they turned to the WIPO and demanded that a fundamental change be made to the international industrial property system in order to respond to their special needs.

The need for a fresh revision of the Paris Convention was emphasised by the UN. In its 1975 resolution, the UNGA decided to review and revise international conventions on industrial property to meet the special needs of the developing countries, in particular, by making these conventions "more satisfactory instruments for aiding developing countries in the transfer and development of technology".[32] Shortly thereafter, WIPO established the Ad Hoc Group of Governmental Experts on the Revision of the Paris Convention (hereafter referred to as "the Ad Hoc Group"). The Ad Hoc Group adopted a Declaration on the Objectives of the Revision of the Paris Convention in December 1975. The Declaration emphasised that the industrial property system should contribute to developing countries' industrialisation, including by promoting technology innovation and the actual working of inventions in developing countries, and by improving the conditions for technology transfer on fair and reasonable terms and conditions.[33]

3.2.1.3 The Unfinished Negotiations for the Revision

In the late 1970s, the WIPO Diplomatic Conference on the Revision of the Paris Convention was expected to consider the then developing countries' concerns "regarding their public interest and their ability to adopt appropriate legislation and policies in that interest".[34] It would decide whether the Paris Convention should maintain the status quo of patent protection or adopt a new system favouring developing countries' access to technologies.[35] Due to the opposition of the Group B countries (the then developed countries), in particular the United States, developing countries' efforts, triggered by an

---

[31] UNCTAD (1974), *The Role of the Patent System in the Transfer of Technology to Developing Countries*, UN Doc. TD/B/AC. 11/19, p. 139.

[32] Development and International Economic Co-operation, UN General Assembly Resolution, A/RES/S-7/3362, 16 September 1975, Part III, p. 3.

[33] WIPO (1979), *Diplomatic Conference on the Revision of the Paris Convention: Basic Proposals*, PR/DC/3, 25 June, WIPO, Geneva, p. 7.

[34] United Nations (1981), *Proceedings of the United Nations Conference on Trade and Development*, 5th Session, Manila, 7 May–3 June 1979, vol. 3, New York, p. 17.

[35] Regina A. Loughran (1981), The United States Position on Revising the Paris Convention: Quid Pro Quo or Denunciation, *Fordham International Law Journal*, vol. 5, no. 2, Article 7, pp. 411–39, at p. 412.

UNCTAD study dealing with the role of the patent system in the transfer of technology, to revise the Paris Convention to serve their own needs and interests more effectively, did not materialise. The negotiations for the revision of the Paris Convention that began in 1980 ended in deadlock.

The arguments made throughout the Conference were characterised by the intense disagreement over the purpose and function of the Paris Convention and the level of patent protection required to optimise technology transfer. The Group of 77 (G77) expected the Paris Convention to be developed into a more satisfactory instrument "for aiding developing countries in the transfer and development of technology".[36] However, the developed countries considered that the main purpose of the Paris Convention was not to promote technology transfer as suggested by the G77 but to protect various forms of industrial property.[37] Developing countries, because of their needs to acquire technology, disagreed with the developed nations' contention that patent protection facilitates rather than impedes developing countries' access to technology.[38] As Drahos et al. (2002) observed, it was almost impossible to reach consensus between the numerous states of the South, which were IP importers, and a few developed countries, which were IP exporters, particularly in the 1970s and 1980s when developing countries claimed that technological knowledge was "the common heritage of mankind".[39]

The fiercest debates took place over Article 5A of the Paris Convention dealing with remedies against non-working and other abuses of patents as developed countries and developing countries have competing demands concerning compulsory licensing. It is observed that the G77 insisted upon exclusivity as an option for compulsory licensing because they considered this would increase the quality of technology transfer, whereas developed countries contended that such proposals would have opposite effects.[40] In particular, the United States considered that developing countries' proposals for exclusive compulsory licensing would amount to a de facto expropriation

---

[36]   Development and International Economic Co-operation, UN General Assembly Resolution, A/RES/S-7/3362, 16 September 1975, part III, p. 3.

[37]   Regina A. Loughran (1981), The United States Position on Revising the Paris Convention: Quid Pro Quo or Denunciation, *Fordham International Law Journal*, vol. 5, no. 2, Article 7, pp 411–39, at p. 424.

[38]   Adrienne Catanese (1985), Paris Convention, Patent Protection, and Technology Transfer, *Boston University International Law Journal*, vol. 3, pp. 209–27, at p. 227.

[39]   Peter Drahos and John Braithwaite (2002), *Information Feudalism: Who Owns the Knowledge Economy?* Earthscan Publications, p. 112.

[40]   See, e.g., Susan K. Sell (1998), *Power and Ideas: North-South Politics of Intellectual Property and Antitrust*, State University of New York Press, p. 139.

of US IP rights.[41] These differences are irreconcilable because of the conflicting interests involved and their divergent ideologies. As Sell (1998) observed, developing countries favour strong state intervention in order to "enhance [their] bargaining power and rectify past injustices" while developed nations favour market mechanisms for technology transfer, depending on "minimal state interference for smooth functioning".[42]

At the revision conference, the United States and its allies defended the status quo and the level of international protection of industrial property as it is expressed in the Stockholm Act (1967) of the Paris Convention.[43] However, soon afterwards, the United States radically changed its position on IP protection due to the industry's desire to remain economically competitive, and went in the opposite direction than what was desired by the developing countries, that is, it sought even stronger IP protection.[44]

The significant North–South divide over intellectual property protection convinced the United States and its industries that they would not succeed in seeking higher patent standards under the auspices of WIPO in which the developing countries' blocs are strong. Thus they shifted their attentions to another forum, the General Agreement on Tariffs and Trade (GATT), where the United States was a more influential player. Commentators observed that it was largely due to the efforts of the United States and its industry community that trade-related aspects of intellectual property rights became the subject of multilateral trade negotiations.[45]

3.2.2 *The Unsuccessful Creation of an International Code of Conduct for the Transfer of Technology*

3.2.2.1 The Major Characteristics of the Latest Draft

The latest version of the Code was prepared in June 1985 and was regarded as "the high benchmark for a model of provisions espousing the 'regulatory'

---

[41] Peter Drahos and John Braithwaite (2002), *Information Feudalism: Who Owns the Knowledge Economy?* Earthscan Publications, p. 81.

[42] Susan K. Sell (1998), *Power and Ideas: North-South Politics of Intellectual Property and Antitrust*, State University of New York Press, p. 140.

[43] Hans Peter Kunz-Hallstein (1989), The United States Proposal for a GATT-Agreement on Intellectual Property and the Paris Convention for the Protection of Industrial Property, *Vanderbilt Journal of Transnational Law*, vol. 22, pp. 265–84, at p. 266.

[44] Susan K. Sell (1998), *Power and Ideas: North-South Politics of Intellectual Property and Antitrust*, State University of New York Press, p. 130.

[45] See, e.g., Peter Drahos (2002), *Developing Countries and International Intellectual Property Standard-Setting*, Commission on Intellectual Property Rights, Study Paper No. 8, p. 10.

approach to technology transfer" by the UNCTAD.[46] The major objective of the Code was to "establish general and equitable standards" as a basis for governing the relations among parties to transfer technology, showing due regard to their legitimate interests and the "special needs of developing countries".[47] A group of provisions were drafted to establish universally applicable standards, thus regulating technology transactions and the conduct of parties. They cover three main areas: (1) identification of "restrictive business practices" to be avoided in the transfer of technology transactions (Chapter 4 of the draft Code); (2) determination of responsibilities and obligations of parties in technology transactions (Chapter 5) and (3) rules governing the applicable law and settlement of disputes (Chapter 9).

The draft Code further recognises States' rights to regulate technology transfer and attempts to "facilitate the formulation, adoption and implementation of national policies, laws and regulations".[48] Chapter 3, dealing with national regulation of technology transfer transactions, specifies general criteria to be followed by States when adopting national regulatory measures. It requires that any importing country's measures should be applied "fairly, equitably, and on the same basis to all parties in accordance with established procedures of law and the principles and objectives of the Code".[49]

Special treatment in favour of developing countries was integrated into the specific objectives of the Code, so as to "increase their participation in world production and trade".[50] Chapter 6 provides for special treatment of the developing countries, and it urges developed countries to "facilitate and encourage the initiation and strengthening of the scientific and technological capacities of developing countries".[51]

Notably, recognition of the protection of intellectual property rights granted under national law is listed as a principle of the draft Code.[52] It provided that each country, before adopting legislation on the protection of intellectual property, should clarify its economic and social development needs, and should "ensure an effective protection of [intellectual] property rights granted under its national law".[53] This again demonstrates the direct and close

---

[46] UNCTAD (2001), *Transfer of Technology*, UNCTAD Series on issues in international investment agreements, New York and Geneva: United Nations, p. 52.

[47] Draft International Code of Conduct on the Transfer of Technology, at the close of the sixth session of Conference on 5 June 1985, Geneva, UN document, No. TD/CODE TOT/47, 20 June 1985, Chapter 2.

[48] Ibid., Chapter 2, 2.1 (vii) and 2.2 (ii).   [49] Ibid., Chapter 3, 3.2.

[50] Ibid., Chapter 2, 2.1 (v) and (vi).   [51] Ibid., Chapter 6, 6.1.   [52] Ibid., Chapter 2, 2.2 (viii).

[53] United Nations (1981), *Proceedings of the United Nations Conference on Trade and Development*, 5th Session, Manila, 7 May–3 June 1979, vol. 3, New York, p. 221.

correlation between the international protection of IPRs and the innovation and transfer of technologies. It also shows that developing countries started to realise the advantages and benefits of a functioning intellectual property system. Special treatment and increased bargaining power alone are insufficient for developing countries to participate fully in the global technology market, and they also need to protect intellectual property.

3.2.2.2 The Failure of the Code and Its Implications

The UN General Assembly, by its resolution 31/159 of December 1976, decided to convene a UN Conference, under the auspices of the UNCTAD, to negotiate a final draft of the Code and to take all decisions necessary for its adoption. The negotiation process began in 1978 and continued until the mid-1980s. Unfortunately, the formal negotiation process was suspended and no final agreement was ever reached. The consolidated text ultimately failed to reconcile the divergent positions taken by the participating parties. Four of the most hotly contested issues that were discussed by the different interest groups, included: first, the legal nature of Code and whether it should be binding or voluntary; second, the scope of its application;[54] third, the treatment of restrictive business practices, and finally, the applicable law and the settlement of disputes. A compromise had been reached regarding most draft chapters in the latest negotiation, with the exception of a number of issues relating to Chapter 4 on restrictive business practices and Chapter 9 on applicable law and the settlement of disputes.[55]

A majority of the member states never agreed on Chapter 4, which deals with the issue of restrictive practices. Fourteen restrictive practices, which prevent technology-receiving countries from extracting the maximum possible value from imported technologies, were identified, including: (1) grant-back

---

[54] For instance, the G77 proposed that the Code would cover all forms of technology transfer transactions, including those between parent companies and their subsidiaries in technology-acquiring countries, whereas the Group B considered that the Code would exclude the transfer between parent and subsidiary enterprises.

[55] There is no agreed draft of Chapter 9. The developing countries favoured a restrictive approach on choice of law under which and forum in which their disputes would be governed in order to "guarantee the application of mandatory national laws". (See Kevin E. Davis (2005), Regulation of Technology Transfer to Developing Countries: The Relevance of Institutional Capacity, *Law & Policy*, vol. 27, pp. 6–32, at p. 12); on the contrary, the Group B countries tended to give parties freedom to choose the proper law provided that it has a genuine connection with the transaction and favoured free choice of arbitration (see Peter Muchlinski (2007), *Multinational Enterprises and the Law*, 2nd edn, New York: Oxford University Press, p. 453).

provisions; (2) preventing the acquiring party from challenging the validity of patents involved in the transfer; (3) exclusive dealing; (4) restricting the freedom of the acquiring party to carry out research and development directed to adapt the transferred technologies to local conditions or to develop new products, processes or equipment; (5) "requiring the acquiring party to use personnel designated by the supplying party"; (6) price fixing; (7) restrictions on adaptations; (8) exclusive sales or representation agreements; (9) tying arrangements; (10) export restrictions; (11) restrictions on "territories, quantities, prices, customers or markets arising out of patent pool or cross-licensing agreements" and other arrangements; (12) restrictions on publicity; (13) "[r] equiring payments or imposing other obligations for continuing the use of industrial property rights" after their expiration and (14) restrictions after the expiration of arrangements.[56]

These restrictive practices are generally those of an anti-competitive nature. Countries could not reach an agreement on how to deal with the issue of restrictive practices. Studies show that the developed countries wished to control such restrictions under their antitrust laws and considered that such practices were "permitted when reasonable", whereas the G77 preferred to ban such restrictive practices outright, believing that these restrictions were unfair in and of themselves and represented "the result of undue influence by a strong supplying party over a weaker acquiring party".[57] Commentators have observed that the G77's disagreement stemmed from two primary concerns: first, a competition-based approach might allow technology suppliers to circumvent the Code because it was not likely to be adopted as a legally binding instrument; and second, developing countries felt that the word "reasonable" would "open the door to the supplying party to enable it to impose restrictions in an arbitrary manner in the face of the Code".[58]

---

[56] Draft International Code of Conduct on the Transfer of Technology, as at the close of the sixth session of the Conference on 5 June 1985, Geneva, UN document, No. TD/CODE TOT/47, 20 June 1985, Chapter 4.

[57] See, e.g., Wolfgang Fikentscher (1980), *The Draft International Code of Conduct on the Transfer of Technology: A Study in Third World Development*, Munich, Germany: Max Planck Institute for Foreign and International Patent, Copyright, and Competition Law, p. 71; Dennis Thompson (2001), An Overview of the Draft Code, in Patel, Roffe and Yusuf (eds.), *International Technology Transfer: The Origins and Aftermath of the United Nations Negotiations on a Draft Code of Conduct*, Kluwer Law International, pp. 51–75, at p. 62.

[58] See, e.g., Peter Muchlinski (2007), *Multinational Enterprises and the Law*, 2nd edn, New York: Oxford University Press, 2007, at p. 453; Dennis Thompson (2001), An Overview of the Draft Code, in Patel, Roffe and Yusuf (eds.), *International Technology Transfer: The Origins and Aftermath of the United Nations Negotiations on a Draft Code of Conduct*, Kluwer Law International, pp. 51–75, at p. 65.

Three main causes leading to the eventual failure of the participating states to agree upon a satisfactory Code have been identified. First, developed countries did not want to impose regulatory control over their MNCs' external commercial activities, and they insisted that the development and transfer of technology should be the result of business transactions between private parties "with minimal government interference".[59] Second, the United States did not see UNCTAD as "an appropriate negotiating forum" and was eager to move discussions over technology transfer into a more hospitable forum, such as the GATT.[60] Last but not least, pressing economic problems such as the debt crisis and a precipitous drop in foreign investment faced by developing countries in the late 1970s and early 1980s forced them to abandon their efforts to establish an international Code of Conduct for technology transfer.[61] As observed by Thomas (1999), "subsequent to the debt crisis, and often as a condition for debt relief", many developing countries' governments set out to liberalise their investment and external trade regimes in the 1980s, which included removing restrictions relating to technology transfer.[62] Meanwhile, many developing countries' policy-makers started to "blame strict laws for the lack of, and decline in, foreign investment" and began to loosen their regulatory control over foreign technology suppliers.[63]

The negotiation process for the draft TOT Code lasted more than ten years. It took so long that the negotiations lost their momentum and the political and economic context had changed. Even the initiators of the draft Code of Conduct – the developing country participants – ultimately abandoned their quest. Yet the eventual non-adoption of the Code did not lessen their concerns about impediments to the transfer of technology that were under discussion. These issues have remained a regular theme in multilateral

---

[59] Draft International Code of Conduct on the Transfer of Technology (1981), UN Doc. TD/CODE TOT/33, at p. 180.

[60] Susan K. Sell (1998), *Power and Ideas: North-South Politics of Intellectual Property and Antitrust*, State University of New York Press, pp. 101 and 102; the then US delegate felt that the UNCTAD Secretariat was not appropriately fulfilling its role as an "international civil service" but rather was acting as a "Third World Club".

[61] Ibid., p. 105.

[62] Thomas Chantal (1999), Transfer of Technology in the Contemporary International Order, *Fordham International Law Journal*, vol. 22, pp. 2096–111, at p. 2108; in Mexico, prior to the debt crisis, for instance, foreign investment regulation authorized the Mexican government to intervene in technology transfer agreements to prohibit "excessive" royalty payments and grant-back and tie-in provisions. As part of its post debt crisis liberalization, Mexico narrowed this authority significantly, giving foreign companies a much freer hand in designing technology transfer agreements.

[63] Susan K. Sell (1998), *Power and Ideas: North-South Politics of Intellectual Property and Antitrust*, State University of New York Press, p. 104.

discussions, as exemplified by the fact that the Multilateral Environmental Agreements (MEAs) concluded since the end of the 1980s often contain provisions on promoting technology transfer.

The Code negotiations continued to "inform, inspire and influence" the scope, content and approach of subsequent instruments relating to innovation and transfer of technologies.[64] When the TRIPS Agreement was negotiated, developing countries managed to add to the agreed text some legitimisation of their national control over anti-competitive licensing practices, e.g., Articles 8.2 and 40 of the TRIPS Agreement.[65] The negotiations have had a major influence on the evolution of national legislation relating to international technology transfer as well. As observed by Galal (2001), many developing countries have adopted or strengthened their national competition laws and institutions since the end of the TOT Code negotiations.[66]

3.3 INTELLECTUAL PROPERTY RIGHTS AND TECHNOLOGY TRANSFER UNDER THE TRIPS AGREEMENT

As the most comprehensive multilateral agreement on IP, the TRIPS Agreement attempts to strike a proper balance between creating incentives for innovation and ensuring competitive access to new technologies. It lays down a set of global minimum standards governing the scope, availability and use of IPRs with the aim of contributing to technological innovation and transfer of technology in a manner that benefits both technology producers and users.[67] This section begins with an introduction of the emergence of the TRIPS Agreement and then moves to the analysis of Members' commitments to global minimum IPR standards followed by a study of technology-transfer-oriented provisions in the TRIPS Agreement.

3.3.1 *The Emergence of the TRIPS Agreement*

Developed countries, led by the United States successfully integrated IP protection into the multilateral trading system in the 1980s, thereby shifting

---

[64] Surendra J. Patel, Pedro Roffe and Abdulqawi A. Yusuf (2001), *International Technology Transfer: The Origins and Aftermath of the United Nations Negotiations on a Draft Code of Conduct*, Kluwer Law International, p. xxiv.

[65] Essam E. Galal (2001), The Developing Countries' Quest for a Code, in Patel, Roffe and Yusuf (eds.), *International Technology Transfer: The Origins and Aftermath of the United Nations Negotiations on a Draft Code of Conduct*, Kluwer Law International, pp. 199–215, at p. 215.

[66] Ibid.   [67] See Articles 1 and 7 of the TRIPS Agreement.

the forum of discussion of trade-related aspects of IP law-making from WIPO to GATT.[68] Commentators observe that many factors have contributed to this forum shifting: the first relates to the pressure from IP-dependent MNCs such as Pfizer and Microsoft, who were worried about their loss of competitiveness and profits due to insufficient foreign IP protection.[69] Their increasing R&D costs as well as the growing levels of piracy and imitation had motivated them to lobby their respective governments to push for strong trade-oriented international IP protection.[70] Second, since the late 1970s, developed countries had shown increasing concern that WIPO treaties failed to adequately protect the interests of their technology-based industries,[71] and they feared that the institutional features of WIPO limited their capacity to impose stringent IP protection standards.[72] Last but not least, the United States was the "single most influential player" in the multilateral trading system where developing countries had limited leverage.[73] This would definitely facilitate the adoption of higher IP protection standards that the industrialised states favoured.

The multilateral trading system was established with the goal of liberalising international trade. Under Article XX(d) of the GATT, IP rights are

---

[68] See, e.g., Laurence R. Helfter (2004), Regime Shifting: The TRIPS Agreement and New Dynamics of International Intellectual Property Lawmaking, *The Yale Journal of International Law*, vol. 29, pp. 1–83, at p. 20.

[69] See, e.g., United States International Trade Commission (1988), *Foreign Protection of Intellectual Property Rights and the Effect on U.S. Industry and Trade*, Report to the US Trade Representative, Investigation No. 332-245, Under Section 332 (g) of the Tariff Act of 1930, USITC Publication 2065, Washington, D.C., at p. H-3 (concluding that "estimated worldwide losses to U.S. industry in 1986 from inadequate foreign protection of intellectual property rights would range from $43 billion to $61 billion").

[70] Robert W. Kastenmeier and David Beier (1989), International Trade and Intellectual Property: Promise, Risks, and Reality, *Vanderbilt Journal of Transnational Law*, vol. 22, pp. 285–307, at p. 286.

[71] UNCTAD and ICTSD (2005), *Resource Book on TRIPS and Development*, Cambridge University Press, at p. 3 (further noting that "the major concerns were that WIPO treaties did not in some cases establish adequate substantive standards of IPR protection and that the WIPO system did not provide adequate mechanism for enforcing obligations").

[72] See, e.g., Andrew J. Grotto (2004), Organizing for Influence: Developing Countries, Non-Traditional Intellectual Property Rights and the World Intellectual Property Organisation, in Armin, Rudiger and Christiane (eds.), *Max Planck Yearbook of United Nations Law*, vol. 8, no. 1, Martinus Nijhoff Publishers, pp. 359–82, at p. 362 (noting that "WIPO, can serve as the hub in a network of developing countries that helps them . . . build stronger coalitions, and produce specific policy recommendations that collectively strengthen their ability to resist new trade rules that are not in their development interests"); it is noted that WIPO has been a specialised agency of the UN since 1974 and is open to all the UN Members.

[73] Peter Drahos (2002), Developing Countries and International Intellectual Property Standard-Setting, *The Journal of World Intellectual Property*, vol. 5, no. 5, pp. 765–89, at p. 769.

recognised as an exception, that is, a legitimate barrier to free trade,[74] and substantive standards for IP protection were not part of the initial multilateral trading law. One initial controversial issue confronting GATT negotiators was whether IP rights were sufficiently related to trade liberalisation to justify their inclusion into the multilateral trading system. Several developed countries asserted that because inadequate protection of IPRs constituted "a major distortion of and impediment to trade", such rights should be dealt with in the GATT framework,[75] and thus comprehensive proposals specifying substantive issues on IPRs should be put forward.[76]

In contrast, developing countries argued that, under the 1986 Punta del Este Declaration,[77] the GATT negotiations should be limited to trade-related aspects such as "trade in counterfeit goods and anti-competitive practices in relation to IPRs".[78] They insisted that the substantive standards and principles of IP protection should be negotiated and implemented

---

[74] The exception was invoked in two GATT disputes: *United States – Imports of Certain Automotive Spring Assemblies* and *United States – Section 337 of the Tariff Act of 1930* where the importance of non-discrimination principle was stressed. For instance, Panel Report, *United States – Section 337 of the Tariff Act of 1930*, L/6439-36 S/345 (7 November 1989), GATT, para. 6.3 (concluding that "the Section 337 of the United States Tariff Act of 1930 is inconsistent with Article III: 4, in that it accords to imported products challenged as infringing US patents treatment less favourable than the treatment accorded to products of US origin similarly challenged, and that these inconsistencies cannot be justified in all respects under Article XX (d)").

[75] Abdulqawi A. Yusuf (1989), Developing Countries and Trade-Related Aspects of Intellectual Property Rights, in UNCTAD (ed.), *Uruguay Round: Papers on Selected Issues*, UN Publication, UN doc. UNCTAD/ITP/10, p. 187.

[76] See, e.g., Suggestion by the United States for Achieving the Negotiating Objective, Negotiating Group on Trade-Related Aspects of Intellectual Property Rights, including Trade in Counterfeit Goods, 20 October 1987, GATT Doc. MTN.GNG/NG11/W/14; Guidelines and Objectives Proposed by the European Community for the Negotiations on Trade-Related Aspects of Substantive Standards of Intellectual Property Rights, Negotiating Group on Trade-Related Aspects of Intellectual Property Rights, including Trade in Counterfeit Goods, 7 July 1988, GATT Doc. MTN.GNG/NG11/W/26; see also Jayashree Watal (2001), *Intellectual Property Rights in the WTO and Developing Countries*, Kluwer Law International, p. 22 (noting that "in October–November 1987 the US and other developed countries, notably Switzerland and Japan, signaled their decision to discuss substantive standards of IPRs ... by making detailed submissions on these matters ... The submission of the EC in November 1987 focused largely on issues relating to the enforcement of such rights").

[77] Draft Ministerial Declaration on the Uruguay Round, 20 September 1986, GATT Doc. MIN (86)/W/19, pp. 14–15. The second mandate for addressing counterfeit issues was "unequivocally mandatory", in comparison to the first one, which made the negotiations on new rules contingent upon "a criterion of appropriateness".

[78] Antony Taubman, Hannu Wager and Jayashree Watal (2012), *A Handbook on the WTO TRIPS Agreement*, Cambridge University Press, p. 6.

in WIPO.[79] Their resistance to incorporating substantive protection of IPRs in the GATT was, however, stymied by threats of unilateral trade sanctions and withdrawal of benefits under the Generalised System of Preferences (GSP) by major developed economies.[80]

In subsequent negotiations, developing countries argued that rigid IPR protection may lead to monopoly situations as well as to the abuse of IPRs, thereby impeding their access to up-to-date technologies.[81] They thus attached great importance to "public interest, exceptions, safeguards, balance of rights and obligations, freedom on scope and level of protection, and access to technology".[82] Developed countries, however, argued that strong IPR protection was essential for stimulating foreign investment flows and technology transfer to, and technological development in, developing countries.[83]

In 1990, a number of developed countries such as the European Community, the United States, Japan, Switzerland and Australia tabled draft legal texts envisaging a single and comprehensive TRIPS Agreement, called "Approach A". The "A" texts covered almost "all IP rights then in existence, even the seldom used *sui generis* protection for computer chips" and included detailed

---

[79] Status of Work in the Negotiating Group: Chairman's Report to the GNG, Negotiating Group on Trade-Related Aspects of Intellectual Property Rights, including Trade in Counterfeit Goods, 23 July 1990, GATT Doc. MTN. GNG/NG11/W/76, p.1.

[80] Jayashree Watal (2001), *Intellectual Property Rights in the WTO and Developing Countries*, Kluwer Law International, pp. 24–6 (noting that "In 1989, ... Brazil and India were identified as priority foreign countries under section "Super 301"; in September 1988, the USTR initiated an investigation into Argentina's pharmaceutical patent protection; In 1989, Thailand was placed on the priority watch list and lost substantive GSP benefits on account of inadequate protection and enforcement of IPRs").

[81] See, e.g., Submission from Brazil, Negotiating Group on Trade-Related Aspects of Intellectual Property Rights, including Trade in Counterfeit Goods, 31 October 1988, GATT Doc. MTN. GNG/NG11/W/30, pp. 3–5; Standards and Principles Concerning the Availability, Scope and Use of Trade-Related Intellectual Property Rights, Communication from India, Negotiating Group on Trade-Related Aspects of Intellectual Property Rights, including Trade in Counterfeit Goods, 10 July 1989, GATT Doc. MTN. GNG/NG11/W/37, p. 2 (arguing that "the essence of the [intellectual property] system is its monopolistic and restrictive characters; its purpose is not to 'liberalise', but to confer exclusive rights on their owners").

[82] Note by the Secretariat, Meeting of Negotiating Group of 5–6 January 1990, Chairman: Ambassador Lars E.R. Anell, Negotiating Group on Trade-Related Aspects of Intellectual Property Rights, including Trade in Counterfeit Goods, 27 February 1990, GATT Doc. MTN. GNG/NG11/18, para. 27.

[83] See, e.g., Suggestion by the United States for Achieving the Negotiating Objective, Negotiating Group on Trade-Related Aspects of Intellectual Property Rights, including Trade in Counterfeit Goods, 20 October 1987, GATT Doc. MTN.GNG/NG11/W/14, p. 2; Trade-Related Aspects of Intellectual Property Rights: Submission from the European Communities, Negotiating Group on Trade-Related Aspects of Intellectual Property Rights, including Trade in Counterfeit Goods, 14 November 1989, GATT Doc. MTN.GNG/NG11/W/49, p. 7.

provisions on enforcement of those rights.[84] In response, a group of developing countries[85] proposed another "legal" text, described as "Approach B". The "B" texts were "much more limited in scope, with few specific normative aspects", highlighting the need to maintain flexibility to achieve development objectives.[86] As observed by Watal (2001), it was, however, "far too general" to counter the detailed "A" texts and "could not form a sound basis" for negotiating the details of the Agreement.[87]

Despite the North–South disagreements over the forum and the content and scope of the TRIPS Agreement during the Uruguay Round negotiations, the TRIPS Agreement was adopted in 1994 and came into effect in 1995 with the establishment of the WTO. According to Gervais (2005), the Agreement largely mirrored the "A" text and as such it "essentially embodied norms that had been accepted by industrialized countries".[88] As a concession, two "B" text provisions – those with respect to "objectives" and "principles", that is, Articles 7 and 8 of TRIPS – were adapted and included in the main body of the Agreement.[89] The Agreement also provided other flexibilities and exceptions, e.g., Articles 13, 27, 29, 30, 31, 40 and 66.2 of TRIPS, to address developing countries' concerns, allowing them to balance private rights with public interest.

As part of a single undertaking, the TRIPS Agreement became a third pillar of the WTO Agreement (Annex 1C).[90] It applies to all WTO Members without exception and with almost no reservation possible.[91] Disputes arising

---

[84] Daniel J. Gervais (2005), Intellectual Property, Trade and Development: The State of Play, *Fordham Law Review*, vol. 74, pp. 505–35, at p. 508.

[85] Argentina, Brazil, Chile, China, Colombia, Cuba, Egypt, India, Nigeria, Peru, Tanzania and Uruguay, and subsequently also sponsored by Pakistan and Zimbabwe. See Communication from Argentina, Brazil, Chile, China, Colombia, Cuba, Egypt, India, Nigeria, Peru, Tanzania and Uruguay, 14 May 1990, GATT Doc. MTN.GNG/NG11/W/71.

[86] Daniel J. Gervais (2005), Intellectual Property, Trade and Development: The State of Play, *Fordham Law Review*, vol. 74, pp. 505–35, at p. 508.

[87] Jayashree Watal (2001), *Intellectual Property Rights in the WTO and Developing Countries*, Kluwer Law International, p. 33.

[88] Daniel J. Gervais (2005), Intellectual Property, Trade and Development: The State of Play, *Fordham Law Review*, vol. 74, pp. 505–35, at p. 508.

[89] Communication from Argentina, Brazil, Chile, China, Colombia, Cuba, Egypt, India, Nigeria, Peru, Tanzania and Uruguay, 14 May 1990, GATT Doc. MTN.GNG/NG11/W/71, pp. 7–8.

[90] The other two pillars are the GATT 1994 (covering rules for trade in goods) and the GATS (General Agreement on Trade in Services).

[91] Marrakesh Agreement, Article XVI:5. It should be noted that LDCs are not bound by the minimum IPR standards before their transitional period expires. The transitional period for LDCs provided for in paragraph 1 of Article 66 of TRPS has been extended until 1 July 2021.

from compliance with the TRIPS obligations are subject to the WTO's integrated dispute settlement procedures.[92]

3.3.2 *Global Minimum IPR Standards and Their Implications*

The TRIPS Agreement covers most forms of IPRs, including patents, copyright and related rights, trademarks, geographical indications, industrial designs, the layout designs (topographies) of integrated circuits, and undisclosed information including trade secrets and test data.[93] It has established a comprehensive set of universal minimum standards of protection and enforcement for virtually all types of IPRs, and extended its application to all WTO Members on a non-discriminatory basis.[94] Some commentators believe that the application of the principles of national treatment and most favoured nation (MFN) treatment to IP as well as the setting of universal minimum standards for the protection and enforcement of IPRs is aimed at "facilitating the transfer and dissemination of technology".[95]

3.3.2.1 Commitments to Global Minimum IPR Standards

It is well accepted that the TRIPS Agreement is a "minimum standards" agreement with respect to intellectual property rights.[96] The TRIPS Agreement intends to function as a minimum standards agreement by providing in Article 1.1 that:

---

[92] See Article 64 of TRIPS; DSU, Understanding on Rules and Procedures Governing the Settlement of Disputes, Marrakesh Agreement Establishing the World Trade Organisation, Annex 2, 1994.

[93] See Part II of the TRIPS Agreement; exceptions include protection for utility models. This is, however, covered by the Paris Agreement.

[94] See, e.g., Graeme B. Dinwoodie and Rochelle C. Dreyfuss (2012), *A Neofederalist Vision of TRIPS: The Resilience of the International Intellectual Property Regime*, Oxford University Press, p. 21 (noting that TRIPS "extended the geographical reach of protection by imposing intellectual property obligations on all members of the WTO including many developing countries that formerly recognized no such rights").

[95] See, e.g., Thomas Cottier and Pierre Véron (2011), *Concise International and European IP Law: TRIPS, Paris Convention, European Enforcement and Transfer of Technology*, 2nd edn, Kluwer Law International, p. 33.

[96] See, e.g., Denis Borges Barbosa (2010), Minimum Standards vs. Harmonization in the TRIPS Context: The Nature of Obligations under TRIPS and Modes of Implementation at the National Level in Monist and Dualist Systems, in Correa (ed.), *Research Handbook on the Protection of Intellectual Property under WTO Rules: Intellectual Property in the WTO*, vol. I, Edward Elgar, pp. 52–109, at p. 71; Panel Report, *Canada – Patent Term*, para. 6.87 (noting that "Article 1.1 confirms that the TRIPS Agreement is a minimum standards agreement in respect of intellectual property right").

Members may, but shall not be obliged to, implement in their law more extensive protection than is required by this Agreement, provided that such protection does not contravene the provisions of this Agreement.

As interpreted by Cottier et al. (2011), Members have "the obligation to implement the minimal standards" of trade-related IP protection provided in TRIPS while they have "the option to provide for more extensive protection" (so-called TRIPS-plus standards of protection).[97] In the view of Kur (2009), the TRIPS Agreement aimed to "create a 'floor' which member states may exceed, but from which they cannot retract".[98] The WTO panel in *China – Intellectual Property Rights* (2009) held that Article 1.1 clarified that "the provisions of the Agreement are minimum standards only, in that it gives Members the freedom to implement a higher standard, subject to a condition".[99] The condition imposed is that the additional level of IP protection shall not go against the provisions of TRIPS, in particular, the objectives and principles of the Agreement. In addition to this condition, as noted by Odman (2000), the extent of the freedom of Members to implement the TRIPS Agreement depends primarily on the policy space inherent in the mandatory provisions of the Agreement.[100]

The TRIPS Agreement lays down obligatory minimum standards for WTO Members, first, by incorporating the main substantive provisions of the pre-existing WIPO-administered Paris Convention and the Berne Convention for the Protection of Literary and Artistic Works (Berne Convention).[101] Second, the TRIPS Agreement introduces a considerable number of additional obligations on matters where pre-existing IP treaties are silent or were perceived as "being inadequate".[102] As observed by Watal (2001), for some developing countries, TRIPS covers new subject matter under pre-existing types of IP such as product patents for pharmaceuticals, food, chemicals or microorganisms; and "creates new categories of rights" such as reversal of burden of proof

---

[97] Thomas Cottier and Pierre Veron (2011), *Concise International and European IP Law: TRIPS, Paris Convention, European Enforcement and Transfer of Technology*, 2nd edn, Kluwer Law International, p. 10.

[98] Annette Kur (2009), International Norm-Making in the Field of Intellectual Property: A Shift towards Maximum Rules? *The WIPO Journal*, no. 1, pp. 27–34, at p. 27.

[99] Panel Report, *China – Intellectual Property Rights*, para. 7.513.

[100] Ayse N. Odman (2000), Using TRIPS to Make the Innovation Process Work, *The Journal of World Intellectual Property*, vol. 3, no. 3, pp. 343–71, at p. 346.

[101] The TRIPS Agreement does not include the provisions of the Berne Convention on moral rights; see Articles 2.1 and 9.1 of the TRIPS Agreement.

[102] Antony Taubman, Hannu Wager and Jayashree Watal (2012), *A Handbook on the WTO TRIPS Agreement*, Cambridge University Press, p. 11.

for process patentees.[103] Last but not least, the TRIPS Agreement obliges WTO Members to provide for effective enforcement mechanisms for IPRs. The TRIPS Agreement "significantly elevated the level of IP protection" beyond what was found in the then existing international conventions, thus occasionally being referred to as a "Berne-plus" or "Paris-plus" Agreement.[104]

In order to fulfil their treaty obligations, most WTO Members had to undertake extensive revisions of their domestic IP law, and judicial as well as administrative systems, thereby incurring significant economic and social costs, in particular, for developing countries.[105] The Council for TRIPS was established to monitor Members' compliance with their TRIPS obligations, including by collecting and reviewing national laws and regulations.[106] Under Article 64, a WTO Member may be challenged under the WTO dispute settlement procedure for an alleged failure to comply with the minimum standards for IP protection and enforcement.

One major consequence of the formal incorporation of IP into the multi-national trading system is that the basic principles of the system – national treatment and MFN treatment – automatically apply to the IP relations between WTO Members.[107] The Appellate Body, in *US – Section 211 Appropriations Act* (2002), has acknowledged the fundamental significance of the principles of national treatment and MFN treatment to ensuring the success of a global rules-based system for trade-related IP rights.[108] National treatment and MFN treatment are two different aspects of the non-discrimination principle. While the national treatment clause calls for equal treatment between foreign right holders and domestic ones, the MFN principle prevents

---

[103] Jayashree Watal (2001), *Intellectual Property Rights in the WTO and Developing Countries*, Kluwer Law International, p. 4.

[104] See, e.g., Jerome H. Reichman (1995), Universal Minimum Standards of Intellectual Property Protection under the TRIPS Component of the WTO Agreement, *The International Lawyer*, vol. 29, no. 2, pp. 345–88, at p. 347 (noting that "the TRIPS Agreement significantly elevates the level of protection beyond that found in existing conventions, as certainly occurs with respect to patents. . ."); Daniel J. Gervais (2007), The TRIPS Agreement and the Doha Round: History and Impact on Economic Development, in Yu (ed.), *Intellectual Property and Information Wealth: Issues and Practices in the Digital Age*, vol. 4, pp. 23–72, at p. 43 (noting that "TRIPS adjusted the level of intellectual property protection to what was the highest common denominator among major industrialized countries as of 1991").

[105] Laurence R. Helfer (2004), Regime Shifting: The TRIPS Agreement and New Dynamics of International Intellectual Property Law-making, *Yale Journal of International Law*, vol. 29, pp. 1–83, at p. 23.

[106] See Articles 63 and 68 of TRIPS.

[107] The preamble of TRIPS recognized the need for new rules and disciplines concerning "the applicability of the basic principles of GATT 1994".

[108] Appellate Body Report, *US – Section 211 Appropriations Act*, paras. 240 and 297.

discrimination between foreigners of different nationalities. National treatment has long been a cornerstone of international IP conventions and the world trading system.[109] Commentators observe that with the adoption of a national treatment clause complemented by a minimum standards requirement, TRIPS has introduced "an effective tool for harmonizing national legislation and tradition" on IPRs, which has codified different views on the need for and level of protection.[110]

Article 4 of the TRIPS Agreement has introduced the MFN obligation for the first time into multilateral IP treaty, requiring non-discrimination among foreign nationals. With regard to IP protection, "any advantage, favour, privilege or immunity" granted by a WTO Member to the nationals of any other Member either through bilateral agreement (e.g. "TRIPS-plus provisions") or unilateral regulation must be extended "immediately and unconditionally" to the nationals of all other Members, with limited exceptions.[111] One potential effect of such a principle within TRIPS would be to elevate the level of IP protection worldwide, which is not always a 'benefit' "in the sense that lower tariffs reduce trade barriers to countries that can take advantage of MFN" in a regime that depends on balancing the interests of IP producers and users.[112]

Having acknowledged that the TRIPS implementation is costly and time-consuming, WTO Members delayed the application of the universal IP standards imposed by TRIPS in whole or in part (with the exception of Articles 3, 4 and 5) to the extent that they benefited from transitional periods that varied in accordance with their respective development status. For example, developed WTO Members had a period of one year, expiring on 1 January 1996, to implement TRIPS whereas developing countries and economies in transition had an extra four years to meet the deadline.[113] In June 2013, WTO Members agreed to extend the deadline for LDCs to protect IP under TRIPS until 1 July 2021, "with a further extension possible when the time comes".[114]

---

[109] Ibid., para. 241.

[110] Peter-Tobias Stoll, Jan Busche and Katrin Arend (2009), *WTO: Trade-Related Aspects of Intellectual Property Rights*, vol. 7, Martinus Nijhoff, p. 151.

[111] See Article 4 of TRIPS.

[112] Graeme B. Dinwoodie and Rochelle C. Dreyfuss (2012), *A Neofederalist Vision of TRIPS: The Resilience of the International Intellectual Property Regime*, Oxford University Press, p. 103 (further stating that "the effect of one country raising the level of protection would be felt by every trader who sought to do business with that country"); it is difficult to apply MFN principle to IP related-FTA provisions as we do not exactly know what is an advantage or a favour in IP.

[113] See Article 65 of TRIPS; it is worth noting that new members acceding to the WTO such as China generally do not benefit from the transitional arrangements; furthermore, the WTO does not provide any official definition regarding the term "developing countries", which are generally defined based on the principle of self-declaration.

[114] Decision of the Council for TRIPS of 11 June 2013: Extension of the Transition Period under Article 66.1 for Least Developed Country Members, WTO Doc. IP/C/64, 12 June 2013.

Despite being temporary, the additional transitional periods for less developed countries reflects, to a certain extent, the special and differential treatment principle enshrined in the multilateral trading system.

3.3.2.2 The Implications of Global Minimum IPR Standards

The "positive integration" approach adopted by TRIPS through imposing numerous positive affirmative obligations on WTO Members to introduce both substantial and procedural standards for IPR protection has at least two significant legal implications: first, WTO Members can no longer exercise their national sovereignty that had been formally guaranteed to them by Article XX(d) of GATT to regulate intellectual property, provided that national laws are non-discriminatory or do not constitute "a disguised restriction of international trade" (chapeau of Article XX).[115] Second, it indicated a controversial shift from negative to positive integration in the WTO's approach to law-making. As Petersmann (2003) observed, the process and structure of GATT was "essentially based on 'negative' prohibitions of tariffs, non-tariff barriers, trade discrimination and other governmental trade distortions".[116] In contrast, the TRIPS Agreement prescribes international minimum standards for IP protection.

However, some scholars have questioned why it is that WTO law has provided positive obligations for IP protection rather than for competition, investment and environmental protection, all of which were left to Members' own legislative discretion together with IP under the GATT.[117] The positive integration of IP standards into the world trading system was essentially due to the powerful political and economic pressures from IP-based industries.[118] In the view of its advocate, in particular, the United States, EC, Japan and their IP industries, stronger international IP protection would increase, on a global

[115] Article XX "Subject to the requirement ... nothing in this Agreement shall be construed to prevent the adoption or enforcement by any contracting party of measures: ... (d) necessary to secure compliance with laws and regulations ... including ... the protection of patents, trademarks and copyrights, and the prevention of deceptive practices ..."; see also Jerome H. Reichman and David Lange (1998), Bargaining around the TRIPS Agreement: The Case for On-Going Public-Private Initiatives to Facilitate Worldwide Intellectual Property Transactions, *Duke Journal of Comparative & International Law*, vol. 9, pp. 11– 68, at p. 20.
[116] Ernst-Ulrich Petersmann (2003), From Negative to Positive Integration in the WTO: The TRIPS Agreement and the WTO Constitution, in Cottier and Mavroidis (eds.), *Intellectual Property: Trade, Competition and Sustainable Development*, The World Trade Forum, vol. 3, University of Michigan Press, pp. 21–52, at p. 22.
[117] Ibid., p. 27.
[118] See, e.g., Peter Drahos (1995), Global Property Rights in Information: The Story of TRIPS at the GATT, *Prometheus*, vol. 13, no. 1, pp. 6–19, at p. 16.

scale, incentives to invest in the research and development of new technologies and facilitate access to the latest emerging world technologies.[119] The
rationale behind this perception is that minimum global IP protection would
prevent the free-riding that the early trade-related IP negotiations aimed to
repress.[120] In order to achieve their goals, the drafters of TRIPS sought to
create a sweeping harmonisation of international IP standards at "relatively
high, rather than minimum levels" by elevating international standards of IP
protection and by introducing detailed enforcement standards that domestic
authorities must comply with.[121]

Logically, as Reichman et al. (1998) observed, the elevated IPR standards tend
to favour the interests of IP holders at the expense of users and consumers in
general, and in particular of those based in technology-importing countries.[122]
In effect, TRIPS has significantly increased the MNCs' freedom to decide
whether, when and where to export their innovative technologies or expand
their R&D efforts.[123] This enhanced bargaining power of technology producers
may be detrimental to the interests of technological users to the extent that the
producers may raise the price of their technologies or simply refuse to deal.

At the global level, the effects of stronger IP rights depend upon the
country's level of economic and technological development. According to
UNIDO (2008), for developed countries – those with advanced scientific and
technological capacities – the evidence suggests that strengthening IPRs
expedited their growth either through improved innovation or increased
diffusion and transfer of technology.[124] Indeed, as predicted by Doane
(1994), the United States was one major beneficiary of TRIPS and has
received significant benefit from it.[125] As shown in Section 2.4.2, an analysis

---

[119] See, e.g., Standards for Trade-Related Intellectual Property Rights: Submission from
Canada, 25 October 1989, GATT Doc. MTN.GNG/NG11/W/47, pp. 5–6; Submission by
United States at Meeting of 25 March 1987, 3 April 1987, GATT Doc. MTN.GNG/NG11/W/2,
p. 1.

[120] See, e.g., Jerome H. Reichman and David Lange (1998), Bargaining around the TRIPS
Agreement: The Case for On-Going Public-Private Initiatives to Facilitate Worldwide
Intellectual Property Transactions, *Duke Journal of Comparative & International Law*, vol. 9,
pp. 11–68, at p. 20 (noting that "the Agreement's minimum standards of intellectual property
protection inhibit free-riders from continuing to engage in wholesale duplication of vulnerable
knowledge goods without making any corresponding investment of their own").

[121] Ibid., at p. 20.   [122] Ibid., at p. 17.

[123] Daniel J. Gervais (2005), Intellectual Property, Trade and Development: The State of Play,
Fordham Law Review, vol. 74, pp. 505–35, at p. 506.

[124] UNIDO (2008), *Public Goods for Economic Development*, UNIDO, Vienna, p. 90.

[125] Michael L. Doane (1994), TRIPS and International Intellectual Property Protection in an Age
of Advancing Technology, *American University International Law Review*, vol. 9, no. 2,
pp. 465–97, at p. 494.

based on the World Bank data of charges for the use of IP (2005–2012) suggests that many developed countries are the major beneficiaries of TRIPS in terms of the "enhanced value" of their intellectual property, with the annual benefit to the United States estimated at around $70 billion.[126]

In assessing the costs and benefits stemming from TRIPS for developing countries, the literature has identified two reasons why the TRIPS Agreement is in the long-term interests of developing countries: first, a high level of IP protection benefits developing countries in the long run because "piracy is detrimental to [their] long-term domestic competitive strategies";[127] and second, with the strengthening of IP rights, developing countries are likely to benefit from increased technology transfer by means of trade, FDI and licensing.[128]

However, TRIPS may be detrimental to the interests of developing countries partly because their adoption of strong IPR standards may not necessarily lead to a sufficient increase of technological innovations to offset their losses resulting from the extension of the exclusive power of innovators, thereby resulting in "a substantial redistribution of income from developing to developed countries".[129] Furthermore, as pointed out by Correa (2009), growing enforcement activities in developing countries may "entail the use of already scarce resources to protect what are substantially [private] commercial interests" in the face of "other competing, and more immediate, public policy priorities" such as public health and combating climate change.[130]

---

[126] World Bank Development Indicator, calculated by author. The calculation is based on the data of the charges for the use of IP for the period of 2005–2012 which are payments and receipts between residents and non-residents for the authorized use of IPRs. Please also refer to Figure 2.5 in Chapter 2: The trend of annual net incomes from licensing fees and royalties of all technologies (1986–2012, in billion US dollars) for further information.

[127] See, e.g., Daniel J. Gervais (2007), The TRIPS Agreement and the Changing Landscape of International Intellectual Property, in Torremans, Shan and Erauw (eds.), *Intellectual Property and TRIPS Compliance in China: Chinese and European Perspectives*, Edward Elgar Publishing, pp. 65–84, at p. 80; Edmund W. Kitch (1994), The Patent Policy of Developing Countries, *Pacific Basin Law Journal*, vol. 13, pp. 166–78, at pp. 168–71.

[128] See, e.g., Ruchi Sharma and K. K. Saxena (2012), Strengthening the Patent Regime: Benefits for Developing Countries – A Survey, *Journal of Intellectual Property Rights*, vol. 17, pp. 122–32, at p. 130; UNCTAD (1996), *The TRIPS Agreement and Developing Countries*, UNCTAD/ITE/1, New York and Geneva: United Nations, p. 2.

[129] Arvind Panagariya (2000), The Millennium Round and Developing Countries: Negotiating Strategies and Areas of Benefits, G-24 Discussion Paper Series: Research Papers for the Intergovernmental Group of Twenty-Four on International Monetary Affairs, New York and Geneva: United Nations, at pp. 5 and 29.

[130] Carlos M. Correa (2009), The Push for Stronger Enforcement Rules: Implications for Developing Countries, in ICTSD (ed.), *The Global Debate on the Enforcement of Intellectual Property Rights and Developing Countries*, Programme on IPRs and Sustainable Development, Issue Paper No. 22, ICTSD, Geneva, pp. 27–80, at pp. x and 31.

Most importantly, through making compliance with the minimum IPR standards a mandatory treaty obligation, the TRIPS Agreement has essentially left few policy options and regulatory flexibilities for developing countries to tailor their own national IPRs systems to their specific needs. According to an UNCTAD–ICTSD Policy Discussion Paper (2003), Japan, Korea, the United States and Western European countries went through a long period of weak IPR protection during their industrial revolutions so as to achieve their present levels of technological capability.[131] As pointed out by Chang (2003), Switzerland turned out to be one of the world's leading technological nations in the nineteenth century without a patent law.[132] However, the TRIPS Agreement obliges WTO Members to set forth minimum standards for IP protection, thereby precluding today's developing countries from taking the same technology development path through imitation or reverse engineering[133] as the developed countries adopted in their early stages of industrialisation.

Moreover, actual IP protection at the national level may go beyond minimum standards of the TRIPS Agreement. Scholars generally agree that the minimum standards obligations create a regulatory "floor", rather than a "ceiling" that cannot be exceeded for international IP law-making, thereby leaving an opening for bilateral or regional agreements to introduce higher levels of IP protection than that is mandated by the TRIPS Agreement (often known as "TRIPS-plus" provisions).[134] Since the adoption of TRIPS, the United States and the EU have negotiated numerous bilateral and regional TRIPS-plus provisions with numerous countries.[135] Typical

---

[131] Linsu Kim (2003), Technology Transfer and Intellectual Property Rights: The Korean Experience, UNCTAD-ICTSD Project on IPRs and Sustainable Development, Issue Paper No. 2, UNCTAD and ICTSD, Geneva, p. 7.

[132] Ha-Joon Chang (2003), *Kicking Away the Ladder: Development Strategy in Historical Perspective*, London: Anthem Press, p. 2.

[133] As discussed in Section 2.2.2.2.5, reverse engineering is a proper way through which a trade secret is made public and enters the public domain.

[134] See, e.g., Sean Baird (2013), Magic and Hope: Relaxing TRIPS-Plus Provisions to Promote Access to Affordable Pharmaceuticals, *Boston College Journal of Law & Social Justice*, vol. 33, no. 1, Article 4, pp. 107–45, at p. 121; James Thuo Gathii (2011), The Neoliberal Turn in Regional Trade Agreements, *Washington Law Review*, vol. 86, pp. 421–74, at p. 466; Antony Taubman (2008), Rethinking TRIPS: "Adequate Remuneration" for Non-Voluntary Patent Licensing, *Journal of International Economic Law*, vol. 11, no. 4, pp. 927–70, at p. 944.

[135] See, e.g., Susan K. Sell (2011), TRIPS Was Never Enough: Vertical Forum Shifting, FTAs, ACTA, and TPP, *Journal of Intellectual Property Law*, vol. 18, pp. 447–78, at p. 455 (noting that "[i]n 2007, just after WIPO adopted the Development Agenda, the U.S., Europe, and Japan announced their plans to negotiate a plurilateral Anti-Counterfeiting Trade Agreement (ACTA) with a smaller group of like-minded countries (many of whom had already signed TRIPS-plus FTAs with the U.S.)". Carsten and Patrick Reichenmiller (2006), Tightening TRIPS: Intellectual Property Provisions of US Free Trade Agreements, in Newfarmer (ed.),

TRIPS-plus provisions include[136] enlargement of the scope of patentable subject matter,[137] requiring the extension of patent term under certain conditions,[138] preventing parallel importation,[139] as well as limiting the grounds on which compulsory licences may be granted.[140] These TRIPS-plus provisions either raise IPR standards or limit the use of the flexibilities or safeguards provided under TRIPS, thereby reducing or eliminating the "policy space [that] TRIPS allows for the implementation of its obligations".[141] Also, TRIPS-plus provisions may further limit developing countries' regulatory flexibilities for innovation and access to technologies. In the TRIPS Council Meeting of June 2010, some developing countries explicitly expressed their concern that

Trade, Doha, and Development: A Window into the Issues, the World Bank, pp. 289–303, at pp. 290 and 291 (noting that some agreements – US–Australia, US–Morocco, US–Bahrain – "extend the scope of patentability by mandating that patents must be available for new uses of known products"; many bilateral agreements prevent marketing approval of a generic drug during the patent term without the consent of the patent holder – an issue on which TRIPS does not impose any obligation).

[136] See, e.g., Frederick M. Abbott (2005), Toward a New Era of Objective Assessment in the Field of TRIPS and Variable Geometry for the Preservation of Multilateralism, *Journal of International Economic Law*, vol. 8, no. 1, pp. 77–100, at pp. 89 and 90; Carsten Fink and Patrick Reichenmiller (2006), Tightening TRIPS: Intellectual Property Provisions of US Free Trade Agreements, in Newfarmer (ed.), *Trade, Doha, and Development: A Window into the Issues*, the World Bank, pp. 289–303, at p. 290; UNCTAD (2010), *Intellectual Property in the World Trade Organisation: Turning It into Developing Countries' Real Property*, New York and Geneva: United Nations, p. 11; Susan K. Sell (2011), TRIPS Was Never Enough: Vertical Forum Shifting, FTAs, ACTA, and TPP, *Journal of Intellectual Property Law*, vol. 18, pp. 447–78, at p. 453.

[137] For example, *US–Bahrain Free Trade Agreement* (FTA), 2006, Article 14.8(2) (providing that "Each party shall make patents available for plant inventions. In addition, the Parties confirm that patents shall be available for any new uses or methods of using a known product, including products to be used for particular medical conditions"); see also *US–Morocco FTA*, 2006, Article 15.9(2).

[138] For example, *US–Chile FTA*, 2004, Article 17.9(6) (providing that "Each Party shall provide for the adjustment of the term of a patent, at the request of the patent owner, to compensate for unreasonable delays that occur in granting the patent"); see also *US–Morocco FTA*, Article 15.9(7).

[139] For example, *US–Morocco FTA*, 2004, Article 15.9(4) (providing that "Each Party shall provide that the exclusive right of the patent owner to prevent importation of a patented product, or a product that results from patented process, without the consent of the patent owner shall not be limited by the sale or distribution of that product outside its territory").

[140] For example, Agreement between the United States of America and the Hashemite Kingdom of Jordan on the Establishment of A Free Trade Area (hereafter, *US–Jordan FTA*), 2010, Article 4(20); *US–Singapore FTA*, 2004, Article 16.7(6). These provisions limit the use of compulsory licensing to emergency situations, anti-trust remedies, and cases of public non-commercial use.

[141] Henning Ruse-Khan Grosse (2011), The International Law Relation between TRIPS and Subsequent TRIPS-Plus Free Trade Agreements: Towards Safeguarding TRIPS Flexibilities? *Journal of Intellectual Property Law*, vol. 18, no. 2, pp. 325–65, at p. 328.

TRIPS-plus standards may undermine the "balance" inherent in TRIPS and constrain the "flexibilities" and "policy space" provided by TRIPS, particularly in areas such as public health, socio-economic development, the promotion of innovation and access to knowledge and transfer of technology.[142]

3.3.3 *Technology Transfer-Oriented Provisions of the TRIPS Agreement*

According to WTO (2008), developing countries perceived technology transfer as "part of the bargain" in which they agreed to, in exchange, introduce high minimum standards for intellectual property rights through TRIPS.[143] The TRIPS Agreement thus introduces a number of provisions that govern or facilitate the innovation and transfer of technology.

Article 7 of the TRIPS Agreement requires, among others, that the protection and enforcement of IP rights "contribute to the promotion of technological innovation and to the transfer and dissemination of technology", thereby making clear that the protection of IP rights is not an end itself, but rather an important means to enhance technological innovation and transfer of technology. The Agreement also recognises that strong protection of IP rights may bring with them market power and the risks of their abuse, thereby allowing Members to adopt rules to restrain or prevent the anti-competitive abuse of IP rights under Articles 8.2, 31 (k) and 40. Furthermore, the Agreement restricts the acquisition and use of patents under some circumstances primarily through the exhaustion of IPRs (Article 6), limitation on patentable subject matter (Article 27), exceptions to patent rights (Article 30) and compulsory licensing (Article 31). Finally, Article 66.2 of the Agreement obliges developed countries to provide incentives for their companies to promote and encourage technology transfer to LDCs. Part II of this book will examine patent-related TRIPS flexibilities and pro-competition provisions in detail. The following section mainly addresses the interpretation and implementation issues related to Article 66.2.

Article 66.2 of TRIPs provides that

> Developed country Members shall provide incentives to enterprises and institutions in their territories for the purpose of promoting and encouraging technology transfer to least-developed country Members in order to enable them to create a sound and viable technological base.

---

[142] Council for Trade-Related Aspects of Intellectual Property Rights, Minutes of Meeting, held on 8–9 June 2010, WTO Doc. IP/C/M/63, 4 October 2010, paras. 264 and 275.

[143] World Trade Organization (2008), *Understanding the WTO*, World Trade Organization, p. 43.

The negotiating history of TRIPS shows that with the understanding that strong IPRs may not necessarily increase the flow of technologies to developing countries, developing countries attempted to create a legal obligation for developed countries to provide incentives for technology transfer as a means to rebalance the final deal. However, as observed by Roffe (2005), developed countries were not keen on this last-minute attempt and they succeeded in limiting the beneficiaries of this obligation to the LDCs only.[144] This provision essentially takes into account the concern that LDCs are less likely to acquire technologies through regular market channels due to their lack of financial means and their insufficient technological base.

The use of the term "shall" in Article 66.2 indicates that it is a positive and binding legal obligation that is being imposed on developed countries for the benefit of LDCs. The 2001 Doha Ministerial Conference has reaffirmed the "mandatory" nature of this obligation.[145] Under Article 66.2, developed countries are not obliged to implement the technology transfer obligations by themselves, but rather, are obliged to "provide incentives" to "enterprises and institutions in their territories" for technology transfer to occur.

Developed countries retain considerable discretion in determining what kind of incentives to provide as the Agreement does not clarify the precise nature of such incentives.[146] Commentators argue that the mere provision of incentives by developed countries is not sufficient to meet their obligation and such incentives have to function effectively.[147] Indeed, the provision of

---

[144] Pedro Roffe (2005), Comment: Technology Transfer on the International Agenda, in Maskus and Reichman (eds.), *International Public Goods and Transfer of Technology under a Globalized Intellectual Property Regime*, Cambridge University Press, pp. 257–64, at p. 263.

[145] Implementation-related Issues and Concerns, Decision of 14 November 2001, WTO Doc., WT/MIN (01)/17, 20 November 2001, para. 11.2.

[146] Peter-Tobias Stoll, Jan Busche and Katrin Arend (2009), *WTO: Trade-Related Aspects of Intellectual Property Rights*, vol. 7, Martinus Nijhoff, at p. 151 (noting that "Incentives for technology transfer can be provided in very different ways, i.e. tax advantages, subsidies, research cooperation, training programmes etc.").

[147] See, e.g., Carlos Correa (2005), Can the TRIPS Agreement Foster Technology Transfer to Developing Countries? in Maskus and Reichman (eds.), *International Public Goods and Transfer of Technology under a Globalized Intellectual Property Regime*, Cambridge University Press, pp. 227–56, at p. 253 (noting that requiring "the submission of reports on 'the functioning in practice' of the incentives provided to their enterprises" would suggest that "the effectiveness of the measures adopted is to be considered in assessing compliance"); Suerie Moon (2008), Does TRIPS Art. 66.2 Encourage Technology Transfer to LDCs?: An Analysis of Country Submissions to the TRIPS Council (1999–2007), UNCTAD-ICTSD Project on IPRs and Sustainable Development, *Policy Brief No. 2*, at p. 2 (arguing that "The obligation may be understood to include not only the provision, but also the effective functioning of such incentives").

incentives is expected to lead to successful technology transfer to LDCs for the purpose of enabling them to "create a sound and viable technological base" as required under Article 66.2. According to Correa (2005), such an explicit purpose provides for a benchmark against which compliance with the obligation under Article 66.2 must be judged or accessed.[148]

Analysts and many developing countries, however, have raised concerns that the effect of Article 66.2 on the promotion of technology transfer to the LDCs has been very limited.[149] The 2001 Decision of the Ministerial Conference on Implementation-Related Issues and Concerns (WT/MIN (01)/17) obliges the TRIPS Council to establish a mechanism for ensuring the monitoring and full implementation of the obligations in Article 66.2.[150] Accordingly, the Decision of the Council for TRIPS of 19 February 2003 (IP/C/28) created an annual reporting obligation for developed countries on their actions taken or envisaged (including any specific regulatory, legislative and policy frameworks) to provide incentives for technology transfer.[151] According to UNCTAD and ICTSD (2005), this decision "constitutes an important step forward in the attempt to operationalise Article 66.2." as it considerably reduces developed countries' implementation discretion.[152]

The extent to which the reporting system has improved the level of compliance with Article 66.2 is not clear. As Moon (2011) observed, many of the policies and programmes reported by developed countries barely target towards LDCs or do not constitute a meaningful technology transfer.[153]

---

[148] Carlos Correa (2005), Can the TRIPS Agreement Foster Technology Transfer to Developing Countries? in Maskus and Reichman (eds.), *International Public Goods and Transfer of Technology under a Globalized Intellectual Property Regime*, Cambridge University Press, pp. 227–56, at p. 253.

[149] See, e.g., Suerie Moon (2011), Meaningful Technology Transfer to the LDCs: A Proposal for a Monitoring Mechanism for TRIPS Article 66.2, UNCTAD-ICTSD Project on IPRs and Sustainable Development, *Policy Brief No. 9, at p.* 1; Minutes of Meeting of the Council for Trade-Related Aspects of Intellectual Property Rights, 8–9 June 2010, WTO Doc., No. IP/C/M/ 63, 4 October 2010; UNCTAD and ICTSD (2005), *Resource Book on TRIPS and Development*, Cambridge University Press, p. 738.

[150] Implementation-Related Issues and Concerns, Decision of 14 November 2001, WTO Doc., WT/MIN (01)/17, 20 November 2001, para. 11.2.

[151] Implementation of Article 66.2 of the TRIPS Agreement, Decision of the Council for TRIPS of 19 February 2003, WTO Doc. IP/C/28, 20 February 2003. See also UNCTAD and ICTSD (2005), *Resource Book on TRIPS and Development*, Cambridge University Press, p. 734.

[152] UNCTAD and ICTSD (2005), *Resource Book on TRIPS and Development*, Cambridge University Press, p. 734.

[153] Suerie Moon (2011), Meaningful Technology Transfer to the LDCs: A Proposal for a Monitoring Mechanism for TRIPS Article 66.2, UNCTAD-ICTSD Project on IPRs and Sustainable Development, *Policy Brief No. 9*, pp. 4–5 (finding that "out of 384 unique programmes or policies reviewed, [only] 33 per cent were targeted specially towards LDC

Accordingly, the current implementation of Article 66.2 may not be sufficient or effective enough to provide meaningful technology transfer to LDCs.

In sum, the TRIPS Agreement has been viewed as a significant revolution in the international IP arena.[154] It surpasses all prior international IP conventions not only in the breadth and depth of its IP protection but also in its requirement for adequate and expeditious enforcement to take place.[155] According to Reichman (1998), the Uruguay Round of multilateral trade negotiations "carried the developed countries well beyond their initial goal", which was to prevent firms in developing countries from free-riding of their companies' invention.[156] By and large, industrialised countries have managed to "impose [their] then most advanced set of norms" on the rest of the world.[157]

However, it would be unfair to simply characterise TRIPS as "a system of exclusion and protection rather than one of diffusion and competition".[158] In exchange for minimum IPR standards, provisions for encouraging international technology transfer are incorporated into TRIPS. Article 7 makes it clear that the TRIPS negotiators sought to maintain "a balanced perspective on the role of intellectual property in society".[159] The protection of IP rights is not a goal in itself but a means to an end: to enhance technological innovation and transfer of technologies. The TRIPS Agreement also provides flexibilities for Members to facilitate innovation of, and access to, technologies. In addition, the TRIPS Agreement provides developing countries, in particular LDCs, with special and differential treatment. Many of them benefit from

---

WTO Members"; and "Of the 128 programmes that specially targeted LDC WTO Members, about one-third (42 programmes) qualified as technology transfer according to the definition we adopted").

[154] See, e.g., Jerome H. Reichman (2000), The TRIPS Agreement Comes of Age: Conflict or Cooperation with the Developing Countries? *Case Western Reserve Journal of International Law*, vol. 32, pp. 441–70, at p. 442; Joost Pauwelyn (2010), The Dog That Barked But Didn't Bite: 15 Years of Intellectual Property Disputes at the WTO, *Journal of International Dispute Settlement*, vol. 1, no. 2, pp. 389–429, at p. 389.

[155] Andres Moncayo von Hase (2008), The Application and Interpretation of the Agreement on Trade-Related Aspects of Intellectual Property Rights, in Correa and Yusuf (eds.), 2nd edn, *Intellectual Property and International Trade: The TRIPS Agreement*, Kluwer Law International, pp. 83–124, at p. 83.

[156] Jerome Reichman H. (1998), Securing Compliance with the TRIPS Agreement after US v. India, *Journal of International Economic Law*, pp. 585–601, at p. 585.

[157] Daniel J. Gervais (2006), The Changing Landscape of International Intellectual Property, *Journal of Intellectual Property Law and Practice*, vol. 1, no. 4, pp. 249–55, at p. 249.

[158] Christopher May (2007), *The World Intellectual Property Organisation: Resurgence and the Development Agenda*, London: Routledge, at p. 32.

[159] UNCTAD and ICTSD (2005), *Resource Book on TRIPS and Development*, Cambridge University Press, at p. 126.

longer transitional periods.[160] Last but not least, developed countries are explicitly obliged to provide incentives for their enterprises to transfer technology to LDCs.

Nevertheless, as observed by Frankel (2010), in comparison with the mandatory IPR standards, these technology transfer-oriented provisions are too vague to produce results that could effectively and meaningfully assist developing countries in their development of indigenous technologies and access to technology produced by developed countries' companies.[161] Under TRIPS, there are neither specific obligations nor operative mechanisms for developed countries to transfer technologies to developing countries other than LDCs. To what extent technology transfer occurs in reality partly depends on the extent to which developing country Members are able to make use of TRIPS flexibilities.

3.4 TECHNOLOGY TRANSFER AND INTELLECTUAL PROPERTY RIGHTS IN INTERNATIONAL CLIMATE FRAMEWORK

With the awareness of the importance of environmental protection increasing across the globe, the issue of development and transfer of ESTs has become a regular feature of the MEAs. Most of them have "adopted an aid-based approach for the supply of sector-specific environment-related technologies to developing countries" with the aim of ensuring developing states' compliance with their treaty obligations.[162] Such agreements mainly address those environmental problems of a truly global nature such as climate change and loss of biodiversity, which present urgent threats to the international community. Examples of such MEAs include the CBD, the Montreal

---

[160] See Article 65 of the TRIPS Agreement (providing that "2. A developing country Member is entitled to delay for a further period of four years the date of application ..."); Article 66.1 (providing that "In view of the special needs and requirements of least-developed country Members, their economic, financial and administrative constraints, and their need for flexibility to create a viable technological base, such Members shall not be required to apply the provisions of this Agreement, other than Articles 3, 4 and 5, for a period of 10 years from the date of application as defined under paragraph 1 of Article 65. The Council for TRIPS shall, upon duly motivated request by a least-developed country Member, accord extensions of this period").

[161] Susy Frankel (2010), The Applicability of GATT Jurisprudence to the Interpretation of the TRIPS Agreement, in Correa (ed.), *Research Handbook on the Interpretation and Enforcement of Intellectual Property Under WTO Rules: Intellectual Property in the WTO*, vol. II, Edward Elgar, pp. 3–23, at p. 4.

[162] Abdulqawi A. Yusuf (2001), Technology Transfer in the Global Environmental Agreements: A New Twist to the North-South Debate, in Patel, Roffe and Yusuf (eds.), *International Technology Transfer: The Origins and Aftermath of the United Nations Negotiations on a Draft Code of Conduct*, Kluwer Law International, pp. 313–20, at p. 319.

Protocol on Substances that Deplete the Ozone Layer (hereafter referred to as "the Montreal Protocol") and the UNFCCC.

However, the effective implementation of the relevant EST transfer clauses has proven to be challenging. The inherent difficulties lie in the fact that ESTs are largely in the hands of private companies, and they require IPRs to protect their innovation.[163] An ideal EST transfer provision is supposed to balance the needs of developing countries with the increasing demands for the protection of IPRs. This section addresses EST transfer commitments under the UNFCCC Agreements, followed by a study of intellectual property rights in the international climate change regime.

3.4.1 *Technology Transfer under the UNFCCC Agreements*

The UNFCCC explicitly recognises that developed countries are largely responsible for historical GHG emissions and have greater financial and technological capabilities to mitigate climate change.[164] The Convention therefore mandates the EST transfer from developed countries to developing countries based on the principle of common but differentiated responsibilities (CBDR).[165] This section describes the establishment and development of EST transfer commitments under the UNFCCC Agreements, examining who should provide technological support, to whom, for what reason and to what extent. It addresses the following questions: who are the obligation-bearers? Are EST transfer commitments binding on Parties? What kinds of mechanisms exist for the implementation of EST transfer obligations and are they adequate? Before answering this question, this part will first discuss the principle of CBDR as it creates the legal and moral basis for developed countries' commitments to transfer ESTs.

3.4.1.1 The Principle of Common but Differentiated Responsibilities

The principle of CBDR has been increasingly recognised in international law since it was enshrined as Principle 7 of the Rio Declaration at the first Earth Summit in 1992.[166] The UNFCCC is the first international treaty to directly

---

[163] Tuula Honkonen (2009), *The Common but Differentiated Responsibility Principle in Multilateral Environmental Agreements: Regulatory and Policy Aspects*, Kluwer Law International, p. 173.

[164] See the Preamble and Article 3.1 of the UNFCCC.

[165] See Articles 3.1 and 4.5 of the UNFCCC.

[166] Rio Declaration on Environment and Development, UN General Assembly, A/CONF.151/26 (Vol. I), 12 August 1992, Principle 7; see also Lavanya Rajamani (2000), The Principle of

refer to CBDR as a principle.[167] Article 3.1 of the Convention makes clear that the obligation of parties to protect the climate system is "on the basis of equity" and "in accordance with their common but differentiated responsibilities and respective capabilities", according to which developed countries should take the lead in tackling climate change. In essence, it points to the fact that problems that are "a common concern of humankind", such as climate change, affect all and are "affected by all nations" to differing degrees, and that "for equity reasons" the resulting "responsibilities" ought to be differentiated.[168]

The principle of CBDR, as applied to international environmental treaties, includes two "related" elements: "the common responsibility of all States for certain international issues", and "differences in the extent of their international obligations to respond to those issues".[169] In the context of climate change, "common responsibilities" arise from the concept of the "common concern of humankind" as the climate system affects and is affected by every nation in the world.[170] This dimension of the principle of CBDR entitles and requires all concerned States to participate in addressing climate change.[171] Article 4.1 of the Convention, which is further enhanced by Article 10 of the Kyoto Protocol, contains a set of commitments for all parties, including their cooperation commitments in the development and transfer of ESTs.

The second dimension of the CBDR principle, differentiated responsibilities, involves a direct response to country differences in their contributions to environmental degradation and their capacity to prevent, reduce and control the threat.[172] Commentators observe that differentiated responsibilities resulting from the application of the equity principle in general international law requires the lawmakers to consider all relevant factors, in particular, the specific needs and special circumstances of developing countries in

Common but Differentiated Responsibility and the Balance of Commitments under the Climate Regime, *RECIEL*, vol. 9, no. 2, pp. 120–31, at p. 120.

[167] The practice of differentiating responsibilities has existed in international law for years, but the UNFCCC is the first multinational environmental agreement to employ the term "common but differentiated responsibilities". See Carlarne Cinnamon Piñon (2010), *Climate Change Law and Policy: EU and US Approaches*, Oxford University Press, p. 337.

[168] Farhana Yamin and Joanna Depledge (2004), *The International Climate Change Regime: A Guide to Rules, Institutions and Procedures*, Cambridge University Press, p. 69.

[169] Philippe Sands (1995), International Law in the Field of Sustainable Development, *British Yearbook of International Law*, vol. 65, no. 1, pp. 303–81, at p. 344.

[170] See the Preamble of the UNFCCC.

[171] See, e.g., Tuula Honkonen (2009), *The Common but Differentiated Responsibility Principle in Multilateral Environmental Agreements: Regulatory and Policy Aspects*, vol. 5, Kluwer Law International, p. 1.

[172] Ibid., p. 2.

allocating responsibilities.[173] Differentiated responsibilities often result in the adoption and implementation of different commitments for States, based on many factors including their historical contribution to the problem, their special circumstances and respective capacities, and their specific developmental needs.[174]

The principle of CBDR is viewed as "a political necessity" to ensure developing countries' participation in the UNFCCC.[175] As a concession, developed countries accepted the CBDR principle and agreed to take the lead in combating climate change under Article 3.1 of the UNFCCC. Yet, there are disagreements over the reasoning of differentiated responsibilities and why developed countries should take the lead in combating climate change. According to Bodansky (1993), developing countries argued that developed countries bore the "main responsibility" for the climate change problem, whereas developed countries (in particular, the United States) opposed this reasoning but "agreed to take the lead because of their greater financial and technical capabilities".[176]

In practical terms, the principle of CBDR has been translated into "specific commitments" under the UNFCCC and the Kyoto Protocol on the mitigation of climate change, but only for developed country parties.[177] The application of this principle has also resulted in the establishment of the obligations on developed countries to provide financial support and to transfer ESTs to developing countries to help them implement their obligations, and to make developing countries' participation contingent on the recipient of their "enabling" finance and technologies.[178]

---

[173] See, e.g., Philippe Sands (1994), The "Greening" of International Law: Emerging Principles and Rules, *Global Legal Studies Journal*, vol. 1, pp. 293–323, at p. 307; Farhana Yamin and Joanna Depledge (2004), *The International Climate Change Regime: A Guide to Rules, Institutions and Procedures*, Cambridge University Press, p. 69.

[174] CISDL (2002), The Principle of Common but Differentiated Responsibilities: Origins and Scope, A *CISDL Legal Brief for the World Summit on Sustainable Development*, available at http://cisdl.org/public/docs/news/brief_common.pdf, p. 1.

[175] See, e.g., Neel Maitra (2010), Access to Environmentally Sound Technology in Developing World: A Proposed Alternative to Compulsory Licensing, *Columbia Journal of Environmental Law*, vol. 35, pp. 407–45, at p. 412.

[176] Daniel Bodansky (1993), The United Nations Framework Convention on Climate Change: A Commentary, *Yale Journal of International Law*, vol. 18, pp. 451–558, at p. 503.

[177] See Article 4 of the UNFCCC and the Kyoto Protocol; see also Philippe Sands (1994), The "Greening" of International Law: Emerging Principles and Rules, *Global Legal Studies Journal*, vol. 1, pp. 293–323, at p. 311.

[178] See Articles 4.3, 4.5 and 4.7 of the UNFCCC; see also Philippe Sands (1994), The "Greening" of International Law: Emerging Principles and Rules, *Global Legal Studies Journal*, vol. 1, pp. 293–323, at p. 311.

3.4.1.2 EST Transfer Commitments under the UNFCCC

In implementing measures to mitigate climate change, development and transfer of ESTs are essential. The most important provisions on development and transfer of technology in the UNFCCC Convention are Articles 4.1(c), 4.3 and 4.5. Article 4.1(c) requires all Parties to "[p]romote and cooperate in the development, application and diffusion, including transfer, of technologies, practices and processes that control, reduce or prevent anthropogenic emissions of greenhouse gases" taking into account their CBDR and their specific national development objectives, priorities and circumstances. Article 4.3 mandates Annex II Parties to provide financial resources for the transfer of technology.[179] The key EST transfer provision is Article 4.5 of the UNFCCC, which obliges developed Parties to transfer technology to developing countries.[180]

Developing countries undertake the general obligations of Article 4.1 in return for financial and technological support that is set out in Articles 4.3 and 4.5.[181] Article 4.7 specifies this trade-off in particular. Yet, it is claimed that there is a lack of actual and effective implementation of these EST transfer provisions.[182] In this context, it is necessary to revisit the developed Parties' commitments to EST transfer and developing countries' conditional commitments to implement the treaty under Article 4.7.

3.4.1.2.1 DEVELOPED PARTIES' COMMITMENTS TO EST TRANSFER. The promise of access to ESTs is often viewed as "the carrot" that has attracted developing countries' participation in contemporary MEAs.[183] Despite the fact

---

[179] According to the UNFCCC website, Annex I Parties include the industrialised countries that were members of the Organisation for Economic Co-operation and Development (OECD) in 1992 whereas Annex II Parties consist of OECD Members in 1992. See the UNFCCC website, available at http://unfccc.int/parties_and_observers/parties/annex_i/items/2774.php

[180] Neither the Convention nor the Kyoto Protocol defines the term "developing country". However, Parties at Subsidiary Body for Implementation-17 (SBI-17), which took place alongside COP-8, agreed that all non-Annex I countries enjoy the status of developing countries. See Draft Conclusions Proposed by the Chair, Request from a Group of Countries of Central Asia and the Caucasus, Albania and the Republic of Moldova Regarding their Status under the Convention, UN Doc. FCCC/SBI/2002/L.14, Subsidiary Body for Implementation, 17th Session, 29 October 2002.

[181] IPCC (2000), *IPCC Special Report: Methodological and Technological Issues in Technology Transfer*, Cambridge University Press, p. 91.

[182] See, e.g., Vicente Paolo B. Yu (2010), The UN Climate Change Convention and Developing Countries: Towards Effective Implementation, in Faundez and Tan (eds.), *International Economic Law, Globalization and Developing Countries*, Cheltenham, UK: Edward Elgar, pp. 379–410, at p. 404.

[183] David Ockwell and Alexandra Mallett (2012), *Low-Carbon Technology Transfer: From Rhetoric to Reality*, London: Routledge, p. 5.

that the wording of EST transfer clauses varies widely across MEAs, it generally uses terms such as "encouraging", "promoting" or "facilitating" transfer of ESTs.[184] The use of these phrases does not affect individual states' freedom to choose how to implement these provisions, however.[185] It is also rather difficult to measure their compliance with such commitments. Verhoosel (1998) thus characterised such EST transfer provisions as "mere diplomatic cosmetics" from a legal angle and considered that their presence in MEAs only reflected "the need to acknowledge new realities in order to close the deal".[186]

Given the fact that the causes and consequences of climate change are global, Article 4.5 of the UNFCCC imposes more far-reaching EST transfer obligations, by providing that:

> The developed country Parties and other developed Parties[187] included in Annex II *shall take all practicable steps* to *promote, facilitate and finance*, as appropriate, the transfer of, or access to, environmentally sound technologies and know-how to other Parties, particularly developing country Parties, to enable them to implement the provisions of the Convention. In this process, the developed country Parties shall support the development and enhancement of endogenous capacities and technologies of developing country Parties. (Emphasis added)

To begin, the use of the term "shall" indicates the intention of the Parties to impose a positive, and legally binding, obligation on developed Parties. The obligation is to "take all practicable steps" to "promote, facilitate and finance"

---

[184] See, e.g., under Article 16 of the CBD, Parties commit themselves to "provide and/or *facilitate* access for and transfer to other Contracting Parties of technologies that are relevant to the conservation and sustainable use of biological diversity or make use of genetic resources"(emphasis added) (Convention on Biological Diversity, 1992, United Nations, Article 16.1); Article 6 of United Nations Convention to Combat Desertification in those Countries Experiencing Serious Drought and/or Desertification, particularly in Africa states that "developed country Parties undertake to: ... (e) *promote* and *facilitate* access by affected country Parties, particularly affected developing country Parties, to appropriate technology, knowledge and know-how" (emphasis added) (United Nations Convention to Combat Desertification in those Countries Experiencing Serious Drought and/or Desertification, Particularly in Africa, United Nations, 14 October 1994); Article 273 of the UNCLOS provides that "States shall cooperate actively with competent international organizations and the Authority to *encourage* and *facilitate* the transfer to developing States, their nationals and the Enterprise of skills and marine technology" (emphasis added) (UN Convention on the Law of the Sea, 10 December 1982, UN Doc. No. A/CONF.62/122, 21 I.L.M.1261).

[185] Gaetan Verhoosel (1998), Beyond the Unsustainable Rhetoric of Sustainable Development: Transferring Environmentally Sound Technologies, *The Georgetown International Environmental Law Review*, vol. 11, pp. 49–76, at p. 58.

[186] Ibid., p. 66.

[187] Other developed parties refer to the European Union. See the UNFCCC website, available at http://unfccc.int/parties_and_observers/parties/annex_i/items/2774.php

the transfer of, or access to, ESTs and know-how to developing countries.[188] In the process of EST transfer, the developed Parties are required to "support the development and enhancement of endogenous capacities and technologies" of the developing country Parties. The EST transfer commitment under Article 4.5 is different from the above-mentioned EST transfer clauses in the following aspects.

First, EST transfer obligations under Article 4.5 go far beyond other "best-endeavour" EST transfer clauses such as Article 16 of the CBD and Article 273 of the United Nations Convention on the Law of the Sea (UNCLOS) by explicitly requiring developed Parties to "finance" such transfers. Article 4.3 of the Convention explicitly requires developed Parties to provide financial resources for the transfer of technology. Article 11.1 of the Convention has established a mechanism for the provision of financial resources "on a grant or concessional basis" for technology transfer. The Global Environment Facility (GEF), established under the auspices of the World Bank, was restructured during the Rio Summit and assigned as the financial mechanism of the Convention.[189] The GEF holds a mandate to provide financial resources to support technology transfer in the context of both mitigation and adaptation under the Guidance of the Conference of the Parties (COP).[190] Its activities help catalyse the transfer of ESTs to meet a variety of development priorities and focus on "removing barriers to the widespread adoption of technologies and practices that enable energy efficiency, renewable energy, and sustainable transport".[191]

Second, developed Parties are obliged to "take all practicable steps" to comply with Article 4.5. This means that to fulfil this commitment, developed countries have to take all practicable steps to transfer technology. What does the term "practicable" mean? We recall that the treaty terms are meant to be interpreted in line with the general rule of treaty interpretation, which is codified in Article 31 of the Vienna Convention, and states that "[a] treaty

---

[188] According to the International Council on Human Rights Policy (2011), the wording "facilitate" refers to "regulatory policies, legislative frameworks, incentives such as subsidies and tax breaks and proactive steps, such as pooling and compulsory licensing" whereas "promote" has the presumably broader implication of actively taking steps to ensure that the objectives of technology transfer are broadly understood and accepted by relevant parties. See International Council on Human Rights Policy (2011), *Beyond Technology Transfer: Protecting Human Rights in a Climate-Constrained World*, International Council on Human Rights Policy, Geneva, p. 37.

[189] GEF website, www.thegef.org/gef/whatisgef, accessed on 14 September 2011.

[190] Global Environment Facility (2010), *Implementing the Poznan Strategic Program on Technology Transfer*, Professional Graphics Printing Co., p. 1.

[191] Ibid.

shall be interpreted in good faith in accordance with the ordinary meaning to be given to the terms of the treaty in their context and in the light of its object and purpose". As to the ordinary meaning, the term "practicable" means "available or useful in practice; able to be used".[192] This has been confirmed by the arbitrators in the *EC – Bananas III* (Ecuador) (Article 22.6 – EC) case (2000) considering "practicability" to be "available for application in practice as well as suited for being used in a particular case".[193] Accordingly, by using the term "practicable", Article 4.5 obliges developed Parties to take all available and suitable action to promote, facilitate and finance EST transfers.

However, it is noted that the EST transfer obligation imposed by Article 4.5 is qualified by the term "as appropriate". The dictionary meaning of the term "appropriate" is "suitable for a particular person, condition, occasion, or place".[194] The use of the term "as appropriate" implies that the commitments should be compatible with the countries' condition, including their legal environments. Thus, developed Parties' commitments should be subject to their international obligations and national legislation, including intellectual property law. Accordingly, as observed by Verhoosel (1998), this EST transfer provision cannot detract from the protection of IPRs as provided for in developed Parties' national legislation.[195]

3.4.1.2.2 CONDITIONS FOR DEVELOPING COUNTRIES TO FULFIL THEIR TREATY COMMITMENTS UNDER ARTICLE 4.7. Article 4.7 directly links developing members' abilities to fulfil their commitments under the Convention to developed Parties' effective implementation of their commitments related to financial resources and transfer of technology by providing that:

> The extent to which developing country Parties will effectively implement their commitments under the Convention will depend on the effective implementation by developed country Parties of their commitments under the Convention related to financial resources and transfer of technology.

In essence, Article 4.7 conditions developing countries' implementation of their commitments upon developed countries' compliance with their

---

[192] *The New Shorter Oxford English Dictionary*, Oxford, 1993, p. 786. See also Decision by the Arbitrators, *EC – Bananas III (Ecuador) (Article 22.6 – EC)*, p. 18.

[193] Ibid.

[194] *American Heritage Dictionary of the English Language*, 5th edn S.v. "appropriate." www.the freedictionary.com/appropriate

[195] Gaetan Verhoosel (1998), Beyond the Unsustainable Rhetoric of Sustainable Development: Transferring Environmentally Sound Technologies, *The Georgetown International Environmental Law Review*, vol. 11, pp. 49–76, at p. 60.

financial and technology transfer commitments.[196] In so doing, this article reinforces "the compact between developing and developed countries" with respect to international climate protection.[197] Commentators observe that this reflects the political reality that developing countries were unlikely to accept any form of commitment to mitigate climate change without developed nations' reciprocal commitment to provide financial and technological support to enable them to develop in a climate-friendly and energy-efficient manner.[198]

The plain meaning of the text reveals that the effectiveness of the implementation by developed-country Parties of their differentiated commitments regarding financial resource and EST transfer determines the extent to which developing country Parties will implement their commitments under the Convention. As confirmed by the UNFCCC Secretariat, this provision "does create a legal relationship insofar as the Convention is legally binding for all the states that ratified it".[199] Some argue that if developed countries fail to fulfil their commitment to provide the necessary financial and technological support, it must be assumed that "developing States will simply have insufficient capacity and resources to meet the commitments imposed upon them".[200] However, others consider that it is only a "factual statement" that merely reflects the economic and political reality of the situation but has no legal implications for developing countries' responsibility.[201] Although the commitments of developed Parties to provide financial resources and technologies to developing countries form "part of the negotiated nexus of rights and responsibilities" between the Parties, this does not imply that sanctions can be imposed on developed countries for their failure to meet their

---

[196] Lavanya Rajamani (2012), Developing Countries and Compliance in the Climate Regime, in Jutta, Meinhard and Lavanya (eds.), *Promoting Compliance in an Evolving Climate Regime*, Cambridge University Press, pp. 367–94, at p. 383.

[197] Ibid.

[198] John H. Barton (2008), *Mitigating Climate Change through Technology Transfer: Addressing the Needs of Developing Countries*, Energy, Environment and Development Programme: Programme Paper 08/02, Chatham House, p. 2.

[199] Mark A. Drumbl (2002), Poverty, Wealth, and Obligation in International Environmental Law, *Tulane Law Review*, vol. 76, no. 4, pp. 843–960, at p. 947, citing e-mail from Seth Osafo, FCCC Secretariat (further stating that "This does not imply, however, that sanctions can be imposed on developed countries for not achieving their commitments in the [FCCC].").

[200] Duncan French (2005), *International Law and Policy of Sustainable Development*, Manchester University Press, p. 94.

[201] See, e.g., Farhana Yamin and Joanna Depledge (2004), *The International Climate Change Regime: A Guide to Rules, Institutions and Procedures*, Cambridge University Press, p. 93; Duncan French (2005), *International Law and Policy of Sustainable Development*, Manchester University Press, p. 94.

commitments under the UNFCCC.[202] In other words, this provision lacks teeth, and breach of such provisions may not lead to sanctions.

3.4.1.3 The Kyoto Protocol

Supplementary protocols are important means on which the Parties to the UNFCCC rely to implement the Convention. The main protocol to the UNFCCC, the Kyoto Protocol, was adopted at COP-3 in 1997 and entered into force in 2005. It imposes a legally binding emission-reduction obligation on developed-country Parties for the first commitment period (2008–2012). It further calls for all parties to advance the implementation of the existing Convention commitments, including the transfer of technology. This section addresses the reaffirmation of the commitments to technology transfer, followed by a brief introduction of the Clean Development Mechanism (CDM), which may facilitate technology transfer.

3.4.1.3.1 THE REAFFIRMATION OF THE COMMITMENTS TO TECHNOLOGY TRANSFER. Article 3.14 of the Kyoto Protocol identifies the transfer of tech-nology as an essential action to minimise the adverse effects of climate change.[203] Articles 10 and 11 of the Kyoto Protocol incorporate the provisions relating to development and transfer of ESTs under Articles 4.1, 4.3 and 4.5 of the Convention (see Box 3.1), while the Protocol strengthens and expands the scope of the EST transfer commitments under the UNFCCC.[204]

As IPCC (2000) observed, the wording on technology transfer in the Protocol, compared to the wording used by the UNFCCC, places a greater emphasis on the role of the private sector and on the actions made by, and in, the developing countries themselves.[205] First, Article 10(c) of the Protocol requires *all Parties* to "take all practicable steps to promote, facilitate and finance, the transfer of, or access to, environmentally sound technologies",

---

[202] Christina Voigt (2009), *Sustainable Development as a Principle of International Law: Resolving Conflicts between Climate Measures and WTO Law*, Leiden, Netherlands: Martinus Nijhoff Publishers, p. 101; Mark A. Drumbl (2002), Poverty, Wealth, and Obligation in International Environmental Law, *Tulane Law Review*, vol. 76, no. 4, pp. 843–960, at p. 947.

[203] Kyoto Protocol to the United Nations Framework Convention on Climate Change (1998), Article 3.14, United Nations.

[204] Farhana Yamin and Joanna Depledge (2004), *The International Climate Change Regime: A Guide to Rules, Institutions and Procedures*, Cambridge University Press, p. 306.

[205] IPCC (2000), *IPCC Special Report: Methodological and Technological Issues in Technology Transfer*, Cambridge University Press, p. 94.

Box 3.1 Kyoto Protocol: Key Provisions Relating to Technology Transfer

Article 3.14 . . . the Conference of the Parties . . . consider what actions are necessary to minimize the adverse effects of climate change and/or the impacts of response measures on Parties referred to in those paragraphs. Among the issues to be considered shall be the establishment of funding, insurance and *transfer of technology*.

Article 10(c) (*All Parties*, taking into account their common but differentiated responsibilities . . ., shall): Cooperate in the promotion of effective modalities for the development, application and diffusion of, and take all practicable steps to promote, facilitate and finance, as appropriate, the transfer of, or access to, *environmentally sound technologies, know-how, practices and processes* pertinent to climate change, in particular to developing countries, including the formulation of policies and programmes for the effective transfer of environmentally sound technologies that are publicly owned or in the public domain and the creation of *an enabling environment for the private sector*, to promote and enhance the transfer of, and access to, environmentally sound technologies;

Article 11.2 . . . the developed country Parties and other developed Parties included in Annex II to the Convention shall:

(b) Also provide such financial resources, including for the transfer of technology, needed by the developing country Parties to meet the agreed full incremental costs of advancing the implementation of existing commitments under Article 4, paragraph 1, of the Convention that are covered by Article 10 and that are agreed between a developing country Party and the international entity or entities referred to in Article 11 of the Convention, in accordance with that Article. (Emphasis added)

---

whereas the Convention's Article 4.5 obliges only Annex II industrialised-country Parties to "take all practicable steps" (emphasis added). This suggests that developing countries will also play a role in promoting, facilitating as well as financing EST transfers, not just act as technology recipients.[206]

A second clear change from the Convention is that the Protocol formally acknowledges the important role of the private sector in the development and transfer of ESTs and demands an "enabling environment" for the

---

[206] Farhana Yamin and Joanna Depledge (2004), *The International Climate Change Regime: A Guide to Rules, Institutions and Procedures*, Cambridge University Press, p. 306.

private sector.[207] During the first COP discussions, Parties to the Convention realised that the main difficulty involving the effective implementation of EST provisions under the Convention was that "property rights to most technologies are held by private sectors" and thus governments have a limited role to play in the process of transferring those technologies.[208] The Protocol thus divides ESTs into three categories: publicly owned ESTs, those in the public domain and ESTs owned by the private sector. It recognises that governments can "take a leading role" in transferring ESTs that are publicly owned or in the public domain but that, for ESTs held by the private sector, creating an enabling environment for private investment could play a more significant role in facilitating EST transfer.[209] Yet, as observed by IPCC (2007) (c), many governments transfer the patents arising out of publicly funded research to private sectors as part of their industrial policy, and then the patented technologies will be transferred in line with the rules applicable to privately owned technologies.[210]

Some commentators perceive the EST transfer provisions of the Protocol to have shifted the principal burden of "promoting, facilitating and financing" the transfer of ESTs from developed-country Parties onto all Parties to the Convention, including the least-developed ones.[211] The shift of the burden towards developing countries mainly lies in creating an enabling environment. This marks a significant evolution of thinking in the UNFCCC process: developing countries that until then had "emphasized the role of developed countries as transferors" are now expected to play a part in creating an environment conducive to market-led technology transfer.[212]

---

[207] Article 10(c) of the Kyoto Protocol; see also IPCC (2000), *IPCC Special Report: Methodological and Technological Issues in Technology Transfer*, Cambridge University Press, p. 94.

[208] Haroldo Machado-Filho and Marcelo Khaled Poppe (2011), Transfer of Technology under the Climate Change Regime, in da Motta et al. (eds.), *Climate Change in Brazil: Economic, Social and Regulatory Aspects*, Institute for Applied Economic Research, pp. 329–48, at p. 333.

[209] Farhana Yamin and Joanna Depledge (2004), *The International Climate Change Regime: A Guide to Rules, Institutions and Procedures*, Cambridge University Press, p. 307.

[210] IPCC (2007)(c), *Mitigation, Contribution of Working Group III to the Fourth Assessment Report of the IPCC*, Metz et al. (eds.), Cambridge University Press, p. 160.

[211] International Council on Human Rights Policy (2011), *Beyond Technology Transfer: Protecting Human Rights in a Climate-Constrained World*, International Council on Human Rights Policy, Geneva, p. 43.

[212] See, e.g., IPCC (2000), *IPCC Special Report: Methodological and Technological Issues in Technology Transfer*, Cambridge University Press, p. 94; Farhana Yamin and Joanna Depledge (2004), *The International Climate Change Regime: A Guide to Rules, Institutions and Procedures*, Cambridge University Press, p. 307.

3.4.1.3.2 CLEAN DEVELOPMENT MECHANISM. Article 12 of the Protocol established the CDM to assist developing country Parties to achieve sustainable development and to help Annex I countries to meet their emission-reduction commitments. CDM is a market-based instrument that allows industrialised nations to invest in clean technology projects in non-Annex I countries, where it is often cheaper to do so, in exchange for carbon credits. The COP-7 extended CDM's mandate to technology transfer by explicitly stating that "clean development mechanism project activities should lead to the transfer of environmentally safe and sound technology and know-how."[213]

Theoretically, CDM may cause a de facto increase in the flow of technologies from developed nations to developing countries by financing emission-reduction projects using technologies that are currently not available in the host countries.[214] Although CDM does not have an explicit technology transfer mandate under the Protocol, it is undisputed that technology transfer occurs through CDM in practice. Empirical studies show that CDM projects contribute significantly to technology transfer.[215] Yet some scholars notice that CDM may not induce large-scale technology transfer in its present form because high transaction costs associated with the project-specific CDM "makes it difficult to create economies of scale and pool risks across projects of the same type".[216] The surveys done by the United Nations University-Maastricht Economic and Social Research Institute on Innovation and Technology (UNU-MERIT) demonstrate that "[s]ince the initiation of the CDM scheme, trends in CDM projects have been showing a reliance mostly

---

[213] Decision 17/CP.7, Modalities and Procedures for a Clean Development Mechanism as Defined in Article 12 of the Kyoto Protocol, UN Doc. FCCC/CP/2001/13/Add.2, 21 January 2002, p. 20.

[214] Stephen Seres (2008), Analysis of Technology Transfer in CDM Projects, Prepared for the UNFCCC Registration and Issuance Unit CDM/SDM, http://cdm.unfccc.int/Reference/Reports/TTreport/TTrepo8.pdf, p. 4.

[215] An empirical study led by Dechezleprêtre examining technology transfers in the CDM projects registered up to May 2007 finds that "technology transfers take place in more than 40 [per cent] of CDM projects". It also shows that "very few [CDM] projects involve the transfer of equipment alone"; instead, "projects often include the transfer of knowledge and operating skills, allowing project implementers to appropriate the technology". See Antoine Dechezleprêtre, Matthieu Glachant and Yann Ménière (2008), The Clean Development Mechanism and the International Diffusion of Technologies: An Empirical Study, *Energy Policy*, vol. 36, no. 4, pp. 1273–83, at p. 1282.

[216] Fei Teng, Wenying Chen and Jiankun He (2008), Possible Development of a Technology Clean Development Mechanism in a Post-2012 Regime, prepared for the Harvard Project on International Climate Agreements, Discussion Paper 08–24, p. 1.

on local sources of technology".[217] Hence, more remains to be done to enable CDM to effectively facilitate such a transfer.

3.4.1.4 Technology Transfer in the Post-Kyoto Climate Regime

3.4.1.4.1 BALI ACTION PLAN. Despite EST transfer being a treaty commitment established under the UNFCCC and repeatedly affirmed by subsequent decisions or protocols, industrialised countries have largely failed to fully and effectively implement and enforce EST transfer provisions.[218] This failure became "the primary bone of contention" during the COP-13 in Bali and has led to the refusal of developing countries to agree to take on specific legally binding emission-reduction commitments in the post-Kyoto period.[219]

Developing country Parties have frequently contended that without sufficient transfers of technology and financial support from Annex II countries, they would not be able to substantially contribute to the mitigation of climate change. The Bali Action Plan, adopted by the COP as decision 1/CP.13, thus identified technology development and transfer as one of the four "building blocks" to establish a new climate framework. The four pillars – mitigation, adaptation, technology development and transfer, and finance – are interdependent and intricately linked while technology plays a central role in all of them. The Bali Action Plan further requires developed countries to provide technology, finances and capacity-building "in a measurable, reportable and

---

[217] Asel Doranova, Ionara Costa and Geert Duysters (2009), Knowledge Base Determinants of Technology Sourcing in the Clean Development Mechanism Projects, UNU-MERIT Working Paper Series 2009-015, p. 23.

[218] See, e.g., South Centre (2009), Accelerating Climate-Relevant Technology Innovation and Transfer to Developing Countries: Using TRIPS Flexibilities under the UNFCCC, SC/IAKP/AN/ENV/1, SC/GGDP/AN/ENV/8, August 2009, Geneva, p. 1 (noting that "the UNFCCC Expert Group on Technology Transfer (EGTT) has pointed out that to date, the UNFCCC's technology transfer-related provisions have not yet been reflected in concrete, practical, results-oriented actions in specific sectors and programs"; Centre for International Environmental Law (CIEL) (2009), Frameworks and Options for Addressing Technology Cooperation in the UNFCCC: National and Multilateral Elements, Background Brief for the Workshop on: Operationalizing of Technology Cooperation in the UNFCCC: Building Civil Society Viewpoints into Copenhagen, 11–15 May 2009, p. 1; UNEP, EPO and ICTSD (2010), *Patents and Clean Energy: Bridging the Gap between Evidence and Policy*, UNEP, EPO and ICTSD, p. 9.

[219] See, e.g., South Centre and CIEL (2008), The Technology Transfer Debate in the UNFCCC: Politics, Patents and Confusion, *IP Quarterly Update*, 4th Quarter, p. 2; Dalindyebo Shabalala (2009), An Introduction to This Issue: Climate Change and Technology Transfer, *Sustainable Development Law & Policy*, vol. 9, no. 3 (Spring): Clean Technology and International Trade, Article 4, p. 4.

verifiable manner" to enable developing country Parties to take nationally appropriate mitigation actions.[220] Hence, the Bali Action Plan reaffirmed that the intensity of developing country Parties' mitigation actions is contingent upon the level of developed countries' compliance with their technological and financial provisions of the Convention.

Responding to the findings of the IPCC Fourth Assessment Report that the delay in reducing emissions significantly constrains opportunities to achieve lower stabilisation levels and increases "the risk of more severe climate change impacts",[221] Parties in COP-13 decided to scale up the efforts to develop, transfer and diffuse low-carbon technologies. The Parties of the Conference decided to strengthen the international framework for technology development and transfer through "[e]nhanced action on technology development and transfer to support action on mitigation and adaptation" (see Box 3.2).[222]

The Bali Action Plan has expanded developed countries' technology transfer obligations under the Convention. Extensive discussions were made as to how to give effect to the objectives established by the Plan. Their role in facilitating technology transfer to developing countries is still unclear. Pueyo and Linares (2012) found that "so far the success of the UNFCCC process in promoting [technology transfer] has been limited because the mechanisms it has created have either failed to materialise in actual [technology transfer] or have led to progress on a project-by-project basis that has been unable to scale-up to the level required".[223]

3.4.1.4.2 TECHNOLOGY TRANSFER MECHANISMS. At the COP-7, the Expert Group on Technology Transfer (EGTT) was established to advance the technology transfer activities under the Convention.[224] It analyses and identifies ways to facilitate technology transfer activities and makes recommendations to the Subsidiary Body for Scientific and Technological Advice (SBSTA).[225]

---

[220] Decision 1/CP.13, Bali Action Plan, UN Doc. FCCC/CP/2007/6/Add.1, 14 March 2008, p. 3.

[221] IPCC (2007) (a), *Synthesis Report, Contribution of Working Groups I, II and III to the Fourth Assessment Report of the IPCC*, Core Writing Team, Pachauri and Reisinger (eds.), Geneva, Switzerland, p. 19.

[222] Decision 1/CP.13, Bali Action Plan, UN Doc. FCCC/CP/2007/6/Add.1, 14 March 2008, pp. 4–5.

[223] Ana Pueyo and Pedro Linares (2012), Renewable Technology Transfer to Developing Countries: One Size Does Not Fit All, *IDS Working Paper*, vol. 2012, no. 412, Institute of Development Studies, p. 6.

[224] Decision 4/CP.7, Development and Transfer of Technologies (Decisions 4/CP.4 and 9/CP.5), UN Doc. FCCC/CP/2001/13/Add.1, 21 January 2002, Annex, p. 22.

[225] Ibid.

Box 3.2 Technology Transfer in Bali Action Plan (Decision 1/CP.13)

The Conference of the Parties ... decides to launch a comprehensive process to enable the full, effective and sustained implementation of the Convention through long-term cooperative action, now, up to and beyond 2012 ... by addressing, inter alia:

(d) Enhanced action on technology development and transfer to support action on mitigation and adaptation, including, inter alia, consideration of:

(i) Effective mechanisms and enhanced means for the removal of obstacles to, and provision of financial and other incentives for, scaling up of the development and transfer of technology to developing country Parties in order to promote access to affordable environmentally sound technologies;

(ii) Ways to accelerate deployment, diffusion and transfer of affordable environmentally sound technologies;

(iii) Cooperation on research and development of current, new and innovative technology, including win-win solutions;

(iv) The effectiveness of mechanisms and tools for technology cooperation in specific sectors.

Yet, because of the limitations of the SBSTA itself, the EGTT is unable to undertake implementation actions.

In Bali, disagreement surrounded the review of the mandate of the EGTT. Developing country Parties wished to establish a new body under the Convention, the Technology Development and Transfer Body, to elevate technology transfer to a level closer in importance to mitigation while industrialised nations advocated the continuation and reinforcement of the EGTT instead.[226] The COP-13 agreed to reconstitute the EGTT for another five years, with the capacity to report to both the SBSTA and the Subsidiary Body for Implementation (SBI).[227] Technology transfer thus became a responsibility of the Convention's main implementation body. In addition to analysing and identifying ways to facilitate and advance the development and transfer of

---

[226] Earth Negotiations Bulletin (2006), Summary of the Twelfth Conference of the Parties to the UN Framework Convention on Climate Change and Second Meeting of the Parties to the Kyoto Protocol: 6–17 November 2006, p. 6.

[227] Earth Negotiations Bulletin (2007), Summary of the Thirteenth Conference of the Parties to the UN Framework Convention on Climate Change and Third Meeting of the Parties to the Kyoto Protocol: 3–15 December 2007, p. 5.

technology, the EGTT shall also develop performance indicators to "monitor and evaluate the effectiveness of the implementation of the technology transfer framework".[228] At the conclusion of COP-16, the Parties decided to terminate the mandate of the EGTT.

Having confirmed the importance of the development and transfer of environmentally sound technologies to developing country Parties, the Cancun Agreement, adopted by the COP-16 in December 2010, established a technology mechanism to boost technology development and transfer. The Technology Mechanism consists of, and operates through, the Technology Executive Committee (TEC) (the policy arm) and the Climate Technology Centre and Network (the implementation component). [229] The overarching goal of the Technology Mechanism is to facilitate the development and transfer of climate-friendly technologies, in particular to developing countries, in support of action on climate mitigation and adaptation.

3.4.1.5 The Adoption of the Paris Agreement

COP 21, also known as the 2015 Paris Climate Change Conference, witnessed the adoption of the historic agreement – the Paris Agreement – by the 196 Parties to the UNFCCC on 12 December 2015. The Agreement became legally binding on 4 November 2016, thirty days after the date on which it was ratified by at least 55 Parties to the Convention representing at least 55 per cent of the total GHG emissions.[230] The Paris Agreement, built upon the foundation of the UNFCCC and the Copenhagen and Cancun Agreements, sets forth an ambitious collective goal to hold the global temperature increase to well below 2 degrees above pre-industrial levels with efforts to limit the increase to 1.5 degrees.[231] To achieve this goal, Parties to the UNFCCC explicitly highlighted "the urgent need to enhance the provision of finance, technology and capacity-building support" by developed countries to enable developing country Parties to mitigate GHG emissions.[232]

---

[228] Decision 3/CP.13, Development and Transfer of Technologies under the Subsidiary Body for Scientific and Technological Advice, UN Doc. FCCC/CP/2007/6/Add.1, 14 March 2008, p. 21.

[229] Cancun Agreements, Report of the Conference of the Parties on Its Sixteenth Session, Part Two: Action Taken by the Conference of the Parties at Its Sixteenth Session, Cancun, UN Doc. FCCC/CP/2010/7/Add.1, 15 March 2011, pp. 18–19.

[230] Paris Agreement, Annex to Decisions Adopted by the Conference of the Parties, Report of the Conference of the Parties on Its Twenty-first Session, held in Paris from 30 November to 13 December 2015, UN Doc. FCCC/CP/2015/10/Add.1, 29 January 2016, Article 21.

[231] Paris Agreement, Article 2.

[232] Decision 1/ CP.21, Adoption of the Paris Agreement, Report of the Conference of the Parties on its Twenty-first Session, held in Paris from 30 November to 13 December 2015, UN Doc. FCCC/CP/2015/10/Add.1, 29 January 2016, p. 2.

On the road to Paris, innovation and transfer of technology had been one of the most contentious issues, as evidenced by various options in the drafts showed. The draft text released after the Bonn intersessional meeting on 23 October 2015 saw the divergent interests of the Parties in innovation and transfer of technology. The draft Article 7 on technology development and transfer, on the one hand, requires all Parties to recognise existing deployment and dissemination efforts and strengthen cooperative action to accelerate and upscale technology development and transfer. On the other hand, it also contains an option that obliges developed countries to provide financial resources to address barriers created by policies and IPRs in line with Article 4.5 of the Convention.[233] The latter option was unlikely to be included in the final text, but it suggested an inherent tension between the need to strengthen IPRs to stimulate innovation of ESTs and the need to access such technologies at an affordable cost.

The Paris Agreement does not explicitly tackle this tension but encourages Parties to "strengthen cooperative action" on development and transfer of ESTs.[234] For this purpose, Parties decide to enhance the Technology Mechanism and request the Technology Executive Committee and the Climate Technology Centre and Network to undertake future work relating to (a) "[t]echnology research, development and demonstration" and (b) "[t]he development and enhancement of endogenous capacities and technologies".[235] To provide overarching guidance to the work of the Technology Mechanism, Article 10.4 of the Paris Agreement establishes a technology framework which is designed to assess technology needs, facilitate financial and technical support and address the barriers to the development and transfer of ESTs.[236] The final text does not provide much more detail, leaving Parties great discretion to design their implementing measures.

With a view to enhancing the development and transfer of ESTs, the COP-22 adopted several decisions in Marrakesh in November 2016, including (1) Decision – / CP.22: Enhancing climate technology development and transfer through the Technology Mechanism[237] and (2) Decision – / CP.22: Linkages between the Technology Mechanism and the Financial Mechanism of

---

[233] Draft Agreement, Work of the ADP Contact Group Incorporating Bridging Proposals by the Co-facilitators, UN Doc. FCCC/ADP/2015/L.6, 5 December 2015, Annex I.
[234] Paris Agreement, Article 10.2.
[235] Decision 1/ CP.21, Adoption of the Paris Agreement, para. 66.
[236] Decision 1/ CP.21, Adoption of the Paris Agreement, para. 67.
[237] Decision – / CP.22, Enhancing climate technology development and transfer through the Technology Mechanism, Marrakesh, November 2016, Advanced unedited version, available at http://unfccc.int/files/meetings/marrakech_nov_2016/application/pdf/auv_cop22_i8a_tm.pdf

the Convention.[238] Meanwhile, on 16 November 2016, Canada, Denmark, the European Union, Germany, Italy, Japan, Korea, Switzerland and the United States pledged more than \$23 million to support technology transfer in developing countries through Climate Technology Centre and Network with a view to accelerating the development and transfer of innovative ESTs.[239]

3.4.2 *Intellectual Property Rights in the International Climate Change Regime*

Private-sector investment, which increasingly plays an important role in innovation and transfer of ESTs,[240] relies heavily on strong and predictable IP protection. While some ESTs are in the public domain, many key ESTs are subject to patents and other IPRs. As will be discussed in Section 4.3.1.1, there are an increasing number of patents on ESTs. Yet, the leading international climate change agreements such as the UNFCCC and the Kyoto Protocol did not explicitly mention IPRs in their provisions for technology transfer. Nevertheless, due to the existing asymmetries in the ownership of EST IP assets, IP issues have remained at the centre of the technology transfer debate in international climate change negotiations.[241] The following sections address the controversy over technology transfer and IPRs in international climate negotiations from Rio to Paris.

3.4.2.1 Technology Transfer and IPRs at the 1992 Rio Summit

The global debate on IPRs and EST transfer can be traced back to the 1992 UNCED. As observed by Khor (2008), in the UNCED negotiating process, the Group 77 countries argued that "IPRs had to be relaxed in the case of

---

[238] Decision – / CP.22: Linkages between the Technology Mechanism and the Financial Mechanism of the Convention, Marrakesh, November 2016, Advanced unedited version, available at http://unfccc.int/files/meetings/marrakech_nov_2016/application/pdf/auv_cop22_i8b_tm_fm.pdf

[239] Climate Change Centre and Network, Countries Pledge Millions for Technology Transfer to Implement Paris Agreement, 16 November 2016, available at V:\10. Personal\oooooo- Book CUP\oo-oo proof reading\Bibiliograph\CH - 3\2016 Countries Pledge Millions to support TT in developing countries.html

[240] The Global Trends in Renewable Energy Investment 2012 Report finds that investment from private entities in R&D of new technologies is almost double that of governments and public bodies. See Eoghan Macguire, 12 June 2012, Who's Funding the Green Energy Revolution? CNN, available at http://edition.cnn.com/2012/06/12/world/renewables-finance-unep

[241] Funding is the other debating point related to technology transfer in the global climate change context.

[ESTs], for otherwise IPRs would hinder the developing countries' access to such technology", whereas developed countries agreed that "concessional terms should be encouraged for the transfer of ESTs" but insisted that "IPRs (such as patents) be applied and that an exception should not be made in IPR regimes on such technologies".[242]

Developing countries' concerns over IPRs during the Rio negotiating process did not come out of a vacuum. They stemmed from the practical experience of several developing countries in obtaining ozone-friendly technology to implement the 1987 Montreal Protocol on Substances that Deplete the Ozone Layer.[243] Firms from developing countries, in particular, India and China, found it extremely difficult to acquire substitute technologies as such technologies are "covered by IPRs and are inaccessible either on account of the high price quoted by the technology suppliers and/or due to the conditions laid down by the suppliers".[244]

The international community's concern over the role of IPRs in transfer of ESTs at the global level had emerged in the early 1990s.[245] Accordingly, Chapter 34 of Agenda 21 explicitly recognises the need to consider the role of IPRs and to examine their impact on the access to, and transfer of, ESTs, in particular with regard to developing countries.[246] Paragraph 34.18 of Agenda 21 calls for countries to adopt measures to prevent the abuse of IPRs, including "rules with respect to their acquisition through compulsory licensing, with the provision of equitable and adequate compensation".[247]

However, it has been alleged that since Rio, little progress has been made in facilitating developing countries' access to ESTs, in particular, those covered by IPRs.[248] The perception that IPRs are possible barriers to EST transfer,

---

[242] Martin Khor (2008), IPRs, Technology Transfer and Climate Change, Third World Network, available at www.un.org/esa/analysis/devplan/egm_climatechange/khor.pdf, p. 1.

[243] A detailed analysis is provided in Section 4.4.2.

[244] Jayashree Watal (2000), India: The Issue of Technology Transfer in the Context of the Montreal Protocol, in Jha and Hoffmann (eds.), Achieving Objectives of Multilateral Environmental Agreements: A Package of Trade Measures and Positive Measures, UNCTAD/ITCD/TED/6, pp. 45–55, at p. 45.

[245] See, e.g., Philippe Sands (1994), The "Greening" of International Law: Emerging Principles and Rules, *Indiana Journal of Global Legal Studies*, vol. 1, no. 2, Article 2, pp. 293–323, at p. 317.

[246] Agenda 21, Chapter 34: Transfer of Environmentally Sound Technology, Cooperation and Capacity-Building, UN Documents Cooperation Circles, available at www.un-documents.net/a21-34.htm, para. 10.

[247] Ibid., para. 18.

[248] See, e.g., South Centre (2009), Accelerating Climate-Relevant Technology Innovation and Transfer to Developing Countries: Using TRIPS Flexibilities under the UNFCCC, SC/IAKP/AN/ENV/1, SC/GGDP/AN/ENV/8, August 2009, Geneva, at p. 4; UNEP, EPO and ICTSD

as suggested by Agenda 21, is not accepted by most developed countries. According to Latif (2012), their general position is that the circumstances that led to the language relating to IPRs in Agenda 21 were "context-specific and have not occurred since".[249] Some authors including Khor (2001) claim that instead of facilitating developing countries' access to ESTs, there has been an emphasis on strengthening the rights of IP holders,[250] which is evidenced by the establishment of global minimum IPR standards under the TRIPS Agreement and various TRIPS-plus provisions in FTAs (as noted in Section 3.3.2.2). As addressed below, such views also surfaced in the UNFCCC negotiations, particularly since 2007 when COP 13 was held in Bali.

3.4.2.2 Divergent Proposals or Unilateral Actions on the Road to Copenhagen

Although the UNFCCC and the Kyoto Protocol are silent on the issue of IPRs, at the end of the Bali Summit, the Parties agreed to include IP language in the Bali Road Map, stating that Parties should "avoid trade and intellectual property rights policies, or lack thereof, restricting transfer of technology" (Decision 3/CP.13 of 2007).[251] Thus, it is now recognised within the UNFCCC context that IPRs are relevant for the development of, and access to, ESTs, and since then the Parties' discussions on this link have been intensified.

In the lead up to the Copenhagen Climate Summit, countries submitted various proposals to the UNFCCC centring on whether and how to reform the IPR regime so as to optimise the development and transfer of ESTs. A notable difference in the desirable level of IP protection exists. Several developing countries, including China, Cuba, India, Indonesia and Tanzania identified IPRs "as a barrier to technology transfer".[252] In contrast, some

---

(2010), *Patents and Clean Energy: Bridging the Gap between Evidence and Policy*, UNEP, EPO and ICTSD, p. 9.

[249] Ahmed Abdel Latif (2012), Intellectual Property Rights and Green Technologies from Rio to Rio: An Impossible Dialogue? *Policy Brief No. 14*, ICTSD, p. 3.

[250] Martin Khor (2001), *Globalisation and the Crisis of Sustainable Development*, Third World Network, p. 26.

[251] Decision 3/CP.13, Development and Transfer of Technologies under the Subsidiary Body for Scientific and Technological Advice, UN Doc. FCCC/CP/2007/6/Add.1, 14 March 2008, p. 18.

[252] Summary of Views Expressed during the First Session of the Ad Hoc Working Group on Long-Term Cooperative Action under the Convention on the Development of the Two-Year Work Programme That Was Mandated under Paragraph 7 of the Bali Action Plan, UN Doc. FCCC/AWGLCA/2008/6, 27 May 2008, available at http://unfccc.int/resource/docs/2008/awglca2/eng/06.pdf, p. 8.

developed countries, including the United States and Australia, considered the protection of IPRs as "key to stimulating and rewarding technology innovation and promoting technology competition".[253]

The following sections will discuss the various UNFCCC submissions on IPRs by developing countries as well as by developed countries.

3.4.2.2.1 DEVELOPING COUNTRIES' PROPOSALS. All Parties to the UNFCCC are represented at the climate negotiations and there are a number of groupings. Developing countries generally work through Group 77 to establish common negotiating positions.[254] However, due to diverse interests on climate change issues, individual developing country alliances such as the group of LDCs and the progressive Latin American Group also intervene in debates.

The emerging countries, assembled in the so-called BASIC Group (Brazil, South Africa, India and China) have shared similar views on matters of IP in the context of climate change. They acknowledge that "innovation plays a central role" in addressing climate change while emphasising "the need for a balanced international intellectual property system" capable of meeting such a challenge "on a truly global scale" and "reducing the technological gap".[255] Immediately preceding the Copenhagen Climate Summit, the BASIC Group insisted that "[t]he existing IPR system does not match the increasing needs for accelerating D&T&D [development, transfer and deployment of ESTs] to meet [the] challenges of climate change",[256] and thus they proposed that new ESTs should be subject to compulsory licensing.[257]

Lesotho, on behalf of the group of LDCs, stated that "[i]ntellectual property rights should not and must not be an excuse [for not] fulfilling commitments under the Convention" and urged developed country Parties to address the IPRs issue in accordance with their commitments under the Convention.[258]

---

[253] Ibid.
[254] Party Groupings, UNFCCC, available at http://unfccc.int/parties_and_observers/parties/ negotiating_groups/items/2714.php
[255] Brasilia Declaration, India-Brazil-South Africa Dialogue Forum, Fourth Summit of Heads of State/Government, 15 April 2010, available at http://ibsa.nic.in/ivsummit.htm
[256] China's Views on Enabling the Full, Effective and Sustained Implementation of the Convention through Long-Term Cooperative Action Now, Up to and Beyond 2012, in *Ideas and Proposals on the Elements Contained in Paragraph 1 of the Bali Action Plan: Submissions from Parties*, UN Doc. FCCC/AWGLCA/2008/MISC.5, 27 October 2008, available at http:// unfccc.int/resource/docs/2008/awglca4/eng/misc05.pdf, pp. 33–8, at p. 36.
[257] Ibid., India (2009), Submission to UNFCCC on Technology Transfer Mechanism, available at http://unfccc.int/files/kyoto_protocol/application/pdf/indiatechtransfer171008.pdf, p. 4.
[258] Lesotho, on behalf of the Least Developed Countries, Fulfilment of the Bali Action Plan and the Components of the Agreed Outcome to be Adopted by the Conference of Parties at its Fifteenth Session, in Ideas and Proposals on the Elements Contained in Paragraph 1 of the Bali

The largest LDC, Bangladesh, argued that LDCs, because of their development needs and lack of capacity, "should be exempted from the obligation of patent protection of climate related technologies for adaptation and mitigation".[259]

The Bolivarian Alliance for the Peoples of Our America (the ALBA Countries), including Bolivia, Cuba, Ecuador, Nicaragua and Venezuela, called for "[t]he establishment of a fund for funding and inventory of appropriate technologies, free from intellectual property rights, particularly patents".[260] They argued that "[r]ather than private monopolies, [the ESTs] should come in the public domain, of ready access and low cost".[261] Bolivia proposed that Parties should take all steps necessary in all fora to mandatorily exclude ESTs from patent protection in developing countries and to revoke all existing patents granted for essential/urgent ESTs in developing countries.[262]

The G77 and China, on behalf of developing countries, stressed the need to address the issue of intellectual property rights and to remove barriers to technology transfer. It lent its support to all proposals made by other developing country groups or individual developing countries, including the ambitious "no patents" proposal put forward by the ALBA countries. Yet, it limited the scope of the proposal to IP-protected technologies held by Annex II countries only. In their text submitted in June 2009, the G77 and China stated that "all necessary steps shall be *immediately* taken in all relevant fora to mandatorily exclude from patenting climate-friendly technologies held by *Annex II countries* which can be used to adapt to or mitigate climate change" (emphasis added).[263] This nuance might reflect diverging interests among developing countries in this area, as patent activity has markedly increased in some developing countries albeit on a small scale basis, as discussed in Section 2.4.

Action Plan: Submissions from Parties, Part II, UN Doc. FCCC/AWGLCA/2009/MISC.4 (Part II), 19 May 2009, pp. 5–10, at p. 7.

[259] Bangladesh, Submission for the Ad Hoc Working Group on Long-Term Cooperative Action on Enhanced National/International Action on Mitigation, in Ideas and Proposals on the Elements Contained in Paragraph 1 of the Bali Action Plan: Submissions from Parties, Part I, UN Doc. FCCC/AWGLCA/2009/MISC.4 (Part I), 19 May 2009, pp. 26–32, at p. 29.

[260] Official Submission of the Bolivian Republic of Venezuela on Behalf of Cuba, Bolivia, Ecuador and Nicaragua; ALBA-PPT Member States, to the UNFCCC Ad Hoc Working Group on Long-Term Cooperative Action, 26 April 2010, available at www.usclimatenetwork .org/resource-database/official-submission-of-the-bolivarian-republic-of-venezuela-on-behalf-of-cuba-bolivia-ecuador-and-nicaragua-alba-ptt-member-states-to-the-unfccc-ad-hoc-working-group-on-long-term-cooperative-action-1/at_download/file, p. 8.

[261] Ibid.

[262] Sangeeta Shashikant (2009), Developing Countries Call for No Patents on Climate-Friendly Technologies, *TWN Bonn News Update* 15, Third World Network, 11 June 2009, p. 1.

[263] Ibid.

In addition, developing countries emphasized their sovereign rights to take measures to tackle climate change, proposing that no international IP agreement shall be "interpreted or implemented in a manner that limits or prevents" such rights.[264] They also called for (1) the "[c]reation of a Global Technology IPR Pool for Climate Change"; (2) the promotion of innovative IPR sharing arrangements for joint development of ESTs; (3) the use of the TRIPS flexibilities, including compulsory licensing; and (4) the reduction of the patent term for ESTs.[265]

In addressing the nexus between IPRs and climate change, developing countries mainly propose to relax IPRs including by permitting compulsory licensing and excluding ESTs from patents. Such proposals are, however, based on a premise that the current IP regime hinders transfer of ESTs to developing countries – a claim that remains to be further substantiated.

3.4.2.2.2 DEVELOPED COUNTRIES' RESPONSE. The "anti-patent" proposals pose a threat to the exclusive rights enjoyed by IP holders under current international patent regime, which especially raise great concerns among the industries of developed countries.

In May 2009, a group of developed countries' companies, including General Electric, Microsoft, Corning, DuPont, Praxair, Daimler, Siemens, 3M, Bendix Commercial Vehicle Systems and Sunrise Solar, launched the Innovation, Development & Employment Alliance (IDEA) to defend IPRs in climate change negotiations.[266] The IDEA aims to advocate the fundamental role of IPRs in promoting the innovation of ESTs.[267] The coalition asserts that robust IP protection is necessary to stimulate R&D investment in ESTs, create green jobs and tackle the global energy and environmental challenges.[268] The IDEA's immediate priority was to urge Congress and the Obama

---

[264] Draft Text, Non-Paper No. 36, Contact Group on Enhanced Action on Development and Transfer of Technology, Ad Hoc Working Group on Long-Term Cooperative Action under the Convention, Barcelona, 2–6 November 2009, on 6 November 2009, p. 9.

[265] Draft Text, Proposed by Co-chairs, Non-Paper No. 36, Contact Group on Enhanced Action on Development and Transfer of Technology, Ad Hoc Working Group on Long-Term Cooperative Action under the Convention, Barcelona, 2–6 November 2009, available at http://unfccc.int/files/kyoto_protocol/application/pdf/technology29091009v03.pdf, p. 20.

[266] U.S. Chamber of Commerce, Companies Launch Coalition to Defend IPR in Climate Change Talks, 22 May 2009, available at www.theglobalipcenter.com/companies-launch-coalition-defend-ipr-climate-change-talks/

[267] Lane Eric, New Alliance's Big IDEA: Strong IP Is Essential for Green Innovation, *Green Patent Blog*, 17 May 2009, available at www.greenpatentblog.com/2009/05/17/new-alliances-big-idea-strong-ip-is-essential-for-green-innovation/

[268] Ibid.

administration to declare their commitment to "maintaining strong IP protection in the UNFCCC treaty talks".[269]

IDEA's lobbying led to quick legislative success. The US politician Kirk, who described compulsory licensing as "authorization for the theft of the US intellectual property", together with Rick Larsen sponsored an IP amendment to the Foreign Relations Authorization Bill.[270] In June 2009, the US House of Representatives voted unanimously (432–0) to pass the legislative amendment to:

> prevent any weakening of, and ensure robust compliance with and enforcement of, existing international legal requirements as of the date of the enactment of this Act for the protection of intellectual property rights related to energy or environmental technology.[271]

The American Clean Energy and Security Act, known as the Waxman-Markey Bill for its sponsors, was approved by the House of Representatives by a vote of 219–212 in June 2009 and reaffirmed the importance of IP protection,[272] while stressing that any weakening of IPR protection poses "a substantial competitive risk" to US companies and jobs.[273] This bill went further by tying US funding to developing countries with regard to exporting clean technology to their robust compliance with, and enforcement of, existing international IP laws.[274] These provisions are supposed to be the policy of the United States,

---

[269] Eric Lane (2010), Clean Tech Reality Check: Nine International Green Technology Transfer Deals Unhindered by Intellectual Property Rights, *Santa Clara Computer and High Technology Law Journal*, pp. 533–57, at p. 541.

[270] A. Peter Buxbaum, Climate Change, Patent Pending, International Relations and Security Network (ISN ETH Zurich), 25 June 2009, available at www.css.ethz.ch/content/specialinterest/gess/cis/center-for-securities-studies/en/services/digital-library/articles/article.html/102425

[271] Foreign Relations Authorization Act, Fiscal Years 2010 and 2011, H.R.2410, 22 June 2009, 111th Congress, Section 1120A. available at www.govtrack.us/congress/bills/111/hr2410/text

[272] American Clean Energy and Security Act of 2009, H.R. 2454, 26 June 2009, 111th Congress, available at www.opencongress.org/bill/111-h2454/text. Section 441 (8) emphasizes "[i]ntellectual property rights are a key driver of investment and research and development in, and the global deployment of, clean technologies".

[273] Ibid. Section 441 (10) states that "Any weakening of intellectual property rights protection poses a substantial competitive risk to U.S. companies and the creation of high-quality U.S. jobs, inhibiting the creation of new 'green' employment and the transformational shift to the 'Green Economy' of the 21st Century".

[274] Ibid. Section 441 (11) stresses that "Any U.S. funding directed toward assisting developing countries with regard to exporting clean technology should promote the robust compliance with and enforcement of existing international legal requirements for the protection of intellectual property rights as formulated in the Agreement on Trade-Related Aspects of Intellectual Property Rights, referred to in section 101(d)(15) of the Uruguay Round Agreements Act (19 U.S.C. 3511(d)(15) and in applicable intellectual property provisions of bilateral trade agreements)".

with respect to the UNFCCC. Despite the fact that neither the amendment nor the Act was ever passed by the US Senate, these legislative activities might suggest that "US policy favours strong IP rights" for ESTs and opposes relaxing IPR rules as part of any climate change treaty.[275] This can be further supported by the US position in subsequent climate negotiations.

The then European Union took a similar position as the United States. A 2009 report commissioned by the European Commission (DG Trade) on the transfer of climate change technology concluded that "dismantling or weakening the intellectual property rights system would not only hinder the access of developing countries to costly technology, it would also hinder the access to low cost technology as IPR protected technology is also to be found among the low abatement cost technologies".[276] As a response to the developing countries' proposals, the Council (Environment) of the European Union adopted on 21 October 2009 a document entitled "EU position for the Copenhagen Climate Conference (7–18 December 2009) – Council conclusions" to assure its industry that such anti-patent activities would not happen. In the document, it stressed "the necessity of protecting and enforcing intellectual property rights (IPRs) for promoting technological innovation and incentivising investments from the private sector".[277]

Overall, developed countries generally consider the protection of IPRs as the key to stimulating and rewarding technological innovation and promoting technology competition.[278] They generally support maintaining or strengthening the current IP regime. On the road to Copenhagen, Japan, Canada, Australia, Switzerland and the United States showed their determination over strong IPR regimes and even opposed the use of compulsory

---

[275] Eric Lane (2010), Clean Tech Reality Check: Nine International Green Technology Transfer Deals Unhindered by Intellectual Property Rights, *Santa Clara Computer & High Technology Law Journal*, pp. 533–57, at p. 541.

[276] Copenhagen Economics (2009), *Are IPR a Barrier to the Transfer of Climate Change Technology?* Report prepared by Copenhagen Economics A/S and the IPR Company ApS, at pp. 38–9.

[277] EU Position for the Copenhagen Climate Conference (7–18 December 2009), Council Conclusions, Document No. 14790/09, General Secretariat of the Council of the European Union, Brussels, 21 October 2009, available at http://register.consilium.europa.eu/pdf/en/09/st14/st14790.en09.pdf, para. 56.

[278] Summary of Views Expressed during the First Session of the Ad Hoc Working Group on Long-Term Cooperative Action under the Convention on the Development of the Two-Year Work Programme That Was Mandated under Paragraph 7 of the Bali Action Plan, UN Doc. FCCC/AWGLCA/2008/6, 27 May 2008, available at http://unfccc.int/resource/docs/2008/awglca2/eng/06.pdf, p. 8; see also ICTSD (2008), Climate Change, Technology Transfer and Intellectual Property Rights, Background paper prepared for the Trade and Climate Change Seminar, International Institute for Sustainable Development, p. 4.

licensing, which is one of the flexibilities permitted by the TRIPS Agreement.[279]

3.4.2.3 The Copenhagen Negotiations and Afterwards

The report (FCCC/AWGLCA/2009/14) released by the Ad Hoc Working Group on Long-Term Co-operative Action provided the foundation for negotiations in Copenhagen in December 2009.[280] It compiled the texts proposed by the parties. Section V of the Report, entitled "Enhanced Action on Development and Transfer of Technology", listed several options related to IPR protection, including (1) urgent and specific measures shall be taken to remove barriers to development and transfer of technologies arising from IPR protection; (2) developing countries' sovereign right to make full use of the TRIPS flexibilities, including compulsory licensing, shall be respected and (3) all necessary steps shall be immediately taken to exclude ESTs from IPR protection or revoke existing IPR protection on ESTs.[281]

Not surprisingly, developed countries strongly opposed these options that were mainly put forward by developing countries. In doing so, they circulated the so-called Danish Text, which was prepared in secret by a group of individuals, known as "the circle of commitment", from nations including the United States, the UK and Denmark.[282] It largely ignored developing countries' proposals and stressed the need to respect IPR regimes and protect innovators' interests.[283]

Undoubtedly, the Danish Text triggered strong resistance from developing countries. The negotiations over IP at the Copenhagen Climate Summit thus

---

[279] Meena Raman (2009), Wide North-South Divide over IPRs and Climate Technologies, *Bonn News Update 13*, 9 June 2009, p.1.

[280] Report of the Ad Hoc Working Group on Long-Term Cooperative Action under the Convention of Its Seventh Session, Held in Bangkok from 28 September to 9 October 2009, and Barcelona from 2 to 6 November 2009, UN Doc. FCCC/AWGLCA/2009/14, 20 November 2009.

[281] Ibid., at pp. 156 and 157.

[282] Vidal John, Copenhagen Climate Summit in Disarray After "Danish Text?" Leak, *The Guardian*, 9 December 2009.

[283] Decision 1/CP.15, Adoption of the Copenhagen Agreement under the United Nations Framework Convention on Climate Change, Draft 271109, 9 December 2009, available at www.elpais.com/elpaismedia/ultimahora/media/200912/09/sociedad/20091209elpepusoc_1_Pes_PDF.pdf, para. 18 states that "Parties commit to enable the accelerated large-scale development, transfer and deployment of environmentally sound and climate friendly technologies across all stages of the technology cycle, respecting IPR regimes including protecting the legitimate interests of public and private innovators".

ended in a stalemate and an impasse. As a result, the Copenhagen Accord did not contain any reference to intellectual property. Owing to developed countries' reluctance to discuss IPRs in the UNFCCC, IPRs issues were mostly ignored during the entire Cancun meeting in 2010. Bolivia consistently asked for intellectual property to be included in the sections on technology transfer.[284] Yet, the adopted Cancun Agreement did not mention any specific IP-related proposals. Despite developing countries' efforts to restore IPRs issues in Durban in 2011, the Durban Agreement was once again silent on IPR issues.[285]

The Lima Draft (1/CP.20, 2014), which contains the views and concerns of all countries, was transformed into the negotiating text in February 2015 and served as the basis for the accord that Parties hoped to reach in Paris at the end of 2015.[286] The Lima Draft[287] proposed three options to facilitate the access to and transfer of ESTs in the post-Kyoto climate change agreement:

Option (a):

a. In accordance with Article 4 of Convention, developed country Parties to provide financial resources to address barriers caused by intellectual property rights (IPRs) and facilitate access to and the deployment of technology . . .;

b. An international mechanism on IPRs to be established to facilitate access to and the deployment of technology to developing country Parties;

c. Other arrangements to be established to address IPRs, such as collaborative research and development, shareware, commitments related to humanitarian or preferential licensing, fully paid-up or joint licensing schemes, preferential rates and patent pools.

Option (b): Parties recognize that IPRs create an enabling environment for the promotion of technology innovation in environmentally sound technologies;

Option (c): IPRs are not to be addressed in this agreement.

---

[284] Catherine Saez (2010), UN Climate Talks Find Make-Do Solution; IP Rights Dismissed, *Intellectual Property Watch*, 14 December 2010.

[285] ICTSD (2012), UNFCCC Technology Executive Committee Seeks More "Clarity" on IPRs, *Biores*, vol. 6, no. 4 (22 November).

[286] UNFCCC Secretariat, Governments Agree the Negotiating Text for the Paris Climate Agreement, Spirit of Lima Transforms into Spirit of Geneva En Route to December Climate Conference, press release, 13 February 2015.

[287] Elements for a Draft Negotiating Text, Annex, Decisions Adopted by the Conference of the Parties, 1/CP.20: Lima Call for Climate Action, FCCC/CP/2014/10/Add.1, 2 February 2015, p. 25.

These various pathways indicate that the issue of IPRs in the climate change context has remained controversial. Options (b) and (c) essentially reflect the *status quo*.

Option (a) outlines three sub-options. Sub-option a. requires developed country Parties to provide financial resources to address barriers caused by IPRs and to facilitate access to, and the deployment of, technology. This option seeks to implement provisions of Articles 4.3 and 4.5 of the UNFCCC, as discussed in Section 3.4.1.2, which require developed country Parties to provide developing countries with financial and technological support. Sub-option b. calls for the establishment of an international mechanism on IPRs to facilitate EST transfer to developing countries. Taking into account the interests of all countries, such an international mechanism has to be established in accordance with the current global IPR rules. Sub-option c. proposes concrete arrangements to address IPRs, including commitments related to humanitarian or preferential licensing, fully paid-up or joint licensing schemes, preferential rates and patent pools. Many of these arrangements cannot be achieved through a business-as-usual approach. Financial support or greater international cooperation is required.

On the way to Paris, developing countries renewed their interest in IPRs and technology transfer. The draft text featured an option calling for developed countries to "provide financial resources to address barriers created by policies and intellectual property rights (IPRs) and facilitate access to and the deployment of technology", including via "utilizing the Financial Mechanism and/or establishing a funding window under the GCF to meet the full costs of IPRs of environmentally sound technologies (ESTs)".[288] Given its contentious nature, the 2015 Paris Agreement is also silent on the issues of the IPRs. However, Parties may continue to discuss this specific issue in the context of development and transfer of technology when countries begin to fully implement the Paris Agreement.

3.5 CONCLUSION

Technology-rich (mainly developed) countries and technology-poor (mainly developing) countries have different interests in shaping the regulations governing innovation and transfer of technology. As Maskus (2004) observed, technology exporters tend to favour reducing the costs and uncertainties of innovation and transfer of technology, along with protecting their rights to profit from such innovation and transfers, whereas technology importers prefer

---

[288] Draft Agreement, Work of the ADP Contact Group Incorporating Bridging Proposals by the Co-facilitators, FCCC/ADP/2015/L.6, 5 December 2015, Article 7.2bis, Option 1.

to acquire technology at a minimal cost and tend to refuse to fully protect the rights of foreign firms to profit from such innovation and transfers, or at least severely restrict their exclusive rights to exploit technological innovation.[289]

Two distinct models for regulating innovation and international technology transfer have thus emerged from these two different groups of countries: the NIEO model and the market-based development model.[290] Some commentators have observed that developing countries used to generally favour the NIEO model that features "relatively loose intellectual property protection and relatively tight technology transfer regulation" and is "designed to require the foreign investment to generate specific benefits to local economic actors".[291] In contrast, developed countries tend to choose a market-based development model that favours strong IP protection and freedom of contract, "tempered in its excesses by competition law".[292] The essential difference between these two models lies in the scope and the level of IP protection and the extent of restrictions placed on IPRs to prevent IPR-related abuses or anti-competitive practices.

The adoption of the TRIPS Agreement in the 1990s seemed to signal that the Market Based Development Model had replaced the NIEO Model as the dominant approach to regulating innovation and transfer of technology. Both the negotiating history of TRIPS and its structure point to an underlying tension between the goal of "promoting and protecting innovation by elevating universal intellectual property standards to the level that the industrialized nations deemed appropriate" and the goal of safeguarding the transfer and dissemination of technologies on terms favourable to developing countries by some rather "vaguely defined and reluctantly conceded" technology transfer-oriented rules.[293]

---

[289] Keith E. Maskus (2004), *Encouraging International Technology Transfer*, ICTSD and UNCTAD Issue Paper No. 7, Geneva, Switzerland, p. 7.

[290] See, e.g., Peter Muchlinski (2007), *Multinational Enterprises and the Law*, 2nd edn, New York: Oxford University Press, pp. 443–54; Thomas Chantal (1999), Transfer of Technology in the Contemporary International Order, *Fordham International Law Journal*, vol. 22, pp. 2096–111, at p. 2109; Kevin E. Davis (2005), Regulation of Technology Transfer to Developing Countries: The Relevance of Institutional Capacity, *Law & Policy*, vol. 27, pp. 6–32, at p. 12; the NIEO Model is also referred to as "the Regulatory Control Model" while the Market-Based Development Model is also named as the "Globalization Model" or the "Bretton Woods Model".

[291] See, e.g., Thomas Chantal (1999), Transfer of Technology in the Contemporary International Order, *Fordham International Law Journal*, vol. 22, pp. 2096–111, at p. 2109.

[292] See, e.g., Peter Muchlinski (2007), *Multinational Enterprises and the Law*, 2nd edn, New York: Oxford University Press, p. 443.

[293] Hanns Ullrich (2004), Expansionist Intellectual Property Protection and Reductionist Competition Rules: A TRIPS Perspective, *Journal of International Economic Law*, pp. 401–30, at p. 413.

In parallel, technology development and transfer has moved to the top of the international environmental law agenda since the 1992 Rio Summit. Coupled with a growing awareness of the global environmental challenges, most MEAs concluded thereafter incorporated provisions for development and transfer of ESTs. In particular, the UNFCCC obliges developed Parties to transfer ESTs to developing countries and links developing members' ability to fulfil their commitments under the Convention to developed Parties' effective implementation of their commitments related to financial resources and the transfer of technology. In the ongoing international climate change negotiations, severe divergences remain between developing and developed countries over the role of the current global IP regime in the development and transfer of ESTs. The following chapter will examine in detail the role of minimum IPR standards shaped by TRIPS in the innovation and transfer of ESTs to developing countries.

4

The Effects of Minimum IPR Standards Shaped by TRIPS on Innovation and Transfer of ESTs

4.1 INTRODUCTION

As discussed in Section 3.4.2, in international climate negotiations, developing countries and leading technology producers disagree over the role of IPRs in innovation and transfer of ESTs. This disagreement stems from their different preferences regarding the trade-off between technological innovation and access to new technologies. Divergent preferences among countries largely based on their level of technological development have shaped two major opposing views: one view is that strong IP rights are needed to incentivise investment in technological innovation, whereas the other is that international IP protection poses an obstacle to access ESTs. The first view primarily focuses on the innovation aspect of the IP balance and argues for the strong protection and enforcement of IPRs to reassure investors that "returns from investments in innovation can be recouped in global markets" whereas supporters of the second view focus primarily on the "dissemination aspect" of the IP balance, criticising "intrinsic and systemic failures in the modern IP system" and arguing for "strong limits on exclusive rights".[1]

In spite of the clear justification of the need to develop and transfer ESTs for mitigating climate change, as demonstrated in Section 3.4, the TRIPS Agreement, as the most comprehensive multilateral agreement on IP rights, does not explicitly seek to facilitate innovation and transfer of ESTs. The text of the Agreement itself says little about environment protection despite its

---

[1] Keith E. Maskus and Ruth L. Okediji (2010), *Intellectual Property Rights and International Technology Transfer to Address Climate Change: Risks, Opportunities and Policy Options*, ICTSD's Programme on IPRs and Sustainable Development, Issue Paper No. 32, ICTSD, Geneva, Switzerland, p. 2.

potential to affect the environment.[2] However, the innovation and transfer of ESTs is a subset of innovation and transfer of technologies under TRIPS. The TRIPS Agreement lists as one of its principles the promotion of public interests in sectors of vital importance to the socio-economic and techno-logical development of its Members.[3] Accordingly, the IPR systems shaped by TRIPS are expected to "complement efforts to protect the environment by encouraging the transfer of environmentally [sound] technology and minim-izing the barriers that IPR might pose to environmental protection".[4]

It is unclear whether the current global IP regime imposed by the TRIPS Agreement has achieved an appropriate and workable balance between tech-nological innovation and access to ESTs. Given the lack of specific EST provisions in the TRIPS Agreement, two questions will be addressed in the context of climate change from a policy perspective: first, whether and, if so, to what extent do the minimum IPR standards facilitate or inhibit innovation and transfer of ESTs; and second, whether and, if so, to what extent can the TRIPS flexibilities help address developing countries' concerns over access to ESTs?[5] This chapter seeks to examine the implications of minimum IPR standards for innovation and transfer of ESTs, in particular, whether the minimum IPR protection is a prerequisite for innovation and transfer of ESTs to developing countries and whether strong IPR protection presents a barrier to EST transfer to developing countries. Prior to answering these questions, the minimum IPR standards imposed by the TRIPS Agreement will be examined.

4.2 MANDATORY MINIMUM IPR STANDARDS UNDER TRIPS

The TRIPS Agreement sets out global minimum standards of protecting and enforcing virtually all forms of IPRs. Part II of TRIPS defines the main elements of protection, including the subject matter to be protected, the scope of the rights to be conferred, permissible exceptions to rights conferred, and, where applicable, the minimum term of protection.[6] Part III stipulates

---

[2]   For example, patents may be granted to technologies that pollute environment. Furthermore as Professor De Werra points out, "IP is technologically neutral – it protects all types of creativity. It is not green in and of itself". See Jacques de Werra (2010), What Color Is IP? in the Green Debate: IP Perspectives, *WIPO Magazine*, pp. 17–19, at p. 17.

[3]   See Article 8.1 of the TRIPS Agreement.

[4]   Simon Walker (2001), The TRIPS Agreement, Sustainable Development and the Public Interest, Discussion Paper, IUCN, Gland, p. xi.

[5]   The second question concerning TRIPS flexibilities is to be addressed in Chapters 6 and 7.

[6]   Antony Taubman, Hannu Wager and Jayashree Watal (2012), *A Handbook on the WTO TRIPS Agreement*, Cambridge University Press, p. 11.

detailed enforcement obligations. The most relevant IP standards for the generation and transfer as well as diffusion of ESTs are found in Section 5 (on patents) and Section 7 (on undisclosed information) of Part II of the TRIPS Agreement, although some of the other forms of IPRs (such as trademarks) could also be relevant. Some commentators have observed that among the substantive minimum standards for all types of IP covered by the Agreement, "the most far-reaching changes brought about by TRIPS concern patents and undisclosed information".[7]

4.2.1 Patents

Patents are not automatically granted for eligible inventions. To obtain a patent in a particular jurisdiction, an application has to be filed. Patents in each jurisdiction are also independent of each other, that is, a patent granted in a particular jurisdiction has no legal effect in another jurisdiction.[8] Though the PCT streamlines the patent application process for multiple jurisdictions, thereby potentially reducing costs, application fees remain applicable in the national phase, which limits actual cost reductions for patent owners. Given the costs, most patent applications are filed in a limited number of countries.[9] There are no restrictions on making, using or selling the patented product in any jurisdiction where no patents have been granted. It might be true that ESTs may not be protected by patents in most developing countries, yet it is observed that where patent protection matters to industry, for example, where there are profitable markets or where there is domestic manufacturing capacity, products will – if possible – be patented.[10]

The Paris Convention was the first key international treaty relating to patents. However, it left key issues for national authorities to regulate, in particular relating to patentability, subject matter, as well as the scope

---

[7]   Pedro Roffe et al. (2010), Intellectual Property Rights in Free Trade Agreements: Moving Beyond TRIPS Minimum Standards, in Correa (ed.), *Research Handbook on the Protection of Intellectual Property under WTO Rules: Intellectual Property in the WTO*, vol. I, Cheltenham, UK: Edward Elgar Publishing, pp. 266–316, at p. 268.

[8]   See Article 4 *bis* of the Paris Convention, incorporated by reference into the TRIPS Agreement.

[9]   Nevertheless, the European Patent Convention provides a legal framework for the granting of European patents, via a single, harmonised procedure before the European Patent Office. See *The European Patent Convention*, 15th edn, September 2013, published by the European Patent Office, Article 2.

[10]   Edwin Cameron (2004), Patents and Public Health: Principle, Politics and Paradox, *SCRIPTed*, vol. 1, no. 4, pp. 517–54, at p. 531.

and duration of patent rights.[11] When incorporating the Paris Convention (Articles 1 to 12 and 19), the TRIPS Agreement filled these gaps with universal minimum standards of protection that largely "reflect the [then] practice of the developed countries".[12] The TRIPS-based national IPR systems have to confer patent holders with exclusive rights to prevent others from making, using or selling relevant technologies, including ESTs, for at least 20 years.[13]

Subject to limited exceptions (see Section 6.2),[14] WTO Members are obliged under Article 27.1 to provide patent protection for "any inventions, whether products or processes, in all fields of technology", provided that they are new, involve an inventive step ("non-obvious") and are capable of industrial application ("useful"). This general obligation of patentability is further enhanced by a non-discrimination requirement regarding the availability of patents and the enjoyment of patent rights.[15] Article 27.1 explicitly requires that patent rights shall be available and enjoyable "without discrimination as to the place of invention, the field of technology and whether products are imported or locally produced". This provision aims to ban *de jure* discrimination in terms of the availability and enjoyment of patent rights. A Member may act inconsistently with the non-discrimination obligation by excluding an entire field of technology from patent grant or by providing for special exceptions to patent rights only in certain fields of technology.[16] Indeed, the *travaux préparatoires* of the TRIPS Agreement confirm that eliminating "blanket exclusions of certain types of patentable subject matter", in particular, pharmaceutical and chemical products, was a primary concern of the negotiators.[17]

---

[11]   Thomas Cottier and Pierre Veron (2011), *Concise International and European IP Law: TRIPS, Paris Convention, European Enforcement and Transfer of Technology*, 2nd edn, Alphen aan den Rijn, The Netherlands: Kluwer Law International, p. 89.

[12]   Jerome H. Reichman (1995), Universal Minimum Standards of Intellectual Property Protection Under the TRIPS Component of the WTO Agreement, *The International Lawyer*, vol. 29, no. 2, pp. 345–88, at p. 351.

[13]   See Articles 28 and 33 of TRIPS.

[14]   For example, Article 27.1 explicitly made this general obligation of patentability subject to three paragraphs: (a) para. 4 of Article 65; (b) para. 8 of Article 70 and (c) para. 3 of Article 27.

[15]   This patent-specific non-discrimination clause is different from the non-discrimination principles with respect to all IPRs, namely national treatment and MFN treatment, which are provided in Articles 3 and 4 of TRIPS and discussed in Section 3.3.2.1.

[16]   Antony Taubman and Jayashree Watal (2010), The WTO TRIPS Agreement – A Practical Overview for Climate Change Policymakers, Documentation used in technical cooperation activities of the WTO's Intellectual Property Division, p. 4, available at www.wto.org/english/tratop_e/trips_e/ta_docs_e/8_3_overviewclimatechange_e.pdf

[17]   Graeme B. Dinwoodie and Rochelle Cooper Dreyfuss (2005), WTO Dispute Resolution and the Preservation of the Public Domain of Science under International Law, in Maskus and Reichman (eds.), *International Public Goods and Transfer of Technology under a Globalized Intellectual Property Regime*, Cambridge University Press, pp. 861–83, at p. 866.

Therefore, Members may not categorically exclude certain fields of technologies such as renewable energy technologies or other sectors of ESTs.

Article 28.1 provides patent holders with certain basic rights, which are intended to prevent others from making, using, offering for sale, selling or importing the patented product or product directly obtained by the patented process or using the patented process without consent.[18] Furthermore, the patent owner enjoys the relative freedom to transfer or assign patent rights (Article 28.2). National legislations that restrict such rights by imposing additional conditions or requirements may violate patent owners' rights, if such conditions "restrict the patent owner's rights unreasonably" or "conflicts with a normal exploitation of the patent rights".[19] The panel in *Canada–Pharmaceutical Patents* (2000) interpreted the term "normal exploitation" as the practice "to exclude all forms of competition that could detract significantly from the economic returns anticipated from a patent's grant of market exclusivity".[20] The scope of "normal exploitation" of patent rights is thus quite broad.

The TRIPS Agreement significantly increased the level and expanded the scope of patent protection. In time, many countries had to increase the duration of the term of the patent protection under TRIPS, for example, even developed countries like Australia increased its standard patent term from 16 to 20 years counting from the date of filing.[21] In scope, TRIPS provides patent protection to (new) subject matters where previous international IP law was either silent or perceived inadequate.[22] The patentee has the exclusive right to import the protected product, subject to the applicable rules of exhaustion, which is left open in the TRIPS Agreement, whereas prior to TRIPS the right of importation was not generally enumerated as an exclusive right.[23] Despite the controversy, patent protection was extended to products directly covered by the patented process.[24] The enforcement of exclusive rights is ensured by

---

[18] The act of making in Article 28.1 is only pertinent to a product patent.

[19] Thomas Cottier and Pierre Veron (2011), *Concise International and European IP Law: TRIPS, Paris Convention, European Enforcement and Transfer of Technology*, 2nd edn, Alphen aan den Rijn, The Netherlands: Kluwer Law International, p. 93.

[20] Panel Report, *Canada – Pharmaceutical Patents*, para. 7.55.

[21] Panel Report, *Canada – Patent Term*, para. 6.61.

[22] Jayashree Watal (2001), *Intellectual Property Rights in the WTO and Developing Countries*, Alphen aan den Rijn, The Netherlands: Kluwer Law International, p. 4.

[23] UNCTAD-ICTSD (2005), *Resource Book on TRIPS and Development*, Cambridge University Press, p. 415.

[24] Daniel Gervais (2012), *The TRIPS Agreement: Drafting History and Analysis*, 4th edn, Hebden Bridge, UK: Sweet & Maxwell, p. 462 (noting that "[t]he inclusion of products obtained by a patented process in the scope of protection of process patents was the result of a long and

civil sanctions and in some cases even by criminal penalties.[25] Through incorporation, the TRIPS Agreement also extends the patent rules of the Paris Convention to all WTO Members, including those who are not a party to the Paris Convention. Thus, the Agreement successfully elevated patent standards universally and is, sometimes, referred to as a "Paris-plus" treaty.

4.2.2 *Trade Secrets*

The TRIPS Agreement provides for the obligation to protect undisclosed information that covers both trade secrets and test data. The Agreement further provides for enforcement, requiring that judicial proceedings be available to protect trade secrets and test data from disclosure.[26] Despite the fact that test data is particularly relevant for certain food- or health-related climate change adaptation technologies,[27] it is not addressed in this book as it is not directly related to climate change mitigation technologies. A trade secret is eligible for protection under TRIPS if it (a) is secret; (b) "has commercial value because it is secret" and (c) has been subject to "reasonable steps" to be kept secret.[28] Article 39.1 of the TRIPS Agreement provides that:

difficult debate. The main argument for the inclusion of this protection was the possibility that a process would be used in a country and the product obtained by the process shipped to another country, thus rending enforcement potentially very complicated").

[25] Article 61 of the TRIPS Agreement provides that "Members shall provide for criminal procedures and penalties to be applied at least in cases of wilful trademark counterfeiting or copyright piracy on a commercial scale ... Members may provide for criminal procedures and penalties to be applied in other cases of infringement of intellectual property rights, in particular where they are committed wilfully and on a commercial scale"; see also UNCTAD (1996), *The TRIPS Agreement and Developing Countries*, New York and Geneva: United Nations, p. 30 (noting that "the provisions on enforcement (Part III of the Agreement) are generally applicable to patent rights, although Member countries need not apply the special requirements of border control measures to patents. Such measures are obligatory for trademarks and copyrights").

[26] See Part III: Enforcement of Intellectual Property Rights of TRIPS.

[27] As pointed out by Taubman and Watal, "[t]est data includes data on safety and efficacy of medicines, and field trial data on the environmental impact of new pesticides. The protection of such data may be relevant to certain climate change adaptation technologies, particularly for food and health, which may need regulatory approval from the perspective of health, efficacy or environmental impact"; see Antony Taubman and Jayashree Watal (2010), The WTO TRIPS Agreement – A Practical Overview for Climate Change Policymakers, Documentation used in technical cooperation activities of the WTO's Intellectual Property Division, p. 12, available at www.wto.org/english/tratop_e/trips_e/ta_docs_e/8_3_overviewclimatechange_e.pdf

[28] See Article 39.2 of the TRIPS Agreement.

In the course of ensuring effective protection against unfair competition as provided in Article 10 *bis* of the Paris Convention (1967), Members shall protect undisclosed information in accordance with paragraph 2.

Protection of trade secrets was listed among the different forms of IP protection albeit of a specific nature, whereas, prior to TRIPS, it was not generally protected by specific intellectual property legislation but by general civil law standards.[29] At the time of the TRIPS negotiations, several developing countries, for example, Brazil, India and Peru, opposed the inclusion of trade secrets into the Agreement on the ground that trade secrets cannot be deemed to be intellectual property rights as they are, by definition, not "disclosable" subject matters.[30] The fact that the "undisclosed information" is deemed to be a type of intellectual property (Article 1.2 of the Agreement) does "not imply the existence of a property right".[31] This is evidenced by the fact that Article 39 does not refer to the "owner" of the undisclosed information but to persons who have "information lawfully within their control", which is in clear contrast to the "ownership" concept in relation to trademarks and patents under Articles 16.1 and 28.1 of the TRIPS Agreement.[32]

Consequently, compared to an intellectual property rights approach, the scope of protection under Article 39 is limited as no exclusive rights are granted to the person that legally controls the undisclosed information.[33]

---

[29] See Article 1.2 of TRIPS (stating that "for the purpose of this Agreement, the term 'intellectual property' refers to all categories of intellectual property that are the subject of Sections 1 through 7 of Part II", suggesting that trade secrets are deemed to be a 'category' of intellectual property); see also Daniel Gervais (2012), *The TRIPS Agreement: Drafting History and Analysis*, 4th edn, Hebden Bridge, UK: Sweet & Maxwell, p. 541 (further noting that "this field is not regulated in multilateral conventions, apart from the general obligations in respect of unfair competition found in art. 10 *bis* of the Paris Convention").

[30] Communication from Brazil, 11 December 1989, GATT Doc. MTN.GNG/NG11/W/57, p. 8 (arguing that "trade secrets are not the object of intellectual property protection since the latter deals only with disclosable subject matters. Therefore, trade secrets should not be subject of discussion in the Negotiating Group."); Standards and Principles Concerning the Availability, Scope and Use of Trade-related Intellectual Property Rights: Communication from India, 10 July 1989, GATT Doc. MTN.GNG/NG11/W/37, p. 18; Guidelines for Negotiations that Strike a Balance between Intellectual Property Rights and Development Objectives: Communication from Peru, 27 October 1989, GATT Doc. MTN.GNG/NG11/W/45, p. 5.

[31] Carlos M. Correa (2007), *Trade Related Aspects of Intellectual Property Rights: A Commentary on the TRIPS Agreement*, Oxford University Press, p. 368.

[32] UNCTAD and ICTSD (2005), *Resource Book on TRIPS and Development*, Cambridge University Press, p. 527.

[33] Carlos M. Correa (2007), *Trade Related Aspects of Intellectual Property Rights: A Commentary on the TRIPS Agreement*, Oxford University Press, at p. 368 (stating that "Article 39 does not imply any obligation to confer exclusive rights on undisclosed information . . .").

Article 39.2 of the TRIPS Agreement specifies the scope of protection, stating that:

> Natural and legal persons shall have the possibility of preventing information lawfully within their control from being disclosed to, acquired by, or used by others without their consent in a manner contrary to honest commercial practices.

In light of this provision, trade secret holders have the right to prevent the disclosure to, the acquisition by or the use by others without their consent. However, such acts are only prohibited if they have been conducted "in a manner contrary to honest commercial practices".[34] This is characterised by Cottier and Veron (2011) as a decisive element for qualifying Article 39 as an unfair competition law provision.[35] Given that the protection of undisclosed information is based on unfair competition law, protection granted by Article 39 is "not enforceable *erga omnes* but applies only against certain third parties which have acted unfairly against the [holder] of the trade secrets".[36]

Footnote 10 to Article 39.2, which is an integral part of TRIPS, provides a non-exhaustive list for defining the concept of "a manner contrary to honest commercial practices". For the purpose of Article 39.2, "a manner contrary to honest commercial practices" shall mean "at least practices such as breach of contract, breach of confidence and inducement to breach", and "includes the acquisition of undisclosed information by third parties who knew, or were grossly negligent in failing to know, that such practices were involved in the acquisition". As observed by De Werra (2010), such a definition "implies the adoption of a subjective standard of analysis (i.e. a standard based on a finding of bad faith)".[37] Whether an act constitutes bad faith or not depends in part upon social and cultural contexts, and is therefore left to the Members to decide under their national laws.

If the acts enumerated by the provision are not performed in bad faith, they may not violate the duty to protect confidential information under TRIPS. In other words, protection of trade secrets is only to prevent non-authorised

---

[34] UNCTAD and ICTSD (2005), *Resource Book on TRIPS and Development*, Cambridge University Press, p. 528.

[35] Thomas Cottier and Pierre Veron (2011), *Concise International and European IP Law: TRIPS, Paris Convention, European Enforcement and Transfer of Technology*, 2nd edn, Alphen aan den Rijn, The Netherlands: Kluwer Law International, p. 116.

[36] Jacques de Werra (2010), How to Protect Trade Secrets in High-Tech Sports? An Intellectual Property Analysis Based on the Experiences at the America's Cup and in the Formula One Championship, *European Intellectual Property Review*, vol. 32, no. 4, pp. 155–64, at p. 156.

[37] Ibid., p. 160.

disclosure, acquisition and use of undisclosed information by unfair means. It is generally accepted that the protection against unfair competition does not exclude the discovery of the trade secret by fair and honest means, for example, independent invention or reverse engineering.[38]

In contrast to patents, for which the term of protection is finite, the protection of a trade secret can, in principle, extend indefinitely, so long as the conditions for its protection are met.[39] Nevertheless, unlike patents, there is no protection against a competitor that develops the same trade secret independently.[40] The competitor is free to use his or her independent discovery at will. Many commentators view reverse engineering as a possible pathway for trade secrets to become public and consequently enter the public domain.[41] US jurisprudence has confirmed that reverse engineering is a legal means to acquire a trade secret as long as the known products are legitimately obtained and there is no contractual constraint.[42] If trade secret law did not allow reverse engineering, it would in effect "convert the Company's trade secret into a state-conferred monopoly akin to the absolute protection that a federal patent affords".[43] The legality of reverse engineering is fundamental to trade secret law, for the likelihood that unpatented objects will be reverse

---

[38] See, e.g., *Kewanee Oil Co. v. Bicron Co.*, 41 U.S. 470, 490 (1974) (noting that "trade secret law does not forbid the discovery of the trade secret by fair and honest means, for example, independent creation or reverse engineering"); Thomas J. McCarthy (1995), *McCarthy's Desk Encyclopaedia of Intellectual Property*, Bureau of National Affairs, p. 452.

[39] Antony Taubman and Jayashree Watal (2010), The WTO TRIPS Agreement – A Practical Overview for Climate Change Policymakers, Documentation used in technical cooperation activities of the WTO's Intellectual Property Division, p. 13, available at www.wto.org/english/tratop_e/trips_e/ta_docs_e/8_3_overviewclimatechange_e.pdf

[40] Mitchel B. Wallerstein, Mary Ellen Mogee and Roberta A. Schoen (1993), *Global Dimensions of Intellectual Property Rights in Science and Technology*, Washington, D.C.: National Academy Press, p. 203.

[41] See, e.g., Rochelle Cooper Dreyfuss and Roberta Rosenthal Kwall (1996), *Intellectual Property: Trademark, Copyright, and Patent Law: Cases and Materials*, Eagan, MN: West Publishing Company, p. 818; UNCTAD and ICTSD (2005), *Resource Book on TRIPS and Development*, Cambridge University Press, p. 529 (stating that "Article 39.2 (a) does not disallow the use of [reverse engineering]; to the extent that the secret information is 'readily accessible', it would not be considered secret under such provision").

[42] See, e.g., *Kewanee Oil Co. v. Bicron Co.*, 41 U.S. 470, 490 (1974) noting that ("trade secret law does not forbid the discovery of the trade secret by fair and honest means, e.g., independent creation or reverse engineering"); *Cataphote Corp. v. Hudson*, 422 F.2d 1290, 1293 (5th Cir. 1970) holding that ("it is not a misappropriation to discover a trade secret by reverse engineering"); Restatement (Third) of Unfair Competition § 43 [Improper Acquisition of Trade Secrets], 1994, para. b. [proper means of acquisition] provides that ("others remain free to analyse products publicly marketed by the trade secret owner and, absent protection under a patent or copyright, to exploit any information acquired through such 'reverse engineering'").

[43] *Chicago Lock Co. v. Fanberg*, 676 F.2d 400, 216 U.S.P.Q. (BNA) 289 (9th Cir. 1982).

engineered is part of the "balance between patent policy and the policy favouring free competition".[44]

Trade secrets play a significant role in technological and scientific advancement, at a level different from (but not necessarily a lower level than) patents.[45] Similar to the patent system, trade secret law provides incentives for innovation and promotes the dissemination of technologies.[46] Yet, trade secret itself has its limits as its non-disclosure nature may slow down the dissemination of know-how to the public in general and to competitors in particular.

4.2.3 *Enforcement of IPRs*

The pre-existing international IP conventions administrated by WIPO were criticised by some commentators for their "lack of effective dispute settlement and enforcement procedures".[47] As observed by Gervais (2012), prior to TRIPS, provisions dealing with the enforcement of IP rights were "basically general obligations to provide for legal remedies" and, in certain cases, the seizure of the infringing goods.[48] The TRIPS Agreement is the first

---

[44] Jay Dratler and Stephen M. McJohn (2004), *Intellectual Property Law: Commercial, Creative, and Industrial Property*, vol. I, Law Journal Press, para. 4.04 [2]. Dratler and McJohn cited from *Acuson Corp* v. *Aloka Co.*, 257 Cal. Rptr. 368, 379 (Cal. App. 1989).

[45] *Kewanee Oil Co.* v. *Bicron Corp.* – 416 U.S. 470 (1974), the US Supreme Court finds that trade secrets "have an important part to play in the technological and scientific advancement of the Nation".

[46] According to Jager (2002), since trade secret laws demand relative, not absolute, secrecy, "a public policy advantage of trade secret protection is the encouragement of technology licensing, while still providing a legal vehicle for protecting the information" and trade secrets "provide incentives to advance technical arts that would not otherwise exist" (see Melvin F. Jager (2002), The Critical Role of Trade Secret Law in Protecting Intellectual Property Assets, in Goldscheider (ed.), *Licensing Best Practices: The LESI Guide to Strategic Issues and Contemporary Realities*, Hoboken, NJ: John Wiley & Sons, pp. 127–38, at p. 130); see also John R. Thomas (2010), *The Role of Trade Secrets in Innovation Policy*, Congressional Research Service (CRS) Report for Congress, Prepared for Members and Committees of Congress, p. 3.

[47] Ernst-Ulrich Petersmann (2003), From Negative to Positive Integration in the WTO: The TRIPS Agreement and the WTO Constitution, in Cottier and Mavroidis (eds.), *Intellectual Property: Trade, Competition and Sustainable Development*, The World Trade Forum, vol. III, University of Michigan Press, pp. 21–52, at p. 28. See also Jayashree Watal (2001), *Intellectual Property Rights in the WTO and Developing Countries*, Alphen aan den Rijn, The Netherlands: Kluwer Law International, p. 22 (noting that "WIPO treaties did not have provisions mandating effective domestic enforcement of IPRs, nor a dispute settlement mechanism to ensure compliance with international obligations").

[48] Daniel Gervais (2012), *The TRIPS Agreement: Drafting History and Analysis*, 4th edn, Hebden Bridge, UK: Sweet & Maxwell, p. 564; see also, arts 9, 10, 10*bis* and 10*ter* (1) of the Paris Convention.

international IP agreement that sets out detailed and comprehensive provisions mandating effective domestic IP rights enforcement.[49]

Despite the acknowledgement that IP rights are private rights in the Preamble to TRIPS, with twenty-one provisions, Part III of TRIPS provides comprehensive international minimum standards on the enforcement of IPRs, including civil, administrative procedures and remedies as well as criminal procedures.[50] As a general principle, Article 41.1 obliges the Members to establish an effective enforcement mechanism against any infringement of IP rights covered by TRIPS, including "expeditious remedies to prevent infringements" and "remedies which constitute a deterrent to further infringements". The reasoning behind this principle is to ensure that effective remedies are available for the right holders. However, as noted by Cottier and Veron (2011) and Stoll et al. (2009), it is not clear to what extent the Members are obliged not only to provide for enforcement remedies but also to ensure their effectiveness in practice.[51]

Nevertheless, the enforcement procedures shall be applied in such a manner as to "avoid the creation of barriers to legitimate trade and to provide for safeguards against abuses".[52] This provision reaffirms the general purpose of the TRIPS Agreement, as enshrined in its Preamble, namely, that it is not only intended to protect and enforce IP rights but also to prevent distortions and impediments to international trade that may result from overprotection.

4.2.4 *Controversy over the Effect of Minimum IPR Standards on Technology Transfer*

To comply with the TRIPS Agreement, many developing countries had to substantially upgrade their IPRs systems. As observed by Reichman and Hasenzahl (2003), the TRIPS Agreement has "blocked further efforts to

---

[49] See, e.g., Monique L. Cordray (1994), GATT v. WIPO, *Journal of the Patent & Trademark Office Society*, vol. 76, pp. 121–44, at p. 135 (considering that "perhaps the most significant milestone in TRIPS is the enforcement provisions").

[50] See Articles 41–61 of the TRIPS Agreement.

[51] Thomas Cottier and Pierre Veron (2011), *Concise International and European IP Law: TRIPS, Paris Convention, European Enforcement and Transfer of Technology*, 2nd edn, Alphen aan den Rijn, The Netherlands: Kluwer Law International, p. 125; Peter-Tobias Stoll, Jan Busche and Katrin Arend (2009), *WTO: Trade-Related Aspects of Intellectual Property Rights*, vol. 7, Leiden, The Netherlands: Martinus Nijhoff, p. 689.

[52] See Article 41.1 of the TRIPS Agreement.

negotiate differential and more favourable treatment for developing countries under the patent provisions of the Paris Convention".[53]

The effects of this revolutionary change in international IP law on technology transfer to developing countries have attracted lots of controversy. It is alleged that the expected increased flows of technology do not seem to have materialised.[54] Particularly during the first few years after the adoption of the TRIPS Agreement, many have claimed that little effort has been devoted to making Article 7 of the Agreement operational.[55] Moreover, some developing countries and commentators expressed their concerns that the strengthening of IPRs in accordance with the TRIPS Agreement may act as an impediment to access to technologies.[56] According to Correa (2001), stronger IP protection has "reinforced the power of private parties to control the use and eventual transfer" of technologies, allowing companies to, for example, raise royalties, impose more onerous conditions or retain their technologies.[57]

---

[53] Jerome H. Reichman and Catherine Hasenzahl (2003), *Non-voluntary Licensing of Patented Inventions: Historical Perspective, Legal Framework under TRIPS, and an Overview of the Practice in Canada and the United States of America*, UNCTAD-ICTSD Project on IPRs and Sustainable Development, Issue Paper No. 5, UNCTAD and ICTSD, Geneva, Switzerland, p. 13.

[54] See, e.g., Ana Pueyo and Pedro Linares (2012), Renewable Technology Transfer to Developing Countries: One Size Does Not Fit All, *IDS Working Paper*, No. 412, p. 6; Carlos M. Correa (2001), *Review of the TRIPS Agreement: Fostering the Transfer of Technology to Developing Countries*, TWN Trade & Development Series 13, Penang, Malaysia: Third World Network, p. 34.

[55] See, e.g., Matthews Stilwell and Elisabeth Tuerk (2001), Towards a Full Review of the WTO's TRIPS Agreement under Article 71.1, Centre for International Environmental Law, p. 4, available at www.ciel.org/Publications/Assessment_Trips_article711.pdf. Preparations for the 1999 Ministerial Conference: Proposals on IPR Issues, Communication from India, WTO Doc., WT/GC/W/147, 18 February 1999, at p. 3 (proposing that "the TRIPS Agreement may be reviewed to consider ways and means to operationalize the objective and principles in respect of transfer and dissemination of technology to developing countries").

[56] See, e.g., Preparations for the 1999 Ministerial Conference: Proposals on IPR Issues, Communication from India, WTO Doc., WT/GC/W/147, 18 February 1999, p. 2 (expressing its concern that "the TRIPS Agreement in its current form might tempt IPR holders to charge exorbitant and commercially unviable prices for transfer or dissemination of technologies held through such IPRs"); Matthews Stilwell and Elisabeth Tuerk (2001), Towards a Full Review of the WTO's TRIPS Agreement under Article 71.1, Centre for International Environmental Law, p. 4, available at www.ciel.org/Publications/Assessment_Trips_article711.pdf, (noting that "developing countries seem to be facing increasing barriers to access to technology as a result of a number of factors including the changing pattern of international economic activity, strengthened intellectual property rights required by the TRIPS Agreement, and inadequate counterbalancing policies and measures to promote technology transfer").

[57] Carlos Correa (2001), Review of the TRIPS Agreement: Fostering the Transfer of Technology to Developing Countries, *TWN Trade & Development Series* 13, Penang, Malaysia: Third World Network, p. 29.

However, further studies are required to substantiate these general observations over the effect of minimum IPR standard on innovation and transfer of technology. The precise effect of strong IPR protection on innovation and transfer of technology is contingent upon the characteristics of the technologies transferred and the level of the technological development of the technology recipients.[58] The following sections conduct an in-depth study of the role of strong IPR protection in innovation and transfer of technologies, in particular, ESTs.

4.3 THE POSITIVE ROLE OF MINIMUM IPR PROTECTION IN FACILITATING INNOVATION AND TRANSFER OF ESTS

If the introduction of high IPR standards was essentially driven by the economic interests of technology producers, would such IPR standard setting also take into account public interests such as the (global) environmental protection? In the context of climate change, despite the urgent need for the wide dissemination and transfer of ESTs, as demonstrated in Section 2.1, the TRIPS Agreement does not provide for special treatment for ESTs. WTO Members are obliged to provide for patent protection for ESTs for at least 20 years as long as they fulfil the specified requirements.[59] ESTs are often protected by trade secrets as well. Trade secrets, coupled with strong patent protection, may provide a strong incentive for the development of ESTs while they may also hinder access to ESTs.

Commentators have observed that the implementation of global minimum IPR standards, especially in the area of patents, directly affects international technology flows,[60] including EST transfer. Divergent views have emerged

---

[58] See, e.g., UNCTAD (2007), *The Least Developed Countries Report 2007: Knowledge, Technological Learning and Innovation for Development*, prepared by the UNCTAD Secretariat, New York and Geneva: United Nations, pp. 106–7 (finding that "the effects of IPRs on technology transfers to developing countries depend on a country's level of development, the specific technological fields involved, the level of individual firms' absorptive capacity, the life cycle of technologies, the sector in which IPRs are applied, the type of technology used and general market conditions").

[59] WTO Members agreed in June 2013 to extend until 1 July 2021 the deadline for LDCs to protect IP under TRIPS, with a further extension possible when the time comes (see Council for Trade-Relate Aspects of Intellectual Property Rights, Extension of the Transition Period under Article 66.1 for Least Developed Country Members, 11 June 2013, WTO Doc., No. IP/C/64).

[60] See, e.g., Danielle L. Tully (2003), Prospects for Progress: The TRIPS Agreement and Developing Countries after the Doha Conference, *Boston College International & Comparative Law Review*, vol. 26, pp. 129–43, at p. 130 (observing that "The implementation and enforcement of these minimum standards, especially in the area of patents, directly affects

among scholars, companies and policy-makers regarding the role of IPRs in facilitating innovation and transfer of ESTs. For the proponents of a patent-based innovation system, IPRs are essential incentives for innovation and transfer of ESTs,[61] whereas some others are concerned about the exclusive effects of IPRs on innovation and transfer of technologies, in particular when the technology is essential for promoting public policy goals, such as mitigating climate change.[62] This section conducts an in-depth study of the enabling role of IPRs in innovation and transfer of ESTs based on the recognition that international transfer of ESTs is a subset of international technology transfer, which may occur through FDI, trade, licensing, imitation and others. A subsequent section, that is Section 4.4, will study the exclusive effects of IPRs on innovation and transfer of ESTs.

4.3.1 *IP Rights as an Enabling Factor for Innovation of ESTs*

Modern IPR legislation has been adopted and implemented with the purported goal of spurring innovation. Even if some studies question the incentivising effect of IPRs on innovation,[63] it is generally agreed that the granting and protection of IPRs, in particular, patents, may contribute to innovation through: (a) "incentive to innovate", that is, providing a critical incentive for

---

transborder technology flows, and, as a result, the course of progress for developing countries");
Ruth L. Gana (1996), Prospects for Developing Countries under the TRIPS Agreement, *Vanderbilt Journal of Transnational Law*, vol. 29, pp. 735–75, at p. 743 (observing that "The allocation and enforcement of intellectual property rights are directly relevant to transborder technology flows which, in turn, have an impact on development objectives").

[61] See, e.g., Copenhagen Economics (2009), *Are IPR a Barrier to the Transfer of Climate Change Technology?* Copenhagen Economics A/S and the IPR Company ApS, p. 38; International Chamber of Commerce (2009), Climate Change and Intellectual Property, ICC Document No. 213/71 and No. 450/1050, p. 9 (stating that "The International Chamber of Commerce (ICC) strongly believes that IPR protection is indispensable in supporting growth in technology innovation, development and dissemination envisioned by proposals for post-2012 action"); Nicholas Stern (2007), *The Economics of Climate Change: The Stern Review*, Cambridge University Press, p. 566.

[62] See, e.g., UNDP (2011), *Technological Cooperation and Climate Change: Issues and Perspectives*, Working papers presented at the Ministry of Environment and Forests, Government of India-UNDP Consultation on Technology Cooperation for Addressing Climate Change, New Delhi, India, pp. 78–86; IPCC (2014), *Climate Change 2014: Mitigation of Climate Change*, Working Group III Contribution to the IPCC 5th Assessment Report, Chapter 15: National and Sub-National Policies and Institutions, p. 1175.

[63] See, e.g., Adam B. Jaffe and Josh Lerner (2004), *Innovation and Its Discontents: How Our Broken Patent System Is Endangering Innovation and Progress, and What to Do about It*, Princeton University Press, p. 52 (finding that IPRs could restrict access to knowledge, discourage attempts to invent around patents and have adverse effects on competition).

innovation by allowing the right holders to reap the rewards of their R&D investment and prevent free-riding; and (b) "incentive to disclose", that is, encouraging disclosure of new and useful inventions into the public domain that would provide the basis for new research and development.[64] Given that existing studies show that the exact role of IPRs in technological innovation is industry- and country- specific,[65] it is necessary to understand whether this generic theory would equally apply to ESTs.

4.3.1.1 The Incentive Effects of IPRs on Innovation of ESTs

The primary justification for IP rights is that they provide incentives to produce socially desirable innovation.[66] IPRs establish legal boundaries that permit technology innovators to control their inventions, "reducing third-party appropriation or free riding", thereby ensuring that the investor can reap the rewards of innovation.[67] Without IP protection, the IP creators who had invested time and money in R&D would tend to lose the economic fruits of their labours, thereby disincentivising the investment necessary to develop the technology in the first place.[68] Therefore, the availability and efficacy of IPRs may provide legal security and confidence for investment in the R&D of new technologies.[69]

---

[64] See, e.g., David Encaoua, Dominique Guellec and Catalina Martinez (2006), Patent Systems for Encouraging Innovation: Lessons from Economic Analysis, *Research Policy* 35, pp. 1423–40, at p. 1425; Christine Greenhalgh and Mark Rogers (2010), *Innovation, Intellectual Property, and Economic Growth*, Princeton and Oxford: Princeton University Press, pp. 32–55; P. Zuniga, D. Guellec, H. Dernis et al. (2009), *OECD Patent Statistics Manual*, Paris: OECD, pp. 21–3.

[65] See, e.g., William Fisher (2001), Intellectual Property and Innovation: Theoretical, Empirical and Historical Perspectives, in *Seminar on Intellectual Property and Innovation in the Knowledge-Based Economy*, The Hague, p. 28; Bronwyn H. Hall and Christian Helmers (2010), The Role of Patent Protection in (Clean/Green) Technology Transfer, *Santa Clara Computer & High Technology Law Journal*, vol. 26, pp. 487–532, at p. 504.

[66] See, e.g., Pugatch Meir Perez (2006), *The Intellectual Property Debate: Perspectives from Law, Economics and Political Economy*, Cheltenham, UK: Edward Elgar Publishing, p. 2; William Fisher (2001), Theories of Intellectual Property, in Munzer (ed.), *New Essays in the Legal and Political Theory of Property*, Cambridge University Press, pp. 168–200.

[67] Frederick M. Abbot (2009), *Innovation and Technology Transfer to Address Climate Change: Lessons from the Global Debate on Intellectual Property and Public Health*, ICTSD's Programme on IPRs and Sustainable Development, Issue Paper No. 24, ICTSD, Geneva, Switzerland, p. 4.

[68] Economics and Statistics Administration and United States Patent and Trademark Office (2012), *Intellectual Property and the U.S. Economy: Industries in Focus*, U.S. Department of Commerce, p. v.

[69] It is also argued that IPRs may increase the value of the innovations themselves. See, e.g., The ICC Commission on Intellectual Property (2011), Intellectual Property: Powerhouse for Innovation and Economic Growth, International Chamber of Commerce, Paris, p. 13.

To what extent can the patent system incentivise the innovation of ESTs? Previous economic studies have failed to provide a clear answer to this question. Various studies suggest that the effectiveness of IPRs in stimulating innovation is contingent on the characteristics of the industry.[70] On the one hand, according to Boldrin and Levine (2013), industrial-level evidence shows that the initial eruption of innovations leading to the emergence of some new industries – from chemicals to information technology, from cars to investment banking – is "seldom, if ever, born out of patent protection and is instead the fruit of a competitive environment".[71] On the other hand, based on survey evidence from a number of countries conducted by various economists, Hall and Helmers (2010) find that "if there is an increase in innovation due to patents, it is likely to be centred in the pharmaceutical, biotechnology, and medical instrument areas, and possibly speciality chemicals".[72] Maskus and Okediji (2010) tend to agree with Hall and Helmers by stating that "outside of these industries [chemical, pharmaceutical and biotechnology], the evidence as to the relative importance of patents for inducing innovation is mixed".[73]

[70] See, e.g., Bronwyn H. Hall and Christian Helmers (2010), The Role of Patent Protection in (Clean/Green) Technology Transfer, *Santa Clara Computer & High Technology Law Journal*, vol. 26, pp. 487–532, at p. 504; Andres Lopez (2009), Innovation and Appropriability, Empirical Evidence and Research Agenda, in WIPO (ed.), *The Economics of Intellectual Property: Suggestions for Further Research in Developing Countries and Countries with Economies in Transition*, WIPO, pp. 1–32, at p. 21; Edwin Mansfield (1986), Patents and Innovation: An Empirical Study, *Management Science*, vol. 32, no. 2, pp. 173–81, at p. 175.
[71] Michele Boldrin and David K. Levine (2013), The Case against Patents, *Journal of Economic Perspectives*, vol. 27, no. 1, pp. 3–22, at p. 3; see also Ove Granstrand (2003), Innovation and Intellectual Property, background paper to the Concluding Roundtable Discussion on IPR at the DRUID Summer Conference 2003 on *Creating, Sharing and Transferring Knowledge: The Role of Geography, Institutions and Organisations*, Copenhagen, 12–14 June, p. 41 (noting that the semi-conductor, telecom and software industries emerged under a lax IPR regime).
[72] Bronwyn H. Hall and Christian Helmers (2010), The Role of Patent Protection in (Clean/Green) Technology Transfer, *Santa Clara Computer & High Technology Law Journal*, vol. 26, pp. 487–532, at p. 504. See, e.g., Edwin Mansfield (1986), Patents and Innovation: An Empirical Study, *Management Science*, vol. 32, no. 2, pp. 173–81, at p. 175 (based on a random sample of firms, finding that the more R&D intensive industries, such as pharmaceuticals and chemicals regarded patents as much more important than the less R&D intensive industries such as office equipment, textiles, motor vehicles, rubber); Stuart J. H. Graham et al. (2010), High Technology Entrepreneurs and the Patent System: Result of the 2008 Berkeley Patent Survey, *Berkeley Technology Law Journal*, vol. 24, no. 4, pp. 1255–328, at p. 1255 (finding "substantial differences between the health-related sectors (biotechnology and medical devices), in which patents are more commonly used and considered important, and the software and Internet fields, in which patents are reported to be less useful").
[73] Keith E. Maskus and Ruth L. Okediji (2010), *Intellectual Property Rights and International Technology Transfer to Address Climate Change: Risks, Opportunities and Policy Options*, ICTSD's Programme on IPRs and Sustainable Development, Issue Paper No. 32, ICTSD, Geneva, Switzerland, p. 16.

It can be seen that all of the above-mentioned patent-sensitive industries share common characteristics identified by Fisher (2001): first, high R&D costs; second, "a high degree of uncertainty concerning whether specific lines of research will prove fruitful"; third, "the content of technological advances can be ascertained easily by competitors through 'reverse engineering'"; and fourth, "technological advances can be mimicked by competitors rapidly and inexpensively".[74] In other words, future outcomes of the private sector's R&D investment in such industries are uncertain and subject to high appropriation risk. Therefore, to what extent patents are necessary for the innovation of ESTs may depend on the degree to which R&D investment in a particular field of ESTs is risky. As Pugatch (2011) observed, "economists agreed on the importance of IPRs in overcoming the substantial uncertainty of investment in environmental innovation".[75] Yet, given the presence of negative environmental externalities, some scholars have questioned whether patent protection is a necessary and/or sufficient incentive for the innovation of ESTs.[76]

As demonstrated in Section 2.2.1, ESTs cover a wide range of different fields of technological innovation, ranging from renewable energy technologies to carbon capture and storage.[77] Some ESTs, such as wind and photovoltaic (PV) solar, are very complex technologies that require considerable investment by manufacturers who tend to be very large and sophisticated companies.[78] Therefore, despite the fact that such complex ESTs may be less susceptible to appropriation than patent-sensitive industries like pharmaceuticals, their manufacturers tend to protect their IP rights so as to be able to better recoup their investment and maintain a competitive advantage.[79]

---

[74] William Fisher (2001), Intellectual Property and Innovation: Theoretical, Empirical and Historical Perspectives, in Seminar on *Intellectual Property and Innovation in the Knowledge-Based Economy*, The Hague, p. 28.

[75] Meir Perez Pugatch (2011), *Intellectual Property & The Transfer of Environmentally Sound Technologies*, Global Challenges Report, WIPO, Geneva, Switzerland, p. 8.

[76] Bronwyn H. Hall and Christian Helmers (2010), The Role of Patent Protection in (Clean/Green) Technology Transfer, *Santa Clara Computer & High Technology Law Journal*, vol. 26, pp. 487–532, at p. 490 (noting that "In the presence of the second (negative) environmental externality, this welfare cost [deriving from IP] is likely to be greater because social welfare is enhanced by rapid diffusion of green technology. Therefore, patents may not be the preferred policy instrument for encouraging innovation in this area").

[77] WIPO, IPC Green Inventory, available at www.wipo.int/classifications/ipc/en/est/index.html

[78] Keith Goldberg, Clean Energy Boom Sets Stage for IP Wars, *Law 360*, New York, 30 October 2013, available at www.law360.com/articles/484594/clean-energy-patent-boom-sets-stage-for-ip-wars

[79] See, e.g., Bernice Lee et al. (2009), *Who Owns Our Low Carbon Future? Intellectual Property and Energy Technologies*, A Chatham House Report, Royal Institute of International Affairs,

The preference of companies for IP protection in certain ESTs is evidenced by the current patent booms in clean energy technologies. As observed by UNEP, EPO and ICTSD (2010), claimed priority patenting (patent applications and granted patents) in the selected clean energy technologies (CETs) (in particular solar PV, wind, carbon capture, hydro/marine and biofuels) has increased by approximately 20 per cent per year since the adoption of the Kyoto Protocol (1997), thereby outpacing the rate of patenting in the traditional energy sources of fossil fuels and nuclear energy.[80] Based on an extensive survey of patents filed throughout the world, Bettencourt et al. (2013) from the Santa Fe Institute and Massachusetts Institute of Technology have found that despite a continued low level of (public) R&D funding, the number of patents issued for renewable energy technologies has risen sharply over the last decade, particularly solar and wind patents, with average annual growth rates during the period of 2004 to 2009 of 13 per cent and 19 per cent, respectively.[81] These two studies used patent statistics, which signify the outputs of the inventive process as an indicator of the innovation of ESTs. Despite several limitations of patents as indicators for innovation,[82] the patent surge in ESTs to a certain extent reflects the increase of EST innovation activities. Nevertheless, patents as indicators for innovation do not imply that they are certainly an enabling factor for innovation.

Different factors have been identified as drivers for the surge of patenting activity in certain ESTs. Due to the fact that the patent boom in clean energy

p. 8 (stating that "regardless of the actual cost associated with royalty, patents provide powerful financial and strategic incentives for companies that can shape the incentive calculus for innovation and diffusion"); Cameron Hutchison (2007), *Does TRIPS Facilitate or Impede Climate Change Technology Transfer into Developing Countries*, *CISDL Legal Working Paper Series on Climate Change Law and Policy*, CISDL, p. 17.

[80] UNEP, EPO and ICTSD (2010), *Patents and Clean Energy: Bridging the Gap between Evidence and Policy*, Munich: Mediengruppe Universal, p. 64; it is noted that when a patent is filed in several countries, the first filing date worldwide is called priority date; accordingly, the first patent application is called the priority application.

[81] Luis M. A. Bettencourt et al. (2013), *Determinants of the Pace of Global Innovation in Energy Technologies*, *Plos One*, vol. 8, no. 10: e67864, p. 2; the authors, using key word searches of the patents themselves, rather than the classifications assigned by patent offices, examined more than 73, 000 patents issued for energy-related technologies.

[82] P. Zuniga et al. (2009), *OECD Patent Statistics Manual*, Paris: OECD, p. 13 (noting patent indicators have several drawbacks, including: (1) "[n]ot all inventions are patented"; (2) "[s]imple counts, which give the same weight to all patents regardless of their value, can [...] be misleading" as some patents have very high technical and economic value whereas many are ultimately never used and (3) "[d]ifferent standards across patent offices and over time affect patent numbers although underlying inventive activities may remain unaffected").

technologies coincided with the adoption of the Kyoto Protocol in 1997, UNEP, EPO and ICTSD (2010) suggest that "political decisions setting adequate frameworks do matter for the development of clean energy technologies".[83] Such policies may help address the environmental externalities of ESTs that result from GHG emissions and pollution.[84] Further, Bettencourt et al. (2013) found that a fast rate of growth in markets for these technologies, together with R&D support, can account for a sharp increase in the patenting of some ESTs observed in recent years.[85]

Last but not least, given the failures associated with the markets for technologies, as discussed in Section 2.3.2, IPRs as a means of protecting technological inventions can serve as incentives for innovation. Many scholars agree that IPRs provide incentives for innovation of ESTs.[86] The latest IPCC report (2014) also finds that IP protection has induced innovation in some areas such as wind energy technology.[87] Firms tend to emphasise the essentiality of IPRs in overcoming the substantial uncertainty of investment in innovation of ESTs; without IP protection, investment in innovation may be diverted elsewhere.

In conclusion, depending on circumstances, IPRs protection may incentivise innovation of ESTs. Nevertheless, the evidence that patents promote innovation is weaker than conventionally alleged and protection of IPRs is not the only driver for investment in the innovation of ESTs.

---

[83] UNEP, EPO and ICTSD (2010), *Patents and Clean Energy: Bridging the Gap between Evidence and Policy*, Munich: Mediengruppe Universal, p. 64.

[84] Bronwyn H. Hall and Christian Helmers (2010), The Role of Patent Protection in (Clean/ Green) Technology Transfer, *Santa Clara Computer & High Technology Law Journal*, vol. 26, pp. 487–532, at pp. 488–9 (pointing out that environmental pollution is an activity producing a negative externality and "the social costs associated with pollution exceed private costs").

[85] Luis M. A. Bettencourt et al. (2013), Determinants of the Pace of Global Innovation in Energy Technologies, *Plos One*, vol. 8, no. 10: e67864, pp. 4–5.

[86] See, e.g., Daniel K. N. Johnson and Kristina M. Lybecker (2009), *Innovating for an Uncertain Market: A Literature Review of the Constraints on Environmental Innovation*, No. 2009-06. Colorado College Working Paper, p. 3 (through reviewing academic literature, concludes that "there is near universal agreement among economists that strong intellectual property rights are an essential prerequisite to the development of environmental technologies"); Ian Harvey (2008), *Intellectual Property Rights: The Catalyst to Deliver Low Carbon Technologies*, briefing paper: breaking the climate deadlock, The Climate Group, p. 6 (stating that "There will be little development, deployment or diffusion of new low-carbon technologies and products unless there are strong and enforceable IPRs. They will be an essential catalyst to driving the development and deployment of low-carbon technologies").

[87] IPCC (2014), *Climate Change 2014: Mitigation of Climate Change*, Working Group III Contribution to the IPCC 5th Assessment Report, Chapter 13: International Cooperation: Agreements and Instruments, p. 1036.

4.3.1.2 The Role of Patent-Induced Information Disclosure in Innovation of ESTs

Another fundamental rationale for the patent system is to stimulate disclosure of technological information that might otherwise be kept secret.[88] One justification for the patent disclosure requirement is known as the "social contract" theory: society concludes a contract with the inventor under which the society grants the inventor a temporary monopoly and in return the inventor discloses technological information to the public; "quid pro quo, this is the very principle of equity".[89] The obligation to disclose the invention is a well-established principle of national patent laws, although national regulations use slightly different terminologies.[90] This principle has been reaffirmed in some national jurisprudence. For instance, in *Bonito Boats, Inc.* v. *Thunder Craft Boats, Inc.*, the US Supreme Court asserted that "the ultimate goal of the patent system is to bring new designs and technologies into the public domain through disclosure".[91] Article 29.1 of the TRIPS Agreement introduces the requirement to disclose the invention in the patent application process by stating that:

> Members shall require that an applicant for a patent shall disclose the invention in a manner sufficiently clear and complete for the invention to be carried out by a person skilled in the art and may require the applicant to indicate the best mode for carrying out the invention known to the inventor at the filing date or, where priority is claimed, at the priority date of the application.

Article 29.1 of the TRIPS Agreement makes it clear that the disclosure of an invention is a mandatory requirement for a patent application and that the

---

[88] Carlos M. Correa (2007), *Trade Related Aspects of Intellectual Property Rights: A Commentary on the TRIPS Agreement*, Oxford University Press, p. 300 (considering the disclosure requirement "as one of the basic trade-offs of patent grants, and even the very reason why patents are issued").

[89] See, e.g., Meir Perez Pugatch (2006), *The Intellectual Property Debate: Perspectives from Law, Economics and Political Economy*, Cheltenham, UK: Edward Elgar Publishing, p. 4 (noting that "When addressing the issue of the incentive to disclose secrets, advocates of the patents system described it as a social contract" between society and the inventor, under which "society grants him a temporary guaranty, he discloses the secret which he could have guarded; quid pro quo, this is the very principle of equity"); Edith Tilton Penrose (1951), *The Economics of the International Patent System*, Baltimore, MD: Johns Hopkins Press, p. 32 (stating "society makes a contract with the inventor by which it agrees to grant him the exclusive use of the invention for a period and in return the inventor agrees to disclose technical information in order that it will later be available to society").

[90] Thomas Cottier and Pierre Veron (2011), *Concise International and European IP Law: TRIPS, Paris Convention, European Enforcement and Transfer of Technology*, 2nd edn, Alphen aan den Rijn, The Netherlands: Kluwer Law International, p. 94.

[91] *Bonito Boats, Inc.* v. *Thunder Craft Boats, Inc.*, 489 U.S. 141 (1989), para. 18.

required disclosure has to be conducted "in a manner sufficiently clear and complete" for the invention to be carried out by "a person skilled in the art". As observed by De Carvalho (2010), failing to disclose the invention in a sufficient manner may lead to "the rejection of the application or the invalidation of the patent".[92] This "enablement" or "sufficiency of disclosure" requirement aims at ensuring that "the patents perform their informative function", by requiring that "the patent specification enable those skilled in the art to make and use the full scope of the invention without undue experimentation".[93]

Member States may go a step further by requiring the applicant to indicate the best mode for carrying out the invention.[94] The best mode requirement obliges the inventor to disclose the best way to put the invention into practice that is known to the inventor at the filing date or at the priority date of application. Accordingly, the best mode practice ensures that "the patent applicant does not withhold information that would be useful to third parties".[95]

Sufficient disclosure is essential for patent examiners to assess the patentability of an invention. Furthermore, the information disclosed in the patent document is identified by WIPO as "the single most valuable and comprehensive source of technological information available in the world".[96] Such technological information, which is accessible to everyone, might serve to stimulate ideas for further innovation. According to OECD (1997), for a number of countries, patent information is viewed as "an essential basis for

[92] Nuno Pires de Carvalho (2010), *The TRIPS Regime of Patent Rights*, 3rd edn, Alphen aan den Rijn, The Netherlands: Kluwer Law International, p. 347.

[93] UNCTAD and ICTSD (2005), *Resource Book on TRIPS and Development*, Cambridge University Press, p. 451 (through study of the English case of *Plimpton* v. *Malcolmson* (1986), further noting that "the directions given in the specification for performing the invention must be such as to enable the invention to be carried into effect without an excessive number of experiments").

[94] See, e.g., 35 United States Code (USC) Section 112: Specification (16 September 2012), provides that "The specification shall ... set forth the best mode contemplated by the inventor or joint inventor of carrying out the invention"; 35 United States Code (USC) Section 282, (b) (3) (A) provides that "any requirement of section 112, except that the failure to disclose the best mode, shall not be a basis on which any claim of a patent may be cancelled or held invalid or otherwise unenforceable".

[95] Commission on Intellectual Property Rights (2002), *Integrating Intellectual Property Rights and Development Policy*, Report of the Commission on Intellectual Property Rights, London, p. 117.

[96] WIPO (1999), The Importance of Technological Information Contained in Patent Documents for Inventors and Industry, WIPO Doc. WIPO/INV/ALP/99/7, p. 7.

transfers of technology and as a way to accelerate R&D efforts".[97] In response to the challenges of global climate change, patent information databases have been proposed as a "quasi-technology transfer" to facilitate EST transfer.[98]

Patent information systems may contribute to the innovation of and access to ESTs in a number of ways. First, the full disclosure requirement would help expand the scope of the existing technical knowledge and also enable others to exploit the invention after patent protection has expired.[99] Second, patent information systems allow competitors to learn details about patents on ESTs, to assess the state of the art, to avoid duplicating R&D effort and improve decision making related to licensing and technology partnerships.[100] Last but not least, studying EST patent documents can help companies to identify where relevant technologies are not protected and to find "holes" where they can operate with immunity.[101]

Yet, there are limits to relying on patent disclosure as a source of information for further innovation. Above all, to the extent that they can protect their trade secrets, companies may "prefer secrecy to avoid the public disclosure of the invention (which patent law requires) or to save the significant fees attached to patent filing".[102] Furthermore, some scholars have questioned the effectiveness of the disclosure requirement for transfer of ESTs.[103] Although a

---

[97] OECD (1997), *Patents and Innovation in the International Context*, OCDE/GD (97) 210, Paris: OECD, p. 7 (further noting that "researchers have access to the latest technological information from all countries and can build upon this universal intellectual 'bank' of specialised knowledge").

[98] WIPO website, WIPO's Contribution to Meeting the Challenges of Climate Change, available at www.wipo.int/about-wipo/en/climate_change_conf_09.html (stating that "WIPO offers tools and services to enhance access to the relevant technologies through its patent information resources, such as its PATENTSCOPE® portal"); see also Cynthia Cannady (2009), Access to Climate Change Technology by Developing Countries: A Practical Strategy, ICTSD's Programme on IPRs and Sustainable Development, Issue Paper No. 25, ICTSD, Geneva, Switzerland, p. 5.

[99] UNCTAD and ICTSD (2005), *Resource Book on TRIPS and Development*, Cambridge University Press, p. 451 (noting that Article 29 concerns "matters relating to the disclosure of the invention for the purposes of examination and of execution of the invention after the expiry of the patent term").

[100] Ibid.; see also WIPO (2009), *WIPO Guide to Using Patent Information*, published by WIPO, Geneva, Switzerland, p. 7.

[101] Cynthia Cannady (2009), Access to Climate Change Technology by Developing Countries: A Practical Strategy, ICTSD's Programme on IPRs and Sustainable Development, Issue Paper No. 25, ICTSD, Geneva, Switzerland, p. 6.

[102] Antoine Dechezleprêtre et al. (2013), What Drives the International Transfer of Climate Change Mitigation Technologies? Empirical Evidence from Patent Data, *Environmental and Resource Economics*, vol. 54, pp. 161–78, at p. 164.

[103] See, e.g., Carlos Correa (2005), Can the TRIPS Agreement Foster Technology Transfer to Developing Countries? in Maskus and Reichman (eds.), *International Public Goods and Transfer of Technology under a Globalized Intellectual Property Regime*, Cambridge University

patent claim is invalid in some jurisdictions if the patent specifications do not fulfil the "enabling requirement", that is, enabling a person skilled in the art to reproduce the invention,[104] patent specifications are not a recipe for reproducing the invention. As observed by Correa (2005), patent specification generally convened "the minimum information required" to have the patent granted and "[s]killed patent agents would normally avoid including information that may help competitors to invent around or rapidly implement the invention, once the patent has expired".[105] Additionally, the actual know-how necessary for operating relevant technologies is generally not available and protected by trade secret and/or unfair competition law.[106]

Furthermore, access to patent information does not amount to a legal right to use the relevant technology. The patent right holders have exclusive rights to make, use, sell, offer for sale or import the patented invention during the patent term, which is usually 20 years from the filling date. A non-right holder may use patent information for experimental purposes under Article 30 of the TRIPS Agreement. In *Canada–Pharmaceutical Products* (2000), the panel makes it clear that "under the policy of the patent laws, both society and the scientist have a 'legitimate interest' in using the patent disclosure to support the advance of science and technology".[107] Nevertheless, such use may be disincentivised, as using the improvement that builds upon the issued patents may infringe on the patents of the underlying invention.[108]

Press, pp. 227–56, at p. 239 (finding that "catching up based on patent documentation is unlikely"); Cynthia Cannady (2009), Access to Climate Change Technology by Developing Countries: A Practical Strategy, ICTSD's Programme on IPRs and Sustainable Development, Issue Paper No. 25, ICTSD, Geneva, Switzerland, p. 6 (concluding that "Patent information . . . is not likely to work as a way to gain access to climate change technology").

[104] For example, *Monsanto Canada Inc. v. Schmeiser*, [2004] 1 S.C.R. 902, 2004 SCC 34, paras. 122–3 (finding that "The scope of the patent protection should be both 'fair' and 'reasonably predictable'; the Inventor may not get exclusive rights to an invention that was not part of the public disclosure of the invention"); in the US, the inventor must disclose the "best mode" for carrying out the invention (see 35 U.S.C. 112 Specification).

[105] Carlos Correa (2005), Can the TRIPS Agreement Foster Technology Transfer to Developing Countries? in Maskus and Reichman (eds.), *International Public Goods and Transfer of Technology under a Globalized Intellectual Property Regime*, Cambridge University Press, pp. 227–56, at p. 239.

[106] WIPO (1999), *The Importance of Technological Information Contained in Patent Documents for Inventors and Industry*, WIPO Doc., WIPO/INV/ALP/99/7, p. 8 (noting that "the information contained in patent documentation provides merely the skeleton of a particular technology, and needs to be supplemented from other sources in order to represent a functional body of technology").

[107] Panel Report, *Canada – Pharmaceutical Patents*, para. 7.69.

[108] Cynthia Cannady (2009), Access to Climate Change Technology by Developing Countries: A Practical Strategy, ICTSD's Programme on IPRs and Sustainable Development, Issue Paper No. 25, ICTSD, Geneva, Switzerland, p. 5 (noting that "[m]aking an improvement that builds upon the issued patent does not necessarily insulate the diligent user of patent information

Overall, we can conclude that access to technologies is not an automatic result of patent disclosure, even where patent information is freely accessible. The disclosed information may not be sufficient to enable further innovation. Companies' preference for maintaining secrecy over certain inventions further reduces the utility of the patent system as a source of technological information. Therefore, the public disclosure of inventions plays a positive role in facilitating innovation of, and access to, technologies including ESTs, but such role should not be overstated.

4.3.2 *Strong IP Rights as a Prerequisite for IP Holders to Transfer ESTs*

From a dynamic point of view, robust IPRs boost innovation in originating countries, thereby increasing future technology flows to other countries.[109] Most importantly, IPRs, particularly patents, can facilitate technology transfer through enabling patent disclosure and reducing the risks of imitation. First, IPRs create incentives for right holders to transfer their technologies through preventing free-riders from appropriating the fruits of private investments in innovation, thereby reducing imitation risk.[110] Without sufficient protection of intellectual property to prevent the leakage of new technological information, right holders may be less willing to transfer their technologies.[111] It has been observed that leading firms often cite weak IP protection in host countries as a major reason for their refusal to transfer their latest technologies to certain markets.[112] Second, IPRs stimulate patent disclosure so as to enable the

---

from liability, as he or she may have to practise one or more claims of the underlying invention in order to use the improvement").

[109] See, e.g., Daniel Alker and Franz Heidhues (2002), Farmers' Rights and Intellectual Property Rights – Reconciling Conflicting Concepts, in Evenson et al. (eds.), *Economic and Social Issues in Agricultural Biotechnology*, Cambridge, MA: CABI Publishing, pp. 61–85, at p. 64; Carsten Fink and Carlos A. Primo Braga (2005), How Stronger Protection of Intellectual Property Rights Affects International Trade Flows, in Fink and Maskus (eds.), *Intellectual Property and Development: Lessons from Recent Economic Research*, a copublication of the World Bank and Oxford University Press, pp. 19–40, at p. 22.

[110] As demonstrated in Section 2.3.3, IPRs, in nature, are exclusive rights that prevent others from free riding on the innovators' investments. See also Jerome Reichman H. (1996), From Free Riders to Fair Followers: Global Competition under the TRIPS Agreement, *N.Y.U. Journal of International Law and Politics*, vol. 29, pp. 11–93, at p. 53 (stating that "international intellectual property standards . . . were supposedly designed to prevent free-riders from appropriating the fruits of private investments in research and development").

[111] See also, Keith E. Maskus (2004), *Encouraging International Technology Transfer*, ICTSD and UNCTAD Issue Paper No. 7, Geneva, Switzerland, p. 22.

[112] See, e.g., Meir Perez Pugatch (2011), Intellectual Property & the Transfer of Environmentally Sound Technologies, Global Challenges Report, WIPO, Geneva, Switzerland, p. 9.

technology recipients to estimate the value of innovation, thereby increasing certainty and lowering the transaction costs.[113] Theoretically, to the extent that the risk taken by one or both parties to a technology transfer agreement can be reduced, expected returns will be increased and an increased transfer of technologies should occur. Yet, the role of IP protection in technology transfer is more of an empirical question. The following subsections address in turn the role of IPRs in FDI, licensing and trade and IPRs as an important factor influencing the transfer of ESTs.

4.3.2.1 IPRs and FDI, Licensing and Trade

Empirical studies suggest that the strengthening of a given country's IPR regime may result in an increased transfer of technologies to that country through increased trade, FDI and licensing dependent on circumstances.[114] First, stronger IPR protection may lead to a larger volume of trade flows, albeit mainly for countries with high imitative capacity and larger markets.[115] As observed by several commentators, a firm may be dissuaded from exporting its IPR-protected goods to a foreign market if potential imitators can undermine the profitability of the firm's business activities in that market because the local IPR regime is not strong enough.[116] Accordingly, strengthening a country's IPR regime would tend to increase the total trade of IPR-protected goods. Various studies confirm that increasing IPRs protection has a significantly

[113] OECD (1989), *Competition Policy and Intellectual Property Rights*, Paris: OECD, p. 11.

[114] See, e.g., Rod Falvey and Neil Foster (2006), *The Role of Intellectual Property Rights in Technology Transfer and Economic Growth: Theory and Evidence*, UNIDO Working Papers, Vienna, Austria, p. x; Michael W. Nicholson (2003), Intellectual Property Rights, Internalization and Technology Transfer, *US Federal Trade Commission Working Paper*, p. 1 (finding that both the volume and the quality of technologies to be transferred tend to rise with the strengthening of IP protection).

[115] Rod Falvey et al. (2009), Trade, Imitative Ability and Intellectual Property Rights, *Review of World Economics*, vol. 145, pp. 373–404, at p. 397; the empirical study concluded that "imitative ability and, to a lesser extent, market size are important in this relationship, with strong evidence of market expansion effects in countries with high imitative ability and larger markets, and rather weaker evidence of market power effects in countries with low imitative ability and small markets".

[116] See, e.g., Daniel Alker and Franz Heidhues (2002), Farmers' Rights and Intellectual Property Rights – Reconciling Conflicting Concepts, in Evenson et al. (eds.), *Economic and Social Issues in Agricultural Biotechnology*, Cambridge, MA: CABI Publishing, pp. 61–85, at p. 63; Carsten Fink and Carlos A. Primo Braga (2005), How Stronger Protection of Intellectual Property Rights Affects International Trade Flows, in Fink and Maskus (eds.), *Intellectual Property and Development: Lessons from Recent Economic Research*, a copublication of the World Bank and Oxford University Press, pp. 19–40, at p. 21.

positive effect on the total trade of IPR-protected goods.[117] However, the study by Fink and Braga (2005) shows that this effect is "surprisingly absent" in the case of high-technology products that are inherently more difficult to imitate than other products.[118] It is highly likely that high-technology MNCs may switch from exporting to direct investment abroad when IPRs protection is strengthened as several studies find that local markets may become more profitable for foreign companies when IP protection is stronger.[119]

Second, the strength of a given country's IPRs protection may positively affect the volume, composition and quality of MNCs' FDI in those countries.[120] As observed by Mansfield (1995), in countries with weak IP protection,

[117] See, e.g., Carsten Fink and Carlos A. Primo Braga (2005), How Stronger Protection of Intellectual Property Rights Affects International Trade Flows, in Fink and Maskus (eds.), *Intellectual Property and Development: Lessons from Recent Economic Research*, a copublication of the World Bank and Oxford University Press, pp. 19–40, at p. 20; Keith E. Maskus and Mohan Penubarti (1995), How Trade-Related Are Intellectual Property Rights? *Journal of International Economics*, vol. 39, pp. 227–48, at p. 227 (finding that "increasing patent protection has a positive impact on bilateral manufacturing imports into both small and large developing economies").

[118] See, e.g., Carsten Fink and Carlos A. Primo Braga (2005), How Stronger Protection of Intellectual Property Rights Affects International Trade Flows, in Fink and Maskus (eds.), *Intellectual Property and Development: Lessons from Recent Economic Research*, a copublication of the World Bank and Oxford University Press, pp. 19–40, at p. 20 (in this study, the term "high-technology products" refers to those products that are inherently more difficult to imitate than other products; examples include engines, gas turbines and electrical machinery and apparatus).

[119] See, e.g., Walter G. Park (2011), Intellectual Property Rights and Foreign Direct Investment: Lessons from Central America, in Lopez and Shankar (eds.), *Getting the Most Out of Free Trade Agreements in Central America*, the International Bank for Reconstruction and Development/ the World Bank, pp. 275–308, at p. 294 (finding that "FDI may rise as IPR levels strengthen . . . as firms shift from exporting to setting up subsidiaries abroad"); Christopher Ngassam (2004), Does the Presence or Lack of Intellectual Property Right Protection Affect International Trade Flows in Emerging Market Economies? An Exploratory Study, *Proceedings of the Academy for Studies in International Business*, vol. 4, no. 2, pp. 5–11, at p. 8 (finding that "stronger IPR regimes may cause high technology firms to serve foreign markets by FDI, in part substituting for trade flows").

[120] See, e.g., Edwin Mansfield (1995), Intellectual Property Protection, Direct Investment and Technology Transfer: Germany, Japan and the United States, International Finance Corporation Discussion Paper No. 27, published by the World Bank and International Finance Corporation, p. 23 (through analysing a survey of major MNCs in Germany, Japan and the US on the importance they attach to IPR protection in making FDI decision, this report concluding that "the strength or weakness of a country's system of intellectual property protection seems to have a substantial effect in relatively high-technology industries like chemicals, pharmaceuticals, machinery and electrical equipment on the kinds of technology transferred to that country and the amount of direct investment in that country"); Peter Nunnenkamp and Julius Spatz (2004), Intellectual Property Rights and Foreign Direct Investment: A Disaggregated Analysis, *Review of World Economics*, vol. 140, no. 3, pp. 393–414, at p. 411.

foreign investors may prefer to invest in sales and distribution outlets or rudimentary production and assembly facilities rather than final production or R&D facilities.[121] This was confirmed by Javorcik (2004), using a unique firm-level dataset from Eastern Europe, which found that "a weak intellectual property regime encourages investors to undertake projects focusing on distribution rather than local production" and "weak protection deters foreign investors in technology-intensive sectors that rely heavily on [IPRs]".[122] As found by Nunnenkamp and Spatz (2004), host countries where local imitative capacity is moderate tends to attract more FDI by strengthening IPR protection; and stronger IPR protection may also raise the quality of FDI with respect to its technology content and the value added in exports created by FDI.[123] Therefore, stronger IPR protection plays a positive role in FDI.

Last but not least, strengthening IPR protection has been found to have a positive effect on licensing, in particular for countries with strong absorptive capacities.[124] Through analysing the number of US firms engaged in FDI or licensing by industry, Nicholson (2007) finds that firms with high capital costs are more likely to engage in FDI when IPRs are weak, and "firms in industries with high investment in [R&D] are more likely to enter a market by licensing to an unaffiliated host firm" when IPRs are strong.[125] This finding is confirmed by Park (2011), which suggests that "if IPRs are not sufficiently strong, firms are

[121] See, e.g., Edwin Mansfield (1995), Intellectual Property Protection, Direct Investment and Technology Transfer: Germany, Japan and the United States, International Finance Corporation Discussion Paper No. 27, published by the World Bank and International Finance Corporation, p. 3 (noting that around 20 per cent of the firms reported that IPRs are important to them for investments in sales and distribution outlets while around 30 per cent viewed IPR protection as important for investment in rudimentary production and assembly facilities; this percentage increased to 70 for investments in facilities to manufacture complete products and to 80 when research and development facilities were involved).

[122] Beata Smarzynska Javorcik (2004), The Composition of Foreign Direct Investment and Protection of Intellectual Property Rights: Evidence from Transition Economies, *European Economic Review*, vol. 48, pp. 39–62, at p. 39.

[123] Peter Nunnenkamp and Julius Spatz (2004), Intellectual Property Rights and Foreign Direct Investment: A Disaggregated Analysis, *Review of World Economics*, vol. 140, no. 3, pp. 393–414, at pp. 411–2.

[124] See, e.g., Walter G. Park and Douglas Lippoldt (2005), International Licensing and the Strengthening of Intellectual Property Rights in Developing Countries during the 1990s, *OECD Economic Studies*, vol. 40, no. 1, pp. 7–48, at p. 37 (based on licensing activities of US multinationals as well as on international licensing alliances between firms in developing/ emerging and developed nations, finding that "the strengthening of IPRs ... has had a net positive effect on the international licensing of technologies between unaffiliated parties during the 1990s").

[125] Michael W. Nicholson (2007), The Impact of Industry Characteristics and IPR Policy on Foreign Direct Investment, *Review of World Economics*, vol. 143, no. 1, pp. 27–54, at p. 27.

more likely to internalise the value of the asset by producing the goods in-house (within a local plant or a subsidiary)"; as the level of IP protection increases further, firms, particularly those in R&D-intensive industries, are more inclined to transfer their technologies through licensing rather than FDI.[126]

Three main findings can be extracted from the above literature. First, IPR protection is only one of many factors that affect decisions by multinational firms on technology transfers. Other important factors include market size and growth and the scientific, industrial and manufacturing capacities of the technology recipient countries. Second, the level of IPR protection may influence companies' choices of their preferred technology transfer mode (FDI, licensing or trade). In case of weak IPR protection, exports are relatively more favoured compared with the other two modes. With increasing IPR protection, preferences shift more towards FDI. When the level of IPR protection increases further, licensing becomes more common.[127] Last but not least, irrespective of the mode, strong IPRs facilitate market-based technology transfer as long as "the IPRs are not used in monopolistic or abusive ways".[128] With the strengths of IP protection, the quality of technology transferred also rises.

In the climate change context, there is still uncertainty, beyond these general findings, regarding the incentive effects of IPR on transfer of technologies, in particular to developing countries. Some studies, for example, Abbott (2009), have pointed out that "IPRs have different effects for different fields of [technologies]".[129] In contrast, other scholars, for example,

---

[126] Walter G. Park (2011), Intellectual Property Rights and Foreign Direct Investment: Lessons from Central America, in Lopez and Shankar (eds.), *Getting the Most Out of Free Trade Agreements in Central America*, the International Bank for Reconstruction and Development/ the World Bank, pp. 275–308, at p. 293 (noting that "If intellectual property rights are strong and very secure, firms that own valuable intangible assets are more likely (and more willing) to license the production and distribution of the product to arm's length parties. The advantage of licensing to other parties is that firms can tap into the sales and distribution capabilities of other agents").

[127] See also Rajesh Asrani (2015), Economic Implications of Intellectual Property Rights in Evolving Markets, in Manimala and Wasdani (eds.), *Entrepreneurial Ecosystem: Perspectives from Emerging Economies*, Springer India, pp. 109–31, at p. 119; Pamela J. Smith (2001), How Do Foreign Patent Rights Affect U.S. Exports, Affiliate Sales, and Licenses? *Journal of International Economics*, vol. 55, pp. 411–39, at p. 434.

[128] Andrew C. Michaels (2009), International Technology Transfer and TRIPS Article 66.2: Can Global Administrative Law Help Least-Developed Countries Get What They Bargained For? *Georgetown Journal of International Law*, vol. 41, pp. 223–61, at p. 235.

[129] Frederick M. Abbott (2009), Innovation and Technology Transfer to Address Climate Change: Lessons from the Global Debate on Intellectual Property and Public Health, ICTSD's Programme on IPRs and Sustainable Development, Issue Paper No. 24, ICTSD, Geneva, Switzerland, p. 2.

Dechezleprêtre et al. (2013), have asserted that ESTs "do not respond differently than the average technology to changes" in IP policies.[130] Given the fact that ESTs involve various fields of technologies, the author tends to agree with the latter view. The subsequent section examines the role of IPRs in the transfer of ESTs.

4.3.2.2 IPRs as an Important Factor Influencing the Transfer of ESTs

A number of studies have been conducted to provide more evidence-based answers regarding the enabling role of IPRs in EST transfer. As one of the first such efforts, Barton (2007) assessed the IP implications for companies developing solar PV, biofuel and wind technologies in China, Brazil and India and found that strengthening IP protection would make foreign investors more willing to transfer technology to scientifically advanced developing nations if they have confidence that their technologies will be protected against illegal copying or free-riding.[131] This has been confirmed by Lee et al. (2009) in a Chatham House Report, which concluded that patent holders of "climate friendly technologies" were often established industrial giants, and their perception of the level of IP protection in developing economies would to a large extent "determine the rate of roll-out of the next generation of low carbon technologies – whether through investment, licensing, joint ventures or other forms of knowledge-sharing".[132]

In a study commissioned by the European Commission in which Copenhagen Economics (2009) evaluated a representative sample of low-income developing countries and emerging market economies over the period 1998 to 2008, similar conclusions were reached by carrying out a more quantitative review of patent protection and ownership relating to waste and biomass, geothermal, ocean, solar, fuel cell and wind energy technologies. On the basis of this patent data, it concluded that IPRs in and of themselves did not constitute the main barrier preventing the transfer of ESTs to developing countries and that the presence of strong IPRs systems was rather

---

[130] Antoine Dechezleprêtre et al. (2013), What Drives the International Transfer of Climate Change Mitigation Technologies? Empirical Evidence from Patent Data, *Environmental and Resource Economics*, vol. 54, pp. 161–78, at p. 163.

[131] John H. Barton (2007), New Trends in Technology Transfer: Implications for National and International Policy, ICTSD, Issue Paper No. 18, pp. 4 and 19.

[132] Bernice Lee et al. (2009), *Who Owns Our Low Carbon Future? Intellectual Property and Energy Technologies*, A Chatham House Report, Royal Institute of International Affairs, p. ix.

"a prerequisite for Western firms to be willing to transfer technology" to the emerging countries.[133]

The fact that the strictness of IPR protection has an influence on transfer of ESTs has been further supported by a recent study by Dechezleprêtre et al. (2013). Using a database of ten climate-related technologies filed in ninety-six countries from 1995 to 2007, obtained from the World Patent Statistical Database (PATSTAT), they found that the impact of strict IPRs on technology transfer was significant, that is, "an increase by one unit of the zero-to-ten rating [brought] about 27 and 60 [per cent] more patent imports".[134] As Dechezleprêtre et al. (2013) observed, this finding is reinforced by the fact that weaker IP protection would prompt innovators to turn to secrecy for the protection of their inventions, which might negatively impact the international transfer of technologies because inventions protected by trade secret law diffuse less extensively and expansively in the recipient country.[135]

Although strong IPRs play an important role in the transfer of ESTs, as the literature shows, it is not the only factor influencing the success of EST transfer. From the perspective of the technology recipient, access to IPRs may be a "necessary but not sufficient requirement" for the successful transfer of ESTs.[136] Citing the example of the light-emitting diode (LED) industry, Ockwell et al. (2007) found that "without improved technological capacity in India in this industry, ownership of relevant IPRs would make little difference to India's ability to manufacture white LEDs".[137] Through conducting surveys over the licensing practices in clean energy technologies in relation to developing countries, UNEP, EPO and ICTSD (2010) concluded that the level of IP protection in the technology recipient country is a significant factor when determining whether to engage in licensing practices, whereas it is not the only important consideration.[138] Similar

---

[133] Copenhagen Economics (2009), *Are IPR a Barrier to the Transfer of Climate Change Technology?* Report prepared by Copenhagen Economics A/S and the IPR Company ApS, p. 38.

[134] Antoine Dechezleprêtre et al. (2013), What Drives the International Transfer of Climate Change Mitigation Technologies? Empirical Evidence from Patent Data, *Environmental and Resource Economics*, vol. 54, pp. 161–78, at p. 174; according to the authors, "[t]he zero-to-10 rating is the share of capital controls levied as a share of the total number of capital controls listed multiplied by 10".

[135] Ibid., p. 176.

[136] David Ockwell et al. (2007), *UK-India Collaboration to Identify the Barriers to the Transfer of Low Carbon Energy Technology*, Final Report, the Department for Environment, Food and Rural Affairs, p. 8.

[137] Ibid., p. 13.

[138] UNEP, EPO and ICTSD (2010), *Patents and Clean Energy: Bridging the Gap between Evidence and Policy*, Munich: Mediengruppe Universal, p. 9.

significance was attached to factors such as favourable market conditions, an investment-friendly environment, scientific and technological infrastructures and human capital.[139]

Therefore, IP protection is an important factor affecting the transfer of ESTs, but it should not be considered in isolation from other factors, in particular, the technological capacities and market conditions of the technology recipient countries. In the WIPO Global Challenge Report (2011), it is recommended that government should "complement effective IPR protection alongside the appropriate policy infrastructure, governance and competition systems" so as to create effective conduits for technology transfer.[140]

4.4 THE POTENTIALLY NEGATIVE EFFECTS OF STRONG IPR PROTECTION ON INNOVATION AND TRANSFER OF ESTS

Newly developed ESTs are often protected by different types of IP rights. In nature, as discussed in Section 2.3.3, IP rights are temporary exclusive rights, also known as a "legal monopoly", granted by States for the exploitation of intellectual creations.[141] Their main legal effect is to grant IP right holders a *ius prohibendi* (i.e. right to prohibit) that can be exercised to prevent all third parties (including actual or potential competitors) from unauthorised use.[142] In consequence, IP rights may confer market power through exclusivity and reduce competition, thereby inhibiting follow-on innovations and restricting the dissemination and use of knowledge and IP-protected ESTs.[143]

---

[139] Ibid., p. 9 (noting that "overall, respondents attached slightly more weight to factors such as scientific infrastructure and human capital, favourable market conditions and investment climates. However, licensing-intensive respondents attached somewhat greater importance to IP protection than to the other above mentioned factors").

[140] Meir Perez Pugatch (2011), *Intellectual Property & the Transfer of Environmentally Sound Technologies*, Global Challenges Report, WIPO, Geneva, Switzerland, p. 17.

[141] See, e.g., Lloyd L. Weinreb (1998), Copyright for Functional Expression, *Harvard Law Review*, vol. 111, no. 5, pp. 1149–254, at p. 1205 (stating that "the most that can be said confidently about copyright or patent is that it confers a monopoly"); Michele Boldrin and David Levine (2002), The Case against Intellectual Property, *The American Economic Review*, vol. 92, no. 2, pp. 209–12, at p. 209 (arguing that intellectual property "creates a socially inefficient monopoly, and what is commonly called intellectual property might be better called 'intellectual monopoly'").

[142] Carlos Correa M. (2000), *Intellectual Property Rights, the WTO and Developing Countries: The TRIPS Agreement and Policy Options*, Zed Books, Third World Network, p. 106.

[143] It is noted that IP rights do not always confer market power as defined under competition law. See Hedvig Schmidt (2009), *Competition Law, Innovation and Antitrust: An Analysis of Tying and Technological Integration*, Cheltenham, UK: Edward Elgar Publishing, p. 161.

The views of commentators on the exclusive effects of IPRs can be summarised as follows: first, "[a]s an intervention in the free market, patents restrict the number of people who could otherwise freely make, use, sell or import the protected products and processes";[144] and second, the exercise of IPRs may give rise to anti-competitive behaviour, whether through unilateral abuses of IPRs which relate to refusal to deal and excessive pricing or by "contractual restraints in international technology transfer agreements".[145]

The above findings equally apply to ESTs. The following subsections will address in turn: (1) the exclusive effects of IPRs on innovation of ESTs and (2) IP rights and abusive or anti-competitive practices in EST transfer.

4.4.1 *The Exclusive Effects of IPRs on Innovation of ESTs*

Some scholars have recently shown their concern over the exclusive effects of IP rights. Jaffe and Lerner (2004) suggested that IPRs could restrict access to knowledge, discourage attempts to invent around patents and have adverse effects on competition.[146] In theory, as Nelson (1992) pointed out, "the going public of new technology not only increases society's ability to use it in its present form, but also widens the range of parties who are in a position to further improve it, variegate it, [and] more generally contribute to its advance".[147] However, granting IPRs enhances the right holder's control over technologies and limits the public's ability to use and improve technologies, thereby inhibiting follow-on innovations and dissemination and transfer of technologies.

In practice, in order to maintain a competitive advantage, IP owners may restrict potential competitors' access to core technologies for follow-on innovation through, for instance, charging a high transaction cost or creating

---

[144] UNCTAD and ICTSD (2003), Intellectual Property Rights: Implications for Development, UNCTAD-ICTSD Project on IPRs and Sustainable Development, Policy Discussion Paper, ICTSD and UNCTAD, Geneva, Switzerland, p. 86.

[145] See, e.g., UNCTAD and ICTSD (2005), *Resource Book on TRIPS and Development*, Cambridge University Press, p. 540; Tú Thanh Nguyãẽn (2010), *Competition Law, Technology Transfer and the TRIPS Agreement: Implications for Developing Countries*, Cheltenham, UK: Edward Elgar Publishing, p. xiv.

[146] Adam B. Jaffe and Josh Lerner (2004), *Innovation and Its Discontents: How Our Broken Patent System Is Endangering Innovation and Progress, and What to Do about It*, Princeton University Press, pp. 56–77.

[147] Richard R. Nelson (1992), What Is "Commercial" and What Is "Public" about Technology, What Should Be? in Rosenberg et al. (eds.), *Technology and the Wealth of Nations*, Stanford University Press, pp. 57–71, at p. 59.

"patent thickets"[148] or refusing to grant licences.[149] A famous example is noted by Shavell and van Ypersele (2001): when James Watt, holder of an early steam engine patent, denied Jonathan Hornblower and Richard Trevithick licences to improve the technology, they "had to wait for Watt's patent to expire in 1800 before they could develop their high-pressure engine".[150] "Using newly-collected data on the sequencing of the human genome by the public Human Genome Project and the private firm Celera", Williams (2010) found evidence that Celera's IP led to reductions in subsequent/follow-on scientific research and product development by 20-30 per cent.[151] Therefore, IPRs may deter innovation in some circumstances, in particular, where "downstream" research or product development relies on access to existing patented technologies. Although this finding is not EST-specific, it equally applies to ESTs. IPCC (2014) warns that "problems could arise if new, very broad patents were granted that impede the development of future, more efficient technologies".[152] This is supported by the study of EST-specific evidence presented in Section 4.4.2.

Historical evidence suggests that many developed countries such as the United States and Japan adopted incomplete and weak IP protection to develop local technological bases in the early stages of their industrialisation, only increasing protection as they became more technologically advanced.[153]

---

[148] The term "patent thicket" refers to "an overlapping set of patent rights requiring that those seeking to commercialize new technology obtain licenses from multiple patentees"; see Carl Shapiro (2002), Navigating the Patent Thicket: Cross Licenses, Patent Pools, and Standard Setting, in Jaffe et al. (eds.), *Innovation Policy and the Economy*, Cambridge, MA: MIT Press, pp. 119–50, at p. 119.

[149] Jerome Reichman et al. (2008), Intellectual Property and Alternatives: Strategies for Green Innovation, Energy, Environment and Development Programme Paper: 08/03, Chatham House, UK, p. 10 (stating that "[m]any of these obstacles [posed by patents] consist of transaction cost problems that can arise in the licensing necessary for follow-on innovation. For example, as a historical matter, progress in the automobile and aircraft industries was hampered by problems in licensing broad patents on foundational platforms ... [t]here is also the possibility that a follow-on inventor will be deterred by the need to clear rights on a 'thicket' of overlapping patents that cover either a research platform or individual components of an end product").

[150] Steven Shavell and Tanguy Van Ypersele (2001), Rewards versus Intellectual Property Rights, *Journal of Law and Economics*, vol. 44, pp. 525–47, at p. 543.

[151] Heidi L. Williams (2010), Intellectual Property Rights and Innovation: Evidence from the Human Genome, NBER *Working Paper Series*, Working Paper 16213, Cambridge, MA: National Bureau of Economic Research, p. 2.

[152] IPCC (2014), *Climate Change 2014: Mitigation of Climate Change*, Working Group III Contribution to the IPCC 5th Assessment Report, Chapter 13: International Cooperation: Agreements and Instruments, p. 1036.

[153] See, e.g., William Kingston (2010), *Beyond Intellectual Property: Matching Information Protection to Innovation*, Cheltenham, UK: Edward Elgar Publishing (through examining the

According to the UK Commission on Intellectual Property Rights (2002), "for those developing countries that have acquired significant technological and innovative capabilities, there has generally been an association with 'weak' rather than 'strong' forms of IP protection in the formative period of their economic development".[154] It further points out that when economies were transformed in Taiwan and Korea between 1960 and 1980, both governments emphasised that imitation and reverse engineering had played a significant role in developing their indigenous technological and innovative capacities.[155]

However, as discussed in Section 3.3.2, today's developing countries have fewer opportunities to follow the imitation-based technological development path as adopted by developed countries during their industrial revolutions. The TRIPS Agreement obliges every country to adopt minimum IPR standards. Empirical studies have suggested that strong IP protection could raise imitation costs and time.[156] According to Falvey and Foster (2006), some even argue that "any imitation unauthorized by the IPR holder is piracy and theft".[157] Strong IP protection may also disincentivise firms from absorbing technologies through reverse engineering. As Graham and Zerbe (1996) observed, reverse engineering the patented product may infringe patent rights if companies make, use or sell products embodying the

economic histories of the United States and some members states of the European Union, noting that these industrialised countries adjusted their level of IP protection to achieve their developmental goals); Fritz Machlup and Edith Penrose (1950), The Patent Controversy in the Nineteenth Century, *The Journal of Economic History*, vol. 10, no. 1, pp. 1–29, at pp. 4–5 (noting during the patent controversy between 1850 and 1875, the Netherlands repealed its patent law and Switzerland refused to enact one); Sanjaya Lall (2003), Indicators of the Relative Importance of IPRs in Developing Countries, UNCTAD-ICTSD Project on IPRs and Sustainable Development, Issue Paper No. 3, published by ICTSD and UNCTAD, Geneva, Switzerland, p. 1 (noting that "[m]any rich countries used weak patent protection in their early stages of industrialisation, increasing protection as they approached the leaders").

[154] The UK Commission on Intellectual Property Rights (2002), *Integrating Intellectual Property Rights and Development Policy*, Report of the Commission on Intellectual Property Rights, London, p. 22.

[155] Ibid., p. 1.

[156] Richard C. Levin et al. (1987), Appropriating the Returns from Industrial Research and Development, *Brookings Papers on Economic Activity*, pp. 783–820, at p. 811 (finding that "patents raise imitation costs by 40 percentage points for both major and typical new drugs, by 30 points for major new chemical products, and by 25 points for typical chemical products. In electronics, our results differed somewhat for semiconductors, computers, and communications equipment, but the range was 7 to 15 percentage points for major products and 7 to 10 for typical products."); these findings are consistent with Mansfield's findings (see Edwin Mansfield (1981), Imitation Costs and Patents: An Empirical Study, *The Economic Journal*, vol. 91, no. 364, pp. 907–18).

[157] Rod Falvey and Neil Foster (2006), *The Role of Intellectual Property Rights in Technology Transfer and Economic Growth: Theory and Evidence*, UNIDO Working Papers, Vienna, Austria, p. 51.

patents.[158] Therefore, strengthened IPR protection has made the process of progressing from imitation and reverse engineering to developing a genuine indigenous innovative capacity very difficult.

There is little clear evidence showing that strong IP protection encourages indigenous innovation in developing countries except in those with high innovation capacities.[159] Regarding the link between the development of ESTs in developing countries and IPRs, Hall and Helmers (2010) conclude that the increased IPR protection will most likely have a positive impact on technological development and innovation in emerging economies such as China, India and Brazil, but the available evidence does not allow drawing a similar conclusion in the case of other developing countries.[160] However, the latest IPCC Report (2014) finds that it is unclear whether the introduction and maintenance of robust IP protection in developing countries will increase the domestic innovation in ESTs, because the evidence that strict and rigid IP protection facilitates indigenous innovation is almost exclusively limited to specific sectors in developed countries.[161]

4.4.2 *IP Rights and Abusive or Anti-Competitive Practices in EST Transfer*

Given the exclusive nature of IPRs, it is acknowledged that certain licensing practices or conditions pertaining to the exercise of IPRs may restrain

---

[158] Lawrence D. Graham and Richard O. Zerbe (1996), Economically Efficient Treatment of Computer Software: Reverse Engineering, Protection, and Disclosure, *Rutgers Computer & Technology Law Journal*, vol. 22, pp. 61–142, at p. 96.

[159] See, e.g., Rod Falvey and Neil Foster (2006), *The Role of Intellectual Property Rights in Technology Transfer and Economic Growth: Theory and Evidence*, UNIDO Working Papers, Vienna, Austria, at pp. x and 21 (through examining the cross-country evidence linking IPRs to domestic innovation, finding that "stronger IPR protection can encourage domestic innovation in countries that have significant domestic capacity for innovation, as measured either by initial GDP per capita or the stock of human capital" whereas "it has little impact on innovation in countries with a small innovative capacity"); Qian Yi (2007), Do National Patent Laws Stimulate Domestic Innovation in a Global Patenting Environment? A Cross-Country Analysis of Pharmaceutical Patent Protection, 1978–2002, *The Review of Economics and Statistics*, vol. 89, no. 3, pp. 436–53, at p. 436 (through evaluating the effects of patent protection on pharmaceutical innovations for 26 countries that established pharmaceutical patent laws during 1978–2002, finding that "[n]ational patent protection alone does not stimulate domestic innovation ... [h]owever, domestic innovation accelerates in countries with higher levels of economic development, educational attainment, and economic freedom").

[160] Bronwyn H. Hall and Christian Helmers (2010), The Role of Patent Protection in (Clean/Green) Technology Transfer, *Santa Clara Computer & High Technology Law Journal*, vol. 26, pp. 487–532, at p. 523.

[161] IPCC (2014), *Climate Change 2014: Mitigation of Climate Change*, Working Group III Contribution to the IPCC 5th Assessment Report, Chapter 15: National and Sub-National Policies and Institutions, p. 1175.

competition and thus impede transfer and dissemination of technology.[162] As pointed out by Roffe and Spennemann (2008), while in most cases licensing is pro-competitive to the extent that it legitimises access to and use of IP-protected technology, these activities may be anti-competitive "where they are a mere sham for a cartel arrangement, where they restrict competition between technologies that are economic substitutes for one another or where they exclude new technologies from the market".[163]

In the context of climate change, potential anti-competitive practices arising from the abuse of IPRs have enhanced developing countries' concerns over the availability and affordability of ESTs.[164] Being profit-oriented, the private sector, particularly the leading technology MNCs, often employs IPR-related anti-competitive practices in the process of EST transfer to maintain its competitive advantage. According to IPCC (2000), various types of abusive or anti-competitive practices ranging from refusal to license[165] to "attaching restrictive or even prohibitive conditions for royalty and equipment sales to maximise the monopolistic rent" had been reported.[166] The high concentration of ESTs in a handful of corporations would increase the risk of such anti-competitive behaviours.[167]

---

[162] WTO Members recognized the adverse effects of IP abuses and IPR-related anti-competitive practices and thus included certain provisions such as Articles 8.2, 31(k) and 40 into the TRIPS Agreement to regulate such practices.

[163] Pedro Roffe and Christoph Spennemann (2008), Control of Anti-competitive Practices in Contractual Licences under the TRIPS Agreement, in Correa and Abdulqawi (eds.), *Intellectual Property and International Trade: The TRIPS Agreement*, Alphen aan den Rijn, The Netherlands: Kluwer Law International, pp. 293–329, at pp. 295 and 296.

[164] See, e.g., UNDP (2011), *Technological Cooperation and Climate Change: Issues and Perspectives*, Working papers presented at the Ministry of Environment and Forests, Government of India-UNDP Consultation on Technology Cooperation for Addressing Climate Change, New Delhi, India, pp. 78–86.

[165] It is noted that in most cases, refusal to license does not, of itself, constitute a violation of law whereas refusal to license may impede, restrict or even eliminate competition in some particular cases such as refusal to license for the purpose of preventing competitors from entering the market. See Xu Shiying (2011), *Intellectual Property Protection and Competition Law*, in Kariyawasam (ed.), *Chinese Intellectual Property and Technology Laws*, Cheltenham, UK: Edward Elgar Publishing, pp. 323–47, p. 325.

[166] IPCC (2000), *IPCC Special Report: Methodological and Technological Issues in Technology Transfer*, Cambridge University Press, p. 99.

[167] See, e.g., Mark Consilvio (2011), The Role of Patents in the International Framework of Clean Technology Transfer: A Discussion of Barriers and Solutions, *American University Intellectual Property Brief*, pp. 7–16, at p. 10; John H. Barton (2007), Intellectual Property and Access to Clean Energy Technologies in Developing Countries: An Analysis of Solar Photovoltaic, Biofuel and Wind Technologies, ICTSD Trade and Sustainable Energy Series Issue Paper No. 2, ICTSD, Geneva, Switzerland, p. 18 (noting "possible risk of anti-competitive behaviour given concentration of industry" in the field of wind energy technologies).

The successive subsections address the practices of patent blockage, high licensing fees, refusal to license and other IPR-related abusive or anti-competitive practices associated with EST transfer.

4.4.2.1 Patent Blockage

Given the urgent need to accelerate the transition to a low-carbon economy, there has been increased investment in the innovation of ESTs since the adoption of the Kyoto Protocol, inducing a proliferation of EST patents. As Correa (2013) pointed out, there are around "400,000 patent documents regarding solar [PV], geothermal, wind and carbon capture".[168] Yet, it is questionable whether this proliferation reveals the real incentive contribution of patents to innovation because of the following reasons: first, an overwhelming majority of patents are granted over incremental development on existing technologies while few patents are given based on core technologies;[169] and second, many patents have no incentive contributions because they are used by companies to limit their competitors' room to operate and to block market entry.[170] "Strategic patenting" has thus, sometimes, been perceived as "the single most important reason" for the patent boom.[171] Such patenting strategies are often used by companies to prevent new domestic and foreign market entrants.[172]

The patent blockage phenomenon occurs in different industrial fields. A recent pharmaceutical sector inquiry conducted by the European Commission (Directorate General Competition) concluded that "[f]iling numerous patent applications for the same medicine (forming so-called 'patent clusters' or 'patent thickets') [was] a common practice" for the originator companies

---

[168] Carlos M. Correa (2013), Innovation and Technology Transfer of Environmentally Sound Technologies, presentation at the Centre for International Environmental Studies of the Graduate Institute of International and Development Studies, 9 October, Geneva, Switzerland, p. 17.

[169] Ibid., p. 10.

[170] According to Correa (2012), the blocking techniques may include "blanketing" (creating a jungle or a minefield of patents), "flooding" (taking out multiple patents, major as well as minor, in a field), "fencing" (acquiring a series of patents that block certain lines or directions of research and development) and "surrounding" (an important central patent is fenced by other less important patents); See Carlos M. Correa (2012), Proliferation of Patents Hurts Public Interest, *IDN-In-Depth News Viewpoint*, 26 July, available at www.indepthnews.info/ index.php/global-issues/1065-proliferation-of-patents-hurts-public-interest

[171] United Nations Conference on Sustainable Development (UNCSD) (2012), Science and Technology for Sustainable Development, *RIO 2012 Issue Briefs*, No. 12, p. 2.

[172] Ibid.

"to delay or block the market entry of generic medicines".[173] For instance, a WIPO *Patent Landscape Report on Ritonavir* (2011) found that there had been more than "800 patents filed since the initial PCT application WO 1994014436 to protect different aspects of Ritonavir and its methods of use".[174] A similar occurrence has taken place in the telecommunications industry; as Correa (2013) noted, Google bought the Motorola's mobile branch to acquire the 17,000 patents from Motorola and to address the patent thicket issue, because they grew tired of litigation.[175]

In the climate change context, various studies have confirmed that patents are often used by companies as a strategy to maintain their competitive advantage through deterring competitors from entering the market or by blocking similar technological innovation.[176] IPCC (2000) observed that "[i]n order to maintain monopoly or competitive advantage, companies [went] after their potential competitors in other countries and [registered] their patents to block similar technological development", and dumped their products to drive the competitors with similar technologies out of the market.[177] According to Lee et al. (2009), some companies have been found to use patents to block other companies' entry into their market space or sales of products that infringe the rights of the patent holders as a complement to their market dominance strategy.[178] A typical example cited by Sovacool (2008) is that General Electric used a 1992 patent on a variable-speed technology for wind turbines to inhibit its competitors from entering into the American wind

[173] European Commission (Directorate General Competition) (2009), Pharma Sector Inquiry-Main Issues Investigated, Human Rights in Patient Care, p.201, available at http://ec.europa.eu/competition/sectors/pharmaceuticals/inquiry/staff_working_paper_part1.pdf

[174] WIPO (2011), *Patent Landscape Report on Ritonavir*, Patent Landscape Reports Project prepared by Landon IP, WIPO, Geneva, Switzerland, p. 58.

[175] Carlos M. Correa (2013), Innovation and Technology Transfer of Environmentally Sound Technologies, presentation at the Centre for International Environmental Studies of the Graduate Institute of International and Development Studies, 9 October, Geneva, Switzerland, p. 18; see also Catherine Saez (2013), Green Innovations, Owned by Developed Countries, Tied Up in Patents, Expert Says, *Intellectual Property Watch*, 14 October, Geneva, Switzerland.

[176] See, e.g., Bernice Lee et al. (2009), *Who Owns Our Low Carbon Future? Intellectual Property and Energy Technologies*, A Chatham House Report, Royal Institute of International Affairs, p. 6; IPCC (2000), *IPCC Special Report: Methodological and Technological Issues in Technology Transfer*, Cambridge University Press, p. 99; Mark Consilvio (2011), The Role of Patents in the International Framework of Clean Technology Transfer: A Discussion of Barriers and Solutions, *American University Intellectual Property Brief*, pp. 7–16, at p. 10.

[177] IPCC (2000), *IPCC Special Report: Methodological and Technological Issues in Technology Transfer*, Cambridge University Press, p. 99.

[178] Bernice Lee et al. (2009), *Who Owns Our Low Carbon Future? Intellectual Property and Energy Technologies*, A Chatham House Report, Royal Institute of International Affairs, p. 6.

power equipment market until the patent expired in 2009.[179] Similarly, Syam (2010) noticed cases where one large US company that held patents in wind energy technology stopped a European firm from entering the market in the United States through patent litigation, until finally the US firm acquired the European firm.[180] As observed by Lewis (2007), since purchasing the European firm in 2002, the US firm filed similar patent infringement suits in Europe, Canada and China with a view to preventing its competitors from entering the US market.[181]

The effects of patent blockage become more severe when numerous separate patents need to be combined to produce a single product, which is the case for many ESTs. For instance, companies producing energy-efficient fluidised combustion technology must invent or purchase "patents relating to combustion dynamics, fluid dynamics, air dynamics, material science, computational controls, and electronics".[182] When those patents are held by different owners, patent blocking may create "the tragedy of anti-commons" problem, that is, as described by Heller and Eisenberg (1998), technological innovation is impeded "when multiple owners [all] have a right to exclude others from scarce resource" giving no single entity "an effective privilege of use".[183] Yet, it is unlikely that multiple patent holders would cooperate because each of them wants to control its IPRs and maintain its competitive advantage unless this is integrated in a standard (i.e. standard essential patents), which has been adopted in certain industries (in particular, the telecom industry).[184]

In addition, the proliferation of low-quality patents in ESTs further exacerbates the problem of patent blockage. Low-quality patents can stem from

[179] Benjamin K. Sovacool (2008), Placing a Glove on the Invisible Hand: How Intellectual Property Rights May Impede Innovation in Energy Research and Development (R&D), *Albany Law Journal of Science & Technology*, vol. 18, no. 2, pp. 381–440, at p. 422.
[180] Nirmalya Syam (2010), Rush for Patents May Hinder Transfer of New Climate-Friendly Technologies, *South Bulletin*, no. 44, 8 March, pp. 11–12, at p. 11.
[181] Joanna I. Lewis (2007), Technology Acquisition and Innovation in the Developing World: Wind Turbine Development in China and India, *Studies in Comparative International Development*, no. 42, pp. 208–32, at p. 224.
[182] Marilyn A. Brown et al. (2008), Carbon Lock-In: Barriers to Deploying Climate Change Mitigation Technologies, Oak Ridge National Laboratory managed by UT-Battelle for the U.S. Department of Energy, ORNL/TM-2007/124, p. 75.
[183] Michael A. Heller and Rebecca S. Eisenberg (1998), Can Patents Deter Innovation? The Anti-Commons in Biomedical Research, *Science*, vol. 280, pp. 698–701, at p. 698.
[184] Guillaume Dufey (2013), Patents and Standardisation: Competition Concerns in New Technology Markets, *Global Antitrust Review*, pp. 7–48, at p. 19 (noting "when a patented technology is used within a standard, the patent owner must agree to license its patent to other members of the organization").

standards of patentability – especially the non-obviousness standards – that are too lax or the failure of patent offices to conform to generally accepted standards for patentability.[185] As Reichman et al. (2008) pointed out, low-quality patents may "cover inventions that are obvious" or "claim too much inventive [scope] or fail to specify exactly what [scope] they cover".[186] The grant of low-quality patents thus may not stimulate innovation of technologies, including ESTs, but rather results in the surge of patent litigation and blocks the entry of potential competitors.[187]

4.4.2.2 High Licensing Fees

High licensing fees may have negative impact on the affordability and availability of ESTs in developing countries. Despite developed countries' commitments to transfer ESTs under the UNFCCC, as discussed in Section 3.4, historical evidence suggests that firms from many developing countries such as India, Brazil, China and Mexico were unable to gain access to ESTs (such as ozone-friendly technology) "on affordable terms".[188] In climate change negotiations, developing countries have expressed their concern that IP protection will make new ESTs excessively costly.[189] Various recent studies have confirmed that the exclusivity afforded by IPRs confers market power on right holders and allows them to charge monopoly prices, which are above marginal costs or socially optimal levels, thereby potentially limiting the availability of technologies.[190]

[185] See, e.g., Stephen A. Merrill et al. (2004), *A Patent System for the 21st Century*, Washington, D.C.: National Academies Press, p. 47; John H. Barton (2000), Reforming the Patent System, *Science*, vol. 287 (5460), pp. 1933–4, at p. 1934.

[186] Jerome Reichman et al. (2008), Intellectual Property and Alternatives: Strategies for Green Innovation, Energy, Environment and Development Programme Paper: 08/03, Chatham House, p. 12.

[187] James Bessen and Michael J. Meurer (2008), *Patent Failure: How Judges, Bureaucrats, and Lawyers Put Innovators at Risk*, Princeton University Press, p. 163; it is noted that while this study is not ESTs-specific, this finding applies to all patented technologies, including ESTs.

[188] Carlos Correa M. (2013), Innovation and Technology Transfer of Environmentally Sound Technologies, presentation at the Centre for International Environmental Studies of the Graduate Institute of International and Development Studies, 9 October, Geneva, Switzerland, p. 26.

[189] Government of India (2013), Submission to the UNFCCC on the Work of the Ad Hoc Working Group on the Durban Platform for Enhanced Action: Workstream I, New Delhi, India, p. 3, available at https://unfccc.int/files/documentation/submissions_from_parties/adp/application/pdf/adp_india_workstream_1_20130913.pdf

[190] See, e.g., Carsten Fink (2013), Intellectual Property Rights: Economic Principles and Trade Rules, in Lukauskas et al. (eds.), *Handbook of Trade Policy for Development*, Oxford University Press, pp. 740–67, at p. 747; Dominique Foray (2009), *Technology Transfer in the TRIPS Age:*

One often-cited example is provided by Watal (2000), who studied the effect of IPRs on technology transfer in the case of India and in the context of the Montreal Protocol. Watal (2000) found that India failed to acquire substitute technologies because the technologies were protected by IPRs and were "inaccessible either on account of the high price quoted by the technology suppliers and/or due to the conditions laid down by the suppliers".[191] The Report of the Energy and Resources Institute (2009) revealed similar experiences in China, Indonesia, Malaysia and Thailand where local companies have terminated negotiations with licensors due to the high costs involved for licences or "have incurred additional costs buying non-related equipment before accessing the desired technology".[192] Therefore, as observed by Ockwell (2008), IPRs may restrict access to new technologies in the first place by enabling owners of patented technologies to "keep prices prohibitively high".[193]

ESTs are often complex technologies protected by different types of IPRs. For instance, a piece of wind energy technology product can be protected by patents, trade secrets, industrial designs, trademarks and copyrights at the same time. As observed by Iliev (2012), in the case of a Suzlon wind turbine, patents on turbine transmission systems have the ability to prevent others from using the technology; the production or installation methods are protected by trade secrets; the word and symbol denoting the origin is protected by trademarks; and control software written by or on behalf of Suzlon is protected by copyright.[194]

The Need for New Types of Partnerships between the Least Developed and Most Advanced Economies, ICTSD programme on IPRs and Sustainable Development, Issue Paper No. 23, ICTSD, Geneva, Switzerland, p. 35; International Council on Human Rights Policy (2011), *Beyond Technology Transfer: Protecting Human Rights in a Climate-Constrained World*, International Council on Human Rights Policy, Geneva, Switzerland, p. 68.

[191] Jayashree Watal (2000), The Issue of Technology Transfer in the Context of Montreal Protocol: Case Study of India, in Jha and Hoffmann (eds.), *Achieving Objectives of Multilateral Environmental Agreements: Lessons from Empirical Studies*, UNCTAD/ITCD/TED/6, pp. 45–55, at p. 45.

[192] The Energy and Resources Institute (2009), *Emerging Asia Contribution on Issues of Technology for Copenhagen*, TERI Report No. 2008 RS09, New Delhi, India, p. 33.

[193] David Ockwell (2008), *Intellectual Property Rights and Low Carbon Technology Transfer to Developing Countries – A Review of the Evidence to Date, UK-India Collaboration to Overcome Barriers to the Transfer of Low Carbon Energy Technology: Phase 2*, University of Sussex, The Energy and Resources Institute and Institute of Development Studies, p. 38.

[194] Ilian Iliev (2012), Role of Patents in Renewable Energy Technology Innovation, Presentation to IRENA Roundtable on Assessment of IPRs for Promoting Renewable Energy, 25 October, Cambridge Intellectual Property, p. 7.

These IPRs can incur significantly high costs for technology producers from developing countries. For example, as observed by Zou et al. (2009), in 1999, Goldwind Global, a Chinese wind turbine producer, got a licence from a small German company named Jacobs to produce 600 KW wind turbines. Under the licensing agreement, Goldwind Global paid Jacobs a 5,000 Euro royalty per machine produced while the technologies transferred included only installation methods and the contents of technical requirements (excluding fan design).[195] A survey conducted by Zhou et al. (2010) on the role of IPRs in low-carbon technology transfer revealed that developed countries' IP owners maintain their monopolistic position by charging high royalty fees and sales commission fees, which together may account for 25 per cent of sales gross profit.[196] While the existing literature indicates that IPRs on ESTs may entail high costs for developing country producers, it cannot be ascertained from such studies that these costs are relatively higher than the IPR costs of non-ESTs (such as pharmaceuticals) or for transfers between developed countries.

Overall, to the extent that IP protection raises the cost and limits the availability of ESTs around the world, IP protection will work to slow down the transfer of new ESTs.[197] There is no doubt that developing countries have to pay licensing fees to get access to IP-protected ESTs. However, unreasonably high licensing fees for developing countries would limit the ability of their manufacturers to access ESTs, thereby inhibiting transfer of ESTs. IPR costs become a bigger concern in some complex technologies that are covered by multiple IPRs, as access to all the necessary IPRs raises the overall costs.

4.4.2.3 Refusal to License

Even if a developing country firm is willing to pay high licensing fees, some multinational companies may refuse to license their patented technologies due to their fear of competition. In most cases, refusal to license does not,

---

[195] Ji Zou et al. (2009), *Proposal on Innovative Mechanism for Development and Transfer of Environmentally Sound Technologies*, [in Chinese], Beijing, China: Economic Science Press, p. 52.

[196] Yuanchun Zhou et al. (2010), How to Conquer the IPR Barriers in the Low Carbon Technologies?", [in Chinese], *Environmental Protection*, vol. 2, pp. 68–70, at p. 69.

[197] IPCC (2014), *Climate Change 2014: Mitigation of Climate Change*, Working Group III Contribution to the IPCC 5th Assessment Report, Chapter 13: International Cooperation: Agreements and Instruments, p. 1036 (noting that "protection of IP works to slow the diffusion of new technologies, because it raises their cost and potentially limits their availability").

in itself, constitute a violation of law,[198] whereas refusal to license may impede, restrict or even eliminate competition in some particular cases such as refusal to license for the purpose of preventing competitors from entering the markets.

Without a doubt, such unilateral refusal to license IPRs to a willing buyer on reasonable commercial terms frustrates the production, diffusion and transfer of ESTs. Studies show that there have been cases where private firms and even public institutions of developed countries have refused to license their IP-protected ESTs to their potential competitors.[199]

The case of ozone-friendly technologies draws particular attention. While implementing the Montreal Protocol, a small group of multinational companies refused to license patented technologies that are used to replace ozone-depleting substances to some developing country firms.[200] As observed by IPCC (2000), at the initial stage of HFC-134a technology development, multinational companies holding IP-protected HFC technologies refused to license or sell the technology to Korean local firms.[201] Occasionally, even public institutions of developed countries were unwilling to license some ESTs, for example, HFC-134a, fuel cell and integrated gasification combined cycle (IGCC), to local producers in Korea.[202] Thus, Korean indigenous firms had to invest more than 10 million dollars in R&D for a period of over six years to develop their own technologies.[203] Yet, when Korea's HFC-134a technology

---

[198] See, e.g., Jay Dratler (1994), *Licensing of Intellectual Property*, ALM Properties, Law Journal Press, para. 3.02 [2] (stating that "[b]ased as it is on strong property rights and the free market, the patent system in the United States has always afforded patentees nearly absolute freedom in deciding unilaterally whether to grant licenses to others"); Katrin Nyman-Metcalf et al. (2014), The Freedom to Conduct Business and the Right to Property: The EU Technology Transfer Block Exemption Regulation and the Relationship between Intellectual Property and Competition Law, in Kerikmäe (ed.), *Protecting Human Rights in the EU: Controversies and Challenges of the Charter of Fundamental Rights*, New York: Springer, pp. 37–70, at p. 56 (stating that "[g]enerally, under EU competition law, a 'mere' refusal to license does not constitute a violation").

[199] See, e.g., IPCC (2000), *IPCC Special Report: Methodological and Technological Issues in Technology Transfer*, Cambridge University Press, p. 99; The Energy and Resources Institute (2009), *Emerging Asia Contribution on Issues of Technology for Copenhagen*, TERI Report No. 2008 RS09, New Delhi, India, p. 34.

[200] Jayashree Watal (2001), *Intellectual Property Rights in the WTO and Developing Countries*, Alphen aan den Rijn, The Netherlands: Kluwer Law International, p. 389.

[201] IPCC (2000), *IPCC Special Report: Methodological and Technological Issues in Technology Transfer*, Cambridge University Press, p. 99.

[202] Ibid.

[203] Rae Kwon Chung (1998), The Role of Government in the Transfer of Environmentally Sound Technology, in Forsyth (ed.), *Positive Measures for Technology Transfer under the Climate Change Convention*, Royal Institute of International Affairs, London, pp. 47–61, at p. 52.

development reached a fairly advanced stage, one multinational company changed its initial policy, that is, blocking the development of similar technology in Korea by registering as many process patents as possible, and approached a Korean company to license its technologies.[204] The case of Korea is only one among many. As Watal (2000) pointed out, given the growing significance of HFC-134a for both domestic and international markets, Indian producers were very keen to purchase the technology for HFC-134a; however, their efforts were ultimately fruitless largely owing to "the high cost and the reluctance among the technology owners to sell the technology to a potential competitor".[205]

The experience of this refusal to deal is not confined to ozone-friendly technology. In other fields of ESTs, leading multinational manufacturers are also inclined to license to would-be competitors in emerging countries such as China and India who have sizable domestic markets, cheap labour and resources.[206] For instance, Lewis (2007) found that developing country manufacturers often have to "obtain technology from second- or third-tier wind power companies that have less to lose in terms of international competition, and more to gain" with regard to licence fees.[207] Therefore, it is difficult for local companies in developing countries to access advanced technologies when foreign manufacturers perceive them as competition threats.

Multinational companies' desire to control becomes stronger in the case of advanced/cutting-edge technologies. A large portion of leading-edge

---

[204] IPCC (2000), *IPCC Special Report: Methodological and Technological Issues in Technology Transfer*, Cambridge University Press, p. 99.

[205] Jayashree Watal (2000), India: The Issue of Technology Transfer in the Context of the Montreal Protocol, in Jha and Hoffmann (eds.), *Achieving Objectives of Multilateral Environmental Agreements: A Package of Trade Measures and Positive Measures*, UNCTAD/ITCD/TED/6, pp. 45–55, at pp. 49 and 54; Watal further observed that "[a]ccording to industry sources, the technology suppliers are concerned that equipped with the alternative technology, India could become a potential competitor in both the sizable Indian market, as well as internationally".

[206] See, e.g., Enabling Environments for Technology Transfer, Technical Paper, UN Doc. FCCC/TP/2003/2, 4 June 2003, p. 22 (concluded that "know-how transfer can prove difficult when foreign manufacturers perceive competition threats. In the China efficient refrigerator project, planned visits of Chinese manufacturers were refused by foreign manufacturers, presumably on market competition grounds . . . Similarly, foreign manufacturers have refused to come to China to train domestic manufacturers"); p. 27 (noting that "although international power plant manufacturers are enthusiastic about closer partnerships with Chinese equipment suppliers, they often feel that licensing will lead to an erosion of their technological position and a loss of revenue").

[207] Joanna I. Lewis (2007), A Comparison of Wind Power Industry Development Strategies in Spain, India and China, prepared for the Centre for Resource Solutions Supported by the Energy Foundation, China Sustainable Energy Program, 19 July, p. 20.

technologies cannot be bought or acquired through licenses. As observed by Barton (2007), firms in emerging countries have difficulty in obtaining most advanced clean energy technologies because the existing strong industry leaders are reluctant to share leading-edge technology due to the fear of creating new competitors.[208] Another example, cited by UNDP (2011), is that the Chinese Yantai Integrated Gasification Combined Cycle demonstration power plants failed to acquire technology from foreign companies due to the unreasonably high cost and the patent holders' reluctance to transfer the key technologies. The project was terminated after prolonged and fruitless negotiations.[209]

Overall, in order to maintain a competitive advantage, MNCs often refuse to license their patented ESTs, which is a strategy enhanced by the global IPR protection. The likelihood for local companies in developing countries to access advanced ESTs is even smaller. A refusal to license under reasonable commercial terms for competitive reasons impedes international technology transfer and may itself constitute an abuse of IPRs under international IP law, in particular TRIPS, which is further addressed in Section 7.

4.4.2.4 Other Abusive or Anti-Competitive Practices

In addition to the above-mentioned patent blockage, high licensing fees and refusal to license, there are many other different ways that MNCs may use IPRs to restrict transfer of ESTs, such as export restrictions, limiting follow-on innovation and exclusive grant back of improved technologies. According to a case study on the experience of Korean companies (UNCTAD: 2000), among 523 technologies introduced in 1994, 122 (23.3 per cent) were accompanied by restrictive conditions. Among 168 Japanese technologies introduced into Korea in the same year, 15 (8.9 per cent) were not allowed to be transferred or reassigned to a third party, and 13 (7.7 per cent) were granted "on a non-exclusive basis" and conditional upon the sharing of improved technologies between the parties during the contract period. Seven (4.2 per cent) were not allowed to be used for export products and three (1.8 per cent) were granted "on the condition that the licensee [would] not deal in

---

[208] John H. Barton (2007), *New Trends in Technology Transfer: Implications for National and International Policy*, ICTSD, Issue Paper No. 18, pp. viii and 18.

[209] UNDP (2011), *Technological Cooperation and Climate Change: Issues and Perspectives*, Working papers presented at the Ministry of Environment and Forests, Government of India-UNDP Consultation on Technology Cooperation for Addressing Climate Change, UNDP, New Delhi, India, p. 84.

competitive products or technologies".[210] Similar restrictions appeared in the process of EST transfers from other developed countries such as the United States. All these conditions were considered unreasonable by Korean firms and reported to impede the effective technology transfer.[211]

A more recent study by Zhou et al. (2009) revealed that there were many anti-competitive practices in the process of the transfer of wind energy technologies to China. According to Zhou et al. (2009), on average, around 5 per cent of royalties per machine produced is charged when the final wind energy product is sold domestically whereas higher licensing fees are charged for products being exported.[212] Such discriminatory requirements make manufacturing companies in developing countries less competitive on the world market. Furthermore, under the licensing agreement, R&D activities in relation to the patented technologies are only possible with the permission of the licensor.[213] This restriction discourages firms from investing in follow-on innovation.

To sum up, the evidence suggests that strong IPR protection enhances the private sector's, in particular the MNCs', market power and leaves room for them to adopt various abusive or anti-competitive practices including patent blockage, high licensing fees, refusal of licensing, export restriction and limiting further innovation. These abusive or anti-competitive practices employed by MNCs may differ depending on the stage of the licensee's technological development. Typically, in the initial stage of technology development, MNCs may refuse to license or sell their technologies to local firms. After the local company launches its technological development programme, MNCs may register as many relevant patents as possible in the licensee's home country so as to block the development of similar technologies.[214] Technologies may be licensed when MNCs feel that they may lose their monopoly position due to their competitors' innovations or when they have more to gain with regard to licence fees. Yet, licensing agreements often contain restrictive conditions such as limiting further innovation, high royalties and restricting or prohibiting exportation.

---

[210] Korean Trade Promotion Agency (2000), Case Study 4: The Republic of Korea and the Montreal Protocol, in Jha and Hoffmann (eds.), *Achieving Objectives of Multilateral Environmental Agreements: A Package of Trade Measures and Positive Measures*, UNCTAD/ ITCD/TED/6, pp. 56–70, at p. 63.

[211] Ibid.

[212] Yuanchun Zhou and Ji Zou (2009), The Intellectual Property Issues in International Development and Transfer of Climate-Friendly Technologies, [in Chinese], Paper presented in PACE Conference, 12–15 July, p. 19.

[213] Ibid.

[214] IPCC (2000), *IPCC Special Report: Methodological and Technological Issues in Technology Transfer*, Cambridge University Press, p. 99.

Being restrictive in nature, these abusive or anti-competitive practices may hinder international transfer of ESTs to developing countries and inhibit follow-on innovation in both developed and developing countries. Such practices may undermine the rationale of granting IPRs and constitute abuse of patents, thereby potentially contravening the spirit of the TRIPS Agreement.[215] Lack of appropriate regulation and control of such practices in developed countries may also lead to the violation of their treaty obligation "to take all practicable steps to promote, facilitate and finance" the transfer of ESTs to developing countries under Article 4.5 of UNFCCC. Chapter 7 explores policy options available under the TRIPS Agreement to address potential abusive or anti-competitive practices.

4.5 CONCLUDING REMARKS

Under the TRIPS Agreement, all fields of technologies, including ESTs, have to be equally protected by IPRs and all developing WTO Members, except LDCs, had to incorporate minimum IPR standards into their national legal systems by 1 January 2000.[216]

Strong IPR protection is a double-edged sword: on the one hand, as exclusive rights, IPRs confer exclusive power on technology creators to exploit their own technologies and prevent the free-riding problems associated with technologies, thereby incentivising innovation and transfer of ESTs as well as patent disclosure. On the other hand, strong IPRs restrict the use of ESTs and are likely to lead to abusive anti-competitive practices, thus hindering follow-on innovation and slowing down the transfer of ESTs. Therefore, IPRs can be incentives as well as barriers in the process of innovation and transfer of ESTs.

The precise role of IPR protection in the innovation and transfer of ESTs is context-specific, depending on the characteristics of different technology sectors and the circumstances of countries, in particular, their level of technological development. As pointed out by IPCC (2014), the evidence that strict and rigid IP protection facilitates indigenous innovation is almost exclusively limited to specific sectors in developed countries.[217] However, the available evidence does support that "the presence of an effective IP regime is a factor in fostering technology transfer into a country".[218] Potential

---

[215] See Articles 8 and 40 of the TRIPS Agreement; for further details, see Section 7.
[216] Products that are not patentable at that date need to be protected from the year 2005.
[217] IPCC (2014), *Climate Change 2014: Mitigation of Climate Change*, Working Group III Contribution to the IPCC 5th Assessment Report, Chapter 15: National and Sub-National Policies and Institutions, p. 1175.
[218] Ibid.

anti-competitive behaviours associated with IP protection in transfer of ESTs have also been observed.

Numerous scholars have expressed their concerns over the shift in the balance between the protection of IPRs and access to technologies in favour of the technology producers and technology-exporting countries as a result of the strengthening of IPRs induced by TRIPS and the lack of an effective international framework ensuring the meaningful transfer of technology.[219] As demonstrated, in reality, innovation of ESTs is highly concentrated in developed countries and these technologies are rarely transferred to developing countries, and if transferred, they primarily go to a small handful of emerging countries.

The concentration of technological innovation and transfer within developed countries suggests that the one-size-fits-all approach adopted by TRIPS may not benefit most developing countries. The strengthening of IPRs in emerging economies may to a certain extent help them access more advanced technologies through market-based channels while this may not be the case for poorer developing countries. Article 66.2 of the TRIPS Agreement obliges the developed countries to provide their enterprises with incentives to transfer technology to LDCs. Despite being a "best endeavour" clause, no such treatment is provided for ESTs or other developing countries.

It is important to strike or maintain a proper balance between the protection of the exclusive rights of technology creators and the social goals of the wider dissemination and transfer of ESTs, as recognised by Article 7 of the TRIPS Agreement. Having acknowledged the incentivising effects of IPRs on innovation and transfer of ESTs, it is important to mitigate the exclusive effects of IPRs and address potential abusive or anti-competitive practices found in EST transfers. Indeed, the TRIPS Agreement has introduced balancing provisions to redress such concerns. To what extent such provisions can be interpreted to address developing countries' concerns in gaining access to ESTs will be explored in subsequent chapters.

---

[219] See, e.g., Keith E. Maskus (2000), *Intellectual Property Rights in the Global Economy*, Institute for International Economics, Washington, D.C., at pp. 237–8 (stating that "[i]t remains to be seen whether such standards excessively tilt the balance . . . toward the private rights of inventors and away from the needs of competitors and users. It is not too early to claim that they are inappropriate for developing economies and net technology importers"); Simon Walker (2001), *The TRIPS Agreement, Sustainable Development and the Public Interest*, Discussion Paper, IUCN, Gland, p. 4 (arguing that "[t]he balance in many IP systems seems to be shifting too far in favour of technology producers . . . [t]he legitimate technological and developmental objectives of developing countries – generally technology users – are not being given due consideration").

PART II

Interpreting the TRIPS Agreement for Facilitating Innovation and Transfer of ESTs

5

Rules Governing Treaty Interpretation and the Elements against Which the TRIPS Agreement Should Be Interpreted

5.1 INTRODUCTION

Chapter 4 makes it clear that while the incentivising aspects of minimum IPR standards established by the TRIPS Agreement may provide a basis for the development and market-based transfer of ESTs, the proprietary nature of IPRs may pose obstacles to the international transfer of ESTs. The TRIPS Agreement recognises that public interest or social and economic welfare may suffer, and therefore includes safeguards, now commonly referred to as "TRIPS flexibilities",[1] allowing WTO Members to address situations where the acquisition and use of IPRs pose or could potentially pose a barrier for their firms or researchers to access ESTs.

The literature indicates that two types of flexibilities inherent to the TRIPS Agreement appear to be relevant to the transfer of ESTs:[2] (1) the "limits to patents" that explicitly restrict the acquisition and use of patents in some circumstances, primarily through the exhaustion of IPRs (Article 6), limitations on patentable subject matter (Article 27), exceptions to patent rights (Article 30) and compulsory licensing (Article 31) and (2) the "pro-competitive measures" that allow WTO Members to adopt rules to restrain

---

[1] Carolyn Deere (2009), *The Implementation Game: The TRIPS Agreement and the Global Politics of Intellectual Property Reform in Developing Countries*, Oxford University Press, p. 27 (further stating that "[t]he widespread use of the term 'flexibilities' to refer to these safeguards and options emerged in the late 1990s in the context of the negotiations leading to the Doha Declaration on TRIPS and Public Health").

[2] See, e.g., Matthew Rimmer (2011), *Intellectual Property and Climate Change: Inventing Clean Technologies*, Cheltenham, UK: Edward Elgar Publishing, pp. 83–119; Ilona Cheyne (2010), Intellectual Property and Climate Change from a Trade Perspective, *Nordic Environmental Law Journal*, vol. 2, pp. 121–30, at p. 127; Matthew Littleton (2008), *The TRIPS Agreement and Transfer of Climate-Change-Related Technologies to Developing Countries*, DESA Working Paper No. 71, ST/ESA/2008/DWP/71, pp. 7–13.

anti-competitive uses of IPRs (Articles 8.2, 31(k) and 40) through competition laws and policies. Authors have argued that these flexibilities were incorporated into TRIPS as a compromise reached between developed countries who demanded the upward harmonization of intellectual property protection and other countries who contended that competing social interests would be best served by setting limits on IPRs.[3]

The complexities of the TRIPS negotiations have at times resulted in rather vague provisions, particularly in the field of TRIPS flexibilities, which establish a "constructive ambiguity" and require extensive interpretation.[4] Part II of this book is dedicated to investigating whether, and to what extent, the limits to patent protection and the competition-related provisions in the TRIPS Agreement, when properly interpreted, could be applied to facilitate innovation and transfer of ESTs – thus contributing to reconciling the public interest in tackling climate change with the private sector's interest in IP protection. WTO Members can certainly take measures to combat climate change, but in doing so they must comply with the WTO Agreements, including the TRIPS Agreement. Lack of precise legal guidance by WTO Members necessitates a proper method to interpret applicable TRIPS provisions, which is essential for the security and predictability of the world trading system.

The TRIPS Agreement itself does not explicitly specify how its provisions should be interpreted. However, as one of the agreements covered by the Understanding on Rules and Procedures Governing the Settlement of Disputes (DSU), the TRIPS Agreement is subject to the dispute settlement rules and procedures contained in the DSU.[5] Article 3.2 of the DSU provides that the purpose of the WTO dispute settlement system is to clarify the existing

---

[3] See, e.g., Robert Howse (2003), Comments on the Papers Presented by Ernst-Ulrich Petersmann and William J. Davey/ Werner Zdouc, in Cottier and Mavroidis (eds.), *Intellectual Property: Trade, Competition and Sustainable Development*, World Trade Forum, Vol. 3, Ann Arbor: University of Michigan Press, pp. 95–9, at p. 98; see also Peter K. Yu (2009), The Objectives and Principles of the TRIPS Agreement, *Houston Law Review*, vol. 46, pp. 979–1046, at p. 981 (stating that "[a]lthough the TRIPS Agreement's one-size-fits-all – or, more precisely, super-size-fits-all – approach is highly problematic, the Agreement includes a number of flexibilities to facilitate development and to protect the public interest").

[4] See Article 1.1 of the TRIPS Agreement providing that "Members shall be free to determine the appropriate method of implementing the provisions of this Agreement within their own legal system and practice". See also UNCTAD-ICTSD (2005), *Resource Book on TRIPS and Development*, Cambridge University Press, p. 694; Jayashree Watal (2001), *Intellectual Property Rights in the WTO and Developing Countries*, The Hague: Kluwer Law International, p. 7 (noting that "TRIPS was the result of bitter North–South negotiations, reflecting strong economic interests on the part of right owners as well as those benefiting from weaker levels of protection for IPRs. This conflict of interests was resolved through 'constructive ambiguity', which each side interprets according to its convenience").

[5] Article 1.1 of the Dispute Settlement Understanding; see also Appellate Body Report, *India – Patents (US)*, para. 29.

provisions of the "covered agreements" in accordance with "customary rules of interpretation of public international law". The WTO Appellate Body has consistently recognised that Articles 31 and 32 of the Vienna Convention on the Law of the Treaties (VCLT) of 1969 form part of the customary rules of interpretation of public international law and it has resorted to them pursuant to Article 3.2 of the DSU.[6] Accordingly, Article 3.2 of the DSU mandates the application of Articles 31 and 32 of the VCLT to the interpretation of the TRIPS Agreement. The Appellate Body in *India – Patent Protection* (1997) made it clear that:

> These rules [as set out in Article 31 of the Vienna Convention] must be respected and applied in interpreting the *TRIPS Agreement* or any other covered agreement . . . Both panels and the Appellate Body must be guided by the rules of treaty interpretation set out in the *Vienna Convention*, and must not add to or diminish rights and obligations provided in the *WTO Agreement*.[7] (Emphasis in the original)

Under Article 31 of the VCLT, the terms of a treaty (including the TRIPS Agreement) shall be interpreted in good faith in accordance with their ordinary meaning in their context and in light of the object and purpose of the treaty.[8] The TRIPS Agreement is an integral part of the Marrakesh Agreement Establishing the World Trade Organization [hereafter, the Marrakesh Agreement], therefore the object and purpose of the Marrakesh Agreement could shed light on the interpretation of the TRIPS Agreement.[9]

This chapter first studies the customary rules governing treaty interpretation and then examines the elements in light of which the TRIPS Agreement

---

[6] See, e.g., Appellate Body Report, *US – Gasoline*, p. 17 (finding that "[t]hat general rule of interpretation [i.e. Article 31 of the VCLT] has attained the status of a rule of customary or general international law. As such, it forms part of the 'customary rules of interpretation of public international law' which the Appellate Body has been directed, by Article 3(2) of the *DSU*, to apply in seeking to clarify the provision of the *General Agreement* and the other 'covered agreements' of the Marrakesh Agreement Establishing the World Trade Organization") (emphasis in the original); Appellate Body Report, *Japan – Alcoholic Beverages II*, p. 10 (stressed that "this general rule of interpretation [i.e. Article 31 of the VCLT,] 'has attained the status of a rule of customary or general international law'. There can be no doubt that Article 32 of the *Vienna Convention*, dealing with the role of supplementary means of interpretation, has also attained the same status") (emphasis in the original); Appellate Body Report, *US – Hot Rolled Steel*, para. 60 (claiming that "the rules of treaty interpretation in Articles 31 and 32 of the *Vienna Convention* apply to *any* treaty, in *any* field of public international law, and not just to the WTO agreements") (emphasis in the original).

[7] Appellate Body Report, *India – Patents (US)*, para. 46.

[8] See Article 31(1) of the Vienna Convention on the Law of the Treaties.

[9] Article II:2 of the Marrakesh Agreement provides that "[t]he agreements and associated legal instruments included in Annexes 1, 2 and 3 are integral parts of this Agreement, binding on all Members."

should be interpreted, including the object and purpose of the treaty, subsequent development as well as relevant rules of public international law.

5.2 RULES GOVERNING TREATY INTERPRETATION

The principal rule of treaty interpretation is enshrined in Article 31(1) of the VCLT, titled "General Rule of Interpretation". It requires that "[a] treaty shall be interpreted in good faith in accordance with the ordinary meaning to be given to the terms of the treaty in their context and in the light of its object and purpose". When the interpretation according to Article 31 of the VCLT "leaves the meaning ambiguous or obscure" or "leads to a result which is manifestly absurd or unreasonable", or "in order to confirm the meaning resulting from the application of [A]rticle 31", the treaty interpreter may have recourse to supplementary means of interpretation under Article 32 of the VCLT, "including the preparatory work of the treaty and the circumstances of its conclusion".

Commentators generally agree that the starting point for treaty interpretation is the actual terms of the text, that is, the words and language of the provision.[10] In *Japan–Alcoholic Beverages* (1996), the Appellate Body confirmed that "Article 31 of the Vienna Convention provides that the words of the treaty form the foundation for the interpretive process: 'interpretation must be based above all upon the text of the treaty'."[11] The International Law Commission (ILC), the original drafter of Article 31, had made similar comments, concluding that "the starting point of interpretation is the elucidation of the meaning of the text, not an investigation *ab initio* into the intention of the parties."[12]

However, there are different views as to the proper sequence in which the treaty interpreter should consider other various elements for interpretation as

---

[10] See, e.g., Georges Abi-Saab (2010), The Appellate Body and Treaty Interpretation, in Fitzmaurice et al. (eds.), *Treaty Interpretation and the Vienna Convention on the Law of Treaties: 30 Years On*, Leiden, Netherlands: Martinus Nijhoff Publishers, pp. 99–109, at p. 104 (stating that "[t]he interpreter has to start with the hard core of the operation, which is the *text* to be interpreted (i.e. the words and language of the provision") (emphasis in the original); Beas Edson Rodrigues (2012), *The General Exception Clauses of the TRIPS Agreement: Promoting Sustainable Development*, vol. 17, Cambridge University Press, p. 31 (stating that "naturally, the starting point should always be the text of the provision, be it ambiguous or seemingly clear").

[11] Appellate Body Report, *Japan – Alcoholic Beverages II*, p. 10.

[12] *Report of the International Law Commission on the Work of Its Eighteenth Session*, 4 May–19 July 1966, Official Reports of the General Assembly, Twenty-First Session, Supplement No. 9, UN Doc. A/6309/Rev. 1, United Nations, p. 220.

specified in Articles 31 and 32.[13] A prevailing approach is to view all these elements for interpretation as "one holistic rule of interpretation rather than a sequence of separate tests to be applied in a hierarchical order".[14] According to the ILC (1996), the title of Article 31 of the VCLT is "General Rule of Interpretation" in the singular, not "General Rules of Interpretation" in the plural, because the Commission sought to emphasise that "the process of interpretation is a unity" and that "the provisions of the article form a single, closely integrated rule".[15] The Appellate Body in *US – Continued Zeroing* (2009) emphasised the notion that treaty interpretation is a holistic exercise by stating that:

> The principles of interpretation that are set out in Articles 31 and 32 are to be followed in a holistic fashion. The interpretative exercise is engaged so as to yield an interpretation that is harmonious and coherent and fits comfortably in the treaty as a whole so as to render the treaty provision legally effective ... it should be kept in mind that treaty interpretation is an integrated operation, where interpretative rules or principles must be understood and applied as connected and mutually reinforcing components of a holistic exercise.[16]

The process of treaty interpretation is, therefore, not a rigid sequence of discrete steps as perceived by some scholars,[17] but "an integrated operation"

---

[13] See, e.g., Georges Abi-Saab (2010), The Appellate Body and Treaty Interpretation, in Fitzmaurice et al. (eds.), *Treaty Interpretation and the Vienna Convention on the Law of Treaties: 30 Years On*, Leiden, Netherlands: Martinus Nijhoff Publishers, pp. 99–109, at pp. 104–5 (perceiving the process of interpretation as "a rigid sequence of autonomous or discrete steps, each of which has to be explicitly addressed and 'exhausted', before moving on to the next one". The order he suggested is as follows: first, the text, second, the context, and the "object and purpose", then subsequent practice, and lastly, the preparatory works and circumstances surrounding the conclusion of the treaty); in contrast, Jeff Waincymer (2002), *WTO Litigation: Procedural Aspects of Formal Dispute Settlement*, London: Cameron May, p. 407 (arguing that "[w]hile Article 32 refers to supplementary means of interpretation this does not imply a temporal prohibition against their use at the outset").

[14] See, e.g., Panel Report, *US – Section 301 Trade Act*, para. 7.22 (finding that "the elements referred to in Article 31 – text, context and object-and-purpose as well as good faith – are to be viewed as one holistic rule of interpretation rather than a sequence of separate tests to be applied in a hierarchical order"); Daniel H. Joyner (2012), *Interpreting the Nuclear Non-Proliferation Treaty*, Oxford University Press, p. 23 (stating that "[t]he primary roles in treaty interpretation which VCLT Article 31 assigns to contextual analysis, and to the object and purpose of the treaty as a whole, are clear evidence of the holistic nature of the approach to treaty interpretation mandated by the VCLT").

[15] *Report of the International Law Commission on the Work of Its Eighteenth Session*, 4 May–19 July 1966, Official Reports of the General Assembly, Twenty-First Session, Supplement No. 9, UN Doc. A/6309/Rev. 1, United Nations, p. 220.

[16] Appellate Body Report, *US – Continued Zeroing*, para. 268.

[17] See, e.g., Georges Abi-Saab (2010), The Appellate Body and Treaty Interpretation, in Fitzmaurice et al. (eds.), *Treaty Interpretation and the Vienna Convention on the Law of Treaties: 30 Years On*, Leiden, Netherlands: Martinus Nijhoff Publishers, pp. 99–109, at p. 104.

and "a holistic exercise". As the panel in *US – Section 301* (1999) observed, "[t]ext, context and object-and-purpose correspond to well-established textual, systemic and teleological methodologies of treaty interpretation, all of which typically come into play when interpreting complex provisions in multilateral treaties."[18]

The following sections deal with the various elements for interpretation respectively. While separate attention is given to each, it is important to remember that they are part of a general methodology of interpretation and subject to the principle of good faith as outlined by Article 31 of the VCLT.

5.2.1 *The Principle of Good Faith*

Article 31(1) of the VCLT stipulates that "[a] treaty shall be interpreted in good faith". The ILC justified the inclusion of the "good faith" principle in the general rule of interpretation by arguing that interpretation in good faith "flows directly from the rule *pacta sunt servanda*", which is restated in Article 26 of the VCLT.[19] Good faith has been viewed as "a core principle of interpretation of the WTO Agreement",[20] including the TRIPS Agreement. On several occasions, the Appellate Body has also considered good faith as a "pervasive" general principle that "underlies all treaties".[21] The principle of good faith interpretation is so fundamental that some scholars believe it is directed to the Members and any judicial organ in their interpretation of a treaty.[22] It "inform[s] a treaty interpreter's task",[23] and applies to the entire interpretation process, including the investigation of the text, purpose and object and the context.

Commentators consider that good faith in treaty interpretation means that a treaty must be interpreted "honestly, fairly and reasonably" and in line with

---

[18] Panel Report, *US – Section 301 Trade Act*, para. 7.22.
[19] *Report of the International Law Commission on the Work of Its Eighteenth Session*, 4 May–19 July 1966, Official Reports of the General Assembly, Twenty-First Session, Supplement No. 9, UN Doc. A/6309/Rev. 1, United Nations, pp. 219 and 221 (further arguing that "the interpretation of treaties in good faith and according to law is essential if the *pacta sunt servanda* rule is to have any real meaning").
[20] Panel Report, *US – Gambling*, para. 6.50.
[21] See, e.g., Appellate Body Report, *US – Cotton Yarn*, para. 81; Appellate Body Report, *US – Shrimp*, para. 158.
[22] See, e.g., Helge Elisabeth Zeitler (2005), "Good Faith" in the WTO Jurisprudence: Necessary Balancing Element or an Open Door to Judicial Activism, *Journal of International Economic Law*, vol. 8, no. 3, pp. 721–58, at p. 726.
[23] Appellate Body Report, *US – Offset Act (Byrd Amendment)*, para. 296.

"the common intention of the parties as expressed in the terms of the treaty".[24] It is generally agreed that good faith underlies the principle that treaty interpretation should not lead to a result that would be "manifestly absurd or unreasonable".[25] In the *Aerial Incident Case* (1959), Judges Sir Hersch Lauterpacht, Wellington Koo and Sir Percy Spender made a classic exposition of the link between the principle of good faith and the test of "reasonableness" in the interpretation of treaties by stating that:

> It is consistent with enlightened practice and principle to apply the test of reasonableness to the interpretation of international instruments – a test which follows from the ever present duty of States to act in good faith.[26]

It follows from the principle of good faith that an interpretation should not lead to obviously absurd or unreasonable results. Although a WTO Member in an early GATT dispute, *U.S. – Lead and Bismuth* (1994), claimed that "a good faith action could be unreasonable" because "good faith concerned motives and intentions, whereas 'reasonableness' concerned rationality and logic", it acknowledged that the concept of "good faith" did not preclude the need for a reasonableness standard with respect to the treaty interpretation.[27] As observed by Mitchell (2007), the reasonableness standard is part of the principle of effective interpretation.[28]

In addition to the principle of effectiveness,[29] the principle of the protection of legitimate expectations also derives from the principle of good faith.[30]

---

[24] See, e.g., Frank Engelen (2004), *Interpretation of Tax Treaties under International Law*, IBFD Publications BV, p. 131; Andrew D. Mitchell (2007), The Legal Basis for Using Principles in WTO Disputes, *Journal of International Economic Law*, vol. 10, no. 4, pp. 795–835, at p. 811.

[25] See, e.g., Shabtai Rosenne (1982), The Election of Five Members of the International Court of Justice in 1981, *The American Journal of International Law*, vol. 76, no. 2, pp. 364–70, at p. 365 (claiming that "[i]t is a cardinal principle of interpretation that a treaty should be interpreted in good faith and not lead to a result that would be manifestly absurd or unreasonable"); Ian McTaggart Sinclair (1984), *The Vienna Convention on the Law of Treaties*, Manchester University Press, p. 120; Asif H. Qureshi (2012), *Interpreting WTO Agreements: Problems and Perspectives*, Cambridge University Press, p. 13 (noting that "good faith is also the basis for the proposition that 'interpretation should not lead to a result which is manifestly absurd or unreasonable'").

[26] Joint Dissenting Opinion by Judges Sir Hersch Lauterpacht, Wellington Koo and Sir Percy Spender, in *Aerial Incident Case* (Israel v. Bulgaria), Preliminary Objections, 1959 I.C.J. Reports, p. 189.

[27] GATT Panel Report, *United States – Imposition of Countervailing Duties on Certain Hot-Rolled Lead and Bismuth Carbon Steel Products Originating in France, Germany and the United Kingdom*, SCM/185, 15 November 1994, para. 104.

[28] Andrew D. Mitchell (2007), The Legal Basis for Using Principles in WTO Disputes, *Journal of International Economic Law*, vol. 10, no. 4, pp. 795–835, at p. 811.

[29] Eirik Bjorge (2014), *The Evolutionary Interpretation of Treaties*, Oxford University Press, p. 72.

[30] See, e.g., Thomas Cottier and Krista Nadakavukaren Schefer (2000), Good Faith and the Protection of Legitimate Expectations in the WTO, in Bronckers and Quick (eds.), *New Directions in International Economic Law: Essays in Honour of John H. Jackson*, Alphen aan

While the use of the principle of effectiveness has been well accepted in WTO jurisprudence, the principle of the protection of legitimate expectations is not.[31] The following sections address the principle of effectiveness and examine the link between the principle of good faith and the protection of legitimate intentions.

5.2.1.1 The Principle of Effectiveness

The principle of effective treaty interpretation, often referred to as *ut res magis valeat quam pereat*, derives from the "good faith" requirement.[32] The ILC viewed it as a true general rule of interpretation embodied in Article 31(1), stating that "[w]hen a treaty is open to two interpretations one of which does and the other does not enable the treaty to have appropriate effects, good faith and the objects and purposes of the treaty demand that the former interpretation should be adopted".[33]

The duty to interpret a treaty as a whole has been clarified by the Permanent Court of International Justice in its Advisory Opinion of 1922 on *Competence of the ILO in regard to International Regulation of the Conditions of the Labour of Persons Employed in Agriculture*, stating that:

> In considering the question before the Court upon the language of the Treaty, it is obvious that the Treaty must be read as a whole, and that its meaning is not to be determined merely upon particular phrases which, if detached from the context, may be interpreted in more than one sense.[34]

---

den Rijn, Netherlands: Kluwer Law International, pp. 47–68, at p. 50 (considering that the principle of good faith encompasses the element of the protection of legitimate expectations); Isabelle Van Damme (2009), *Treaty Interpretation by the WTO Appellate Body*, Oxford University Press, p. 65 (arguing that "[i]t is generally well accepted that the principle of legitimate expectations is derived from the principle of good faith").

[31] Panel Report, *India – Patents (US)*, para. 7.18 (stating that "good faith interpretation requires the protection of legitimate expectations derived from the protection of intellectual property rights provided for in the Agreement"). However, the Appellate Body rejected the use of "legitimate expectations" as a principle of WTO law. See Appellate Body Report, *India – Patents (US)*, para. 45.

[32] Panel Report, *US – Gambling*, para. 6.46 (finding that the principle of effective treaty interpretation "derives from the requirement that treaties be interpreted in good faith").

[33] *Report of the International Law Commission on the Work of Its Eighteenth Session*, 4 May–19 July 1966, Official Reports of the General Assembly, Twenty-First Session, Supplement No. 9, UN Doc. A/6309/Rev. 1, United Nations, p. 219.

[34] Permanent Court of International Justice, *Competence of the ILO in regard to International Regulation of the Conditions of the Labour of Persons Employed in Agriculture*, Advisory Opinion of 12 August 1922, p. 23.

This approach has been followed by the International Court of Justice, for instance, highlighting in the Interpretation of Peace Treaties with Bulgaria, Hungary and Romania (1950) that the rule of effectiveness cannot justify attributing a meaning to a provision that is contrary to the letter and spirit of the instrument.[35]

The WTO Appellate Body has recognised, on numerous occasions, the principle of effectiveness in the interpretation of treaties applying in connection with the WTO covered agreements,[36] and thus this principle is applicable to the TRIPS Agreement. In *US – Gasoline* (1996), the Appellate Body considered the principle of effectiveness as one corollary of the 'general rule of interpretation' in the VCLT and found that this principle requires interpretation to "give meaning and effect to all the terms of the treaty" and does not allow an interpreter to "adopt a reading that would result in reducing whole clauses or paragraphs of a treaty to redundancy or inutility".[37] It is suggested that the principle of effective interpretation requires that all provisions of a treaty must be read in a harmonious fashion and applied in a cumulative and simultaneous manner.[38]

Built upon this principle, in *Canada – Pharmaceutical Patents* (2000), Canada criticised the EU for having construed the TRIPS provisions in isolation, maintaining that:

> The principle of effectiveness required that account be taken of both the contextual provisions, which indicated that intellectual property rights were not intended to be unlimited, and the objectives provision, which made it clear that the TRIPS Agreement sought a balance of rights and obligations. To fail to take those provisions into account, and to read Article 30 as if it were intended that the TRIPS Agreement should be 'neutral vis-à-vis societal values', . . . would be to render Articles 7, 8.1 and 30 inutile.[39]

---

[35] International Court of Justice, Advisory Opinion, *Interpretation of Peace Treaties with Bulgaria, Hungary and Romania (Second Phase)*, 1950, ICJ Reports, 221, p. 229.

[36] See, e.g., Appellate Body Report, *US – Gasoline*, p. 23; Appellate Body Report, *Japan – Alcoholic Beverages II*, pp. 11 and 16.

[37] Appellate Body Report, *US – Gasoline*, p. 23; see also Appellate Body Report, *Japan – Alcoholic Beverages II*, p. 12.

[38] See, e.g., Gabrielle Marceau (2006), The WTO Is NOT a Closed Box, *Proceedings of the Annual Meeting (American Society of International Law)*, vol. 100, pp. 29–31, at p. 30; Miguel Rodriguez Mendoza and Marie Wilke (2011), Revisiting the Single Undertaking: Towards a More Balanced Approach to WTO Negotiations, in Birkbeck (ed.), *Making Global Trade Governance Work for Development: Perspectives and Priorities from Developing Countries*, Cambridge University Press, pp. 486–506, at p. 496.

[39] Panel Report, *Canada – Pharmaceutical Patents*, para. 4.41.

Accordingly, the interpretive principle of effectiveness requires a treaty interpreter to read all TRIPS provisions in a way that gives meaning to all of them harmoniously and prevents reading the TRIPS provisions in an isolated manner.[40] Also, Articles 7, 8.1 and 30 of TRIPS provide rights and other provisions of the TRIPS Agreement should not be interpreted and applied so as to nullify the exercise of such rights.[41]

Furthermore, the Appellate Body in *Korea – Dairy Safeguards* (1999) built upon its statement in *US – Gasoline* (1996) and found that:

> An important corollary of this [effectiveness] principle is that a treaty should be interpreted as a whole, and in particular, its sections and parts should be read as a whole. Article II: 2 of the *WTO Agreement* expressly manifests the intention of the Uruguay Round negotiators that the provisions of the *WTO Agreement* and the Multilateral Trade Agreements included in its Annexes 1, 2 and 3 must be read as a whole.[42] (Emphasis in the original)

This shows that the principle of effective interpretation in the context of the WTO "Single Undertaking" requires the "harmonious interpretation and application of all WTO provisions".[43] Therefore, the fact that the TRIPS Agreement is an integral part of the WTO Marrakesh Agreement indicates that the provisions of the TRIPS Agreement should be read together with other WTO Agreements.

Accordingly, the principle of effectiveness requires that a specific TRIPS provision be read in its context and in the light of the objects and purposes of both the TRIPS Agreement and the Marrakesh Agreement. The balance of rights and obligations contained in the TRIPS Agreement should not be nullified by an interpretation of a specific TRIPS provision.

5.2.1.2 The Link between Good Faith and Legitimate Expectations

The principle of good faith is considered by some courts as the "corollary in public international law of the principle of the protection of legitimate expectations".[44] In contrast, others argue that the principle of the protection

---

[40] Appellate Body Report, *Korea – Dairy*, para. 81.   [41] Ibid.   [42] Ibid.

[43] Gabrielle Marceau and Joel P. Trachtman (2014), A Map of the World Trade Organization Law of Domestic Regulation of Goods: The Technical Barriers to Trade Agreement, the Sanitary and Phytosanitary Measures Agreement, and the General Agreement on Tariffs and Trade, *Journal of World Trade*, vol. 48, no. 2, pp. 351–432, at p. 418.

[44] See, e.g., *Opel Austria GmbH* v. *Council of the European Union*, Case T-115/94, Judgment of the Court of First Instance (Fourth Chamber), 22 January 1997, at paras. 90 and 93.

of legitimate expectations is the corollary of the good faith principle.[45] There is no doubt that these two principles are closely related to each other.

The latter link between good faith and legitimate expectations was supported by several early dispute panels in the WTO. The panel in *India – Patents (US)* (1997) considered that the good-faith interpretation necessitated the protection of legitimate expectations derived from the TRIPS Agreement.[46] Similarly, another panel, in *EC – Computer Equipment* (1998), asserted that legitimate expectations shall be protected so as to maintain the security and predictability of the multilateral trading system and emphasised that "[t]his is consistent with the principle of good faith interpretation under Article 31 of the Vienna Convention".[47] In their analysis, both panels referred to an earlier Panel Report in *US – Underwear* (1997), stating that:

> [T]he relevant provisions [of the Agreement on Textiles and Clothing] have to be interpreted in good faith. Based upon the wording, the context and the overall purpose of the Agreement, exporting Members can ... legitimately expect that market access and investments made would not be frustrated by importing Members taking improper recourse to such action.[48]

However, the Appellate Body found that both panels misapplied Article 31 of the VCLT and overruled their attempts to invoke legitimate expectations for treaty interpretation.[49] First, the Appellate Body made it clear that "[t]he legitimate expectations of the parties to a treaty are reflected in the language of the treaty itself".[50] Accordingly, treaty interpreters should not consider legitimate expectations separately from the words of the treaties because such legitimate expectations had been incorporated in the text of the treaty.[51] Furthermore, the duty of treaty interpreters is to "ascertain common intentions of the parties".[52] Such common intentions cannot be ascertained "on the basis of the subjective and unilaterally determined 'expectations' of one of the parties to a treaty".[53] This should be done in line with the principles of treaty

---

[45] See, e.g., Jan Wouters et al. (2011), *The Influence of General Principles of Law*, Working Paper No. 70, Leuven Centre for Global Governance Studies, p. 16.

[46] Panel Report, *India – Patents (US)*, para. 7.18.

[47] Panel Report, *EC – Computer Equipment*, para. 8.25.

[48] Panel Report, *US – Underwear*, para. 7.20.

[49] Appellate Body Report, *India – Patents (US)*, para. 45; Appellate Body Report, *EC – Computer Equipment*, para. 83.

[50] Appellate Body Report, *India – Patents (US)*, para. 45.

[51] Helge Elisabeth Zeitler (2005), 'Good Faith' in the WTO Jurisprudence: Necessary Balancing Element or an Open Door to Judicial Activism, *Journal of International Economic Law*, vol. 8, no. 3, pp. 721–58, at p. 728.

[52] Appellate Body Report, *EC – Computer Equipment*, para. 84.   [53] Ibid.

interpretation set out in Article 31 of the VCLT, which "neither require nor condone the imputation into a treaty of words that are not there or the importation into a treaty of concepts that were not intended".[54] According to Zeitler (2005), the Appellate Body's restrictive approach in applying the good faith principle indicates "signs of judicial restraint".[55]

Overall, the WTO jurisprudence suggests that legitimate expectations should not be used *per se* as a principle of interpretation for the WTO Agreements including the TRIPS Agreement. Further, using legitimate expectations in the interpretation of the WTO Agreements may run contrary to the textual approach to treaty interpretation, which is found in the WTO practice.

5.2.2 *Determining Ordinary Meaning under Article 31*

5.2.2.1 Ordinary Meaning

Article 31(1) of the VCLT requires a treaty to be interpreted "in accordance with the ordinary meaning to be given to the terms of the treaty". The ILC viewed this principle as "the very essence of the textual approach": the ordinary meaning of the treaty terms is presumed to have embodied the parties' common intentions.[56] Scholars have endorsed this textual approach by arguing that the ordinary meaning tends to reflect what the parties intended unless the contrary is established.[57] This approach reveals the inherent limitations of treaty interpretation: as observed by Pauwelyn (2008), "interpretation must be limited to giving meanings to rules of law", and it cannot add new rules or diminish the rights and obligations provided in the treaty.[58]

---

[54] Appellate Body Report, *India – Patents (US)*, para. 45.

[55] Helge Elisabeth Zeitler (2005), 'Good Faith' in the WTO Jurisprudence: Necessary Balancing Element or an Open Door to Judicial Activism, *Journal of International Economic Law*, vol. 8, no. 3, pp. 721–58, at p. 755.

[56] *Report of the International Law Commission on the Work of Its Eighteenth Session*, 4 May–19 July 1966, Official Reports of the General Assembly, Twenty-First Session, Supplement No. 9, UN Doc. A/6309/Rev. 1, United Nations, p. 221.

[57] See, e.g., Anthony Aust (2007), *Modern Treaty Law and Practice*, Cambridge University Press, p. 235 (stating that "it is reasonable to assume, at least until the contrary is established, that the ordinary meaning is most likely to reflect what the parties intended"; Alexander Orakhelashvili (2008), *The Interpretation of Acts and Rules in Public International Law*, Oxford University Press, p. 318 (arguing that "[t]he primacy [of] plain and ordinary meaning follows directly from the need for an interpreter to establish and preserve the original consensus between States-parties").

[58] Joost Pauwelyn (2008), *Conflict of Norms in Public International Law: How WTO Law Relates to other Rules of International Law*, Cambridge University Press, p. 245.

Therefore, treaty interpretation cannot impute words or concepts into WTO rules, including TRIPS rules, that "goes either beyond or against the 'clear meaning of the terms'" of the relevant rule.[59]

Scholars and interpreters agree that one natural way to identify the ordinary meaning of a term is to use recognised dictionary definitions.[60] The Appellate Body has observed that "dictionaries are a 'useful starting point' for the analysis of 'ordinary meaning' of a treaty term".[61] Nevertheless, it has cautioned against equating the "ordinary meaning" of a term with its dictionary definition because "dictionary meanings leave many interpretive questions open".[62] In *China – Publications and Audiovisual Products* (2009), the Appellate Body affirmed that dictionaries are "not dispositive of the meanings appearing in treaties" and the "ordinary meaning" of treaty terms should be ascertained only in their context and in accordance with the treaty's object and purpose.[63]

The Appellate Body's approach to determining ordinary meaning is consistent with Article 31(1) of the VCLT, under which the "ordinary meaning" of a treaty term cannot be determined in the abstract but in its context and in light of the object and purpose of the treaty.[64] The ILC considered this rule as both "common sense" and "good faith".[65] In *Land, Island and Maritime Frontier Dispute* (1992), Judge Torres Bernardez in his separate opinion affirmed that the term ordinary meaning is not "in the absolute or in the abstract", but is

---

[59] Ibid.

[60] See, e.g., Jeff Waincymer (2002), *WTO Litigation: Procedural Aspects of Formal Dispute Settlement*, London: Cameron May, p. 410 (further noting that "[d]ictionaries utilised by Panels have included Websters Third New International Dictionary, Black's Law Dictionary and the New Shorter Oxford English Dictionary").

[61] Appellate Body Report, *EC – Chicken Cuts*, para. 175.

[62] See, e.g., Appellate Body Report, *Canada – Aircraft*, para. 153; Appellate Body Report, *China – Publications and Audiovisual Products*, para. 348 (noting that "dictionaries alone are not necessarily capable of resolving complex questions of interpretation because they typically catalogue all meanings of words. Dictionaries are important guides to, but not dispositive of, the meaning of words appearing in treaties").

[63] Appellate Body Report, *China – Publications and Audiovisual Products*, para. 348.

[64] See, e.g., A v. *Minister for Immigration & Ethnic Affairs* [1997] HCA 4 (24 February 1997) 190 CLR 225; 71 ALJR 381; 142 ALR 331 finding that ("the ordinary meaning of the words [is] not to be determined in a vacuum removed from the context of the treaty or its object and purpose"); *Report of the International Law Commission on the Work of Its Eighteenth Session*, 4 May–19 July 1966, Official Reports of the General Assembly, Twenty-First Session, Supplement No. 9, UN Doc. A/6309/Rev. 1, United Nations, p. 221 (stating that "the ordinary meaning of a term is not to be determined in the abstract but in the context of the treaty and in the light of the object and purpose").

[65] *Report of the International Law Commission on the Work of Its Eighteenth Session*, 4 May–19 July 1966, Official Reports of the General Assembly, Twenty-First Session, Supplement No. 9, UN Doc. A/6309/Rev. 1, United Nations, p. 221.

"fully qualified" by its connection with the treaty's context, object and purpose.[66] The rule of interpretation according to ordinary meaning is, thus, not an absolute one, as the ICJ in *South West Africa Cases* (1962) found:

> Where such a method of interpretation results in a meaning incompatible with the spirit, purpose and context of the clause or instrument in which the words are contained, no reliance can be validly placed on it.[67]

Accordingly, if the ordinary meaning of a treaty term is to be reliable, it has to be confirmed by its context and the object and purpose of the treaty.[68]

5.2.2.2 "In the Light of Its Object and Purpose"

Article 31(1) of the VCLT provides that the terms of a treaty shall be interpreted in the light of the object and purpose of the treaty. According to Sinclair (1984), it is in light of the object and purpose of the treaty that the ordinary meaning of the words "must be tested and either confirmed or modified".[69]

Commentators have correctly pointed out that while "consideration of a treaty's object and purpose ensures the effectiveness of its terms", the purposive interpretation is limited by the treaty text itself.[70] The WTO panels and Appellate Body often use a treaty's object and purpose as an interpretive factor but have avoided relying on it too heavily.[71] In an early WTO dispute, the

---

[66] Separate Opinion by Bernardez Torres, in *Land, Island and Maritime Frontier Dispute* (El Salvador/Honduras: Nicaragua Intervening), Judgment, 11 September 1992, at pp. 371–2 (stating that "[f]or treaty interpretation rules there is no 'ordinary meaning' in the absolute or in the abstract. That is why Article 31 of the Vienna Convention refers to 'good faith' and to the ordinary meaning 'to be given' to the terms of the treaty 'in their context and in the light of its object and purpose". It is, therefore, a fully qualified 'ordinary meaning'); see also Andreas Zimmermann (2011), *The 1951 Convention Relating to the Status of Refugees and Its 1967 Protocol: A Commentary*, Oxford University Press, p. 83.

[67] *South West Africa Cases* (*Ethiopia* v. *South Africa; Liberia* v. *South Africa*), Preliminary Objections, Judgment of 21 December 1962, I.C.J. Reports, p. 336.

[68] Richard K. Gardiner (2008), *Treaty Interpretation*, Cambridge University Press, p. 165 (stating that "[t]he ordinary meaning might have a determinative role but only if the context confirmed this and if there were no other factors leading away from the conclusion").

[69] Ian McTaggart Sinclair (1984), *The Vienna Convention on the Law of Treaties*, Manchester University Press, p. 130.

[70] Mark E. Villiger (2011), The Rules on Interpretation: Misgivings, Misunderstandings, Miscarriage? The 'Crucible' Intended by the International Law Commission, in Enzo Cannizzaro (ed.), *The Law of Treaties Beyond the Vienna Convention*, Oxford University Press, pp. 105–22, at p. 110.

[71] See, e.g., Appellate Body Report, *US – Shrimp*, para. 114 (stating that "[a] treaty interpreter must begin with, and focus upon, the text of the particular provision to be interpreted . . . Where the

Appellate Body made it clear that the object and purpose of the treaty is "to be referred to in determining the meaning of the 'terms of the treaty' and not as an independent basis for interpretation".[72] Therefore, just as other Article 31(1) interpretative elements, the object and purpose cannot exclusively determine the meaning of the treaty terms.[73]

Scholars generally agree that the object and purpose of a treaty is ascertained from the text of the treaty, in particular its preamble.[74] As pointed out by Ehlermann (2003), "it is risky to ascertain the object and purpose that the parties pursued if they are not expressed in the treaty itself", because when agreeing on a certain text, parties often have different objects and purposes in mind.[75] It is well established that the use of the singular word "its" in the term "its object and purpose" under Article 31(1) of the VCLT makes it clear that "the starting point for ascertaining 'object and purpose' is the treaty itself, in its entirety".[76]

However, as the Appellate Body pointed out in *EC – Chicken Cuts* (2005), Article 31(1) does not exclude considering the object and purpose of a particular treaty provision, insofar as it helps the treaty interpreter ascertain the object and purpose of the treaty as a whole.[77] The Appellate Body further cautioned against the interpretation of the WTO law in accordance with the "object and purpose" of specific provisions, paragraphs or terms of the WTO agreements in isolation from the treaty's object and purpose on the whole.[78]

Accordingly, under Article 31 of the VCLT, the meaning of a term has to be determined in light of the overall object and purpose of the entire treaty.

---

meaning imparted by the text itself is equivocal or inconclusive, or where confirmation of the correctness of the reading of the text itself is desired, light from the object and purpose of the treaty as a whole may usually be sought."); Panel Report, *US – Section 301 Trade Act*, para. 7.22 (finding that "[c]ontext and object-and-purpose may often appear simply to confirm an interpretation seemingly derived from the 'raw' text").

[72] Appellate Body Report, *Japan – Alcoholic Beverages II*, p. 10.

[73] Isabelle van Damme (2009), *Treaty Interpretation by the WTO Appellate Body*, Oxford University Press, p. 263.

[74] See, e.g., Alexander Orakhelashvili (2008), *The Interpretation of Acts and Rules in Public International Law*, Oxford University Press, p. 343; Frank Engelen (2004), *Interpretation of Tax Treaties under International Law*, IBFD Publications BV, p. 176.

[75] Claus-Dieter Ehlermann (2003), Reflections on the Appellate Body of the WTO, *Journal of International Economic Law*, vol. 6, no. 3, pp. 695–708, at p. 699.

[76] Appellate Body Report, *EC – Chicken Cuts*, para. 238 (also stating that "the use of the singular word 'its' preceding the term 'object and purpose' in Article 31(1) of the Vienna Convention indicates that the term refers to the treaty as a whole").

[77] Ibid.   [78] Ibid., para. 239.

5.2.2.3 "In Their Context"

The terms of a treaty must be interpreted "in their context" under Article 31(1) of the VCLT. As observed by Gardiner (2008), context is "an aid to selection of ordinary meaning" and "a modifier of any over-literal approach to interpretation".[79] It is relevant for treaty interpretation to the extent that it may "shed light" on the meaning of the term.[80] According to Waincymer (2002), contextual interpretation is even more relevant when a set of rules is adopted as a complete package which is the case for the WTO Agreements.[81] As demonstrated, the Appellate Body in *Korea – Dairy Safeguards* (1999) stressed the "single undertaking" nature of the WTO Agreements and confirmed that Members must comply with their WTO obligations cumulatively and "simultaneously".[82]

Article 31(2) of the VCLT has identified the material that is considered to be "part" of the context by stating that:

> The context for the purpose of the interpretation of a treaty shall comprise, in addition to the text, including its preamble and annexes:
>
> (a) Any agreement relating to the treaty which was made between all the parties in connection with the conclusion of the treaty;
> (b) Any instrument which was made by one or more parties in connection with the conclusion of the treaty and accepted by the other parties as an instrument related to the treaty.

As pointed out by ILC (1966), it is well established that the preamble and annexes form part of a treaty for the purposes of its interpretation.[83] In this sense, the preamble and annexes of treaties, as elements of the general rule of interpretation, should be distinguished from "the preparatory work of the treaty" and "the circumstances of its conclusion" which are "supplementary means of interpretation" to be referred to for further confirmation of the treaty interpretation or in cases of ambiguity or obscurity under Article 32.

---

[79] Richard K. Gardiner (2008), *Treaty Interpretation*, Cambridge University Press, p. 177.
[80] Appellate Body Report, *China – Auto Parts*, para. 151.
[81] Jeff Waincymer (2002), *WTO Litigation: Procedural Aspects of Formal Dispute Settlement*, London: Cameron May, p. 418.
[82] Appellate Body Report, *Korea – Dairy Safeguards*, para. 74 (supported the statement of the Panel that: "[i]t is now well established that the WTO Agreement is a 'Single Undertaking' and therefore all WTO obligations are generally cumulative and Members must comply with all of them simultaneously").
[83] *Report of the International Law Commission on the Work of Its Eighteenth Session*, 4 May–19 July 1966, Official Reports of the General Assembly, Twenty-First Session, Supplement No. 9, UN Doc. A/6309/Rev. 1, United Nations, p. 221.

The question is to what extent other documents related to the treaty can be considered as part of the "context" for treaty interpretation purposes. Article 31 (2) of the VCLT identifies two types of documents that shall be regarded as part of the context: (a) any such "agreement *relating to* the treaty which was made between all the parties in connection with the conclusion of the treaty" and (b) any such "instrument which was made by one or more parties in connection with the conclusion of the treaty and accepted by the other parties as an instrument *related to* the treaty" (emphasis added).

The ILC explains in its commentary on draft articles on VCLT that this provision is based on the principle that a unilateral document cannot be considered as forming part of the "context" within the meaning of Article 31 "unless not only was it made in connection with the conclusion of the treaty but its relation to the treaty was accepted in the same manner by the other parties".[84] Accordingly, for an instrument to qualify as part of the "context" under Article 31 of the VCLT, the following criteria must be fulfilled: first, it is "essential" that the agreement or instrument should be "related to the treaty".[85] For an agreement or instrument to be "related" to the treaty, a leading international law commentator suggests that "[i]t must be concerned with the substance of the treaty and clarify certain concepts in the treaty or limit its field of application" and "[i]t must equally be drawn up on the occasion of the conclusion of the treaty".[86] The WTO panels have applied this test in WTO disputes on numerous occasions such as in *EC – Chicken Cuts* (2005) and *US – Section 110(5) Copyright Act* (2000).[87]

Second, to qualify as "context", such a document has to constitute an "agreement" between the parties or an instrument "accepted by the parties".[88] Therefore, interpretative or explanatory statements made by members of a drafting committee in their personal capacity should not be considered as part of the "context".[89] However, as the panel pointed out in *US – Section 110(5) Copyright Act* (2000), "uncontested interpretations given at a conference,

---

[84] Ibid.

[85] Ian McTaggart Sinclair (1984), *The Vienna Convention on the Law of Treaties*, Manchester University Press, p.129.

[86] Ibid.

[87] See, e.g., Panel Report, *EC – Chicken Cuts (Brazil)*, para. 7.154; Panel Report, *US – Section 110(5) Copyright Act*, para. 6.45.

[88] See, e.g., Appellate Body Report, *US – Gambling*, para. 175 (making it clear that "documents can be characterized as context only where there is sufficient evidence of their constituting an 'agreement relating to the treaty' between the parties or of their 'accept[ance by the parties] as an instrument related to the treaty'").

[89] Panel Report, *US – Section 110(5) Copyright Act*, para. 6.46.

e.g., by a chairman of a drafting committee, may constitute an 'agreement' forming part of the 'context'".[90]

For the purpose of interpreting TRIPS, the panel in *Canada – Pharmaceutical Patents* (2000) made it clear that in addition to the text, Preamble and Annexes to the TRIPS Agreement, the context also includes the provisions of other international IP treaties that were incorporated into the TRIPS Agreement, and any agreement between the parties or any instrument accepted by the parties relating to these agreements within the meaning of Article 31(2) of the VCLT.[91]

5.2.2.4 "Elements to Be Considered Together with the Context"

Article 31(3) of the VCLT "contains the rules relevant to the adaptation of a treaty based on changed circumstances",[92] providing that:

There shall be taken into account, together with the context:

(a) Any subsequent agreement between the parties regarding the interpretation of the treaty or the application of its provisions;

(b) Any subsequent practice in the application of the treaty which establishes the agreement of the parties regarding its interpretation;

(c) Any relevant rules of international law applicable in the relations between the parties.

The use of the term "shall" in the chapeau of Article 31(3) of the VCLT suggests that the elements for interpretation in paragraphs (a), (b) and (c) of Article 31(3) are "an integral part of the general rule of interpretation set forth in Article 31" (UN Doc. A/68/10).[93] Article 31(3) mandates a treaty interpreter to take into account the three interpretative elements, and "it does not merely give a treaty interpreter the option of doing so".[94] This view is supported by the negotiating history of the VCLT. The ILC in its commentary to Article 27(3) of the draft Vienna Convention [currently Article 31(3)] stated that "these three elements are all of obligatory character and by their very nature could not be considered to be norms of interpretation in any way inferior to those which precede them".[95] These three elements are discussed below.

[90] Ibid.   [91] Panel Report, *Canada – Pharmaceutical Patents*, para. 7.14.

[92] Rudiger Wolfrum and Nele Matz (2003), *Conflicts in International Environmental Law*, vol. 164, Heidelberg, Germany: Springer-Verlag Berlin Heidelberg, p. 139.

[93] *Report of the International Law Commission, General Assembly Official Records*, Sixty-Eighth Session, Supplement No. 10, UN Doc. A/68/10, 6 May–7 June and 8 July–9 August 2013, p. 16.

[94] Panel Reports, *EC – Approval and Marketing of Biotech Products*, para. 7.69.

[95] *Report of the International Law Commission on the Work of Its Eighteenth Session*, 4 May–19 July 1966, Official Reports of the General Assembly, Twenty-First Session, Supplement No. 9, UN Doc. A/6309/Rev. 1, United Nations, p. 220.

5.2.2.4.1 SUBSEQUENT AGREEMENT. Article 31(3)(a) of the VCLT mandates treaty interpreters to consider "[a]ny subsequent agreement between the parties regarding the interpretation of the treaty or the application of its provisions" in applying the general rule of interpretation. The text of Article 31(3)(a) of the VCLT suggests that the definition of "subsequent agreement" within the meaning of Article 31(3)(a) contains three elements: firstly, it is an agreement between "the parties"; secondly, the terms and content of the agreement have to relate to either the interpretation or the application of the treaty; and thirdly, in a temporal sense, this agreement is adopted subsequent to the conclusion of the treaty.[96]

As to the first element, ILC (2014) has clarified that the term "agreement" in Article 31(3)(a) of the VCLT neither implies a particular degree of formality nor establishes a requirement as to the form which a "subsequent agreement between the parties" should take.[97] The Appellate Body in *US – Clove Cigarettes* (2012) further made clear that the term "agreement" in Article 31 (3)(a) of the VCLT "refers, fundamentally, to substance rather than to form".[98] The use of the term "agreement" in Article 31(3)(a) is said to suggest that the preconditions for a "subsequent agreement" are less demanding than for a "treaty".[99] As pointed out by Wolfrum and Matz (2003), the subsequent agreement may be "a declaration of the parties or a resolution of the treaty's organs concerning the meaning of unclear provisions" and it "does not have to take the form of an international treaty".[100] The difference between a

---

[96] See, e.g., Marina Foltea (2012), *International Organisations in WTO Dispute Settlement: How Much Institutional Sensitivity?* , Cambridge University Press, p. 106; Ulf Linderfalk (2007), *On the Interpretation of Treaties: The Modern International Law as Expressed in the 1969 Vienna Convention on the Law of Treaties*, Houten: Springer Netherlands, p. 162. Appellate Body Report, *US – Clove Cigarettes*, para. 262.

[97] International Law Commission (2014), *Second Report on Subsequent Agreements and Subsequent Practice in Relation to the Interpretation of Treaties*, UN Doc. A/CN.4/671, p. 26.

[98] Appellate Body Report, *US – Clove Cigarettes*, para. 267.

[99] See, e.g., Georg Nolte (2013), Subsequent Agreements and Subsequent Practice of States Outside of Judicial or Quasi-judicial Proceedings, in Nolte (ed.), *Treaties and Subsequent Practice*, Oxford University Press, pp. 307–86, at p. 309; Marina Foltea (2012), *International Organisations in WTO Dispute Settlement: How Much Institutional Sensitivity?* Cambridge University Press, p. 106 (points out that "there is no requirement for an agreement in a written form, nor that it should conform to the definition of a treaty enshrined in VCLT Article 2, although documentary evidence might be needed").

[100] Rudiger Wolfrum and Nele Matz (2003), *Conflicts in International Environmental Law*, vol. 164, Heidelberg, Germany: Springer-Verlag Berlin Heidelberg, p. 140; see also Steve Charnovitz (2002), The Legal Status of the Doha Declarations, *Journal of International Economic Law*, vol. 5, no. 1, pp. 207–11, at p. 211 (stating that "[w]hile a Ministerial Conference's pronouncement [declaration] is not treaty language or a treaty interpretation, it might be a subsequent agreement between the parties regarding 'the application' of a treaty's

subsequent agreement under Article 31(3)(a) and a subsequent practice which "establishes the agreement" of the parties under Article 31(3)(b) is that, as pointed out by ILC (2014), subsequent agreement presupposes a "single common act".[101] Apart from this minimal degree of formality in the requirement, ILC (2014) considers "any identifiable agreement of the parties" to be sufficient.[102]

Turning to the second element, Article 31(3)(a) of the VCLT provides that a subsequent agreement has to relate to either the interpretation or the application of the treaty. According to ILC (2014), conduct "regarding the interpretation" of the treaty and conduct "in the application" of the treaty both imply that one or more State parties assume, or are attributed to, a position regarding the interpretation of the treaty.[103] For a subsequent agreement regarding the interpretation of a treaty, the position in relation to the interpretation of a treaty is "specifically and purposefully *assumed*", whereas in the case of a subsequent agreement with respect to the application of its provisions, "an assumption of a position regarding interpretation 'by application' is *implied* in simple acts of application of the treaty" (emphasis added).[104] In *EC – Bananas III (Article 21.5 – Ecuador II) / EC – Bananas III (Article 21.5 – US)* (2008), the Appellate Body has clarified that the term "application" relates to "the situation where an agreement specifies how existing rules or obligations in force are to be 'applied'".[105] The ILC describes a subsequent agreement within the meaning of Article 31(3)(a) of the VCLT as an "authentic element of interpretation" to be considered together with the context.[106] Based on the ILC's reference to "authentic interpretation", the Appellate Body considers that the ILC has interpreted Article 31(3)(a) as referring to "agreements bearing specifically upon the interpretation of a treaty".[107]

Finally, in a temporal sense, the agreement must be "subsequent" to "the conclusion of the treaty". As pointed out by Linderfalk (2007), the earliest

provisions, which is recognized by the Vienna Convention on the Law of Treaties, Article 31.3 (a), as a proper consideration in treaty interpretation").

[101] International Law Commission (2014), *Second Report on Subsequent Agreements and Subsequent Practice in Relation to the Interpretation of Treaties*, UN Doc. A/CN.4/671, p. 26.

[102] Ibid.   [103] Ibid., p. 5.   [104] Ibid.

[105] Appellate Body Report, *EC – Bananas III (Article 21.5 – Ecuador II) / EC – Bananas III (Article 21.5 – US)*, para. 391.

[106] *Report of the International Law Commission on the Work of Its Eighteenth Session*, 4 May–19 July 1966, Official Reports of the General Assembly, Twenty-First Session, Supplement No. 9, UN Doc. A/6309/Rev. 1, United Nations, p. 221.

[107] Appellate Body Report, *EC – Bananas III (Article 21.5 – Ecuador II) / EC – Bananas III (Article 21.5 – US)*, para. 390.

existence of a "subsequent" agreement "cannot be traced further back than to the point in time when the interpreted treaty was established as definite".[108]

In the context of the TRIPS Agreement, the Doha Declaration is generally accepted as a "subsequent agreement" within the meaning of Article 31(3)(a) of the VCLT.[109] The factors that support the Declaration's status as a subsequent agreement are explored in Section 5.4.1.

5.2.2.4.2 SUBSEQUENT PRACTICE. Article 31(3)(b) of the VCLT requires a treaty interpreter to take into account "any subsequent practice in the application of the treaty which establishes the agreement of the parties regarding its interpretation". The ILC has confirmed its importance as an authentic element of interpretation by arguing that subsequent practice "constitutes objective evidence of the understanding of the parties as to the meaning of the treaty".[110] Thus, as found by the Appellate Body in *EC – Chicken Cuts* (2005), the interpretation of a treaty provision based on subsequent practice is "binding on all parties to the treaty, including those that have not actually engaged in such practice".[111]

---

[108] Ulf Linderfalk (2007), *On the Interpretation of Treaties: The Modern International Law as Expressed in the 1969 Vienna Convention on the Law of Treaties*, Houten: Springer Netherlands, p. 163.

[109] See, e.g., Susy Frankel (2006), WTO Application of "the Customary Rules of Interpretation of Public International Law" to Intellectual Property, *Virginia Journal of International Law*, vol. 46, pp. 366–431, at p. 400 (stating that "[a]n example of a subsequent agreement occurred at Doha, where the members of the WTO expressly addressed concerns that a strict interpretation of Article 31 of the TRIPS Agreement might make medicines unavailable"); Cynthia M. Ho (2009), Patent Breaking or Balancing?: Separating Strands of Fact from Fiction under TRIPS, *North Carolina Journal of International Law and Commercial Regulation*, vol. 34, pp. 371–469, at pp. 391 and 392 (noting that "scholars who have analysed this issue generally conclude that the Declaration is, in fact, a subsequent agreement. There are a number of factors that support the Declaration's status as a subsequent agreement"); Carlos M. Correa (2002), Implications of the Doha Declaration on the TRIPS Agreement and Public Health, World Health Organization, p. 45 (arguing that "the Declaration can be regarded as a 'subsequent agreement' between the parties regarding the interpretation of a treaty or the application of its provisions, under Article 31.3 (a) of the Vienna Convention on the Law of Treaties"); Nattapong Suwan-in (2012), Compulsory Licensing, a Long Debate on TRIPS Agreement Interpretation: Discovering the Truth of Thailand's Imposition on Pharmaceutical Patents, *Asian Journal of WTO & International Health Law and Policy*, vol. 7, pp. 225–61, at p. 237 (concluding that "the Doha Declaration is ... deserved and logical to be recognized as a subsequent agreement, though Ministerial Declaration requires no signatory like general or common treaty where all parties agreed upon").

[110] *Report of the International Law Commission on the Work of Its Eighteenth Session*, 4 May–19 July 1966, Official Reports of the General Assembly, Twenty-First Session, Supplement No. 9, UN Doc. A/6309/Rev. 1, United Nations, p. 221; this is also confirmed by the Appellate Body in *EC – Chicken Cuts* (2005). See Appellate Body Report, *EC – Chicken Cuts*, para. 255.

[111] Appellate Body Report, *EC – Chicken Cuts*, para. 273.

In *Japan – Alcoholic Beverages* (1996), the panel held that panel reports adopted by the GATT Contracting Parties and WTO Members "constitute subsequent practice in a specific case by virtue of the decision to adopt them".[112] The Appellate Body disagreed and, in overruling the panel's findings on this issue, characterised "subsequent practice" as "a 'concordant, common and consistent' sequence of acts or pronouncements" that is cable of establishing a discernible pattern implying the parties' agreement in relation to the treaty interpretation. The Appellate Body further clarified that "[a]n isolated act is generally not sufficient to establish subsequent practice; it is a sequence of acts establishing the agreement of the parties that is relevant".[113]

The Appellate Body in *US – Gambling* (2005) further made clear that establishing "subsequent practice" within the meaning of Article 31(3)(b) involves two elements: first, "there must be a common, consistent, discernible pattern of acts or pronouncements"; and second, "those acts or pronouncements must imply agreement on the interpretation of the relevant provision".[114]

As to the first element, the Appellate Body in *EC – Chicken Cuts* (2005) clarified that it does not require all parties to have engaged in a particular practice for it to constitute a "common" and "concordant" practice.[115] It is generally accepted that to establish a "subsequent practice", there is no need to show that each party has engaged in a particular practice, only that "all have accepted it, albeit tacitly".[116] Therefore, consistent practice among some Members is sufficient to establish a subsequent practice within the meaning of Article 31(3)(b) of the VCLT.[117] The term "some Members" is understood to mean "more than one or very few parties". The Appellate Body clarified that "it would be difficult to establish a 'concordant, common and discernible pattern' on the basis of acts or pronouncements of one or very few parties to a multilateral treaty, such as the WTO Agreement".[118]

---

[112] Panel Report, *Japan – Alcoholic Beverages II*, para. 6.10.

[113] Appellate Body Report, *Japan – Alcoholic Beverages II*, pp. 11–13.

[114] Appellate Body Report, *US – Gambling*, para. 192.

[115] Appellate Body Report, *EC – Chicken Cuts*, para. 259 (finding that "not each and every party must have engaged in a particular practice for it to qualify as a 'common' and 'concordant' practice").

[116] See, e.g., Anthony Aust (2007), *Modern Treaty Law and Practice*, Cambridge University Press, p. 91; Appellate Body Report, *EC – Chicken Cuts*, para. 272 (stating that "[w]e do not exclude that, in specific situations, the 'lack of reaction' or silence by a particular treaty party may, in the light of attendant circumstances, be understood as acceptance of the practice of other treaty parties").

[117] See also Ping Xiong (2012), *An International Law Perspective on the Protection of Human Rights in the TRIPS Agreement: An Interpretation of the TRIPS Agreement in Relation to the Right to Health*, Leiden, Netherlands: Martinus Nijhoff Publishers, p. 123.

[118] Appellate Body Report, *EC – Chicken Cuts*, para. 259.

Notably, the findings of the Appellate Body suggest that the common understanding of all the parties rather than specific engagement of every party is more essential in establishing a "subsequent practice" of a particular treaty. Such findings are consistent with the negotiating history of Article 31(3)(b) of the VCLT. When Article 31(3)(b) was drafted, the ILC (1966) stated that:

> The text [of Article 31(3)(b) VCLT] provisionally adopted in 1964 spoke of a practice which "establishes the understanding of all the parties". By omitting the word 'all', the Commission did not intend to change the rule. It considered that the phrase "the understanding of the parties" necessarily means "the parties as a whole". It omitted the word "all" merely to avoid any possible misconception that every party must individually have engaged in the practice where it suffices that it should have accepted the practice.[119]

With regard to the second element, the Appellate Body has been very cautious in finding the agreement of the parties regarding the interpretation of a treaty term, in particular when these parties have not engaged in a practice. The Appellate Body in *EC – Chicken Cuts* (2005) clarified that "agreement may be deduced from the affirmative reaction of a treaty party"; however, it should not be lightly inferred from a party's "lack of reaction" without further inquiry into the attendant circumstances of a case.[120] In case of "lack of reaction" or silence, acceptance may be inferred if a particular party has become or been aware of the practice of other parties, including by means of notification or participation in a relevant forum, but fails to react to it. However, "lack of protest" against one Member's practice might not be understood as establishing agreement with that particular practice by other WTO Members.[121]

In the context of the TRIPS Agreement, subsequent acts concerning the TRIPS flexibilities by WTO Members may constitute "subsequent practice" within the meaning of Article 31(3)(b) of the VCLT as long as they are common, consistent and discernible and they imply agreement on the interpretation of the relevant provision. Section 5.4.2 addresses relevant subsequent practice in the interpretation of the TRIPS flexibilities.

5.2.2.4.3 RELEVANT RULES OF INTERNATIONAL LAW. Article 31(3)(c) of the VCLT mandates a treaty interpreter to take into account "[a]ny relevant rules of international law applicable in the relations between the parties", when

---

[119] *Report of the International Law Commission on the Work of Its Eighteenth Session*, 4 May–19 July 1966, Official Reports of the General Assembly, Twenty-First Session, Supplement No. 9, UN Doc. A/6309/Rev. 1, United Nations, p. 222.
[120] Appellate Body Report, *EC – Chicken Cuts*, para. 272.   [121] Ibid.

interpreting treaty obligations. As Marceau (2001) points out, this rule seeks to ensure the treaty at issue and other relevant rules of international law are interpreted in a mutually supportive manner, thereby promoting "coherence" and avoiding conflict in the interpretation of treaty obligations.[122] Similarly, ILC (2006) clarifies that the underlying rationale of Article 31(3)(c) is the principle of "systemic integration", according to which treaties should be interpreted "by reference to their normative environment ('system')" in a manner that integrates "a sense of coherence and meaningfulness" into the process of interpretation.[123]

Support for the legitimacy of the principle of systemic integration can also be found in international jurisprudence. The ICJ in its Advisory Opinion on Namibia (1970) stated that a treaty must be "interpreted and applied within the framework of the entire legal system prevailing at the time of the interpretation".[124] In *Bankovic v. Belgium and others* (2001), the European Court of Human Rights found that a treaty "cannot be interpreted and applied in a vacuum" and should be interpreted "as far as possible in harmony with other principles of international law of which it forms part".[125] In the WTO context, the Appellate Body in *US – Gasoline* (1996), in its first decision, clarified that the WTO Agreements are "not to be read in clinical isolation from public international law".[126] In *US – Shrimp* (1998), the Appellate Body, relying on Article 31(3)(c) of the VCLT, endorsed the importance of "seeking additional interpretative guidance, as appropriate, from the general principles of international law" in interpreting a specific WTO provision.[127]

Article 31(3)(c) of the VCLT contains three elements: first, this provision refers to the "rules of international law"; second, the rules must be "relevant"; and third, such rules must be "applicable in the relations between the

---

[122] Gabrielle Marceau (2001), Conflicts of Norms and Conflicts of Jurisdictions: The Relationship between the WTO Agreement and MEAs and Other Treaties, *Journal of World Trade*, vol. 35, no. 6, pp. 1081–1131, at p. 1089.

[123] Report of the Study Group of the International Law Commission (ILC), *Fragmentation of International Law: Difficulties Arising from the Diversification and Expansion of International Law*, UN Doc. A/CN.4/L.682, 13 April 2006, paras. 413 and 419; this argument finds confirmation in Appellate Body Report, *EC and Certain Member States – Large Civil Aircraft*, WT/DS 316/AB/R, 18 May 2011, para. 845.

[124] Advisory Opinion of the International Court of Justice, *Legal Consequences for States of the Continued Presence of South Africa in Namibia* (South West Africa) Notwithstanding Security Council Resolution 276 (1970), ICJ Report, 21 June 1971, p. 19, para. 53.

[125] European Court of Human Rights Grand Chamber Decision as to the Admissibly of Application No. 52207/99, *Bankovic v. Belgium and Others*, 12 December 2001, ECHR 2001-XII, p. 351, para. 57.

[126] Appellate Body Report, *US – Gasoline*, p. 17.

[127] Appellate Body Report, *US – Shrimp*, para. 158.

parties".[128] Controversies exist regarding the meaning of the "parties" in the third requirement, which is to be addressed in greater detail below.

As to the first requirement, the reference to "rules of international law", in the words of the Appellate Body, "corresponds to the sources of international law in Article 38(1) of the Statute of the International Court of Justice"[129] and thus includes "all generally accepted sources of public international law, that is to say, (i) international conventions (treaties), (ii) international custom (customary international law), and (iii) the recognized general principles of international law".[130]

Turning to the second element, in order for a rule to be "relevant", the Appellate Body in *US – Anti-Dumping and Countervailing Duties (China)* (2011) considered that such a rule "must concern the same subject matter as the treaty terms being interpreted".[131] Some scholars consider that such an interpretation may be overly restrictive to the extent that "a rule could be relevant but [does] not involve the same subject matter".[132] The Appellate Body in its subsequent report clarified that a rule is "relevant" in the sense of Article 31(3)(c) of the VCLT as long as "it concerns the subject matter of the provision at issue".[133] In addition, Marceau (2001) points out that, absent specific guidance, the meaning of "relevant" in Article 31(3)(c) should be determined on a "case-by-case basis, by examining criteria such as the subject of the dispute and the content (i.e. subject-matter) of the rules under consideration".[134]

The third requirement is that the rules in question are "applicable in the relations between the parties". As pointed out by the ILC study group, Article 31(3)(c) of the VCLT does not specify whether the term "parties" refers to all parties to the treaty in question, or merely the parties to

---

[128] Appellate Body Report, *US – Anti-Dumping and Countervailing Duties (China)*, para. 307.
[129] Appellate Body Report, *US – Anti-Dumping and Countervailing Duties (China)*, para. 308; see also United Nations, Statute of the International Court of Justice, 18 April 1946, Article 38; Mark Eugen Villiger (2009), *Commentary on the 1969 Vienna Convention on the Law of Treaties*, Leiden, Netherlands: Martinus Nijhoff Publishers, p. 433.
[130] Panel Reports, *EC – Approval and Marketing of Biotech Products*, para. 7.67.
[131] Appellate Body Report, *US – Anti-Dumping and Countervailing Duties (China)*, para. 308.
[132] See, e.g., Asif H. Qureshi (2012), *Interpreting WTO Agreements: Problems and Perspectives*, 2nd edn, Cambridge University Press, p. 47.
[133] Appellate Body Report, *EC and Certain Member States – Large Civil Aircraft*, para. 846. See also Mark Eugen Villiger (2009), *Commentary on the 1969 Vienna Convention on the Law of Treaties*, Leiden, Netherlands: Martinus Nijhoff Publishers, p. 433.
[134] Gabrielle Marceau (2001), Conflicts of Norms and Conflicts of Jurisdictions: The Relationship between the WTO Agreement and MEAs and Other Treaties, *Journal of World Trade*, vol. 35, no. 6, pp. 1081–131, at p. 1087.

the dispute.[135] In practice, the exact scope of "the parties" in Article 31(3)(c) of the VCLT has been the subject of much debate.

A clear but narrow interpretation adopted by some scholars is that all parties to the treaty being interpreted should be parties to the treaty referred to via Article 31(3)(c) of the VCLT.[136] In this vein, for a non-WTO treaty to be relied upon to interpret WTO obligations under Article 31(3)(c), all WTO Members should be parties to the non-WTO treaty.[137] The WTO panel adopted this approach in *EC – Approval and Marketing of Biotech Products* (2006). On the basis of the definition of the term "party" provided by Article 2.1(g) of the VCLT, that is, "'Party' means 'a State which has consented to be bound by the treaty and for which the treaty is in force'", the panel inferred that the rules under Article 31(3)(c) are rules of international law applicable in relations between the parties "which have consented to be bound by the treaty [that] is being interpreted, and for which that treaty is in force".[138] Following this understanding of the term "the parties", the panel logically concluded that the rules of international law to be taken into account for the interpretation of the WTO Agreements via Article 31(3)(c) of the VCLT are the rules that are "applicable in the relations between the WTO Members".[139]

In the panel's view, requiring consideration of rules of international law that are applicable in the relations between all parties to the interpreted treaty could avoid conflicts between relevant rules and ensure or enhance the consistency of the rules of international law applicable to these States.[140] However, this approach requiring non-WTO treaties relied upon via Article 31(3)(c) to be applicable to all WTO Members could be problematic. In reality, few international treaties, if any, could include all WTO Members as parties because non-State actors such as customs territories could become

---

[135] Report of the Study Group of the International Law Commission (ILC), *Fragmentation of International Law: Difficulties Arising from the Diversification and Expansion of International Law*, UN Doc. A/CN.4/L.682, 13 April 2006, para. 426.

[136] Michael Lennard (2002), Navigating by the Stars: Interpreting the WTO Agreements, *Journal of International Economic Law*, vol. 5, no. 1, pp. 17–89, at p. 36 (considering that "the 'parties' referred to are the parties to the WTO Agreement generally, not the parties to a dispute or some other subset of those whose relationships are being examined"); see also Campbell McLachlan (2005), The Principle of Systemic Integration and Article 31(3)(c) of the Vienna Convention, *International and Comparative Law Quarterly*, vol. 54, no. 2, pp. 279–320, at p. 314.

[137] Gabrielle Marceau (1999), A Call for Coherence in International Law: Praises for the Prohibition against "Clinical Isolation" in WTO Dispute Settlement, *Journal of World Trade*, vol. 33, no. 5, pp. 87–152, at p. 124.

[138] Panel Reports, *EC – Approval and Marketing of Biotech Products*, para. 7.68.   [139] Ibid.

[140] Ibid., para. 7.70.

WTO Members but may not have treaty-making power.[141] Therefore, under this approach, it would become unlikely that non-WTO treaties could be used to interpret WTO obligations via Article 31(3)(c) of the VCLT, resulting in the "isolation" of WTO Agreements as "islands".[142] In this sense, the requirement that relevant rules of international law be "applicable between all WTO Members" would go against the spirit of the principle of systemic integration. In the view of the ILC study group, this would also presumably contradict the intention of most treaty makers.[143] This approach is, thus, not desirable.

Some authors such as Palmeter and Mavroidis (1998) interpret the term "parties" to mean "the parties to the dispute".[144] This method has its limits, because the Vienna Convention is not applied exclusively in case of disputes.[145] In practice, this approach is explicitly rejected by the WTO panel in *EC – Approval and Marketing of Biotech Products* (2006), as it notes that Article 31 of the VCLT does not purport to specify rules of interpretation that are "applicable solely in the context of international (quasi-) judicial proceedings".[146] Moreover, as pointed out by the ILC's study group, this restrictive interpretation may result in divergent interpretations, depending on which States are parties to the dispute.[147]

The Appellate Body in *EC and Certain Member States – Large Civil Aircraft* (2011), however, opted for a third approach that seeks to strike a balance between the aforementioned two approaches. In interpreting

[141] See also Margaret Young (2007), The WTO's Use of Relevant Rules of International Law: An Analysis of the Biotech Case, *The International and Comparative Law Quarterly*, vol. 56, no. 4, pp. 907–30, at p. 916 (arguing that "[t]he Panel's conception that treaties must be applicable to all WTO Members requires parallels in treaty membership that are mostly unrealistic, especially when the treaty under interpretation extends to non-State actors, as does the WTO").

[142] See, e.g., Gabrielle Marceau (2002), WTO Dispute Settlement and Human Rights, *European Journal of International Law*, vol. 13, no. 4, pp. 753–814, at p. 781; Margaret Young (2007), The WTO's Use of Relevant Rules of International Law: An Analysis of the Biotech Case, *The International and Comparative Law Quarterly*, vol. 56, no. 4, pp. 907–30, at p. 916.

[143] Report of the Study Group of the International Law Commission (ILC), *Fragmentation of International Law: Difficulties Arising from the Diversification and Expansion of International Law*, UN Doc. A/CN.4/L.682,13 April 2006, para. 471.

[144] David Palmeter and Petros Mavroidis (1998), The WTO Legal System: Sources of Law, *The American Journal of International Law*, vol. 92, pp. 398–413, at p. 411.

[145] Gabrielle Marceau (1999), A Call for Coherence in International Law: Praises for the Prohibition against "Clinical Isolation" in WTO Dispute Settlement, *Journal of World Trade*, vol. 33, no. 5, pp. 87–152, at p. 125.

[146] Panel Reports, *EC – Approval and Marketing of Biotech Products*, para. 7.68 and footnote 241.

[147] Report of the Study Group of the International Law Commission (ILC), *Fragmentation of International Law: Difficulties Arising from the Diversification and Expansion of International Law*, UN Doc. A/CN.4/L.682,13 April 2006, para. 472.

"the parties" in Article 31(3)(c), the Appellate Body, guided by the purpose of the treaty interpretation that is "to establish the common intention of the parties to the treaty", exercised "caution in drawing from an international agreement to which not all WTO Members are party" while emphasising the importance of the "principle of systemic integration".[148] It accordingly found that:

> In a multilateral context such as the WTO, when recourse is had to a non-WTO rule for the purposes of interpreting provisions of the WTO agreements, a delicate balance must be struck between, on the one hand, taking due account of an individual WTO Member's international obligations and, on the other hand, ensuring a consistent and harmonious approach to the interpretation of WTO law among all WTO Members.[149]

Some scholars share a similar view and suggest that the "parties" in Article 31(3)(c) of the VCLT may refer to a subset of all the parties to the treaty being interpreted, which is more than one or several but may be fewer than all the parties.[150] This approach thus requires the non-WTO treaty to be relied upon via Article 31(3)(c) in interpreting the WTO Agreements be applicable to a large number of WTO Members.

For the interpretation of the terms used in the TRIPS Agreement, rules of international treaties such as MEAs may qualify under Article 31(3)(c) of the VCLT if such rules are applicable to a large number of WTO Members and they are "relevant", that is, they concern the subject matter of the treaty term at issue.

5.2.3 *Supplementary Means of Interpretation under Article 32*

Article 32 of the VCLT, entitled "Supplementary Means of Interpretation", stipulates that:

> Recourse may be had to supplementary means of interpretation, including the preparatory work of the treaty and the circumstances of its conclusion, in

---

[148] Appellate Body Report, *EC and Certain Member States – Large Civil Aircraft*, para. 845.
[149] Ibid.
[150] Gabrielle Marceau (1999), A Call for Coherence in International Law: Praises for the Prohibition against "Clinical Isolation" in WTO Dispute Settlement, *Journal of World Trade*, vol. 33, no. 5, pp. 87–152, at p. 125; Holger Hestermeyer (2007), *Human Rights and the WTO: The Case of Patents and Access to Medicines*, Oxford University Press, p. 221 (stating that "the reference to 'all the parties' in Article 31(2)(a) of the Vienna Convention and to 'one or more parties' in Article 31(2)(b) can only mean that the term 'the parties' used in Article 31(3)(c) implies more than one, but less than all the parties. It therefore demands that the international law rule binds at least a large number of the WTO Members").

order to confirm the meaning resulting from the application of article 31, or to determine the meaning when the interpretation according to article 31:

(a) Leaves the meaning ambiguous or obscure or
(b) Leads to a result which is manifestly absurd or unreasonable.

The use of the term "supplementary" in Article 32 reveals its "subsidiary" status vis-à-vis Article 31.[151] The ILC in its commentary has confirmed its subsidiary nature by arguing that Article 32 "does not provide for alternative or autonomous means of interpretation but only for means to aid an interpretation" governed by the principles contained in Article 31.[152] The panel in *Japan – Alcoholic Beverages* (1996) noted that a supplementary means of interpretation does not have the same "authentic character" as an element of interpretation in Article 31 of the VCLT, no matter how valuable it may sometimes be in aiding the interpretation of the treaty text.[153]

Article 32 of the VCLT provides for circumstances under which supplementary means of interpretation may be utilised. The Appellate Body has on numerous occasions confirmed that it is logical to resort to the supplementary means of interpretation specified in Article 32, if the interpretation under Article 31 has left the meaning of the term "ambiguous or obscure", or has led to a "manifestly absurd or unreasonable" result.[154] Furthermore, the ILC felt that it would be "unrealistic and inappropriate" to lay down the rule that no recourse whatsoever may be had to any "extrinsic means of interpretation" until after the application of the rules contained in Article 31 had disclosed no clear or reasonable meaning.[155] In practice, international courts and tribunals, including the WTO panels and the Appellate Body, have frequently had recourse to supplementary means of interpretation such as *travaux préparatoires* for the purpose of "confirming" the interpretation arrived at under Article 31.[156]

---

[151] J. Romesh Weeramantry (2012), *Treaty Interpretation in Investment Arbitration*, Oxford University Press, p. 99.

[152] *Report of the International Law Commission on the Work of Its Eighteenth Session*, 4 May–19 July 1966, Official Reports of the General Assembly, Twenty-First Session, Supplement No. 9, UN Doc. A/6309/Rev. 1, United Nations, p. 223.

[153] Panel Report, *Japan – Alcoholic Beverages II*, para. 6.16 and footnote 87.

[154] See, e.g., Appellate Body Report, *EC – Computer Equipment*, para. 86; Appellate Body Report, *EC – Chicken Cuts*, para. 282.

[155] *Report of the International Law Commission on the Work of Its Eighteenth Session*, 4 May–19 July 1966, Official Reports of the General Assembly, Twenty-First Session, Supplement No. 9, UN Doc. A/6309/Rev. 1, United Nations, p. 223.

[156] See, e.g., Panel Report, *China – Publications and Audiovisual Products*, para. 7.1221 (considering that "recourse to such supplementary means is useful to confirm the Panel's preliminary conclusion"); Appellate Body Report, *Canada – Periodicals*, p. 34 (stating that "the object and purpose of Artic III:8(b) is confirmed by the drafting history of Article III").

Nevertheless, the inclusion of the word "may" in Article 32 of the VCLT indicates that the use of supplementary means for interpretation is not mandatory. Accordingly, in a number of cases, the Appellate Body has considered it unnecessary to have recourse to supplementary means of interpretation.[157]

With regard to the preparatory work of the treaty, as the ILC explained, the VCLT did not define the term so as to avoid "the possible exclusion of relevant evidence".[158] The term "preparatory work" or *travaux préparatories*, commonly also referred to as the "negotiating history", has been given a very broad meaning.[159] For example, Van Damme (2009) considers that preparatory work "encompasses all materials relating to the treaty negotiations prior to the conclusion of the treaty [including] unpublished but accessible materials".[160]

There is no officially recorded negotiating history, however, indicating the intention of the WTO Members regarding the final form of the WTO Agreements.[161] Thus, both dispute settlement panels and the Appellate Body have attributed little importance to the "preparatory work of the treaty" in the process of their interpretation of the WTO Agreements. In particular, they have exercised caution with respect to "various country-specific and often conflicting negotiating proposals" and given limited weight to "the often contradictory and self-serving personal recollections of negotiations".[162] In

---

[157] See, e.g., Appellate Body Report, *US – Carbon Steel*, para. 89 (stating that "we do not consider it strictly necessary to have recourse to the supplementary means of interpretation identified in Article 32 of the Vienna Convention"); Panel Report, *US – Corrosion Resistant Steel Sunset Review*, para. 7.84 (arguing that "[t]his provision [Article 32] of the Vienna Convention limits recourse to the negotiating history of a treaty to two instances: (i) to confirm the meaning of the treaty's provisions or in cases where either a meaning cannot be derived from the treaty or (ii) where the interpretation would lead to absurd results. Neither is the case here. Therefore, there is no need to have recourse to the negotiating history of the Anti-Dumping Agreement").

[158] *Report of the International Law Commission on the Work of Its Eighteenth Session*, 4 May–19 July 1966, Official Reports of the General Assembly, Twenty-First Session, Supplement No. 9, UN Doc. A/6309/Rev. 1, United Nations, p. 223.

[159] See e.g., Arnold Duncan McNair (1961), *The Law of Treaties*, Oxford: Clarendon Press, p. 411 (describing preparatory work as "an omnibus expression which is used rather loosely to indicate all documents, such as memoranda, minutes of conferences, and drafts of the treaty under negotiations").

[160] Isabelle Van Damme (2009), *Treaty Interpretation by the WTO Appellate Body*, Oxford University Press, p. 309.

[161] Peter Van den Bossche and Werner Zdouc (2013), *The Law and Policy of the World Trade Organization*, 3rd edn, Cambridge University Press, p. 193 (further noting that "[i]n *India – Quantitative Restrictions* (1999), for example, the Appellate Body explicitly noted 'the absence of a record of the negotiations' on the 1994 WTO understanding at issue in that case"). See also, Appellate Body Report, *India – Quantitative Restrictions*, para. 94.

[162] Peter Van den Bossche and Werner Zdouc (2013), *The Law and Policy of the World Trade Organization*, 3rd edn, Cambridge University Press, p. 193; for example, in *US – Line Pipe*, the

US – Carbon Steel (2002), the Appellate Body considered that selective reliance on the preparatory work prepared by certain negotiating groups in interpreting a relevant treaty could lead to an unreliable conclusion.[163] Accordingly, the preparatory work could play a role in the treaty interpretation only if it shows the common intentions of all rather than one or more negotiating parties as to the meaning of a given treaty term.[164]

Turning to the "circumstances of the conclusion" of a treaty, the Appellate Body and panels consider that the reference to this term in Article 32 "permits, in appropriate cases, the examination of the historical background against which the treaty was negotiated".[165] The "circumstance of conclusion" under Article 32 of the VCLT is described as "[t]he historical background that comprises the collection of events which led the parties to conclude the treaties".[166] The Appellate Body in *EC – Chicken Cuts* (2005) clarified that "not only 'multilateral' sources, but also 'unilateral' acts, instruments, or statements of individual negotiating parties may be useful in ascertaining 'the reality of the situation which the parties wished to regulate by means of the treaty' and, ultimately, for discerning the common intentions of the parties".[167] It further pointed out that "'relevance', as opposed to 'direct

---

Appellate Body concluded that the negotiating history of Article XIX of the GATT 1947 and of the Agreement on Safeguards "does not provide guidance as to whether the Members intended to establish a requirement of a discrete determination of serious injury or of the threat of serious injury". See Appellate Body Report, *US – Line Pipe*, para. 175.

[163] Appellate Body Report, *US – Carbon Steel*, para. 78.

[164] Beas Edson Rodrigues (2012), *The General Exception Clauses of the TRIPS Agreement: Promoting Sustainable Development*, vol. 17, Cambridge University Press, p. 88.

[165] See, e.g., Appellate Body Report, *EC – Computer Equipment*, para. 86; Panel Report, *EC – Chicken Cuts (Brazil)*, para. 7.340 (noting that "for the purpose of Article 32 of the Vienna Convention, the 'circumstances of conclusion' may provide insights into the historical background against which EC Schedule was negotiated"). Such finding is partially based on the view of Sinclair (1984) that "the reference in Article 32 [of the Convention] to the circumstances of the conclusion of a treaty may have some value in emphasising the need for the interpreter to bear constantly in mind the historical background against which the treaty has been negotiated" (see Ian McTaggart Sinclair (1984), *The Vienna Convention on the Law of Treaties*, Manchester University Press, p. 141).

[166] Mustafa Kamil Yasseen (1976), *L'interprétation des Traités d'après la Convention de Vienne sur le Droit des Traités*, Leiden, Netherlands: Martinus Nijhoff Publishers, p. 90, para. 3 (stating that "Il s'agit du cadre historique que forme l'ensemble des événements qui ont porté les parties à conclure le traité pour maintenir ou confirmer le statu quo ou apporter un changement qu'une nouvelle conjoncture nécessite"); See also Panel Report, *EC – Chicken Cuts (Brazil)*, para. 7.340.

[167] Appellate Body Report, *EC – Chicken Cuts*, para. 289; see also Ian McTaggart Sinclair (1984), *The Vienna Convention on the Law of Treaties*, Manchester University Press, p. 141 (adding that it may also be necessary to take into account "the individual attitude of the parties – their economic, political and social conditions, their adherence to certain groupings or their status,

influence' [on the common intentions] or 'genuine link' [to the treaty text], is the 'more appropriate criterion' to judge the extent to which a particular event, act, or other instrument should be relied upon or taken into account when interpreting a treaty provision in the light of the 'circumstances of its conclusion'".[168]

In practice, the Appellate Body in *EC – Computer Equipment* (1998) has explicitly recognised that the WTO Members' classification practices during the Uruguay Round negotiations and legislation on customs classification at that time were part of "the circumstances of the conclusion" of the WTO Agreement and "may be used as a supplementary means of interpretation" within the meaning of Article 32 of the Vienna Convention.[169] In *EC – Poultry* (1998), the Appellate Body considered a bilateral agreement negotiated under Article XXVIII of the GATT 1947 (i.e. the *Oilseeds Agreement*) as a supplementary means of interpretation under Article 32 of the VCLT because it forms part of the historical background in interpreting relevant WTO obligations.[170]

As far as the TRIPS Agreement is concerned, not only the negotiating history and the historical background of the TRIPS Agreement but also those of the treaties incorporated into the TRIPS Agreement (such as the Paris Convention and the Berne Convention) may be taken into account.[171] The WTO panel in *Canada – Pharmaceutical Patents* (2000) pointed out that an analysis of the negotiating history of the TRIPS Agreement also needs to "inquire into that of the incorporated international instruments on intellectual property".[172]

In addition, Article 32 of the VCLT refers explicitly to the preparatory work of the treaty and the circumstances of its conclusion as supplementary means

---

for example, as importing or exporting country in the particular case of a commodity agreement – in seeking to determine the reality of the situation which the parties wished to regulate by means of the treaty").

[168] Appellate Body Report, *EC – Chicken Cuts*, para. 290.
[169] Appellate Body Report, *EC – Computer Equipment* , paras. 92 and 94.
[170] Appellate Body Report, *EC – Poultry*, paras. 79 and 83.
[171] See, e.g., Carlos M. Correa (2005), The TRIPS Agreement and Developing Countries, in Macrory et al. (eds.), *The World Trade Organization: Legal, Economic and Political Analysis*, New York: Springer, pp. 420–55, at p. 430 (stating that "[o]ne interesting feature is that the negotiating history may include not only the negotiating history of the TRIPS Agreement as such but also the history of the Conventions that are specifically referred to by the TRIPS Agreement, such as the Paris Convention and the Berne Convention"); Nuno Pires De Carvalho (2011), *The TRIPS Regime of Trademarks and Designs*, Alphen aan den Rijn, Netherlands: Kluwer Law International, p. 123 (stating that "it should be noted that the history of negotiations of the treaties incorporated into the TRIPS Agreement may also be taken into account for the purpose of interpreting the TRIPS Agreement itself").
[172] Panel Report, *Canada – Pharmaceutical Patents*, para. 7.15.

of treaty interpretation by using the term "including", suggesting that these two elements are "meant to be examples", rather than an exclusive list.[173] Notably, the Appellate Body in *EC – Chicken Cuts* (2005) clarified that the list of supplementary means is not exhaustive and considered that a treaty interpreter has the discretion to take into account other relevant supplementary means for the purpose of "ascertaining the common intentions of the parties".[174]

The Arbitral Tribunal in *The Canadian Cattlemen for Fair Trade* v. *United States of America* found that:

> Article 32 VCLT permits, as supplementary means of interpretation, not only preparatory work and circumstances of conclusion of the treaty, but indicates by the word "including" that, beyond these two means expressly mentioned, other supplementary means may be applied. Article 38 [paragraph 1.d.] of the Statute of the International Court of Justice provides that judicial decisions are applicable for the interpretation of public international law as "supplementary means". Therefore, they must be understood to be also supplementary means of interpretation in the sense of Article 32 VCLT.[175]

Some critics believe that this statement distorted Article 32 because it leaped from the "supplementary means" in Article 32 of the VCLT to the term "subsidiary means" in Article 38(1)(d) of the ICJ Statute, and introduced "judicial decisions and awards" in the treaty interpretation.[176]

Turning to the text of Article 38(1) of the Statute, it states that "the Court, whose function is to decide in accordance with international law such disputes as are submitted to it, shall apply: … d. subject to the provisions of Article 59, judicial decisions and the teachings of the most highly qualified publicists of the various nations, as subsidiary means for the determination of rules of law". The dictionary meaning of the term "determine" is "to conclude or ascertain, as after reasoning, observation".[177] According to Borda (2013), "determination" in Article 38(1)(d) refers to the process of verification of the

---

[173] Oliver Dörr and Kirsten Schmalenbach (2012), *Vienna Convention on the Law of Treaties: A Commentary*, Springer-Verlag Berlin Heidelberg, p. 574.

[174] Appellate Body Report, *EC – Chicken Cuts*, para. 283.

[175] *The Canadian Cattlemen for Fair Trade* v. *United States of America*, Award on Jurisdiction, 28 January 2008, para. 50.

[176] Michael W. Reisman (2009), Opinion with Respect to Selected International Legal Problems in LCIA Case No. 7941, *United States of America* v. *Canada*, London Court of International Arbitration (LCIA), LCIA Case No. 81010, para. 15.

[177] Determine. Dictionary.com. Dictionary.com Unabridged. Random House, http://dictionary .reference.com/browse/determine

existence and state as well as the proper interpretation of rules of law.[178] Some commentators note that judicial decisions and the teachings of publicists could "provide the best possible evidence regarding the content and scope of legal rules".[179] Thus, both the judicial decisions and the teachings of publicists have an interpretative value in the determination of rules of law.

Accordingly, in interpreting the TRIPS Agreement, relevant judicial decisions, in particular, the rulings of the WTO panels and the Appellate Body, as well as the teachings of publicists such as the 2014 Max Planck Declaration on Patents Protection, which was drafted in collaboration with forty well-known international patent scholars from twenty-five countries and under the auspices of the Max Planck Institute for Innovation and Competition, may be used as subsidiary means to determine the meaning and scope of the TRIPS rules.[180]

5.3 THE OBJECT AND PURPOSE OF WTO AND TRIPS

The interpretive rule set out in Article 31 of the VCLT requires the terms of an international treaty, including the TRIPS Agreement, to be interpreted in light of the object and purpose of the treaty. The Declaration on the TRIPS Agreement and Public Health (WT/MIN(01)/DEC/2) (hereafter referred to as Doha Declaration) reaffirms this rule by stating that "in applying the customary rules of interpretation of public international law, each provision of the TRIPS Agreement shall be read in the light of the object and purpose of the Agreement as expressed, in particular, in its objectives and principles".[181]

In the context of the WTO, the Marrakesh Agreement is a constitutional-like agreement governing the entire WTO system.[182] Article XVI:3 of the Marrakesh Agreement establishes a legal priority of the Marrakesh Agreement

---

[178] Aldo Zammit Borda (2013), A Formal Approach to Article 38(1)(d) of the ICJ Statute from the Perspective of the International Criminal Courts and Tribunals, *The European Journal of International Law*, vol. 24, no. 2, pp. 649–61, at p. 650.

[179] See, e.g., Georg Schwarzenberger (1965), *The Inductive Approach to International Law*, Stevens & Sons, Oceana Publications, p. 21; Todd Weiler (2013), *The Interpretation of International Investment Law: Equality, Discrimination and Minimum Standards of Treatment in Historical Context*, Leiden, Netherlands: Koninklijke Brill NV, p. 53.

[180] Max Planck Institute for Innovation and Competition (2014), Declaration on Patent Protection: Regulatory Sovereignty under TRIPS, available at www.ip.mpg.de/files/pdf2/Patent_Declaration1.pdf

[181] Declaration on the TRIPS Agreement and Public Health, WT/MIN (01)/DEC/2, Adopted on 14 November 2001, para. 5(a).

[182] See, e.g., Robert L. Howse and Mutua Makau (2001), Protecting Human Rights in a Global Economy Challenges for the World Trade Organization, in Hugo Stokke and Anne Tostensen (eds.), *Human Rights in Development Yearbook 1999/2000*, Alphen aan den Rijn, Netherlands:

over the TRIPS Agreement.[183] As Petersmann (2000) argued, the Marrakesh Agreement enjoys "legal supremacy" over the WTO covered agreements listed in its annexes.[184] Thus, the object and purpose of the Marrakesh Agreement must "stand at the apex of the configuration of objects and purposes set in the WTO Agreements".[185] In *US – Shrimp* (1998), the Appellate Body recognised that the objectives included in the preamble to the Marrakesh Agreement, in particular, the sustainable development objective, inform all the covered agreements.[186] Accordingly, the TRIPS Agreement shall also respect and promote the object and purpose of the Marrakesh Agreement and not run counter to it.

The following sections will first examine the objective of the Marrakesh Agreement and then study the object and purpose of the TRIPS Agreement.

5.3.1 *The Sustainable Development Objective of the WTO*

It is generally understood that the preamble to an international treaty typically "set[s] out the motives for the conclusion of the treaty" and thus helps identify its object and purpose.[187] The Preamble to the Marrakesh Agreement makes

Kluwer Law International, pp. 51–82, at p. 64 (stating that "[t]he Marrakesh Agreement is the framework agreement for the entire WTO system"); Yan Luo (2010), *Anti-Dumping in the WTO, the EU and China: The Rise of Legalization in the Trade Regime and Its Consequences*, vol. 69, Alphen aan den Rijn, Netherlands: Kluwer Law International, p. 38 (stating that "[t]he new WTO treaty system integrated the fruits of all previous multilateral negotiation rounds – about sixty agreements, understandings and decisions – into a comprehensive treaty network, supported by a constitutional-like agreement: the Marrakesh Agreement Establishing the WTO").

[183] Marrakesh Agreement Establishing the World Trade Organization, 15 April 1994, The Legal Texts: The Results of the Uruguay Round of the Multilateral Trade Negotiations 4 (1999), 1867 U.N.T.S.154, 33 I.L.M. 1144 (1994) [hereafter Marrakesh Agreement], Article XVI: 3 provides that "[i]n the event of a conflict between a provision of this Agreement and a provision of any of the Multilateral Trade Agreements, the provision of this Agreement shall prevail to the extent of the conflict".

[184] Ernst-Ulrich Petersmann (2000), The WTO Constitution and Human Rights, *Journal of International Economic Law*, vol. 3, no. 1, pp. 19–25, at p. 20 (noting that "WTO law already serves 'constitutional functions' ... The WTO Agreement asserts legal supremacy over the more than 20 worldwide trade agreements list in the WTO Annexes. It also provides a legal framework for the periodic negotiation of new WTO Agreements").

[185] Asif H. Qureshi (2012), *Interpreting WTO Agreements: Problems and Perspectives*, Cambridge University Press, p. 19.

[186] Appellate Body Report, *US – Shrimp*, para. 129 (stating that "The preamble of the WTO Agreement – which informs not only the GATT 1994, but also the other covered agreements – explicitly acknowledges 'the objective of sustainable development'").

[187] See, e.g., Roger O'Keefe and Christian J. Tams (2013), *The United Nations Convention on Jurisdictional Immunities of States and Their Property: A Commentary*, Oxford University Press,

explicit reference to the objective of sustainable development. As pointed out by some leading international trade law practitioners, this suggests that the WTO is not only about trade liberalisation as it also shows regard for "the sustainability of economic development, environmental degradation and global poverty".[188]

This section will first address sustainable development as an objective of the WTO and then analyse its role in interpreting the WTO Agreements, in particular the TRIPS Agreement.

5.3.1.1 Sustainable Development as an Objective of the WTO

The objectives of the WTO are enshrined in the Preamble to the Marrakesh Agreement. According to the Preamble, the Parties to the WTO Agreement explicitly recognise that:

> their relations in the field of trade and economic endeavour should be conducted with a view to raising standards of living, ensuring full employment and a large and steadily growing volume of real income and effective demand, and expanding the production of and trade in goods and services, while allowing for the optimal use of the world's resources in accordance with the objective of sustainable development, seeking both to protect and preserve the environment and to enhance the means for doing so in a manner consistent with their respective needs and concerns at different levels of economic development.[189]

In recognition of "the importance of continuity with the previous GATT [The General Agreement on Tariffs and Trade] system", the preamble to the Marrakesh Agreement largely reiterated the objectives of GATT, including: (1) the increase of standards of living; (2) the attainment of full employment; (3) the steady growth of real income and effective demand and (4) the expansion of the production of and trade in goods and services.[190]

---

p. 28; Michael Blakeney (2012), *Intellectual Property Enforcement: A Commentary on the Anti-Counterfeiting Trade Agreement (ACTA)*, Cheltenham, UK: Edward Elgar Publishing, p. 81.

[188] Peter Van den Bossche and Werner Zdouc (2013), *The Law and Policy of the World Trade Organization*, 3rd edn, Cambridge University Press, p. 83.

[189] Marrakesh Agreement, para. 1 of the Preamble.

[190] General Agreement on Tariffs and Trade 1994, 15 April 1994, Marrakesh Agreement Establishing the World Trade Organization, Annex 1A, The Legal Texts: The Results of the Uruguay Round of Multilateral Trade Negotiations 17 (1999), 1867, U.N.T.S. 187, 33 I.L.M.1153 (1994) [hereafter GATT 1994], the Preamble; Appellate Body Report, *US – Shrimp*, para. 152 (noting that "in recognition of the importance of continuity with the previous GATT system, negotiators used the preamble of the GATT 1947 as the template for the preamble of the new WTO Agreement").

However, the Preamble to the New WTO Agreement qualifies the original objectives of the GATT 1947 with the objective of sustainable development. In *US – Shrimp* (1998), the Appellate Body pointed out that WTO negotiators evidently believed that "the objective of 'full use of the resources of the world' set forth in the preamble of the GATT 1947 was no longer appropriate to the world trading system of the 1990's" and thus called for the optimal use of the world's resources in line with the sustainable development objective.[191]

In order to confirm the changes of the goals of the multilateral trading system, ministers, relying on the preamble to the Marrakesh Agreement, pronounced a separate 1994 Decision on Trade and Environment.[192] They acknowledged the outcomes of the 1992 Rio Conference including the Rio Declaration as well as Agenda 21, and expressed the view that "there should not be, nor need be, any policy contradiction between upholding and safe-guarding an open, non-discriminatory and equitable multilateral trading system on the one hand, and acting for the protection of the environment, and the promotion of sustainable development on the other".[193] Under this decision, the WTO Committee on Trade and Environment was established with a mandate, inter alia, of identifying the relationship between trade and the environment to promote sustainable development.[194]

The inclusion of the sustainable development objective into the preamble to the Marrakesh Agreement "widens the scope of interpretative policy space to balance economic and public interests".[195] Based on the preambular statements of the objectives of the WTO, the Appellate Body in *China – Raw Materials* (2012) considered that "the WTO Agreement, as a whole, reflects the balance struck by WTO Members between trade and non-trade-related concerns".[196]

Turning to the legal status of sustainable development, there is much debate in the context of public international law in general. Some scholars argue that sustainable development is a vague concept with no

---

[191] Appellate Body Report, *US – Shrimp*, para. 152 and 153.
[192] Marrakesh Ministerial Decision on Trade and Environment, Decision of 14 April 1994, MTN.TNC/45 (MIN), 6 May 1994, p. 16.
[193] Ibid.
[194] Ibid.; see also World Trade Organization, "The Committee on Trade and Environment ('regular' CTE)", available at www.wto.org/english/tratop_e/envir_e/wrk_committee_e.htm
[195] Henning Grosse Ruse-Khan (2011), Assessing the Need for a General Public Interest Exception in the TRIPS Agreement, in Kur and Levin (eds.), *Intellectual Property Rights in a Fair World Trade System: Proposal for Reforms of TRIPS*, Cheltenham, UK: Edward Elgar Publishing, pp. 167–207, at p. 201.
[196] Appellate Body Reports, *China – Raw Materials*, para. 306.

normative status.[197] Cassese (2001) characterised "sustainable development as a 'general guideline' laid down in 'soft law' documents".[198] In contrast, some others are of the view that sustainable development is "more than a mere concept, but as a principle with normative value".[199] According to Judge Weeramantry, the 'normative value' of sustainable development derives from "its wide and general acceptance", as evidenced by the recognition of it in multilateral treaties, international declarations or state practice.[200]

In the WTO context, sustainable development is an already established overarching objective as enshrined in the Preamble to the Marrakesh Agreement. In the 2001 Doha Ministerial Declaration, WTO Members strongly reaffirmed their "commitment to the objective of sustainable development, as stated in the Preamble to the Marrakesh Agreement".[201] The WTO Secretariat describes the concept of sustainable development as

---

[197] See, e.g., Vaughan Lowe (1999), Sustainable Development and Unsustainable Arguments, in Alan Boyle and David Freestone (eds.), *International Law and Sustainable Development: Past Achievements and Future Challenges*, Oxford University Press, pp. 19–38, at p. 24 (expressly arguing that "[t]here is, in the catalogue of treaty provisions, declarations, and so on that use the term 'sustainable development', a lack of clear evidence that the authors regarded the concept as having the force of a rule or principle of customary international law"); Alhaji B. M. Marong (2003), From Rio to Johannesburg: Reflections on the Role of International Legal Norms in Sustainable Development, *The Georgetown International Environmental Law Review*, vol. 16, pp. 21–76, at p. 76 (arguing that "while sustainable development is a legally significant notion, the concept is not yet a binding norm of international law").

[198] Antonio Cassese (2001), *International Law*, Oxford University Press, p. 384; see also Ian Brownlie (2008), *Principles of Public International Law*, Oxford University Press, p. 278.

[199] See, e.g., Separate Opinion of Vice-President Weeramantry, *Gabčíkovo-Nagymaros Project (Hungary/Slovakia)*, Judgment of 25 September 1997, ICJ Reports 1997, p. 85; David Luff (1996), An Overview of International Law of Sustainable Development and a Confrontation between WTO Rules and Sustainable Development, *Revue Belge de Droit International*, vol. 29, no.1, pp. 91–144, at p. 94 (arguing that "[a]s a legal institution, sustainable development is obviously a source of obligations for both developed and developing countries").

[200] Separate Opinion of Vice-President Weeramantry, *Gabčíkovo-Nagymaros Project (Hungary/Slovakia)*, Judgment of 25 September 1997, ICJ Reports 1997, p. 90 (citing the following examples: the United Nations Convention to Combat Desertification, 1994, Preamble, Article 9(1); the United Nations Framework Convention on Climate Change, 1992, Articles 2 and 3; the Convention on Biological Diversity, 1992, Preamble, Articles 1 and 10; the Rio Declaration on Environment and Development, 1992; the Copenhagen Declaration, 1995; … and in 1990, the Dublin Declaration by the European Council on the Environmental Imperative stated that there must be an acceleration of effort to ensure that economic development in the Community is "sustainable and environmentally sound" (Bulletin of the European Communities, 6, 1990, Ann. II, p. 18); at p. 92, further arguing that (sustainable development is "a part of modern international law by reason not only of its inescapable logical necessity, but also by reason of its wide and general acceptance by the global community").

[201] Doha Ministerial Declaration, WT/MIN (01)/DEC/1, Adopted on 14 November 2001, para. 6.

"a central principle",[202] and noted that sustainable development is "an object-ive running through all subjects in current Doha negotiations".[203] The former WTO Director General Pascal Lamy (2007) pointed out that "sustainable development was placed right at the heart of its founding charter" and recommended that sustainable development should be "the cornerstone of our approach to globalization and to the global governance architecture that we create".[204] Accordingly, sustainable development is viewed as a central element of international trade law and the WTO.[205]

5.3.1.2 The Role of Sustainable Development in Interpreting TRIPS

The inclusion of the sustainable development objective into the WTO Agree-ment should be reflected in the interpretation and application of its rules. The Appellate Body in *US – Shrimp* (1998) noted that the objective of sustainable development "reflects the intentions of the negotiators of the WTO Agreements" and accordingly concluded that the objective of sustainable development "must add colour, texture and shading to [the] interpretation of the agreements annexed to the WTO Agreement", including the TRIPS Agreement.[206] As Voigt (2009) commented, sustainable development should inform all decisions and developments within the world trading system.[207] In this sense, treaty interpreters should give effect to the objective of sustainable development as required by the principle of effectiveness, when reading the WTO Agreements, including the TRIPS Agreement.

---

[202] World Trade Organization, "Sustainable Development", available at www.wto.org/english/ tratop_e/envir_e/sust_dev_e.htm. It is noted that the views of the WTO Secretariat do not necessarily represent the views of its Member States, even though WTO is a Member-driven organization.

[203] World Trade Organization, "Sustainable Development", available at www.wto.org/english/ tratop_e/envir_e/sust_dev_e.htm

[204] Lamy Pascal (2007), "Globalization and the Environment in a Reformed UN: Charting a Sustainable Development Path", Speech at the Twenty-Fourth Session of the Governing Council/Global Ministerial Environmental Forum, Nairobi, 5 February 2007, available at www.wto.org/english/news_e/sppl_e/sppl54_e.htm

[205] See, e.g., Christina Voigt (2009), *Sustainable Development as a Principle of International Law: Resolving Conflicts between Climate Measures and WTO Law*, Leiden, Netherlands: Martinus Nijhoff Publishers, p. 126; Gary P. Sampson (2005), *The WTO and Sustainable Development*, United Nation University, p. 2 (stating that "[t]he WTO has unquestionably gravitated towards become a Word Trade and Sustainable Development Organisation").

[206] Appellate Body Report, *US – Shrimp*, para. 153.

[207] Christina Voigt (2009), *Sustainable Development as a Principle of International Law: Resolving Conflicts between Climate Measures and WTO Law*, Leiden, Netherlands: Martinus Nijhoff Publishers, p. 127.

The WTO Agreement, however, does not define the concept of sustainable development. The panel in *US – Shrimp (Article 21.5 – Malaysia)* (2001) referred to the well-accepted definition provided by the World Commission on Environment and Development's (WCED) 1987 Brundtland Report,[208] also known as 'Our Common Future', that is:

> Sustainable development is development that meets the needs of the present without compromising the ability of future generations to meet their own needs.[209]

The Brundtland Report also laid out the concept of sustainable development as containing economic growth, social development and environmental protection. Thus, giving effect to the WTO's sustainable development objective means that its core principle of integration and reconciliation of economic, social and environmental interests should guide the interpretation of WTO Agreements, including the TRIPS Agreement.[210] This can be ascertained from the relevant international legal instruments and international jurisprudence.

Above all, various documents such as the Rio Declaration (1992) and the Johannesburg Declaration (2002), the New Delhi Declaration of Principles of International Law Relating to Sustainable Development and the Rio+20 outcome documents show that the principle of integration and reconciliation lies at the core of the principle of sustainable development. The 1992 Rio Declaration confirms that the integration of economic and social development and environmental protection is an indispensable requirement for sustainable development.[211] In the Johannesburg Declaration on Sustainable

---

[208] Panel Report, *US – Shrimp (Article 21.5 – Malaysia)*, para. 5.54.
[209] *Report of the World Commission on Environment and Development: Our Common Future*, Annex to UN document A/42/427-Development and International Co-operation: Environment, 1987, p. 54.
[210] See, e.g., Henning Grosse Ruse-Khan (2010), Sustainable Development in International Intellectual Property Law – New Approaches from EU Economic Partnership Agreements? ICTSD's Programme on IPRs and Sustainable Development, Issue Paper No. 29, ICTSD, Geneva, p. viii (arguing that "giving effect to sustainable development as a treaty objective means that its core principle of integration guides the interpretation of individual treaty provisions"); Virginie Barral (2012), Sustainable Development in International Law: Nature and Operation of an Evolutive Legal Norm, *The European Journal of International Law*, vol. 23, no. 2, pp. 377–400, at p. 381 (describing reconciliation of environmental protection and economic and social development, through their integration "as the core philosophy underlying the concept [of sustainable development]").
[211] The Rio Declaration on Environment and Development, UN Doc. A/CONF.151/26, Vol. I, 12 August 1992, available at www.un.org/documents/ga/conf151/aconf15126-1annex1.htm; relevant principles including: Principle 4 stating that "[i]n order to achieve sustainable development, environmental protection shall constitute an integral part of the development process and cannot be considered in isolation from it"; Principle 5 stating that "[a]ll States and

Development, adopted in 2002 at the World Summit on Sustainable Development, States assumed "a collective responsibility to advance and strengthen the interdependent and mutually reinforcing pillars of sustainable development – economic development, social development and environmental protection – at the local, national, regional and global levels."[212] The 2002 New Delhi Declaration of Principles of International Law Relating to Sustainable Development calls for the implementation of the "principle of integration and interrelationship, in particular in relation to human rights and social, economic and environmental objectives" at all levels of governance and describes the principle of integration as "essential to the achievement of sustainable development".[213] The Rio+20 outcome document, "The Further We Want" (UN Document A/66/L.56), adopted by the world's heads of states and governments in 2012, reaffirmed "the need to further mainstream sustainable development at all levels, integrating economic, social and environmental aspects and recognizing their interlinkages, so as to achieve sustainable development in all its dimensions".[214] All these legal instruments have confirmed that the principle of integration of economic, social development and environmental protection is a central element of sustainable development.

Moreover, international jurisprudence has witnessed the invocation of sustainable development to justify the principle of the integration and reconciliation of economic and social development and environmental protection. Sustainable development has performed such a legal function to reconcile competing interests in the *Gabčíkovo-Nagymaros Project* case decided by the ICJ,[215] in the arbitration regarding the *Iron Rhine*,[216] and in the *US – Shrimp* dispute in the WTO.[217]

---

all people shall cooperate in the essential task of eradicating poverty as an indispensable requirement for sustainable development, in order to decrease the disparities in standards of living and better meet the needs of the majority of the people of the world"; and Principle 25 stating that "[p]eace, development and environmental protection are interdependent and indivisible".

[212] Johannesburg Declaration on Sustainable Development, UN Doc. A/CONF: 199/20, 4 September 2002, available at www.un-documents.net/jburgdec.htm, para. 5.

[213] International Law Association (2002), Declaration of Principles of International Law Related to Sustainable Development, Resolution 3/2002 adopted at the 70th Conference of the International Law Association, held in New Delhi, India, 2–6 April 2002, UN Do. A/CONF.199/8, 9 August 2002.

[214] The Future We Want, UN Doc. A/66/L.56, UNGA Sixty-Sixth Session, 24 July 2012, para. 3.

[215] *Gabčíkovo-Nagymaros Project (Hungary/Slovakia)*, Judgment of 25 September 1997, ICJ Reports 1997.

[216] Arbitration Regarding the Iron Rhine (Ijzeren Rijn) Railway, *Belgium v. Netherlands*, Award of the Arbitral Tribunal, 24 May 2005, The Hague.

[217] Appellate Body Report, *US – Shrimp*.

The *Gabčíkovo-Nagymaros Project* (1997) is the first case where the International Court of Justice invoked the concept of sustainable development to strike a balance between the traditional development-oriented rules and emerging environmental norms.[218] The Court found it necessary to consider the new environmental norms in interpreting the treaty aimed at the construction of the Gabčíkovo-Nagymaros system of locks on the Danube River[219] by stating that "this need to reconcile economic development with the protection of the environment is aptly expressed in the concept of sustainable development".[220] Judge Weeramantry clarified this statement in his separate opinion by arguing that the principle of sustainable development "necessarily contains within itself the principle of reconciliation" to balance the competing demands of development and environmental protection.[221] However, unlike Judge Weeramantry, the Court described "sustainable development" as a concept not as a principle. Nevertheless, as pointed out by Sands and Peel (2012), the invocation of "sustainable development" indicates that the term has a legal function: from a procedural/temporal perspective, it obliges the parties to "'look afresh' at the environmental consequences of the operation of the plant"; and from a substantive perspective, it seeks to "ensure that a 'satisfactory volume of water' be released from the bypass canal into the main river and its original side arms".[222]

Referring to the integration principle in international and EU law as well as the interpretation of the concept of sustainable development by the ICJ, the Arbitral Tribunal, established under the rules of the Permanent Court of

---

[218] See, e.g., Philippe Sands (2003), International Courts and the Application of the Concept of "Sustainable Development", in Hatchard and Perry-Kessaris (eds.), *Law and Development: Facing Complexity in the 21st Century*, London: Cavendish Publishing, pp. 147–57, at p. 148; Stephen Stec and Gabriel E. Eckstein (1997), Of Solemn Oaths and Obligations: The Environmental Impact of the ICJ's Decision in the Case Concerning the Gabčíkovo-Nagymaros Project, *Yearbook of International Environmental Law*, vol. 8, pp. 41–50, at p.41; Jessica Howley (2009), The Gabčíkovo-Nagymaros Case: The Influence of the International Court of Justice on the Law of Sustainable Development, *Queensland Law Student Review*, vol. 2, no. 1, pp. 1–19, at p. 3.

[219] *Gabčíkovo-Nagymaros Project (Hungary/Slovakia)*, Judgment of 25 September 1997, ICJ Reports 1997, p. 78 (noting that "[o]wing to new scientific insights and to a growing awareness [of environmental effects] ... new norms and standards have been developed ... Such new norms have to be taken into consideration, and such new standards given proper weight, not only when States contemplate new activities but also when continuing with activities begun in the past").

[220] Ibid.

[221] Separate Opinion of Vice-President Weeramantry, *Gabčíkovo-Nagymaros Project* (Hungary/ Slovakia), Judgment of 25 September 1997, ICJ Reports 1997, p. 87.

[222] Philippe Sands and Jacqueline Peel (2012), *Principles of International Environmental Law*, Cambridge University Press, p. 208.

Arbitration, in the *Iron Rhine* case (2005) confirmed the need to integrate "appropriate environmental measures in the design and implementation of economic development activities".[223] As found by the Tribunal, "[e]nvironmental law and the law on development stand not as alternatives but as *mutually reinforcing, integral* concepts, which require that where development may cause significant harm to the environment there is a duty to prevent, or at least mitigate, such harm. This duty, in the opinion of the Tribunal, has now become a principle of general international law" (emphasis added).[224] In this case, the Arbitral Tribunal, thus, relied on sustainable development and the integration principle to reconcile the competing norms and interests.

In *US – Shrimp* (1998), the Appellate Body expressly acknowledged the objective of sustainable development and confirmed that sustainable development has been "generally accepted as integrating economic and social development and environmental protection".[225] The objective of sustainable development informed the finding of the Appellate Body that sea turtles are "exhaustible natural resources" within the meaning of Article XX (g).[226] It also played a significant role in justifying the environmental measures under Article XX (g).[227] Therefore, while the WTO Agreements govern international trade and economic relations, the WTO's sustainable development objective allows its Members to comply with the WTO Agreements in accordance with their respective environmental and social needs and concerns.[228] However, this does not mean that the objective of sustainable development can be invoked as a basis to deviate from the requirements of specific WTO provisions.[229]

In sum, various international legal instruments and decisions by international courts and tribunals indicate that the principle of sustainable development provides a legal basis for integrating and reconciling potentially

---

[223] Arbitration Regarding the Iron Rhine (Ijzeren Rijn) Railway, *Belgium* v. *Netherlands*, Award of the Arbitral Tribunal, 24 May 2005, The Hague, para. 59 (observed that "today, both international and EC law require the integration of appropriate environmental measure in the design and implementation of economic development activities").

[224] Arbitration Regarding the Iron Rhine (Ijzeren Rijn) Railway, *Belgium* v. *Netherlands*, Award of the Arbitral Tribunal, 24 May 2005, The Hague, para. 59.

[225] Appellate Body Report, *US – Shrimp*, para. 129.   [226] Ibid., paras. 129–131.

[227] Ibid., para. 153.

[228] See, e.g., Robert L. Howse and Makau Mutua (2001), Protecting Human Rights in a Global Economy Challenges for the World Trade Organization, in Stokke and Tostensen (eds.), *Human Rights in Development Yearbook 1999/2000*, Alphen aan den Rijn, Netherlands: Kluwer Law International, pp. 51–82, at pp. 64–5.

[229] Panel Reports, *China – Rare Earths*, para. 7.261.

conflicting legal norms relating to economic and social development and environmental protection.[230] Sands and Peel (2012) went a step further by asserting that "[t]here can be little doubt that the concept of 'sustainable development' has entered the corpus of international customary law, requiring different streams of international law to be treated in an integrated manner".[231] In my view, it may be too early to characterise sustainable development as part of international customary law since its legal status is still subject to debate, as discussed in the previous section. However, the principle of integration required by sustainable development does play a significant legal role not only in the decision-making and implementation process but also in the resolution of disputes.[232]

Accordingly, in the WTO context, its overarching sustainable development objective "allows and obliges" a treaty interpreter to take into account all relevant economic, social and environmental concerns in interpreting the WTO Agreements, including the TRIPS Agreement.[233] This is consistent with the common intentions of the WTO Members, as expressed in the 2001 Doha Ministerial Declaration, that "the aims of upholding and safeguarding an open and non-discriminatory multilateral trading system, and acting for the protection of the environment and the promoting of sustainable development *can* and *must be* mutually supportive" (emphasis added).[234]

However, when applying the integrated approach, there lacks a benchmark to determine how to "balance and weigh" different competing interests and to

---

[230] See also, Christina Voigt (2009), *Sustainable Development as a Principle of International Law: Resolving Conflicts between Climate Measures and WTO Law*, Leiden, Netherlands: Martinus Nijhoff Publishers, p. 162 (stating that "the normative potential of sustainable development [may] facilitate and require a balance and reconciliation between conflicting legal norms relating to environmental protection, social justice and economic development"); Alhaji B. M. Marong (2003), From Rio to Johannesburg: Reflections on the Role of International Legal Norms in Sustainable Development, *The Georgetown International Environmental Law Review*, vol. 16, pp. 21–76, at p. 47; Vaughan Lowe (1999), Sustainable Development and Unsustainable Arguments, in Boyle and Freestone (eds.), *International Law and Sustainable Development: Past Achievements and Future Challenges*, Oxford University Press, pp. 19–38, at p. 24 (arguing that "sustainable development appears to entail what has been called a 'holistic' approach to the resolution of disputes").

[231] Philippe Sands and Jacqueline Peel (2012), *Principles of International Environmental Law*, Cambridge University Press, p. 208.

[232] See, e.g., Marcos A. Orellana (2009), Evolving WTO Law Concerning Health, Safety and Environmental Measures, *Trade, Law and Development*, vol. 1, pp. 103–44, at pp. 105 and 106.

[233] See also Henning Grosse Ruse-Khan (2011), Assessing the Need for a General Public Interest Exception in the TRIPS Agreement, in Kur and Levin (eds.), *Intellectual Property Rights in a Fair World Trade System: Proposal for Reforms of TRIPS*, Cheltenham, UK: Edward Elgar Publishing, pp. 167–207, at p. 202.

[234] Doha Ministerial Declaration, WT/MIN (01)/DEC/1, Adopted on 14 November 2001, para. 6.

what extent other relevant competing interests can be considered. Some optimistic scholars such as Lowe predicted in 1999 that "[a] tribunal might one day assert, on the basis of the principle of sustainable development, a power to modify not only the application of primary norms of customary law but also treaty obligations".[235] Nevertheless, as articulated in Section 5.2.2, treaty interpretation in the WTO dispute settlement body is bound by the "ordinary meaning" and "context" of the relevant treaty. Thus, interpreting the TRIPS provisions in light of the objective of sustainable development does not include modifying treaty obligations.

However, where the norms are sufficiently open and ambiguous, which is often the case of TRIPS flexibilities provisions, the objective of sustainable development can direct treaty interpreters to reconcile and integrate economic, social and environmental concerns affected by the operation of the norms.[236] As pointed out by Grosse Ruse-Khan (2011), "[w]ith its concept of integrating and reconciling economic, social and environmental interests, it further emphasises the need to interpret and implement the TRIPS provisions in a way which not only reflects the rights holders' interests but [also] equally takes competing public interests into account".[237] In this way, the sustainable development objective enshrined in the Preamble to the Marrakesh Agreement provides a legal basis for WTO Members to consider their respective environmental and social needs and concerns in interpreting the TRIPS Agreement.

5.3.2 *The Object and Purpose of the TRIPS Agreement*

The object and purpose of the TRIPS Agreement are found primarily in its preamble and in its Article 7, entitled "Objectives" and Article 8, entitled "Principles".[238]

---

[235] Vaughan Lowe (1999), Sustainable Development and Unsustainable Arguments, in Boyle and Freestone (eds.), *International Law and Sustainable Development: Past Achievements and Future Challenges*, Oxford University Press, pp. 19–38, at pp. 36–7.
[236] Henning Grosse Ruse-Khan (2010), Sustainable Development in International Intellectual Property Law – New Approaches from EU Economic Partnership Agreements? ICTSD's Programme on IPRs and Sustainable Development, Issue Paper No. 29, ICTSD, Geneva, p. 6.
[237] Henning Grosse Ruse-Khan (2011), Assessing the Need for a General Public Interest Exception in the TRIPS Agreement, in Kur and Levin (eds.), *Intellectual Property Rights in a Fair World Trade System: Proposal for Reforms of TRIPS*, Cheltenham, UK: Edward Elgar Publishing, pp. 167–207, at p. 202.
[238] See, e.g., Susy Frankel (2009), Challenging TRIPS-Plus Agreements: The Potential Utility of Non-Violation Disputes, *Journal of International Economic Law*, vol. 12, no. 4, pp. 1023–65, at p. 1027 (noting that "[t]he preamble to the TRIPS Agreement and its articles entitled 'principle'

The Preamble of TRIPS confirmed that one main objective of the Agreement is "to reduce distortions and impediments to international trade".[239] It is generally accepted that trade distortions could be caused by "insufficient, as well as excessive" IP protection.[240] Accordingly, WTO Members recognise "the need to promote effective and adequate protection of intellectual property rights" while at the same time stressing that IP protection should not in itself become a barrier to legitimate trade.[241] These objectives were originally set out in the Punta del Este Declaration (which is the ministerial declaration launching the Uruguay Round)[242] and are often labelled as "trade-oriented".[243]

Nevertheless, the Preamble also addresses the need to promote development and technology transfer. The fifth recital of the Preamble recognises the

and 'objectives' provide some guidance about the object and purpose of the Agreement"); Antony Taubman et al. (2012), *A Handbook on the WTO TRIPS Agreement*, Cambridge University Press, p. 13 (stating that "[t]he Preamble and Articles 7 and 8 express the general goals, objectives and principles of the Agreement").

[239] See the first recital of the Preamble of TRIPS, starting with the word "desiring" and thus being viewed as an expression of objectives.

[240] See, e.g., Thomas Cottier and Pierre Veron (2011), *Concise International and European IP Law: TRIPS, Paris Convention, European Enforcement and Transfer of Technology*, 2nd edn, Alphen aan den Rijn, Netherlands: Kluwer Law International, p. 6; Daniel Gervais (2012), *The TRIPS Agreement: Drafting History and Analysis*, 4th edn, Hebden Bridge, UK: Sweet & Maxwell, p. 160 (stating that "insufficient protection of intellectual property (which is otherwise an exception in art. XX (d) of GATT 1947) will distort trade by allowing piracy and counterfeiting but that excessive protection can be counter-productive when measured in terms of innovation outcomes").

[241] See the first recital of the Preamble of TRIPS.

[242] Draft Ministerial Declaration on the Uruguay Round, 20 September 1986, GATT Doc. MIN (86)/W/19, pp. 14–15 (stating that "(a) In order to reduce the distortions and impediments to international trade, and taking into account the need to promote effective and adequate protection of intellectual property rights, and to ensure that measures and procedures to enforce intellectual property rights do not themselves become barriers to legitimate trade, the negotiations shall aim to clarify GATT provisions and elaborate as appropriate new rules and disciplines. (b) Negotiations shall aim to develop a multilateral framework of principles, rules and disciplines dealing with international trade in counterfeit goods, taking into account work already undertaken in the GATT").

[243] See, e.g., Annette Kur (2011), Limitations and Exceptions under the Three-step-test – How Much Room to Walk the Middle Ground? in Kur and Levin (eds.), *Intellectual Property Rights in a Fair World Trade System: Proposal for Reforms of TRIPS*, Cheltenham, UK: Edward Elgar Publishing, pp. 208–61, at p. 243 (noting that "[w]ith TRIPS being an element of the WTO Agreement, its object and purpose are primarily trade-oriented"); Martin Senftleben (2004), *Copyright, Limitations, and the Three-step Test: An Analysis of the Three-Step Test in International and EC Copyright Law*, Alphen aan den Rijn, Netherlands: Kluwer Law International, p. 17 (arguing that "[t]he TRIPS Agreement ... primarily desiring to reduce 'distortions and impediments to international trade', points in the direction of utilitarian considerations, such as the economic rationale of copyright and corresponding industry policy").

"underlying public policy objectives" of national IP systems including "developmental and technological objectives", while paragraph 6 emphasises the LDCs' special needs with respect to "maximum flexibility in the domestic implementation". The integration of public policy objectives into the TRIPS Agreement was requested by developing countries, and was initially included in the preamble of the "B" text, that is, Group 14's proposals.[244]

The Preamble thus underscores the need to strike a balance between the private rights of IP holders on the one hand and the objective of public policy on the other hand.[245] Within TRIPS, public policy objectives are largely enshrined in Articles 7 and 8.[246] These two articles are, thus, fundamental to an analysis of the balancing objective and purpose of the TRIPS Agreement.

The following sections will address these two articles in turn, followed by an analysis of the interpretation of the TRIPS Agreement in light of its objectives and principles.

5.3.2.1 Article 7: "Objectives"

IPRs are often described as a means to "benefit society by providing incentives to introduce new inventions and creations".[247] Article 7 of the TRIPS Agreement confirms that "IPRs are not an end in themselves" by setting out the objectives that Member States should be able to reach through the protection and enforcement of such rights,[248] providing that:

> The protection and enforcement of intellectual property rights should contribute to the promotion of technological innovation and to the transfer and dissemination of technology, to the mutual advantage of producers and users

---

[244] Communication from Argentina, Brazil, Chile, China, Colombia, Cuba, Egypt, India, Nigeria, Peru, Tanzania and Uruguay, (subsequently sponsored by Pakistan and Zimbabwe) 14 May 1990, GATT Doc. MTN.GNG/NG11/W/71, p. 2.

[245] See Daniel Gervais (2012), *The TRIPS Agreement: Drafting History and Analysis*, 4th edn, Hebden Bridge, UK: Sweet & Maxwell, p. 163.

[246] Abdulqawi A.Yusuf (2008), TRIPS: Background, Principles and General Provisions, in Correa and Yusuf (eds.), *Intellectual Property and International Trade: The TRIPS Agreement*, 2nd edn, Alphen aan den Rijn, Netherlands: Kluwer Law International, pp. 3–21, at p. 11.

[247] See, e.g., Carlos M. Correa (2003), Formulating Effective Pro-Development National Intellectual Property Policies, in Bellmann et al. (eds.), *Trading in Knowledge: Development Perspectives on TRIPS, Trade and Sustainability*, Earthscan Publications Ltd, pp. 209–17, at p. 209; UNCTAD and ICTSD (2005), *Resource Book on TRIPS and Development*, Cambridge University Press, p. 125.

[248] UNCTAD and ICTSD (2005), *Resource Book on TRIPS and Development*, Cambridge University Press, p. 126.

of technological knowledge and in a manner conducive to social and economic welfare, and to a balance of rights and obligations.

Although Article 7 is merely a "should" provision, it authoritatively states the objectives of the TRIPS Agreement.[249] Thus, this provision has to be taken into consideration during the process of interpreting and applying the TRIPS Agreement so as to ensure the outcomes are conducive to its objectives.[250] This has been reaffirmed by WTO Members in their Doha Declaration.[251]

Article 7 makes it clear that IPRs should be protected and enforced to promote innovation and the transfer and dissemination of technology. These objectives formalise a "utilitarian public policy rationale for granting patents",[252] which has long been present in national patent laws. It can be seen that TRIPS negotiators chose "a balanced perspective" on the role of IPRs in society at the multilateral level.[253] Looking back at the TRIPS negotiating history, some scholars consider that Article 7 reflects a compromise between industrialised countries that emphasised the role of IPRs as an incentive for innovation, and some developing countries that were concerned about the impact that IPRs might have on their access to technologies.[254] To reconcile these potentially conflicting interests, Article 7 requires that IPRs be protected and enforced "in mutually beneficial ways" for IPR holders and users of technological knowledge.[255]

The objectives of promoting innovation and transfer of technology have to be pursued in a way that respects "a balance of rights and obligations", with

---

[249] See, e.g., Holger Hestermeyer (2007), *Human Rights and the WTO: The Case of Patents and Access to Medicines*, Oxford University Press, p. 51; Antony Taubman (2011), *A Practical Guide to Working with TRIPS*, Oxford University Press, p. 83 (arguing that "Article 7 is an authoritative statement of the public policy role of the IP system, unprecedented in multilateral law").

[250] Thomas Cottier and Pierre Veron (2011), *Concise International and European IP Law: TRIPS, Paris Convention, European Enforcement and Transfer of Technology*, 2nd edn, Alphen aan den Rijn, Netherlands: Kluwer Law International, p. 29; see also Carlos M. Correa (2007), *Trade-Related Aspects of Intellectual Property Rights: A Commentary on the TRIPS Agreement*, Oxford University Press, p. 93 (arguing that "these provisions [Article 7] are to be systematically applied in the implementation and interpretation of the Agreement").

[251] Declaration on the TRIPS Agreement and Public Health, WT/MIN (01)/DEC/2, Adopted on 14 November 2001, para. 5(a).

[252] Holger Hestermeyer (2007), *Human Rights and the WTO: The Case of Patents and Access to Medicines*, Oxford University Press, p. 51.

[253] UNCTAD-ICTSD (2005), *Resource Book on TRIPS and Development*, Cambridge University Press, p. 126.

[254] Carlos M. Correa (2007), *Trade-Related Aspects of Intellectual Property Rights: A Commentary on the TRIPS Agreement*, Oxford University Press, pp. 91–2.

[255] Beas Edson Rodrigues (2012), *The General Exception Clauses of the TRIPS Agreement: Promoting Sustainable Development*, vol. 17, Cambridge University Press, p. 43.

"the overall goal of promoting social and economic welfare".[256]These require-ments are considered to be "consonant with the overall goals" of the WTO, as established in the Preamble to the Marrakesh Agreement.[257] Such provisions essentially stress the "balanced nature" of the overall agreement. In *Canada – Pharmaceutical Patents* (2000), both parties to the dispute agreed that such text shows that one main goal of the TRIPS Agreement is to achieve a balance between IP rights and other important socio-economic objectives of the WTO Members.[258] As observed by Hestermeyer (2007), the TRIPS Agreement is not intended to solely protect IP holders' commercial interests, but also to impose limits on IP rights so as to promote social and economic welfare.[259] Mitigating climate change is one of the important societal interests that can be brought into the balance within the TRIPS Agreement.

5.3.2.2 Article 8: "Principles"

Article 8 of TRIPS, entitled "Principles", complements the philosophy under-lying Article 7 by recognising Members' sovereign discretion to adopt meas-ures on public interest grounds and to prevent rights holders from abusing their IP rights within the bounds of the TRIPS Agreement.[260] Article 8.2 of TRIPS allows Members to take appropriate measures against the abuse of IP rights or unreasonable restriction of international trade or transfer of technol-ogy. This is examined in greater detail in Chapter 7. This section focuses on the analysis of Article 8.1 of TRIPS, which provides that:

> Members may, in formulating or amending their laws and regulations, adopt measures necessary to protect public health and nutrition, and to promote the public interest in sectors of vital importance to their socio-economic and technological development, provided that such measures are consistent with the provisions of this Agreement.

[256] Antony Taubman et al. (2012), *A Handbook on the WTO TRIPS Agreement*, Cambridge University Press, p. 13.
[257] See, e.g., Daniel Gervais (2012), *The TRIPS Agreement: Drafting History and Analysis*, 4th edn, Hebden Bridge, UK: Sweet & Maxwell, p. 230; Thomas Cottier and Pierre Veron (2011), *Concise International and European IP Law: TRIPS, Paris Convention, European Enforcement and Transfer of Technology*, 2nd edn, Alphen aan den Rijn, Netherlands: Kluwer Law International, p. 29.
[258] Panel Report, *Canada – Pharmaceutical Patents*, paras. 7.24–7.25.
[259] Holger Hestermeyer (2007), *Human Rights and the WTO: The Case of Patents and Access to Medicines*, Oxford University Press, p. 51.
[260] Thomas Cottier and Pierre Veron (2011), *Concise International and European IP Law: TRIPS, Paris Convention, European Enforcement and Transfer of Technology*, 2nd edn, Alphen aan den Rijn, Netherlands: Kluwer Law International, p. 31.

Article 8.1 of TRIPS recognises Members' rights to take specific measures that respond to particular public health and other public interests, thus being described by some scholars as a "public interest principle".[261] Similar to Article XX(b) of the GATT 1994, this provision forms a legal basis for WTO Members to adopt internal measures. However, contrary to Article XX(b), which is used to justify GATT-inconsistent measures that are necessary to achieve its policy goal, Article 8.1 of TRIPS provides that measures necessary to protect or promote public interest must be TRIPS-consistent.[262]

The policy objectives of the measures referred to under Article 8.1 include: (a) the protection of public health and nutrition and (b) the promotion of the "public interest in sectors of vital importance to their socio-economic and technological development". The use of the term "socio-economic and technology development" suggests that "all vital interests and sectors are captured",[263] not only public health and nutrition. The implications of making reference to "measures to promote public interest" are two-fold: first, as interpreted by Correa (2007), WTO Members that invoke this provision "need not prove that such measures actually achieve their intended objectives, but that they are suitable to do [so] in the particular context where they apply"; second, the concerned Member States have the right to define what constitutes the "public interest".[264] One such elaboration on the concept of public interest states that:

> Whether a particular act is 'in the public interest' ... is probably not subject to any objective tests. Inherent in the noble motive of the public good is the notion that, in certain circumstances, the needs of the majority override those

---

[261] See, e.g., Abdulqawi A. Yusuf (2008), TRIPS: Background, Principles and General Provisions, in Correa and Yusuf (eds.), *Intellectual Property and International Trade: The TRIPS Agreement*, 2nd edn, Alphen aan den Rijn, Netherlands: Kluwer Law International, pp. 3–21, at p. 13; Peter Yu (2009), Objectives and Principles of the TRIPS Agreement, *Houston Law Review*, vol. 46, pp. 979–1046, at p. 1009.

[262] UNCTAD-ICTSD (2005), *Resource Book on TRIPS and Development*, Cambridge University Press, p. 126.

[263] Thomas Cottier and Pierre Veron (2011), *Concise International and European IP Law: TRIPS, Paris Convention, European Enforcement and Transfer of Technology*, 2nd edn, Alphen aan den Rijn, Netherlands: Kluwer Law International, p. 32; see also Carlos M. Correa (2007), *Trade-Related Aspects of Intellectual Property Rights: A Commentary on the TRIPS Agreement*, Oxford University Press, p. 106 (arguing that "the concept of 'socio-economic and technological development' is broad enough to encompass any sector, socially, economically, or technologically relevant").

[264] Carlos M. Correa (2007), *Trade-Related Aspects of Intellectual Property Rights: A Commentary on the TRIPS Agreement*, Oxford University Press, p. 105.

of the individual, and that the citizen should relinquish any thoughts of self-interest in favour of the common good of society as a whole.[265]

Members also retain substantial discretion regarding "the kinds and subject matter of measures" that they may adopt in accordance with Article 8.1.[266] This interpretation reaffirms Members' intentions to respect "the underlying public policy objectives of national systems for the protection of intellectual property", as outlined in the fifth recital of the Preamble.

However, such measures would be subject to a test of "necessity" and of "consistency" with the provisions of the TRIPS Agreement, both of which were "added at the request of developed countries in the last stages of negotiations".[267]

The first constraint requires that the measure referred to must be "necessary". This necessity requirement has not been examined by dispute settlement panels or the Appellate Body so far. It is noted that the core concepts of the necessity requirement in Article 8.1 of TRIPS are similar to those used in Article XX(b) of the GATT. Both the TRIPS Agreement and the GATT are "integral parts" of the same treaty, that is the Marrakesh Agreement. Thus, the "necessity" requirement in Article XX of the GATT and its WTO jurisprudence may provide the basis for interpreting the term "necessary" in Article 8.1 of the TRIPS Agreement.[268] Notably, in the first case dealing with Article XIV of the General Agreement on Trade in Services (GATS), US – Gambling (2005), the Appellate Body found previous decisions regarding the necessity requirement under Article XX of the GATT 1994 relevant for their analysis under Article XIV of the GATS.[269]

---

[265] Gillian Davies (2002), *Copyright and the Public Interest*, 2nd edn, Hebden Bridge, UK: Sweet & Maxwell, p. 4; see also Peter Yu (2009), The Objectives and Principles of the TRIPS Agreement, *Houston Law Review*, vol. 46, pp. 797–1046, at p. 1011; Carlos M. Correa (2007), *Trade-Related Aspects of Intellectual Property Rights: A Commentary on the TRIPS Agreement*, Oxford University Press, pp. 105–6.

[266] UNCTAD-ICTSD (2005), *Resource Book on TRIPS and Development*, Cambridge University Press, p. 127.

[267] See, e.g., Peter Yu (2009), The Objectives and Principles of the TRIPS Agreement, *Houston Law Review*, vol. 46, pp. 797–1046, at p.1013; Abdulqawi A. Yusuf (2008), TRIPS: Background, Principles and General Provisions, in Correa and Yusuf (eds.), *Intellectual Property and International Trade: The TRIPS Agreement*, 2nd edn, Alphen aan den Rijn, Netherlands: Kluwer Law International, pp. 3–21, at p. 14; Daniel Gervais (2012), *The TRIPS Agreement: Drafting History and Analysis*, 4th edn, Hebden Bridge, UK: Sweet & Maxwell, p. 238.

[268] Beas Edson Rodrigues (2012), *The General Exception Clauses of the TRIPS Agreement: Promoting Sustainable Development*, vol. 17, Cambridge University Press, p. 46; see also Carlos M. Correa (2007), *Trade-Related Aspects of Intellectual Property Rights: A Commentary on the TRIPS Agreement*, Oxford University Press, p. 106.

[269] Appellate Body Report, US – Gambling, para. 291.

The current popular approach to determining whether a measure is necessary was introduced by the Appellate Body's ruling in *Korea – Various Measures on Beef* (2001),[270] and developed by its ruling on *Brazil – Retreaded Tyres* (2007). It requires a "weighing and balancing" of all factors such as "the contribution of the measure to the achievement of its objective", "the importance of the interests or values at stake", the trade restrictiveness of the measure, and "the comparison of the possible alternatives, including associated risks".[271] The Appellate Body emphasised that "[t]he weighing and balancing is a holistic operation that involves putting all the variables of the equation together and evaluating them in relation to each other after having examined them individually, in order to reach an overall judgment".[272] Therefore, the review under the principle of necessity of Article 8.1 entails difficult issues of "weighing and balancing" a series of factors, including the "proportionality of measures", "whether there is a proper relationship of means and ends", and "whether the measure is suitable to achieve the goal".[273]

Even if the measure designed to promote public interest passes the "necessity" test, Article 8.1 requires that the measure must be consistent with the provisions of the TRIPS Agreement. This consistency requirement is introduced to "find a balance between various public policy goals".[274] The consistency provision is subject to divergent interpretations. Some scholars consider that it implies that "the policy space in the pursuit of welfare is defined by the operational provisions throughout the [TRIPS] agreement".[275] In contrast, some other scholars argue that this consistency requirement should be assessed in the light of "Article 7 and of the Preamble, that is, taking the balance of rights and obligations and the social and economic welfare into

---

[270] Peter Van den Bossche and Werner Zdouc (2013), *The Law and Policy of the World Trade Organization*, 3rd edn, Cambridge University Press, pp. 556 and 565 (further noting that "this case law on the 'necessity' requirement did not cease to evolve"); see also Appellate Body Report, *Korea – Various Measures on Beef*, para. 164 (finding that "determination of whether a measure, which is not 'indispensable', may nevertheless be 'necessary' within the contemplation of Article XX(d), involves in every case a process of weighing and balancing a series of factors which prominently include the contribution made by compliance measure to the enforcement of the law or regulation at issue, the importance of the common interests or values protected by the law or regulation, and the accompanying impact of the law or regulation on imports or exports").

[271] Appellate Body Report, *Brazil – Retreaded Tyres*, paras. 178–9 and 182; see also WTO (2012), *WTO Analytical Index: Guide to WTO Law and Practice*, 3rd edn, vol. 1, Cambridge University Press, p. 324.

[272] Appellate Body Report, *Brazil – Retreaded Tyres*, para. 182.

[273] Thomas Cottier and Pierre Veron (2011), *Concise International and European IP Law: TRIPS, Paris Convention, European Enforcement and Transfer of Technology*, 2nd edn, Alphen aan den Rijn, Netherlands: Kluwer Law International, p. 33.

[274] Ibid., p. 32.   [275] Ibid.

account".[276] A third interpretation is more in line with the interpretation rules established by the VCLT as discussed in Section 5.2, which states that "[i]n evaluating the consistency of public interest measures with the TRIPS Agreement, consideration should be given to the provisions of the agreement as a whole, including its preamble, objectives and principles".[277] Therefore, the "consistency" requirement has to be assessed in line with the basic balance of rights and obligations within the TRIPS Agreement.[278]

As Correa (2007) pointed out, "nothing in the TRIPS Agreement should be read as preventing Members from adopting measures to protect public health", or from pursuing public policies as defined in Article 8.[279] This is consistent with Members' common intentions as expressed in paragraph 4 of the Doha Declaration, which states that "[w]e agree that the TRIPS Agreement does not and should not prevent Members from taking measures to protect public health". Such public-health-specific interpretation could be extended to other sectors of vital importance to Members' socio-economic and technological developments as defined in Article 8.1 of TRIPS. ESTs that tackle climate change – which is a common concern of humankind – are of vital importance to social-economic and technological development. Therefore, in accordance with Article 8.1, WTO Members may adopt measures to promote public interest in EST sectors, provided that such measures are consistent with the TRIPS provisions.

5.3.2.3 Interpreting the TRIPS Agreement in Light of Its Objectives and Principles

It is well accepted that the objectives and principles of the TRIPS Agreement enshrined in Articles 7 and 8 provide guidance for the interpretation and

---

[276] Carlos M. Correa (2007), *Trade-Related Aspects of Intellectual Property Rights: A Commentary on the TRIPS Agreement*, Oxford University Press, p. 104.

[277] Abdulqawi A. Yusuf (2008), TRIPS: Background, Principles and General Provisions, in Correa and Yusuf (eds.), *Intellectual Property and International Trade: The TRIPS Agreement*, 2nd edn, Alphen aan den Rijn, Netherlands: Kluwer Law International, pp. 3–21, at p. 14 (further arguing that "even though certain public interest measures may be inconsistent with some of the specific standards laid down in the TRIPS Agreement, it is their overall consistency with the agreement that should be taken into account").

[278] Henning Grosse Ruse-Khan (2011), Assessing the Need for a General Public Interest Exception in the TRIPS Agreement, in Kur and Levin (eds.), *Intellectual Property Rights in a Fair World Trade System: Proposal for Reforms of TRIPS*, Cheltenham, UK: Edward Elgar Publishing, pp. 167–207, at p. 176.

[279] Carlos M. Correa (2007), *Trade-Related Aspects of Intellectual Property Rights: A Commentary on the TRIPS Agreement*, Oxford University Press, p. 104.

implementation of the entire Agreement.[280] Under the general rules of treaty interpretation, Articles 7 and 8 as objectives and principles of the TRIPS Agreement shall guide or inform the interpretation of each provision of the TRIPS Agreement.[281] Paragraph 19 of the Doha Ministerial Declaration, adopted on 14 November 2001, highlights their importance by providing that "[i]n undertaking [the work referred to in that paragraph], the TRIPS Council shall be guided by the objectives and principles set out in Articles 7 and 8 of the TRIPS Agreement".[282] Paragraph 5(a) of the Doha Declaration also obliges a treaty interpreter to read each provision of the TRIPS Agreement in the light of Articles 7 and 8.[283] The WTO panel in *Canada – Pharmaceutical Patents* (2000), acknowledged the interpretative role of these provisions by stating that:

> Both the goals and the limitations stated in Articles 7 and 8.1 must obviously be borne in mind when [interpreting the words of Article 30] as well as those of other provisions of the TRIPS Agreement which indicate its object and purposes.[284]

Thus, the objectives and principles of TRIPS play a vital role in the interpretation and implementation of the entire agreement.[285]

---

[280] See, e.g., Antony Taubman (2011), *A Practical Guide to Working with TRIPS*, Oxford University Press, p. 84 (noting that "these two provisions [Articles 7 and 8] have continued to guide both the political and legal context of international IP law, even though some specific interpretative questions remain open to debate"); Peter Yu (2010), The Objectives and Principles of the TRIPS Agreement, in Correa (ed.), *Research Handbook on the Protection of Intellectual Property under WTO Rules: Intellectual Property in the WTO*, Vol. I, Cheltenham, UK: Edward Elgar Publishing, pp. 146–91, at p. 191 (finding that "politically, they [Articles 7 and 8] provide the much-needed balance to make the Agreement a legitimate bargain between developed and less developed countries. Structurally, the two provisions bridge the gap between the TRIPS regime and other international regimes. Globally, they have sowed the seeds for the development of new international norms both within and without the TRIPS regime").

[281] See also Henning Grosse Ruse-Khan (2011), Assessing the Need for a General Public Interest Exception in the TRIPS Agreement, in Annette Kur and Marianne Levin (eds.), *Intellectual Property Rights in a Fair World Trade System: Proposal for Reforms of TRIPS*, Cheltenham, UK: Edward Elgar Publishing, pp. 67–207, at p. 200.

[282] Ministerial Declaration, WT/MIN (01)/DEC/1, Doha, adopted on 14 November 2001, para. 19.

[283] Declaration on the TRIPS Agreement and Public Health, WT/MIN (01)/DEC/2, adopted on 14 November 2001, para. 5 (a).

[284] Panel Report, *Canada – Pharmaceutical Patents*, para. 7.26.

[285] See also Denis Barbosa Borges (2010), Minimum Standards vs. Harmonization in the TRIPS Context: The Nature of Obligations under TRIPS and Modes of Implementation at the National Level in Monist and Dualist System, in in Correa (ed.), *Research Handbook on the Protection of Intellectual Property under WTO Rules: Intellectual Property in the WTO*, Vol. I, Cheltenham, UK: Edward Elgar Publishing, pp. 52–109, at p. 93 (concluding that "the

The interpretative role of the objectives and principles of the TRIPS Agreement becomes more important when there is a need to clarify ambiguities in the existing treaties, or to alleviate tension between IP rights and competing public values.[286] It is recognised that Articles 7 and 8 provide "objective clues" as to how ambiguous or vague TRIPS provisions are to be interpreted.[287] As Correa (2007) pointed out, Articles 7 and 8 are of particular significance to properly interpret several ambiguous exceptions and flexibilities in TRIPS, such as "legitimate interests" in Article 30, and "abuse" in Article 40, among others.[288] When conflicting values are at issue, the two provisions can serve as an interpretive tool to reconcile the tension.[289] As observed by Harris (2006), private rights of IP owners may be circumscribed with the competing public interests embodied in Articles 7 and 8.[290] The interpretation of the TRIPS provisions should therefore be informed by the balancing objectives of the TRIPS Agreement, as identified in the previous two sections; the protection and enforcement of IP rights should facilitate innovation and transfer of technology while at the same time promoting social and economic welfare and public policy objectives.

objectives and principles of TRIPS should play a central role in the interpretation of the entire agreement"); Carlos M. Correa (2007), *Trade-Related Aspects of Intellectual Property Rights: A Commentary on the TRIPS Agreement*, Oxford University Press, p. 108 (stating that "Article 8 . . . constitutes jointly with Article 7, a central piece for the implementation and interpretation of the TRIPS Agreement").

[286] Peter Yu (2009), Objectives and Principles of the TRIPS Agreement, *Houston Law Review*, vol. 46, pp. 979–1046, at pp. 1045–6 (stating that "[i]t would indeed be no surprise if drafters in other fora or interpreters of non-intellectual property treaties look to Articles 7 and 8 to help resolve ambiguities in existing treaties, alleviate tension between and among the various treaties, or even to provide a starting point for new treaties and initiatives").

[287] Peter Yu (2009), Objectives and Principles of the TRIPS Agreement, *Houston Law Review*, vol. 46, pp. 979–1046, at p. 1022; see also Thomas Cottier and Pierre Veron (2011), *Concise International and European IP Law: TRIPS, Paris Convention, European Enforcement and Transfer of Technology*, 2nd edn, Alphen aan den Rijn, Netherlands: Kluwer Law International, p. 32 (noting "[t]he provision is of particular importance in defining the scope of rights, fair use exemptions, compulsory licensing and the relationship to competition law").

[288] Carlos M. Correa (2007), *Trade-Related Aspects of Intellectual Property Rights: A Commentary on the TRIPS Agreement*, Oxford University Press, pp. 94–5.

[289] Denis Borges Barbosa et al., Slouching towards Development in International Intellectual Property, *Michigan State Law Review*, vol. 2007, pp. 71–141, at p. 109 (stating that "[t]he norms expressed in the preamble and articles 7 and 8 indicate opposing interests that should be given due respect and reconciliation").

[290] Donald P. Harris (2006), Carrying a Good Joke Too Far: TRIPS and Treaties of Adhesion, *Journal of International Law*, vol. 27, no. 3, at p. 743; see also Daniel Gervais (2012), *The TRIPS Agreement: Drafting History and Analysis*, Fourth Edition, Hebden Bridge, UK: Sweet & Maxwell, p. 163. (recognizing that "[the object and purpose of the TRIPS] confirm the need to achieve a balance . . . between the private rights of intellectual property owners and cases where the public interest may trump some aspects of the protection of intellectual property").

The objective of environmental protection, in particular, climate change mitigation, is within the scope of public interest in Articles 7 and 8 of TRIPS. Furthermore, as discussed in Section 5.3.1, environmental protection is one of the pillars of "sustainable development" which is the WTO's objective. While the TRIPS Agreement does not prescribe how this objective should be attained, increasing innovation and transfer of ESTs is essential for environmental protection, in particular, climate change mitigation (see Section 2.1). Measures adopted by a WTO Member to facilitate the innovation, transfer and dissemination of ESTs in order to mitigate climate change undoubtedly benefit public interest and contribute to sustainable development. Therefore, both the WTO's sustainable development objective and the overarching object and purpose of the TRIPS Agreement provide a legal basis for a balanced and tailored interpretation of IP-related obligations for addressing climate change concerns. In other words, WTO Members may resort to these objectives to enlarge their domestic policy space in tailoring the IP regime to their needs to address climate change.

However, those balancing objectives should not be used to alter the meaning of particular TRIPS provisions. As pointed out by Yu (2009), the extent to which they can be "a true blessing" will depend on whether the WTO Members "can use them effectively, to their advantage, and to the fullest possible extent".[291]

5.4 CONTEXTUAL ELEMENTS FOR INTERPRETING THE TRIPS AGREEMENT

As discussed in Section 5.2.2.4, subsequent agreements and practices in relation to the interpretation of treaties as well as any relevant rules of international law are "primary, obligatory sources of treaty interpretation" according to Article 31(3) of the VCLT.[292] By describing these three elements as the authentic means of interpretation, it is recognised that the common intentions of the parties possess "a specific authority regarding the identification of the meaning of the treaty [terms], even after the conclusion of the treaty".[293]

---

[291] Peter Yu (2009), Objectives and Principles of the TRIPS Agreement, *Houston Law Review*, vol. 46, pp. 979–1046, at p. 1046.

[292] Robert Howse (2007), *The WTO System: Law, Politics & Legitimacy*, London: Cameron May, p. 231.

[293] *Report of the International Law Commission, General Assembly Official Records*, Sixty-Eighth Session, Supplement No. 10, UN Doc. A/68/10, 6 May–7 June and 8 July–9 August 2013, at p. 21.

Subsequent agreement and subsequent practice are designated as "the main tools for determining the consent of parties to evolving interpretations of treaty obligations".[294] In the WTO context, these elements exclusively cover instruments adopted after the entry into force of the WTO Agreements, and they link the WTO treaties, in our case, the TRIPS Agreement, to modernity.[295] Article 31(3)(c) of the VCLT demands reference to other relevant rules of international law when interpreting the WTO Agreements, thereby opening the door to non-WTO law including international environmental law.

The following sections address, in turn, the relevant subsequent agreements and subsequent practices and rules of international law for interpreting the TRIPS Agreement to facilitate the innovation and transfer of ESTs.

5.4.1 *Subsequent Agreement: The Doha Declaration*

5.4.1.1 The Doha Declaration as a Subsequent Agreement under Article 31(3)(a) of the VCLT

This section considers whether the Doha Declaration[296] may constitute a "subsequent agreement" on the interpretation of a provision of a covered agreement, in this case, the TRIPS Agreement, under Article 31(3)(a) of the VCLT. As demonstrated in Section 5.2.2.4.1, based on the text of Article 31(3)(a) of the VCLT, a declaration adopted by WTO Members may qualify as a "subsequent agreement" regarding the interpretation of the TRIPS Agreement or the application of its provisions if: (1) the declaration is an agreement between the parties; (2) the terms and content of the declaration express an agreement between WTO Members on the interpretation or application of a TRIPS provision and (3) the declaration is, in a temporal sense, adopted subsequent to the TRIPS Agreement.[297]

With regard to the first element, it is noted that the Doha Declaration, as a ministerial declaration, was adopted on 14 November 2001 by consensus of all WTO Members at the Ministerial Conference, described by the WTO

---

[294] Alexander M. Feldman (2009), Evolving Treaty Obligations: A Proposal for Analysing Subsequent Practice Derived from WTO Dispute Settlement, *International Law and Politics*, vol. 41, pp. 655–706, at pp. 657 and 662 (further noting that "[t]he concepts of subsequent agreement and subsequent practice are premised on the idea that over time, parties can informally consent to new and different interpretations of treaty obligations").

[295] Mitsuo Matsushita et al. (2006), *The World Trade Organization: Law, Practice, and Policy*, 2nd edn, Oxford University Press, pp. 33–4.

[296] See also Appendix : Declaration on the TRIPS Agreement and Public Health.

[297] See also Appellate Body Report, *US – Clove Cigarettes*, para. 262.

Secretariat as "the topmost decision-making body of the WTO".[298] In particular, the text of the Doha Declaration was explicitly written using terms such as "we agree that ..." and "we reaffirm that ...".[299] Therefore, the Doha Declaration constitutes "an agreement between 'the parties'" within the meaning of Article 31(3)(a) of the VCLT.

As regards the second element, the key question to be answered is whether the Doha Declaration expresses an agreement between Members on the interpretation or application of the terms of the TRIPS Agreement. It has generally been accepted that the content of the Doha Declaration adequately represents an interpretation of the TRIPS Agreement or an application of its provisions.[300] This is evidenced from the text of the Doha Declaration. For instance, in paragraph 4 of the Doha Declaration, WTO Members explicitly agree that "the [TRIPS] Agreement can and should be *interpreted* and *implemented* in a manner supportive of WTO members' right to protect public health and, in particular, to promote access to medicines for all" (emphasis added). In addition, Haugen (2007) considered that the intention of the Declaration "must be understood as clarifying specific provisions of TRIPS with regard to how these provisions shall be interpreted and applied".[301]

It was at the Ministerial Conference that WTO Members were able to agree on the manner in which the terms of the TRIPS Agreement "can and should be interpreted and implemented". It can be noted that under Article IX: 2 of the Marrakesh Agreement, the Ministerial Conference has the authority to

---

[298] Declaration on the TRIPS Agreement and Public Health, WT/MIN (01)/DEC/2, adopted on 14 November 2001; see also "Ministerial Conferences", WTO website, available at www.wto .org/english/thewto_e/minist_e/minist_e.htm

[299] Declaration on the TRIPS Agreement and Public Health, WT/MIN (01)/DEC/2, adopted on 14 November 2001, paras. 4 and 7.

[300] See, e.g., Joost Pauwelyn (2008), *Conflict of Norms in Public International Law: How WTO Law Relates to Other Rules of International Law*, Cambridge University Press, p. 47; Asif H. Qureshi (2012), *Interpreting WTO Agreements: Problems and Perspectives*, Cambridge University Press, p. 35; Hans Morten Haugen (2007), *The Right to Food and the TRIPS Agreement: With a Particular Emphasis on Developing Countries' Measures for Food Production and Distribution*, Leiden, Netherlands: Martinus Nijhoff Publishers, p. 77; Frederick M. Abbott (2004), WTO Dispute Settlement Practice Relating to the Agreement on Trade-Related Intellectual Property Rights, in Federioo Ortino and Petersmann Ernst-Ulrich (eds.), *The WTO Dispute Settlement System 1995–2003*, Alphen aan den Rijn, Netherlands: Kluwer Law International, pp. 421–53, at p. 445 (stating that "the Doha Declaration should from a jurisprudential standpoint be considered to authoritatively interpret the TRIPS Agreement").

[301] Hans Morten Haugen (2007), *The Right to Food and the TRIPS Agreement: With a Particular Emphasis on Developing Countries' Measures for Food Production and Distribution*, Leiden, Netherlands: Martinus Nijhoff Publishers, p. 77.

adopt interpretations of the TRIPS Agreement.[302] Furthermore, it can be observed that the Doha Declaration does not modify, add to or diminish legal rights and obligations of the Members as it simply clarifies the application or the interpretation of the TRIPS Agreement.[303] Some scholars thus consider the Doha Declaration to constitute an "authoritative interpretation" within the meaning of Article IX: 2 of the Marrakesh Agreement.[304]

However, Article IX: 2 requires that an authoritative interpretation shall be made "on the basis of a recommendation by the Council overseeing the functioning of that Agreement". In the case of the Doha Declaration, some scholars submit that the Declaration was negotiated with the TRIPS Council, which is the Council overseeing the functioning of the TRIPS Agreement, and the Ministerial Conference adopted what had been agreed upon in the TRIPS Council, and thus "there was an implied recommendation".[305] However, other scholars consider that the TRIPS Council does not seem to have made a recommendation to the Ministerial Conference as is required by Article IX: 2.[306] Thus, it is debatable whether the

---

[302] Article IX: 2 of the Marrakesh Agreement provides that: "The Ministerial Conference and the General Council shall have the exclusive authority to adopt interpretations of this Agreement and of the Multilateral Trade Agreements. In the case of an interpretation of a Multilateral Trade Agreement in Annex 1, they shall exercise their authority on the basis of a recommendation by the Council overseeing the functioning of that Agreement."

[303] See, e.g., Joost Pauwelyn (2008), *Conflict of Norms in Public International Law: How WTO Law Relates to Other Rules of International Law*, Cambridge University Press, p. 47 (stating that "[t]he language of the Declaration seems to imply that it simply interprets the TRIPS Agreement"); Asif H. Qureshi (2012), *Interpreting WTO Agreements: Problems and Perspectives*, Cambridge University Press, p. 35 (arguing that "[the Declaration] is considered to be a subsequent agreement between the members of the WTO regarding the application of the TRIPS Agreement").

[304] See, e.g., Daya Shanker (2002), The Vienna Convention on the Law of Treaties, the Dispute Settlement System of the WTO and the Doha Declaration on the TRIPS Agreement, *Journal of World Trade*, vol. 36, no. 4, pp. 721–2, at p. 722 (stating that "the most significant part of this Declaration is that for the first time . . . the Ministerial Conference used Article IX(b) of the Marrakesh Agreement to arrive at an interpretation of a Multilateral Trade Agreement").

[305] See, e.g., Susan Isiko Štrba (2012), *International Copyright Law and Access to Education in Developing Countries: Exploring Multilateral Legal and Quasi-Legal Solutions*, Leiden, Netherlands: Martinus Nijhoff Publishers, p. 169.

[306] See e.g., Joost Pauwelyn (2008), *Conflict of Norms in Public International Law: How WTO Law Relates to Other Rules of International Law*, Cambridge University Press, p. 47 (noting that "[t]his 'declaration' does not specify the legal basis pursuant to which it was adopted . . . This formality [on the basis of a recommendation by the Council overseeing the functioning of that Agreement] does not seem to be complied with"); see also Frederick M. Abbott (2002), The Doha Declaration on the TRIPS Agreement and Public Health: Lighting a Dark Corner at the WTO, *Journal of International Economic Law*, vol. 5, no. 2, pp. 469–505, at p. 492 (stating that "paragraph 4 [of the Doha Declaration] is not an 'interpretation' in the technical

Doha Declaration constitutes an authoritative interpretation under Article IX: 2 of the Marrakesh Agreement.

Even if the Doha Declaration does not constitute an "authoritative interpretation", there is no doubt that it relates to the interpretation or the application of the TRIPS Agreement. Therefore, the Doha Declaration meets the second requirement for being considered a "subsequent agreement". [307]

With regard to the third element, it is noted that the Doha Declaration was adopted by consensus on 14 November 2001 on the occasion of the fourth Ministerial Conference of the WTO. Thus, it is beyond dispute that the Doha Declaration was adopted subsequent to the TRIPS Agreement.

For the foregoing reasons, the Doha Declaration can be considered as a "subsequent agreement" between WTO Members in interpreting the TRIPS Agreement or applying its provisions under Article 31(3)(a) of the VCLT. As pointed out by Frankel (2006), the Doha Declaration qualifies as a subsequent agreement between the parties in relation to the interpretation of the TRIPS Agreement, and thus it constitutes a guide to interpreting TRIPS by virtue of Article 31(3)(a) of the VCLT.[308] According to the ILC, "an agreement as to the interpretation of a provision reached after the conclusion of the treaty represents an authentic interpretation by the parties which must be read into the treaty for the purposes of its interpretation".[309] Thus, as a subsequent agreement between WTO Members on the interpretation of the TRIPS Agreement, the Doha Declaration must be read into the TRIPS Agreement for the purpose of its interpretation. The extent to which the Doha Declaration will inform the interpretation or application of a term or provision of the TRIPS Agreement, however, will depend on the degree to which it "bears specifically" on the interpretation or application of the respective term or

---

sense of Article IX:2 of the WTO Agreement since it was not based on a recommendation of the TRIPS Council").

[307] This is confirmed by the WTO jurisprudence. For example, in *US – Clove Cigarettes* (2012), the Appellate Body found that a decision by the Ministerial Conference regarding the interpretation of a provision of a covered agreement, namely the Doha Ministerial Decision on Implementation-Related Issues and Concerns constituted a subsequent agreement between the parties, within the meaning of Article 31.3(a), despite that it is not adopted pursuant to Article IX.2 of the Marrakesh Agreement; see Appellate Body Report, *US – Clove Cigarettes*, paras. 259 and 268.

[308] Susy Frankel (2006), WTO Application of "the Customary Rules of Interpretation of Public International Law" to Intellectual Property, *Virginia Journal of International Law*, vol. 46, pp. 366–431, at p. 400.

[309] *Report of the International Law Commission on the Work of Its Eighteenth Session*, 4 May–19 July 1966, Official Reports of the General Assembly, Twenty-First Session, Supplement No. 9, UN Doc. A/6309/Rev. 1, United Nations, p. 221.

its provision.[310] The following sections examine the background, content and the implications of the Doha Declaration.

5.4.1.2 The Doha Declaration: Its Context and Content

It is observed that patents may lead to higher prices for pharmaceuticals, thus reducing the affordability and accessibility of the medicine for the poor.[311] As early as the late 1980s when the TRIPS Agreement was being negotiated, developing countries expressed great concern over subjecting inventions related to public health and nutrition such as pharmaceuticals, chemicals and foodstuffs to strict patenting rules.[312] It is true that the TRIPS Agreement does provide safeguards to remedy the negative effects of patent protection, or patent abuse, in order to address such concerns.[313] However, as noted by Taubman et al. (2012), there was a particular concern over "the extent to

---

[310] Appellate Body Report, *US – Tuna II (Mexico)*, para. 372 (finding that "[t]he extent to which this Decision [TBT Committee Decision] will inform the interpretation and application of a term or provision of the TBT Agreement in a specific case, however, will depend on the degree to which it 'bears specifically' on the interpretation and application of the respective term or provision").

[311] See, e.g., WHO, WIPO and WTO (2012), *Promoting Access to Medical Technologies and Innovation: Intersections between Public Health, Intellectual Property and Trade*, published by WHO, WIPO and WTO, p. 87 (in order to understand the effect of pharmaceutical product patents, citing a finding by Chaudhuri et al. (2006) that "the introduction of product patents on pharmaceuticals in just one therapeutic subsegment in India would lead to significantly higher prices and welfare losses, which are estimated to range from US \$145 million to US \$450 million per year"); Shubham Chaudhuri et al. (2006), Estimating the Effects of Global Patent Protection in Pharmaceuticals: A Case Study of Quinolones in India, *American Economic Review*, vol. 96, no. 5, pp. 1477–514; Holger Hestermeyer (2007), *Human Rights and the WTO: The Case of Patents and Access to Medicines*, Oxford University Press, pp. 148–52 (through empirical studies and extrapolations, finding that patents lead to higher prices for pharmaceuticals and reduce the accessibility of the medicine for the poor; patents impede access is not negated by the fact that other factors impede access ever more); The UK Commission on Intellectual Property Rights (2002), *Integrating Intellectual Property Rights and Development Policy*, Report of the Commission on Intellectual Property Rights, London, pp. 36–8 (finding that "the introduction of patent regimes into [lower and middle income] developing countries has, or is predicted to have, the effect of raising prices. The estimates range widely depending on drugs and countries being considered – from 12 [per cent] to over 200 [per cent], but even the lower estimates imply very substantial costs for consumers").

[312] Note by the Secretariat, Meeting of Negotiating Group of 12–14 July 1989, Negotiating Group on Trade-Related Aspects of Intellectual Property Rights, including Trade in Counterfeit Goods, 12 September 1989, GATT Doc. MTN.GNG/NG11/14, para. 79.1; see also Frederick M. Abbott (2002), The Doha Declaration on the TRIPS Agreement and Public Health: Lighting a Dark Corner at the WTO, *Journal of International Economic Law*, vol. 5, no. 2, pp. 469–505, at p. 470.

[313] See Articles 7, 8, 30, 31 and 40 of the TRIPS Agreement.

which governments would feel free to use, to the full, these flexibilities without the fear of coming under pressure from their trading partners".[314]

In practice, different views were expressed regarding "the nature and scope" of the TRIPS flexibilities.[315] As Gathii (2002) observed, while developing countries have considered that the TRIPS Agreement does not limit their regulatory sovereignty to address public interest concerns, some developed countries have argued that the only TRIPS flexibility is "the staggered implementation periods" that developing countries enjoy under the Agreement.[316] Developing Members' concerns over the effects of patents on access to medicine were intensified as the United States, EU and their research-based pharmaceutical companies initiated aggressive campaigns or litigations against countries that threatened to make use of TRIPS flexibilities.[317]

In this context, a special session on the TRIPS Agreement and access to medicine was held in 2001 by the TRIPS Council at the request of the African Group, that is, all African members of the WTO.[318] The then WTO Director-General, Mike Moore, supported this special session by delivering a statement, entitled "Countries Must Feel Secure That They Can Use TRIPS' Flexibility", stating that:

> The WTO's TRIPS Agreement plays a vital role in tackling these [access to medicine] problems. It strikes a carefully-negotiated balance between

---

[314] Antony Taubman et al. (2012), *A Handbook on the WTO TRIPS Agreement*, Cambridge University Press, p. 180 (further noting that "questions were raised as to whether these flexibilities would be interpreted by the WTO and its Members in a broad, pro-public health way").

[315] Ibid.

[316] James Thuo Gathii (2002), The Legal Status of the Doha Declaration on TRIPS and Public Health under the Vienna Convention on the Law of the Treaties, *Harvard Journal of Law & Technology*, vol. 15, no. 2, pp. 292–317, at p. 292.

[317] Frederick M. Abbott (2002), The Doha Declaration on the TRIPS Agreement and Public Health: Lighting a Dark Corner at the WTO, *Journal of International Economic Law*, vol. 5, no. 2, pp. 469–505, at p. 471 (further noting that "[t]he most visible case involved a multi-pronged attack against the government of the Republic of South Africa that combined government threats to impose trade and economic sanctions with private Pharma litigation to delay the implementation of health reform legislation"); see also Holger Hestermeyer (2007), *Human Rights and the WTO: The Case of Patents and Access to Medicines*, Oxford University Press, p. 256.

[318] Minutes of Meeting, Council for Trade-Related Aspects of Intellectual Property Rights, WTO Doc. IP/C/M/30, 1 June 2001, para. 229 (The representative of Zimbabwe, speaking on behalf of the African Group, saying that "the African Group would like to bring into the TRIPS Council an issue that had aroused public interest and was being actively debated outside the WTO, but one which the Council could not afford to ignore especially given the need to clarify the role of intellectual property rights protection in dealing with pandemics such as the one caused by AIDS and other life-threatening diseases").

providing intellectual property protection – which is essential if new medicines and treatments are to be developed – and allowing countries the flexibility to ensure that treatments reach the world's poorest and most vulnerable people.

Countries must feel secure that they can use this flexibility. The work started today in the TRIPS Council should reinforce that security.[319]

The special session of the TRIPS Council, held in June 2001, sought to clarify the TRIPS flexibilities to which Members are entitled to and examine the relationship between IPRs and access to medicines. The developing countries' submission (IP/C/W/296, 2001) aimed to give primacy to public health over private IP rights by arguing that "[n]othing in the TRIPS Agreement should prevent Members from taking measures to protect public health" and suggesting that "where the provisions of the Agreement may be considered insufficient to protect public health, Members may wish to bring further proposals for modifications in the Agreement, with a view to [increasing] its flexibility".[320] By contrast, the delegations of Australia, Canada, Japan, Switzerland and the United States (IP/C/W/313, 2001) submitted that "strong, effective and balanced protection for intellectual property is a necessary incentive for research and development of life-saving drugs", therefore recognising that intellectual property contributes to public health objectives globally.[321] The negotiations were contentious, but Members managed to adopt the Doha Declaration on the TRIPS Agreement and Public Health by consensus on 14 November 2001.

The title of the Doha Declaration, "Declaration on the TRIPS Agreement and Public Health", incorporates the general term "public health" that was used in the initial developing country Members' submission (IP/C/W/296, 2001) rather than restricting its scope to "medicine for HIV/AIDS and other pandemics" as was suggested by some developed countries (IP/C/W/313, 2001).[322] The text of Doha Declaration, for example, the first paragraph, recognised the gravity of the public health problems being faced by the

---

[319] Mike Moore (2001), Countries Must Feel Secure That They Can Use TRIPS' Flexibility, 20 June, available at www.wto.org/english/news_e/news01_e/dg_trips_medicines_010620_e.htm

[320] Submission by the African Group, Barbados, Bolivia, Brazil, Cuba, Dominican Republic, Ecuador, Honduras, India, Indonesia, Jamaica, Pakistan, Paraguay, Philippines, Peru, Sri Lanka, Thailand and Venezuela, Council for Trade-Related Aspects of Intellectual Property Rights, WTO Doc. IP/C/W/296, 29 June 2001, p. 1.

[321] Preambular Language for Ministerial Declaration: Contribution from Australia, Canada, Japan, Switzerland and the United States, Council for Trade-Related Aspects of Intellectual Property Rights, WTO Doc. IP/C/W/313, 4 October 2001, p. 1.

[322] See WTO Doc. IP/C/W/296, p. 1 and WTO Doc. IP/C/W/313, p. 1.

developing countries in general, while emphasising "those resulting from HIV/AIDS, tuberculosis, malaria and other epidemics" in particular.[323] As Abbott (2002) observed, this signals that the Doha Declaration applies to a wide set of public health concerns, and not limited to certain special circumstances.[324] The reference to the term "public health" is thus significant in that it shows the intention of WTO Members to address public health concerns in general rather than target only certain diseases.

The entire Doha Declaration is composed of seven paragraphs. The first three paragraphs are preambular in nature, acknowledging the gravity of the public health problems while stressing the role of TRIPS in the context of public health.[325] In paragraph 3, while WTO Members stress that IP protection is essential for the development of new medicines, they acknowledge "the concerns about its effects on prices". This consensus is significant, as it reflects WTO Members' common understanding that IP protection has dual effects and that it "can, indeed, be an impediment to access to medicine".[326]

The fourth paragraph of the Doha Declaration is of great significance. It reveals all WTO Members' agreement that the TRIPS Agreement "does not and should not prevent Members from taking measures to protect public health". However, WTO Members immediately qualified this provision by reiterating their commitment to the TRIPS Agreement. This paragraph is understood by UNCTAD and ICTSD (2005) as directed to elaborate on the meaning of Article 8.1 in the context of public health.[327] Accordingly, paragraph 4 does not constitute a rebalance of the Agreement in the sense that

---

[323] Declaration on the TRIPS Agreement and Public Health, WT/MIN (01)/DEC/2, adopted on 14 November 2001.

[324] Frederick M. Abbott (2002), The Doha Declaration on the TRIPS Agreement and Public Health: Lighting a Dark Corner at the WTO, *Journal of International Economic Law*, vol. 5, no. 2, pp. 469–505, at p. 490; see also Holger Hestermeyer (2007), Human Rights and the WTO: The Case of Patents and Access to Medicines, Oxford University Press, p. 258.

[325] See, e.g., Carlos Correa (2002), Implications of the Doha Declaration on the TRIPS Agreement and Public Health, World Health Organization, p. 5; Frederick M. Abbott (2002), at p. 490 (stating that "[t]he first three paragraphs (1–3) of the Declaration are in the nature of preambles to the operative paragraphs 4–7").

[326] Holger Hestermeyer (2007), *Human Rights and the WTO: The Case of Patents and Access to Medicines*, Oxford University Press, p. 258; see also Carlos Correa (2002), Implications of the Doha Declaration on the TRIPS Agreement and Public Health, World Health Organization, p. 7 (stating that "[t]he consensus achieved on patent protection's impact on drug prices may be considered one of the major political achievements of the developing countries in the Doha Ministerial Declaration").

[327] UNCTAD and ICTSD (2005), *Resource Book on TRIPS and Development*, Cambridge University Press, p. 131.

public health overrides the private interests of IP holders.[328] Nevertheless, this paragraph offers an interpretative guideline by further stating that:

> we affirm that the Agreement can and should be interpreted and implemented in a manner supportive of WTO Members' right to protect public health and, in particular, to promote access to medicines for all.
>
> In this connection, we affirm the right of WTO Members to use, to the full, the provisions in the TRIPS Agreement, which provide flexibility for this purpose.

"Members' right to protect public health, and, in particular, to promote access to medicines for all", introduced by the first part of the fourth paragraph, is not explicitly derived from the TRIPS Agreement, but is "exercisable in light of contemporary international concern" regarding the public health crisis.[329] As to the second part of the fourth paragraph, the WTO Secretariat views these important statements as a signal from all WTO Members that "they will not try to prevent each other from using [TRIPS flexibilities]".[330] Therefore, "in cases of ambiguity, or where more than one interpretation [is] possible", a treaty interpreter should "opt for the interpretation that is effectively 'supportive of WTO Members' right to protect public health'".[331]

Accordingly, in light of paragraph 4, the fifth paragraph of the Doha Declaration enumerates, in a non-exhaustive manner, the TRIPS flexibilities that can be used for the purposes of adopting measures to protect public health.[332] Its chapeau embraces a balance of rights and obligations, and while maintaining their commitments in the TRIPS Agreement, Members recognise the existence of TRIPS flexibilities. Paragraph 5(a) highlights the importance of the objectives and principles of the TRIPS Agreement in interpreting the TRIPS provisions. This provision is a mere reminder that the rules established by Article 31(1) of the VCLT apply to the interpretation of TRIPS provisions as well. Subparagraphs (b), (c) and (d) of paragraph 5 explicitly

---

[328] Carlos Correa (2002), Implications of the Doha Declaration on the TRIPS Agreement and Public Health, World Health Organization, p. 11.

[329] James Thuo Gathii (2002), The Legal Status of the Doha Declaration on TRIPS and Public Health under the Vienna Convention on the Law of the Treaties, *Harvard Journal of Law & Technology*, vol. 15, no. 2, pp. 292–317, at pp. 301 and 302.

[330] WTO Secretariat, The Separate Declaration Explained, available at www.wto.org/english/ tratop_e/trips_e/healthdeclexpln_e.htm

[331] See, e.g., Holger Hestermeyer (2007), *Human Rights and the WTO: the Case of Patents and Access to Medicines*, Oxford University Press, p. 258; Carlos Correa (2002), Implications of the Doha Declaration on the TRIPS Agreement and Public Health, World Health Organization, p. 12.

[332] The chapeau of paragraph 5 of the TRIPS Agreement.

confirm that Members have the right to grant compulsory licences, the freedom to determine the grounds for such licences and what constitutes a "national emergency and other circumstances of extreme urgency" as well as the right to establish their own exhaustion regime. As discussed in the beginning of this section, interpretations regarding these flexibilities have been the subject of heated debates.[333] Paragraph 5 offers clarification regarding the nature and scope of these flexibilities. Accordingly, as Correa (2002) notes, the attempts to prevent the use of available flexibilities would "run counter to the spirit and purpose of the TRIPS Agreement".[334]

In order to ensure that all Members can "make effective use of compulsory licenses", paragraph 6 of the Doha Declaration instructs the TRIPS Council to find an expeditious solution to address the problems that exist for Members with "insufficient or no manufacturing capacities in the pharmaceutical sectors". Consequently, a decision regarding the implementation of paragraph 6 of the Doha Declaration (WT/L/540) was adopted by the General Council on 30 August 2003.[335]

The last paragraph of the Doha Declaration is LDC-specific, first reaffirming "the commitment of developed country Members to provide incentives to their enterprises and institutions to promote and encourage technology transfer" to LDCs and then instructing the TRIPS Council to extend the transition period for LDC Members with respect to pharmaceutical products until 1 January 2016.

5.4.1.3 The Implications of the Doha Declaration

It should be noted that there are voices emanating from the pharmaceutical industry and scholars objecting to the Doha Declaration as they perceive it to be "a threat to vital incentives for research and development".[336] However, in

---

[333] See also Antony Taubman et al. (2012), *A Handbook on the WTO TRIPS Agreement*, Cambridge University Press, p. 180 (noting that "different views were expressed about the nature and scope of the flexibilities in the TRIPS Agreement, for example, in regard to compulsory licensing and parallel imports").

[334] Carlos Correa (2002), Implications of the Doha Declaration on the TRIPS Agreement and Public Health, World Health Organization, p. 13.

[335] Decision of 30 August 2003: Implementation of paragraph 6 of the Doha Declaration on the TRIPS Agreement and Public Health, WTO Doc. WT/L/540, 2 September 2003.

[336] Holger Hestermeyer (2007), *Human Rights and the WTO: The Case of Patents and Access to Medicines*, Oxford University Press, p. 261; see also Alan O. Sykes (2002), TRIPS, Pharmaceuticals, Developing Countries, and the Doha "Solution", *Chicago Journal of International Law*, vol. 3, pp. 47–68, at p. 49 (stating that "the Doha Declaration casts great doubt on the future credibility of patent rights for pharmaceuticals in developing nations. The

general, the Doha Declaration has been labelled as "a breakthrough" in addressing the tension between IP rights and public health policies.[337]

In essence, the Doha Declaration is a mere clarification of some TRIPS provisions, and therefore it neither adds nor diminishes the rights and obligations set out in the Agreement.[338] As a result, the Doha Declaration does not establish any new rights that override the TRIPS obligations.[339]

However, the implications of the Doha Declaration are significant: firstly, it clears up some of the uncertainty in the interpretation of the TRIPS Agreement and reaffirms Members' regulatory sovereignty to authorise compulsory licensing and permit international exhaustion. It, thus, provides a legal basis for and guidance to governments who want to make use of the TRIPS flexibilities at the national level.[340] Accordingly, in the words of Barratt (2008), a major "political obstacle" was established for some Members to initiate WTO challenges against those countries that, in order to protect

---

result may be quite unfortunate for research incentives, especially those relating to particular diseases").

[337] See, e.g., Thomas A. Haag (2002), TRIPS Since Doha: How Far Will the WTO Go toward Modifying the Terms for Compulsory Licensing? *Journal of the Patent & Trademark Office Society*, vol. 84, pp. 945–81, at p. 952 (noting that "[t]he Doha Declaration was received by those advocating the position of the developing world, with great enthusiasm and hailed as a leap toward correcting the social injustice allegedly resulting from the high price of patented drugs"); Ellen 't Hoen (2002), TRIPS, Pharmaceutical Patents, and Access to Essential Medicines: A Long Way From Seattle to Doha, *Chicago Journal of International Law*, vol. 3, no. 1, pp. 27–46, at p. 28 (noting that "[p]ublic health advocates welcomed the Doha Declaration as an important achievement ... the Doha Declaration broke new ground in guaranteeing Member's access to medical products"); Susan K. Sell and Aseem Prakash (2004), Using Ideas Strategically: The Contest between Business and NGO Networks in Intellectual Property Rights, *International Studies Quarterly*, vol. 48, pp. 143–75, at p. 167 (describing the Doha Declaration as "a key victory for the NGO campaign"); see also Holger Hestermeyer (2007), *Human Rights and the WTO: The Case of Patents and Access to Medicines*, Oxford University Press, p. 261; Jean-Frederic Morin and Richard E. Gold (2010), Consensus-Seeking, Distrust and Rhetorical Entrapment: The WTO Decision on Access to Medicines, *European Journal of International Relations*, vol. 16, no. 4, pp. 563–87, at p. 564.

[338] See, e.g., Eric Noehrenberg (2003), TRIPS, the Doha Declaration and Public Health, *The Journal of World Intellectual Property*, vol. 6, pp. 379–83, at p. 379 (noting that "the Doha Declaration did not add anything new; it did not weaken TRIPS; it did not change any of its obligations").

[339] See, e.g., Peter Drahos (2007), Four Lessons for Developing Countries from the Trade Negotiations Over Access to Medicines, *Liverpool Law Review*, vol. 28, pp. 11–39, at p. 23; Holger Hestermeyer (2007), *Human Rights and the WTO: The Case of Patents and Access to Medicines*, Oxford University Press, p. 261.

[340] Roger Kampf and Hannu Wager (2011), The Role of the TRIPS Agreement in the Global Health Policy, *Stanford Journal of Law, Science & Policy*, pp. 17–41, at p. 26 (noting that "[s]ince its adoption, the Doha Declaration has served as a landmark and benchmark for all stakeholders, including international organizations, governments, the private sector and civil society. It has been referred to in numerous instruments, including many WHO solutions").

public health, grant the compulsory licensing or permit the parallel imports of patented drugs.[341]

Moreover, the most important value of the Doha Declaration lies in that it has reinforced the common understanding that the TRIPS Agreement represents a balanced and flexible IP framework that is responsive to the broader public interest needs and public policy objectives.[342] The Doha Declaration reaffirmed the flexibilities provided under the TRIPS Agreement. When properly applied, these flexibilities facilitate the dissemination and transfer of patented technologies to meet certain public interests such as those mentioned in the Preamble of the Marrakesh Agreement or in Articles 7 and 8 of the TRIPS Agreement.[343]

As discussed in Section 5.2.2.4.1, as a subsequent agreement to the TRIPS Agreement, the Doha Declaration must "shed light on" the interpretation of the TRIPS Agreement. Further, although it was adopted to facilitate access to medicine for public health purposes, the Doha Declaration sets a precedent for developing issue-specific interpretation to address other common concerns of humankind, such as climate change. The Appellate Body's ruling in *US – Shrimp* (1998) also supports reading the terms of the TRIPS Agreement "in the light of contemporary concerns of the community of nations" when dealing with environmental protection such as climate change.[344] Thus, the Doha Declaration could serve as a model for the Members to adopt a Ministerial Declaration for climate change with a view to clarifying flexibilities to promote innovation and transfer of ESTs.

5.4.2 *Relevant Subsequent Practices in the Interpretation of the TRIPS Agreement*

In the TRIPS context, the WTO jurisprudence is not very consistent with regard to whether individual countries' subsequent acts concerning the TRIPS flexibilities constitute subsequent practices under Article 31.3(b) of

---

[341] Amanda Barratt (2008), *The Battle for Policy Space: Strategic Advantages of a Human Rights Approach in International Intellectual Property Negotiations*, PhD dissertation, University of Cape Town, p. 128.

[342] Roger Kampf and Hannu Wager (2011), The Role of the TRIPS Agreement in the Global Health Policy, *Stanford Journal of Law, Science & Policy*, pp. 17–41, at p. 26.

[343] See, e.g., Beas Edson Rodrigues (2012), *The General Exception Clauses of the TRIPS Agreement: Promoting Sustainable Development*, vol. 17, Cambridge University Press, p. 77; Henning Grosse Ruse-Khan (2008), A Comparative Analysis of Policy Space in WTO Law", Research Paper Series no. 08-02, Max Planck Institute for Intellectual Property, Competition and Tax Law, p. 68.

[344] Appellate Body Report, *US – Shrimp*, para. 129.

the VCLT. The panel in *Canada – Pharmaceutical Patents* (2000) did not accord any weight to Canada's argument that "the subsequent practices of certain WTO Member governments supported the view that Article 30 was understood to permit regulatory review exceptions". In the panel's view, individual countries' subsequent acts did not constitute "practice in the application of the treaty which establishes the agreement of the parties regarding its interpretation" under Article 31.3(b) of the Vienna Convention.[345]

However, the panel in *US – Section 110(5) Copyright Act* (2000) states that:

> State practice as reflected in the national copyright laws of Berne Union members before and after 1948, 1967 and 1971, as well as of WTO Members before and after the date that the TRIPS Agreement became applicable to them, confirms our conclusion about the minor exceptions doctrine.[346]

Nevertheless, in footnote 68, the panel explicitly refused to take any position on whether these examples of state practice are sufficient to constitute "subsequent practice" for the purpose of Article 31(3)(b) of the VCLT.[347]

It is thus debatable whether state practices in providing flexibilities such as the exceptions and limitations based on the TRIPS Agreement can be deemed as "subsequent practice" within the meaning of Article 31(3)(b) of the VCLT. As discussed in Section 5.2.2.4.2, a state practice in relation to the TRIPS flexibilities may qualify as a "subsequent practice" regarding the interpretation of the TRIPS Agreement or the application of its provisions if: (1) the state practice is a common, consistent, discernible pattern of acts or pronouncements and (2) those acts or pronouncements imply agreement on the interpretation of the relevant provision.

As regards the first element, it is common practice for countries to provide for TRIPS flexibilities such as exceptions and limitations to patents. This has been confirmed by WIPO member states' responses to the Standing Committee on the Law of Patents (SCP) Questionnaire on Exceptions and Limitations to Patent Rights.[348] The Experts' Study on Exclusion from Patentable Subject Matter and Exceptions and Limitations to the Rights (SCP/15/3)

---

[345] Panel Report, *Canada – Pharmaceutical Patents*, para. 7.47.
[346] Panel Report, *US – Section 110(5) Copyright Act*, para. 6.55.   [347] Ibid., footnote 68.
[348] WIPO, Questionnaire on Exceptions and Limitations to Patent Rights: Tables and Links to the replies received from member states and regional offices to the SCP, available at: www.wipo.int/scp/en/exceptions/

prepared by the WIPO Secretariat further reveals countries' common and consistent practices in providing exceptions and limitations to patent rights based on the TRIPS flexibilities.[349] The author also recalls that to establish a "subsequent practice", there is no need to show that each party has engaged in a particular practice, only that "all have accepted it, albeit tacitly".[350] Thus, when certain TRIPS flexibilities are incorporated into the national laws of various WTO Members, state practices (as reflected in their national legislations) may constitute a "common, consistent and discernible pattern" of acts or pronouncements.

The second element concerns whether the utilisation of certain TRIPS flexibilities by various WTO Members in their domestic laws implies agreement on the interpretation of the relevant TRIPS provisions. With regard to the nature and scope of the TRIPS flexibilities, considerable disagreements existed during the TRIPS negotiations among negotiating parties. However, the ultimate adoption of the TRIPS Agreement has signalled that an agreement among WTO Members was reached in relation to certain limitations and exceptions to IP rights. Thus, it can be inferred that WTO Members' practices in providing such limitations and exceptions based on the TRIPS flexibilities may constitute the agreement of the parties regarding the interpretation of such flexibilities. When different views as to the nature and scope of some limitations and exceptions were observed, the Doha Declaration was adopted to further clarify certain specific flexibilities. It is noted that the Doha Declaration adopted by the WTO Ministerial Conference represents Members' common understanding regarding the interpretation of specific TRIPS flexibilities. Thus, WTO Members' utilisation of specific flexibilities on the basis of the Doha Declaration establishes their agreement regarding the interpretation of these flexibilities.

Accordingly, to the extent that specific limitations or exceptions to IP rights are commonly and consistently utilised by WTO Members on the basis of their common understanding regarding the interpretation of TRIPS such as the Doha Declaration, they constitute a subsequent practice within the meaning of Article 31(3)(b) of the VCLT that shall be taken into account in interpreting the TRIPS Agreement.[351]

---

[349] WIPO Standing Committee on the Law of Patents (2010), *Experts' Study on Exclusions from Patentable Subject Matter and Exceptions and Limitations to the Rights*, SCP/15/3.
[350] See Section 5.2.2.4.2.
[351] See also James Thuo Gathii (2002), The Legal Status of the Doha Declaration on TRIPS and Public Health under the Vienna Convention on the Law of the Treaties, *Harvard Journal of Law & Technology*, vol. 15, no. 2, pp. 292–317, at p. 311.

5.4.3 *Article 4.5 of the UNFCCC as Relevant Rules of International Law*

Article 31(3)(c) of the VCLT directly addresses "the issue of the relevance of other rules of international law to the interpretation of a treaty".[352] Article 31(3)(c) is considered particularly relevant when interpreting the obligations of the WTO Agreements because they interact with various multilateral treaties.[353] The question before us is whether the commitment to the transfer of ESTs under Article 4.5 of the UNFCCC, as discussed in Section 3.4.1.2, could be relevant under the VCLT to the interpretation of the TRIPS terms and provisions for facilitating innovation and transfer of ESTs.

As discussed in Section 5.2.2.4.3, to qualify under Article 31(3)(c) of the VCLT, Article 4.5 of the UNFCCC would have to be a "rule of international law", which is "relevant" and "applicable in the relations between the parties". First, the UNFCCC is an international convention or treaty between parties. As discussed in Section 5.2.2.4.3, such a convention is among the "rules of international law" within the meaning of Article 31(3)(c).

Second, in order to be "relevant", Article 4.5 of the UNFCCC must "concern the subject-matter of the treaty term at issue".[354] This means that the relevant provisions of the UNFCCC have to be applicable to the facts of the case examined under the TRIPS Agreement.[355] The subject matter at issue is the facilitation of the innovation and transfer of ESTs. Article 4.5 of the UNFCCC explicitly obliges developed country Parties to take all practicable steps to promote, facilitate and finance the transfer of ESTs to developing countries. Similarly, the TRIPS Agreement contains several provisions that seek to facilitate the innovation and transfer of technologies, including ESTs. For instance, Article 7 requires that the protection and enforcement of IP

---

[352] Panel Reports, *EC – Approval and Marketing of Biotech Products*, para. 7.67.

[353] Gabrielle Marceau (2001), Conflicts of Norms and Conflicts of Jurisdictions: The Relationship between the WTO Agreement and MEAs and Other Treaties, *Journal of World Trade*, vol. 35, no.6, pp. 1081–131, at p. 1087.

[354] Mark Eugen Villiger (2009), *Commentary on the 1969 Vienna Convention on the Law of Treaties*, Leiden, Netherlands: Martinus Nijhoff Publishers, p. 433; see also Gabrielle Marceau (2001), Conflicts of Norms and Conflicts of Jurisdictions: The Relationship between the WTO Agreement and MEAs and Other Treaties, *Journal of World Trade*, vol. 35, no. 6, pp. 1081–131, at p. 1087 (stating that "[i]n the absence of specific guidance, the determination of what rules are 'relevant' would need to be made on a case-by-case basis, by examining criteria such as the subject of the dispute and the content (i.e. subject matter) of the rules under consideration"); this argument finds confirmation in Appellate Body Report, *EC and Certain Member States – Large Civil Aircraft*, para. 846.

[355] See also Holger Hestermeyer (2007), *Human Rights and the WTO: The Case of Patents and Access to Medicines*, Oxford University Press, p. 221.

rights should contribute to the promotion of technological innovation and to the transfer and dissemination of technology. Further, as discussed in Sections 4.3 and 4.4, the innovation and transfer of ESTs are closely linked to the patent protection of technologies and the control of anti-competitive practices. Thus, both Article 4.5 of the UNFCCC and certain TRIPS provisions affect the innovation and transfer of ESTs. Accordingly, even though the EST transfer commitments under UNFCCC are formulated in the climate change context, this rule is relevant for the interpretation of the TRIPS provisions for facilitating innovation and transfer of ESTs.

The third requirement essentially concerns whether Article 4.5 of the UNFCCC is applicable in the relations between the parties to the TRIPS Agreement. As discussed in Section 5.2.2.4.3, for the interpretation of the terms used in the TRIPS Agreement, rules of international treaties such as MEAs may qualify under Article 31(3)(c) of the VCLT if such rules are applicable to a large number of WTO Members.

As of 1 January 2017, with 197 Parties including 196 States and the European Union, the UNFCCC is close to achieving universal participation. At the same time, WTO has 164 Members including 160 States and three separate customs territories (i.e. Hong Kong, Macau and Chinese Taipei) and the European Union. There is no doubt that Article 4.5 of the UNFCCC applies to all WTO Members that are States and the European Union because all of them are parties to the UNFCCC.

As to the separate customs territories, the UNFCCC is applicable to Hong Kong and Macau in accordance with the Basic Law of Hong Kong Special Administrative Region of the People's Republic of China and the Basic Law of Macao Special Administrative Region of the People's Republic of China. There is no explicit legal provision governing the applicability of the UNFCCC to Chinese Taipei. However, this should not constitute a barrier for relevant rules of international law to be considered in interpreting the WTO Agreements. Indeed, as noted by the panel in *EC – Approval and Marketing of Biotech Products* (2006), the term "parties" in Article 31(3)(c) refers to "States" as informed by Article 2.1(g) of the VCLT.[356] Thus, to the extent that relevant rules of international law are applicable to all WTO Member States, such rules fall within the scope of Article 31(3)(c) of the VCLT.

Accordingly, Article 4.5 of the UNFCCC, which is applicable to all WTO Member States, constitutes a relevant rule of international law within the meaning of Article 31(3)(c) of the VCLT in interpreting the TRIPS provisions for facilitating the innovation and transfer of ESTs.

---

[356] Panel Reports, *EC – Approval and Marketing of Biotech Products*, para. 7.68.

The UNFCCC enjoys near universal membership. According to Marceau (2001), this provides "a strong indication that a genuine environmental problem [, in this case climate change,] exists, and that the international community has agreed that a certain response is required".[357] The Appellate Body in *US – Shrimp* (1998) obliges a treaty interpreter to read the WTO Agreements "in the light of contemporary concerns of the community of nations about the protection and preservation of the environment".[358] Therefore, the TRIPS Agreement should be read in the light of global contemporary concerns such as the climate change. This further supports the need to take into account the relevant rules provided by the UNFCCC, including obligations to transfer ESTs, when interpreting the TRIPS Agreement for facilitating innovation and transfer of ESTs.

5.5 CONCLUSION

The TRIPS Agreement does not itself contain any specific provision for the innovation and transfer of ESTs. However, several provisions, in particular the patent-related flexibilities and pro-competition provisions of the TRIPS Agreement, could be interpreted to facilitate innovation and transfer of ESTs in order to address climate change concerns.

Under Article 3.2 of the DSU, the TRIPS Agreement is to be interpreted in accordance with Articles 31 and 32 of the VCLT. This means that the terms of the TRIPS Agreement shall be interpreted in good faith in accordance with their ordinary meaning in their context and in the light of the object and purpose of both the WTO Agreement and the TRIPS Agreement. Bearing in mind that "the purpose of treaty interpretation is to establish the common intention of the parties to the treaty",[359] the interpretation cannot alter the meaning of particular TRIPS provisions.[360] Nevertheless, some open-textured TRIPS provisions require extensive and in-depth interpretation which takes into account all relevant elements.

The sustainable development objective enshrined in the Preamble to the Marrakesh Agreement has provided the discretion required for WTO Members to consider their respective environmental and social needs and concerns when interpreting the TRIPS Agreement. The balancing

---

[357] Gabrielle Marceau (2001), Conflicts of Norms and Conflicts of Jurisdictions: The Relationship between the WTO Agreement and MEAs and Other Treaties, *Journal of World Trade*, vol. 35, no. 6, pp. 1081–131, at p. 1097.

[358] Appellate Body Report, *US – Shrimp*, para. 129.

[359] Appellate Body Report, *EC – Computer Equipment*, para. 93.

[360] Joost Pauwelyn (2008), *Conflict of Norms in Public International Law: How WTO Law Relates to Other Rules of International Law*, Cambridge University Press, p. 245.

objective of the TRIPS Agreement also demands the consideration of "non-trade concerns". Environmental protection, in particular climate change mitigation, is within the scope of public interest in Articles 7 and 8 of TRIPS. Measures adopted by WTO Members to facilitate the innovation and transfer of ESTs which are essential for climate change mitigation undoubtedly promote public interest and contribute to sustainable development. Therefore, both the WTO's sustainable development objective and the overarching objective and purpose of the TRIPS Agreement provide a legal basis for a balanced and tailored interpretation of IP-related obligations for facilitating innovation and transfer of ESTs.

As a subsequent agreement to the TRIPS Agreement, the Doha Declaration has reinforced WTO Members' common understanding that the TRIPS Agreement represents a balanced and flexible IP framework that is responsive to the broader public interest needs and public policy objectives. It must "shed light on" the interpretation of the TRIPS Agreement. Although it reiterated and clarified relevant TRIPS' flexibilities for the purpose of protecting public health, such flexibilities should be applicable to the ESTs in a similar manner for the purpose of mitigating climate change. The Doha Declaration could also serve as a model for the Members to adopt a Ministerial Declaration for climate change, clarifying flexibilities to facilitate innovation and transfer of ESTs. The Doha Declaration also explicitly enumerates some of the flexibilities available to WTO Members such as compulsory licences and parallel imports. To the extent that such flexibilities are consistently utilised by WTO Members, they may constitute "subsequent practice" within the meaning of Article 31(3)(b) of the VCLT that shall be considered when interpreting the TRIPS Agreement.

As part of the WTO legal system, the TRIPS Agreement is "not to be read in clinical isolation from public international law".[361] The use of open-textured provisions that call on areas of law outside of IP protection, such as public health and environmental protection, is an implicit recognition that relevant applicable international law is important for interpreting the TRIPS Agreement. The commitments to transfer ESTs under Article 4.5 of the UNFCCC as relevant rules of international law that are applicable in the relations between the parties under Article 31(3)(c) of the VCLT shall be taken into account in the interpretation of the TRIPS Agreement for facilitating innovation and transfer of ESTs so as to mitigate climate change, which is a common concern of humankind.

---

[361] Appellate Body Report, *US – Gasoline*, p. 17.

6

Interpreting Patent–Related Flexibilities in the TRIPS Agreement for Facilitating Innovation and Transfer of ESTs

6.1 INTRODUCTION

The purpose of this chapter is to explore the regulatory space that the TRIPS Agreement leaves for WTO Members to implement or interpret its patent-related provisions within their own legal system and practice in a manner that facilitates the innovation and transfer of ESTs.

Prior to TRIPS, countries were allowed to adjust the levels of their patent protection in accordance with their national development strategies, provided that national treatment was secured,[1] whereas under the TRIPS Agreement, states' discretion to tailor the level and scope of their patent protection to suit their individual circumstances and development priorities is much more restrictive and further bound by the minimum standards for patents, as discussed earlier in Section 4.2. Opponents of TRIPS have thus claimed that the TRIPS Agreement leaves little or no room for national policy space or public policy objectives.[2] Taking such an approach to the interpretation of

---

[1] WIPO, "Advice on Flexibilities under the TRIPS Agreement", available at www.wipo.int/ip-development/en/legislative_assistance/advice_trips.html, (stating that "[u]nder the Paris Convention, the national treatment principle allowed for what was usually called the 'asymmetries', that is, the adoption of different standards of protection by different countries in accordance with different levels of national development [provided that national treatment was secured]").

[2] See, e.g., Laurence R. Helfer (2009), Regime Shifting: The TRIPS Agreement and New Dynamics of International Intellectual Property Lawmaking, *The Yale Journal of International Law*, vol. 29, pp. 1–83, at p. 46 (noting that "intellectual property protection rules codified in the TRIPS Agreement have been framed by NGOs, independent experts, and developing states as a threat to economic, social, and cultural rights"); Joost Pauwelyn (2010), The Dog That Barked But Didn't Bite: 15 Years of Intellectual Property Disputes at the WTO, *Journal of International Dispute Settlement*, vol. 1, no. 2, pp. 389–429, at p. 392 (stating that "[o]n the 'fear' side, conversely, many developing countries and non-governmental organizations [NGOs] expected merciless WTO enforcement of ever stricter IP rights with little or no room left for

TRIPS is, however, extreme and flawed. It is true that Part II of the TRIPS Agreement imposes mandatory obligations on WTO Members to establish minimum standards for IP protection for all technologies including ESTs. Nevertheless, the TRIPS Agreement also provides for considerable flexibilities in terms of the patentability requirement, the limits to patent rights, and the transitional period for LDCs allowing members to adapt their patent systems to their socio-economic needs including by facilitating their innovation of and access to ESTs.[3]

It is, however, obvious that in contrast with the mandatory minimum patent standards, these patent-related exceptions and flexibilities are merely permissive and not mandatory.[4] Furthermore, the open-textured nature or vagueness of such flexibilities, as discussed in Section 5.1, makes it difficult for developing countries to utilise them in pursuit of their public policy objectives. In the view of Frankel (2010), the TRIPS flexibilities have failed to produce the desired results that "really assist in development of local innovation and technology transfer".[5] In practice, developing countries' attempts to use some TRIPS flexibilities such as compulsory licensing to address climate change concerns has met strong opposition from some developed countries and their industries.[6] Accordingly, similar to the case of access to medicine as discussed in Section 5.4.1.2, questions have been raised with regard to the extent to which a WTO Member would feel free to use the TRIPS flexibilities to the fullest extent to facilitate their access to ESTs without fearing pressure from their trading partners.

At the international level, many countries have expressed their concern over the availability, sufficiency and effectiveness of the TRIPS flexibilities to address public interest concerns such as climate change. For example, at the WTO, as early as the third meeting of the WTO Committee on Trade and Environment (WT/CTE/M/3, 1995), the Korean delegation proposed

---

national policy space or social objectives in an organization, originally GATT now the WTO, reputed for its trade or economic-first approach").

[3] This chapter will not address the transitional period for LDCs as it is not patent-specific.

[4] See, e.g., Articles 27.2, 27.3 and 30 of the TRIPS Agreement use the word "may" when describing Members' right to use exceptions to patentability or patent rights.

[5] Susy Frankel (2010), The Applicability of GATT Jurisprudence to the Interpretation of the TRIPS Agreement, in Correa (ed.), *Research Handbook on the Interpretation and Enforcement of Intellectual Property Under WTO Rules: Intellectual Property in the WTO*, Vol. II, Cheltenham, UK: Edward Elgar Publishing, pp. 3–23, at p. 5.

[6] See, e.g., Tessa Schwartz and Tierney Sarah Niyogi (2009), Technology Transfer and Intellectual Property Issues Take Centre Stage in UNFCCC Negotiations, *Cleantech Update*, p. 2; Meena Raman (2009), Wide North-South Divide over IPRs and Climate Technologies, *TWN Bonn News Update* No. 13.

that the TRIPS provisions relating to patentable subject matter, compulsory licences and anti-competitive practices should be reviewed to confirm whether they were "sufficient to strike a balance between the protection of patent holders and users [that] would ensure a wider diffusion of [ESTs]".[7] More recently, Ecuador initiated a proposal (IP/C/W/585, 2013) in the TRIPS Council to evaluate the TRIPS Agreement from the stand-point of mitigating environmental problems with a view to reaffirming and enhancing the existing TRIPS flexibilities related to ESTs.[8] Within the UNFCCC framework, developing countries have pushed for the full use of the TRIPS flexibilities, including compulsory licences, to facilitate EST transfer.[9]

The TRIPS Agreement was negotiated to ensure that countries could take various kinds of measures to qualify and limit patent rights for the sake of public interest. These built-in limits to patents under TRIPS, representing the flexibilities, cannot be interpreted in such a manner that defeats the objectives of either the TRIPS Agreement or the WTO. The implementation of the patent-related flexibilities, thus, must accommodate environmental protection and technological and scientific progress,[10] as informed by the WTO's sus-tainable development objective as well as Articles 7 and 8 of the TRIPS Agreement. In this respect, the 2014 Max Planck Declaration on Patents Protection states that sovereign states should "retain the discretion to adopt a patent system that best suits their technological capabilities as well as their social, cultural and economic needs and priorities".[11] Combating climate change, which is "a common concern of mankind", as discussed in Section 1.1, is firmly in the public interest. As demonstrated in Section 2, the innov-ation and transfers of ESTs are essential for mitigating climate change. Therefore, the limits to patentability and patent rights in the TRIPS

[7]   Report of the Meeting Held on 21–22 June 1995, Committee on Trade and Environment, 18 July 1995, WTO Doc. No. WT/CTE/M/3, para. 30.

[8]   Contribution of Intellectual Property to Facilitating the Transfer of Environmentally Rational Technology, Council for Trade-Related Aspects of Intellectual Property Rights, 27 February 2013, WTO Doc. No. IP/C/W/585, para. 16.

[9]   See, e.g., Draft Text (2009), Proposed by Co-chairs, Non-Paper No. 36, Contact Group on Enhanced Action on Development and Transfer of Technology, Ad Hoc Working Group on Long-Term Cooperative Action under the Convention, Barcelona, 2–6 November 2009, available at http://unfccc.int/files/kyoto_protocol/application/pdf/technology 29091009v03.pdf, p. 20.

[10]   Ibid.

[11]   Max Planck Institute for Innovation and Competition (2014), Declaration on Patent Protection: Regulatory Sovereignty under TRIPS, available at www.ip.mpg.de/files/pdf2/Patent_ Declaration1.pdf, p. 1.

Agreement should be interpreted and applied in a manner that facilitates innovation and transfer of ESTs.

This chapter examines to what extent such patent-related flexibilities can be interpreted to facilitate the innovation and transfer of ESTs so as to address global climate change concerns. It seeks to interpret the equivocal patent-related flexibilities in accordance with the customary rules of interpretation of public international law. In addition to the objectives of both the WTO and the TRIPS Agreement, subsequent developments, such as the Doha Declaration, as well as non-WTO norms, such as EST transfer commitments under Article 4.5 of the UNFCCC, will be taken into account. As outlined in Section 5.2.3, relevant judicial decisions as well as the "teachings of publicists", such as the 2014 Max Planck Declaration on Patents Protection, may be used to confirm or determine the meaning and scope of certain patent-related flexibilities.

This chapter will first address the interpretative issues regarding patentable subject matter under Article 27 and then examine the limits to patent rights in the TRIPS Agreement, followed by a study of compulsory licensing under Article 31. Their relevance for the innovation and transfer of ESTs will be addressed respectively.

6.2 PATENTABLE SUBJECT MATTER UNDER ARTICLE 27

The Paris Convention leaves it to the discretion of its Members to define the patentability requirements in their domestic laws and to exclude areas from patentability.[12] In contrast, Article 27 of the TRIPS Agreement delineates the scope of patentable subject matter and sets out boundaries to patentability. This article substantially harmonised patentable subject matter requirements at a nearly universal level through the principle that patents shall be available for both product and process inventions in

---

[12] Article 1 of the Paris Convention is drafted in "very general and liberal terms". Article 1(4), specially dealing with patents, provides that: "Patents shall include the various kinds of industrial patents, recognized by the laws of the countries of the Union, such as patents of importation, patents of improvement, patents and certificates of addition". See Chidi Oguamanam (2003), The Convention on Biological Diversity and Intellectual Property Rights: The Challenge of Indigenous Knowledge, *Southern Cross University Law Review*, vol. 7, pp. 89–141, at p. 109; see also Joseph Straus (1996), Implications of the TRIPS Agreement in the Field of Patent Law, in Beier and Schricker (eds.), *From GATT to TRIPS: The Agreement on Trade-Related Aspects of Intellectual Property Rights*, Hoboken, NJ: Wiley, pp. 160–215, at p. 171.

"all fields of technologies", with few exceptions.[13] Significantly, this provision introduces an obligation of non-discrimination as to "the place of invention, the field of technology and whether products are imported or locally produced". According to a WIPO Document (SCP/15/3), such provisions would "dramatically alter the number and nature of the exclusions from patentability".[14]

The scope of patentable subject matter is vast, and read literally, Article 27 does not permit WTO Members to exclude ESTs from patent protection. Nevertheless, Article 27.1 provides some flexibility and Articles 27.2 and 27.3 contain explicit exceptions that are highly relevant in relation to ESTs. The following sections address the non-discrimination principle and ESTs, followed by patent eligibility requirements, and then explore the permissible exclusions for ESTs.

6.2.1 *Non-Discrimination (Article 27.1) and ESTs*

6.2.1.1 The Principle of Non-Discrimination under Article 27.1

The non-discrimination clause of Article 27.1 is patent-specific, as there is no comparable provision in other sections of TRIPS. It is also an innovative element in both international and national patent systems. As observed by UNCTAD and ICTSD (2005), "[n]either the Paris Convention nor national laws contained a provision comparable to Article 27.1".[15] The implication of this non-discrimination clause is, however, vital as it may affect what type of regulatory flexibility would be permissible under TRIPS.[16]

The second sentence of Article 27.1 prescribes that:

> Subject to paragraph 4 of Article 65, paragraph 8 of Article 70 and paragraph 3 of this Article, patents shall be available and patent rights enjoyable without

---

[13] Jeremy H. Reichman (1995), Universal Minimum Standards of Intellectual Property Protection under the TRIPS Component of the WTO Agreement, *The International Lawyer*, vol. 29, no. 2, pp. 345–88, at p. 352.

[14] WIPO Standing Committee on the Law of Patents (2010), Exclusions from Patentability and Exceptions and Limitations to Patentees' Rights, A study prepared by Prof. Bently Lionel et al., SCP/15/3, Annex I, p. 23.

[15] UNCTAD-ICTSD (2005), *Resource Book on TRIPS and Development*, Cambridge University Press, at p. 369.

[16] See, e.g., Jonathan Michael Berger (2002), Tripping over Patents. AIDS, Access to Treatment and the Manufacturing of Scarcity, *Connecticut Journal of International Law*, vol. 17, pp. 157–248, at p. 199 (stating that "[t]he issue of discrimination is key to the question of what type of regulatory framework would be permissible under TRIPS").

discrimination as to the place of invention, the field of technology and whether products are imported or locally produced.[17]

Judging from the text, the scope of application of this non-discrimination clause covers both the availability of patents, that is patentability, as well as the enjoyment of patent rights. Despite broad coverage, Article 27.1 only prohibits discrimination on the basis of the three factors explicitly indicated in the provision: (1) the place of invention, (2) the field of technology and (3) whether products are imported or locally manufactured. The second element will be examined in detail in Section 6.2.1.2, whereas another two factors will be discussed in subsequent paragraphs.

With regard to the first element, discrimination based on the place of invention is prohibited under Article 27.1. This is to ensure equal treatment for all inventions irrespective of the place of invention. As interpreted by various commentators, Members may act inconsistently with this non-discrimination requirement in Article 27.1 when they refuse to grant patents on an invention on the grounds that it is invented in certain countries; or when they impose limitations on patent rights under certain circumstances solely for the inventions made in specific countries.[18]

Turning to the third element, Article 27.1 prohibits discrimination on the basis of "whether products are imported or locally produced". This clause seeks to ban discrimination based on the origin of products (locally produced or imported). It reflects a delicate compromise reached during the TRIPS negotiations between developing countries insisting on limiting the meaning of patent working requirement to local manufacturing and developed countries contending that importation satisfies the local working requirement.[19] It essentially stemmed from the debate regarding "whether exploitation of a

---

[17] There are three basic exceptions to the basic obligations set forth in Article 27.1, including: first, Article 65.4 allowing developing Members to delay product patent protection in areas that they did not protect on the general date of application of the Agreement for those Members (i.e. 1 January 2000) for an additional period of five years; second, Article 70.8 establishing the "mailbox" system for pharmaceutical and agricultural chemical products; and third, Article 27.3 permitting exclusion from patentability of (a) diagnostic, therapeutic and surgical methods for the treatment of humans or animals; and (b) certain plants and animals.

[18] See, e.g., Antony Taubman and Jayashree Watal (2010), The WTO TRIPS Agreement – A Practical Overview for Climate Change Policymakers, Documentation used in technical cooperation activities of the WTO's Intellectual Property Division, available at www.wto.org/english/tratop_e/trips_e/ta_docs_e/8_3_overviewclimatechange_e.pdf, p. 4; Carlos M. Correa (2007), *Trade Related Aspects of Intellectual Property Rights: A Commentary on the TRIPS Agreement*, Oxford University Press, p. 282.

[19] Yamane Hiroko (2011), *Interpreting TRIPS: Globalisation of Intellectual Property and Access to Medicines*, Oxford, UK: Hart Publishing, p. 122.

patent through importing the patented product rather than through local production should be admissible as a ground for compulsory licences".[20]

Article 27.1 does not explicitly prohibit local working requirements, however, the interpretation of this provision is quite controversial. On the one hand, UNCTAD (2003) points out that the local working requirement may "create a distinction between imported and locally produced products", but it does not necessarily amount to discrimination.[21] On the other hand, some countries contend that the local working requirement is inconsistent with the non-discrimination obligation as to "whether products are imported or locally produced" in Article 27.1. For instance, in 2001, the United States filed a WTO complaint against Brazil with respect to those provisions of Brazil's 1996 industrial property law and other related measures, establishing a "local working" requirement that can only be fulfilled by the local manu-facturer and not the importation of the patented product.[22] The United States explicitly claimed that the local working requirement is inconsistent with Brazil's obligations under Article 27 of the TRIPS Agreement.[23] Given fierce pressure from health activists and international non-governmental organiza-tions (NGOs), the United States eventually withdrew its WTO complaint because of the potential detrimental effect on Brazil's HIV/AIDS program.[24] The parties to the dispute reached a mutually satisfactory solution in 2000,[25] thereby leaving unanswered the question as to whether local working require-ments are compatible with Article 27.1. This issue is addressed in more detail in Section 6.4 concerning compulsory licensing under Article 31.

6.2.1.2 "Non-Discrimination as to the Field of Technology" and ESTs

This section focuses on the prohibition of discrimination regarding the field of technology, also referred to as "the technological neutrality principle" by

---

[20] Antony Taubman et al. (2012), *A Handbook on the WTO TRIPS Agreement*, Cambridge University Press, p. 107.

[21] UNCTAD (2003), *Course on Dispute Settlement: International Centre for Settlement of Investment Disputes*, Vol. III, United Nations, p. 20.

[22] Request for Consultations by the United States, *Brazil – Measures Affecting Patent Protection*, WT/DS199/1, G/L/385, IP/D/23, 8 June 2000.

[23] Ibid.

[24] See, e.g., Ellen't Hoen (2002), TRIPS, Pharmaceutical Patents, and Access to Essential Medicines: A Long Way From Seattle to Doha, *Chicago Journal of International Law*, vol. 3, no. 1, pp. 27–46, at p. 33; Thomas Cottier et al. (2013), Use It or Lose It? Assessing the Compatibility of the Paris Convention and TRIPS with Respect to Local Working Requirements, *Working Paper* No. 2012/11, p. 5.

[25] Notification of Mutually Agreed Solution (2001), *Brazil – Measures Affecting Patent Protection*, WT/DS199/4, G/L/454, IP/D/23/Add.1.

some scholars.[26] The *travaux préparatoires* of the TRIPS Agreement show that the objective of this provision was to guarantee protection for certain subject matters, particularly pharmaceutical products, previously left unprotected by patents in many countries.[27] This provision first reinforces the principle established in the first sentence of Article 27.1, requiring that patents shall be available "in all fields of technology". WTO Members are thus forbidden from excluding any field of technology from patentability (apart from specific exceptions in TRIPS, which are discussed below). Furthermore, this provision imposes an explicit ban on discrimination based on the "field of technology" as to the enjoyment of patent rights. This means that broadening or reducing rights available to patent holders pertaining to certain fields of technology could be found as such to be inconsistent with Article 27.1 because it constitutes discrimination either against or in favour of patent owners in other fields of technologies.[28] Accordingly, patent legislations that discriminate between fields of technology may not be compatible with Article 27.1 of the TRIPS Agreement.

To what extent does this non-discrimination clause preclude Members from legislating exceptions for the entire category of inventions pertaining to ESTs? According to Taubman and Watal (2010), excluding an entire field of technology from patentability, or providing exceptions to patent rights only for certain fields of technology would be in violation of the non-discrimination obligation of Article 27.1.[29] However, it is debatable whether exceptions or differential treatment for inventions pertaining to all ESTs would constitute

---

[26] See, e.g., Graeme B. Dinwoodie and Rochelle C. Dreyfuss (2012), A *Neofederalist Vision of TRIPS: The Resilience of the International Intellectual Property Regime*, Oxford University Press, p. 67.

[27] See, e.g., UNCTAD-ICTSD (2005), *Resource Book on TRIPS and Development*, Cambridge University Press, p. 353 (noting that prior to TRIPS, about 50 countries excluded pharmaceutical products from patentability and "[m]any also excluded food and other products from patentability"); Carlos M. Correa (2007), *Trade Related Aspects of Intellectual Property Rights: A Commentary on the TRIPS Agreement*, Oxford University Press, p. 271 (pointing out that "from the outset of the [Uruguay] Round the extension of patentability, particularly to pharmaceuticals, in those countries that did not recognize it, was a major objective of the proponents of GATT disciplines on intellectual property"); Graeme B. Dinwoodie and Rochelle C. Dreyfuss (2012), A *Neofederalist Vision of TRIPS: The Resilience of the International Intellectual Property Regime*, Oxford University Press, p. 105.

[28] Carlos M. Correa (2000), Integrating Public Health Concerns into Patent Legislation in Developing Countries, Geneva: South Centre Working Papers, p. 7.

[29] Antony Taubman and Jayashree Watal (2010), The WTO TRIPS Agreement – A Practical Overview for Climate Change Policymakers, Documentation used in technical cooperation activities of the WTO's Intellectual Property Division, available at www.wto.org/english/tratop_e/trips_e/ta_docs_e/8_3_overviewclimatechange_e.pdf, p. 4.

discrimination "as to the field of technology" within the meaning of Article 27.1 of the TRIPS Agreement.

First, not everyone agrees that all types of ESTs would constitute one field of technology.[30] In fact, ESTs covers various fields of technologies ranging from renewable energy technologies to carbon storage, from emissions abatement and fuel efficiency in transportation to energy efficiency in buildings and lighting. Thus, it can be argued that differential treatment vis-à-vis ESTs covering various fields of technologies falls outside the scope of Article 27.1. Indeed, the text of Article 27.1 clearly shows that non-discrimination should extend to "the field of technology" rather than "the fields of technology". This reading is consistent with the principle of *expressio unius est exclusio alterius* holding that "to express or include one thing implies the exclusion of the other".[31] Furthermore, even if there is discrimination in favour of ESTs, the basis of such discrimination does not pertain to "the field of technology" but to a certain particular function of the technology, which, in the case of ESTs, is mitigating climate change.

Nevertheless, the first sentence of Article 27.1 of TRIPS makes clear that patents shall be available for any inventions "in all fields of technologies", unless they are specially excluded by Articles 27.2 and 27.3. This leaves little room for WTO Members to exclude ESTs as a whole from patentability. Furthermore, as pointed out in Section 4.3, patent protection has incentivising effects on innovation and transfer of ESTs. Therefore, excluding ESTs from patentability may discourage investment in R&D for ESTs and may not facilitate the dissemination of technological information in the area of ESTs, thereby frustrating the objectives of the TRIPS Agreement. Accordingly, the proposal made by some states in the UN climate change negotiations to exclude all ESTs from patent eligibility or revoke existing patents on essential ESTs in developing countries[32] is inconsistent with the TRIPS Agreement and runs counter to the spirit and objectives of the TRIPS Agreement. As observed by Maskus (2010), such an anti-patent proposal would require a significant

---

[30] See, e.g., Antony Taubman and Jayashree Watal (2010), p. 4 (considering "biofuels", which is only one type of renewable energy technologies, as one field of technology).

[31] Panel Reports, *China – Publications and Audiovisual Products*, para. 7.60; *China – Raw Materials*, para. 7.49.

[32] See, e.g., Draft Decision Text on Technology Transfer and Intellectual Property Rights (2012), submission by the Bolivarian Republic of Venezuela, available at http://unfccc.int/files/bodies/application/pdf/venezuela_tt_ipr_040912.pdf, para. 5(h); Draft Text, Proposed by Co-chairs, Non-Paper no. 36, Contact Group on Enhanced Action on Development and Transfer of Technology, Ad Hoc Working Group on Long-Term Cooperative Action under the Convention, Barcelona, 2–6 November 2009, available at http://unfccc.int/files/kyoto_protocol/application/pdf/technology29091009v03.pdf, p. 20.

amendment to Article 27 of TRIPS that would contradict WTO Members' "fundamental intentions".[33]

Second, even if ESTs as a whole were considered a "field of technology", not all differential treatment would constitute "discrimination" within the meaning of Article 27.1. The concept of "discrimination" has been subject to diverging interpretations.

Some authors interpret "discrimination" expansively as "any form of differential treatment".[34] According to this view, any differential treatment or exception applied to one field of technology but not another would be inconsistent with the non-discrimination clause in Article 27.1. Such interpretation has been endorsed by some commentators, several developed countries and their industry groups.[35] For example, when Australia amended the US Free Trade Agreement Implementation Bill 2004 by permitting a penalty "for drug patent litigation in bad faith" so as to discourage the "ever-greening" of pharmaceutical patents, the United States threatened Australia with a WTO challenge under the non-discrimination rule of Article 27.1 on the ground that the amendment did not apply to non-drug patents.[36] Also, pharmaceutical industries have consistently contended that WTO Members would act inconsistently with Article 27.1 by adopting compulsory licensing legislation that

---

[33] Keith E. Maskus (2010), Differential Intellectual Property Regimes for Environmental and Climate Technologies, *OECD Environment Working Papers*, no. 17, OECD, p. 25.

[34] See, e.g., Maria Victoria Stout (2008), Crossing the TRIPS Non-Discrimination Line: How CAFTA Pharmaceutical Patent Provisions Violate TRIPS Article 27.1, *Boston University Journal of Science and Technology Law*, vol. 14, pp. 177–200, at p. 180.

[35] See, e.g., Rajnish Kumar Rai (2008), Patentable Subject Matter Requirements: An Evaluation of Proposed Exclusions to India's Patent Law in Light of India's Obligations under the TRIPS Agreement and Options for India, *Chicago-Kent Journal of Intellectual Property*, vol. 8, pp. 41–84, at p. 82 (concluding that "[b]y denying patent protection solely on the grounds that the invention is a micro-organism or certain type of pharmaceutical substance, India's amendments would also violate the [non-discrimination] requirement in TRIPS Article 27.1"); Edson Beas Rodrigues and Bryan Murphy (2006), Brazil's Prior Consent Law: A Dialogue between Brazil and the United States Over Where the TRIPS Agreement Currently Sets the Balance between the Protection of Pharmaceutical Patents and Access to Medicines, *Albany Law Journal of Science and Technology*, vol. 16, pp. 423–56, at p. 453 (arguing that "the additional delay in examination of pharmaceutical applications imposed by ANVISA's [Brazil's National Sanitary Supervision Agency] review does raise issues of discrimination under Article 27.1 because no other area of technology is susceptible to the extra delay").

[36] See, e.g., Carlos M. Correa (2007), *Trade Related Aspects of Intellectual Property Rights: A Commentary on the TRIPS Agreement*, Oxford University Press, p. 283; Bryan Mercurio (2005), The Impact of the Australia–United States Free Trade Agreement on the Provision of the Health Services in Australia, *Whittier Law Review*, vol. 26, pp. 1051–1100, at p. 1094 (noting that "the International Federation of Pharmaceutical Manufacturers (IFPMA) felt that the amendments violated the TRIPS Agreement by discriminating against pharmaceutical patent holders and dissuading holders from seeking to protect and enforce their rights").

only applies to the pharmaceutical sector and not to other sectors.[37] As observed by Stout (2008), this interpretative approach requires that a Member "establish a 'one-size-fits-all' patent system that does not treat patents protecting food and medicines any differently than those protecting mechanical devices or software".[38] Under this view, national regulations that differentiate fields of ESTs from other fields of technology would thus be inconsistent with Article 27.1.

Alternatively, a more normative interpretation of this term is that discrimination is not mere differentiation but "unjustified differential treatment". The panel in *Canada – Pharmaceutical Patents* (2000) adopted this approach by stating that:

> [Discrimination] is a normative term, pejorative in connotation, referring to results of the unjustified imposition of differentially disadvantageous treatment.[39]

According to this interpretation, even differential treatment or exceptions confined to particular technological fields would be allowed under Article 27.1 of the TRIPS Agreement when there are "merit-based" reasons for such exceptions.[40] In other words, only arbitrary or unjustifiable distinctions would be prohibited by Article 27.1. More specifically, the non-discrimination requirement in Article 27.1 "only bars unjustified distinctions in patent law among technological areas and does not bar differences in legislation and processes based on legitimate policy preferences".[41] This interpretation is consistent with the widely accepted view shared by economists and legal scholars that "IPRs should be differentiated by field" to reflect varying industry characteristics and to achieve different trade-offs between innovation and imitation in different industries.[42] In practice, many major patenting powers –

---

[37] See, e.g., Frederick M. Abbott (2001), The TRIPS-Legality of Measures Taken to Address Public Health Crises: A Synopsis, *Widener Law Symposium Journal*, vol. 7, pp. 71–85, at p. 75.

[38] Maria Victoria Stout (2008), Crossing the TRIPS Non-Discrimination Line: How CAFTA Pharmaceutical Patent Provisions Violate TRIPS Article 27.1, *Boston University Journal of Science and Technology Law*, vol. 14, pp. 177–200, at p. 180.

[39] Panel Report, *Canada – Pharmaceutical Patents*, para. 7.94.

[40] See, e.g., WIPO Standing Committee on the Law of Patents (2010), Exclusions from Patentability and Exceptions and Limitations to Patentees' Rights, A study prepared by Prof. Bently Lionel et al., SCP/15/3, Annex I, p. 41; Keith E. Maskus (2010), Differential Intellectual Property Regimes for Environmental and Climate Technologies, *OECD Environment Working Papers*, no. 17, OECD, p. 20.

[41] Keith E. Maskus (2010), Differential Intellectual Property Regimes for Environmental and Climate Technologies, *OECD Environment Working Papers*, no. 17, OECD, p. 20.

[42] See, e.g., Michael Trebilcock et al. (2013), *The Regulation of International Trade*, 4th edn, New York: Routledge, p. 517 (arguing that "a rational country would have different levels of

the European Union, the United States and Japan – and innovative emerging countries have been treating different fields of technologies differently in their national patent systems.[43]

In addition, the WTO panel found that "the anti-discrimination rule of Article 27.1 does apply to exceptions of the kind authorized by Article 30."[44] In the panel's view, even exceptions to patent owners' rights must be technologically neutral. Such an interpretation would confer a "structural effect" on the non-discrimination provision of Article 27.1, making it applicable to all patent rules under TRIPS.[45] Although the panel report was not appealed, the panel's interpretation that even exceptions to patent rights must operate in a technology-neutral manner has been heavily criticized. According to the 2014 Max Planck Declaration on Patents Protection, "[t]he principle of *in dubio mitius* precludes an interpretation to that effect".[46] Indeed, as pointed out by some critics, if any exception to patent rights must extend to all fields of

---

protection for different industries, representing different trade-offs between innovation and imitation in each industry, depending upon where its comparative advantage lies"); Holger Hestermeyer (2007), *Human Rights and the WTO: The Case of Patents and Access to Medicines*, Oxford University Press, p. 53 (arguing that "differences between fields of technology indubitably require responses tailored to the field of technology"); Keith E. Maskus (2010), Differential Intellectual Property Regimes for Environmental and Climate Technologies, *OECD Environment Working Papers*, no. 17, OECD, p. 20 (noting that "[e]conomists and legal scholars have long argued that IPRs should be differentiated by field to reflect varying industry-innovation characteristics and the relative power of IPRs to influence activity in different sectors"); Frederick M. Abbott (2009), *Innovation and Technology Transfer to Address Climate Change: Lessons from the Global Debate on Intellectual Property and Public Health*, ICTSD's Programme on IPRs and Sustainable Development, Issue Paper No. 24, Geneva: ICTSD, p. 2 (stating that "[i]t is well accepted among IPRs experts in the fields of law and economics that IPRs have different effects for different fields of technology, whether those effects concern rates of innovation, economic and/or social welfare impacts").

[43] Frederick M. Abbott (2009), *Innovation and Technology Transfer to Address Climate Change: Lessons from the Global Debate on Intellectual Property and Public Health*, ICTSD's Programme on IPRs and Sustainable Development, Issue Paper No. 24, Geneva: ICTSD, p. 3 (further noting that "[a] specific provision in the U.S. Patent Act establishes a broad exemption for research regarding pharmaceutical products that does not, by its terms, apply to other fields of technology" [U.S. Patent Act, 35 US § 271(e)(1)]; [t]he European Patent Convention, at Article 52(2), expressly excludes computer programs from the subject matter scope of patent protection as distinguished, for example, from patent practice in the United States").

[44] Panel Report, *Canada – Pharmaceutical Patents*, para. 7.93.

[45] Graeme B. Dinwoodie and Rochelle C. Dreyfuss (2012), *A Neofederalist Vision of TRIPS: The Resilience of the International Intellectual Property Regime*, Oxford University Press, p. 105 (noting that "the Canada-Pharmaceuticals panel treated Article 27.1 as a structural provision and equivalent in operation to the [non-discrimination] guarantees in Articles 3 and 4").

[46] Max Planck Institute for Innovation and Competition (2014), Declaration on Patent Protection: Regulatory Sovereignty under TRIPS, available at www.ip.mpg.de/files/pdf2/Patent_Declaration1.pdf, p. 4.

technologies, it would be almost impossible to meet the requirement in Article 30 that exceptions be "limited".[47]

Moreover, the panel in *Canada – Pharmaceutical Patents* (2000) further clarified that:

> [I]t is not true that Article 27 requires all Article 30 exceptions to be applied to all products. Article 27 prohibits only discrimination as to the place of invention, the field of technology, and whether products are imported or produced locally. Article 27 does not prohibit bona fide exceptions to deal with problems that may exist only in certain product areas.[48]

The panel, however, does not provide any guidance as to the precise meaning and scope of "certain product areas". It does not draw a clear distinction between the terms "field of technology" and "certain product areas" either. Nevertheless, some commentators suggest that patent laws that draw distinctions on the basis of narrow categories of products, rather than broader fields of technologies, may be compatible with Article 27.1.[49] For instance, Correa (2008) considered that a justified differentiation may be permitted with respect to "a particular type of processes or products belonging to a given area of technology".[50] In the view of Cann (2004), even if a limited exception targeting an entire industry would not be allowed, an exception could be made for certain particular products, such as HIV/AIDS medicines.[51]

In conclusion, the non-discrimination principle in Article 27.1 may impose constraints on WTO Members' discretion to tailor their patent systems to meet the perceived needs of specific fields of technology. Nevertheless, it also leaves WTO Members space to provide differential treatment for ESTs by permitting bona fide exceptions for "certain product areas", as held by the panel in *Canada – Pharmaceutical Patents* (2000). In theory, some scholars such as Maskus (2010) have proposed differentiated IP regimes for global innovation

---

[47] See, e.g., John R. Thomas (2015), Tailoring the Patent System for Specific Industries, *Congressional Research Service Report* 7-5700, p. 11; Graeme B. Dinwoodie and Rochelle C. Dreyfuss (2012), *A Neofederalist Vision of TRIPS: The Resilience of the International Intellectual Property Regime*, Oxford University Press, p. 105.

[48] Panel Report, *Canada – Pharmaceutical Patents*, para. 7.92.

[49] John R. Thomas (2015), Tailoring the Patent System for Specific Industries, *Congressional Research Service Report* 7-5700, p. 12.

[50] Carlos M. Correa (2008), Patent Rights, in Correa and Yusuf (eds.), Intellectual Property and International Trade: The TRIPS Agreement, New York: Kluwer Law International, pp. 227–57, at p. 239.

[51] Wesley A. Cann (2004), On the Relationship between Intellectual Property Rights and the Need of Less-Developed Countries for Access to Pharmaceuticals: Creating a Legal Duty to Supply Under a Theory of Progressive Global Constitutionalism, *University of Pennsylvania Journal of International Economic Law*, vol. 25, no. 3, pp. 755–944, at p. 815.

and diffusion of ESTs as an option to address climate change concerns.[52] In practice, ESTs have enjoyed differential treatment vis-à-vis other technologies in some countries. Notably, several national IP offices, including those in Australia, Canada, Israel, Japan, Korea, the UK and the United States have established fast-track mechanisms for patent applications in respect of ESTs so as to facilitate the adoption and transfer of such technologies.[53]

6.2.2 *Patent Eligibility Requirements*

The general obligation of patentability in the first sentence of Article 27.1 does not mean that a WTO Member has to grant patents for new inventions in all circumstances because patent eligibility requirements and other conditions such as appropriate patent disclosure have to be met. The condition of patent disclosure is addressed in Section 4.3.1.2. This section will first interpret the patentability requirements in the first sentence of Article 27.1 and then study the potential relevance of this flexibility for WTO Members to facilitate further development and transfer of ESTs.

6.2.2.1 Interpretation of the Patentability Requirements

Patentability is a prerequisite for claiming patent protection for any invention, including inventions pertaining to ESTs. The first sentence of Article 27.1 sets forth the general rule of patentability, providing that:

> Subject to the provisions of paragraphs 2 and 3, patents shall be available for any inventions, whether products or processes, in all fields of technology, provided that they are new, involve an inventive step and are capable of industrial application.[54]

Above all, the text of Article 27.1 shows that to be eligible for patent protection, the relevant ESTs have to be "inventions". The TRIPS Agreement does not define the term "invention". Its dictionary meaning is "the discovery

---

[52] Keith E. Maskus (2010), Differential Intellectual Property Regimes for Environmental and Climate Technologies, *OECD Environment Working Papers*, no. 17, OECD, p. 20.

[53] Antoine Dechezleprêtre (2013), Fast-Tracking Green Patent Applications: An Empirical Analysis, ICTSD Programme on Innovation, Technology and Intellectual Property, Issue Paper No. 37, Geneva: ICTSD, p. viii.

[54] A footnote to the provision makes it clear that "[f]or the purposes of this Article, the terms 'inventive step' and 'capable of industrial application' may be deemed by a Member to be synonymous with the terms 'non-obvious' and 'useful' respectively".

or production of some new or improved process or machine that is both useful and is not obvious to persons skilled in the particular field".[55] The WIPO Model Law for Developing Countries on Inventions (1979) describes invention as "an idea of an inventor which permits in practice the solution to a specific problem in the field of technology".[56] Some national patent laws contain different definitions of invention.[57] As pointed out by Taubman et al. (2012), many national laws exclude such material as "scientific theories, aesthetic creations, schemes, and rules and methods for performing mental acts" from patentability because "[t]hese activities do not aim at any direct technical result but are rather of an abstract and intellectual character".[58]

Moreover, under Article 27.1 of the TRIPS Agreement, to be patentable, an invention pertaining to ESTs must (1) be new, (2) involve an inventive step ("non-obvious") and (3) be capable of industrial application ("useful"). These requirements contained in Article 27.1 mirrors the terminology in national patent laws, but the TRIPS Agreement itself does not clarify the meaning of these criteria. First, to meet the novelty requirement, an invention must be "new" as compared to the available state of the art or the prior art.[59] It is observed that most WTO Members define the relevant prior art as "any publicly available knowledge".[60] Some members, such as China, which previously applied a somewhat broader definition of "new", according to

---

[55] invention. Dictionary.com. *Dictionary.com Unabridged*. New York: Random House, http://dictionary.reference.com/browse/invention

[56] WIPO (1979), *WIPO Model Law for Developing Countries on Inventions*, Vol. 1: Patents, Geneva: WIPO, Section 112: Inventions, p. 19.

[57] For example, *US Patent Law*, 35 U.S. Code § 100 (a) (2013) (defining the term "invention" as "invention or discovery"); *Patent Law of the People's Republic of China* (2008 Amendment), adopted at the Sixth Meeting of the Standing Committee of the Eleventh National People's Congress on 27 December 2008, Article 2 (defining the term "inventions" as "new technical solutions proposed for a product, a process or the improvement thereof").

[58] Antony Taubman et al. (2012), *A Handbook on the WTO TRIPS Agreement*, Cambridge University Press, p. 95; see also WIPO Standing Committee on the Law of Patents (2010), Exclusions from Patentability and Exceptions and Limitations to Patentees' Rights, A Study Prepared by Bently Lionel et al., SCP/15/3, Annex 1, p. 21.

[59] Regulations under the Patent Cooperation Treaty (2013), WIPO, Rule 33.1 (providing that "[f]or the purposes of Article 15 (2), relevant prior art shall consist of everything which has been made available to the public anywhere in the world by means of written disclosure (including drawings and other illustrations) and which is capable of being of assistance in determining that the claimed invention is or is not new").

[60] See, e.g., Thomas Cottier and Pierre Véron (2011), *Concise International and European IP Law: TRIPS, Paris Convention, European Enforcement and Transfer of Technology*, 2nd edn, New York: Kluwer Law International, p. 90 (further noting that "other member states only consider inventions published in writing"); Holger Hestermeyer (2007), *Human Rights and the WTO: The Case of Patents and Access to Medicines*, Oxford University Press, p. 66.

which the mere use or knowledge of an invention outside China did not destroy novelty, have recently enlarged the scope of prior art by eliminating the territorial requirement.[61] As observed by Taubman et al. (2012), this criterion of "novelty" seeks to prevent patenting of publicly available technologies, and to "ensure that a patented invention is a genuine contribution to existing knowledge".[62]

Second, an invention must "involve an inventive step" or be "non-obvious". The dictionary meaning of "obvious" is "easy to see or understand; evident".[63] In the context of patents, the "obviousness" requirement is defined by WIPO to mean that the invention must represent a significant or essential advance or progress in relation to the state of the art, that is, it should not be obvious to a person ordinarily skilled in the art.[64] Many jurisdictions have adopted a similar test. For instance, under Article 56 of the European Patent Convention (2013), "an invention shall be considered as involving an inventive step if, having regard to the state of the art, it is not obvious to a person skilled in the art".[65] US patent law negates "non-obviousness" if "the claimed invention as a whole would have been obvious before the effective filing date of the claimed invention to a person having ordinary skill in the art".[66] In essence, this criterion is a "safeguard", in the words of Taubman et al. (2012), against patents being granted for inventions that "only represent a trivial or routine advance in existing knowledge, reserving patents for inventions that represent a clear and non-obvious advance [over] the state of the art".[67]

---

[61] See *Patent Law of the People's Republic of China (2000 Amendment)*, Standing Committee of the National People's Congress, 25 August 2000, Article 22); the 2008 Amendment defines prior art as any technology known to the public both in China and abroad before the filing date (see *Patent Law of the People's Republic of China (2008 Amendment)*, adopted at the Sixth Meeting of the Standing Committee of the Eleventh National People's Congress on 27 December 2008, Article 22).

[62] Antony Taubman et al. (2012), A *Handbook on the WTO TRIPS Agreement*, Cambridge University Press, p. 99.

[63] Obvious. *Dictionary.com Unabridged*. New York: Random House, http://dictionary.reference.com/browse/obvious

[64] WIPO (2004), *WIPO Intellectual Property Handbook*, WIPO Publication No. 489 (E), 2nd edn, reprinted 2008, p. 20.

[65] European Patent Convention (Convention on the Grant of European Patents) of 5 October 1973 as revised by the Act revising Article 63 EPC of 17 December 1991 and the Act revising the EPC of 29 November 2000, European Patent Office, Munich. It is noted that the membership of the European Patent Convention currently includes all the countries from the European Union, plus others.

[66] 35 U.S. Code § 103 (a).

[67] Antony Taubman et al. (2012), A *Handbook on the WTO TRIPS Agreement*, Cambridge University Press, p. 99.

A third requirement of patentability is that an invention has to be "capable of industrial application", being deemed as synonymous with "useful" under the TRIPS Agreement.[68] National laws concerning this requirement vary significantly. European countries, where the requirement of industrial applicability originated, regard this requirement as being fulfilled if the invention is "susceptible of practical use" in any field of industry, including agriculture.[69] The standard of "usefulness" as adopted in US patent law is somewhat broader, and only requires an invention to be capable of producing a positive benefit to society.[70] Some commentators have expressed concern that the latter approach may allow the patenting of "purely experimental inventions that cannot be made or used in an industry or do not produce a technical effect", as illustrated by the fact that the United States has granted a large number of patents on the methods of doing business and research tools.[71]

The TRIPS Agreement does not provide concrete definitions for these three requirements, thereby leaving WTO Members considerable discretion in designing and applying patentability criteria. It is noted that the way inventions are understood, and how to further define these criteria, may "have a major impact on where countries draw the line between private exclusive rights and the public domain",[72] thereby influencing the follow-on innovation and transfer of patented technologies, including ESTs.

---

[68] See footnote 5 to Article 27.1 of the TRIPS Agreement.

[69] Holger Hestermeyer (2007), *Human Rights and the WTO: The Case of Patents and Access to Medicines*, Oxford University Press, p. 67; Antony Taubman et al. (2012), *A Handbook on the WTO TRIPS Agreement*, Cambridge University Press, p. 100.

[70] WIPO (2007), *WIPO Patent Drafting Manual*, WIPO Publication No. 867 (E), Geneva: WIPO, p. 21.

[71] See, e.g., Rajnish Kumar Rai (2008), Patentable Subject Matter Requirements: An Evaluation of Proposed Exclusions to India's Patent Law in Light of India's Obligations under the TRIPS Agreement and Options for India, *Chicago–Kent Journal of Intellectual Property*, vol. 8, no. 1, Article 2, pp. 41–84, at p. 50; Donal O'Connell (2011), *Harvesting External Innovation: Managing External Relationships and Intellectual Property*, Surrey, UK: Gower Publishing, p. 50; UNCTAD-ICTSD (2005), *Resource Book on TRIPS and Development*, Cambridge University Press, p. 361. It should be noted that the term "technical effect" has no official definition.

[72] Pedro Roffe et al. (2010), Intellectual Property Rights in Free Trade Agreements: Moving beyond TRIPS Minimum Standards, in Correa (ed.), *Resource Handbook on the Protection of Intellectual Property under WTO Rules: Intellectual Property in the WTO*, Vol. I, Cheltenham, UK: Edward Elgar Publishing, pp. 266–316, at p. 270. Notably, the dictionary meaning of the term "public domain" is "the status of a published work or invention upon which the copyright or patent has expired or which has not been patented or subject to copyright. It may thus be freely used by the public". See "public domain", *Dictionary.com Unabridged*. New York: Random House, http://dictionary.reference.com/browse/public domain

6.2.2.2 The Relevance of the Patentability Requirements for WTO Members to Facilitate Innovation and Transfer of ESTs

The TRIPS Agreement does not weigh factors such as the importance of environmental protection in its patentability equation. In other words, the TRIPS Agreement does not differentiate between the patentability criteria of inventions pertaining to ESTs and other inventions. Therefore, the precise levels of novelty, inventive step and industrial applicability set by WTO Members affect the quantity and quality of patent grants in general and patents pertaining to ESTs in particular.[73]

A patent regime based on low standards of patentability may "subject to private control both genuine inventions and minor/incremental innovations" that occur in different fields of technology.[74] As a consequence, a low requirement of patentability risks blocking follow-on innovation through exclusive control of knowledge that ought to be in the public domain.[75] Furthermore, broader interpretations of the patentability standards lead to the proliferation of patents on minor developments in a given technology, often used by companies to keep competitors out of the market, thereby restraining competition.[76] Critics have noted that the low benchmark for patentability set by some countries, including the United States, has allowed for a large number of patents on minor or trivial developments that could potentially block competition and raise transaction costs, thereby undermining the benefits of improved

---

[73] Centre for International Environmental Law (2010), *Technology Transfer in the UNFCCC and Other International Legal Regimes: The Challenges of Systemic Integration*, Background Paper, International Council on Human Rights Policy, p. 11.

[74] Carlos M. Correa (2007), *Trade Related Aspects of Intellectual Property Rights: a Commentary on the TRIPS Agreement*, Oxford University Press, p. 277.

[75] See, e.g., Pedro Roffe et al. (2010), Intellectual Property Rights in Free Trade Agreements: Moving Beyond TRIPS Minimum Standards, in Correa (ed.), *Resource Handbook on the Protection of Intellectual Property under WTO Rules: Intellectual Property in the WTO*, Vol. I, Cheltenham, UK: Edward Elgar Publishing, pp. 266–316, at p. 270; Carlos M. Correa (2007), *Trade Related Aspects of Intellectual Property Rights: A Commentary on the TRIPS Agreement*, Oxford University Press, p. 277 (further noting that "the public will be bound to pay monopoly prices for access to knowledge and product that should be, and remain, in the public domain").

[76] See, e.g., Peter Drahos (2008), "Trust Me": Patent Offices in Developing Countries, *American Journal of Law and Medicine & Ethics*, pp. 151–74, at pp. 169–70; Carlos M. Correa (2011), Pharmaceutical Innovation, Incremental Patenting and Compulsory Licensing, Research Paper No. 41, p. 3 (noting that "large firms with experienced teams of patent lawyers are much better prepared, financially and technically, than domestic firms to exploit a patent regime with a low patentability threshold; there is a risk of blocking innovation and competition, rather than promoting it").

knowledge and diffusion of technology.[77] As discussed in Section 4.4.2.1, low standards of patentability applied in some countries have led to a large number of low-quality EST patents that have made little incentivising contribution but are often used by companies to restrain competition in a relevant EST market.

On the other hand, applying strict patentability standards allows patents only for genuine inventions, thus preserving a larger public domain for follow-on research and development.[78] Furthermore, high patent requirements reduce the number of incremental patents granted, thereby mitigating the strategic use of patents by multinational companies and allowing competition.[79] According to UNCTAD (2011), in principle, countries with weaker technological capabilities will benefit more from a relatively high standard of patentability.[80] In fact, various studies such as the UK Commission on Intellectual Property Rights (2002), World Bank (2002) and Reichman (2009) have recommended that developing countries adopt more stringent standards of patentability than those currently applied in many developed countries.[81]

---

[77] See, e.g., Keith E. Maskus and Ruth L. Okediji (2010), *Intellectual Property Rights and International Technology Transfer to Address Climate Change: Risks, Opportunities and Policy Options*, ICTSD Issue Paper No. 32, p. 16 (noting that "widespread criticism of the number and quality of patents issued by the US Patent and Trademark Office (USPTO) has led some scholars to suggest that weakened standards of patentability have undermined the benefits of improved technical knowledge and diffusion of technology"); Carlos M. Correa (2007), *Trade Related Aspects of Intellectual Property Rights: A Commentary on the TRIPS Agreement*, Oxford University Press, pp. 276–77; Holger Hestermeyer (2007), *Human Rights and the WTO: The Case of Patents and Access to Medicines*, Oxford University Press, p. 66; UNCTAD-ICTSD (2005), *Resource Book on TRIPS and Development*, Cambridge University Press, p. 360; John H. Barton (2000), Intellectual Property Rights: Reforming the Patent System, *Science*, vol. 287, no. 5460, pp. 1933–4, at p. 1933.

[78] Christoph Spennemann (2010), TRIPS Pre-Grant Flexibilities: Patentable Subject Matter, UNCTAD presentation, available at www.ictsd.org/downloads/2010/01/patentability-criteria-rev.pdf, p. 9.

[79] See, e.g., Boyan Konstantinov et al. (2013), The Shifting Sands of Intellectual Property Law and Policy: Implications for the Future of HIV Treatment and Public Health, in Smith (ed.), *Global HIV/AIDS Politics, Policy, and Activism: Persistent Challenges and Emerging Issues*, Praeger, vol. 2, pp. 3–22, at pp. 7 and 8; Carlos M. Correa (2011), Pharmaceutical Innovation, Incremental Patenting and Compulsory Licensing, *Research Paper* No. 41, p. 16.

[80] UNCTAD (2011), *Using Intellectual Property Rights to Stimulate Pharmaceutical Production in Developing Countries: A Preference Guide*, Geneva and New York: United Nations, p. 72.

[81] See, e.g., The UK Commission on Intellectual Property Rights (2002), *Integrating Intellectual Property Rights and Development Policy, Report of the Commission on Intellectual Property Rights*, London, p. 118; World Bank (2002), *Global Economic Prospects and Developing Countries: Making Trade Work for the World's Poor*, World Bank, p. 143 (suggesting that "countries could set high standards for the inventive step, thereby preventing routine discoveries from being patented"); Jerome H. Reichman (2009), Intellectual Property in the Twenty-First Century: Will the Developing Countries Lead or Follow? *Houston Law Review*, vol. 46, pp. 1115–85, at pp. 1132–3 (suggesting that "developing countries could help to

In practice, some developing countries such as India and the Members of the Andean Community have opted for high standards of patentability in their patent laws including by precluding new or second uses of patents.[82]

Accordingly, from the perspective of ensuring innovation of and access to patented ESTs, developing countries should adopt stricter patentability requirements within the boundaries of the TRIPS Agreement. If such high criteria for patentability are strictly applied by the patent office, it could remediate the perceived threat of low-quality patents. However, the trade-off associated with such a policy is that local innovators, in particular small and medium enterprises (SMEs), in developing countries would find it more difficult to obtain patents.[83] Nevertheless, developing countries could introduce utility models to protect their minor inventions, which is an approach common to the East Asian countries (including China) and Germany, and combine "a lower standard of inventiveness, with registration rather than examination, and a shorter protection period".[84]

accommodate international minimum standards of patent protection to their national development goals by adopting relatively stringent eligibility standards covering subject matter, novelty, non-obviousness, and disclosure").

[82] Carolyn Deere (2009), *The Implementation Game: The TRIPS Agreement and the Global Politics of Intellectual Property Reform in Developing Countries*, Oxford University Press, p. 79. For instance, Indian Patents Act 1970, Section 2 (stating that "[t]he following are not inventions within the meaning of this Act: (d) the mere discovery of a new form of a known substance which does not result in the enhancement of the known efficacy of that substance or the mere discovery of any new property or new use for a known substance or of the mere use of a known process, machine or apparatus unless such known process results in a new product or employs at least one new reactant"); Andean Community, Decision 486: Common Intellectual Property Regime, 2000, Article 21 (providing that "[p]roducts or processes that are already patented and included in the state of the art within the meaning of Article 16 of this Decision may not form the subject matter of a new patent owing to the fact of having a use ascribed to them different from that originally provided for in the first patent").

[83] See, e.g., UNCTAD (2011), *Using Intellectual Property Rights to Stimulate Pharmaceutical Production in Developing Countries: A Preference Guide*, Geneva and New York: United Nations, p. 72.

[84] The UK Commission on Intellectual Property Rights (2002), *Integrating Intellectual Property Rights and Development Policy*, Report of the Commission on Intellectual Property Rights, London, pp. 21 and 116. With respect to the definition of utility model, WIPO (2004), *WIPO Intellectual Property Handbook*, WIPO Publication No. 489 (E), 2nd edn, reprinted 2008, p. 40 (stating that "[i]n essence 'utility model' is merely a name given to certain inventions, namely – according to the laws of most countries which contain provisions on utility models – inventions in the mechanical field. This is why the objects of utility models are sometimes described as devices or useful objects. Utility models differ from inventions for which patents for invention are available mainly in two respects. First, the technological progress required is smaller than the technological progress ('inventive step') required in the case of an invention for which a patent for invention is available. Second, the maximum term of protection provided in the law

6.2.3 *Permissible Exclusions for ESTs?*

In case an invention pertaining to ESTs meets the patentability criteria, a question arises as to whether patent protection could be denied for such invention under Article 27.2 of TRIPS. This provision states that:

> Members may exclude from patentability inventions, the prevention within their territory of the commercial exploitation of which is necessary to protect *ordre public* or morality, including to protect human, animal or plant life or health or to avoid serious prejudice to the environment, provided that such exclusion is not made merely because the exploitation is prohibited by law.

Article 27.2 recognises the right of WTO Members to protect the public interest and "allows (but not mandates) two potential exceptions to patentability, based on *ordre public* and morality".[85] However, read literally, such exceptions are subject to the condition set out in Article 27.2 that the prohibition of the commercial exploitation of such invention must be necessary to protect *ordre public* and morality. According to UNCTAD and ICTSD (2005), this suggests that "a Member cannot refuse a patent on *ordre public* and morality grounds and, at the same time, permit the commercialisation of the invention".[86] Accordingly, in order to be justified under Article 27.2, the exclusion of ESTs from patentability has to meet the following three requirements: (1) the exclusion of ESTs from patentability contributes to protecting *ordre public* and morality (2) the commercial exploitation of this invention must be prevented and (3) such prevention is necessary to protect *ordre public* or morality. The following sections address these three elements in turn.

First, the exclusion of ESTs from patentability must contribute to protecting *ordre public* and morality. According to Taubman et al. (2012), the French term "*ordre public*" can be literally translated into English as "public order" and has been understood to "represent ideas such as the general security and core values of society".[87] Article 27.2 clarifies that protection of *ordre public* or morality includes the protection of human, animal or plant life or health or avoiding serious prejudice to the environment. The use of the word "including" in Article 27.2 suggests a non-exhaustive enumeration. Hence, some

---

for a utility model is generally much shorter than the maximum term of protection provided in the law for an invention for which a patent for invention is available").

[85] UNCTAD-ICTSD (2005), *Resource Book on TRIPS and Development*, Cambridge University Press, p. 375.

[86] Ibid., p. 376.

[87] Antony Taubman et al. (2012), *A Handbook on the WTO TRIPS Agreement*, Cambridge University Press, p. 102.

scholars such as Gervais (2012) go further, arguing that the French concept *ordre public* is tantamount to "public policy" and thus the term *"ordre public"* could include the protection of environment.[88] Accordingly, Article 27.2 is applicable not only for the purpose of avoiding serious prejudice to the environment but also for the purpose of protecting the environment in general.

As discussed in Sections 4.3 and 4.4, patent protection provides incentives for innovation and transfer of ESTs but it could also restrict access to ESTs. Thus, in a broad interpretation of *ordre public*, where it is understood to include "environmental protection", to the extent that the restrictive effects of patents exceed their incentivising effects, the exclusion of ESTs from patentability could contribute to protecting *ordre public* in the sense of Article 27.2. However, in a restrictive reading of Article 27.2, where *ordre public* does not include environmental protection, the exclusion from patentability is only permitted for polluting technologies that actually may cause serious prejudice to the environment, rather than ESTs.[89] This is because no matter whether ESTs are patented or not, they will eventually contribute positively to the environment and are unlikely to cause serious prejudice to the environment. Therefore, in a broad interpretation of *ordre public*, excluding ESTs from patentability might contribute to protecting *ordre public*, whereas in a more restrictive definition, this is not the case.

The second element concerns the requirement to prohibit commercial exploitation of a relevant invention. As pointed out by Taubman and Watal (2010), Article 27.2 does not permit exclusions from patentability of inventions that are actually allowed to be "commercially exploited in a Member's jurisdiction".[90] According to Hestermeyer (2007), the term "commercial exploitation" of the invention within the meaning of Article 27.2 refers to "the marketing of the invention for profit".[91] Prevention of commercial exploitation of ESTs thus means that such inventions are not allowed to be disseminated to or transacted in the marketplace, which obviously would not

[88] Daniel Gervais (2012), *The TRIPS Agreement: Drafting History and Analysis*, 4th edn, New York: Thomson Reuters, pp. 435–6.

[89] Estelle Derclaye (2008), Intellectual Property Rights and Global Warming, *Marquette Intellectual Property Law Review*, vol. 12, no. 2, pp. 264–97, at pp. 272–73.

[90] Antony Taubman and Jayashree Watal (2010), The WTO TRIPS Agreement – A Practical Overview for Climate Change Policymakers, Documentation used in technical cooperation activities of the WTO's Intellectual Property Division, available at www.wto.org/english/tratop_e/trips_e/ta_docs_e/8_3_overviewclimatechange_e.pdf, p. 5.

[91] Holger Hestermeyer (2007), *Human Rights and the WTO: The Case of Patents and Access to Medicines*, Oxford University Press, p. 56.

facilitate the innovation and transfer of ESTs. Consequently, such prohibition would frustrate the objective of intellectual property protection as established by Article 7 of the TRIPs Agreement, that is to promote technological innovation and the transfer and dissemination of technology.

As regards the third element, the prevention of commercial exploitation needs to pass a "necessity" test. The WTO dispute settlement panels and the Appellate Body have yet to clarify the term "necessary" in Article 27.2 of TRIPS. However, their interpretation concerning the general exceptions of GATT and GATS may provide important guidance. As to the determination of whether a measure is "necessary" within the meaning of Article XX of the GATT 1994, the Appellate Body in *Brazil – Retreaded Tyres* (2007) found that it is "a process involving, first, the examination of the contribution of [the measure at issue] to the achievement of its objective against its trade restrictiveness in the light of the interests at stake, and second, the comparison of the possible alternative including associated risks, with [the measure at issue]".[92] Regarding the second step, the Appellate Body further clarified that:

> If . . . the measure is necessary, this result must be confirmed by comparing the measure with its possible alternatives, which may be less trade restrictive while providing an equivalent contribution to the achievement of the objective pursued.[93]

It is obvious that the prevention of commercial exploitation of ESTs is trade restrictive. Alternatively, commercialisation of ESTs is less trade restrictive. Furthermore, wide use of ESTs, whether commercial or not, is necessary to address climate change concerns. In practice, to access more ESTs, Members need to open their market for ESTs rather than prevent their commercialisation. Therefore, we can conclude that the prevention of commercialisation of "green" inventions is not "necessary" to achieve the intended environmental protection goals but would rather run counter to such goals.

In conclusion, Article 27.2 cannot be invoked to justify excluding ESTs from patentability because: (1) exclusion of inventions pertinent to ESTs from patentability does not necessarily contribute to the protection of *ordre public* or morality, (2) it is not desirable to prevent the commercial exploitation of such inventions and (3) the prevention of commercial exploitation of such inventions is not necessary to protect *ordre public* or morality. This finding is consistent with the view of Taubman and Watal (2010) that Article 27.2

---

[92] Appellate Body Report, *Brazil – Retreaded Tyres*, para. 182.
[93] Appellate Body Report, *Brazil – Retreaded Tyres*, para. 156.

"does not allow exclusions, on environmental or other public policy grounds, from patent grants for inventions that are beneficial or desirable".[94]

As previously mentioned, in the current international climate change negotiations, some developing countries proposed to exclude "essential" or "urgent" ESTs from patentability in developing countries (see Section 3.4.2.2.1).[95] As discussed in this section, such a proposed measure is also inconsistent with Article 27.2 of the TRIPS Agreement. To the extent that compliance with WTO standards is desired, the implementation of such measure would require a fundamental change in the TRIPS Agreement (Article 27). This type of amendment would demand a high level of political cost and its feasibility could be questioned, especially considering that it took almost twelve years for the only TRIPS amendment (2005) to enter into force.[96] Accordingly, for national legislatures, rather than blanket exclusions of ESTs from patent protection, it is better to adopt stricter standards for patentability, as recommended in Section 6.2.2.2, so as to increase the quality of patents on ESTs.

6.3 LIMITS TO PATENT RIGHTS IN THE TRIPS AGREEMENT

6.3.1 *Introduction*

As discussed in Section 3.3.2, the TRIPS Agreement mandates minimum standards for IP protection (e.g., minimum standards on the subject matter of protection, the exclusive rights granted and the duration of the protection) and enforcement and allows countries to offer more extensive protection.[97] Articles 28 and 33 of the TRIPS Agreement oblige WTO Members to grant patent owners exclusive rights to prevent third parties from making, using,

---

[94] Antony Taubman and Jayashree Watal (2010), The WTO TRIPS Agreement – A Practical Overview for Climate Change Policymakers, Documentation used in technical cooperation activities of the WTO's Intellectual Property Division, available at www.wto.org/english/tratop_e/trips_e/ta_docs_e/8_3_overviewclimatechange_e.pdf, p. 5.

[95] Draft Decision Text on Technology Transfer and Intellectual Property Rights, submission by the Bolivarian Republic of Venezuela, 4 September 2012, available at http://unfccc.int/files/bodies/application/pdf/venezuela_tt_ipr_040912.pdf, para. 5(h); draft text, proposed by co-chairs, Non-Paper No. 6, Contact Group on Enhanced Action on Development and Transfer of Technology, Ad Hoc Working Group on Long-Term Cooperative Action under the Convention, Barcelona, 2–6 November 2009, available at http://unfccc.int/files/kyoto_protocol/application/pdf/technology29091009v03.pdf, p. 20.

[96] The Amendment to the TRIPS Agreement entered into force on 23 January 2017.

[97] See Article 1.1 of the TRIPS Agreement (stating that "Members may, but shall not be obliged to, implement in their law more extensive protection than is required by this Agreement").

selling, or importing the patented technology without the owner's consent for at least twenty years from the filing date. However, under the TRIPS Agreement, patent rights are not absolute but can be subject to a number of limitations or exceptions that "aim to balance the legitimate interests of right holders and users".[98] As Cottier and Véron (2011) noted, these limitations and exceptions "form part of the effort to achieve an overall balance" between competing public policy interests and contribute to the operationalisation of Articles 7 and 8 of the TRIPS Agreement.[99]

In an attempt to accommodate the diverging interests of the WTO Members,[100] the exceptions and limitations to patent rights are incorporated into the TRIPS Agreement but framed in permissive language. This means that WTO Members have the right (but no obligation) to provide for an exception to patent rights. In other words, the simple recognition of Member's rights to take measures to qualify and limit patent rights for public interest purposes does not necessarily mean that Members' national laws have to provide for such limits. Furthermore, Members' right to introduce exceptions to patent rights is subject to certain conditions and limitations imposed by the TRIPS Agreement.[101] However, this does not mean that the limitations and exceptions are less important than IP protection or that the TRIPS Agreement prioritises the interests of patent owners over public interests. Indeed, exceptions and limitations to IP rights, characterised by Taubman (2011) as "the art of the policy balance", "have long been critical issues in domestic and international standard-setting on IP", and the diplomatic history of international IP treaties "shows an evolving debate, responding to shifts in technology and public interest concerns".[102]

---

[98] Antony Taubman et al. (2012), *A Handbook on the WTO TRIPS Agreement*, Cambridge University Press, p. 4.

[99] Thomas Cottier and Pierre Véron (2011), *Concise International and European IP Law: TRIPS, Paris Convention, European Enforcement and Transfer of Technology*, 2nd edn, New York: Kluwer Law International, p. 95.

[100] See, e.g., Christopher Garrison (2006), Exceptions to Patent Rights in Developing Countries, UNCTAD-ICTSD Project on IPRs and Sustainable Development, Issue Paper No. 17, UNCTAD and ICTSD, p. 1 (noting that "[m]any WTO Members ("Members") are convinced of the utility of the patent system in encouraging research and development activity for new inventions. Many other Members are less confident of the benefits of the patent system and indeed are concerned about the dangers that the patent system poses, in terms of, for example, the impact that it and other intellectual property right systems will have on their economic and social welfare").

[101] See Articles 30, 31 and 40 of the TRIPS Agreement; see also Henning Grosse Ruse-Khan (2009), Time for a Paradigm Shift? Exploring Maximum Standards in International Intellectual Property Protection, *Trade, Law and Development*, vol. 1, pp. 56–102, at p. 58.

[102] Antony Taubman (2011), *A Practical Guide to Working with TRIPS*, Oxford University Press, p. 88.

It is noted that the TRIPS drafters attempted, but ultimately failed, to enumerate a set of designated limitations and exceptions to patent rights in the Uruguay Round negotiations.[103] Accordingly, the limits to patent rights are to be effected through national legislation, in order to facilitate innovation and transfer of technologies, including ESTs. According to UNCTAD and ICTSD (2005), "[t]he purpose of the exceptions as well as their scope may vary significantly among national laws, depending on the policy objectives pursued in each country".[104]

However, some uncertainty has arisen pertaining to whether the limits to patent rights in the TRIPS Agreement and their interpretation are adequate to ensure that it is supportive of public interest, particularly in promoting innovation and transfer of ESTs.[105] With a view to addressing this concern, one task of this book is to clarify the provisions regarding limits to patent rights in line with customary rules of interpretation of public international law, taking into account the objectives and purposes of the TRIPS Agreement and the WTO Agreement, as demonstrated in Section 5.

The most relevant limits to patent rights include parallel importation, exceptions to patent rights, compulsory licensing as well as control of anti-competitive practices. This section seeks to interpret the provisions governing the exhaustion of rights (Article 6 of the TRIPS Agreement) and the exceptions to patent rights (Article 30 of the TRIPS Agreement). Compulsory licensing is addressed in the following section and the interpretation of provisions governing anti-competitive practices are elaborated in Section 7.

6.3.2 *Limited Exceptions to Patent Rights under Article 30*

This section first examines the conditions imposed by Article 30 for the limited exceptions in general. It then conducts a detailed analysis of the

---

[103] Jerome H. Reichman and Ruth L. Okediji (2012), When Copyright Law and Science Collide: Empowering Digitally Integrated Research Methods on a Global Scale, *Minnesota Law Review*, vol. 96, pp. 1362–480, at p. 1389; Antony Taubman (2011), *A Practical Guide to Working with TRIPS*, Oxford University Press, p. 89.

[104] UNCTAD-ICTSD (2005), *Resource Book on TRIPS and Development*, Cambridge University Press, p. 430.

[105] See, e.g., Marianne Levin (2011), The Pendulum Keeps Swinging-Present Discussions on and around the TRIPS Agreement, in Kur and Levin (eds.), *Intellectual Property Rights in a Fair World Trade System: Proposals for Reform of TRIPS*, Cheltenham, UK: Edward Elgar Publishing, pp. 3–60, at p. 17 (describing "the uncertain scope of flexibilities"); Antony Taubman et al. (2012), *A Handbook on the WTO TRIPS Agreement*, Cambridge University Press, p. 180 (further noting that "different views were expressed about the nature and scope of the flexibilities in the TRIPS Agreement, for example in regard to compulsory licensing and parallel imports).

interpretation of the three-step test developed by the WTO panel in *Canada – Pharmaceutical Patents* (2000) and where necessary and appropriate, the terms of Article 30 will be interpreted in accordance with Article 31 of the VCLT with a view to facilitating innovation and transfer of ESTs. Subsequently, this section identifies relevant exceptions for ESTs.

6.3.2.1 Conditions in General

Article 30 of the TRIPS Agreement, entitled "Exceptions to Rights Conferred", allows Members to provide for limited exceptions to the exclusive patent rights, that is, "to define acts that would not be deemed as infringing when made without the authorization of the patent owner".[106] It stipulates that:

> Members may provide limited exceptions to the exclusive rights conferred by a patent, provided that such exceptions do not unreasonably conflict with a normal exploitation of the patent and do not unreasonably prejudice the legitimate interests of the patent owner, taking account of the legitimate interests of third parties.

The text of Article 30 shows that patent rights are not absolute or unlimited. As pointed out by the panel in *Canada – Pharmaceutical Patents* (2000), "Article 30's very existence amounts to a recognition that the definition of patent rights contained in Article 28 would need certain adjustments".[107] Garrison (2006) describes "exceptions to patent rights" as "'safe harbour' areas of activity where the rights of a patent holder do not extend".[108]

The exceptions to patent rights within the meaning of Article 30 "operate automatically" in the sense that the user does not need to "obtain a specific authorisation from a governmental body or judicial court, as it is the case with compulsory licences", or from the patent holder to perform the exempted act.[109] Thus, the exceptions or limitations in Article 30 may be invoked by any patent user "as a defence in case of alleged infringement" at any point during the lifetime of the patent.[110] Accordingly, such limits to patent rights can serve

---

[106] Carlos M. Correa (2002), Implications of the Doha Declaration on the TRIPS Agreement and Public Health, *Health Economics and Drugs EDM Series* No. 12, WHO, p. 28.

[107] Panel Report, *Canada – Pharmaceutical Patents*, para. 7.26.

[108] Christopher Garrison (2006), Exceptions to Patent Rights in Developing Countries, UNCTAD-ICTSD Project on IPRs and Sustainable Development, Issue Paper No. 17, UNCTAD and ICTSD, p. 1.

[109] UNCTAD-ICTSD (2005), *Resource Book on TRIPS and Development*, Cambridge University Press, p. 430.

[110] Ibid.

to mitigate the exclusive effects of patents and thereby increase the availability and affordability of patented technologies to a certain degree.[111]

The permissible scope of the exceptions to patent rights under Article 30 is "expressed in terms of general principles", known as the "three-step test", which are derived from Article 9.2 of the Berne Convention that delineates permissible exceptions to the exclusive right to control the reproductions of copyright protected works.[112] The "three-step test" in Article 30 of TRIPS contains three conditions: (1) the exception must be "limited", (2) it must not "unreasonably conflict with the normal exploitation of the patent" and (3) it must not "unreasonably prejudice the legitimate interests of the patent owner, taking account of the legitimate interests of third parties".[113] While these general principles are phrased in relatively vague language, Taubman (2011) posits that the three-step test contains "compelling legal ideas that go to the heart of fairness and equity in the IP system and its public policy settings".[114]

Commentators note that the addition of the phrase "taking account of the legitimate interests of third parties" to Article 30 could expand the scope of permissible exceptions to patent rights as compared with its Berne "parent" as well as Article 13 of the TRIPS Agreement, which describes the limitations and exceptions to copyright, leaving room for public policy considerations.[115] Accordingly, the requirement to take into account the interests of third parties possibly provides an apt entry point for WTO Members to design patent laws that could promote the interests of both producers and users of ESTs. Bearing in mind that the three-step test is worded in a very general manner, it might not be an easy task for national legislators or adjudicators to determine the

---

[111] Holger Hestermeyer (2007), *Human Rights and the WTO: The Case of Patents and Access to Medicines*, Oxford University Press, p. 234.

[112] Berne Convention for the Protection of Literary and Artistic Works, 9 September 1886, as revised at Stockholm on 14 July 1971, 1161 U.N.T.S. 30, Article 9.2 (Providing that "[i]t shall be a matter for legislation in the countries of the Union to permit the reproduction of such works in certain special cases, provided that such reproduction does not conflict with a normal exploitation of the work and does not unreasonably prejudice the legitimate interests of the author"); see also Antony Taubman (2011), *A Practical Guide to Working with TRIPS*, Oxford University Press, p. 89.

[113] Lionel Bently (2011), Exclusions from Patentability and Exceptions to Patentees' Rights: Taking Exceptions Seriously, *Current Legal Problems*, pp. 1–33, at p. 20; see also Panel Report, *Canada – Pharmaceutical Patents*, para. 7.20.

[114] Antony Taubman (2011), *A Practical Guide to Working with TRIPS*, Oxford University Press, p. 89.

[115] See, e.g., Daniel Gervais (2012), *The TRIPS Agreement: Drafting History and Analysis*, 4th edn, New York: Thomson Reuters, p. 472; Hiroko Yamane (2011), *Interpreting TRIPS: Globalisation of Intellectual Property Rights and Access to Medicines*, Oxford, UK: Hart Publishing, p. 229.

precise scope of the exceptions and limitations to patent rights, including on how to take into account the interests of the users of ESTs.

In practice, the interpretation and application of Article 30 by WTO Members vary considerably. For instance, according to the proposal of the African Group in the WTO (2002), exports of necessary pharmaceutical products to any countries that need support to address public health concerns "could be permitted as a limited and reasonable exception to patent rights under Article 30".[116] However, in the view of the United States (2002), Article 30 is only "intended to apply to statutory exceptions already provided for in many countries' laws at the time the TRIPS Agreement was negotiated, situations such as non-commercial experimental use, use aboard vessels temporarily in the territory of a Member, and prior use rights", and therefore it disagrees that the interpretation of Article 30 would justify such exports.[117] Such divergent interpretations pose a threat to legal certainty and predictability. Unfortunately, no authoritative interpretation of the terms of Article 30 has ever been given.

Notably, Article 30 was interpreted in considerable detail by a WTO dispute panel in *Canada – Pharmaceutical Patents* (2000). In interpreting Article 30 of the TRIPS Agreement, the panel explicitly referred to the rules of treaty interpretation codified in Articles 31 and 32 of the VCLT as governing rules.[118] This infers the panel's acknowledgement that the terms of Article 30 should be interpreted in good faith in line with their ordinary meaning in their context and in the light of the object and purpose of the treaty. Yet, some critics consider that the panel failed to apply the customary rules of interpretation in an appropriate manner.[119]For example, Hestermeyer (2007) points out that the panel erred in failing to take account of third parties' right to access to medicine in interpreting Article 30, even though it did consider the objectives

---

[116] Joint Communication from the African Group in the WTO, Proposal on Paragraph 6 of the Doha Declaration on the TRIPS Agreement and Public Health, WTO Doc. IP/C/W/351, 24 June 2002, para. 6 (a).

[117] Second Communication from the United States, Paragraph 6 of the Doha Declaration on the TRIPS Agreement and Public Health, WTO Doc. IP/C/W/358, 9 July 2002, para. 31 (arguing that "[i]nterpreting Article 30 to allow Members to amend their patent laws to permit compulsory licences to be granted to authorize their manufacturers to produce and export patented pharmaceutical products to other countries would both unreasonably conflict with the normal exploitation of a patent and unreasonably prejudice the legitimate interests of the patent owner").

[118] Panel Report, *Canada – Pharmaceutical Patents*, para. 7.13.

[119] See, e.g., Edson Beas Rodrigues (2012), *The General Exception Clauses of the TRIPS Agreement: Promoting Sustainable Development*, Vol. XVII, Cambridge University Press, p. 90.

of the TRIPS Agreement enshrined in Articles 7 and 8.[120] For the sake of legal predictability, WTO Members could seek to adopt a detailed authoritative interpretation of the terms of Article 30.

6.3.2.2 Interpretation of the "Three-Step" Test

This section examines the interpretation of the three-step test developed by the WTO panel in *Canada – Pharmaceutical Patents* (2000) and where necessary and appropriate, the terms of Article 30 will be interpreted taking account of the context, objective and purpose of the TRIPS Agreement and the WTO with a view to facilitating innovation and transfer of ESTs.

Turning to the *Canada – Pharmaceutical Patents* (2000) case, the measures at issue were two provisions of Canada's Patent Act: (1) the "regulatory review exception" (Section 55.2 (1) of the Patent Act), also known as the "Bolar exemption", allowing a patent owner's potential competitors to use the patented invention without the patent owner's authorisation during the patent term, for the purposes of obtaining government marketing approval, "so that they will have the regulatory permission to sell in competition with the patent owner by the date on which the patent expires"[121] and (2) "the stockpiling exception" (Section 55.2(2)), permitting competitors to manufacture and stockpile but preventing selling patented goods before the patent expiration date.[122]

The panel found that Canada's regulatory review provision meets all three criteria of Article 30 and thus is not inconsistent with the requirements of Article 28.1 of the TRIPS Agreement.[123] However, the panel also found that the stockpiling exception constitutes "a substantial curtailment" of the exclusive rights, which are required to be granted to patent owners under Article 28.1, to such an extent that it cannot be considered to be a "limited exception" under Article 30 of the TRIPS Agreement.[124]

In this case, the panel considered that the three steps are cumulative and clarified the interpretation of the individual steps. The following subsections will revisit the panel's interpretation of these elements in turn.

6.3.2.2.1 THE "CUMULATIVE" STRUCTURE OF THE THREE-STEP TEST. In analysing the basic structure of Article 30, the panel made clear that the three conditions apply on a cumulative basis, with "each being a separate and

---

[120] Holger Hestermeyer (2007), *Human Rights and the WTO: The Case of Patents and Access to Medicines*, Oxford University Press, p. 235.
[121] Panel Report, *Canada – Pharmaceutical Patents*, para. 7.2.   [122] Ibid., para. 7.7.
[123] Ibid., para. 7.84.   [124] Ibid., para.7.36.

independent requirement that must be satisfied."[125] This view suggests that failure to comply with any one of the three criteria would render an Article 30 exception TRIPS-inconsistent, "regardless of how well it meets the concerns expressed in the other prongs".[126] Relying on the principle of effective treaty interpretation explicitly recognised by the Appellate Body in *US – Gasoline* (1996), the panel requires a treaty interpreter to presume each of the three conditions in Article 30 of the TRIPS Agreement to mean something different from the other two to avoid redundancy.[127] In the panel's view, the syntax of Article 30 suggests that an exception may be "limited", yet it may "unreasonably conflict with the normal exploitation" and/or "unreasonably prejudice the legitimate interests of the patent owner".[128] Accordingly, for an Article 30 exception to be WTO-consistent, such exception has to pass all three requirements contained in Article 30 in a cumulative manner.

When interpreting the three-step test for exceptions to copyright, the panel in *US – Section 110 (5) Copyright Act* (2000) reiterated the view that the three-step test imposes three cumulative conditions.[129] This interpretation is also endorsed by some commentators such as Pires de Carvalho (2010), Cottier et al. (2011) and Taubman et al. (2012).[130] However, some critics have shown their concern over treating the three steps of the exception test in patent systems in a cumulative manner.[131] As observed by Dinwoodie and Dreyfuss

[125] Ibid., para.7.20.

[126] Graeme B. Dinwoodie and Rochelle C. Dreyfuss (2012), *A Neofederalist Vision of TRIPS: The Resilience of the International Intellectual Property Regime*, Oxford University Press, p. 60.

[127] Panel Report, *Canada – Pharmaceutical Patents*, para. 7.21; see also Panel Report, *US – Section 110(5) Copyright Act*, para. 6.97; Appellate Body Report, *US – Gasoline*, p. 23 (clarifying that "[a]n interpreter is not free to adopt a reading that would result in reducing whole clauses or paragraphs of a treaty to redundancy or inutility").

[128] Ibid., para. 7.21; see also Thomas Cottier and Pierre Véron (2011), *Concise International and European IP Law: TRIPS, Paris Convention, European Enforcement and Transfer of Technology*, 2nd edn, New York: Kluwer Law International, p. 96.

[129] Panel Report, *US – Section 110(5) Copyright Act*, para. 6.97.

[130] See, e.g., Nuno Pires de Carvalho (2010), *The TRIPS Regime of Patent Rights*, 3rd edn, New York: Kluwer Law International, p. 418; Antony Taubman et al. (2012), *A Handbook on the WTO TRIPS Agreement*, Cambridge University Press, p. 108; Thomas Cottier and Pierre Véron (2011), *Concise International and European IP Law: TRIPS, Paris Convention, European Enforcement and Transfer of Technology*, 2nd edn, New York: Kluwer Law International, p. 96.

[131] See, e.g., Henning Grosse Ruse-Khan (2011), Assessing the Need for a General Public Interest Exception in the TRIPS Agreement, in Kur and Levin (eds.), *Intellectual Property Rights in a Fair World Trade System: Proposals for Reform of TRIPS*, Cheltenham, UK: Edward Elgar Publishing, pp. 167–207, at p. 183; Christophe Geiger et al. (2008), Declaration on a Balanced Interpretation of the "Three-Step Test" in Copyright Law, *IIC*, vol. 39, pp. 707–13, at p. 709 (stating that "[w]hen correctly applied, the Three-Step Test requires a comprehensive overall assessment, rather than the step-by-step application that its usual, but misleading, description implies. No single step is to be prioritized").

(2012), the cumulative application of the three individual steps would lead to a situation in which public interests may never be taken into account for exceptions that cannot pass the first two tests.[132]

The 2014 Max Planck Institute's "Declaration on Patents Protection: Regulatory Sovereignty under TRIPS" proposes a different interpretation, stating that "[c]ontrary to what a panel of the WTO's Dispute Settlement Body seemed to assume (cf. WT/DS114/R of 17 March 2000), the three conditions are not cumulative".[133] The leading scholars in the field of patent law further contend that "[t]he three-step test may be understood to require a comprehensive overall assessment rather than a separate and independent assessment of each criterion".[134] Indeed, this interpretation allows the treaty interpreter to take into account public interests in interpreting the three conditions in Article 30 under all circumstances. Thus, the interests between the public and the patent right holders would be better balanced if no single criterion is prioritised. Accordingly, an overall assessment of all the three steps could better serve the public interest, thereby contributing to the achievement of the objectives and purpose of the TRIPS Agreement.

Furthermore, the latter interpretation is consistent with the principle of effectiveness in treaty interpretation, requiring all terms of relevant provisions be read as a whole in a harmonious fashion (see Section 5.2.1.1). Thus, a good-faith interpretation of Article 30 requires a holistic assessment rather than a separate and independent assessment of each constituent criterion of the three-step test. Such interpretation could help ensure that the public interest in mitigating climate change is not left out in determining the WTO-compatibility of the exceptions to patent rights designed to promote the innovation and transfer of ESTs.

6.3.2.2.2 "LIMITED" EXCEPTION. The panel in *Canada – Pharmaceutical Patents* (2000) found that the second and third conditions in Article 30 address the issue of "the economic impact of an exception" while the first condition concerns the extent to which the exception curtails the rights of the patent owners.[135]

---

[132] Graeme B. Dinwoodie and Rochelle C. Dreyfuss (2012), *A Neofederalist Vision of TRIPS: the Resilience of the International Intellectual Property Regime*, Oxford University Press, p. 195.

[133] Max Planck Institute for Innovation and Competition (2014), Declaration on Patent Protection: Regulatory Sovereignty under TRIPS, available at www.ip.mpg.de/files/pdf2/Patent_Declaration1.pdf, p. 8.

[134] Ibid.; see also Christophe Geiger et al. (2008), Declaration on a Balanced Interpretation of the "Three-Step Test" in Copyright Law, *IIC*, vol. 39, pp. 707–13, at p. 709.

[135] Panel Report, *Canada – Pharmaceutical Patents*, para. 7.31.

Turning to the first condition, "limited exception", the dictionary meaning of "limited" is "confined within limits; restricted or circumscribed".[136] This meaning has been endorsed by many scholars such as Correa (2007) and Abbott (2004).[137] Similarly, in *Canada – Pharmaceutical Patents* (2000), relying on conventional dictionary meaning, Canada interpreted the word "limited" as "confined within definite limits", or "restricted in scope, extent, amount".[138] In contrast, the EU interpreted the word "limited" in Article 30 to "connote a narrow exception, one that could be described by words such as 'narrow, small, minor, insignificant or restricted'". [139] The panel agreed with the EU, finding that a narrower definition of the term "limited" is more appropriate when it is used together with the term "exception" because "[t]he word 'exception' by itself connotes a limited derogation".[140] Exceptions in Article 30 are narrowed further by the word "limited", and thus, in the panel's view, "limited exceptions" within the meaning of Article 30 should make "only a small diminution of the rights in question".[141]

Some scholars have criticised the panel's interpretation of the term "limited exception" for being unduly narrow.[142] For certain commentators, the panel's interpretation of limited exception may be simply too restrictive on public policy choices or have a chilling effect on policy flexibility.[143] In the view of

---

[136] Limited. Dictionary.com Unabridged. New York: Random House, http://dictionary.reference
.com/browse/limited

[137] See, e.g., Frederick M. Abbott (2004), WTO Dispute Settlement Practice Relating to the
Agreement on Trade-related Intellectual Property Rights, in Ortino and Petersmann (eds.), *The
WTO Dispute Settlement System 1995–2003*, New York: Kluwer Law International, pp. 421–53,
at p. 426; Carlos M. Correa (2007), *Trade Related Aspects of Intellectual Property Rights:
A Commentary on the TRIPS Agreement*, Oxford University Press, p. 306; see also Panel Report,
Canada – Pharmaceutical Patents, para. 4.14.

[138] Panel Report, *Canada – Pharmaceutical Patents*, para. 7.27.

[139] Panel Report, *Canada – Pharmaceutical Patents*, para. 7.28.

[140] Panel Report, *Canada – Pharmaceutical Patents*, para. 7.30; see also Panel Report, *US –
Section 110(5) Copyright Act*, para. 6.107 (viewing that "exceptions were in and by themselves
'limited' in that they derogated from an exclusive right provided under national legislation").

[141] Ibid., para. 7.30.

[142] See, e.g., Robert Howse (2000), The Canadian Generic Medicines Panel: A Dangerous
Precedent in Dangerous Time, *The Journal of World Intellectual Property*, vol. 3, no. 4,
pp. 493–507, at p. 496; Holger Hestermeyer (2007), *Human Rights and the WTO: The Case of
Patents and Access to Medicines*, Oxford University Press, p. 235.

[143] See, e.g., Cynthia M. Ho (2007), A New World Order for Addressing Patent Rights and Public
Health, *Chicago – Kent Law Review*, vol. 82, pp. 1469–1515, at p. 1481 (stating that "[a]lthough
member states initially had varied interpretations of the scope of flexibility of this provision,
such interpretations have been largely limited by a WTO panel decision interpreting the scope
of Article 30"); UNDP (2003), *Making Global Trade Work for People*, Earthscan Publications,
p. 212 (noting that "[i]n the only dispute on article 30, (*Canada – Generic Pharmaceuticals*),
the panel followed a much more restrictive interpretation of 'limited exception'. While Article

Rodrigues (2012), in the light of the panel's interpretation, the patent right holders' commercial interests would be hierarchically placed above other interests pursued by the TRIPS Agreement and the WTO.[144]

Given its potential far-reaching implications, a careful examination of the panel's interpretation is needed. Notably, the panel's reasoning underlying its interpretation of the term "limited exception" is problematic in two aspects: first, such interpretation contradicts the well-established interpretative principle of *in dubio mitius*, under which in case of ambiguity, "that meaning is to be preferred which is less onerous to the party assuming an obligation"; [145] second, the panel's interpretation is inconsistent with the Appellate Body's finding in *EC – Hormones* (1998), that is,

merely characterizing a treaty provision as an "exception" does not by itself justify a "stricter" or "narrower" interpretation of that provision than would be warranted by examination of the ordinary meaning of the actual treaty words, viewed in context and in the light of the treaty's object and purpose, or, in other words, by applying the normal rules of treaty interpretation.[146]

Thus, the term "limited exceptions" does not by itself justify a "stricter" or "narrower" interpretation. As discussed in Section 5, the term "limited exceptions" in Article 30 should be read in conjunction with the WTO's sustainable development objective, Articles 7 and 8 of the TRIPS Agreement, and in its context, including the commitments to transfer ESTs under Article 4.5 of the UNFCCC. In practice, the limiting effect of the exception on a given patent should be evaluated on a case-by-case basis, in light of the acts involved, the purpose of the exception, and other criteria such as "the duration of the exception, the limitation on the volume of the production allowed or on the market destinations of such products".[147] Accordingly, it could be argued

30 has the potential to resolve the access to drugs problem, it has not been interpreted in a development-friendly manner as yet and is open to legal challenge"); Edson Beas Rodrigues (2012), *The General Exception Clauses of the TRIPS Agreement: Promoting Sustainable Development*, vol. 17, Cambridge University Press, p. 91 (pointing out that "[t]he Panel Report embraced an interpretation that restricted the leeway available for WTO Member States to adopt exceptions to patent rights").

[144] Edson Beas Rodrigues (2012), *The General Exception Clauses of the TRIPS Agreement: Promoting Sustainable Development*, vol. 17, Cambridge University Press, p. 99.

[145] Appellate Body Report, *EC – Hormones*, footnote 154 (stating "[t]he principle of *in dubio mitius* applies in interpreting treaties, in deference to the sovereignty of states. If the meaning of a term is ambiguous, that meaning is to be preferred which is less onerous to the party assuming an obligation, or which interferes less with the territorial and personal supremacy of a party, or involves less general restrictions upon the parties" and further noting that this principle has been widely cited in international case law).

[146] Ibid., para. 104.

[147] See, e.g., Thomas Cottier and Pierre Véron (2011), *Concise International and European IP Law: TRIPS, Paris Convention, European Enforcement and Transfer of Technology*, 2nd edn,

that Article 30, if properly interpreted, would allow WTO Members to retain certain policy flexibility with respect to the extent to which the exception curtails the rights of the patent owners.

6.3.2.2.3 NO UNREASONABLE CONFLICT WITH THE NORMAL EXPLOIT-ATION OF THE PATENT. The second criterion in Article 30 requires that exceptions must not "unreasonably conflict with a normal exploitation of the patent". According to the panel, the term "exploitation" refers to "the commercial activity by which patent owners employ their exclusive patent rights" listed in Article 28 to extract economic value from their patents.[148] The normal practice of exploitation by patent owners is "to exclude all forms of competition that could detract significantly from the economic returns anticipated from a patent's grant of market exclusivity".[149] The panel further stressed that "protection of all normal exploitation practices is a key element of the policy reflected in all patent laws" and stated that:

> Patent laws establish a carefully defined period of market exclusivity as an inducement to innovation, and the policy of those laws cannot be achieved unless patent owners are permitted to take effective advantage of that inducement once it has been defined.[150]

The panel went further and regarded a certain period of market exclusivity following patent expiration to be part of normal exploitation.[151] In the panel's view, patent holders enjoy the separate right to prevent competitors from producing the patented products during the patent term, thereby forbidding the competitors to stockpile the patented products needed to enter a market immediately after the patent expiration.[152]

However, the panel held that "the additional period of *de facto* market exclusivity created by using patent rights to preclude submissions for regulatory authorisation should not be considered 'normal'",[153] because such market exclusivity is not "a natural or normal consequence of enforcing patent rights".[154] The panel further pointed out that most patent holders in fact do not employ this type of patent exclusivity because only certain patented products are subject to regulatory approval.[155] Accordingly, the panel concluded that a Bolar exemption does not conflict with the normal exploitation of the patent,[156]

New York: Kluwer Law International, p. 96; Carlos M. Correa (2007), *Trade Related Aspects of Intellectual Property Rights: A Commentary on the TRIPS Agreement*, Oxford University Press, p. 307.
[148] Panel Report, *Canada – Pharmaceutical Patents*, para. 7.54.   [149] Ibid., para. 7.55.
[150] Ibid.   [151] Ibid., para. 7.56.   [152] Ibid.   [153] Ibid., para. 7.57.   [154] Ibid.   [155] Ibid.
[156] Ibid., para. 7.59.

without further considering the legitimate interests of third parties or the object and purpose of the TRIPS Agreement.

Critics point out that the panel's approach to interpret the term "normal exploitation" is "surprisingly one-sided", that is solely from the perspective of patent right holders.[157] While emphasising the role of patent protection in stimulating innovation, the panel seems to have failed to consider other essential objectives of the TRIPS Agreement such as the dissemination and transfer of technologies.[158] The panel's one-sided approach can be remedied by a proper interpretation of the term "normal exploitation" in light of Article 31 of the VCLT. The object and purpose of the TRIPS Agreement demands the consideration of the public interest and of both innovation and transfer of technologies. The use of the term "not unreasonably" to qualify the "conflict with a normal exploitation" by the TRIPS negotiators suggests their intention to balance the "normal exploitation" with the interests that a WTO Member seeks to protect by allowing for the exception.[159]

6.3.2.2.4 LEGITIMATE INTERESTS. The third criterion for an Article 30 exception is that the exception must not "unreasonably prejudice the legitimate interests of the patent owner, taking account of the legitimate interests of third parties". The panel in *Canada – Pharmaceutical Patents* (2000) noted the dictionary meaning of the word "legitimate" is commonly defined as "(a) Conformable to, sanctioned or authorized by, law or principle: lawful; justifiable; proper. (b) Normal, regular, conformable to a recognized standard type".[160]

---

[157] See, e.g., Robert Howse (2000), The Canadian Generic Medicines Panel: A Dangerous Precedent in Dangerous Time, *The Journal of World Intellectual Property*, vol. 3, no. 4, pp. 493–507, at p. 499 (stating that "In interpreting 'normal', the Panel looked exclusively at the expectations of rights holders as to the 'economic returns anticipated from a patent's grant of market exclusivity'. This again reflects its overall bias in viewing the TRIPS Agreement as having, as its overarching goal, the protection of the rights of innovators, not a balance of rights and obligations between different relevant social and economic interests"); Holger Hestermeyer (2007), *Human Rights and the WTO: The Case of Patents and Access to Medicines*, Oxford University Press, p. 236.

[158] See also Carlos M. Correa (2007), *Trade Related Aspects of Intellectual Property Rights: A Commentary on the TRIPS Agreement*, Oxford University Press, p. 309.

[159] See also Thomas Cottier and Pierre Véron (2011), *Concise International and European IP Law: TRIPS, Paris Convention, European Enforcement and Transfer of Technology*, 2nd edn, New York: Kluwer Law International, p. 97 (stating that "The qualification that the conflict must not be unreasonable requires the interpreter to strike a balance between that 'normal exploitation' and the interests which a Member protects by the exception").

[160] Panel Report, *Canada – Pharmaceutical Patents*, para. 7.68.

The panel explicitly rejected the EU's interpretative approach to equate "legitimate interests" in Article 30 with "a full respect of legal interests pursuant to Article 28.1" largely on the following grounds: (1) the EU's definition would effectively reduce the condition "[must] not unreasonably prejudice the legitimate interests of the patent owner" to a simple requirement that the proposed exception must not be "unreasonable" because in line with the EU's definition, every Article 30-type exception would cause "prejudice" to some legal rights in Article 28; and (2) the definition equating "legitimate interests" with legal interests protected under Article 28 does not make sense when applied to the term "legitimate interests of third parties" in Article 30.[161]

The panel noted the attempt to illustrate limited exceptions in the TRIPS negotiation process and stressed the explicit reference to "the legitimate interests of third parties" in Article 30 as opposed to Article 13, seemingly suggesting "a more 'balanced' test" in determining the scope of "legitimate interests" in Article 30.[162] The panel, thus, interpreted the term "legitimate interests" to mean "interests that are 'justifiable' in the sense that they are supported by relevant public policies or other social norms".[163] Accordingly, the panel concluded that the patent holder's interests in obtaining compensatory patent term extensions for the time it lost in acquiring regulatory approval was "neither so compelling nor so widely recognized" that it could be considered as a "legitimate interest" under Article 30.[164]

However, the panel's reasoning seems to have exclusively focused on inquiring whether the interests of the patent holder are compelling rather than weighing the interests of the patent holders against "the legitimate interests of third parties".[165] Therefore, the panel appeared to have avoided ruling on Canada's assertion that third-party interests include "general societal interests".[166] Accordingly, some commentators are concerned that competing social and economic interests might be ignored where the right holder's interests are compelling.[167]

---

[161] Panel Report, *Canada – Pharmaceutical Patents*, para. 7.68.

[162] Ibid., paras. 7.70–7.71; see also Daniel Gervais (2012), *The TRIPS Agreement: Drafting History and Analysis*, 4th edn, New York: Thomson Reuters, p. 475.

[163] Ibid., para. 7.69.   [164] Ibid., para. 7.82.   [165] Ibid.   [166] Ibid., para. 7.67.

[167] See, e.g., Robert Howse (2000), The Canadian Generic Medicines Panel: A Dangerous Precedent in Dangerous Time, *The Journal of World Intellectual Property*, vol. 3, no. 4, pp. 493–507, at p. 501 (stating that "one can silence competing social and economic interests entirely by starting off with defining the rights holder's interests as so weighty or fundamental that other legitimate interests cannot possibly outweigh the prejudice to right holder's interests"); Holger Hestermeyer (2007), *Human Rights and the WTO: The Case of Patents and Access to Medicines*, Oxford University Press, p. 237.

In fact, the definition and the open-ended nature of "legitimate interests of third parties" should have opened the doors to the societal interests and public policy considerations underlined in the Preamble of the Marrakesh Agreement and in Articles 7 and 8 of the TRIPS Agreement which constitute part of the context of Article 30 of the TRIPS Agreement.[168] These interests include, inter alia, "sustainable development" (the Preamble of the Marrakesh Agreement), "the mutual advantage of producers and users of technological knowledge" (Article 7) and "the public interest in sectors of vital importance to socio-economic and technological development" (Article 8).[169] All these interests shall be taken into account in interpreting Article 30 of the TRIPS Agreement in accordance with Article 31 of the VCLT.

In the context of climate change, public interests in general and societal interests in combating climate change in particular fall within the scope of the "legitimate interests of third parties" under Article 30. As argued in Section 2.1, innovation and transfer of ESTs are vital for mitigating climate change. Therefore, relevant public and societal interests shall be taken into account when determining the scope of legitimate exceptions in Article 30 designed to facilitate innovation and transfer of ESTs.

6.3.2.3 Examples of Relevant Exceptions under Article 30 for ESTs

This subsection seeks to identify relevant Article 30-type exceptions for facilitating innovation and transfer of ESTs.

Article 30 does not provide for concrete exceptions to patent rights. Notably, treaty drafters did not agree to an approach in which Members would enumerate specific acts that may be exempted in the TRIPS Agreement.[170]

---

[168] Panel Report, *Canada – Pharmaceutical Patents*, para. 7.67 (noting that in support of the consideration of general societal interests, "Canada, together with several of the third party participants in this proceeding, relied most heavily on the statements of objectives and principles stated in Articles 7 and 8.1 of the TRIPS Agreement").

[169] See also Robert Howse (2000), The Canadian Generic Medicines Panel: A Dangerous Precedent in Dangerous Time, *The Journal of World Intellectual Property*, vol. 3, no. 4, pp. 493–507, at p. 502.

[170] Chairman's Report to the GNG, Status of Work in the Negotiating Group, GATT Doc. MTN. GNG/NG11/W/76, 23 July 1990, pp. 31–32 (stating "limited exceptions to the exclusive rights conferred by a patent may be made for certain acts, such as rights based on prior use, acts done privately and for non-commercial purposes, acts done for experimental purposes and preparation in a pharmacy in individual cases of a medicine in accordance with a prescription, or acts carried out with a medicine so prepared"); Panel Report, *Canada – Pharmaceutical Patents*, para. 7.70 (noting that "eventually, [the] illustrative list approach was abandoned in favour of a more general authorization following the outlines of the present Article 30. The negotiating records of the TRIPS Agreement give no explanation of the reason for this decision").

According to the panel in *Canada – Pharmaceutical Patents* (2000), despite an attempt to illustrate exceptions such as "private use, scientific use, prior use, a traditional exception for pharmacists, and the like", TRIPS negotiators eventually opted for "a more general authorisation following the outlines of the present Article 30".[171] However, in practice, it is well-accepted that limitations to patent rights cover "the use of the patented invention for private, non-commercial purposes and for research or experimental purposes (to varying degrees according to national [laws] and jurisprudence)".[172]

A research or an experimental use exception is one of the most commonly used Article 30-type exceptions found in national patent laws.[173] The panel in *Canada – Pharmaceutical Patent* (2000) defined the term as "the exception under which use of the patented product for scientific experimentation, during the term of the patent and without consent, is not an infringement".[174] The panel further found that:

this exception is based on the notion that a key public policy purpose underlying patent laws is to facilitate the dissemination and advancement of technical knowledge and that allowing the patent owner to prevent experimental use during the term of the patent would frustrate part of the purpose of the requirement that the nature of the invention be disclosed to the public.[175]

This panel's finding has been endorsed by many commentators.[176] Indeed, one of the purposes of the patent system is to stimulate the dissemination of

---

[171] Panel Report, *Canada – Pharmaceutical Patents*, para. 7.70.

[172] See, e.g., Antony Taubman and Jayashree Watal (2010), The WTO TRIPS Agreement – A Practical Overview for Climate Change Policymakers, Documentation used in technical cooperation activities of the WTO's Intellectual Property Division, available at www.wto.org/english/tratop_e/trips_e/ta_docs_e/8_3_overviewclimatechange_e.pdf, p. 8; CIEL (2010), *Technology Transfer in the UNFCCC and Other International Legal Regimes: The Challenge of Systemic Integration*, International Council on Human Rights Policy, p. 13; Thomas Cottier and Pierre Véron (2011), *Concise International and European IP Law: TRIPS, Paris Convention, European Enforcement and Transfer of Technology*, 2nd edn, New York: Kluwer Law International, p. 97.

[173] See, e.g., WIPO (2010), Patent Related Flexibilities in the Multilateral Legal Framework and Their Legislative Implementation at the National and Regional Levels, CDIP/5/4, Annex II, pp. 43–52 (having identified 98 countries that provide varying levels of exceptions for acts carried out for experimental purposes or scientific research); WHO, WIPO and WTO (2013), *Promoting Access to Medical Technologies and Innovation: Intersections between Public Health, Intellectual Property and Trade*, p. 134.

[174] Panel Report, *Canada – Pharmaceutical Patents*, para. 7.69.   [175] Ibid.

[176] See, e.g., Edson Beas Rodrigues (2012), *The General Exception Clauses of the TRIPS Agreement: Promoting Sustainable Development*, vol. 17, Cambridge University Press, p. 181; Evans Misati and Kiyoshi Adachi (2010), The Research and Experimentation Exceptions in Patent Law: Jurisdictional Variations and the WIPO Development Agenda, UNCTAD-ICTSD Project on IPRs and Sustainable Development, *Policy Brief* No.7, p. 1; Rebecca

the technological knowledge, thereby facilitating follow-on scientific research and technological innovation. It thus makes no sense to prevent experimental use of the patented inventions. Accordingly, under the TRIPS Agreement, both society and the scientists have a "legitimate interest" in using an experimental use exception to support the dissemination and advancement of technology.[177]

Exceptions relating to research or experimental use can create an enabling environment for technology innovation and dissemination.[178] As pointed out by Correa (2003), the adoption of such exceptions may expedite innovation and technological progress based on "inventing around" or improving a patented invention, as well as allow for evaluation of an invention for legitimate purposes such as requesting a licence or testing whether the invention works.[179] Although patent disclosure provides some basis for "inventing around", it is often inadequate to serve as a basis for reproducing or improving the technology (as also discussed in Section 4.3.1.2). Further research and experimentation are thus required for complex technologies such as ESTs. According to the Commonwealth Secretariat (2009), an experimental use exception will allow researchers to gain access to the technological knowledge of patented ESTs and permit firms to "invent around" the EST patents.[180] Thus, countries should make use of research and experimental exception with a view to facilitating innovation and transfer of ESTs.

6.3.2.4 Conclusion

In conclusion, Article 30 requires a holistic assessment rather than a separate and independent assessment of each constituent criterion of the "three-step test". As to the first element, "limited exceptions", WTO Members retain certain policy flexibility under Article 30 with respect to the extent to which

S. Eisenberg (1989), Patents and the Progress of Science: Exclusive Rights and Experimental Use, *The University of Chicago Law Review*, vol. 56, no. 3, pp. 1017–86, at pp. 1061–5.

[177] Panel Report, *Canada – Pharmaceutical Patents*, para. 7.69.

[178] WIPO (2010), *Patent Related Flexibilities in the Multilateral Legal Framework and their Legislative Implementation at the National and Regional Levels*, CDIP/5/4 Rev., at p. 22; WHO, WIPO and WTO (2013), *Promoting Access to Medical Technologies and Innovation: Intersections between Public Health, Intellectual Property and Trade*, p. 134.

[179] Carlos M. Correa (2003), Intellectual Property Rights and the Protection of Public Health in Developing Countries, *The World Bank Legal Review: Law and Justice for Development*, vol. 1, pp. 161–205, at p. 186.

[180] Moustapha Kamal Gueye et al. (2009), *Trade, Climate Change and Sustainable Development: Key Issues for Small States, Least Developed Countries and Vulnerable Economics*, Commonwealth Secretariat, DOI: http://dx.doi.org/10.14217/9781848590007-en, p. 92.

the exception curtails the rights of the patent owners. With respect to the second criterion, the use of the term "not unreasonably" to qualify the "conflict with a normal exploitation" suggests WTO Members' intention to strike a balance between the "normal exploitation" and the interests protected by an exception. The third criterion requires that the legitimate interests of third parties be taken into account.

All these criteria shall be read in accordance with the WTO's sustainable development objective, Articles 7 and 8 of the TRIPS Agreement, and in their context, including the commitments to transfer ESTs under Article 4.5 of the UNFCCC. Public interests in general and societal interests in combating climate change in particular fall within the scope of "legitimate interests of third parties" in Article 30. Thus, such interests shall be considered when determining the scope of legitimate exceptions for ESTs. Notably, experimental use exceptions could be adopted under Article 30 of the TRIPS Agreement to facilitate innovation of ESTs and disseminate technological knowledge, thereby contributing to climate change mitigation.

6.3.3 *Exhaustion of Rights and Parallel Imports*

6.3.3.1 Exhaustion of Rights

One of the limits on the exclusive patent rights is the exhaustion of patent rights. The concept of "the exhaustion of IPRs", or "first sale" (US doctrine) refers to the point at which "the right holder ceases to control a tangible good based on the [IPRs] that are embodied in it".[181] Under the doctrine of patent exhaustion, the right holders' exclusive right to control a patented item lapses after the initial authorised sale of the item.[182] In effect, if one has legitimately obtained an article incorporating patents, she or he is entitled to use, sell or transfer it without seeking further authorisation from the patent right holder or paying an additional royalty.

It is well-accepted that the rationale behind the doctrine of exhaustion is that the exclusive control over the first sale of goods embodying the patent is

---

[181] Thomas Cottier and Pierre Véron (2011), *Concise International and European IP Law: TRIPS, Paris Convention, European Enforcement and Transfer of Technology*, 2nd edn, New York: Kluwer Law International, p. 24.

[182] See, e.g., Antony Taubman et al. (2012), *A Handbook on the WTO TRIPS Agreement*, Cambridge University Press, p. 18; Supreme Court of the United States, *Quanta Computer, Inc. v. LG Electronics, Inc.* (No. 06 – 937), 453 F. 3d 1364, 2008, (stating that "[t]he longstanding doctrine of patent exhaustion limits the patent rights that survive the initial authorized sale of a patented item").

sufficient to provide incentives to invest in technological innovation.[183] As pointed out by UNCTAD and ICTSD (2005), without an exhaustion doctrine, the original patent owner would "perpetually exercise control over the sale, transfer or use" of an article embodying a patent, thereby restricting the free movements of goods in the marketplace and stifling competition.[184]

There is a broad consensus that patent rights are exhausted within the jurisdiction where the first sale takes place whereas a question arises over whether such rights are exhausted when the first sale occurs outside the jurisdiction in question.[185] The answer to this question depends on the type of exhaustion regimes adopted by the country in question: "national", "regional" or "international" and thereby determines whether parallel imports are legal or not.[186] It is observed that, at the regional level, with few exceptions, the Court of Justice of the European Union (CJEU) has applied the regional exhaustion doctrine to the entire EU and to all types of IPRs, in order to "unite national markets into a single market" and "prevent market segmentation".[187] Under this doctrine, parallel imports coming from non-EU territories would be denied.

---

[183] See, e.g., Margreth Barrett (2000), United States' Doctrine of Exhaustion: Parallel Imports of Patented Goods, *Northern Kentucky Law Review*, vol. 27, no. 5, pp. 911–84, at p. 913 (stating that "an intellectual property owner will have exclusive control over the first sale of goods embodying the intellectual property, and that this should be sufficient to ensure that there is a financial incentive to invest in the creative process"); Daniel Erlikhman (2003), Jazz Photo and the Doctrine of Patent Exhaustion: Implications to TRIPS and International Harmonization of Patent Protection, *Hastings Communications and Entertainment Law Journal*, vol. 25, pp. 307–42, at p. 308.

[184] UNCTAD-ICTSD (2005), *Resource Book on TRIPS and Development*, Cambridge University Press, p. 93; see also Seungwoo Son (2002), Selective Refusals to Sell Patented Goods: The Relationship between Patent Rights and Antitrust Law, *Journal of Law, Technology & Policy*, vol. 2002, no. 1, pp. 109–91, at p. 126 (stating that "[e]xtending legal rights to control goods beyond their first sale is unnecessary to accomplish the inventive function, and may unduly interfere with competition and the free movement of goods in the marketplace").

[185] See, e.g., Antony Taubman et al. (2012), *A Handbook on the WTO TRIPS Agreement*, Cambridge University Press, p. 19; Jayashree Watal (2003), Parallel Imports and IPR-Based Dominant Positions: Where Do India's Interests Lie? in Cottier and Mavroidis (eds.), *Intellectual Property: Trade, Competition and Sustainable Development*, Ann Arbor: The University of Michigan Press, pp. 199–210, at p. 201.

[186] Antony Taubman et al. (2012), *A Handbook on the WTO TRIPS Agreement*, Cambridge University Press, p. 19.

[187] See e.g., Carlos M. Correa (2000), *Integrating Public Health Concerns into Patent Legislation in Developing Countries*, Geneva: South Centre, p. 74 (further noting that "[i]n the case of the United Kingdom, however, the principle of international exhaustion has been admitted in some cases"); Fink Carsten (2005), Entering the Jungle of Intellectual Property Rights Exhaustion and Parallel Importation, in Fink and Maskus (eds.), *Intellectual Property and Development: Lessons from Recent Economic Research*, World Bank and Oxford University Press, pp. 173–91, at p. 175.

At the national level, developed countries such as the United States have adopted national exhaustion of patent rights and thus protect their patent owners from parallel imports.[188] In contrast, many developing countries such as India and Brazil favour international exhaustion of patent rights and thus allow parallel trade. In the view of Ganslandt and Maskus (2008), this reflects in part "the absence of broader competition policies and the existence of stricter limitations on the exercise of intellectual property rights than are found in the United States and EU".[189]

At the global level, despite widespread acknowledgement during the Uruguay Round negotiations that the concept of parallel import "fitted perfectly within the goal of international free trade advocated by GATT", the TRIPS negotiators failed to agree upon a proper scope of the exhaustion doctrine.[190] As a compromise, Article 6 of TRIPS was added to exclude the issue of the exhaustion of IPRs from WTO dispute settlement, provided that MFN and national treatment obligations are to be complied with, stating that:

> For the purposes of dispute settlement under this Agreement, subject to the provisions of Articles 3 and 4 nothing in this Agreement shall be used to address the issue of the exhaustion of intellectual property rights.

According to Watal (2003), this provision implicitly allows WTO Members to adopt their own regimes on exhaustion of IPRs in a non-discriminatory manner, thus neither barring nor encouraging parallel imports.[191] In other words, the TRIPS Agreement leaves it entirely up to the WTO Members to choose their own regime of exhaustion of rights, thereby determining the legality of parallel imports themselves.

Footnote 6 of TRIPS clarifies that the patent holders' right to prevent third parties from importing the product is "subject to the provisions of Article 6". Therefore, the international exhaustion rule adopted by WTO Members may

---

[188] See, e.g., Keith E. Maskus (2002), Benefiting from Intellectual Property Protection, in Hoekman et al. (eds.), *Development, Trade and the WTO: A Handbook*, World Bank, pp. 369–81, at p. 377; Scott C. Bradford and Robert Z. Lawrence (2004), *Has Globalization Gone Far Enough?: The Costs of Fragmented Markets*, Washington, D.C.: Peterson Institute, p. 14.

[189] Mattias Ganslandt and Keith E. Maskus (2008), Intellectual Property Rights, Parallel Imports and Strategic Behaviour, in Maskus (ed.), *Intellectual Property, Growth and Trade*, Bingley, UK: Emerald Group Publishing, pp. 263–88, at p. 268.

[190] Rajnish Kumar Rai and Sirnath Jagannathan (2012), Parallel Imports and Unparallel Laws: An Examination of the Exhaustion Doctrine through the Lens of Pharmaceutical Products, *Information and Communications Technology Law*, vol. 21, no. 1, pp. 53–89, at p. 65.

[191] Jayashree Watal (2003), Parallel Imports and IPR-Based Dominant Positions: Where Do India's Interests Lie? in Cottier and Mavroidis (eds.), *Intellectual Property: Trade, Competition and Sustainable Development*, Ann Arbor: The University of Michigan Press, pp. 199–210, at p. 201.

not be challenged on the basis of the patent holder's exclusive right to importation in Article 28.[192] The Doha Declaration has further confirmed that the effect of the TRIPS provisions that are relevant to the exhaustion of IPRs is to "leave each Member free to establish its own regime for such exhaustion without challenge", subject to the MFN and national treatment provisions of TRIPS.[193] It is therefore clear that the TRIPS Agreement does not prohibit WTO Members from permitting parallel imports.

6.3.3.2 Parallel Imports for Patented ESTs

Some commentators observe that parallel imports may help some developing countries obtain ESTs "at more affordable prices".[194] This section addresses the relevance of parallel imports to the innovation and transfer of patented ESTs.

It is well-accepted that Article 6 of the TRIPS Agreement gives WTO Members broad leeway to introduce parallel import policies.[195] In particular, this provision allows WTO Members to incorporate in their national laws the principle of international exhaustion of rights which is "the underlying justification for parallel imports".[196] Parallel imports, also called grey-market imports, refer to a situation "[w]hen a product made legally (i.e. not pirated) abroad is imported without the permission of the intellectual property right-holder (e.g. the trademark or patent owner)".[197] Such imports allow a third party, without the patent holder's authorisation, to import legitimate products from a foreign market, thereby permitting direct competition between the third party and the patent right holder.[198]

---

[192] UNCTAD-ICTSD (2005), *Resource Book on TRIPS and Development*, Cambridge University Press, p. 106.

[193] Declaration on the TRIPS Agreement and Public Health, adopted on 14 November 2001, 20 November 2001, WTO Doc. No. WT/MIN (01)/DEC/2, para. 5(d).

[194] See, e.g., Jerome H. Reichman (2014), Intellectual Property in the Twenty-First Century: Will the Developing Countries Lead or Follow? in Mario et al. (eds.), *Intellectual Property Rights: Legal and Economic Challenges for Development*, Oxford University Press, pp. 111–81, at p. 126.

[195] See, e.g., Ping Xiong (2012), *An International Law Perspective on the Protection of Human Rights in the TRIPS Agreement: An Interpretation of the TRIPS Agreement in Relation to the Right to Health*, Leiden, Netherlands: Martinus Nijhoff Publishers, p. 186.

[196] Carlos M. Correa (2003), Intellectual Property Rights and the Protection of Public Health in Developing Countries, *The World Bank Legal Review: Law and Justice for Development*, vol. 1, pp. 161–205, at p. 192.

[197] WTO, glossary term, available at www.wto.org/english/thewto_e/glossary_e/parallel_imports_e.htm

[198] Sisule F. Musungu et al. (2004), *Utilizing TRIPS Flexibilities for Public Health Protection through South – South Regional Frameworks*, Geneva: South Centre, p. 13.

Proponents of international exhaustion of rights believe that parallel imports increase competition, thereby lowering prices and making technology more accessible and affordable in developing countries.[199] There are, however, concerns that parallel imports may limit IPR holders' profits and discourage investment in research and development thus, ultimately, leading to a decrease in innovation and transfer of technology.[200] As observed by Cottier et al. (2011), "[r]ight holders quite naturally support restrictive regimes of exhaustion" while "considerations of competition and consumer protection are in favour of an extensive regime".[201]

In order to increase consumer welfare and maintain free competition in a scenario of full compliance with the TRIPS Agreement, the UK Commission on Intellectual Property Rights (2002) recommended that "parallel imports should be allowed whenever the patentee's rights have been exhausted in the foreign country".[202] In the case of access to medicine, WHO (2006) suggested that less developed countries "should retain the possibilities to benefit from differential pricing, and the ability to seek and parallel import lower priced medicines".[203] Similarly, in the context of combating climate change, this book recommends that countries with low level of technological advancement should allow parallel imports to ensure the lowest cost source of supply of patented ESTs for combating climate change.

---

[199] See, e.g., Jerome H. Reichman (2009), Intellectual Property in the Twenty-first Century: Will the Developing Countries Lead or Follow? *Houston Law Review*, vol. 46, no. 4, pp. 1115–85, at p.1147.

[200] See, e.g., Claude E. Barfield and Mark A. Groombridge (1999), Parallel Trade in the Pharmaceutical Industry: Implications for Innovation, Consumer Welfare, and Health Policy, *Fordham Intellectual Property, Media and Entertainment Law Journal*, vol. 10, pp. 185–265, at p. 221 (considering that "to the extent that international exhaustion threatens parallel exports from low priced developing countries, patent holders will be less likely to transfer technology and production capacity to them through direct investment and licensing"); WIPO Standing Committee on the Law of Patents (2010), Transfer of Technology, SCP/14/4, 11 December 2009, p. 32 (noting that "wide availability of parallel imported products may discourage foreign right holders from investing in the domestic market, since the parallel importer could free ride on the investments made by authorized distributors").

[201] Thomas Cottier and Pierre Véron (2011), *Concise International and European IP Law: TRIPS, Paris Convention, European Enforcement and Transfer of Technology*, 2nd edn, New York: Kluwer Law International, p. 24.

[202] The UK Commission on Intellectual Property Rights (2002), *Integrating Intellectual Property Rights and Development Policy*, Report of the Commission on Intellectual Property Rights, London, at p. 42.

[203] See, e.g., WHO (2006), *Public Health: Innovation and Intellectual Property Rights*, Report of the Commission on Intellectual Property Rights, Innovation and Public Health, published by WHO, at p. 142.

6.4 COMPULSORY LICENSING UNDER ARTICLE 31

Compulsory licensing is another instrument that may limit the exclusive patent rights when needed to protect public interest or "fulfil certain public policy objectives" including mitigating climate change.[204] The TRIPS Agreement gives considerable leeway to WTO Members to impose compulsory licences "for any legitimate purpose", including mitigating climate change, and "without undue constraints".[205] The following sections will address in turn: first, the concept of compulsory licensing; second, grounds for granting compulsory licences; third, conditions for the granting of compulsory licences; and finally, compulsory licensing as a policy lever for EST transfer.

6.4.1 *The Concept of Compulsory Licensing*

Compulsory licences are licences granted by a government authority, permitting a person other than the patent owner (or the government itself, which is then called "government use") to produce, import, sell or use the patent-protected product or use the patented process "without the consent of the patent owner".[206] In these cases, the public interest pertaining to a broader access to the patented invention is deemed to supersede the patent owner's private interests in fully exploiting its exclusive rights.[207] Nonetheless, under

---

[204] See, e.g., Carlos M. Correa (2002), Implications of the Doha Declaration on the TRIPS Agreement and Public Health, Health Economics and Drugs EDM Series No. 12, WHO, p. 15 (noting that "Developing countries have identified compulsory licensing as one of the key instruments that may limit the exclusive rights of the patent owner when needed to fulfil certain objectives of public policy, particularly in order to ensure the availability of alternative sources for the supply of medicines at lower prices"); The UK Commission on Intellectual Property Rights (2002), *Integrating Intellectual Property Rights and Development Policy*, Report of the Commission on Intellectual Property Rights, London, at p. 42 (stating that "We do not regard compulsory licensing as a panacea, but rather as an essential insurance policy to prevent abuses of the IP system"); Australian Productivity Commission (2013), *Compulsory Licensing of Patents*, Inquiry Report No. 61, Commonwealth of Australia, at p. 47 (categorizing compulsory licensing as *ex post* safeguards that are invoked when "exercising the exclusive right associated with the patent is not in the interest of the community as a whole").

[205] See also Jerome H. Reichman and Catherine Hasenzahl (2003), Non-voluntary Licensing of Patented Inventions: Historical Perspective, Legal Framework under TRIPS, and an Overview of the Practice in Canada and the USA, UNCTAD-ICTSD Issue Paper No. 5, p. 15.

[206] See, e.g., Antony Taubman et al. (2012), *A Handbook on the WTO TRIPS Agreement*, Cambridge University Press, p. 109; Holger Hestermeyer (2007), *Human Rights and the WTO: The Case of Patents and Access to Medicines*, Oxford University Press, p. 239.

[207] Jerome H. Reichman and Catherine Hasenzahl (2003), *Non-Voluntary Licensing of Patented Inventions: Historical Perspective, Legal Framework under TRIPS, and an Overview of the Practice in Canada and the USA*, UNCTAD-ICTSD Issue Paper No. 5, p. 10; see also Cristian

the current global IP regime, patent holders are entitled to an "adequate remuneration" if States infringe upon their exclusive rights.[208] It is well documented that compulsory licences can serve several goals, including but not limited to: (1) protecting compelling public interest such as public health or the environment; (2) preserving healthy competition between firms, promoting "more competitive use of patented technology", including remedying anti-competitive practices; and (3) safeguarding "the supply of the domestic market" with a patented product.[209]

A compulsory licensing system is a typical feature of current national patent laws. It is observed that almost all countries throughout the world allow for compulsory licences in one form or another.[210] At the international level, Article 5A(2) of the Paris Convention, an amendment of 1925, permits the contracting States to grant compulsory licences to remedy the abuses of patent rights, including failure to work.[211] However, as observed by UNCTAD and ICTSD (2005), the Paris Convention neither limits the grounds upon which compulsory licences may be granted, nor does it establish a right of

Timmermann and Henk van den Belt (2013), Intellectual Property and Global Health: From Corporate Social Responsibility to the Access to Knowledge Movement, *Liverpool Law Review*, vol. 34, no. 1, pp. 47–73, at p. 51 (considering that the affirmation of compulsory licenses in the TRIPS Agreement and the Doha Declaration suggests that the drafters of the Agreement agreed that "in case of conflict, urgent public health interests supersede private interests").

[208] Article 31(h) of the TRIPS Agreement; see also Antony Taubman (2008), Rethinking TRIPS: "Adequate Remuneration" for Non-voluntary Patent Licensing, *The Journal of International Economic Law*, vol. 11, no. 4, pp. 927–70.

[209] See, e.g., WIPO (2011), *Survey on Compulsory Licenses Granted by WIPO Member States to Address Anti-Competitive Uses of Intellectual Property Rights*, WIPO Doc. CDIP/4/4 Rev./ Study/INF/5, p. 7 (noting that compulsory licenses were often invoked on the grounds of anti-competitive uses (practices) of IP rights, national or public interests; and failure to work or insufficient working of a patented invention); Eric Keller (2008), Time-varying Compulsory License: Facilitating License Negotiation for Efficient Post-Verdict Patent Infringement, *Texas Intellectual Property Law Journal*, vol. 16, pp. 427–51, at p. 436 (noting that "Compulsory licensing of patents [in the United States] has been used in [two] narrow cases: for government use pursuant to 28 U.S.C. § 1498 (a), to protect compelling public needs such as public health, and as an antitrust remedy"); Antony Taubman (2008), Rethinking TRIPS: "Adequate Remuneration" for Non-voluntary Patent Licensing, *The Journal of International Economic Law*, vol. 11, no. 4, pp. 927–70, at p. 931; Holger Hestermeyer (2007), *Human Rights and the WTO: The Case of Patents and Access to Medicines*, Oxford University Press, p. 239.

[210] See, e.g., WIPO (2011), Survey on Compulsory Licenses Granted by WIPO Member States to Address Anti-Competitive Uses of Intellectual Property Rights, WIPO Doc. CDIP/4/4 Rev./ Study/INF/5; Carlos M. Correa (2007), *Trade Related Aspects of Intellectual Property Rights: A Commentary on the TRIPS Agreement*, Oxford University Press, p. 313; UNCTAD and ICTSD (2005), *Resource Book on TRIPS and Development*, Cambridge University Press, p. 462.

[211] Paris Convention for the Protection of Industrial Property, Article 5(A)(2), 1883, WO020EN.

compensation for patent holders.[212] It is observed that the controversy regarding "the appropriate scope of compulsory licensing" is one of the reasons that developed countries shifted the crucial forum for global IP standard setting from WIPO to GATT in the 1980s.[213] Undoubtedly, compulsory licensing constituted one of the most controversial issues during the Uruguay Round negotiations. Notably, many developed countries were in favour of minimising the grant of compulsory licences and listing specific and limited grounds on which licenses might be granted.[214] In contrast, developing countries preferred to give governments broader powers to grant compulsory licences and thus strongly resisted the strict limits regarding grounds for compulsory licensing.[215] Ultimately, the two sides compromised and the final TRIPS text (Article 31 of the TRIPS Agreement) does not list or define permissible grounds for granting compulsory licences (except for semiconductor technology), but sets strict conditions for the granting of such licences.[216]

---

[212] UNCTAD and ICTSD (2005), *Resource Book on TRIPS and Development*, Cambridge University Press, p. 463.

[213] See, e.g., Jerome H. Reichman(2009), Compulsory Licensing of Patented Pharmaceutical Inventions: Evaluating the Options, *Journal of Law, Medicine & Ethics*, vol. 37, no. 2, pp. 247–63, at p. 247 (pointing out that "[t]hose efforts [to revise Paris Convention] broke down, largely because developed and developing countries could not agree on the powers that governments should retain to issue compulsory licenses or on the grounds for which these powers could be exercised"); Jerome H. Reichman and Catherine Hasenzahl (2003), Non-voluntary Licensing of Patented Inventions: Historical Perspective, Legal Framework under TRIPS, and an Overview of the Practice in Canada and the USA, UNCTAD-ICTSD Issue Paper No. 5, pp. 12-13; UNCTAD and ICTSD (2005), *Resource Book on TRIPS and Development*, Cambridge University Press, p. 463.

[214] Chairman's Report to the GNG, Status of Work in the Negotiating Group, Negotiating Group on Trade-Related Aspects of Intellectual Property Rights, including Trade in Counterfeit Goods, GATT Doc. MTN.GNG/NG11/W/76, 23 July 1990, pp. 34–6 (the so-called A text proposed by developed countries stating that "Parties shall minimise the grant of compulsory licences in order not to impede adequate protection of patent rights" and "[a] compulsory licence may [only] be granted for the following purposes: 5A.2.1 to remedy an adjudicated violation of competition laws; 5A.2.2a to address, only during its existence, a declared national emergency").

[215] See, e.g., Chairman's Report to the GNG, Status of Work in the Negotiating Group, Negotiating Group on Trade-Related Aspects of Intellectual Property Rights, including Trade in Counterfeit Goods, GATT Doc. MTN.GNG/NG11/W/76, 23 July 1990, at p. 36 (stating that: "Nothing in this Agreement shall be construed to prevent any Party from taking any action necessary: (i) for the working or use of a patent for governmental purposes; or (ii) where a patent has been granted for an invention capable of being used for the preparation or production of food or medicine, for granting to any person applying for the same a licence limited to the use of the invention for the purposes of the preparation or production and distribution of food and medicines"); UNCTAD and ICTSD (2005), *Resource Book on TRIPS and Development*, Cambridge University Press, p. 465.

[216] Article 31 of the TRIPS Agreement; see also Daniel Gervais (2012), *The TRIPS Agreement: Drafting History and Analysis*, 4th edn, New York: Thomson Reuters, p. 493.

Article 31 of the TRIPS Agreement, entitled "Other Use Without Authorization of the Right Holder", covers:

> other use of the subject matter of a patent without the authorization of the right holder, including use by the government or third parties authorized by the government.

This article covers both compulsory licences granted to third parties for their own use and use by or on behalf of governments without the consent of the patent holder. In the view of Watal (2001), such a provision has followed the Indian proposal in the TRIPS negotiations to combine both government use and compulsory licensing under "the same set of conditions" while the United States argued for "broader government use provisions but strict grounds for compulsory licences".[217] It is further noted that Article 31 does not use the concept of "compulsory licences" but rather the phrase "other use without authorization of the right holder". The footnote to Article 31 clarifies that "other use" refers to "use other than that [is] allowed under Article 30".[218] As observed by UNCTAD and ICTSD (2005), Article 31 addresses the patent holders' interests in specific cases – "a compulsory licence is directed to an identified patent and authorised party" – whereas Article 30 exceptions often involve "legislation of more general effect on patent holders and authorised parties".[219] Nevertheless, both Articles 30 and 31 are permissible exceptions to the exclusive rights conferred on patent owners.

Under Article 31 of the TRIPS Agreement, as reaffirmed by the Doha Declaration on the TRIPS Agreement and Public Health, compulsory licences can be issued to address access concerns for essential goods through, inter alia, the granting of licences to correct anti-competitive practices, and the authorisation for use of the patented item in situations of "national emergency or other circumstances of extreme urgency" or "in cases of public non-commercial use".[220] In the context of public health, compulsory licences have been identified as a "valuable tool" in promoting access to essential medicines.[221] Similarly, compulsory licensing can be used as a policy

---

[217] Jayashree Watal (2001), *Intellectual Property Rights in the WTO and Developing Countries*, New York: Kluwer Law International, p. 320.

[218] See footnote 7 of the TRIPS Agreement.

[219] UNCTAD and ICTSD (2005), *Resource Book on TRIPS and Development*, Cambridge University Press, p. 462.

[220] Article 31 of the TRIPS Agreement; see also Jakkrit Kuanpoth (2010), *Patent Rights in Pharmaceuticals in Developing Countries: Major Challenges for the Future*, Cheltenham, UK: Edward Elgar Publishing, p. 169.

[221] See, e.g., Holger Hestermeyer (2007), *Human Rights and the WTO: The Case of Patents and Access to Medicines*, Oxford University Press, p. 240; Charles R. McManis and Jorge

lever for facilitating transfer of ESTs to the extent allowed under the TRIPS Agreement. Section 6.4.4 discusses this issue in a detailed manner.

6.4.2 *Grounds for Granting Compulsory Licences*

6.4.2.1 Grounds for Granting Compulsory Licences in General

The compulsory licensing system was first adopted under the UK Patents Act of 1883, on the grounds that (1) "the patent is not being worked in the United Kingdom", or (2) "the reasonable requirements of the public with respect to the invention cannot be supplied" or (3) "any person is prevented from working or using to the best advantage an invention of which he is possessed".[222] It can be seen that the compulsory licences were originally related to local working and public interests.

Nonetheless, compulsory licences were later gradually extended to other situations, such as anti-competitive behaviour. In the United States, compulsory licences may be ordered by the court to remedy anti-competitive practices.[223] For instance, the US Supreme Court in *United States* v. *Glaxo Group Ltd. et al.* (1973) found that "compulsory patent licensing at reasonable charges" is a recognised anti-trust remedy.[224] Moreover, the US law permits the issuance of compulsory licensing to facilitate the access to certain technological inventions, thereby meeting specific objectives such as "national security" and "air pollution control".[225] For example, compulsory licensing is allowed under the 1992 Atomic Energy Act if "the invention or discovery covered by the patent is of primary importance in the production or utilization of special nuclear material or atomic energy".[226] Similarly, the 1994 US Clean Air Act provides for compulsory licences of the patented invention that is needed to achieve emission limitations under certain conditions.[227] It seems difficult to track the application of these

---

L. Contreras (2014), Compulsory Licensing of Intellectual Property: A Viable Policy Lever for Promoting Access to Critical Technologies, in Ghidini et al. (eds.), *TRIPS and Developing Countries: Towards a New IP World Order?* Cheltenham, UK: Edward Elgar Publishing, pp. 109–31, at p. 112.

[222] Joseph Edwin Crawford Munro (1884), *The Patents, Designs, and Trade Marks Act, 1883,* Stevens and Sons, Section 22.

[223] Nitya Nanda (2009), Diffusion of Climate-Friendly Technologies: Can Compulsory Licensing Help? *Journal of Intellectual Property Rights,* vol. 14, pp. 241–6, at p. 243.

[224] *United States* v. *Glaxo Group Ltd. et al.*, 410 U.S. 52 (1973), para. 64.

[225] John C. Miller et al. (2005), *The Handbook of Nanotechnology: Business, Policy and Intellectual Property Law,* Hoboken, NJ: John Wiley & Sons, p. 80.

[226] 42 USC § 2183 (Atomic Energy Act, 1992).

[227] 42 USC § 7608 (Clean Air Act, 1994); Mandatory Patent Licenses Under Section 308 of the Clean Air Act Federal Register Notice, 30 December 1994; other conditions include (1) the

particular compulsory licensing provisions in practice. Even if the use of such compulsory licences is limited, the mere existence of such provisions could have a deterrent effect on the refusal to transfer relevant essential technologies on reasonable commercial terms. In addition, the United States is observed to have extensively resorted to government use under 28 USC § 1498 (a).[228]

Article 31 of the TRIPS Agreement does not contain any explicit limitations on the grounds upon which compulsory licences may be granted (except in the case of semiconductor technology).[229] This is viewed as "quite a significant achievement for developing countries" because the United States had insisted in the TRIPS negotiations that there should be only two grounds for the issuance of compulsory licences: "to remedy an adjudicated violation of competition laws or to address a declared national emergency".[230] Countries' freedom to determine the grounds for granting compulsory licences has been reaffirmed in the Doha Declaration.[231] Therefore, the TRIPS Agreement allows WTO Members to issue compulsory licences for the general public interest including environmental protection, as recommended by Agenda 21,[232] and provided for under the US Clean Air Act.

6.4.2.2 Local Working Requirements and Non-Discrimination under Article 27

As discussed in Section 6.4.2.1, the birth of the system of compulsory licences is related to the obligation to locally work a patented invention.[233] Under the

---

patented technology is not otherwise reasonably available and no reasonable alternatives are available and (2) the patent reduces competition or creates a monopoly.

[228] Holger Hestermeyer (2007), *Human Rights and the WTO: The Case of Patents and Access to Medicines*, Oxford University Press, p .240.

[229] UNCTAD-ICTSD (2005), *Resource Book on TRIPS and Development*, Cambridge University Press, p. 462. Notably, in the case of semiconductor technology, the grounds for compulsory licenses are limited (1) to public non-commercial use or (2) to remedy an adjudicated violation of competition laws (see Article 31 (c) of TRIPS).

[230] Jayashree Watal (2001), *Intellectual Property Rights in the WTO and Developing Countries*, New York: Kluwer Law International, p. 320.

[231] Doha Declaration on the TRIPS Agreement and Public Health, Doha WTO Ministerial 2001, adopted on 14 November 2001, WTO Doc. WT/MIN(01)/DEC/2, 20 November 2001, para. 5 (b).

[232] Agenda 21, United Nations Conference on Environment & Development, Rio de Janerio, Brazil, 3 to 14 June 1992, United Nations, CH 34.18 (iv), available at http://sustainable development.un.org/content/documents/Agenda21.pdf

[233] See also Carlos M. Correa (1999), Intellectual Property Rights and the Use of Compulsory Licenses: Options for Developing Countries, *South Centre Working Papers*, p. 3 (noting that "The birth of the concept of compulsory licenses is linked to the obligation, introduced by the UK Statute of Monopolies in 1623 and recognized in many national patent laws during the XIX century, to work locally a patented invention").

UK Patents Act of 1883, if "the patent is not being worked in the United Kingdom", a compulsory licence can be imposed.[234] According to Correa (1999), this provision influenced the development of the Paris Convention, and the 1925 Hague Conference ultimately "adopted compulsory licensing as the main means to ensure the exploitation of a patent".[235] Article 5(A)(2) of the Paris Convention explicitly authorises compulsory licences in cases of failure to work a patent.

It is claimed that the primary goal of local working requirements is to facilitate the transfer of technology, thereby accelerating indigenous innovation capacity building.[236] However, neither the TRIPS Agreement nor the Paris Convention defines what constitutes a local working requirement. It is thus left to individual Member States to determine the exact content of this requirement. The Guide to the Application of the Paris Convention for the Protection of Industrial Property (1969) state that "working" in the 1967 revision means "working it industrially, namely, by manufacture of the patented product, or industrial application of a patented process".[237] Commentators note that at the time of the TRIPS negotiations, such a local working requirement was a feature of many countries' patent regimes, "where it was viewed, much like the disclosure requirement, as one of the quid pro quos of patent protection".[238] The classical definition of local working, thus, requires local

---

[234] Joseph Edwin Crawford Munro (1884), *The Patents, Designs, and Trade Marks Act, 1883,* Stevens and Sons, Section 22.

[235] Carlos M. Correa (1999), Intellectual Property Rights and the Use of Compulsory Licenses: Options for Developing Countries, *South Centre Working Papers,* at p. 3.

[236] See, e.g., G. B. Reddy and Harunrashid A. Kadri (2013), Local Working of Patents-Law and Implementation in India, *Journal of Intellectual Property Rights,* vol. 18, pp. 15–27, at p. 16 (stating that "local working has an unequivocal role in transfer of technology and socio-economic welfare of the state, which itself is the ultimate objective of the patent privilege"); Michael Halewood (1997), Regulating Patent Holders: Local Working Requirements and Compulsory Licences at International Law, *Osgoode Hall Law Journal,* vol. 35, no. 2, p. 246 (stating that "[local working requirement] has the effect of forcing foreign patentees to situate production facilities within the patent granting country. Such transfers of technology are desirable from the patent granting country's point of view"); WIPO (2004), *WIPO Intellectual Property Handbook,* 2nd edn, WIPO Publication No. 489, pp. 35 and 247 (noting that the underlying rationale behind local working requirements is that "patents for invention should not be used merely to block the working of the invention in the country or to monopolize importation of the patented article by the patent owner", but "should rather be used to introduce the use of the new technology into the country").

[237] G.H.C. Bodenhausen (1969), *Guide to the Application of the Paris Convention for the Protection of Industrial Property* (as revised at Stockholm in 1967), United International Bureaux for the Protection of Intellectual Property, p. 71.

[238] Graeme B. Dinwoodie and Rochelle C. Dreyfuss (2012), *A Neofederalist Vision of TRIPS: The Resilience of the International Intellectual Property Regime,* Oxford University Press, p. 44; see also Cynthia M. Ho (2011), *Access to Medicine in the Global Economy: International*

manufacturing to take place; and hence, the mere importation of a patented product does not seem to satisfy this requirement.[239]

However, a review of the national laws of selected WTO Members by Cottier et al. (2014) shows that at the present time countries such as Ghana, Jordan, Mexico, Philippines, South Africa and Uruguay view that "importation meeting local demand for a patented product [also] satisfies local working requirements".[240] In the current era, globalisation placed a stronger emphasis on "maintaining healthy competition and access to technology, rather than favouring domestic manufacturers"; and thus, the importation of the patented technology that generally passes the test of "reasonably meeting the domestic market need" could satisfy local working requirement.[241] This definition is particularly relevant for countries lacking the infrastructure to manufacture the patented products.

Nevertheless, for countries with relatively strong manufacturing capacities, they may insist that a "local working" requirement can only be met by local production and not the importation of the patented subject matter.[242] For instance, Article 68(1) of Brazil's 1996 Industrial Property Law provides that a patent shall be subject to a compulsory licence in case of the following:

Agreements on Patents and Related Rights, Oxford University Press, p. 238 (noting that "many nations historically imposed compulsory licenses if the patent owner failed to 'work' its invention in the patent-granting country by manufacturing it locally"); Paul Champ and Amir Attaran (2002), Patent Rights and Local Working Under the WTO TRIPS Agreement: An Analysis of the *U.S. – Brazil Patent Dispute, The Yale Journal of International Law*, vol. 27, pp. 365–93, at p. 366 (stating that "such [production based] local working requirements, coupled with the remedy of compulsory licensing for failure to work locally, are a fixture in the patent regimes of many countries in the world and have been since the advent of the patent system").

[239] See, e.g., Holger Hestermeyer (2007), *Human Rights and the WTO: The Case of Patents and Access to Medicines*, Oxford University Press, p. 242; Cynthia M. Ho (2011), *Access to Medicine in the Global Economy: International Agreements on Patents and Related Rights*, Oxford University Press, p. 393.

[240] Thomas Cottier et al. (2014), Use It or Lose It: Assessing the Compatibility of the Paris Convention and TRIPS Agreement with Respect to Local Working Requirements, *Journal of International Economic Law*, pp. 1–35, at p. 5.

[241] Antony Taubman (2011), *A Practical Guide to Working with TRIPS*, Oxford University Press, p. 104; Antony Taubman (2008), Rethinking TRIPS: "Adequate Remuneration" for Non-voluntary Patent Licensing, *The Journal of International Economic Law*, vol. 11, no. 4, pp. 927–70, at p. 934.

[242] Thomas Cottier et al. (2014), Use It or Lose It: Assessing the Compatibility of the Paris Convention and TRIPS Agreement with Respect to Local Working Requirements, *Journal of International Economic Law*, pp. 1–35, at p. 6 (noting that "In fact, until the 1990s, almost every country had legislated local working requirements to be satisfied by local production, importation or both and today," the laws of many developing countries continue to impose local working requirements for patented invention).

I. non–exploitation of the object of the patent within the Brazilian territory for failure to manufacture or incomplete manufacture of the product, or also failure to make full use of the patented process, except cases where this is not economically feasible, when importation shall be permitted.[243]

As briefly discussed in Section 6.2.1.1, this Brazilian legislation establishing a local manufacturing requirement was challenged by the United States at the WTO in 2000.[244] However, this dispute was settled prior to the convening of the panel,[245] leaving the question of the legality of local working requirements unaddressed by the WTO's dispute settlement panels and Appellate Body. The negotiating history of TRIPS, as observed by UNCTAD and ICTSD (2005), shows that "Members differed strongly on the issue of local working", with several delegations favouring a direct prohibition while others opposing it.[246] The TRIPS Agreement itself does not explicitly prohibit or permit local working requirements. Instead, it prohibits discrimination on the basis of whether products are imported or locally produced under Article 27.1.

There has been considerable controversy over the legality of production-based local working requirements under the TRIPS Agreement. The United States and some commentators have interpreted Article 27.1 of TRIPS to rule out a production-based local working requirement, thereby outlawing compulsory licences based on non-working of the invention.[247] It is argued that the

---

[243] Brazil, Law No. 9.279 of 14 May 1996 (Industrial Property Law), reproduced by WIPO, available at www.wipo.int/edocs/lexdocs/laws/en/br/br003en.pdf, Article 68, no. 1.

[244] Request for Consultations by the United States, *Brazil–Measures Affecting Patent Protection*, WT/DS199/1, G/L/385, IP/D/23, 8 June 2000.

[245] Notification of Mutually Agreed Solution, *Brazil – Measures Affecting Patent Protection*, WT/DS199/4, G/L/454, IP/D/23/Add.1, 19 July 2001.

[246] UNCTAD-ICTSD (2005), *Resource Book on TRIPS and Development*, Cambridge University Press, p. 482.

[247] See, e.g., Request for Consultations by the United States, *Brazil–Measures Affecting Patent Protection*, WT/DS199/1, G/L/385, IP/D/23, 8 June 2000; Jakkrit Kuanpoth (2010), *Patent Rights in Pharmaceuticals in Developing Countries: Major Challenges for the Future*, Cheltenham, UK: Edward Elgar Publishing, p. 33 (stating that "Article 27.1 ... requires equal treatment for both imported and locally-manufactured products, and so seems to prohibit the imposition of local working requirements"); Nuno Pires de Carvalho (2010), *The TRIPS Regime of Patent Rights*, 3rd Edition, New York: Kluwer Law International, at p. 287 (stating "What Article 27.1 states ... is that WTO Members may not make the granting of patents dependent on their local exploitation or on a promise in that senses"); Gustavo Ghidini (2010), *Innovation, Competition and Consumer Welfare in Intellectual Property Law*, Cheltenham, UK: Edward Elgar Publishing, p. 250 (considering that Article 27.1 of the TRIPS Agreement expressly sanctioned "the historical principle (enshrined in the Paris Convention 1883, article 5A.2, and adopted by the vast majority of the emerging industrial states of the nineteenth century) that allowed Member States granting a patent to request that said patent be (industrially) worked *in situ* [the so-called local working requirement]").

local production requirement could have a detrimental impact on the patent holder's enjoyment of the patent rights on the basis of whether the products are locally produced.[248]

However, other commentators argue that TRIPS does not totally rule out the local working requirements on several grounds. First, as observed by Kuanpoth (2010), "TRIPS does not limit the right of countries to establish compulsory licences on grounds other than those explicitly mentioned in the Agreement".[249] This is confirmed by paragraph 5(b) of the 2001 Doha Declaration, emphasising that each member has the "freedom to determine the grounds upon which such licences are granted". Thus, the TRIPS Agreement does not rule out compulsory licensing based on a failure to work the invention. Second, some scholars believe that the direct incorporation of Article 5A (2) of the Paris Convention into TRIPS by virtue of Article 2.1 supports the view that a local working requirement is consistent with the TRIPS Agreement.[250] As demonstrated in Section 3.2.1, Article 5A(2) of the Paris Convention permits the contracting parties to grant compulsory licences to prevent failure to work, but it did not define the term "work". Therefore, WTO Members have regulatory discretion to define the term "work" as including the requirement of local production of the patented technology.[251] Last but not least, some commentators, relying on the panel's ruling in *Canada – Pharmaceutical Patents* (2000), argued that a *bona fide* distinction (between locally produced products and imported products) may not constitute discrimination within the meaning of Article 27.1, thereby leaving room for local working requirements to be adopted for *bona fide* purposes.[252]

---

[248] Bryan Mercurio and Mitali Tyagi (2010), Treaty Interpretation in WTO Dispute Settlement: The Outstanding Question of the Legality of Local Working Requirements, *Minnesota Journal of International Law*, vol. 19, no. 2, pp. 275–326, at p. 286.

[249] Jakkrit Kuanpoth (2010), *Patent Rights in Pharmaceuticals in Developing Countries: Major Challenges for the Future*, Cheltenham, UK: Edward Elgar Publishing, p. 33.

[250] See, e.g., Holger Hestermeyer (2007), *Human Rights and the WTO: The Case of Patents and Access to Medicines*, Oxford University Press, p. 243; Carlos M. Correa (2007), *Trade Related Aspects of Intellectual Property Rights: A Commentary on the TRIPS Agreement*, Oxford University Press, p. 286; Thomas Cottier and Pierre Véron (2011), *Concise International and European IP Law: TRIPS, Paris Convention, European Enforcement and Transfer of Technology*, 2nd edn, New York: Kluwer Law International, p. 100.

[251] See also Saad Abughanm (2012), *The Protection of Pharmaceutical Patents and Data under TRIPS and US – Jordan FTA: Exploring the Limits of Obligations and Flexibilities: A Study of the Impact on the Pharmaceutical Sector in Jordan*, SJD thesis, University of Toronto, p. 190.

[252] See, e.g., Antony Taubman (2008), Rethinking TRIPS: "Adequate Remuneration" for Non-voluntary Patent Licensing, *Journal of International Economic Law* 11 (4), pp. 927–70, at p. 933 (noting that "a *bona fide* intervention to promote local working may be defensible if it can be made out to be non-discriminatory"); Frederick M. Abbott (2008), Intellectual Property Rights in World Trade, in Guzman and Sykes (eds.), *Research Handbook in International Economic*

As demonstrated in Section 5, the provisions of the TRIPS Agreement shall be interpreted in good faith in accordance with their ordinary meaning in their context and in the light of the object and purpose of both the WTO Agreement and the TRIPS Agreement. Accordingly, Article 27.1 of TRIPS cannot be read in isolation; rather it should be interpreted in line with the object and purpose of the TRIPS Agreement and the WTO Agreement, taking into account other relevant provisions and subsequent agreements. It is noted that both Article 7, entitled "Objectives", and Article 8, entitled "Principles" stress the need to contribute to technology transfer and technological development. Therefore, a purposive interpretation of Article 27.1 supports the permissibility of a local working requirement that could contribute to technology transfer and indigenous innovation.[253] Furthermore, Article 8.2 of TRIPS specifically allows countries to adopt measures to prevent the abuse of patents, which is defined to include failure to work the patent by Article 5 of the Paris Convention.[254] Therefore, countries have the regulatory right to take certain measures such as the issuing of compulsory licences to remedy any failure to locally work the patent. This is supported by paragraph 4 of the 2001 Doha Declaration, which explicitly reaffirms the right of WTO members to use, to the full, the TRIPS flexibility for public interest purposes.

In the climate change context, the WTO's sustainable development objective supports facilitating the innovation and transfer of ESTs through permitting the local working of the patented ESTs. Requiring local production of certain EST-related inventions may create a differential treatment between imported and locally produced ESTs. However, such a requirement plays a significant role in mitigating climate change by stimulating the transfer of ESTs and indigenous innovation in certain countries. In this sense, local production requirement may constitute a *bona fide* distinction rather than "discrimination" within the meaning of Article 27.1. Thus, the issuance of compulsory licences for failure to locally work the EST patents

---

Law, Cheltenham, UK: Edward Elgar Publishing, pp. 444–84, at p. 475 (stating that "Under this jurisprudence of the *Canada–Generic Pharmaceuticals* case, this leaves room for local working requirements adopted for bona fide [i.e. non-discriminatory] purposes"); Carlos M. Correa (2008), Patent Rights, in Correa and Yusuf (eds.), *Intellectual Property and International Trade: The TRIPS Agreement*, New York: Kluwer Law International, pp. 227–57, at p. 240 (arguing that "Article 27 (1) would not prohibit local production obligations, but just the discrimination in the exercise of rights against infringing goods, whether imported or locally produced").

[253] See also Holger Hestermeyer (2007), *Human Rights and the WTO: The Case of Patents and Access to Medicines*, Oxford University Press, p. 244.

[254] Graeme B. Dinwoodie and Rochelle C. Dreyfuss (2012), *A Neofederalist Vision of TRIPS: The Resilience of the International Intellectual Property Regime*, Oxford University Press, p. 44.

is not necessarily inconsistent with Article 27.1. Accordingly, a good faith interpretation of Article 27.1 does not outlaw compulsory licences for failure to work the EST patents in the patent granting country.

6.4.2.3 Enumerated Grounds for Compulsory Licences under Article 31

It is well-accepted that the TRIPS Agreement does not limit the grounds for which a compulsory licence may be issued.[255] At the Doha Ministerial Conference, WTO Members explicitly affirmed that each Member has "the freedom to determine the grounds upon which such licences are granted".[256] According to Taubman and Watal (2010), this clarification has effectively rejected the view held by some commentators that "some form of public health emergency was an essential pre-condition for any compulsory licensing".[257]

However, the TRIPS Agreement does indirectly list certain grounds that may be used to justify compulsory licensing: (1) national emergencies or other

---

[255] See, e.g., Daniel Gervais (2012), *The TRIPS Agreement: Drafting History and Analysis*, 4th edn, New York: Thomson Reuters, p. 492 (stating that "It sets specific conditions for the grant of [compulsory] licences, but does not list or define exhaustively the cases where a licence may be granted [except for semiconductor technology]. Negotiators weighed both options and preferred to leave open the cases where compulsory licensing may be allowed"); Paul Champ and Amir Attaran (2002), Patent Rights and Local Working Under the WTO TRIPS Agreement: An Analysis of the U.S. – Brazil Patent Dispute, *The Yale Journal of International Law*, vol. 27, pp. 365–93, at p. 384 (noting that "the United States tried and failed to limit the grounds of compulsory licensing ... The fact that Article 31 does not generally prohibit any grounds for compulsory licensing means that national discretion to compel a licence is implicitly wide-ranging"); Anke Dahrendorf (2010), Global Proliferation of Bilateral and Regional Trade Agreements: A Threat for the World Trade Organisation and/or for Developing Countries? in Hertwig and Maus (eds.), *Global Risks: Constructing World Order Through Law, Politics and Economics*, Frankfurt, Germany: Peter Lang GmbH, pp. 39–66, at p. 56 (stating that "Article 31 of the TRIPS Agreement ... does not contain an exhaustive list of grounds and therefore offers some discretion for WTO Members to add other grounds").

[256] Declaration on the TRIPS Agreement and Public Health, WT/MIN (01)/DEC/2, adopted on 14 November 2001, para. 5(b).

[257] Antony Taubman and Jayashree Watal (2010), *The WTO TRIPS Agreement: A Practical Overview for Climate Change Policymakers*, Documentation used in technical cooperation activities of the WTO's Intellectual Property Division, available at www.wto.org/english/tratop_e/trips_e/ta_docs_e/8_3_overviewclimatechange_e.pdf, p. 8; see also Tim Wilson (2008), Undermining Mitigation Technology: Compulsory Licensing, Patents and Tariffs, *Melbourne: Institute of Public Affairs Backgrounder*, vol. 21, no. 1, p. 5 (arguing that "the compulsory licensing of heart medications is deemed to be an abuse of the obligation to only issue compulsory licenses in cases of 'national emergency or other circumstances of extreme urgency'").

circumstances of extreme urgency (Article 31(b)), (2) public non-commercial use (Article 31(b)) and (3) "to remedy a practice determined after judicial or administrative process to be an anti-competitive practice" (Article 31(k)). However, such enumeration is not exhaustive and only serves to indicate that, in these circumstances, some of the general conditions do not apply, such as the need to seek a voluntary licence first.[258]

All these listed grounds are relevant in the context of the transfer of patented ESTs, which will be addressed in detail in Section 6.4.4.2. It can be inferred that the TRIPS Agreement allows WTO Members to issue compulsory licences on the grounds of environmental protection or general public interest, thereby permitting the grant of compulsory licences where certain patented ESTs play an essential role in climate change mitigation.[259] As demonstrated in Section 6.4.2.1, compulsory licences are permitted under the US Clean Air Act if the patented invention is needed to mitigate GHG emissions.[260] In practice, according to South Centre (2009), US courts have authorised a considerable number of compulsory licences for ESTs: for instance, in 2006, a US court "granted Toyota a compulsory licence on three Paice patents, which involved a hybrid electric vehicle improvement, for a royalty of $25" per car.[261] Members' right to grant compulsory licences for ESTs is supported by the WTO's sustainable development objective and the innovation and technology transfer objective in Article 7 of the TRIPS Agreement. It can also find legal support in Article 8 of TRIPS, allowing Members to adopt measures necessary to promote the public interest in sectors of vital importance to their socio-economic and technological development, including the EST sector.

---

[258] WTO (2006), Under TRIPS, What Are Member Governments' Obligations on Pharmaceutical Patents? available at www.wto.org/english/tratop_e/trips_e/factsheet_pharm02_e.htm

[259] See also Carlos M. Correa (1999), Intellectual Property Rights and the Use of Compulsory Licenses: Options for Developing Countries, *South Centre Working Papers*, p. 8 (stating that "The TRIPS Agreement does not limit the Members' right . . . to establish compulsory licences on grounds other than those explicitly mentioned therein, for instance, in order to protect the environment (as recommended by the "Agenda 21"), or for reasons of "public interest" (as provided for by the German patent law)").

[260] 42 USC § 7608 (Clean Air Act, 1994); Mandatory Patent Licenses Under Section 308 of the Clean Air Act Federal Register Notice, 30 December 1994.

[261] *Paice, LLC v. Toyota Motor Corp.*, ___ F. 3d ___, Nos. 2006-1680, - 1631 (Fed. Cir. Oct. 18, 2007) (Lourie, Rader (concurring), Prost); see also South Centre (2009), Accelerating Climate-Relevant Technology Innovation and Transfer to Developing Countries: Using TRIPS Flexibilities under the UNFCCC, Analytical Note, SC/IAKP/AN/ENV/1, SC/GGDP/AN/ENV/8, Geneva: South Centre p. 19.

6.4.3 *Conditions for the Grant of Compulsory Licences*

While not limiting the grounds or underlying reasons for the granting of a compulsory licence, Article 31 codifies a list of conditions and procedural requirements for such a grant. These conditions have been characterized as "strict safeguards" by Gervais (2012).[262] In essence, Article 31 recognizes that the practice of compulsory licensing is itself susceptible to abuse and should thus be subject to "stringent legal constraints".[263]

6.4.3.1 Procedural Requirements

Under Article 31 of TRIPS, the issuance of a compulsory licence shall generally meet the following procedural requirements: (1) authorisation on its individual merits (Article 31(a)); (2) prior negotiation with the right holder (Article 31(b)); and (3) review of the decisions (Article 31(i) and (j)). The following sub-sections examine, in turn, these procedural requirements.

6.4.3.1.1 AUTHORISATION ON ITS INDIVIDUAL MERITS. The first TRIPS procedural requirement is that each licence must be considered "on its individual merits", that is, on a case-by-case basis (Article 31(a)). It is well-accepted that such a requirement would appear to exclude or at least to render very difficult the granting of compulsory licences for a particular field or a whole class of patents, e.g., those related to clean energy technologies.[264] However, Correa (2007) points out that "this would not be an impediment to establish parameters for the granting of compulsory licences, regarding, for instance, certain categories of products that are needed to address a specific need".[265] This view is supported by some national legislations such as the

---

[262] Daniel Gervais (2012), *The TRIPS Agreement: Drafting History and Analysis*, 4th edn, New York: Thomson Reuters, p. 492 (stating that "Negotiators preferred to leave open the cases where compulsory licensing may be allowed. Instead, they established strict safeguards").

[263] Charles R. McManis and Jorge L. Contreras (2014), Compulsory Licensing of Intellectual Property: A Viable Policy Lever for Promoting Access to Critical Technologies, in Ghidini et al. (eds.), *TRIPS and Developing Countries: Towards a New IP World Order?* Cheltenham, UK: Edward Elgar Publishing, pp. 109–31, at p. 120.

[264] See, e.g., Thomas Cottier and Pierre Véron (2011), *Concise International and European IP Law: TRIPS, Paris Convention, European Enforcement and Transfer of Technology*, 2nd edn, New York: Kluwer Law International, p. 102; Antony Taubman et al. (2012), *A Handbook on the WTO TRIPS Agreement*, Cambridge University Press, p. 112; Jay Dratler and Stephen M. McJohn (2006), *Intellectual Property Law: Commercial, Creative, and Industrial Property*, ALM Properties, Law Journal Press, p. 1 A-45.

[265] Carlos M. Correa (2007), *Trade Related Aspects of Intellectual Property Rights: A Commentary on the TRIPS Agreement*, Oxford University Press, p. 320.

compulsory licensing provisions of the US Atomic Energy Act and Section 308 of the US Clean Air Act which establish conditions for compulsory licensing of patents that are needed to meet a specific policy objective.[266] Therefore, the requirement that each licence be considered "on its individual merits" does not prevent WTO Members from setting parameters for the granting of compulsory licences regarding certain categories of technologies that are needed to mitigate climate change.

6.4.3.1.2 PRIOR NEGOTIATIONS WITH THE RIGHT HOLDER. Under Article 31(b), prior to the application for a compulsory licence, an "unsuccessful" attempt must be made to obtain the authorisation from the right holder "on reasonable commercial terms and conditions" "within a reasonable period of time". This provision does not define the term "reasonable". The dictionary meaning of the term "reasonable" is "within the limits of reason, not greatly less or more than might be thought likely or appropriate".[267] The open-textured nature of the term "reasonable" makes the requirement at issue "inherently flexible", allowing the context of the case in question to be taken into account.[268] Commentators note that this reasonableness requirement varies from technology to technology, and within each field, depending on the nature of the particular invention involved.[269] This flexibility may also provide an entry point for facilitating the transfer of ESTs; deliberate delay of negotiations or unduly cumbersome conditions imposed by the patent holders may not meet the reasonableness requirement in Article 31(b).[270]

It is noted that Article 31(b) and (k) allows for three circumstances in which a WTO Member can waive the prior negotiation requirement: (a) in the case of a national emergency or other circumstances of extreme urgency (instead, the right holder shall be notified "as soon as reasonably practicable"); (b) in the case of public non-commercial use (instead, the right holder shall be informed promptly "where the government or contractor, without making a patent search, knows or has demonstrable grounds to know that a valid patent

---

[266] See Section 6.4.2.1.

[267] *Shorter Oxford English Dictionary* (2007), 6th edn, vol. 2, Stevenson (ed.), Oxford University Press, p. 2481.

[268] UNCTAD-ICTSD (2005), *Resource Book on TRIPS and Development*, Cambridge University Press, p. 469.

[269] See, e.g., Daniel Gervais (2012), *The TRIPS Agreement: Drafting History and Analysis*, 4th edn, New York: Thomson Reuters, p. 494; Holger Hestermeyer (2007), *Human Rights and the WTO: The Case of Patents and Access to Medicines*, Oxford University Press, p. 246.

[270] See also Holger Hestermeyer (2007), *Human Rights and the WTO: The Case of Patents and Access to Medicines*, Oxford University Press, p. 246 (elaborating such flexibilities in the context of access to medicines).

is or will be used by or for the government") and (c) "where such use is permitted to remedy a practice determined after judicial or administrative process to be anti-competitive".[271] All three of these exceptions are relevant for facilitating access to patented ESTs and are elaborated further in Section 6.4.4.2.

6.4.3.1.3 REVIEW OF THE DECISIONS. Under Article 31(i) and (j), the legal validity of any decision concerning the authorisation of such use or the remuneration provided in respect of such use is subject to independent review, including review by a distinct higher authority. As observed by Correa (2007), such review, however, will not prevent a Member from giving immediate effect to a decision granting a compulsory licence. This is of particular importance "in cases involving public interests or the correction of anti-competitive practices".[272]

6.4.3.2 Substantive Requirements

Under Article 31 of TRIPS, the main substantive requirements for the granting of a compulsory licence are as follows: (1) adequate remuneration (Article 31 (h)), (2) limits to the scope and duration (Article 31(c), (d) and (e)) and (3) predominant supply of the domestic market (31(f)). The following sub-sections examine, in turn, these substantive requirements.

6.4.3.2.1 ADEQUATE REMUNERATION. Article 31(h) of TRIPS provides that "the right holder shall be paid adequate remuneration in the circumstances of each case, taking into account the economic value of the authorization."

The ambiguity on the issue of determining the proper "economic value of the authorization" has led to different interpretations of this provision. In the view of Dratler and McJohn (2006), under Article 31(h), "royalty rates or other compensation must be determined on a commercial basis; members are prohibited from establishing a royalty rate schedule in advance, without consideration of the value of the technology at issue".[273] In contrast, some commentators consider that this provision embodies substantial flexibility as a

---

[271] See Article 31 (b) and (k) of TRIPS.
[272] Carlos M. Correa (2007), *Trade Related Aspects of Intellectual Property Rights: A Commentary on the TRIPS Agreement*, Oxford University Press, p. 323.
[273] Jay Dratler and Stephen M. McJohn (2006), *Intellectual Property Law: Commercial, Creative, and Industrial Property*, New York: ALM Properties, Law Journal Press, p. 1A–46.

result of the use of the phrase "in the circumstances of each case", indicating that the determination of the level of compensation should consider other factors such as "the circumstances of the licensee and of the country where it operates, as well as the purpose of the licence".[274]

The text of Article 31(h) makes clear that the payment of adequate remuneration should be based upon the circumstances in each case rather than "the economic value of the authorization" which is merely to be taken into account. The term "taking into account" in Article 31(h) of the TRIPS Agreement has not been interpreted by dispute settlement panels or the Appellate Body so far. However, given the single undertaking nature of the WTO Agreements, the interpretation of the term "take account of" contained in other WTO Agreements could provide guidance in interpreting the term "taking into account" in Article 31(h) of the TRIPS Agreement.

Notably, two dispute settlement panels have interpreted the phrases "take account of", contained in Article 10.1 of the Agreement on the Application of Sanitary and Phytosanitary Measures (SPS Agreement) and Article 11.3 of the Technical Barriers to Trade Agreement (TBT), respectively. The panel in *EC – Approval and Marketing of Biotech Products* (2006), guided by a dictionary meaning, defined the expression "take account of" as "consider along with other factors before reaching a decision" and accordingly concluded that "Article 10.1 does not prescribe a specific result to be achieved."[275] The panel in *US – Clove Cigarettes* (2011) adopted a similar interpretation. In interpreting Article 12.3 of the TBT Agreement, it found that "to 'take account of' the special financial, development and trade needs of a developing country does not necessarily mean that the Member preparing or applying a technical regulation must agree with or accept the developing country's position and desired outcome".[276]

These panels' findings provide guidance with respect to the interpretation of the phrase "taking into account" found in Article 31(h). In the same vein, Members authorising compulsory licences are not necessarily bound to pay the remuneration commensurate to the economic value of the authorisation. Instead, Members will be guided by other relevant factors present in a particular case. Furthermore, Article 31(h) does not necessarily mean that the Member authorising a compulsory licence must agree with or accept the patent holder's position and desired outcome regarding the level of remuneration.

---

[274] See, e.g., Carlos M. Correa (2007), *Trade Related Aspects of Intellectual Property Rights: A Commentary on the TRIPS Agreement*, Oxford University Press, p. 322; UNCTAD-ICTSD (2005), *Resource Book on TRIPS and Development*, Cambridge University Press, p. 475.

[275] Panel Reports, *EC – Approval and Marketing of Biotech Products*, para. 7.1620.

[276] Panel Report, *US – Clove Cigarettes*, para. 7.646.

In conclusion, Article 31(h) embodies substantial flexibilities in determining the level of, and the basis upon which, adequate remuneration is paid. For example, in the case of compulsory licences for ESTs, the need for the transfer of ESTs could be an important consideration in establishing the level of compensation.

6.4.3.2.2 LIMITS TO THE SCOPE AND DURATION. Article 31(c) obliges WTO Members to limit the scope and duration of a compulsory licence to the purpose for which the licence is granted. Under Article 31(g), if and when the circumstances which led to the licence cease to exist and are deemed unlikely to recur, the compulsory licence has to be terminated, subject to sufficient protection of "the legitimate interests of the persons so authorized".[277] Some analysts are concerned that this provision may discourage potential licensees from requesting compulsory licences as they may lack adequate time to recoup their investments.[278] However, Article 31(g) makes clear that the legitimate interest of the compulsory licensee, in particular, its "reasonable investment",[279] should be considered before revocation of the licence is decided. In the view of Correa (2007), the protection of legitimate interest may be interpreted as meaning that a person could not be deprived of his or her right to the licence once he or she "has made serious preparations for putting the invention into use, or established productive or marketing capabilities".[280] It is, thus, recommended that WTO Members should carefully interpret and implement Article 31(g) in a manner that does not undermine the incentives for private sectors to apply for a compulsory licence.[281]

---

[277] See Article 31(g) of TRIPS (further providing that "[t]he competent authority shall have the authority to review, upon motivated request, the continued existence of these circumstances").

[278] See, e.g., Carlos M. Correa (2005), Can the TRIPS Agreement Foster Technology Transfer to Developing Countries? in Maskus and Reichman (eds.), *International Public Goods and Transfer of Technology under a Globalized Intellectual Property Regime*, Cambridge University Press, pp. 227–56, at p. 248; Niranjan C. Rao (2009), TRIPS and Public Health, in Dasgupta (ed.), *The WTO at the Crossroads*, New Delhi, India: Ashok Kumar Mittal Concept Publishing, pp. 81–100, at p. 83 (stating that "[o]ne of the provisions which make compulsory licences unattractive, is Article 31(g)[which] introduces such an uncertainty that no prospective licensee will come forward to ask for a compulsory licence").

[279] Daniel Gervais (2012), *The TRIPS Agreement: Drafting History and Analysis*, 4th edn, New York: Thomson Reuters, p. 494.

[280] Carlos M. Correa (2007), *Trade Related Aspects of Intellectual Property Rights: A Commentary on the TRIPS Agreement*, Oxford University Press, p. 322.

[281] See, e.g., Kong Qingjiang (2011), China in the WTO: Enforcement of the TRIPS Agreement and the Doha Agenda, in Rohan (ed.), *Chinese Intellectual Property and Technology Laws*, Cheltenham, UK: Edward Elgar Publishing, pp. 348–66, at p. 354; Holger Hestermeyer (2007), *Human Rights and the WTO: The Case of Patents and Access to Medicines*, Oxford University Press, p. 250.

Moreover, the rights of a compulsory licensee are further limited by the requirement that the licence shall be non-exclusive (Article 31(d)), and "non-assignable, except with that part of the enterprise or goodwill which enjoys such use" (Article 31(e)). The non-exclusive requirement, that is, allowing the patent holder to continue to use and license the patent, may raise difficulties for compulsory licensees because "patent holders and possibly other licensees will seek to undercut them in the market", thereby reducing their incentive to invest.[282]

6.4.3.2.3 PREDOMINANT SUPPLY OF THE DOMESTIC MARKET. Another limitation to the scope of compulsory licences is contained in Article 31(f), providing that "any such use shall be authorized predominantly for the supply of the domestic market of the Member authorizing such use". Notably, this provision is not applicable in cases where a compulsory licence is granted to remedy anti-competitive practices (Article 31(k)).

The word "predominantly" is not defined but is generally interpreted as meaning "more than 50 per cent".[283] The requirement to predominantly supply the domestic market necessarily means that compulsory licences should not be issued primarily for supplying foreign markets. In consequence, this requirement may prevent WTO Members with insufficient manufacturing capacities from relying on imports of goods manufactured under a compulsory licence granted in a foreign country.[284] As a result, it is observed that this provision may become a major obstacle for poor countries to access public goods such as essential medicines and ESTs since they may not have sophisticated manufacturing capacity and would have to rely on a more developed country to issue a compulsory licence for export.[285]

In the context of public health, WTO Members have recognised that this restriction needed to be relaxed so that poorer countries would be able to make meaningful use of compulsory licences, so they instructed the Council

---

[282] UNCTAD-ICTSD (2005), *Resource Book on TRIPS and Development*, Cambridge University Press, p. 473.

[283] See, e.g., Cynthia M. Ho (2011), *Access to Medicine in the Global Economy: International Agreements on Patents and Related Rights*, Oxford University Press, at p. 135; Carlos M. Correa (2007), *Trade Related Aspects of Intellectual Property Rights: A Commentary on the TRIPS Agreement*, Oxford University Press, p. 321.

[284] Tú Thanh Nguyãên (2010), *Competition Law, Technology Transfer and the TRIPS Agreement: Implications for Developing Countries*, Cheltenham, UK: Edward Elgar Publishing, p. 31.

[285] See, e.g., Suerie Moon and Wolfgang Hein (2013), *Informal Norms in Global Governance: Human Rights, Intellectual Property Rules and Access to Medicines*, Farnham, UK: Ashgate Publishing Limited, p. 79; Ping Xiong (2012), *An International Law Perspective on the Protection of Human Rights in the TRIPS Agreement: An Interpretation of the TRIPS Agreement in Relation to the Right to Health*, Leiden, Netherlands: Martinus Nijhoff Publishers, p. 204.

for TRIPS to find an expeditious solution to this problem before the end of 2002 (the Doha Declaration, para. 6).[286] A waiver of the requirement to predominantly supply the domestic market was adopted in 2003,[287] and replaced by the amendment to the TRIPS Agreement that makes the waiver permanent from 23 January 2017 for members who have accepted the amendment. Section 6.4.4.1 further discusses this issue.

Such public-health-specific waiver or amendment should be extended to "other sectors of vital importance to socio-economic and technological development" in Article 8.1 of TRIPS which is of equal importance to humankind. In the context of climate change, a similar waiver or amendment is recommended in Section 8.4.1.

6.4.4 *Compulsory Licensing as a Policy Lever for EST Transfer*

Compulsory licences may be issued to ensure that patent-protected ESTs are accessible, available and affordable for the public. In the field of public health, the use of compulsory licences or the threat thereof has to a certain extent improved access to essential medicines in developing countries, as will be further discussed in Section 6.4.4.1. Similarly, compulsory licensing for patented essential ESTs should be used to the extent allowed under the TRIPS Agreement.

The interpretative rules set out in Article 31 of the VCLT require treaty interpreters to read Article 31 of TRIPS in its context and in accordance with the object and purpose of the TRIPS Agreement and the WTO. Several provisions of the TRIPS Agreement such as Articles 7, 8 and 31, and Article 5(A) of the Paris Convention, which is incorporated into TRIPS by virtue of Article 2.1, provide contextual support for the use of compulsory licences to facilitate access to ESTs, thereby addressing the concern of climate change. The objectives and principles of the TRIPS Agreement as provided in Articles 7 and 8, allowing WTO Members to pursue specific public interest objectives, must shed light on the interpretation of the terms used in Article 31 of TRIPS.[288] When read in accordance with the WTO's sustainable

---

[286] Doha Declaration on the TRIPS Agreement and Public Health, Doha WTO Ministerial 2001, adopted on 14 November 2001, WTO Doc. WT/MIN(01)/DEC/2, 20 November 2001, para. 6.
[287] Decision of the General Council of 30 August 2003, Implementation of Paragraph 6 of the Doha Declaration on the TRIPS Agreement and Public Health, WTO Doc. WT/L/540, 1 September 2003.
[288] Thomas Cottier and Pierre Véron (2011), *Concise International and European IP Law: TRIPS, Paris Convention, European Enforcement and Transfer of Technology*, 2nd edn, New York: Kluwer Law International, p. 100.

development objective, Article 31 of TRIPS also provides regulatory space for Members to promote public policy objectives, including the mitigation of climate change.

The following sections address, in turn, the feasibility, opportunities and challenges of compulsory licences for EST transfer following a brief study of the case of improved access to medicine and compulsory licences.

6.4.4.1 The Case of Improved Access to Medicine and Compulsory Licences

Even though there are limits to their effectiveness, compulsory licences are considered a valuable tool for governments to facilitate access to medicines through the prevention of patent abuses as well as the "encouragement of domestic capacities for manufacturing pharmaceuticals".[289] According to the UNDP Human Development Report (2001), after the adoption of the TRIPS Agreement, compulsory licences were initially mainly used in Canada, Japan, the UK and the United States for products such as pharmaceuticals – particularly as a remedy to address anti-competitive practices and prevent higher prices – while no compulsory licence was issued then in developing countries largely due to pressure from Europe and the United States and the fear of long and expensive litigation against the pharmaceutical industry.[290] As demonstrated in Section 5.4.1.2, in order to address developing countries' concern, the 2001 Doha Declaration explicitly reaffirmed the right of countries to issue compulsory licences where necessary, in the interests of public health.

In order to enable countries with insufficient manufacturing capacity in the pharmaceutical sector to benefit from the compulsory licensing system, the WTO General Council adopted the Decision of 30 August 2003 on the implementation of paragraph 6 of the Doha Declaration on the TRIPS Agreement and public health (the so-called paragraph 6 system).[291] This decision essentially expanded the TRIPS flexibilities, involving two waivers: (1) with respect to the exporting country, a "waiver" of obligations to use the authorised compulsory licence predominantly for the supply of the domestic market under

[289] Submission by the African Group, Barbados, Bolivia, Brazil, Cuba, Dominican Republic, Ecuador, Honduras, India, Indonesia, Jamaica, Pakistan, Paraguay, Philippines, Peru, Sri Lanka, Thailand and Venezuela, Council for Trade-Related Aspects of Intellectual Property Rights, WTO Doc. IP/C/W/296, 29 June 2001, p. 1.
[290] UNDP (2001), *Human Development Report 2001: Making New Technologies Work for Human Development*, Oxford University Press, p. 107.
[291] Decision of the General Council of 30 August 2003, Implementation of Paragraph 6 of the Doha Declaration on the TRIPS Agreement and Public Health, WTO Doc. WT/L/540, 1 September 2003.

Article 31(f); and (2) with regard to the importing country, a waiver of the adequate remuneration requirement under Article 31(h) when remuneration is paid in the exporting Member. "Where a compulsory licence is granted by an exporting Member under the system set out in this Decision, adequate remuneration pursuant to Article 31(h) of the TRIPS Agreement shall be paid in that Member taking into account the economic value to the importing Member of the use that has been authorised in the exporting Member".[292]

In 2005, WTO Members agreed to make the waivers permanent by amending the TRIPS Agreement.[293] With the approval of two-thirds of the WTO Members, the amendment entered into force on 23 January 2017. As the very first legal amendment to a WTO multilateral agreement, it was said to have shown that "[M]embers are determined to ensure the WTO's trading system contributes to humanitarian and development goals".[294] Likewise, such amendment could be extended to address other global concerns such as climate change in accordance with the WTO's sustainable development objective and Articles 7 and 8 of the TRIPS Agreement.

In effect, the compulsory licensing system established within the WTO framework is not a panacea, but rather a legal guarantee of rights and ability to make effective use of compulsory licences. Since the adoption of the Doha Declaration, a number of developing countries (e.g., Thailand, Brazil, Ecuador, India and Indonesia) have issued compulsory licences to lower the price of patented medicines such as HIV/AIDS drugs.[295] Additionally, in 2007, Rwanda became the first country without sufficient manufacturing capacities to use the WTO "paragraph 6 system" to import Apo-TriAvir from Apotex, a Canadian firm.[296] Commentators note that since the Doha Declaration was

---

[292] Ibid., paras. 2 and 3.

[293] Decision of 6 December 2005, Amendment of the TRIPS Agreement, WTO Doc. WT/L/641, 8 December 2005.

[294] WTO (2005), Members OK amendment to make health flexibility permanent, Press/426, 6 December 2005, available at www.wto.org/english/news_e/pres05_e/pr426_e.htm

[295] Manica Balasegaram et al. (2014), The Fight for Global Access to Essential Health Commodities, in Brown et al. (eds.), *The Handbook of Global Health Policy*, Hoboken, NJ: John Wiley & Sons, pp. 245–66, at p. 258 (noting that "In 2007, Thailand issued a compulsory license to bring down the price of lopinavir/ritonavir, and in the same year, Brazil overcame a patent on efavirenz, enabling the government to import a generic version from India at one third of the originator company price. A compulsory license in Ecuador in 2010 halved the cost of lopinavir/ritonavir to the public health system. India … issued the first compulsory license in 2012 [which] brought down the price of a patented anticancer drug, sorafenib tosylate, from more than $5,500 per month to $175 per month – a 97 per cent reduction in price").

[296] WTO (2007), Patents and Health: WTO Receives First Notification under "Paragraph 6" System, TRIPS and Public Health, available at www.wto.org/english/news_e/news07_e/public_health_july07_e.htm

adopted in 2001, the threat of compulsory licences has motivated multi-national companies to "voluntarily make proactive efforts to realistically make their drugs accessible" either through dramatically lowering the price or by offering voluntary licences on favourable terms.[297] Meanwhile, many countries have successfully used the threat of compulsory licences as leverage in drug price negotiations with pharmaceutical companies.[298]

The positive role of compulsory licences and the threat thereof in promoting access to medicines could inspire WTO Members to use the compulsory licensing instrument to pursue other public policy objectives such as mitigating climate change. Despite being public-health-specific, the Doha Declaration and the TRIPS Amendment set a welcome precedent in guaranteeing Members' right and ability to make effective use of the compulsory licensing for the protection of other general public interests such as environmental protection. Bearing this in mind, the following sections examine the feasibility, opportunities and challenges of compulsory licences for EST transfer.

6.4.4.2 Compulsory Licences for Transfer of ESTs: Feasibilities and Opportunities

The TRIPS Agreement does not contain any explicit limitations on the grounds upon which compulsory licences may be granted.[299] This is reaffirmed by Paragraph 5(b) of the Doha Declaration, emphasising that each Member has the right to grant compulsory licences upon the grounds it

---

[297] See, e.g., Subhasis Saha (2009), Patent Law and TRIPS: Compulsory Licensing of Patents and Pharmaceuticals, *Journal of the Patent and Trademark Office Society*, vol. 91, pp. 364–74, at p. 372; Kevin Outterson (2005), Pharmaceutical Arbitrage: Balancing Access and Innovation in International Prescription Drug Markets, *Yale Journal of Health Policy, Law, and Ethics*, vol. 5, pp. 193–291, at pp. 226–7 (noting that "[since the adoption of the Doha Declaration,] there have been many announcements of dramatic price cuts or voluntary programs"; as responses to the looming threat of compulsory licensing, Merck granted voluntary no-royalty licenses to South African-Indian company Thembalami Pharmaceuticals).

[298] Ha-Joon Chang (2008), *Bad Samaritans: The Guilty Secrets of Rich Nations and the Threat to Global Prosperity*, New York: Random House, p. 123 (noting that "in the aftermath of the anthrax terror scare in 2001, the US government used the public interest provision to maximum effect – it used the threat of compulsory licensing to extract a whopping 80 per cent discount for Cipro, the patent-protected anti-anthrax drug from Bayer, the German pharmaceutical company"); Micheal A. Gollin (2008), *Driving Innovation: Intellectual Property Strategies for a Dynamic World*, Cambridge University Press, p. 314 (noting that "South Africa, Brazil, Thailand, and Taiwan have used the threat of compulsory licensing proceedings as leverage in drug price negotiations with pharmaceutical manufacturers, as has the United States"; and that "Brazil's health minister [in 2001] threatened compulsory licensing and negotiated a price reduction of about 50 per cent from the approximately $100 million per year paid to Abbott").

[299] Article 31(c) establishes an exception for semiconductor technology.

determines. As discussed in Section 1.1, climate change is "a common concern of mankind" and tackling climate change is clearly in the public interest. Thus, WTO Members have the power to grant compulsory licences for patented ESTs on the ground that such ESTs are needed to achieve climate change mitigation. This view has been endorsed by many commentators, considering that climate change mitigation could provide a valid ground for compulsory licence of ESTs.[300]

As previously demonstrated, read in accordance with the WTO's sustainable development objective and Articles 7 and 8 of the TRIPS Agreement, Article 31 provides regulatory space for Members to use compulsory licences to facilitate the transfer of ESTs. Members' right and discretion to use compulsory licences in the context of climate change is further supported by developed countries' commitments to transfer ESTs under Article 4.5 of the UNFCCC which serve as a contextual element for the interpretation Article 31. Specially speaking, WTO Members not only enjoy great discretion to grant compulsory licences for EST patents on different grounds but also have certain flexibilities in applying the conditions for the granting of compulsory licences.

As to the grounds for compulsory licensing, first, Members may issue compulsory licences for the lack of local working of certain EST patents. To the extent that local production of certain patented ESTs is needed to mitigate climate change, such local working requirements constitute a *bona fide* distinction rather than discrimination as to whether products are imported or locally produced in Article 27.1. As demonstrated in Section 6.4.2.2, some countries, such as Brazil, permit compulsory licences in cases where the invention is not (sufficiently) exploited locally.[301]

Second, Members may issue compulsory licences to address IP-related abuses and anti-competitive practices in the process of the transfer of ESTs.

---

[300] See, e.g., Maria Julia Oliva (2009), Technologies for Climate Change and Intellectual Property: Issues for Small Developing Countries, *Information Note No. 12*. p. 6 (stating that "climate mitigation or adaptation could provide valid grounds for compulsory licensing, and could even be considered to be included in general references to 'public interest'"); Martin Khor (2011), Climate Change, Technology and IPR, in UNDP (2011), Technological Cooperation and Climate Change: Issues and Perspectives, working papers presented at the Ministry of Environment and Forests, Government of India – UNDP Consultation on Technology Cooperation for Addressing Climate Change, pp. 71–94, at p. 87 (stating that "certainly the fact that a country requires a product or technology in order to meet its objectives or responsibilities to mitigate climate change or to adapt to climate change is a valid ground for compulsory licensing").

[301] See also Maria Julia Oliva (2009), Technologies for Climate Change and Intellectual Property: Issues for Small Developing Countries, *Information Note No. 12*, p. 6.

As pointed out by Reichman et al. (2008), compulsory licences for anti-competitive practices afford countries another set of options to facilitate the access to patented ESTs, "especially when foreign firms refuse to deal with local firms or refuse to make technologies available at prices that local firms can afford".[302] In this case, compulsory licensing may proceed without prior negotiation efforts and the licensee may exploit the patent at issue regardless of the location of the predominant market.[303]

Third, WTO Members may consider climate change as a "national emergency or other circumstances of extreme urgency" within the meaning of Article 31(b), thereby permitting compulsory licensing for certain EST-related patents. The TRIPS Agreement neither defines the concept of "national emergency" or "other circumstances of extreme urgency" nor does it provide guidance for what is meant by these concepts. Again the Doha Declaration affirms that "[e]ach member has the right to determine what constitutes a national emergency or other circumstances of extreme urgency", but added that "public health crises, including those relating to HIV/AIDS, tuberculosis, malaria and other epidemics, can represent a national emergency or other circumstances of extreme urgency".[304] According to Correa (2002), the reference to "HIV/AIDS, tuberculosis, malaria and other epidemics" suggests that an "emergency" may not be restricted to a short-term problem, but can also be a long-lasting situation, and such recognition implies that "specific measures to deal with an emergency may be adopted and maintained as long as the underlying situation persists, without temporal constraints".[305] The Rio+20 Outcome Document (A/RES/66/288) reaffirms that "climate change is one of the greatest challenges of our time" and stresses that combating climate change represents "an immediate and urgent global priority".[306] The preamble of the 2015 Paris Agreement explicitly recognises that climate change poses an "urgent threat".[307] Accordingly, WTO Members, in particular, those countries suffering the most from climate change, may well argue that climate change constitutes "a national emergency" or another circumstance of

---

[302] Jerome Reichman et al. (2008), Intellectual Property and Alternatives: Strategies for Green Innovation, *Energy, Environment and Development Programme Paper*, vol. 8, no. 3, p. 30.

[303] See Article 31(k) of the TRIPS Agreement.

[304] Declaration on the TRIPS Agreement and Public Health, WT/MIN (01)/DEC/2, adopted on 14 November 2001, para. 5(c).

[305] Carlos M. Correa (2002), Implications of the Doha Declaration on the TRIPS Agreement and Public Health, *Health Economics and Drugs EDM Series* No. 12, WHO, p. 17.

[306] The Future We Want, Resolution Adopted by the General Assembly on 27 July 2012, UN Doc. A/RES/66/288, 11 September 2012, para. 190.

[307] Paris Agreement, para. 4 of the Preamble.

"extreme urgency" within the meaning of Article 31(b) of the TRIPS Agreement, therefore permitting compulsory licences for certain EST-related patents. No prior negotiations are needed for such licences, which would therefore promote rapid access to critical ESTs by the countries concerned.

Turning to the conditions for the granting of compulsory licences, although these conditions are strict, interpreting these clauses in their context in accordance with the WTO's sustainable development objective and Articles 7 and 8 of the TRIPS Agreement would provide Members some policy space to facilitate the transfer of patented ESTs. As discussed in Section 6.4.3.1.1, the procedural requirement that a licence must be considered "on its individual merits" (Article 31(a)) does not prevent WTO Members from setting parameters for the granting of compulsory licences regarding certain categories of technologies that are needed to mitigate climate change. As discussed in Section 6.4.3.2.1, Article 31(h) embodies substantial flexibilities in determining the level of, and the basis upon which, adequate remuneration is paid and, in particular, the need for the transfer of ESTs could be an important consideration in establishing the level of compensation.

In general, compulsory licensing is seen as a means of ensuring easy access to, and wide dissemination of, ESTs throughout the world.[308] The use of compulsory licences and the threat thereof to ensure the availability and affordability of essential medicines have provided a powerful precedent supporting that such licences could be used to facilitate access to essential ESTs.[309] As is the case with essential medicines described above, not only compulsory licences are indispensable when an EST-patent holder refuses to

---

[308] See, e.g., Neel Maitra (2010), Access to Environmentally Sound Technology in the Developing World: A Proposed Alternative to Compulsory Licensing, *Columbia Journal of Environmental Law*, vol. 35, pp. 408–45, at p. 409; Robert Fair (2009), Does Climate Change Justify Compulsory Licensing of Green Technology? *International Law & Management Review*, vol. 6, p. 29; Martin Khor (2011), Climate Change, Technology and IPR, in UNDP (2011), *Technological Cooperation and Climate Change: Issues and Perspectives*, working papers presented at the Ministry of Environment and Forests, Government of India-UNDP Consultation on Technology Cooperation for Addressing Climate Change, pp. 71–94, at p. 87.

[309] See, e.g., Robert Fair (2009), Does Climate Change Justify Compulsory Licensing of Green Technology? *International Law & Management Review*, vol. 6, p. 29 (stating that "use, or threatened use [of compulsory licenses] to provide lower-priced medication to the developing world provides a helpful precedent supporting the argument that such licensing can be used for green technology"); Nitya Nanda (2009), Diffusion of Climate Friendly Technologies: Can Compulsory Licensing Help? *Journal of Intellectual Property Rights*, vol. 14, pp. 241–6, at p. 245 (concluding that "It would be useful to explore the idea of according protection of environment the same status as that of protecting the public health in the context of TRIPS"; and that "A public health type exemption to issue compulsory license to foreign firms would certainly be a welcome move").

transfer the essential technologies at all, but often the mere threat to impose a compulsory licence may compel the EST-patent holder to engage in voluntary licensing or lower the price of the patented ESTs.[310] As mentioned in Section 6.4.2.1, using compulsory licences to facilitate access to ESTs have been recommended by Agenda 21 and incorporated into the US Clear Air Act. Therefore, countries, at least those with sufficient technological capabilities, can facilitate access to patented ESTs by using or threatening to use compulsory licences in accordance with the relevant rules set forth in the TRIPS Agreement.[311]

In international negotiations, many developing countries have strongly supported the use of compulsory licences to facilitate access to and transfer of ESTs. As discussed in Section 3.4.2.2.1, despite opposition from some developed countries, emerging countries such as China, India and Brazil have proposed in post-Kyoto climate negotiations that patented green technologies should be subject to "compulsory licensing" so as to accelerate the development and transfer of ESTs needed to address climate change concerns.[312] Overall, the compulsory licensing system is a well-recognised, yet controversial, "policy lever" for promoting transfer of ESTs, in particular to developing countries.[313]

6.4.4.3 Compulsory Licences for Transfer of ESTs: Challenges

Despite developing countries' advocacy and the support of many scholars and civil society activists, the idea of using compulsory licences to facilitate transfer

---

[310] See e.g., Jerome Reichman et al. (2008), Intellectual Property and Alternatives: Strategies for Green Innovation, *Energy, Environment and Development Programme Paper*, vol. 8, no. 3, p. 30; Claire Topal (2014), The Globalization of China's Life Sciences Industry: Flashpoints in Sino-U.S. Trade Relations: An Interview with Ka Zeng, The National Bureau of Asian Research, available at www.nbr.org/research/activity.aspx?id=413

[311] Tú Thanh Nguyễn (2010), *Competition Law, Technology Transfer and the TRIPS Agreement: Implications for Developing Countries*, Cheltenham, UK: Edward Elgar Publishing, at p. 31.

[312] See, e.g., China's Views on Enabling the Full, Effective and Sustained Implementation of the Convention through Long-Term Cooperative Action Now, Up to and Beyond 2012, in Ideas and Proposals on the Elements Contained in Paragraph 1 of the Bali Action Plan: Submissions from Parties, UN Doc. FCCC/AWGLCA/2008/MISC.5, 27 October 2008, available at http://unfccc.int/resource/docs/2008/awglca4/eng/misc05.pdf, pp. 33–38, at p. 36; India (2009), Submission to UNFCCC on Technology Transfer Mechanism, available at http://unfccc.int/files/kyoto_protocol/application/pdf/indiatechtransfer171008.pdf, p.4.

[313] Charles R. McManis and Jorge L. Contreras (2014), Compulsory Licensing of Intellectual Property: A Viable Policy Lever for Promoting Access to Critical Technologies, in Ghidini et al. (eds.), *TRIPS and Developing Countries: Towards a New IP World Order?* Cheltenham, UK: Edward Elgar Publishing, pp. 109–31, at p. 115.

of ESTs attracts considerable opposition from developed countries and their multinational companies. As discussed in Section 3.4.2.2.2, in the UNFCCC negotiations, some developed countries such as the United States have strongly opposed the use of compulsory licensing, while being an inbuilt flexibility in the TRIPS Agreement, by asserting that such a measure will discourage private companies from investing in innovation of ESTs.[314] As a response, developing countries such as Brazil have suggested that a declaration or decision similar to the Doha Declaration should be adopted in the climate change context to ensure WTO Members' right to use compulsory licences to facilitate the transfer of ESTs needed to address climate change concerns.[315]

However, the appropriateness and effectiveness of compulsory licensing as a means to facilitate access to and transfer of ESTs are said to have been undermined by a number of factors.[316] First, some scholars are concerned that compulsory licensing may deter private investment in ESTs and discourage entry of international firms that would otherwise transfer ESTs to local firms.[317]

---

[314] Tessa Schwartz and Sarah Tierney Niyogi (2009), Technology Transfer and Intellectual Property Issues Take Centre Stage in UNFCCC Negotiations, *Cleantech Update*, p. 2. See also Meena Raman (2009), Wide North-South Divide over IPRs and Climate Technologies, *TWN Bonn News Update* No. 13.

[315] ICTSD (2008), Climate Change, Technology Transfer and Intellectual Property Rights, *Paper Prepared for Trade and Climate Change Seminar*, 18–20 June 2008, Copenhagen, ICTSD, Geneva, at p. 7.

[316] See, e.g., Robert Fair (2009), Does Climate Change Justify Compulsory Licensing of Green Technology? *International Law & Management Review*, vol. 6, pp. 24–25 (arguing that "the wide implementation of [compulsory licensing system] would have serious negative ramifications. Increased use of compulsory licensing would almost certainly elicit a harmful backlash from the owners of the appropriated patents, as well as from their respective states"); Alexander Adam (2009), Technology Transfer to Combat Climate Change: Opportunities and Obligations under TRIPS and Kyoto, *Journal of High Technology Law*, vol. 9, no. 1, pp. 1–20, at p. 20 (concluding that "[e]ven when export restrictions under the TRIPS Agreement were waived, as they are for compulsory licensing of pharmaceuticals, the hurdles of the system apparently outweigh its benefits, since only one compulsory license for export manufacture of a drug has been notified to the WTO so far").

[317] See, e.g., Tim Wilson (2008), Undermining Mitigation Technology: Compulsory Licensing, Patents and Tariffs, *Melbourne: Institute of Public Affairs Backgrounder*, vol. 21, no. 1, p. 6 (stating that "[u]ndermining IP on CO_2 mitigation technologies would cause irreparable damage to the development of technologies necessary to reduce emissions"); Keith E. Maskus (2010), Differentiated Intellectual Property Regimes for Environmental and Climate Technologies, *OECD Environment Working Papers*, no. 17, p. 25 (stating that "unless there are offsetting commercial advantages in a market widespread resort to compulsory licensing may deter entry of international firms that would otherwise transfer technology to local partners"); Thomas J. Bollyky (2009), Intellectual Property Rights and Climate Change: Principles for Innovation and Access to Low-Carbon Technology, Centre for Global Development (CGD) Notes, p. 5 (arguing that "[w]hile a multilateral agreement calling for widespread use of

Second, it is noted that compulsory licensing under Article 31 of the TRIPS Agreement cannot mandate the transfer of associated know-how that is necessary to adopt or employ ESTs.[318] As highlighted in a Background Paper for the UNDP Human Development Report (2007), "access to key patents by developing country firms is not a sufficient condition for effective technology transfer" because "[m]uch of the knowledge relevant to working a patent is tacit".[319] Thus, to make full use of the licensed invention, licensees may need to access a variety of associated know-how or tacit technological knowledge and invest in the learning of related skills.

Last but not least, as is the case with essential medicines, the requirement that compulsory licensing be used to predominantly supply the domestic market under Article 31(f) makes it difficult for countries with insufficient manufacturing capacities, which have to rely on another country to issue a compulsory licence for export, to use a compulsory licensing arrangement to facilitate access to ESTs.[320] As demonstrated in Section 6.4.4.1, a waiver was adopted with regard to Article 31(f) of the TRIPS Agreement but is limited to public health needs. A certain WTO Member has called for a review of the restrictive effect of Article 31(f) on "access to and dissemination of ESTs", with a view to introducing an international system of compulsory licensing similar to the "Paragraph 6 system" to facilitate access to ESTs for countries with insufficient manufacturing capacities. [321] Such proposals, however, have triggered strong opposition from some developed countries, in particular the United States.

If Article 31(f) could restrict the ability of poor countries to make effective use of compulsory licences in the pharmaceutical sector, there is no reason to

---

compulsory licensing might have modest benefits increasing access, it would deter foreign direct investment and technology transfer in emerging markets where IP can support such transfer").

[318] See, e.g., Thomas J. Bollyky (2009), Intellectual Property Rights and Climate Change: Principles for Innovation and Access to Low-Carbon Technology, Centre for Global Development (CGD) Notes, p. 5; Keith E. Maskus (2010), Differentiated Intellectual Property Regimes for Environmental and Climate Technologies, *OECD Environment Working Papers*, no. 17, p. 25.

[319] Jim Watson et al. (2007), Technology and Carbon Mitigation in Developing Countries: Are Cleaner Coal Technologies a Viable Option? *Background Paper for Human Development Report 2007*, UNDP, p. 7.

[320] See, e.g., Nitya Nanda (2009), Diffusion of Climate-Friendly Technologies: Can Compulsory Licensing Help? *Journal of Intellectual Property Rights*, vol. 14, pp. 241–6, at p. 245; Thomas J. Bollyky (2009), Intellectual Property Rights and Climate Change: Principles for Innovation and Access to Low-Carbon Technology, Centre for Global Development (CGD) Notes, p. 5.

[321] Communication from Ecuador: Contribution of Intellectual Property to Facilitating the Transfer of Environmentally Sound Technology, Council for Trade-Related Aspects of Intellectual Property Rights, WTO Doc. IP/C/W/585, 27 February 2013, p. 4.

not recognize that countries with insufficient manufacturing capacities also have difficulty in using compulsory licences to facilitate access to ESTs that are needed to address climate change concerns. Indeed, ESTs are generally more complex and require greater manufacturing capacity than pharmaceuticals. As discussed in Section 2.2.1, virtually all ESTs are a combination of technologies, or "system technologies". For example, a wind turbine is made up of several components including a tower and foundation, rotor and rotor blades, gearbox, generator and others. A transmission belt used in wind turbines is merely one component that has to operate with the other components of a system so as to constitute an EST product that is "less polluting" or that "uses all resources in a more sustainable manner". In contrast, products in the fields of pharmaceuticals, chemicals and biotechnology (e.g. the human genome) are usually more easily replicated once the formula, active substance or sequence is known. Therefore, in general, the production of ESTs is more difficult, demanding stronger manufacturing capacities. In practice, as observed by Nanda and Srivastava (2011), "even a least developed country like Bangladesh has capacities to produce pharmaceutical products", but a relatively advanced developing country may not have sufficient manufacturing capacity to produce certain ESTs needed to mitigate climate change.[322]

Accordingly, many countries may lack sufficient manufacturing capacities to produce ESTs and thus, they have to import relevant ESTs to meet their local needs. However, Article 31(f) may limit their ability to benefit from the compulsory licensing system established by the TRIPS Agreement. To address this concern, a waiver of Article 31(f) should be adopted with a view to facilitate access to ESTs that are needed to address climate change concerns. Specific recommendation is addressed in Section 8.4.1.

6.5 CONCLUSION

The TRIPS Agreement contains many patent-related flexibilities to enable WTO Members to take the measures necessary to facilitate innovation and transfer of ESTs that are needed to address climate change concerns. However, the extent to which innovation and transfer of ESTs will occur in reality partly depends on how WTO Members interpret and implement the TRIPS flexibilities in order to facilitate innovation of, and access to, ESTs.

[322] Nitya Nanda and Nidhi Srivastava (2011), Facilitating Technology Transfer for Climate Change Mitigation and Adaptation, prepared for the 17th Conference of Parties to the United Nations Framework Convention on Climate Change, 28 November–9 December 2011, The Energy and Resources Institute, p. 11.

In accordance with the general interpretative rules established by Article 31 of the VCLT, this chapter seeks to interpret patent-related flexibilities in good faith in the context and in line with the objectives of the WTO and the TRIPS Agreement, taking into account non-WTO norms such as EST transfer commitments under Article 4.5 of the UNFCCC as well as subsequent agreements to TRIPS, in particular the Doha Declaration. The WTO's sustainable development objective requires that patent-related flexibilities should be interpreted with a view to promoting environmental protection including by facilitating innovation and transfer of ESTs. Article 7 of the TRIPS Agreement informs the WTO Members that their interpretation of patent-related provisions should be conducive to both technological innovation and the transfer and dissemination of technology including ESTs. The public interest principle established by Article 8 of the TRIPS Agreement requires that the interpretation of the TRIPS terms shall take into account the fact that combating climate change is in the public interest.

As to the non-discrimination principle established by Article 27.1, it may impose constraints on WTO Members' discretion to tailor their patent systems to meet the perceived needs of specific fields of technology. Nevertheless, it also leaves WTO Members room to provide differential treatment for ESTs by permitting bona fide exceptions for "certain product areas". In practice, ESTs have enjoyed differential treatment vis-à-vis other technologies in some countries. Some national IP offices have established fast-track mechanisms for patent applications in respect of ESTs so as to facilitate the adoption and transfer of such technologies.

With regard to patent eligibility, a low requirement of patentability risks blocking follow-on innovation through the exclusive control of knowledge that ought to be in the public domain. From the perspective of ensuring innovation of and access to patented ESTs, developing countries should adopt stricter patentability requirements within the boundaries of the TRIPS Agreement. If such high criteria for patentability are strictly applied by the patent office, it could remediate the perceived threat of low-quality patents. However, the trade-offs associated with such a policy is that local innovators in developing countries would find it more difficult to obtain patents. Nevertheless, developing countries could introduce utility models to protect their minor inventions.

Furthermore, Article 27.2 cannot be invoked to justify excluding ESTs from patentability because: (1) exclusion of inventions pertinent to ESTs from patentability does not necessarily contribute to the protection of *ordre public* or morality, (2) it is not desirable to prevent the commercial exploitation of such inventions and (3) the prevention of commercial exploitation of such inventions is not necessary to protect *ordre public* or morality. Accordingly, the proposal to exclude from patentability "essential" or "urgent" ESTs in the current international climate change negotiations is inconsistent with Article 27.2 of the TRIPS Agreement. To the extent that compliance with WTO standards is desired, the implementation of such measure would require a fundamental change in the TRIPS Agreement (Article 27). This type of amendment would demand a high level of political cost and its feasibility could be questioned, especially considering that it took almost twelve years for the only TRIPS amendment (2005) to enter into force. Accordingly, for national legislatures, rather than blanket exclusions of ESTs from patent protection, it is better to adopt stricter standards for patentability so as to increase the quality of EST patents

Turning to limits on patent rights, the limitations or exceptions under Article 30 have the potential to safeguard public interests. Through limiting patent rights, the exceptions can mitigate the exclusive effects of a patent and thereby increase the availability of the patented product. Article 30 requires a holistic assessment rather than a separate and independent assessment of each constituent criterion of the "three-step test". Public interests in general and societal interests in combating climate change in particular fall within the scope of "legitimate interests of third parties" in Article 30. Thus, such interests shall be considered when determining the scope of legitimate exceptions for ESTs. Notably, experimental use exceptions could be adopted under Article 30 of the TRIPS Agreement to facilitate innovation of ESTs and disseminate technological knowledge, thereby contributing to climate change mitigation. Countries with low level of technological advancement should also make use of the flexibility provided by Article 6 and allow parallel imports to ensure the lowest cost source of supply of patented ESTs for combating climate change.

Moreover, climate change as a "common concern of mankind" provides a valid ground for the compulsory licensing of patented ESTs that are needed to address climate change concerns. WTO Members, in particular those countries suffering the most from climate change, may well argue that climate change constitutes "a national emergency" or another circumstance of "extreme urgency" within the meaning of Article 31(b) of the TRIPS Agreement, therefore permitting compulsory licences for certain EST-related patents. A good faith interpretation of Article 27.1 does not outlaw compulsory licences for failure to work the patented ESTs in the patent-granting country. The use of compulsory licensing and the mere threat thereof can serve as a means of ensuring access to ESTs throughout the world, in particular, when foreign firms refuse to deal with local firms or refuse to make technologies available at prices that local firms can afford.

However, there are inherent restrictions to prevent WTO Members from making full use of all the patent-related flexibilities. For instance, compulsory licensing cannot compel the transfer of know-how necessary to adapt and employ patented ESTs. The requirement that compulsory licensing be used to predominantly supply the domestic market under Article 31(f) makes it difficult for countries with insufficient manufacturing capacity to make effective use of the compulsory licensing system to facilitate access to patented ESTs that play an important role in tackling climate change concerns. The remedies to these insufficiencies go beyond the interpretation of the TRIPS provisions and may demand amendment despite high political cost.

7

Interpreting Competition-Related Flexibilities in the TRIPS Agreement for Facilitating Innovation and Transfer of ESTs

7.1 INTRODUCTION

It is evident that IPRs can be abused despite the limits and boundaries placed upon them, as discussed in Section 4.4.[1] The exclusive rights inherent in IPRs can be exercised in an abusive or anti-competitive manner either through unilateral conduct or contractual restraints. In the context of ESTs, Section 4.4 found that the MNCs controlling ESTs may refuse to license their patented ESTs to other producers so as to maintain a competitive advantage; that companies may exercise their exclusive rights to deter competitors from entering the market or block similar technological innovation; and that firms may grant access to their patented ESTs on restrictive conditions. Such IPR-related practices may adversely affect competition on the market, and in fact impede innovation and transfer of technology.[2]

---

[1] See, e.g., Barry J. Rodger and Angus MacCulloch (2015), *Competition Law and Policy in the EU and UK,* New York: Routledge, p. 123 (stating that "Intellectual property rights encourage innovation by rewarding the innovator with exclusivity, but that may in turn become statutory dominance which may be abused"; and that "It has always been held that the ownership of an intellectual property right was not, in itself, an abuse but that the use of such a right may amount to one"); Jae Hun Park (2010), *Patents and Industry Standards,* Cheltenham, UK: Edward Elgar Publishing, p. 169 (stating that "it is argued that the exclusivity of patent rights can be used in anti-competitive ways. The owner of property rights can prevent others from using the subject matters protected by the rights and thus the owner of systems technology may exercise the property rights to exclude competitors by refusing to grant licences or to expand market power from one market to another market by means of tie-in"); Graeme B. Dinwoodie and Rochelle C. Dreyfuss (2012), *A Neofederalist Vision of TRIPS: The Resilience of the International Intellectual Property Regime,* Oxford University Press, p. 187.

[2] See, e.g., Tú Thanh Nguyãẽn (2010), *Competition Law, Technology Transfer and the TRIPS Agreement: Implications for Developing Countries,* Cheltenham, UK: Edward Elgar Publishing, p. xiii.

Competition law is viewed as a legal instrument to correct a non-optimal IP policy and prevent or control the anti-competitive behaviour, thereby promoting the public interest in access to IP-protected subject matter and facilitating a dynamic and innovative economy.[3] Accordingly, whereas the TRIPS Agreement requires all WTO Members to provide minimum standards of IPRs, it leaves considerable discretion to its Members in the adoption and implementation of competition laws. According to Ullrich (2005), this reservation of IPR-related competition policy to a Member's regulatory sovereignty represents a concession that developed countries made during the Uruguay Round negotiations in response to developing countries' unsuccessful attempt to enact a global Code of Conduct for the Transfer of Technology in the late 1970s.[4]

The TRIPS Agreement contains three provisions that expressly address the issue of competition: that is, Articles 8.2, 31(k) and 40. Articles 8.2 and 40 primarily define the boundaries of a Member's freedom to formulate competition-oriented restrictions on IPRs. While Article 8.2 represents a general recognition that appropriate measures may be needed to deal with abuse of IPRs or "practices which unreasonably restrain trade or adversely affect the international transfer of technology", Article 40 deals specifically with the "control of anti-competitive practices in contractual licensing". Another operative provision, Article 31(k), allows Members to impose compulsory licences to remedy anti-competitive practices.

The existence of the foregoing provisions reflects the concerns articulated by some countries, in particular, developing countries during the Uruguay Round negotiations (1986–94), that "exploitation of IPRs could give rise to anti-competitive behaviour".[5] These provisions grant WTO Members broad

[3] See, e.g., Josef Drexl (2005), The Critical Role of Competition Law in Preserving Public Goods in Conflict with Intellectual Property Rights, in Maskus and Reichman (eds.), *International Public Goods and Transfer of Technology under a Globalized Intellectual Property Regime*, Cambridge University Press, pp. 707–25, at p. 716; Carsten Fink (2005), Comment: Competition Law as a Means of Containing Intellectual Property Rights, in Maskus and Reichman (eds.), *International Public Goods and Transfer of Technology under a Globalized Intellectual Property Regime*, Cambridge University Press, pp. 770–3, at p. 770.
[4] Hanns Ullrich (2005), Expansionist Intellectual Property Protection and Reductionist Competition Rules: A TRIPS Perspective, in Maskus and Reichman (eds.), *International Public Goods and Transfer of Technology under a Globalized Intellectual Property Regime*, Cambridge University Press, pp. 726–57, at p. 730.
[5] See, e.g., UNCTAD-ICTSD (2005), *Resource Book on TRIPS and Development*, Cambridge University Press, p. 540; Tú Thanh Nguyãễn (2010), *Competition Law, Technology Transfer and the TRIPS Agreement: Implications for Developing Countries*, Cheltenham, UK: Edward Elgar Publishing, p. 42; Standards and Principles Concerning the Availability Scope and Use of Trade-related Intellectual Property Rights, Communication from India, Negotiating Group

regulatory discretion to formulate their own competition policies concerning IPR-related anti-competitive and abusive practices. As such, they represent a central aspect of the flexibility inherent in the TRIPS Agreement, ensuring it is applied in a manner consistent with the protection of public interests, which also include combating climate change.[6]

Nevertheless, the competition-related provisions of the TRIPS Agreement are quite vague and limited, leaving important questions unanswered. They do not define the standards under which practices may be deemed to be abusive or anti-competitive; and they provide little guidance "regarding the remedies that may be adopted in particular cases", beyond the general requirement of consistency with other provisions of the TRIPS Agreement.[7] In practice, finding an optimal solution under specific circumstances for the application of competition law to facilitate innovation and transfer of technology is not an easy task, and thus, most countries do not dispose of effective IPR-related competition rules.[8]

In the context of climate change, given the fact that competition policy plays an important role in facilitating innovation of and ensuring access to ESTs that are needed to mitigate climate change, a preliminary question for analysis arises regarding whether the relevant provisions of the TRIPS Agreement provide sufficient policy space and guidance for Members to regulate anti-competitive practices. This chapter examines to what extent such competition-related flexibilities can be interpreted in line with Articles 31 and 32 of the VCLT to facilitate innovation and transfer of ESTs so as to address global climate change concerns.

---

on Trade-Related Aspects of Intellectual Property Rights, including Trade in Counterfeit Goods, 10 July 1989, GATT Doc. MTN. GNG/NG11/W/37, p. 8.

[6] Robert D. Anderson (2010), Competition Policy and Intellectual Property in the WTO: More Guidance Needed? in Drexl (ed.), *Research Handbook on Intellectual Property and Competition Law*, Cheltenham, UK: Edward Elgar Publishing, pp. 451–73, at p. 457.

[7] Robert D. Anderson and Hannu Wager (2006), Human Rights, Development and the WTO: The Case of Intellectual Property Rights and Competition Policy, *Journal of International Economic Law*, vol. 9, no. 3, pp. 707–47, at p. 742; Robert D. Anderson (2010), Competition Policy and Intellectual Property in the WTO: More Guidance Needed? in Drexl (ed.), *Research Handbook on Intellectual Property and Competition Law*, Cheltenham, UK: Edward Elgar Publishing, pp. 451–73, at p. 452; Antony Taubman, Hannu Wager and Jayashree Watal (2012), *A Handbook on the WTO TRIPS Agreement*, Cambridge University Press, p. 133.

[8] See, e.g., Thomas Cottier and Pierre Véron (2011), *Concise International and European IP Law: TRIPS, Paris Convention, European Enforcement and Transfer of Technology*, 2nd edn, New York: Kluwer Law International, p. 35; Tú Thanh Nguyẽn (2010), *Competition Law, Technology Transfer and the TRIPS Agreement: Implications for Developing Countries*, Cheltenham, UK: Edward Elgar Publishing, p. xiv.

The following sections examine, in turn, the interpretative issues of the basic principle established under Article 8.2, control of anti-competitive practices in contractual licences under Article 40, and compulsory licensing as a remedy to anti-competitive practices under Article 31(k). Their application to the innovation and transfer of ESTs will be addressed correspondingly.

7.2 ARTICLE 8.2: BASIC PRINCIPLE

Article 8.2 of the TRIPS Agreement, as a "Basic Principle", provides WTO Members with the freedom to adopt appropriate measures to combat the abuse of IPRs and to deal with practices that unreasonably restrain trade or adversely affect the international transfer of technology, stating that:

> Appropriate measures, provided that they are consistent with the provisions of this Agreement, may be needed to prevent the abuse of intellectual property rights by right holders or the resort to practices which unreasonably restrain trade or adversely affect the international transfer of technology.

Although Article 8 bears the title "Principles", some scholars perceive Article 8.2 as a mere "policy statement" that explains the rationale underlying the measures taken in accordance with Articles 31 and 40.[9] Other observers disagree with this view and have read this provision as establishing an "overarching, constitutional principle" that confers authority on Members to rule on IPR-related practices that are abusive, that "unreasonably restrain trade or adversely affect international transfer of technology".[10] Indeed, the explicit

---

[9]   See, e.g., Daniel Gervais (2012), *The TRIPS Agreement: Drafting History and Analysis*, 4th edn, New York: Thomson Reuters, p. 238; Peter Yu (2009), The Objectives and Principles of the TRIPS Agreement, *Houston Law Review*, vol. 46, pp. 797–1046, at p. 1017 (endorsing the argument of Professor Gervais).

[10]   See, e.g., UNCTAD-ICTSD (2005), *Resource Book on TRIPS and Development*, Cambridge University Press, p. 546 (observing that "As indicated by its heading, Article 8.2 states a 'principle', which is different from a mere 'policy statement'"); Thomas Cottier and Pierre Véron (2011), *Concise International and European IP Law: TRIPS, Paris Convention, European Enforcement and Transfer of Technology*, 2nd edn, New York: Kluwer Law International, p. 32 (stating that "The principles of art. 8, together with art. 7, read like overarching, constitutional principles defining the relationship of international obligations and domestic policies in the field"); UNCTAD (1996), *The TRIPS Agreement and Developing Countries*, UNCTAD/ITE/1, New York and Geneva: United Nations, p. 53 (stating that "As this provision [Article 8.2], which relates to all intellectual property covered by the TRIPS Agreement, is set out under the heading of Principles and as it forms part of Part I (General Provisions and Basic Principles), it must be construed broadly"); Mark D. Janis (2005), "Minimal" Standards for Patent-related Antitrust Law under TRIPS, in Maskus and Reichman (eds.), *International Public Goods and Transfer of Technology under a Globalized Intellectual Property Regime*, Cambridge University Press, pp. 774–92, at p. 777.

reference to "principle" in the heading of Article 8.2 distinguishes it from a mere policy statement or a specific rule. Despite significant legal weight, this provision is of limited normative value and mainly serves an interpretative function. According to Correa (2014), together with Article 7, this provision constitutes "a central element for the interpretation and implementation of the TRIPS Agreement, particularly with regard to those provisions that leave flexibilities to legislate at the national level".[11]

Article 8.2 acknowledges that appropriate measures "may be needed" to prevent the practices mentioned, thus allowing room for the argument that "Members agree that there are such practices and that they have to be remedied".[12] However, Article 8.2 sets limits on Members' sovereign power to prevent or control the said practices by requiring that the appropriate measures be "consistent with the provisions of this Agreement" (the "consistency requirement").[13]

The following sections address, in turn, the scope of Article 8.2, the meaning of its consistency requirement and how the terms of Article 8.2 can be interpreted in accordance with the VCLT with a view to facilitating innovation and transfer of ESTs.

7.2.1 *Scope of Application*

Judging from its text, Article 8.2 applies to three types of practices: (1) the abuse of IPRs by right holders, (2) the practices that unreasonably restrain trade and (3) the practices that adversely affect the international transfer of technology. Notably, this provision refers only to "trade" and "international" technology transfer, and thus, purely domestic practices may not be subject to the limits provided by Article 8.2.[14] The following sections examine the

---

[11] Carlos M. Correa (2014), Intellectual Property and Competition – Room to Legislate under International Law, in Frederick Abbott et al. (eds.), *Using Competition Law to Promote Access to Health Technologies: A Guidebook for Low- and Middle-Income Countries*, New York: United Nations Development Programme, pp. 35–57, at p. 46.

[12] UNCTAD-ICTSD (2005), *Resource Book on TRIPS and Development*, Cambridge University Press, p. 546.

[13] See Article 8.2 of the TRIPS Agreement; see also Tú Thanh Nguyãẽn (2010), *Competition Law, Technology Transfer and the TRIPS Agreement: Implications for Developing Countries*, Cheltenham, UK: Edward Elgar Publishing, p. 48.

[14] UNCTAD (1996), *The TRIPS Agreement and Developing Countries*, UNCTAD/ITE/1, New York and Geneva: United Nations, p. 54 (further stating that "it applies only to anti-competitive conduct related to IPRs, not to anti-competitive conduct in general. Consequently, control of the exercise or the exploitation of IPRs that forms part of a broader and distinct restrictive practice or agreement (such as joint ventures, bid-rigging, or distribution agreements) is not covered by the TRIPS Agreement"); see also UNCTAD-ICTSD (2005), *Resource Book on*

three IPR-related abuse or practices covered by Article 8.2 in turn, beginning with the abuse of IP rights.

7.2.1.1 Abuse of IP Rights

Under Article 8.2, the abuse of IP rights by right holders may be subject to competition laws. Cottier and Véron (2011) observe that the prevention of abuse of rights is inherent in the restricting provisions found throughout the Agreement and that "it is a principle in international law based upon the precepts of equity".[15]

Article 8.2 does not define the term "abuse of IP rights", thereby leaving WTO Members considerable flexibility in its interpretation. The dictionary meaning of the verb "abuse" is "misuse, make a bad use of; wrongly take advantage of".[16] Wrongly taking advantage of a legal right constitutes an abuse of rights, which may harm the public interest or the interests of third parties. The prohibition of the abuse of rights has long been accepted as a general principle of law that plays an important role in certain limited contexts by imposing restrictions on, or mediating between, different actors' rights.[17] In *US – Shrimp* (1998), the Appellate Body clarified the content of this legal principle:

> [The principle of good faith], at once a general principle of law and a general principle of international law, controls the exercise of rights by states. One application of this general principle, the application widely known as the doctrine of *abus de droit*, prohibits the abusive exercise of a state's rights and enjoins that whenever the assertion of a right "impinges on the field covered by [a] treaty obligation, it must be exercised bona fide, that is to say, reasonably." An abusive exercise by a Member of its own treaty right thus

---

TRIPS and Development, Cambridge University Press, p. 547 (further stating that "the assessment of broader restrictive agreements or arrangements, which involve IPRs, but which, under general principles of competition law, are dealt with as separate categories of possible antitrust law violations, may not be subject to the limits set by Article 8.2").

[15] Thomas Cottier and Pierre Véron (2011), *Concise International and European IP Law: TRIPS, Paris Convention, European Enforcement and Transfer of Technology*, 2nd edn, New York: Kluwer Law International, p. 35.

[16] *Shorter Oxford English Dictionary* (2007), 6th edn, Vol. 2, Stevenson (ed.), Oxford University Press, p. 11.

[17] See, e.g., Michael Byers (2002), Abuse of Rights, An Old Principle, A New Age, *McGill Law Journal*, vol. 47, pp. 389–431, at p. 431; Aidan O'Neill (2011), *EU Law for UK Lawyers*, Oxford, UK: Hart Publishing, p. 1959 (noting that "The concept of 'abuse of rights' has also been accepted in the jurisprudence of the CJEU as being a general principle of EU law").

results in a breach of the treaty rights of the other Members and, as well, a violation of the treaty obligation of the Member so acting."[18]

According to Cheng (1953), a bona fide exercise of a right is one that is "in furtherance of the interests which the right is intended to protect" and "compatible with the obligation".[19] The same holds true for the exercise of IP rights. Guided by the general principle of good faith and the legal doctrine of *abus de droit*, the term "the abuse of IP rights" can be interpreted as exercising IP rights in an unreasonable manner that may harm the interests of third parties or the public interest.[20] The abuse of IP rights tends to go against the objective of IPR protection that is to promote innovation and technology transfer.

Article 5A(2) of the Paris Convention, incorporated into the TRIPS Agreement via Article 2.1, provides contextual support for interpreting "the abuse of intellectual property rights" in Article 8.2, by labelling failure to work a patented invention as an example of an "abuse" of the patent right.[21] This also shows that the term an "abuse" of IP rights in Article 8.2 is independent of whether or not the IP owner enjoys "a dominant position".[22] Thus, the abuses of IP rights within the meaning of Article 8.2 do not necessarily cover the same types of conduct as anti-competitive practices.[23]

WTO Members enjoy broad discretion to determine what constitutes an abuse of IP rights in Article 8.2.[24] In the United States, the Supreme Court has developed "the doctrine of patent misuse which denies relief to patentees who attempt to extend the patent beyond the scope of the lawful grant" in

---

[18] Appellate Body Report, *US – Shrimp*, para. 158.

[19] Bin Cheng (1953), *General Principles of Law as Applied by International Courts and Tribunals*, Stevens and Sons, p. 125.

[20] Edson Beas Rodrigues (2012), *The General Exception Clauses of the TRIPS Agreement: Promoting Sustainable Development*, Vol. 17, Cambridge University Press, p. 38.

[21] Article 5A(2) of the Paris Convention states that "Each country of the Union shall have the right to take legislative measures providing for the grant of compulsory licenses to prevent the abuses which might result from the exercise of the exclusive rights conferred by the patent, for example, failure to work".

[22] See also Carlos M. Correa (2014), Intellectual Property and Competition – Room to Legislate under International Law, in Frederick Abbott et al. (eds.), *Using Competition Law to Promote Access to Health Technologies: A Guidebook for Low- and Middle-Income Countries*, New York: United Nations Development Programme, pp. 35–57, at p. 47.

[23] Carlos M. Correa (2007), *Trade Related Aspects of Intellectual Property Rights: A Commentary on the TRIPS Agreement*, Oxford University Press, p. 111.

[24] UNCTAD-ICTSD (2005), *Resource Book on TRIPS and Development*, Cambridge University Press, p. 548; Beatriz Conde Gallego (2010), Intellectual Property Rights and Competition Policy, in Correa (ed.), *Research Handbook on the Protection of Intellectual Property under WTO Rules: Intellectual Property in the WTO*, Vol. I, Cheltenham, UK: Edward Elgar Publishing, pp. 226–65, at p. 234.

accordance with the principle that "equity will deny use of its powers to a wrongdoer".[25] Some examples of patent misuse are tying, "refusal to license, resale price maintenance, price discrimination and mandatory package licensing".[26]

In the context of climate change, Section 4.4.2.1 found that companies have used patents as a strategic tool to block similar technological innovation and to prevent market entry by potential competitors. In particular, the boom of low-quality patents or strategic patents has resulted in the surge of patent litigation rather than to stimulate innovation of ESTs. Such use of a patent may constitute an "abuse" of IP rights within the meaning of Article 8.2 because it could defeat the objective of IP protection enshrined in Article 7 and prejudice the public interest outlined in Article 8.1. Under Article 8.2, WTO Members have the right to regulate such abuse of IP rights to promote the innovation and transfer of ESTs that are needed to mitigate climate change. Article 48.1 of the TRIPS Agreement, "which regulates compensation for the injury of a third party caused by abuses of IPR enforcement procedure", provides contextual support for the interpretation that Article 8.2 allows Members to address the abuse in the enforcement of IP rights such as sham litigation and strategic litigation.[27]

7.2.1.2 Practices That Unreasonably Restrain Trade

Article 8.2 allows Members to take measures to prevent "the resort to practices which unreasonably restrain trade". However, the TRIPS Agreement does not clarify which practices could unreasonably restrain trade. Therefore the

---

[25] Larry R. Fisher (1967), The Misuse Doctrine and Expiration-Discriminatory-and Exorbitant Patent Royalties, *Indiana Law Journal*, vol. 43, no.1, art. 6, pp. 106–29, at p. 106.

[26] Hiroko Yamane (2014), Competition Analyses of Licensing Agreements: Considerations for Developing Countries under TRIPS, Discussion Paper, ICTSD Innovation, Technology and Intellectual Property, Geneva: International Centre for Trade and Sustainable Development, p. 39.

[27] Article 48.1 of the TRIPS Agreement provides that "The judicial authorities shall have the authority to order a party at whose request measures were taken and who has abused enforcement procedures to provide to a party wrongfully enjoined or restrained adequate compensation for the injury suffered because of such abuse. The judicial authorities shall also have the authority to order the applicant to pay the defendant expenses, which may include appropriate attorney's fees"; see also Tú Thanh Nguyãẽn (2010), *Competition Law, Technology Transfer and the TRIPS Agreement: Implications for Developing Countries*, Cheltenham, UK: Edward Elgar Publishing, p. 43; Carlos M. Correa (2014), Intellectual Property and Competition-Room to Legislate under International Law, in Frederick Abbott et al. (eds.), *Using Competition Law to Promote Access to Health Technologies: A Guidebook for Low- and Middle-Income Countries*, New York: United Nations Development Programme, pp. 35–57, at p. 48.

crucial question here is the point at which "restraint" may be considered to have reached an "unreasonable" level.

The term "unreasonable" means "going beyond what is reasonable, or equitable; excessive".[28] The ordinary meaning of the term "reasonable" is "within the limits of reason, not greatly less or more than might be thought likely or appropriate", or "of a fair, average or considerable amount or size".[29] Furthermore, the interpretation of "unreasonably" in other provisions of the TRIPS Agreement could provide contextual support and helpful guidance for the interpretation of "unreasonably" in Article 8.2 of the TRIPS Agreement. In interpreting the phrase "unreasonably prejudice the legitimate interests of the right holder" in Article 13 of the TRIPS Agreement, the panel in *US – Section 110(5) Copyright Act* (2000) found that:

> [P]rejudice to legitimate interests of right holders reaches an unreasonable level if an exception or limitation causes or has the potential to cause an unreasonable loss of income to the copyright owner.[30]

Similarly, when a restraint of trade either causes or has the potential to cause an unreasonable loss to society or to third parties, such restraint may be deemed unreasonable. According to Abbott (2004), the question of whether a particular practice "unreasonably" restrains trade "involves a classical balancing test that takes into account the effect of the conduct on consumers or on industrial policy interests".[31] The objectives and principles enshrined in Articles 7 and 8.1 also support the interpretation that the reasonableness determination, in essence, requires a weighing of the competing interests and a balancing of all pertinent factors involved in the particular circumstances.

In doing so, Article 8.2 seeks to discourage Members from outlawing "practices that are inherently beneficial, such as contractual clauses facilitating the productive use of the intellectual property".[32] However, "this provision may not be read as excluding rules of *a priori* illegality of certain restrictive practices (so-called *per se* rules)" and in practice, many WTO Members

---

[28] *Shorter Oxford English Dictionary* (2007), 6th edn, Vol. 2, Stevenson (ed.), Oxford University Press, p. 3455.

[29] *Shorter Oxford English Dictionary* (2007), 6th edn, Vol. 2, Stevenson (ed.), Oxford University Press, p. 2481.

[30] Panel Report, *US – Section 110(5) Copyright Act*, para. 6.229.

[31] Frederick M. Abbott (2004), Are the Competition Rules in the WTO TRIPS Agreement Adequate? *Journal of International Economic Law*, vol. 7, no. 3, pp. 687–703, at p. 692.

[32] UNCTAD-ICTSD (2005), *Resource Book on TRIPS and Development*, Cambridge University Press, p. 548.

submit some anti-competitive practices to *per se* rules.[33] Furthermore, commentators observe that the "practices which unreasonably restrain trade" mentioned in Article 8.2 are not limited to licensing practices that restrain trade, which are specially addressed in Article 40 of the TRIPS Agreement, but to "any behaviour that may unreasonably restrain trade".[34]

Section 4.4.2.1 found that sham litigation or strategic litigation based on low-quality patents has delayed the entry of certain ESTs that are needed to mitigate climate change into the market. Such practices restricting market entry of technologies that are needed to promote the public interest appear to contradict the objectives set forth in Article 7 and the public interest principle enshrined in Article 8. They do not appear to be compliant with the rationale of the TRIPS Agreement that is embodied in the first recital of the Preamble, stressing Members' desire to "reduce distortions and impediments to international trade". Such behaviours thus constitute "practices that unreasonably restrain trade" within the meaning of Article 8.2 and should be addressed by WTO Members.

7.2.1.3 Practices That Adversely Affect the International Transfer of Technology

Article 8.2 of the TRIPS Agreement entitles Members to take measures to prevent the resort to practices which "adversely affect the international transfer of technology". Read textually, this provision only covers the international transfer of technology, and thus, domestic technology transfer, such as from the national research institutions to domestic industry, may not be subject to Article 8.2.[35]

---

[33] See, e.g., UNCTAD-ICTSD (2005), *Resource Book on TRIPS and Development*, Cambridge University Press, p. 549; Tú Thanh Nguyãẽn (2010), *Competition Law, Technology Transfer and the TRIPS Agreement: Implications for Developing Countries*, Cheltenham, UK: Edward Elgar Publishing, pp. 68–71; Robert D. Anderson (1998), The Interface between Competition Policy and Intellectual Property in the Context of the International Trading System, *Journal of International Economic Law*, pp. 655–78 (providing an overview of national antitrust laws relating to IPRs' exploitation).

[34] Carlos M. Correa (2014), Intellectual Property and Competition-Room to Legislate under International Law, in Frederick Abbott et al. (eds.), *Using Competition Law to Promote Access to Health Technologies: A Guidebook for Low- and Middle-Income Countries*, New York: United Nations Development Programme, pp. 35–57, at p. 49; see also Thomas Cottier and Pierre Véron (2011), *Concise International and European IP Law: TRIPS, Paris Convention, European Enforcement and Transfer of Technology*, 2nd edn, New York: Kluwer Law International, p. 36.

[35] UNCTAD-ICTSD (2005), *Resource Book on TRIPS and Development*, Cambridge University Press, p. 550.

As discussed in Section 3.3.1, this provision reflects developing countries' concern during the Uruguay Round negotiations that the IPR-related restrictive practices may hinder their access to technologies.[36] By the broad reference to practices adversely affecting the international transfer of technology, Article 8.2 goes well beyond the confines of competition law.[37] Commentators observe that Article 8.2 covers not only contractual restrictive practices affecting international technology transfer, but also unilateral practices such as "abusive refusals to license" and imposing unreasonably high royalties.[38]

Recalling that Article 8.1 expressly authorises Members to promote the public interest in sectors of vital importance to their technological development, UNCTAD (1996) contends that "Article 8.2 may not be presumed to overrule a measure that Article 8.1 expressly allows, at least within certain limits".[39] Read together with Article 8.1, Article 8.2 allows WTO Members to control practices adversely affecting international technology transfer to pursue a public-interest objective such as mitigating climate change. This interpretation is also supported by the objective of IPR protection enshrined in Article 7, that is, to promote technological innovation and transfer.

Section 4.4.2.1 found that depending on the stage of the licensee's technological development, MNCs may employ different abusive or anti-competitive practices such as patent blockage, high licensing fees, and refusal of licensing to maintain their competitive advantage. Such practices adversely affect the international transfer of ESTs that are needed to meet the climate change mitigation objective, thereby going against the objectives and principles set forth in Articles 7 and 8 of the TRIPS Agreement. Under Article 8.2, Members have broad discretion to take action to address such practices. As suggested by Correa (2014), as many developing countries did in the past, WTO Members may establish policies to guide "technology pricing and other

---

[36] See, e.g., Standards and Principles Concerning the Availability Scope and Use of Trade-Related Intellectual Property Rights, Communication from India, Negotiating Group on Trade-Related Aspects of Intellectual Property Rights, including Trade in Counterfeit Goods, 10 July 1989, GATT Doc. MTN. GNG/NG11/W/37, p. 2 (arguing that "the essence of the [intellectual property] system is its monopolistic and restrictive characters; its purpose is not to 'liberalise', but to confer exclusive rights on their owners").

[37] Daniel Gervais (2012), *The TRIPS Agreement: Drafting History and Analysis*, 4th edn, New York: Thomson Reuters, p. 240.

[38] See, e.g., Carlos M. Correa (2007), *Trade Related Aspects of Intellectual Property Rights: A Commentary on the TRIPS Agreement*, Oxford University Press, p. 112; UNCTAD-ICTSD (2005), *Resource Book on TRIPS and Development*, Cambridge University Press, p. 550.

[39] UNCTAD (1996), *The TRIPS Agreement and Developing Countries*, UNCTAD/ITE/1, New York and Geneva: United Nations, p. 54.

aspects of transfer of technology transactions".[40] However, Members' regulatory sovereignty to prevent practices adversely affecting international technology transfer is, again, subject to the consistency requirement, which is addressed in the following section.

7.2.2 *The Requirement That Appropriate Measures*
Be TRIPS-Consistent

Articles 8.2 and 40.2 require that appropriate measures for preventing or controlling IPR-related abusive or anti-competitive practices must be taken in a manner consistent with the provisions of the TRIPS Agreement.[41] This consistency requirement limits the Members' sovereign power to prescribe IPR-related national competition policy, thus precluding an excessive exercise of these rules that would weaken the minimum standards of IP protection guaranteed by the TRIPS Agreement.[42] As argued by Abbott (2004), this caveat suggests that "competition law should not be used as a disguised mechanism for undermining the basic rights accorded under it".[43]

The consistency requirement, incorporated into the TRIPS Agreement at the last stage of Uruguay Round negotiations, seeks to find a balance between IP protection and competition policy.[44] However, the text of Article 8.2 does not specify the meaning and scope of this requirement. WTO dispute

---

[40] Carlos M. Correa (2014), Intellectual Property and Competition-Room to Legislate under International Law, in Frederick Abbott et al. (eds.), *Using Competition Law to Promote Access to Health Technologies: A Guidebook for Low- and Middle-Income Countries*, New York: United Nations Development Programme, pp. 35–57, at p. 49.

[41] Article 8(1) of the TRIPS Agreement also requires that measures may only be taken consistently with the provision of the TRIPS Agreement; this has been briefly addressed in Section 5.3.2.2. Furthermore, the appropriateness requirement in Article 8.2 is a well-established principle in national competition laws (see UNCTAD-ICTSD (2005), *Resource Book on TRIPS and Development*, Cambridge University Press, p. 553). Thus, this section focuses only on the consistency requirement.

[42] See, e.g., Beatriz Conde Gallego (2010), Intellectual Property Rights and Competition Policy, in Correa (ed.), *Research Handbook on the Protection of Intellectual Property under WTO Rules: Intellectual Property in the WTO*, Vol. I, Cheltenham, UK: Edward Elgar Publishing, pp. 226–65, at p. 237; Hanns Ullrich (2005), Expansionist Intellectual Property Protection and Reductionist Competition Rules: A TRIPS Perspective, in Maskus and Reichman (eds.), *International Public Goods and Transfer of Technology under a Globalized Intellectual Property Regime*, Cambridge University Press, pp. 726–57, at p. 736.

[43] Frederick M. Abbott (2004), Are the Competition Rules in the WTO TRIPS Agreement Adequate? *Journal of International Economic Law*, vol. 7, no. 3, pp. 687–703, at p. 692.

[44] Thomas Cottier and Pierre Véron (2011), *Concise International and European IP Law: TRIPS, Paris Convention, European Enforcement and Transfer of Technology*, 2nd edn, New York: Kluwer Law International, p. 32.

settlement panels and the Appellate Body have so far not had the opportunity to clarify how the consistency requirement in Article 8.2 could be met.

In reality, the consistency requirement has been subject to divergent interpretations among commentators. On the one hand, some scholars maintain that the TRIPS-consistency requirement of Article 8.2 could be best fulfilled by applying the operational provisions in TRIPS that allow IPR-related national competition measures, notably Articles 31 and 40.[45] Supporters of this view consider that the policy space to adopt and implement national competition laws is defined by the "operational provisions" of the TRIPS Agreement.[46]

On the other hand, other commentators emphasize that the objectives and principles enshrined in the preamble and Articles 7 and 8 of the TRIPS Agreement are of particular relevance in determining whether the consistency requirement is met.[47] For instance, Correa (2007) observes that the consistency requirement "should be assessed in light of Articles 7 and 8.1 and of the Preamble, that is, taking social and economic welfare into account"; and that nothing in the TRIPS Agreement should be read as preventing Members from "pursuing the overarching policies defined in Article 8".[48] Yusuf (2008) goes even further by arguing that "even though certain [national] measures may be inconsistent with some of the specific standards laid down in the TRIPS Agreement, it is their overall consistency with the agreement that should be taken into account".[49]

The gulf between these interpretations can be reduced by returning to the general rule of treaty interpretation as set out in the VCLT. Recalling the analysis in Section 5, the terms of the TRIPS provisions shall be interpreted in accordance with their ordinary meaning in their context and in the light of the object and purpose of both the TRIPS Agreement and the WTO Agreement.

---

[45] See, e.g., Daniel Gervais (2012), *The TRIPS Agreement: Drafting History and Analysis*, 4th edn, New York: Thomson Reuters, p. 240.

[46] See, e.g., Thomas Cottier and Pierre Véron (2011), *Concise International and European IP Law: TRIPS, Paris Convention, European Enforcement and Transfer of Technology*, 2nd edn, New York: Kluwer Law International, p. 32 (in interpreting the TRIPS-consistency requirement of Article 8, arguing that "the policy space in the pursuit of welfare is defined by the operational provisions throughout the Agreement").

[47] See, e.g., Abdulqawi A. Yusuf (2008), TRIPS: Background, Principles and General Provisions, in Correa and Abdulqawi (eds.), *Intellectual Property and International Trade: The TRIPS Agreement*, 2nd edn, New York: Kluwer Law International, pp. 3–21, at p. 14.

[48] Carlos M. Correa (2007), *Trade Related Aspects of Intellectual Property Rights: A Commentary on the TRIPS Agreement*, Oxford University Press, p. 110.

[49] Abdulqawi A. Yusuf (2008), TRIPS: Background, Principles and General Provisions, in Correa and Abdulqawi (eds.), *Intellectual Property and International Trade: The TRIPS Agreement*, 2nd edn, New York: Kluwer Law International, pp. 3–21, at p. 14.

On this basis, whether national competition measures are consistent with the TRIPS Agreement should be assessed in line with the sustainable development objective of the WTO Agreement and the Preamble, Articles 7 and 8 as well as other specific provisions of the TRIPS Agreement. Accordingly, the consistency requirement in Article 8.2 has two implications: (1) national competition laws and regulations must be in furtherance of the objectives and principles of the TRIPS Agreement and the WTO Agreement; and (2) they must not add to or diminish the rights and obligations provided in the TRIPS Agreement.[50]

The third approach to the interpretation of the TRIPS-consistency requirement is confirmed by its negotiating history. It is noted that the corresponding provision of the Anell Draft (MTN.GNG/NG11/W/76, July 1990) proposed by the Group B countries (developing countries) did not include any such limitation.[51] Contrastingly, the Brussels Ministerial Text (MTN.TNC/W/35/Rev.1, December 1990) of Article 8.2 requires that appropriate measures must "not derogate from the obligations arising under this Agreement".[52] According to Gallego (2010), the final TRIPS text is a compromise between the aforementioned two texts, and the consistency requirement clarifies that "Article 8.2 merely allows the prevention of individual excesses within the system".[53] Despite this limitation, WTO Members retain broad regulatory sovereignty in the formulation and application of their IPR-related competition rules.[54]

---

[50] Tú Thanh Nguyễn (2010), Competition Law, *Technology Transfer and the TRIPS Agreement: Implications for Developing Countries*, Cheltenham, UK: Edward Elgar Publishing, p. 48.

[51] Status of Work in the Negotiating Group: Chairman's Report to the GNG, Negotiating Group on Trade-Related Aspects of Intellectual Property Rights, including Trade in Counterfeit Goods, 23 July 1990, GATT Doc. MTN.GNG/NG11/W/76, Art. 8B.4 (providing that "Each PARTY will take the measures it deems appropriate with a view to preventing the abuse of intellectual property rights or the resort to practices which unreasonably restrain trade or adversely affect the international transfer of technology. PARTIES undertake to consult each other and to co-operate in this regard").

[52] Draft Final Act Embodying the Results of the Uruguay Round of Multilateral Trade Negotiations, Multilateral Trade Negotiations, The Uruguay Round, 3 December 1990, GATT Doc. MTN.TNC/W/35/Rev.1, Article 8.2 (providing that "Appropriate measures, provided that they do not derogate from the obligations arising under this Agreement, may be needed to prevent the abuse of intellectual property rights by right holders or the resort to practices which unreasonably restrain trade or adversely affect the international transfer of technology").

[53] Beatriz Conde Gallego (2010), Intellectual Property Rights and Competition Policy, in Correa (ed.), *Research Handbook on the Protection of Intellectual Property under WTO Rules: Intellectual Property in the WTO*, Vol. I, Cheltenham, UK: Edward Elgar Publishing, pp. 226–65, at p. 237.

[54] Ibid.; Frederick M. Abbott (2004), Are the Competition Rules in the WTO TRIPS Agreement Adequate? *Journal of International Economic Law*, vol. 7, no. 3, pp. 687–703, at p. 692.

7.2.3 *Relevance of Article 8.2 for EST Transfer*

As documented and observed in Section 4.4, IPRs have been used by some MNCs to maintain their competitive advantage, through charging unreasonably high licensing fees, refusing to deal on reasonable terms and using patents as commercial strategies to block market entries, and the like. Such practices may either constitute an "abuse of intellectual property rights" or unreasonably restrain trade or adversely affect the international transfer of ESTs, thereby falling within the scope of Article 8.2 of the TRIPS Agreement.

These behaviours appear to contradict the objective of IP protection enshrined in Article 7 and the public interest principle established by Article 8.1 of the TRIPS Agreement. Article 8.2 makes clear that Members are entitled to adopt appropriate measures to address such IPR-related abusive or anticompetitive practices. Interpreting Article 8.2 in accordance with the objectives and principles of the TRIPS Agreement seems to imply the need for Members to adopt appropriate measures to deal with such abusive or anticompetitive practices in the furtherance of the transfer of ESTs. The need to adopt IPR-related competition policies in developed countries to facilitate the transfer of ESTs that are needed to mitigate climate change is further supported by their commitment "to take all practicable steps to promote, facilitate and finance" the transfer of ESTs to developing countries in Article 4.5 of UNFCCC.

As such, Article 8.2, as a "Basic Principle", provides WTO Members with broad discretion and strong incentives to adopt appropriate measures to combat the IPR-related abusive practices in the transfer of ESTs and to deal with practices unreasonably restraining trade in EST goods or adversely affecting the international transfer of ESTs.

Specifically speaking, WTO Members enjoy broad discretion to determine what constitute an abuse of IP rights in Article 8.2. They are not only permitted but also encouraged to regulate the abuse of IP rights to promote the innovation and transfer of ESTs that are needed to mitigate climate change. Furthermore, WTO Members have regulatory sovereignty to determine when a restraint of trade may be deemed unreasonable. The determination of reasonableness essentially requires a weighing of the competing interests and a balancing of all pertinent factors involved in the particular circumstances. Thus, in determining whether a restraint of trade in patented ESTs is unreasonable or not, the public interest in combating climate change should be taken into account. Finally, Article 8.2 explicitly allows Members to address the adverse effects of IP rights that are detrimental to the transfer of technology, including ESTs. Thus, WTO Members may establish policies to regulate technology pricing and other aspects involved in transfer-of-technology transactions with a view to facilitating the transfer of ESTs that are needed to mitigate climate change.

However, Members' regulatory sovereignty to adopt appropriate IPR-related competition laws and regulations is subject to the consistency requirement. Such measures must be in the furtherance of the objectives and principles of the TRIPS Agreement and the WTO Agreement, whereas they must not derogate from the minimum IPR standards established by the TRIPS Agreement. Nevertheless, such a consistency requirement does "not prevent Members from determining the types of abuses and practices that may be subject to control, nor the remedies to be applied".[55] Furthermore, Article 8.2 does not set clear-cut parameters regarding the measures that Members can adopt, leaving Members with ample policy room to introduce a range of appropriate measures to address IPR-related abusive and anti-competitive practices in the process of EST transfer.

7.3 ARTICLE 40: CONTROL OF ANTI-COMPETITIVE PRACTICES IN CONTRACTUAL LICENCES

Article 40, found in Part II of TRIPS, entitled "Standards Concerning the Availability, Scope and Use of Intellectual Property Rights", constitutes an entire section (Section 8) dealing with the "Control of Anti-Competitive Practices in Contractual Licences". Its title makes clear that this article relates to anti-competitive practices in contractual licences and thus has a narrower scope of application than Article 8.2.

Article 40 covers both substantive laws and procedural rules. The text of Article 40.1 explicitly recognises that some licensing practices or conditions pertaining to IPRs "may have adverse effects on trade and may impede the transfer and dissemination of new technology". To address this concern, Article 40.2 gives members the freedom to adopt "appropriate" measures to control or prevent such practices, on condition that such measures are consistent with other TRIPS provisions. In order to "enable effective enforcement of competition rules in cross-border contexts", Articles 40.3 and 40.4 impose on the Members an obligation of consultation (upon request) and

---

[55] Carlos M. Correa (2014), Intellectual Property and Competition-Room to Legislate under International Law, in Frederick Abbott et al. (eds.), *Using Competition Law to Promote Access to Health Technologies: A Guidebook for Low- and Middle-Income Countries*, New York: United Nations Development Programme, pp. 35–57, at p. 57.

cooperation in resolving issues relating to the violation of laws concerning anti-competitive practices.[56]

The following sections will address: first, the legal effects of Article 40.1; second, Members' sovereign power to regulate anti-competitive licensing practices under Article 40.2; and third, their relevance to EST transfer.

7.3.1 *Legal Effects of Article 40.1*

Whereas Article 8.2 is limited to recognising that appropriate measures may be needed to prevent certain abusive or anti-competitive practices, Article 40.1 contains the Members' "unanimous and affirmative" agreement that some licensing practices or conditions pertaining to IPRs may have adverse effects on trade and technology transfer because they restrain competition.[57] Article 40.1 of the TRIPS Agreement provides that:

> Members agree that some licensing practices or conditions pertaining to intellectual property rights which restrain competition may have adverse effects on trade and may impede the transfer and dissemination of technology.

A question has arisen as to whether such a unanimous and affirmative agreement would impose upon Members an obligation to regulate under Article 40.1. Commentators have expressed different opinions regarding the legal effects of Article 40.1. Some scholars view Article 40.1 as a non-committal declaration or a non-binding "chapeau" to this section.[58] According to Heinemann (1996), "Article 40.1 is not a classical legal norm containing an example of conduct and a suitable legal remedy, but constitutes a declaration of the Members' common opinion regarding the detrimental consequences of certain conditions of license"; such language is generally

---

[56] Peter-Tobias Stoll, Jan Busche and Katrin Arend (2009), *WTO: Trade-Related Aspects of Intellectual Property Rights*, Vol. VII, Leiden, Netherlands: Martinus Nijhoff Publishers, p. 659.

[57] Hanns Ullrich (2005), Expansionist Intellectual Property Protection and Reductionist Competition Rules: A TRIPS Perspective, in Maskus and Reichman (eds.), *International Public Goods and Transfer of Technology under a Globalized Intellectual Property Regime*, Cambridge University Press, pp. 726–57, at p. 733.

[58] See, e.g., Tú Thanh Nguyãẽn (2010), *Competition Law, Technology Transfer and the TRIPS Agreement: Implications for Developing Countries*, Cheltenham, UK: Edward Elgar Publishing, p. 47; Daniel Gervais (2012), *The TRIPS Agreement: Drafting History and Analysis*, 4th edn, New York: Thomson Reuters, p. 554; Andreas Heinemann (1996), Antitrust Law of Intellectual Property in the TRIPS Agreement of the World Trade Organisation, in Beier and Schricker (eds.), *From GATT to TRIPS – The Agreement on Trade-Related Aspects of Intellectual Property Rights*, IIC Studies, Munich: Max Planck Institute for Foreign and International Patent, Copyright and Competition Law, pp. 239–47, at p. 245.

found in the Preamble.[59] Gervais (2012) contends that Article 40.1 "has to be read as an introduction or chapeau to this Section" because examples of practices and nature of remedies are described in other paragraphs.[60]

In contrast, other observers contend that Article 40.1 imposes an affirmative obligation on WTO Members to address the described practices and conditions.[61] UNCTAD and ICTSD (2005) maintain that "[r]eading Article 40.1 in conjunction with Article 7 may well be understood as imposing an obligation on Members to address certain forms of anti-competitive practices in licensing agreements".[62] In their view, "[i]f Members have indeed agreed that certain licensing practices should be addressed, it is difficult to see why TRIPS would allow Members to remain inactive with respect to such practices, since these run directly contrary to the objectives of Article 7". Furthermore, under Article 1.1, first sentence, Members are obliged "to give effect to the provisions of this Agreement".[63] This view has been described by Correa (2007) as constituting an authoritative interpretation.[64] Following such a strict interpretation, WTO Members may arguably act inconsistently with the TRIPS Agreement by failing to provide or enforce competition rules against anti-competitive practices as contemplated under Article 40.1.[65]

[59] Andreas Heinemann (1996), Antitrust Law of Intellectual Property in the TRIPS Agreement of the World Trade Organisation, in Beier and Gerhard (eds.), *From GATT to TRIPS – The Agreement on Trade-Related Aspects of Intellectual Property Rights*, IIC Studies, Munich: Max Planck Institute for Foreign and International Patent, Copyright and Competition Law, pp. 239–47, at p. 245.

[60] Daniel Gervais (2012), *The TRIPS Agreement: Drafting History and Analysis*, 4th edn, New York: Thomson Reuters, p. 554.

[61] See, e.g., UNCTAD (2010), *Intellectual Property in the World Trade Organisation: Turning It into Developing Countries' Real Property*, New York and Geneva: United Nations, p. 67; UNCTAD-ICTSD (2005), *Resource Book on TRIPS and Development*, Cambridge University Press, at p. 555; George Yijun Tian (2012), Consumer Protection and IP Abuse Prevention under the WTO Framework, in Malcolm (ed.), *Consumers in the Information Society: Access, Fairness and Representation*, Kuala Lumpur: Consumers International, p. 21; Carlos M. Correa (2007), *Trade Related Aspects of Intellectual Property Rights: A Commentary on the TRIPS Agreement*, Oxford University Press, p. 400.

[62] UNCTAD-ICTSD (2005), *Resource Book on TRIPS and Development*, Cambridge University Press, p. 555.

[63] Ibid.

[64] Carlos M. Correa (2007), *Trade Related Aspects of Intellectual Property Rights: A Commentary on the TRIPS Agreement*, Oxford University Press, p. 400; it is noted that this authoritative interpretation is different from the one within the meaning of Article IX:2 of the WTO Agreement.

[65] See, e.g., Thomas Cottier and Pierre Véron (2011), *Concise International and European IP Law: TRIPS, Paris Convention, European Enforcement and Transfer of Technology*, 2nd edn, New York: Kluwer Law International, p. 121; UNCTAD-ICTSD (2005), *Resource Book on TRIPS and Development*, Cambridge University Press, p. 556 (stating that "Members may be considered to contradict the spirit of Article 40.1 if they systematically abstain from taking measures against practices which directly offend the basis and the objectives of TRIPS

Bearing in mind that the terms of WTO Agreements are to be interpreted in accordance with the general rules of treaty interpretation set forth in Articles 31 and 32 of the VCLT, the author seeks to read the provision of Article 40.1 in good faith in its context and in line with the object and purpose of the TRIPS Agreement. The anti-competitive practices that adversely affect trade or impede the transfer and dissemination of technology within the meaning of Article 40.1 would contradict the objective of the IP protection enshrined in Article 7 and undermine the public interest principle contained in Article 8.1. To the extent that compliance with the TRIPS Agreement is desired, WTO Members should take action to control or regulate the anti-competitive practices in Article 40.1. According to Cottier and Véron (2011), read in conjunction with Article 7, Article 40.1 can be understood as "offering a strong incentive for, if not imposing an actual obligation on Members to address anti-competitive practices in licensing agreements".[66]

In my view, the overriding objective of a balance of rights and obligations enshrined in Article 7 would compel WTO Members to address IPR-related anti-competitive practices falling within the scope of Article 40.1. The need to achieve a specific public policy objective such as mitigating climate change would also provide a compelling reason under Article 8.1 for WTO Members to adopt measures to control practices prescribed in Article 40.1. Accordingly, interpreting Article 40.1 in good faith in accordance with the object and purpose of the TRIPS Agreement in its context, compels, if not obliges, WTO Members to adopt competition laws to address IPR-related abusive or anti-competitive licensing practices or conditions in licensing agreements. In the case of ESTs that are needed to mitigate climate change, the commitment to EST transfer in Article 4.5 of UNFCCC would provide additional contextual support for such interpretation.

7.3.2 *Members' Sovereign Power to Regulate Anti-Competitive Licensing Practices under Article 40.2*

Article 40.2 explicitly permits Members to specify certain licensing practices and conditions constituting abuses of IP rights (first sentence), and then goes on to recognise Members' authority to take appropriate measures to prevent or

---

provisions and/or principles, or if they systematically fail to enforce existing national rules on competition regarding such practices").

[66] Thomas Cottier and Pierre Véron (2011), *Concise International and European IP Law: TRIPS, Paris Convention, European Enforcement and Transfer of Technology*, 2nd edn, New York: Kluwer Law International, p. 121.

control anti-competitive licensing practices consistently with other provisions of the TRIPS Agreement (second sentence). It provides that:

> Nothing in this Agreement shall prevent Members from specifying in their legislation licensing practices or conditions that may in particular cases constitute an abuse of intellectual property rights having an adverse effect on competition in the relevant market. As provided above, a Member may adopt, consistently with the other provisions of this Agreement, appropriate measures to prevent or control such practices, which may include for example exclusive grantback conditions, conditions preventing challenges to validity and coercive package licensing, in the light of the relevant laws and regulations of that Member.

The second sentence of Article 40.2 is closely linked to Article 8.2 via the opening clause "as provided above" and the resembling language that "a Member may adopt, consistently with other provisions of this Agreement, appropriate measures". Thus, the analysis of the consistency requirement in Article 8.2 conducted in Section 7.2.2 applies *mutatis mutandis* to the consistency requirement within the meaning of Article 40.2.

Article 40.2 essentially responds to the need to regulate embodied in Article 40.1 by providing guidance regarding the measures that Members may adopt.[67] It has been viewed as a "source of international law that permits competition law to address certain abusive licensing practices" and conditions.[68] The following sections first address Members' competition approach to regulate IPR-related abusive or anti-competitive licensing practices and conditions, followed by a study of some examples of anti-competitive practices.

7.3.2.1 A Competition Approach to Regulate IPR-Related Abusive or Anti-Competitive Licensing Practices and Conditions

The first sentence of Article 40.2 reiterates Members' sovereign power to regulate licensing practices or conditions that may "in particular cases constitute an abuse of intellectual property rights having an adverse effect on competition in the relevant market". The main elements or conditions embodied in this provision are addressed as follows.

---

[67] UNCTAD-ICTSD (2005), *Resource Book on TRIPS and Development*, Cambridge University Press, 558.

[68] See, e.g., Hiroko Yamane (2014), Competition Analyses of Licensing Agreements: Considerations for Developing Countries under TRIPS, *Discussion Paper*, ICTSD Innovation, Technology and Intellectual Property, Geneva: International Centre for Trade and Sustainable Development, p. vii.

First, the reference to "an adverse effect on competition" in Article 40.2 places the control of licensing practices and conditions directly within the scope of competition law, and thus confirms "a competition law approach to the control of technology transfer".[69] However, reading Article 40.2 in light of Articles 7 and 8.2, which single out technology transfer as one of the TRIPS objectives, Article 40.2 does not "elevate competition as such" to the exclusion of the promotion of technology transfer.[70]

Second, the language "particular cases" in Article 40.2 appears to support a case-based rule of reason approach but it "cannot plausibly" be interpreted to prevent the adoption of *per se* rules; in particular, such a restrictive interpretation would render the existing legislation in some countries inconsistent with the TRIPS Agreement.[71] According to Abbott (2004), the phrase "particular cases" in Article 40.2, representing "less than ideal drafting", is intended to require Members to "define such practices on the basis of their competitive merits, rather than in an overly abstract manner" and not to preclude legislation that renders certain licensing conditions or practices *per se* unlawful.[72]

Moreover, read textually, the first sentence of Article 40.2 shows that "an abuse of IP rights" and an "adverse effect on competition" are two cumulative conditions. The accumulation of these two conditions suggests that IPRs may "be the basis of, or reinforce, dominant market positions".[73] Members are thus

---

[69] UNCTAD-ICTSD (2005), *Resource Book on TRIPS and Development*, Cambridge University Press, p. 559.

[70] Ibid.

[71] See, e.g., Mark D. Janis (2005), "Minimal" Standards for Patent-Related Antitrust Law under TRIPS, in Maskus and Reichman (eds.), *International Public Goods and Transfer of Technology under a Globalized Intellectual Property Regime*, Cambridge University Press, pp. 774–92, at p. 779 (arguing that "Article 40.2 refers to "particular cases", suggesting application of a case-based rule of reason approach, but it cannot plausibly be read to preclude altogether legislation that would identify some licensing practices as per se competition law violations; such a reading would run counter to practice in some developed countries"); Pedro Roffe (1998), Control of Anti-Competitive Practices in Contractual Licences under the TRIPS Agreement, in Correa and Yusuf (eds.), *Intellectual Property and International Trade: The TRIPS Agreement, Kluwer Law International*, pp. 261–96, at p. 284 (suggesting that "the Article 40.2 'particular cases' language may be a reaction to calls from developing countries to include presumptions of per se unlawful practices, and that the language therefore may be construed to call for a rule of reason approach").

[72] Frederick M. Abbott (2004), Are the Competition Rules in the WTO TRIPS Agreement Adequate? *Journal of International Economic Law*, vol. 7, no. 3, pp. 687–703, at p. 692; see also UNCTAD-ICTSD (2005), *Resource Book on TRIPS and Development*, Cambridge University Press, p. 559.

[73] Thomas Cottier and Pierre Véron (2011), *Concise International and European IP Law: TRIPS, Paris Convention, European Enforcement and Transfer of Technology*, 2nd edn, New York: Kluwer Law International, p. 122.

entitled to use competition legislation to limit the effects of IPRs "in cases of abuse of such dominant positions".[74] Jurisprudence has confirmed Members' rights and authority to regulate IPR-related abuses of their dominant position through competition law. For instance, in *Microsoft* v. *Commission*, the Court of First Instance (CFI) of the EU found that:

> In any event, there is nothing in the provisions of the TRIPS Agreement to prevent the competition authorities of the members of the WTO from imposing remedies which limit or regulate the exploitation of intellectual property rights held by an undertaking in a dominant position where that undertaking exercises those rights in an anti-competitive manner. Thus, as the Commission correctly observes, it follows expressly from Article 40(2) of the TRIPS Agreement that the members of the WTO are entitled to regulate the abusive use of such rights in order to avoid effects which harm competition.[75]

This is the very first judgment made by a WTO Member's court that relies on Article 40.2 of the TRIPS Agreement to justify the application of domestic competition rules to the exercise of IP rights.[76] This finding was subsequently cited by the European Commission Decision of 29.04.2014 addressed to Motorola Mobility LLC relating to the enforcement of general packet radio service (GPRS) standard essential patents.[77] Commentators consider that the invocation of the TRIPS competition flexibilities in *Microsoft* v. *Commission* may inspire developing countries to "enact and apply national competition law to the IPR-related area" so as to serve their public interests and protect their consumer welfare.[78]

Notably, drawing on the legislative and judicial experience of developed countries, the State Administration for Industry and Commerce (SAIC) of

---

[74] Ibid.

[75] Judgment of the Court of the First Instance (Grand Chamber), in Case T-201/04 *Microsoft* v. *Commission* [2007] ECR II-3601, 17 September 2007, para. 1192. In this dispute, Microsoft was accused of abuse of its dominant position through refusal to supply and authorise the use of interoperability information as well as tying of the Windows client PC operating system and Windows Media Player. The Court ordered Microsoft to license interface information to its competitors on reasonable terms and to supply a fully functioning version of Windows Personal Computer Operating System without Windows Media Player.

[76] Tú Thanh Nguyãẽn and Hans Henrik Lidgard (2008), The CFI Microsoft Judgment and TRIPS Competition Flexibilities, *Currents: International Trade Law Journal*, vol. 16, no. 3, pp. 41–51, at p. 41.

[77] Commission Decision, Case AT.39985, *Motorola-Enforcement of GPRS Standard Essential Patents*, 29 April 2014, para. 498. "GPRS" refers to "general packet radio service".

[78] Tú Thanh Nguyãẽn and Hans Henrik Lidgard (2008), The CFI Microsoft Judgment and TRIPS Competition Flexibilities, *Currents: International Trade Law Journal*, vol. 16, no. 3, pp. 41–51, at p. 49.

China released in 2015 the "Provisions on Prohibition of Abuse of Intellectual Property Rights to Eliminate or Restrict Competition" (hereafter, 2015 Regulation on Prohibition of Abuse of IPRs).[79] Article 6 of this regulation explicitly prevents a company from abusing its dominant position in the course of exercising IPRs. This article further clarifies that ownership of IPRs can be one factor, but not necessarily the determining one, in holding an undertaking to have a dominant market position. Though this regulation does not explicitly refer to the competition-related TRIPS flexibilities, it constitutes an example of using TRIPS flexibilities in particular Article 40.2 by regulating IPR-related abusive practices through competition rules. The adoption of the 2015 Regulation on Prohibition of Abuse of IPRs provides a helpful precedent for developing Members to enact and apply competition rules to address IPR-related abusive and anti-competitive practices in the process of transfer of technologies including ESTs.

7.3.2.2 Examples of Anti-Competitive Practices

Although Article 40 is entitled "Control of Anti-Competitive Practices in Contractual Licences", it does not define the phrase "anti-competitive practices". Based on the dictionary meaning of the terms "practices" and "competitive", the panel in *Mexico – Telecoms* (2004) found that "the term 'anti-competitive practices' is broad in scope, suggesting actions that lessen rivalry or competition in the market".[80] However, this definition is not IPR-specific.

In the context of TRIPS, Article 40.2 itself specifies certain criteria for determining IPR-specific anti-competitive practices. Article 40.2 makes clear that such practices may "in particular cases" have "an adverse effect on competition" in the "relevant market". As discussed in Section 7.3.2.1, the textual reference to "particular cases" and the need to examine the effect on competition appear to support a case-by-case based "rule of reason" approach for determining whether a practice is anti-competitive or not but do not necessarily preclude the adoption of *per se* rules.[81] The rule of reason doctrine, developed by the US Supreme Court in its interpretation of the Sherman Act,

---

[79] Provisions on Prohibition of Abuse of Intellectual Property Rights to Eliminate or Restrict Competition, promulgated by Decree No. 74 of the State Administration for Industry and Commerce on 7 April 2015, effective as of 1 August 2015.

[80] Panel Report, *Mexico – Telecoms*, para. 7.230.

[81] See, e.g., Justin Malbon, Charles Lawson and Mark Davison (2014), *The WTO Agreement on Trade-Related Aspects of Intellectual Property Rights: A Commentary*, Cheltenham, UK: Edward Elgar Publishing, p. 607; Mark D. Janis (2005), "Minimal" Standards for Patent-related Antitrust Law under TRIPS, in Maskus and Reichman (eds.), *International Public Goods and*

requires weighing and balancing different factors and circumstances to determine whether a practice "unreasonably" restrains competition.[82] Therefore, under the rule of reason doctrine, a competent authority is required to conduct a fact-specific inquiry to weigh the pro- and anti-competitive effects of a practice within a relevant market, namely, "a market of competing (substitute) technologies or products established as 'relevant'".[83]

In the TRIPS negotiation process, Article 43 (para. 2B) of the Chairman's Draft Text of 23 November 1990 listed a series of licensing clauses which may be considered to be abusive or anti-competitive:

> 2B. [. . .]The following practices and conditions may be subject to such measures where they are deemed to be abusive or anti-competitive: (i) grant-back provisions; (ii) challenges to validity; (iii) exclusive dealing; (iv) restrictions on research; (v) restrictions on use of personnel; (vi) price fixing; (vii) restrictions on adaptations; (viii) exclusive sales or representation agreements; (ix) tying arrangements; (x) export restrictions; (xi) patent pooling or cross-licensing agreements and other arrangements; (xii) restrictions on publicity; (xiii) payments and other obligations after expiration of industrial property rights; (xiv) restrictions after expiration of an arrangement.[84]

This draft text essentially incorporated the list of restrictive practices contained in Chapter 4 of the Draft International Code of Conduct on the Transfer of Technology (see Section 3.2.2.2). It arguably permits Members to hold the listed restrictive practices to be unlawful *per se*, thereby resulting in the rejection of this proposal and the ultimate adoption of the text of Article 40.2.[85] The second sentence of Article 40.2 allows a Member to adopt appropriate measures to prevent and control such practices "which may include for

---

Transfer of Technology under a Globalized Intellectual Property Regime, Cambridge University Press, pp. 774–92, at p. 779.

[82] See, e.g., Giorgio Monti (2007), *EC Competition Law: Law in Context*, Cambridge University Press, pp. 29–31; Barry J. Rodger and Angus MacCulloch (2001), *Competition Law and Policy in the European Community and United Kingdom*, 2nd edn, London: Cavendish Publishing, pp. 178–80; Anne C Witt (2016), *The More Economic Approach to EU Antitrust Law*, Oxford and Portland, Oregon: Hart Publishing, at p. 65.

[83] Hiroko Yamane (2014), Competition Analyses of Licensing Agreements: Considerations for Developing Countries under TRIPS, Discussion Paper, ICTSD Innovation, Technology and Intellectual Property, Geneva: International Centre for Trade and Sustainable Development, p. 6.

[84] Draft Final Act Embodying the Results of the Uruguay Round of Multilateral Trade Negotiations, Trade Negotiations Committee, GATT Doc. MTN.TNC/W/35/Rev. 1, 3 December 1990, p. 215.

[85] See, e.g., Pedro Roffe and Christoph Spennemann (2008), Control of Anti-competitive Practices in Contractual Licences under the TRIPS Agreement, in Correa and Abdulqawi (eds.), *Intellectual Property and International Trade: The TRIPS Agreement*, New York: Kluwer

example exclusive grantback conditions, conditions preventing challenges to validity and coercive package licensing". The use of the term "include" suggests that the list is not exhaustive, leaving Members with the freedom to treat other practices as anti-competitive in their national legislation.

7.3.3 *Relevance for EST Transfer*

As discussed in Section 4.4.2, anti-competitive practices are not uncommon in licensing agreements relating to ESTs, including but not limited to: grant-back conditions, export restrictions and limitation to follow-on innovation. Such practices restrain competition and have adverse effects on trade and the transfer of technology, thus constituting "anti-competitive practices" in Article 40. Articles 40.1 and 40.2 allow WTO Members to adopt competition laws to address abusive licensing practices or conditions with a view to facilitating the transfer of technologies, in particular, ESTs.

Interpreting Article 40 in good faith in accordance with the object and purpose of the TRIPS Agreement in its context, compels, if not obliges, WTO Members to adopt competition laws to address IPR-related anti-competitive licensing practices in the process of transfer of ESTs. The commitment to EST transfer in Article 4.5 of UNFCCC would provide additional contextual support for the interpretation that competition laws and regulations should be enacted and applied to address anti-competitive practices in furtherance of the transfer of ESTs that are needed to mitigate climate change.

Under Article 40.2, the measures taken by WTO Members to prevent or control anti-competitive practices must be consistent with other provisions of the TRIPS Agreement. As argued in Section 7.2.3, this means that such measures must be in the furtherance of the objectives and principles of the TRIPS Agreement and the WTO Agreement whereas they must not derogate from the minimum IPR standards established by the TRIPS Agreement. Nevertheless, such a consistency requirement does not limit Members' discretion to determine the types of licensing practices or conditions that may be subject to control, "nor the remedies to be applied".[86] Members thus have broad discretion to introduce a range of measures to address anti-competitive practices that may arise in the process of EST licensing.

Law International, pp. 293–329, at p. 320; UNCTAD-ICTSD (2005), *Resource Book on TRIPS and Development*, Cambridge University Press, p. 546.

[86] Carlos M. Correa (2014), Intellectual Property and Competition-Room to Legislate under International Law, in Frederick Abbott et al. (eds.), *Using Competition Law to Promote Access to Health Technologies: A Guidebook for Low- and Middle-Income Countries*, New York: United Nations Development Programme, pp. 35–57, at p. 57.

Moreover, Members should adopt laws and policies including guidelines to prevent and correct anti-competitive practices in contractual licences because regulating anti-competitive practices in licensing agreements is essential to promoting the public interest in gaining access to global public goods such as patented ESTs.[87] However, studies show that many developing countries do not apply competition laws to prevent or control anti-competitive uses of IPRs, largely due to "the lack of legislation, weak implementation or absence of policies to deal with the IP-competition relationship".[88]

Notably, Article 67 of TRIPS obliges developed country Members to provide technical and financial cooperation to support developing country Members. This article provides that:

> Such cooperation shall include assistance in the preparation of laws and regulations on the protection and enforcement of intellectual property rights as well as *on the prevention of their abuse*, and shall include support regarding the establishment or reinforcement of domestic offices and agencies relevant to these matters, including the training of personnel. (Emphasis added)

It is clear that technical cooperation under Article 67 extends to the preparation and implementation of laws and regulations on the prevention of the abuse of IPRs, including anti-competitive practices.[89] Upon request and based "on mutually agreed terms and conditions", developed countries have the obligation to provide such technical assistance and thus help developing countries overcome their internal obstacles, as listed above. Developing countries, in particular those with insufficient legislative experience and capacities in the field of competition law, should request developed countries to assist in the preparation of competition laws and regulations to address

---

[87] Josef Drexl (2005), The Critical Role of Competition Law in Preserving Public Goods in Conflict with Intellectual Property Rights, in Maskus and Reichman (eds.), *International Public Goods and Transfer of Technology under a Globalized Intellectual Property Regime*, Cambridge University Press, pp. 707–25, at p. 716.

[88] See, e.g., Carlos M. Correa (2007), Intellectual Property and Competition Law: Exploring Some Issues of Relevance to Developing Countries, ICTSD IPRs and Sustainable Development Programme Issue Paper No. 21, Geneva: International Centre for Trade and Sustainable Development, p. 1; Sangeeta Shashikant and Martin Khor (2010), *Intellectual Property and Technology Transfer Issues in the Context of Climate Change*, Jelutong, Malaysia: Jutaprint, p. 52.

[89] See also Marco Ricolfi (2006), Is There an Antitrust Antidote against IP Overprotection within TRIPS? *Marquette Intellectual Property Law Review*, vol. 10, no. 2, Art. 6, pp. 305–67, at pp. 313 and 318; Jens Schovsbo (2011), Fire and Water Make Steam – Redefining the Role of Competition Law, in Kur and Levin (eds.), *Intellectual Property Rights in a Fair World Trade System: Proposal for Reforms of TRIPS*, Cheltenham, UK: Edward Elgar Publishing, pp. 308–58, at p. 331.

IPR-related abusive and anti-competitive practices so as to facilitate their access to global public goods such as ESTs.

One of the objectives of compulsory licensing as a remedy to correct anti-competitive practices is to restore competition in the relevant market in cases involving the abuse of IP rights.[90] The basic rationale underlying the conferral of such a compulsory licence is that "although the patent holder is entrusted with exclusive rights, he cannot overreach his privilege as to intrude upon the right of the public".[91]

Article 31(k) permits WTO Members to grant compulsory licences to remedy patent-related anti-competitive practices, providing that:

> Members are not obliged to apply the conditions set forth in subparagraphs (b) and (f) where such use is permitted to remedy a practice determined after judicial or administrative process to be anti-competitive. The need to correct anti-competitive practices may be taken into account in determining the amount of remuneration in such cases. Competent authorities shall have the authority to refuse termination of authorization if and when the conditions which led to such authorization are likely to recur.

As Section 6.4 has examined compulsory licensing under Article 31 in detail, the following sections address, in turn, the interpretative issues of Article 31(k), and its relevance for the innovation and transfer of ESTs.

7.4.1 *Interpretation of Article 31(k)*

It can be seen from the text of Article 31(k) that patent-related anti-competitive practices may constitute grounds for granting compulsory licences. This provision subjects the granting of compulsory licences to remedy anti-competitive

---

[90] See, e.g., Carlos M. Correa (2014), Intellectual Property and Competition – Room to Legislate under International Law, in Frederick Abbott et al. (eds.), *Using Competition Law to Promote Access to Health Technologies: A Guidebook for Low- and Middle-Income Countries*, New York: United Nations Development Programme, pp. 35–57, at p. 50 (Noting that "Compulsory licences have been used by competition authorities in some countries, notably in the United States, to restore competition in cases involving the exercise of IP rights").

[91] Ida Madieha bt Abdul Ghani Azmi (2015), Scope and Duration of Compulsory Licensing: Lessons from National Experiences, in Hilty and Liu (eds.), *Compulsory Licensing: Practical Experiences and Ways Forward*, MPI Studies on Intellectual Property and Competition Law 22, Berlin and Heidelberg, Germany: Springer-Verlag , pp. 207–20, at p. 214.

practices to less rigid conditions compared to compulsory licences on other grounds. Under Article 31(k), WTO Members are not obliged to meet the requirements set forth in subparagraphs (b) and (f), including: (1) the requirement to seek a voluntary licence from the right holder under Article 31(b) and (2) the requirement that use shall be authorised "predominantly for the supply of the domestic market" under Article 31(f). This provision also modifies the obligation in Article 31(h) to provide adequate remuneration by allowing Members to adjust the level of compensation to reflect the need to correct anti-competitive practices, including "the need to remedy past misconduct and to affirmatively promote the entry of new competitors in the market".[92]

By subjecting compulsory licensing for competition reasons to less stringent requirements than conditions set forth for compulsory licensing on other grounds, it arguably suggests that the TRIPS Agreement accords "a high status to the protection of competition".[93] This is further supported by the last sentence of Article 31(k), which explicitly affirms the competent authorities' right to refuse termination of authorisation if and when the anti-competitive conditions that led to the initial grant of the compulsory licences are likely to recur.

While Article 31(k) requires anti-competitive practices to be determined after due judicial and administrative processes, it does not specify the criteria for such determination, thereby leaving it to the Members' discretion to define what constitutes anti-competitive practices. In the United States, the grounds for granting compulsory licensing under competition law have included "the use of patents as a basis for price-fixing or entry-restricting cartels, the consummation of market-concentrating mergers in which patents played an important role, and practices that extended the scope of patent restrictions beyond the bounds of the patented subject matter".[94]

In the EU, under competition law, compulsory licensing may be granted in cases of abuses of a dominant position to facilitate access to IP-protected essential goods, which is an example of the application of the "essential facility

[92] UNCTAD-ICTSD (2005), *Resource Book on TRIPS and Development*, Cambridge University Press, at p. 476.
[93] Beatriz Conde Gallego (2010), Intellectual Property Rights and Competition Policy, in Correa (ed.), *Research Handbook on the Protection of Intellectual Property under WTO Rules: Intellectual Property in the WTO*, Vol. I, Cheltenham, UK: Edward Elgar Publishing, pp. 226–65, at p. 246.
[94] Frederic M. Scherer and Watal Jayashree (2002), Post-TRIPS Options for Access to Patented Medicines in Developing Nations, *Journal of International Economic Law*, vol. 5, no. 4, pp. 913–39, at p. 917.

doctrine".[95] Given its importance to accessing IP-protected essential goods, including EST products, the relevance of the essential facility doctrine for EST transfer will be addressed in the following section.

7.4.2 *Relevance for the Innovation and Transfer of ESTs*

A competition law-based compulsory licence is very important for facilitating the follow-on innovation of, and access to, essential IP-protected technologies, including ESTs. It is often used as a remedy in the context of refusal to license.[96]

In principle, a patent holder has the right to refuse to license his or her patented invention, which essentially derives from his or her right to exclude others from making, using or selling products protected by patents.[97] However, a patent holder's right to refuse to license is not absolute. Under exceptional circumstances, refusal to license may constitute anti-competitive practices to the extent that such a refusal constitutes "an attempt to monopolize or to maintain a monopoly in a relevant market or, in broader terms, it constitutes an abusive expression of a market dominant position".[98]

Different views are found in diverse jurisdictions regarding whether, and if so, under what circumstances, a unilateral refusal to license patent rights may violate competition laws.[99] According to WIPO (2013), "[i]n general, the anti-

[95] WIPO (2011), Survey on Compulsory Licences Granted by WIPO Member States to Address Anti-competitive Uses of Intellectual Property Rights, CDIP/4/4 Rev./Study/INF/5, 4 October 2011, p. 9.

[96] See, e.g., Beatriz Conde Gallego (2010), Intellectual Property Rights and Competition Policy, in Correa (ed.), *Research Handbook on the Protection of Intellectual Property under WTO Rules: Intellectual Property in the WTO*, Vol. I, Cheltenham, UK: Edward Elgar Publishing, pp. 226–65, at p. 258.

[97] See, e.g., Jay Dratler (1994), *Licensing of Intellectual Property*, ALM Properties, Inc., Law Journal Press, § 3.02[2] (stating that "Based as it is on strong property rights and the free market, the patent system in the United States has always afforded patentees nearly absolute freedom in deciding unilaterally whether to grant licenses to others"); Katrin Nyman-Metcalf, Pawan Kumar Dutt and Archil Chochia (2014), The Freedom to Conduct Business and the Right to Property: The EU Technology Transfer Block Exemption Regulation and the Relationship between Intellectual Property and Competition Law, in Kerikmäe (ed.), *Protecting Human Rights in the EU: Controversies and Challenges of the Charter of Fundamental Rights*, Berlin, Germany: Springer, pp. 37–70, at p. 56 (stating that "Generally, under EU competition law, a 'mere' refusal to license does not constitute a violation").

[98] WIPO (2013), Refusals to License IP Rights – A Comparative Note on Possible Approaches, prepared by the Secretariat, available at: www.wipo.int/export/sites/www/ipcompetition/en/studies/refusals_license_IPRs.pdf, p. 11.

[99] Antony Taubman, Hannu Wager and Jayashree Watal (2012), *A Handbook on the WTO TRIPS Agreement*, Cambridge University Press, p. 134.

competitive nature of refusals to license IPRs is associated with the concept of essential facilities".[100] US jurisprudence defines a facility as essential if it is "otherwise unavailable" and cannot be "reasonably or practically duplicated".[101] The essential facility doctrine was developed under case law as an exception to the general principle that firms have a right to refusal to deal.[102] In the context of IPRs, the essential facility doctrine imposes an obligation on right holders to provide competitors with reasonable access to IP-protected products in a relevant market.[103]

The landmark judgment in *Magill* (1995) is viewed as an implicit adoption by the CJEU of the doctrine of essential facilities in the context of IPRs. In this case, the Court upheld the European Commission's imposition of compulsory licensing on right holders to correct an anti-competitive practice which had prevented potential competitors from entering the market.[104] In this case, the Court found that the "refusal to grant a licence, even if it is the act of an undertaking holding a dominant position, cannot in itself constitute abuse of a dominant position";[105] however, "the exercise of an exclusive right by the proprietor may, in exceptional circumstances, involve abusive conduct".[106] These circumstances included that: (1) the refusal concerned a product, the supply of which was indispensable for carrying on the business in question,[107] (2) such refusal prevented the appearance of new products,[108] (3) "there was no justification for such refusal"[109] and (4) it was likely to exclude all competition on the secondary market because access to indispensable product is denied.[110] This "exceptional circumstances" test clearly restricts IP right

---

[100] WIPO (2013), Refusals to License IP Rights – A Comparative Note on Possible Approaches, prepared by the Secretariat, available at: www.wipo.int/export/sites/www/ipcompetition/en/studies/refusals_license_IPRs.pdf, p. 13.

[101] See, e.g., *City of Anaheim* v. *Southern Calif. Edison Co.*, 955 F.2d 1373, 1380 n. 5 (9th Cir. 1992), at 1380; *Metronet Services Corporation* v. *Qwest Corporation*, 383 F3d 1124, United States Court of Appeals, Ninth Circuit, 24 September 2004, para. 16.

[102] Mariateresa Maggiolino (2011), *Intellectual Property and Antitrust: A Comparative Economic Analysis of US and EU Law*, Cheltenham, UK: Edward Elgar Publishing, p. 147 (noting that "a general principle is in force in US and EU: even dominant firms are free to contract, by choosing whether and with whom to make a deal").

[103] Joseph M. Purcell (2014), The "Essential Facilities" Doctrine in the Sunlight: Stacking Patented Genetic Traits in Agriculture," *St. John's Law Review*, vol. 85, no. 3, Art. 9, pp. 1251–74, at pp. 1253 –4 (stating that "Under the essential facilities doctrine, a monopolist has a duty to provide competitors with reasonable access to essential facilities, facilities under the monopolist's control and without which one cannot effectively compete in a given market").

[104] Judgment of the Court of 6 April 1995, *Radio Telefís Eireann (RTE) and Independent Television Publications Ltd (ITP)* v. *Commission of the European Communities*, Joined cases C-241/91 P and C-242/91 P., 1995 I-00743.

[105] Ibid., para. 49.   [106] Ibid., para. 50.   [107] Ibid., paras. 52 and 53.   [108] Ibid., para. 54.
[109] Ibid., para. 55.   [110] Ibid., para. 56.

holders' freedom to refuse to license. However, the test is not exhaustive, allowing the possibility that there are other circumstances that are also sufficient to justify the imposition of compulsory licences in case of refusal to license.

In *IMS* (2004), in determining whether the refusal by an IPR owner in a dominant position to grant a licence for a brick structure protected by an IP right which it owns is abusive, the Court found that the criteria of the "exceptional circumstances" as stated in *Magill* (1995) constituted cumulative conditions.[111] Furthermore, the Court emphasised the importance of consumer welfare when balancing the interest in protecting IP rights and the economic freedom of its owner against the interest in protecting free competition, holding that the latter can prevail only when a refusal to license "prevents the development of the secondary market to the detriment of consumers".[112] The Court elaborated on the "new product" criterion and found that the licensee should not intend to essentially limit itself to duplicating the goods or services, but should intend to produce new goods or services "for which there is a potential consumer demand".[113] This new product requirement may discourage potential competitors from free-riding on dominant firms' innovations but encourage them to increase investment in R&D to make further improvements and upgrade the current level of innovation in order to produce a new product on the basis of the required IPRs.[114]

The Court of the First Instance in the *Microsoft* (2007) case, relying on Article 82(b) of the EC Treaty,[115] found that prejudice to consumers may arise where "there is a limitation not only of production or markets, but also of technical development".[116] The addition of limitation of technical development as a

[111] Judgment of the Court (Fifth Chamber) of 29 April 2004, *IMS Health GmbH & Co. OHG* v. *NDC Health GmbH & Co. KG.*, Case C-418/01, para. 38 (stating that "in order for the refusal by an undertaking which owns a copyright to give access to a product or service indispensable for carrying on a particular business to be treated as abusive, it is sufficient that three cumulative conditions be satisfied, namely, that the refusal is preventing the emergence of a new product for which there is a potential consumer demand, that it is unjustified and such as to exclude any competition on a secondary market").
[112] Ibid., para. 48.   [113] Ibid., para. 49.
[114] See also Tú Thanh Nguyễn (2010), *Competition Law, Technology Transfer and the TRIPS Agreement: Implications for Developing Countries*, Cheltenham, UK: Edward Elgar Publishing, p. 123.
[115] Article 82 of the EC Treaty, provides that: "Any abuse by one or more undertakings of a dominant position within the common market or in a substantial part of it shall be prohibited as incompatible with the common market insofar as it may affect trade between Member States. Such abuse may, in particular, consist in: ... (b) limiting production, markets or technical development to the prejudice of consumers".
[116] Judgment of the Court of First Instance (Grand Chamber) of 17 September 2007, *Microsoft Corp.* v. *Commission of the European Communities*, Case T-201/04, para. 647.

relevant notion under the new product criterion broadens the scope of the harm to consumers and places greater emphasis on the users' interests by focusing on the impact of the refusal to license on incentives for dominant firms' competitors to innovate.[117]

As a result of the CJEU's decisions in *Magill* (1995), *IMS* (2004) and *Microsoft* (2007), the essential facilities doctrine can be applied in relation to IP-protected essential goods in the EU. Following the EU's approach, the 2015 Regulation on Prohibition of Abuse of IPRs has extended the "essential facilities" doctrine to IPRs in China, requiring a patent owner with a dominant market position to license its IPRs on reasonable terms when its IPRs "constitute an essential facility for production and operation activities".[118] Notably, Article 7 of the 2015 Regulation sets forth three conditions for the application of the essential facility doctrine: (1) relevant IP right is not reasonably substitutable in the relevant market and is essential for other undertakings to compete in the relevant market; (2) refusal to license such IP right will have an adverse effect on competition or innovation in the relevant market, and be detrimental to consumer benefits or public interests and (3) the licensing of such IPRs will not result in unreasonable damages to the owner of IPRs. It can be seen that the Chinese essential facility doctrine has a much broader scope than the EU doctrine, which is based on the "exceptional circumstances" test. Further, the essential facility doctrine contained in the 2015 Regulation places a greater emphasis on public interests compared to the doctrine developed in the EU jurisprudence.

As discussed in Section 4.4.2.3, the owners of ESTs sometimes refuse to license their IPRs to their (potential) competitors on reasonable terms. Such practices unreasonably restraining competition could constitute a ground for the grant of a compulsory licence under Article 31(k). As discussed above, refusals to license IPRs that constitute "essential facilities" are in

---

[117] See, e.g., Thomas Cottier and Pierre Véron (2011), *Concise International and European IP Law: TRIPS, Paris Convention, European Enforcement and Transfer of Technology*, 2nd edn, New York: Kluwer Law International, at p. 122; Nicholas Banasevic and Per Hellstrom (2010), Windows into the World of Abuse of Dominance: An Analysis of the Commission's 2004 Microsoft Decision and the CFI's 2007 Judgment, in Rubini (ed.), *Microsoft on Trial: Legal and Economic Analysis of a Transatlantic Antitrust Case*, Cheltenham, UK: Edward Elgar Publishing, pp. 47–75, at p. 57.
[118] Provisions on Prohibition of Abuse of Intellectual Property Rights to Eliminate or Restrict Competition, promulgated by Decree No. 74 of the State Administration for Industry and Commerce on 7 April 2015, effective as of 1 August 2015, Article 7 (providing that "An undertaking with a dominant market position, being aware that its intellectual property rights constitute an essential facility for production and operation activities, shall not, without any justification, refuse to license other undertakings to use its intellectual property rights on reasonable terms to eliminate or restrict competition").

general anti-competitive in nature. Using the essential facilities doctrine to impose a duty on IP right holders to license could lead to lower prices and greater innovation, thereby contributing to "the promotion of technological innovation and to the transfer and dissemination of technology", as provided in Article 7 of the TRIPS Agreement.

Developing Members could follow, for instance, the EU's approach to apply the essential facility doctrine to facilitate the access to, and further development of, essential ESTs. Under the EU essential facility doctrine, relevant EST IPRs may be subject to compulsory licences, when a refusal to license meets the following conditions, including (1) the product in question is indispensable, (2) the refusal limits the appearance of new products or limits technical development, (3) it is unjustified and (4) it excludes all competition in a downstream market.

Members, however, have the discretion to define their own criteria for the application of the essential facility doctrine in their domestic competition law or intellectual property law. Nevertheless, the condition that relevant IP right is "not reasonably substitutable" appears to be an essential element. In specifying relevant conditions, Members should take into account the objectives of the TRIPS Agreement enshrined in Article 7 and the public interest principle in Article 8.1.

Further, to the extent that compliance with TRIPS is desired, the granting of a compulsory licence for patented ESTs needs to be consistent with the procedural requirements as set forth in Article 31. However, as discussed in the previous section, compared with other compulsory licences granted under Article 31, a competition-law-based compulsory licence under Article 31(k) has the advantage that it neither requires prior negotiations with the patent owner nor is it necessary that the licence be authorized predominantly for the supply of domestic market. Also Members can adjust their level of compensation to reflect the need to remedy anti-competitive practices.

7.5 CONCLUSION

In the process of the transfer of ESTs, Members are faced with IPR-related abusive or anti-competitive practices. Articles 8.2, 31(k) and 40 of the TRIPS Agreement give WTO Members leeway to enact and apply national competition laws to control and correct these practices. In accordance with the general interpretive rules set out by the VCLT, such competition-related provisions can be interpreted to facilitate innovation and transfer of ESTs that are needed to address global climate change concerns.

Article 8.2, as a "Basic Principle", provides WTO Members with broad discretion and strong incentives to adopt appropriate measures to combat the

IPR-related abusive practices in the transfer of ESTs and to deal with practices unreasonably restraining trade in EST goods or adversely affecting the international transfer of ESTs. In particular, WTO Members enjoy broad discretion to determine what constitutes an abuse of IP rights and when a restraint of trade may be deemed unreasonable in Article 8.2. In determining whether a restraint of trade in patented ESTs is unreasonable or not, the public interest in combating climate change should be taken into account. Further, Article 8.2 explicitly allows Members to address the adverse effects of IP rights that are detrimental to the transfer of technology, including ESTs. Thus, WTO Members may establish policies to regulate technology pricing and other aspects involved in transfer of technology transactions with a view to facilitating the transfer of ESTs that are needed to mitigate climate change.

Interpreting Article 40 in good faith in accordance with the object and purpose of the TRIPS Agreement in its context, compels, if not obliges, WTO Members to adopt competition laws to address IPR-related anti-competitive licensing practices in the process of transfer of ESTs. The commitment to EST transfer in Article 4.5 of UNFCCC would provide additional contextual support for the interpretation that competition laws and regulations should be enacted and applied to address anti-competitive practices in furtherance of the transfer of ESTs that are needed to mitigate climate change.

A competition law-based compulsory licence under Article 31(k) is essential for facilitating the follow-on innovation of, and access to, essential IP-protected technologies, including ESTs. In case of refusals to license essential IPRs, using the essential facilities doctrine to impose IP right holders a duty to license could lead to lower prices and greater innovation. Members have the discretion to define their own criteria for the application of the essential facility doctrine in their domestic competition law or intellectual property law. In specifying relevant conditions, Members should take into account the objectives of the TRIPS Agreement enshrined in Article 7 and the public interest principle in Article 8.1.

However, Members' regulatory sovereignty to adopt appropriate measures is subject to the consistency requirement. In accordance with Article 31 of the VCLT, whether national competition measures are consistent with the TRIPS Agreement should be assessed in line with the sustainable development objective of the WTO Agreement and the Preamble, Articles 7 and 8 and as well as other specific provisions of the TRIPS Agreement. Therefore, such measures must be in the furtherance of the objectives and principles of the TRIPS Agreement and the WTO Agreement, whereas they must not derogate from the minimum IPR protection standards established by the TRIPS Agreement.

Nevertheless, such a consistency requirement does not prevent Members from determining the types of abuses and practices that may be subject to control, or the remedies to be applied. Also, the TRIPS Agreement does not establish clear-cut parameters pertaining to the measures that Members can adopt, thereby leaving Members with broad discretion to introduce a range of appropriate measures to address IPR-related abusive and anti-competitive practices in the process of EST transfer.

Many developing countries may lack the technical and institutional capacity to adopt and implement measures to correct the abusive or anti-competitive use of IPRs. Article 67 of the TRIPS Agreement extends technical cooperation and assistance to the preparation and implementation of laws and regulations on the prevention of the abuse of IPRs, including anti-competitive practices. Upon request, and "on mutually agreed terms and conditions", developed countries have the obligation to provide such technical assistance and thus help developing countries overcome their internal obstacles. Developing countries, in particular those with insufficient legislative experience and capacities in the field of competition law, should request developed countries to assist in the preparation of competition laws and regulations to address IPR-related abusive and anti-competitive practices so as to facilitate their access to global public goods such as ESTs.

8

Conclusions and Recommendations

8.1 INTRODUCTION

As the most comprehensive multilateral agreement on IP rights, the TRIPS Agreement attempts to balance the need to provide incentives for innovation with the need to ensure fair access to new technologies. It obliges WTO Members to comply with minimum standards governing the scope, availability and use of IPRs that should contribute to the promotion of both technological innovation and the transfer of technology. However, as mentioned in Section 1.1, its role in facilitating innovation and transfer of ESTs, which are essential to combat climate change, has been questioned.

This book seeks to make the TRIPS Agreement a more efficient and effective instrument for facilitating innovation and transfer of ESTs, mainly through legal interpretative devices. It addresses two main research questions: first, whether, and if so to what extent, strong IPR protection is a prerequisite for or presents a barrier to innovation and transfer of ESTs; and second, whether the limits to patent protection and the competition provisions of the TRIPS Agreement, when properly interpreted, could be applied to facilitate innovation and transfer of ESTs, thus contributing to reconciling the public interest in tackling climate change with the private sector's interest in IP protection.

Taking into account the WTO's sustainable development objective and the object and purpose of the TRIPS Agreement, this book proposes a balanced and pro-competitive interpretation of the relevant TRIPS provisions for ESTs. The inadequacy of the treaty interpretation further drives the author to briefly explore the possible remedies.

The following sections summarize the main findings contained in Sections 1 to 7 and subsequently, in order to remedy the insufficiency of the treaty interpretation, propose (1) the adoption of a Doha-Type Declaration on

Intellectual Property Rights and Climate Change and (2) the creation of international guidelines for licensing of IP-protected ESTs.

8.2 PROBLEMS IDENTIFIED

Climate change has been characterised by the UN General Assembly as "a common concern of mankind". Innovation and transfer of technologies play an essential role in creating an effective and meaningful global response to climate change. Part I of this book finds that: (1) significant global asymmetries exist in the innovation and transfer of ESTs; (2) the role of IPRs has been a contentious issue in international climate change negotiations; and (3) the minimum IPR standards shaped by TRIPS have mixed effects on innovation and transfer of ESTs.

8.2.1 *Global Asymmetries in the Innovation and Transfer of ESTs*

On the basis of an extensive literature review and empirical evidence, Section 2.4 concludes that ESTs needed to mitigate climate change are asymmetrically distributed at the global level. In particular, innovation and development of selected ESTs are highly concentrated in developed countries (around 80 per cent); emerging countries such as China, Brazil, Russia and India own a significant amount of patents in selected ESTs, yet the economic value of their invention is generally relatively low. International transfer of ESTs primarily occurs between developed countries whereas ESTs are seldom transferred to developing countries, in particular, LDCs. Among developing countries, emerging countries (China in particular) are the main beneficiaries in terms of patent filing and out-licensing destinations.

Section 2.4.2.1 finds that innovation of ESTs, as measured by patent filing under PCT by inventors residing in the same country, is concentrated in developed countries whereas developing countries hold a marginal share of world EST patents. Notably, the concentration of EST patenting activities mirrors overall global patenting trends in all fields of technologies; and the unbalanced global pattern of innovation of ESTs partially derives from the asymmetries in global R&D investment.

Section 2.4.2.2 observes that the concentration of technologies has led to a significant volume of international technology transfer, as indicated by the large cross-border flows of licence fees and royalties. Relying on the World Bank data on charges for the use of IPRs for the period of 1986 to 2012, this section finds that developing countries are net technology importers, with BRIC countries being the main recipients among them and international technology transfer is mainly occurring among OECD countries. This information is not EST-specific. However, given that ESTs involve various fields of technologies, it can be inferred that the transfer of ESTs to developing countries as required by Article 4.5 of the UNFCCC is far from being adequate to respond to the need for mitigating climate change.[1]

8.2.2 *The Role of IPRs as a Contentious Issue in International Climate Change Negotiations*

In examining the fundamental issues in innovation and transfer of ESTs, Section 2.3 observes that ESTs capable of mitigating climate change are global public goods. The markets for ESTs are inherently subject to two independent failures: the first refers to uncompensated spillovers associated with technological innovation; and the second is the external cost associated with GHG emissions.[2] IP rules are primary policy interventions to correct the first failure in the markets for ESTs. Under the utilitarian philosophy, IP rights that proportionately remedy market failure can create incentives for innovation.

Section 3.3 shows that the TRIPS Agreement significantly elevated the level of IP protection globally by establishing a comprehensive set of minimum standards of protection and enforcement for virtually all types of IPRs irrespective of the field of technology. In particular, the TRIPS Agreement does not provide any differential treatment for global public goods such as essential medicine and the ESTs that are needed to mitigate climate change.

Section 3.4 finds that to the extent that ESTs are protected by IPRs, the role played by global IPR regimes established by the TRIPS Agreement in innovation and transfer of ESTs has been one particularly contentious issue in international climate change negotiations. Policy-makers in developing countries contend that the global IPR regime constitutes a (potential) barrier to the transfer of ESTs and thus advocates the use and expansion of the TRIPS flexibilities and push for stronger language on compulsory licensing or even the exclusion of ESTs from patentability. In contrast, MNCs owning advanced ESTs often cite insufficient IPR protection as a barrier to innovation and transfer of technology and suggest stronger IP protection. Many developed nations believe that only strong IP regimes will facilitate the necessary innovation, diffusion and transfer of such technologies.

---

[1] Different factors such as tax minimisation strategies used by firms may affect the accuracy of the findings.

[2] IPCC (2012), *Renewable Energy Sources and Climate Change Mitigation: Special Report of the Intergovernmental Panel on Climate Change*, Cambridge University Press, p. 870.

However, neither side has fully proved its case. The divergence over the role of IPR in innovation and transfer of technology threatens the long-term prospects for a comprehensive international solution to mitigate climate change. There is an urgent need to conduct an in-depth study on the interface between the TRIPS Agreement and innovation and transfer of ESTs. The remaining sections of the book seek to fill this gap.

8.2.3 *The Mixed Effects of Minimum IPR Standards Shaped by TRIPS on Innovation and Transfer of ESTs*

Section 4 seeks to conduct an in-depth study on the implications of minimum IPR standards for innovation and transfer of ESTs, in particular, whether and, if so, to what extent the minimum IPR standards could facilitate or inhibit innovation and transfer of ESTs.

This section finds that strong protection of IPRs is a double-edged sword: on the one hand, as exclusive rights, IPRs confer exclusive power on technology creators to exploit their own technologies and prevent the free-riding problems associated with technologies, thereby incentivising innovation and transfer of ESTs as well as stimulating the patent disclosure. On the other hand, strong IPRs restrict the use of ESTs and are likely to lead to abusive anti-competitive practices, thereby hindering follow-on innovation and slowing down the transfer of ESTs. Therefore, IPRs can be an incentive as well as a barrier in the process of innovation and transfer of ESTs.

The precise role of IPR protection in innovation and transfer of ESTs is, however, context-specific, depending on the characteristics of different technology sectors and the individual circumstances of countries, in particular, their level of technological development. As pointed out by IPCC (2014), the available evidence does support that "the presence of an effective IP regime is a factor in fostering technology transfer into a country".[3] However, the evidence that strict and rigid IP protection facilitates indigenous innovation is almost exclusively limited to specific sectors in developed countries.[4]

Furthermore, potential anti-competitive behaviours associated with IP rights in the transfer of ESTs have been observed in Section 4.4. For instance, MNCs controlling ESTs may unreasonably refuse to license their patented ESTs to other producers so as to maintain a competitive advantage; companies

---

[3] Ibid.
[4] IPCC (2014), *Climate Change 2014: Mitigation of Climate Change*, Working Group III Contribution to the IPCC 5th Assessment Report, Chapter 15: National and Sub-National Policies and Institutions, p. 1175.

may exercise their exclusive rights to deter competitors from entering the market or block similar technological innovation; and firms may grant access to their IPR-protected ESTs on restrictive conditions. Such IPR-related practices may adversely affect competition and innovation, and hinder the transfer of ESTs.

8.3 A BALANCED AND PRO-COMPETITIVE INTERPRETATION OF THE TRIPS FLEXIBILITIES

Despite the long-standing debate surrounding the role of strong IPR protection, the TRIPS Agreement does leave policy space for WTO Members to accommodate public interest concerns. Indeed, while setting forth mandatory minimum IPR standards, the TRIPS Agreement provides WTO Members with the flexibility to design their IP laws in order to mitigate the exclusive effects of IPRs or to adopt appropriate measures to address the IPR-related abusive and anti-competitive practices existing in the process of EST transfer. With a view to making the TRIPS Agreement a more efficient and effective instrument for facilitating innovation and transfer of ESTs, Part II of this book seeks to propose a balanced and pro-competitive interpretation of the TRIPS Agreement.

The following subsections summarize the methodology of legal interpretation (Section 5) and the interpretation of patent-related flexibilities (Section 6) as well as competition-related flexibilities under the TRIPS Agreement (Section 7).

8.3.1 *The Methodology of Legal Interpretation*

Under Article 3.2 of the DSU, the TRIPS Agreement is to be interpreted in accordance with Articles 31 and 32 of the VCLT. This means that the terms of the open-textured TRIPS flexibilities shall be interpreted in good faith in accordance with their ordinary meaning in their context and in the light of the object and purpose of both the WTO Agreement and the TRIPS Agreement.

Section 5.3 finds that the sustainable development objective enshrined in the Preamble to the Marrakesh Agreement provides the discretion required for WTO Members to consider their respective environmental and social needs and concerns when interpreting the TRIPS Agreement. The balancing objective of the TRIPS Agreement also demands the consideration of "non-trade concerns". Environmental protection, in particular, climate change mitigation, is within the scope of public interest enshrined in Articles 7 and 8 of TRIPS. Measures adopted by WTO Members to facilitate the innovation and transfer of ESTs, which are essential for climate change mitigation, undoubtedly benefit public interest and contribute to sustainable development. Therefore, both the WTO's sustainable development objective and the overarching object and purpose of the TRIPS Agreement provide a legal basis for a balanced and tailored interpretation of IPR-related obligations for facilitating innovation and transfer of ESTs.

As found in Section 5.4, as a subsequent agreement to the TRIPS Agreement, the Doha Declaration on the TRIPS Agreement and Public Health reinforces WTO Members' common understanding that the TRIPS Agreement represents a balanced and flexible IP framework responsive to the broader public interest needs and public policy objectives. Although it reiterated and clarified relevant TRIPS flexibilities with a view to protecting public health, such interpretation should be *mutatis mutandis* applicable to the ESTs for the purpose of mitigating climate change. In cases in which the IPR standards affect the innovation and transfer of ESTs, the Doha Declaration must "shed light on" the interpretation of relevant TRIPS flexibilities. The Doha Declaration also explicitly enumerates some of the flexibilities available to WTO Members such as compulsory licences and parallel imports. To the extent that such flexibilities are consistently utilized by WTO Members, they may constitute "subsequent practice" within the meaning of Article 31(3)(b) of the VCLT that shall be taken into account when interpreting the TRIPS Agreement for ESTs.

As part of the WTO legal system, the TRIPS Agreement is "not to be read in clinical isolation from public international law".[5] The use of open-textured provisions that call on areas of law outside IP protection, such as public health and environmental concerns, is an implicit recognition that relevant applicable international law is important for interpreting the TRIPS Agreement. Section 5.4.3 observes that the commitment to transfer ESTs under Article 4.5 of the UNFCCC, which constitutes "relevant rules of international law applicable in the relations between the parties" under Article 31(3)(c) of the VCLT shall be taken into account in the interpretation of the TRIPS Agreement for facilitating innovation and transfer of ESTs so as to mitigate climate change, which is a common concern of humankind.

In addition, Section 5.2.3 finds that relevant judicial decisions as well as the teachings of publicists, such as the 2014 Max Planck Declaration on Patents Protection, may be used to confirm or determine the meaning and scope of certain patent-related flexibilities.

---

[5] Appellate Body Report, *US – Gasoline*, p. 17.

8.3.2 *Interpretation of Patent-Related Flexibilities*

The TRIPS Agreement contains various patent-related flexibilities to enable WTO Members to take the measures necessary to facilitate innovation and transfer of ESTs that are needed to address climate change concerns. However, the extent to which innovation and transfer of ESTs will occur in reality partly depends on how WTO Members interpret and implement the TRIPS flexibilities for ESTs. Section 6 seeks to interpret the patent-related flexibilities in accordance with general interpretative rules established by Articles 31 and 32 of the VCLT.

The WTO's sustainable development objective requires that patent-related flexibilities should be interpreted with a view to promoting environmental protection including by facilitating innovation and transfer of ESTs. Article 7 of the TRIPS Agreement informs the WTO Members that their interpretation of patent-related provisions should be conducive to both technological innovation and the transfer and dissemination of technologies including ESTs. The public interest principle established by Article 8 of the TRIPS Agreement requires that the interpretation of the TRIPS terms should take into account the fact that combating climate change is in the public interest.

As to the non-discrimination principle established by Article 27.1, Section 6.2.1 finds that it may impose constraints on WTO Members' discretion to tailor their patent systems to meet the perceived needs of specific fields of technology. Nevertheless, it also leaves WTO Members room to provide differential treatment for ESTs by permitting *bona fide* exceptions for "certain product areas". In practice, ESTs have enjoyed differential treatment vis-à-vis other technologies in some countries. Some national IP offices have established fast-track mechanisms for patent applications in respect of ESTs so as to facilitate the adoption and transfer of such technologies.

With regard to patent eligibility, Section 6.2.2 finds that a low requirement of patentability risks blocking follow-on innovation through the exclusive control of knowledge that ought to be in the public domain. From the perspective of ensuring access to patented ESTs, developing countries should adopt stricter patentability requirements within the boundaries of TRIPS. If such high criteria for patentability are strictly applied by the patent office, it could remediate the perceived threat of low-quality patents. However, the trade-off associated with such a policy is that local innovators in developing countries would find it more difficult to obtain patents. Nevertheless, developing countries could introduce utility models to protect their minor inventions.

Furthermore, Section 6.2.3 concludes that Article 27.2 cannot be invoked to justify excluding ESTs from patentability because: (1) exclusion of inventions pertinent to ESTs from patentability does not necessarily contribute to the protection of *ordre public* or morality, (2) it is not desirable to prevent the commercial exploitation of such inventions and (3) the prevention of commercial exploitation of such inventions is not necessary to protect *ordre public* or morality. Accordingly, the proposal to exclude from patentability "essential" or "urgent" ESTs in international climate change negotiations is inconsistent with Article 27.2 of the TRIPS Agreement. To the extent that compliance with WTO standards is desired, the implementation of such measure would require a fundamental change in the TRIPS Agreement (Article 27). This type of amendment would demand a high level of political cost and its feasibility could be questioned, especially considering that it took almost 12 years for the only TRIPS Agreement (2005) to enter into force. Accordingly, for national legislatures, rather than blanket exclusions of ESTs from patent protection, it is better to adopt stricter standards for patentability so as to increase the quality of EST patents.

Turning to limits on patent rights, Section 6.3 finds that the limitations or exceptions under Article 30 have the potential to safeguard public interests. Through limiting patent rights, the exceptions can mitigate the exclusive effects of a patent and thereby increase the availability of the patented product. As observed by the 2014 Max Planck Declaration on Patents Protection, Article 30 requires a holistic assessment rather than a separate and independent assessment of each constituent criterion of the "three-step test". Public interests in general and societal interests in combating climate change in particular fall within the scope of "legitimate interests of third parties" in Article 30. Thus, such interests shall be considered when determining the scope of legitimate exceptions for ESTs. Notably, experimental use exceptions could be adopted under Article 30 to allow firms to "invent around" patent claims and to gain access to patented EST technological knowledge. In addition, Section 6.3.3 recommends that countries with the low level of technological advancement should make full use of the flexibility provided by Article 6 and allow parallel imports so as to ensure the lowest cost source of supply of patented ESTs for combating climate change.

Moreover, Section 6.4 finds that climate change provides a valid ground for the compulsory licensing of patented ESTs that are needed to address climate change concerns. WTO Members, in particular those countries suffering the most from climate change, may well argue that climate change constitutes "a national emergency" or another circumstance of "extreme urgency" within the meaning of Article 31(b) of the TRIPS Agreement, therefore justifying compulsory licences for certain EST-related patents. A good faith interpretation of Article 27.1 does not outlaw compulsory licences for failure to work the patented ESTs in the patent-granting country. The use of compulsory licensing and the mere threat thereof can serve as a means of ensuring access to ESTs throughout the world, in particular, when foreign firms refuse to deal with local firms or refuse to make technologies available at prices that local firms can afford.

8.3.3 *Interpretation of Competition-Related Flexibilities*

According to Section 4.4, in the process of the transfer of ESTs, Members are faced with IPR-related abusive or anti-competitive practices. Articles 8.2, 31(k) and 40 of the TRIPS Agreement give WTO Members leeway to enact and apply national competition laws to control and correct these practices. In accordance with the general interpretive rules set out by the VCLT, Section 7 finds that such competition-related provisions can be interpreted to facilitate innovation and transfer of ESTs to address global climate change concerns.

Section 7.2 finds that Article 8.2, as a "Basic Principle", provides WTO Members with broad discretion and strong incentives to adopt appropriate measures to combat the IPR-related abusive practices in the transfer of ESTs and to deal with practices unreasonably restraining trade in EST goods or adversely affecting the international transfer of ESTs. In particular, WTO Members enjoy broad discretion to determine what constitutes an abuse of IP rights and when a restraint of trade may be deemed unreasonable in Article 8.2. In determining whether a restraint of trade in patented ESTs is unreasonable or not, the public interest in combating climate change should be taken into account. Further, Article 8.2 explicitly allows Members to address the adverse effects of IP rights that are detrimental to the transfer of technology, including ESTs. Thus, WTO Members may establish policies to regulate technology pricing and other aspects involved in transfer-of-technology transactions with a view to facilitating the transfer of ESTs that are needed to mitigate climate change.

Section 7.3 observes that interpreting Article 40 in good faith in accordance with the object and purpose of the TRIPS Agreement in its context, compels, if not obliges, WTO Members to adopt competition laws to address IPR-related anti-competitive licensing practices in the process of transfer of ESTs. The commitment to EST transfer in Article 4.5 of UNFCCC would provide additional contextual support for the interpretation that competition laws and regulations should be enacted and applied to address anti-competitive practices in furtherance of the transfer of ESTs that are needed to mitigate climate change.

Section 7.4 finds that a competition law-based compulsory licence under Article 31(k) plays an important role in facilitating the follow-on innovation of, and access to, essential IP-protected technologies, including ESTs. In case of refusals to license essential IPRs, using the essential facilities doctrine to impose IP right holders a duty to license could lead to lower prices and greater innovation. Members have the discretion to define their own criteria for the application of the essential facility doctrine in their domestic competition law or intellectual property law. In specifying relevant conditions, Members should take into account the objectives of the TRIPS Agreement enshrined in Article 7 and the public interest principle in Article 8.1.

However, as observed in Section 7.2.2, Members' regulatory sovereignty to adopt appropriate measures is subject to the consistency requirement. In accordance with Article 31 of the VCLT, whether national competition measures are consistent with the TRIPS Agreement or not should be assessed in line with the sustainable development objective of the WTO Agreement, the Preamble, Articles 7 and 8 as well as other specific provisions of the TRIPS Agreement. Therefore, such measures must be in the furtherance of the objectives and principles of the TRIPS Agreement and the WTO Agreement, whereas they must not derogate from the minimum IPR standards established by the TRIPS Agreement.

Nevertheless, such a consistency requirement does not prevent Members from determining the types of abuses and practices that may be subject to control, or the remedies to be applied. Also, the TRIPS Agreement does not establish clear-cut parameters pertaining to the measures that Members can adopt, thereby leaving Members with broad discretion to introduce a range of appropriate measures to address IPR-related abusive and anti-competitive practices in the process of EST transfer.

8.4 THE INSUFFICIENCY OF TREATY INTERPRETATION AND POSSIBLE REMEDIES

The mere treaty interpretation may not be sufficient for Members to make effective use of the TRIPS flexibilities for the protection of public interest such as environmental protection. This section first examines the factors affecting the effectiveness and sufficiency of a balanced and pro-competitive interpretation. With a view to effectively addressing relevant concerns, the author subsequently recommends (1) the adoption of a Doha-Type Declaration on

Intellectual Property Rights and Climate Change and (2) the creation of international guidelines for the licensing of IPR-protected ESTs.

8.4.1 *Factors Affecting the Sufficiency of Treaty Interpretation*

As observed in Sections 5 to 7, factors affecting the effectiveness and adequacy of a balanced and pro-competitive interpretation of the TRIPS Agreement include but are not limited to: (1) the inherent limits of treaty interpretation; (2) the vagueness of certain TRIPS flexibilities, leaving ample room for divergent interpretations and (3) countries' technical and institutional capacity.

Above all, treaty interpretation is subject to inherent limits because it cannot go either beyond or against the clear meaning of the terms of the TRIPS rule in question.[6] Section 6 finds that there are inherent restrictions within the TRIPS provisions themselves to prevent (certain) WTO Members from making full use of all TRIPS flexibilities. For instance, as pointed out in Section 6.4.4.3, compulsory licensing cannot compel the transfer of know-how necessary to adapt and employ patented ESTs. The requirement that compulsory licensing be used to predominantly supply the domestic market under Article 31(f) makes it difficult for countries with insufficient manufacturing capacity to make effective use of the compulsory licensing system to facilitate access to patented ESTs that play an important role in tackling climate change.

The remedies to such insufficiencies go beyond the interpretation of the TRIPS provisions and may demand an amendment despite high political costs. In this respect, the TRIPS Amendment – a waiver of Article 31(f) for access to medicine – sets a welcome precedent in guaranteeing Members' ability to make effective use of the compulsory licensing for the protection of other general public interests such as environmental protection.

Further, as discussed in Section 5.1, the flexibilities are often vaguely worded in the TRIPS Agreement, leaving ample room for divergent interpretations. In theory, WTO Members may interpret the existing TRIPS flexibilities in a balanced and pro-competitive manner in accordance with Articles 31 and 32 of the VCLT to facilitate innovation and transfer of ESTs. However, in practice, different views have been expressed regarding the nature and scope of the TRIPS flexibilities, for example, with respect to

---

[6] Joost Pauwelyn (2008), *Conflict of Norms in Public International Law: How WTO Law Relates to Other Rules of International Law*, Cambridge University Press, p. 245.

compulsory licensing.[7] There are also concerns over the extent to which WTO Members would feel free to use, to the fullest, these flexibilities without pressures from their trading partners.[8] For instance, as discussed in Section 3.4.2.2, in the current international climate change negotiations, developing countries proposed to use compulsory licensing to facilitate access to patented ESTs, whereas some developed countries and their industries strongly opposed such proposals.

As demonstrated in Section 5.4.1, in order to address developing countries' concern with respect to the TRIPS flexibilities in the case of access to medicine, the 2001 Doha Declaration explicitly reaffirmed Members' regulatory sovereignty to make full use of the TRIPS flexibilities in the interests of public health. It not only clears up some uncertainty in the interpretation of the TRIPS Agreement, but also reinforced the common understanding that the TRIPS Agreement represents a balanced and flexible IP framework that is responsive to the broader public interest needs and public policy objectives.[9] Despite being public health specific, the Doha Declaration could also serve as a model for the Members to adopt a Ministerial Declaration for climate change, clarifying flexibilities to facilitate innovation and transfer of ESTs.

Additionally, countries' technical and institutional capacity may affect their ability to interpret and implement the TRIPS flexibilities. As found in Section 7, many developing countries may lack the technical and institutional capacity to adopt and implement measures to correct the abusive or anti-competitive use of IPRs in the process of licensing ESTs. Such technical and institutional constraints equally affect their ability to make full use of patent-related flexibilities. In fact, as observed in Section 3.3.2.2, such countries may be forced by some developed countries to limit the TRIPS flexibilities by adopting TRIPS-plus provisions in bilateral or regional FTAs.

Nevertheless, Article 67 of the TRIPS Agreement extends the obligations of technical cooperation and assistance to the preparation and implementation of laws and regulations on the TRIPS flexibilities. Upon request, and "on mutually agreed terms and conditions", developed countries have the obligation to provide such technical assistance and thus help developing countries overcome their internal obstacles. Developing countries, in particular those with insufficient legislative experience and capacities, should request

---

[7] Antony Taubman et al. (2012), *A Handbook on the WTO TRIPS Agreement*, Cambridge University Press, p. 180.

[8] Ibid.

[9] Roger Kampf and Hannu Wager (2011), The Role of the TRIPS Agreement in the Global Health Policy, *Stanford Journal of Law, Science & Policy*, pp. 17–41, at p. 26.

developed countries to assist in the preparation of laws or regulations to make full use of the TRIPS flexibilities so as to facilitate their access to global public goods such as ESTs.

8.4.2 A Doha-Type Declaration on Intellectual Property Rights and Climate Change

Even if the TRIPS flexibilities are capable of being interpreted in a balanced and pro-competitive manner in furtherance of the innovation and transfer of ESTs, such theoretical possibility may not necessarily be translated into a full opportunity for WTO Members to make full use of the TRIPS flexibilities for the reasons outlined in Section 8.4.1. With a view to making the balanced and pro-competitive interpretation of the TRIPS flexibilities more authoritative, this section seeks to propose a Doha-type Declaration on Intellectual Property Rights and Climate Change following the precedent set by the 2001 Doha Ministerial Conference of the WTO in the field of public health.

In fact, many developing country delegations and commentators have proposed the adoption of a declaration on IPRs and climate change comparable to the Doha Declaration on the TRIPS Agreement and Public Health.[10] At the Bali Climate Summit (2008), Brazil highlighted the need to introduce new approaches to IPR protection that facilitate technological sharing, "bearing in mind the example set by decisions in other relevant international fora related to intellectual property rights, such as the Doha Declaration on the TRIPS Agreement and Public Health".[11] This proposal was echoed by other Parties and subsequently included in the UNFCCC negotiating text (FCCC/AWGLCA/2009/INF.1) which calls for "adoption of a Declaration on IPRs and environmentally sound technologies in relevant fora to, inter alia, reaffirm the flexibilities in the TRIPS Agreement and enhance the enabling environment for implementing these flexibilities".[12]

---

[10] See, e.g., Matthew Rimmer (2011), *Intellectual Property and Climate Change: Inventing Clean Technologies*, Cheltenham, UK: Edward Elgar Publishing, p. 117; Frederick M. Abbott (2009), Innovation and Technology Transfer to Address Climate Change: Lessons from the Global Debate on Intellectual Property and Public Health, ICTSD's Programme on IPRs and Sustainable Development, Issue Paper No. 24, Geneva: International Centre for Trade and Sustainable Development, pp. 26–8.

[11] Brazil (2008), Views on Elements From the Terms of Reference For the Review and Assessment of the Effectiveness of the Implementation of Article 4, paras. 1(c) and 5, of the Convention, 28th Session, Boon, 4–13 June 2008, FCCC/SBI/2008/MISC.1, 5, available at http://unfccc.int/resource/docs/2008/sbi/eng/misc01.pdf

[12] Revised negotiating text, Note by the Secretariat, Ad Hoc Working Group on Long-Term Cooperative Action under the Convention, FCCC/AWGLCA/2009/INF.1, 22 June 2009, p. 185.

However, given that the difficulty in having access to ESTs appears to be greater than that of getting access to medicine as observed in Section 6.4.4.3, a direct transposition of the Doha Declaration to the climate change context may not be sufficient to address countries' concerns with respect to the innovation of and access to ESTs. Drawing on the experience of the Doha Declaration, the following subsections explore potential elements for a declaration on IPRs and climate change and identify potential challenges and solutions.

8.4.2.1 Potential Elements of the Declaration

Following the sprit and essence of the Doha Declaration, the Declaration on Intellectual Property Rights and Climate Change (hereafter "the Climate Change Declaration" or "the Declaration") should seek to clarify the TRIPS flexibilities rather than modify the rights or obligations set out in the Agreement. Section 5.4.1 observes that the Doha Declaration mainly clarifies patent-related flexibilities, reaffirming Members' right to adopt measures to mitigate the adverse effects of patent rights in furtherance of access to essential medicine. In the context of climate change, in addition to the exclusive effects of patent rights on innovation and transfer of ESTs, Section 4.4.2 finds that companies are often faced with IPR-related abusive or anti-competitive practices in the process of international transfer of ESTs. Thus, the Climate Change Declaration should offer clarifications regarding the nature and scope of both the patent-related flexibilities and the competition-related provisions.

Similar to the first three preambular paragraphs of the Doha Declaration, the Climate Change Declaration could start with the acknowledgement of the gravity of the global climate change while stressing the role of TRIPS in the context of climate change. Further, the Declaration should recognize both the incentivising and the exclusive effects of IPRs on the innovation and transfer of ESTs as found in Section 4. Overall, the Declaration should reaffirm Members' regulatory sovereignty to make full use of the TRIPS flexibilities so as to address climate change concerns in line with the findings contained in Sections 6 and 7 (and summarized in Sections 8.3.2 and 8.3.3).

Moreover, Section 5.4.1.2 makes clear that the central element of the Doha Declaration is the unanimous agreement among WTO Members that the TRIPS Agreement "does not and should not prevent Members from taking measures to protect public health" (the Doha Declaration, para. 4). This paragraph is understood as an elaboration of the meaning of Article 8.1 in the context of public health.[13] Notably, Article 8.1 has equally stressed the

---

[13] UNCTAD and ICTSD (2005), *Resource Book on TRIPS and Development*, Cambridge University Press, p. 131.

need to protect the public interest in "sectors of vital importance to socio-economic and technological development" that would undoubtedly include the EST sector. Such statement could thus be transposed to the climate change context. Further, similar to the second sentence of paragraph 4 of the Doha Declaration, Members should affirm that the TRIPS Agreement can and should be interpreted and implemented in a manner supportive of WTO Members' right to protect the environment and, in particular, to mitigate climate change, including through facilitating innovation and transfer of ESTs.

With respect to the compulsory licensing system within the meaning of Article 31, the following flexibilities should be highlighted in the light of paragraph 5(b) and (c) of the Doha Declaration: first, each member has the freedom to grant compulsory licences and determine the grounds for granting such licenses; and second, each member has the right to define what constitutes "a national emergency or other circumstances of extreme urgency". As argued in Section 6.4.4.2, countries suffering the most from climate change may well argue that climate change constitutes "a national emergency or other circumstances of extreme urgency" within the meaning of Article 31(b), thereby permitting compulsory licences for certain ESTs-related patents.

With respect to the competition-related flexibilities, the Declaration should compel, if not oblige, WTO Members to adopt national competition laws or regulations to address IPR-related abusive or anti-competitive licensing practices in the process of transfer of ESTs. The Declaration could further clarify that the TRIPS Agreement does not preclude the adoption of *per se* rules; and that in determining whether a restraint of competition with respect to the patented ESTs is unreasonable or not, the public interest in combating climate change should be taken into account in the weighing and balancing process.[14]

Despite the fact that such a declaration does not create new rights or obligations, WTO Members may find it useful as they would face less political constraints and have greater confidence in making full use of the TRIPS flexibilities. Thus, such a declaration could "reinforce" the trend towards balancing innovation of, and access to, ESTs at the international level.[15]

[14] See Section 7.3.2.1.
[15] Frederick M. Abbott (2009), Innovation and Technology Transfer to Address Climate Change: Lessons from the Global Debate on Intellectual Property and Public Health, ICTSD's Programme on IPRs and Sustainable Development, Issue Paper No. 24, Geneva: International Centre for Trade and Sustainable Development, p. 26.

8.4.2.2 Potential Challenges and Solutions

Two main challenges may emerge with respect to the Climate Change Declaration: the first is pertinent to the nature and limits of the Climate Change Declaration itself; and the second relates to the external political obstacles and the institutional constraints faced by countries to adopt and implement such a declaration.

First, the mere clarification of the TRIPS provisions through the Doha-type Declaration on the IPRs and Climate Change may not be sufficient for some WTO Members to fully use the TRIPS flexibilities in pursuing the public interest in climate change mitigation. As pointed out in Section 8.4.1, there are inherent restrictions within the TRIPS provisions that prevent (certain) WTO Members from making full use of all the TRIPS flexibilities available to them: the first relates to the requirement that compulsory licensing be used to predominantly supply the domestic market under Article 31(f); and the second is associated with the know-how that is necessary for the adoption of the patented ESTs.

With respect to the restrictions contained in Article 31(f), the solution to a similar problem in the context of access to medicine could provide a powerful precedent. As observed in Section 6.4.4.1, to enable countries with insufficient manufacturing capacity in the pharmaceutical sector to benefit from the compulsory licensing system, WTO Members decided to waive exporting countries' obligations under Article 31(f) in 2003 and agreed to make this waiver permanent by amending the TRIPS Agreement in 2005. Significantly, the amendment – the very first amendment to a WTO agreement – entered into force on 23 January 2017, signaling Members' determination to contribute to "humanitarian and development goals".[16]

Section 6.4.4.3 finds that the requirements in Article 31(f) tend to create more obstacles for poor countries to access patented ESTs because compared to medicines, ESTs are generally more complex and the production of ESTs is more difficult, demanding stronger manufacturing capacities. Further, the public interest in mitigating climate change is equally, if not more, important than that in access to medicine. Thus, if the requirements in Article 31(f) are waived to promote access to medicine, there is no reason to not eliminate such restrictions vis-à-vis ESTs that are needed to mitigate climate change. Accordingly, the amendment to the TRIPS Agreement should be extended to address global climate change concerns. Such amendment would be

---

[16] WTO (2005), Members OK amendment to make health flexibility permanent, Press/426, 6 December 2005, available at www.wto.org/english/news_e/pres05_e/pr426_e.htm

supported by the WTO's sustainable development objective and Articles 7 and 8 of the TRIPS Agreement.

With respect to essential know-how, Section 6.4.4.3 finds that in order to fully use the licensed invention, licensees may need to access a variety of associated know-how or tacit technological knowledge that is necessary to adopt or employ ESTs. Article 4.5 of the UNFCCC thus explicitly obliges developed countries to facilitate the transfer of know-how together with the ESTs. However, in the case of refusal to license the associated know-how, compulsory licences within the meaning of Article 31 of the TRIPS Agreement cannot compel the holders of ESTs to do so.

Nevertheless, as observed by Correa (2016), the US Courts have issued compulsory licences to facilitate access to know-how in antitrust proceedings.[17] To the extent that access to know-how is of equal importance, there is no reason to exclude the associated know-how from the subject matter of compulsory licences. In fact, the TRIPS Agreement does not limit the possibility of issuing compulsory licences for essential know-how. Further, Section 7.4.2 finds that compulsory licences are permitted in many jurisdictions such as the EU, the United States and China in cases of refusals to license IPRs, including trade secrets, that constitute "essential facilities". Thus, Members are not prohibited by the TRIPS Agreement from issuing compulsory licences for know-how protected as trade secret.

To maintain a proper balance between the private rights and public interest, requirements contained in Article 31 of the TRIPS Agreement should be *mutatis mutandis* applicable to compulsory licences for know-how associated with ESTs. In particular, the right holder should be paid reasonable compensation. Prior to the authorization of such licences, Members can also provide incentives to induce the trade secret holders to engage in voluntary licensing.

Second, some countries have initiated proposals to formulate and adopt a Doha-type declaration in both the UNFCCC and the WTO; however, both initiatives have failed after several years of efforts due to political obstacles and

---

[17] Carlos M. Correa (2016), Intellectual Property Rights under the UNFCCC: Without Response to Developing Countries' Concerns, in Sarnoff (ed.), *Research Handbook on Intellectual Property and Climate Change*, Cheltenham, UK: Edward Elgar Publishing, pp. 74–91, at p. 80 (observing that "[The requirement to transfer know-how] has been established in the case of some compulsory licenses granted in the US in the framework of anti-trust procedures. Requirements of this kind were imposed on American Home Products on occasion of the acquisition of Solvay S.A.'s animal health division (1997), on Dow Chemical in relation to the production of dicycolmine (1994), and in the case of the merger between Ciba-Geigy and Sandoz Ltd. These companies were required to license a large portfolio of patents, data and know-how relating to HSV-tk products, hemophilia gene rights and other products to Rhone-Poulenc Rorer (2001)").

institutional constraints. As pointed out in Section 3.4.2.2.2, in international climate change negotiations, developed countries have insisted on strong protection of IP rights and opposed the use of certain TRIPS flexibilities, in particular compulsory licences, for access to ESTs. As a result, the 2015 Paris Agreement is silent on the issues of the IPRs. Given its contentious nature, the UNFCCC may not be an appropriate forum for the adoption of the Doha-type Declaration for the time being.

At the WTO, Ecuador initiated a proposal (IP/C/W/585, 2013) in the TRIPS Council to evaluate the TRIPS Agreement from the standpoint of mitigating environmental problems with a view to reaffirming and enhancing the existing TRIPS flexibilities related to ESTs.[18] Although this proposal gained support from some developing countries, several developed countries, particularly the United States, strongly opposed such a proposal in the TRIPS Council. It has not led to any concrete outcome. Given the Member-driven nature of the WTO, it would be difficult for the WTO to accommodate a declaration on intellectual property rights and climate change in the near future.

It appears less challenging to adopt a declaration on IP rights and climate change within the UN framework, in particular, the UN General Assembly. Notably, in the 69th annual UN General Assembly, the Secretary-General called upon all Member States to "(e) ensure that our global intellectual property regimes and the application of the flexibilities of the Agreement on Trade-Related Aspects of Intellectual Property Rights are fully consistent with and contribute to the goals of sustainable development" and "(g) promote the acceleration of the innovation-to-market-to-public-good cycle of clean and environmentally sound technologies".[19] The UN General Assembly Resolution on Transforming Our World: the 2030 Agenda for Sustainable Development adopted on 25 September 2015 provides contextual support for the adoption of the Climate Change Declaration by, inter alia, reaffirming developing countries' right to make full use of the TRIPS flexibilities in furtherance of access to medicines and emphasising the need to facilitate development, transfer and dissemination of relevant technologies.[20]

---

[18] Contribution of Intellectual Property to Facilitating the Transfer of Environmentally Rational Technology, Council for Trade-Related Aspects of Intellectual Property Rights, 27 February 2013, WTO Doc. No. IP/C/W/585, para. 16.

[19] UNGA (2014), The Road to Dignity by 2030: Ending Poverty, Transforming All Lives and Protecting the Planet, Synthesis Report of the Secretary-General on the Post-2015 Sustainable Development Agenda, A/69/700, at p. 27.

[20] Transforming Our World: the 2030 Agenda for Sustainable Development, Resolution adopted by the United Nations General Assembly on 25 September 2015, A/RES/70/1, 21 October 2015, p. 17 and p. 26.

However, the cooperation from the WTO in formulating and implementing such a declaration is indispensable because the TRIPS Agreement is an international agreement administrated by the WTO, and the WTO has a potent dispute settlement mechanism.

8.4.3 *International Guidelines for Licensing of IPR-Protected ESTs*

In response to the need to regulate IPR-related anti-competitive practices implied in Article 40 of the TRIPS Agreement, this Section seeks to propose international guidelines for licensing of IPR-protected ESTs (hereafter, International Guidelines).

An industry-specific international guideline to address anti-competitive practices is not innovative in the WTO context. In 1996, the WTO Negotiating Group on Basic Telecommunications created the Reference Paper on Regulatory Principles (hereafter "Reference Paper") to prevent the anti-competitive practices in the telecommunications sector. The Reference Paper codified the then "best practices" in national telecom regulation, specifying a set of pro-competitive regulatory principles: (1) competitive safeguards, (2) interconnection, (3) universal service, (4) public availability of licensing criteria, (5) independent regulators and (6) allocation and use of scare resources.[21] As of 17 February 2017, 82 WTO Members have committed in full or in part to the regulatory principles contained in the Reference Paper by integrating the commitments into their schedules,[22] thereby making such commitments an integral part of the GATS Agreement,[23] and enforceable through the WTO dispute settlement mechanism. To the extent that WTO Members have incorporated the Reference Paper in their schedules, the Reference Paper provides contextual support for creating international guidelines to prevent anti-competitive licensing practices for ESTs under Article 40 of TRIPS.

The following subsections examine in turn (1) the need to create international guidelines for licensing of IPR-protected ESTs, (2) the potential elements of such guidelines and (3) potential benefits and challenges.

---

[21] Reference Paper, Negotiating group on basic telecommunications, 24 April 1996, available at www.wto.org/english/tratop_e/serv_e/telecom_e/tel23_e.htm

[22] Telecommunications Services, WTO website, available at www.wto.org/english/tratop_e/ serv_e/telecom_e/telecom_e.htm

[23] GATS, Article XX:3 (providing that "Schedules of specific commitments shall be annexed to this Agreement and shall form an integral part thereof").

8.4.3.1 The Need for International Guidelines for
Licensing of IPR-Protected ESTs

Licensing guidelines for ESTs are needed to address IPR-related anti-competitive licensing practices and conditions in the EST industry. As discussed in Section 2.4, the majority of the patented ESTs are owned by private sectors and such ESTs are mainly transferred through market-based channels such as licensing. Indeed, access to existing IPR-protected technologies through licences will often be a cheaper and faster option than re-engineering or re-inventing those technologies.[24] However, Section 4.4.2 finds that IPR-related abusive and anti-competitive practices are not uncommon in the process of licensing ESTs. Guidelines on licensing practices should thus be adopted to encourage the appropriate exercise of IP rights by private sectors.[25]

Unfortunately, as pointed out in Section 7.1, the competition-related provisions in TRIPS provide little guidance for WTO Members with regard to how to regulate or control IPR-related anti-competitive practices beyond the consistency requirement. In 2013, Ecuador requested the TRIPS Council to evaluate the licensing regulations and conditions from the perspectives of the pressing needs of vulnerable developing countries in the context of climate change but largely failed to achieve its objective.[26] In practice, as found in Section 7.3.3, many WTO Members lack legislative and technical capacities to enact and implement laws and regulations to address IPR-related anti-competitive practices. Though they may request developed Members to assist in the preparation of such laws or regulations under Article 67 of the TRIPS Agreement, international guidelines appear to better serve their needs.

International guidelines for licensing of IPR-protected ESTs could promote regulatory harmonisation and coherence among WTO Members. Through reducing the divergence in the licensing regulatory requirements imposed in different Members, such international guidelines could also mitigate the cost

---

[24] John H. Barton (2007), New Trends in Technology Transfer: Implications for National and International Policy, Issue Paper No. 18, Geneva: International Centre for Trade and Sustainable Development, p. 22.

[25] WTO (2012), Options for a Technology Facilitation Mechanism, Rio +20 – WTO Secretariat Contribution Regarding "A Facilitation Mechanism That Promotes the Development, Transfer and Dissemination of Clean and Environmentally Sound Technologies", available at https://sustainabledevelopment.un.org/index.php?page=view&type=111&nr=1243&menu=35, p. 10.

[26] Contribution of Intellectual Property to Facilitating the Transfer of Environmentally Rational Technology, Council for Trade-Related Aspects of Intellectual Property Rights, 27 February 2013, WTO Doc. No. IP/C/W/585, para. 17.

and difficulty of access to IPR-protected ESTs for licensees.[27] Accordingly, to avoid undue distortions that licensing requirements may introduce, international guidelines, codifying the "best practices" in national licensing regulations, should be introduced.

8.4.3.2 Potential Elements for Guidelines on Licensing IP-Protected ESTs

Following the precedent set forth by WTO Members in the telecommunications sector and considering the fact that facilitating the licensing of ESTs may play a vital role in contributing to climate change mitigation, the International Guidelines should introduce regulatory principles for licensing ESTs with a view to addressing IPR-related anti-competitive licensing practices. In accordance with Article 7 of the TRIPS Agreement, the licensing guidelines should balance the interests between IP right holders and IP users in the context of combating climate change. Their ultimate objective is to facilitate meaningful transfer and follow-on innovation of ESTs.

As a starting point, the guidelines need to explore options to identify EST-related IP assets and make such assets more visible to other stakeholders in order to promote their exploitation through, inter alia, licensing. Notably, WIPO GREEN was created in 2013 to connect providers of IPR-protected ESTs with users through a publicly available database of various IP assets.[28] It also seeks to identify EST needs in different regions.[29] Thus, the International Guidelines could refer to the WIPO GREEN as one of the sources of IP assets.

The central principle of the guidelines would be that the licensing terms should be fair, reasonable and non-discriminatory (FRAND). This means that all licensees and licensors should be treated equally and that newcomers should not be discriminated. Also, the cost-oriented rate should not be unreasonably high. This principle finds contextual support in paragraph 2.2

---

[27] Peter Van den Bossche and Werner Zdouc (2013), *The Law and Policy of the World Trade Organization*, 3rd edn, Cambridge University Press, p. 851 (finding that "the divergence in the regulatory requirements imposed in different countries increases the cost and difficulty of granting market access for exporters").

[28] WIPO (2013), WIPO GREEN: New Online Marketplace Seeks Environmentally Sustainable Solutions for Climate Change, PR/2013/749, available at www.wipo.int/pressroom/en/articles/2013/article_0025.html

[29] Yesim Baykal (2013), WIPO GREEN: The Sustainable Technology Marketplace, presented at the Conference on Climate Change in Africa: Advancing Knowledge, Technology, Policy and Practice, available at www.wipo.int/edocs/mdocs/africa/en/wipo_kenya_cic_jpo_inn_nbo_13/wipo_kenya_cic_jpo_inn_nbo_13_t_1.pdf, p. 4.

of the Reference Paper which explicitly requires that the interconnection be provided in a timely fashion, under non-discriminatory terms and on cost-oriented rates that are reasonable, having regard to economic feasibility. This FRAND principle has been widely used in the context of standard setting.[30] With respect to ESTs, the FRAND principle is of particular relevance in the following two circumstances as identified in Section 4.4: first, some ESTs such as smart grid require standard setting; and second, some ESTs, for example, electric and hybrid cars, may be very complex and covered by many essential IPRs, which may be owned by different parties.

Further, the International Guidelines should codify the essential facilities doctrine. Section 7.4.2 finds that the essential facilities doctrine has been adopted by many jurisdictions such as the EU, the United States and China in cases of refusals to license IPRs. WTO Members have also provided a definition of "essential facilities" for the telecommunications sector and explicitly characterised the failure to make available to other service suppliers on a timely basis technical information about essential facilities as an "anti-competitive practice" (Reference Paper, para. 1.2). In the same vein, WTO Members should adopt the essential facilities doctrine to correct certain anti-competitive practices in the EST industry.

Last but not least, the International Guidelines should take into account the importance of ESTs and the special needs and circumstances of developing countries, in particular, LDCs and small island developing countries (SIDCs), which are often the biggest victims of climate change. In the UN climate change negotiations, negotiators have proposed in the 2015 Draft Negotiating Text to establish commitments related to humanitarian or preferential licensing.[31] As an exception, companies or research institutes from LDCs and SIDCs should be entitled to access the EST-related IPRs for free or buy IPR-protected ESTs at a lower price.

In order not to undermine the private sector's incentive in the innovation and transfer of ESTs, the Green Climate Fund, which was established by the Parties to the UNFCCC in 2011 with the mandate of promoting a paradigm shift towards low-carbon development pathways by providing financial support

---

[30] One example is 3G Patent Platform Partnership which was created in 1999 to allow for "fair, reasonable, and non-discriminatory" (FRAND) access to rights essential for implementing the Wideband Code Division Multiple Access third Generation (W-CDMA 3G) PP standard. See David Serafino (2007), Survey of Patent Pools Demonstrates Variety of Purposes and Management Structures, *KEI Research Note* 2007, vol. 6, pp. 1–2.

[31] Elements for a Draft Negotiating Text, Annex, Decisions adopted by the Conference of the Parties, 1/CP.20: Lima Call for Climate Action, FCCC/CP/2014/10/Add.1, 2 February 2015, para. 56.3.

to developing countries to mitigate their GHG emissions,[32] should finance preferential licensing to meet the special needs of LDCs and SIDCs.

8.4.3.3 Potential Benefits and Challenges of the Licensing Guidelines

International Guidelines, designed to address IPR-related anti-competitive licensing practices related to ESTs could facilitate the transfer of IPR-protected ESTs and bring relatively reliable royalties to IP right holders, thereby further incentivising private sectors to invest in research, development and innovation of such ESTs. Moreover, implementing the "fair, reasonable and non-discrimination" licensing policies may help remedy the failures in private markets for ESTs caused by information asymmetries or non-competitive markets as identified in Section 3.2.2.2. In addition, the International Guidelines would increase commercial predictability and security.

Although well-designed licensing guidelines may bring the above-mentioned benefits to EST industry, we should not overlook potential challenges. The central challenge facing the guidelines may be the voluntary adoption and implementation of the pro-competitive licensing principles by IP holders, in particular, the major EST MNCs. Firms may lack incentives to implement the licensing guidelines. For instance, as observed in Section 4.4, they may refuse to license essential IPRs on reasonable commercial terms. Under such circumstances, as pointed out in Section 7.4.2.2, a compulsory licence or the threat thereof may motivate IP holders to license its IPR-protected ESTs on FRAND terms and conditions.

However, it may be difficult to determine the "reasonableness" of the licensing fees. In determining the reasonableness, relevant stakeholders or administrators should take into account many different factors such as the value of the EST-related IP rights, their competition status in the relevant market and an ordinary licensee's affordability. The proposed licensing fees should be evaluated and adjusted in a regular manner to reflect the changes of relevant factors.

Among other issues, one question is what body should create such International Guidelines.[33] The UNFCCC, whose mandate is to combat climate

---

[32] UNFCCC (2014), Report of the Green Climate Fund to the Conference of the Parties to the United Nations Framework Convention on Climate Change, UN Doc. FCCC/CP/2014/8, Annex, at p. 12.

[33] Many other issues should be examined in depth for the purpose of creating international guidelines for the licensing of IPR-protected ESTs. However, a detailed analysis in this respect would fall outside the scope of this book.

change, and WIPO, which accepts international patent application and provides patent information services, should take the initiative. Cooperation from WTO, which addresses trade-related aspects of IP rights, is needed. As observed in Section 3.2.1.3, UNCTAD also has a mandate to promote innovation and transfer of technology. Accordingly, UNCTAD, UNFCCC, WIPO and WTO could work together to design the content of the International Guidelines. They could co-organise expert meetings involving the major stakeholders, such as EST companies, universities, manufacturers and country delegations, with a view to identifying a set of pro-competitive regulatory principles for the licensing of the IPR-protected ESTs. Following the Reference Paper precedent, the International Guidelines could be incorporated into the WTO Agreements, thereby making them enforceable through the WTO dispute settlement mechanism.

Appendix

WORLD TRADE ORGANIZATION

WT/MIN(01)/DEC/2
20 November 2001
(01-5860)

MINISTERIAL CONFERENCE
Fourth Session
Doha, 9 – 14 November 2001

DECLARATION ON THE TRIPS AGREEMENT AND PUBLIC HEALTH
Adopted on 14 November 2001

1. We recognize the gravity of the public health problems afflicting many developing and least-developed countries, especially those resulting from HIV/AIDS, tuberculosis, malaria and other epidemics.

2. We stress the need for the WTO Agreement on Trade-Related Aspects of Intellectual Property Rights (TRIPS Agreement) to be part of the wider national and international action to address these problems.

3. We recognize that intellectual property protection is important for the development of new medicines. We also recognize the concerns about its effects on prices.

4. We agree that the TRIPS Agreement does not and should not prevent Members from taking measures to protect public health. Accordingly, while reiterating our commitment to the TRIPS Agreement, we affirm that the Agreement can and should be interpreted and implemented in a manner supportive of WTO Members' right to protect public health and, in particular, to promote access to medicines for all.

In this connection, we reaffirm the right of WTO Members to use, to the full, the provisions in the TRIPS Agreement, which provide flexibility for this purpose.

5. Accordingly and in the light of paragraph 4 above, while maintaining our commitments in the TRIPS Agreement, we recognize that these flexibilities include:

(a) In applying the customary rules of interpretation of public international law, each provision of the TRIPS Agreement shall be read in the light of the object and purpose of the Agreement as expressed, in particular, in its objectives and principles.

(b) Each Member has the right to grant compulsory licences and the freedom to determine the grounds upon which such licences are granted.

(c) Each Member has the right to determine what constitutes a national emergency or other circumstances of extreme urgency, it being understood that public health crises, including those relating to HIV/AIDS, tuberculosis, malaria and other epidemics, can represent a national emergency or other circumstances of extreme urgency.

(d) The effect of the provisions in the TRIPS Agreement that are relevant to the exhaustion of intellectual property rights is to leave each Member free to establish its own regime for such exhaustion without challenge, subject to the MFN and national treatment provisions of Articles 3 and 4.

6. We recognize that WTO Members with insufficient or no manufacturing capacities in the pharmaceutical sector could face difficulties in making effective use of compulsory licensing under the TRIPS Agreement. We instruct the Council for TRIPS to find an expeditious solution to this problem and to report to the General Council before the end of 2002.

7. We reaffirm the commitment of developed-country Members to provide incentives to their enterprises and institutions to promote and encourage technology transfer to least-developed country Members pursuant to Article 66.2. We also agree that the least-developed country Members will not be obliged, with respect to pharmaceutical products, to implement or apply Sections 5 and 7 of Part II of the TRIPS Agreement or to enforce rights provided for under these Sections until 1 January 2016, without prejudice to the right of least-developed country Members to seek other extensions of the transition periods as provided for in Article 66.1 of the TRIPS Agreement. We instruct the Council for TRIPS to take the necessary action to give effect to this pursuant to Article 66.1 of the TRIPS Agreement.

Bibliography

REPORTS

Australian Productivity Commission (2013). *Compulsory Licensing of Patents*, Inquiry Report No. 61, Commonwealth of Australia.

Copenhagen Economics (2009). *Are IPR a Barrier to the Transfer of Climate Change Technology?* Copenhagen Economics A/S and the IPR Company ApS.

Economics and Statistics Administration and United States Patent and Trademark Office (2012). *Intellectual Property and the U.S. Economy: Industries in Focus*, Washington, D.C.: US Department of Commerce.

International Council on Human Rights Policy (2011). Beyond Technology Transfer: Protecting Human Rights in a Climate-Constrained World, Geneva: International Council on Human Rights Policy.

IPCC (2000). IPCC Special Report: Methodological and Technological Issues in Technology Transfer. Cambridge University Press.

(2007a). Synthesis Report, Contribution of Working Groups I, II and III to the Fourth Assessment Report of the IPCC, Core Writing Team. R. K. Pachauri and A. Reisinger (eds.). Geneva, Switzerland: Intergovernmental Panel on Climate Change.

(2007b). Climate Change 2007: The Physical Science Basis: Contribution of Working Group I to the Fourth Assessment Report of the IPCC. S. D. Solomon et al. (eds.). Cambridge University Press.

(2007c). Mitigation, Contribution of Working Group III to the Fourth Assessment Report of the IPCC. B. Metz, O. R. Davidson, P. R. Bosch, R. Dave, and L. A. Meyer (eds.). Cambridge University Press.

(2012). Renewable Energy Sources and Climate Change Mitigation: Special Report of the Intergovernmental Panel on Climate Change. Cambridge University Press.

(2014a). *Climate Change 2014 Synthesis Report: Summary for Policymakers*, available at www.ipcc.ch/pdf/assessment-report/ar5/syr/SYR_AR5_SPM_Final.pdf

(2014b). *Climate Change 2014: Mitigation of Climate Change*, Working Group III Contribution to the IPCC 5th Assessment Report, Chapter 13: International Cooperation: Agreements and Instruments.

(2014c). *Climate Change 2014: Mitigation of Climate Change*, Working Group III Contribution to the IPCC 5th Assessment Report, Chapter 15: National and Sub-National Policies and Institutions.

Lee, B., L. Iliev, and F. Preston (2009). *Who Owns Our Low Carbon Future?*, Intellectual Property and Energy Technologies, A Chatham House Report.

Ockwell, David (2008). *Intellectual Property Rights and Low Carbon Technology Transfer to Developing Countries – A Review of the Evidence to Date*, UK-India Collaboration to Overcome Barriers to the Transfer of Low Carbon Energy Technology: Phase 2, University of Sussex, Energy and Resources Institute and Institute of Development Studies.

Ockwell, David, Jim Watson, Gordon Mackerron, Prosanto Pal, Farhana Yamin, N. Vasudevan and Parimita Mohanty, (2007). *UK-India Collaboration to Identify the Barriers to the Transfer of Low Carbon Energy Technology*, Final Report, Department for Environment, Food and Rural Affairs.

OECD (2002). Foreign Direct Investment for Development: Maximising Benefits, Minimising Costs. Paris: Organisation for Economic Co-operation and Development Publishing.

Pugatch, Meir Perez (2011). Intellectual Property and the Transfer of Environmentally Sound Technologies, Global Challenges Report. Geneva: World Intellectual Property Organization.

Report of the World Commission on Environment and Development: Our Common Future (1987, March 20). Transmitted to the General Assembly as an Annex to Document A/42/427 – Development and International Co-operation: Environment.

The Energy and Resources Institute (2009). Emerging Asia Contribution on Issues of Technology for Copenhagen, TERI Report No. 2008 RS09. New Delhi.

The UK Commission on Intellectual Property Rights (2002). Integrating Intellectual Property Rights and Development Policy, Report of the Commission on Intellectual Property Rights. London.

Thomas, John R. (2010). *The Role of Trade Secrets in Innovation Policy*, Congressional Research Service (CRS) Report for Congress, Prepared for Members and Committees of Congress.

UNCTAD (1974a). *The Role of the Patent System in the Transfer of Technology to Developing Countries*, UN Doc. TD/B/AC.11/19.

   (1974b). *The Possibility and Feasibility of an International Code of Conduct on Transfer of Technology*, UN Doc. TD/B/AC.11/22.

   (1996). The TRIPS Agreement and Developing Countries, UNCTAD/ITE/1. New York and Geneva: United Nations.

   (2001). Transfer of Technology, UNCTAD Series on Issues in International Investment Agreements. New York and Geneva: United Nations.

   (2007). The Least Developed Countries Report 2007: Knowledge, Technological Learning and Innovation for Development, prepared by the UNCTAD Secretariat. New York and Geneva: United Nations.

   (2010). Intellectual Property in the World Trade Organisation: Turning It into Developing Countries' Real Property. New York and Geneva: United Nations.

   (2011). Using Intellectual Property Rights to Stimulate Pharmaceutical Production in Developing Countries: A Preference Guide. New York and Geneva: United Nations.

   (2014). Transfer of Technology and Knowledge Sharing for Development: Science, Technology and Innovation Issues for Developing Countries, UNCTAD/DTL/STICT/2013/8. Geneva: United Nations.

UNCTC (1987). Transnational Corporations and Technology Transfer: Effects and Policy Issues, ST/CTC/86. New York: United Nations.

UNEP, EPO and ICTSD (2010). Patents and Clean Energy: Bridging the Gap between Evidence and Policy. Munich: Mediengruppe Universal.

UNFCCC (2014). *Report of the Green Climate Fund to the Conference of the Parties to the United Nations Framework Convention on Climate Change*, UN Doc. FCCC/CP/2014/8, Annex.

UNGA (2014). *The Road to Dignity by 2030: Ending Poverty, Transforming All Lives and Protecting the Planet*, Synthesis Report of the Secretary-General on the Post-2015 Sustainable Development Agenda, A/69/700.

UNIDO (2008). Public Goods for Economic Development. Vienna: United Nations Industrial Development Organisation.

United Nations (1981). Proceedings of the United Nations Conference on Trade and Development, Fifth Session, Manila, 7 May–3 June 1979, Vol. III, New York.

United States International Trade Commission (1988). *Foreign Protection of Intellectual Property Rights and the Effect on U.S. Industry and Trade*, Report to the United States Trade Representative, Investigation No. 332–245, Under Section 332 (g) of the Tariff Act of 1930, USITC Publication 2065, Washington, D.C.

WHO (2006). *Public Health: Innovation and Intellectual Property Rights*, Report of the Commission on Intellectual Property Rights, Innovation and Public Health, Geneva: World Health Organization.

WHO, WIPO and WTO (2012). Promoting Access to Medical Technologies and Innovation: Intersections between Public Health, Intellectual Property and Trade. Geneva: WHO, WIPO and WTO.

(2013). Promoting Access to Medical Technologies and Innovation: Intersections between Public Health, Intellectual Property and Trade. Geneva: WHO, WIPO and WTO.

WIPO (1979, 25 June). Diplomatic Conference on the Revision of the Paris Convention: Basic Proposals, PR/DC/3, Geneva: World Intellectual Property Organization.

(1979). WIPO Model Law for Developing Countries on Inventions, Vol. I: Patents, Geneva: World Intellectual Property Organization.

(2011). Patent Landscape Report on Ritonavir, Patent Landscape Reports Project prepared by Landon IP, Geneva: World Intellectual Property Organization.

World Bank (2002). Global Economic Prospects and Developing Countries: Making Trade Work for the World's Poor, Washington, D.C.: World Bank.

(2008). Global Economic Prospects: Technology Diffusion in the Developing World, Washington, D.C.: World Bank.

World Economic Forum (2013, December). *The Global Energy Architecture Performance Index Report 2014*, World Economic Forum and Accenture.

BOOKS

Anderman Steven (2007). *The Interface between Intellectual Property Rights and Competition Policy*, Cambridge University Press.

Andersen Birgitte (2006). *Intellectual Property Rights: Innovation, Governance and the Institutional Environment*, Cheltenham, UK: Edward Elgar Publishing.

Aust Anthony (2007). *Modern Treaty Law and Practice*, Cambridge University Press.

Barro Robert J. and Xavier Sala-i-Martin (2004). *Economic Growth*, 2nd edn, Cambridge, MA: Massachusetts Institute of Technology.

Bessen James and Michael J. Meurer (2008). *Patent Failure: How Judges, Bureaucrats, and Lawyers Put Innovators at Risk*, Princeton University Press.

Bjorge Eirik (2014). *The Evolutionary Interpretation of Treaties*, Oxford University Press.

Blakeney Michael (2012). *Intellectual Property Enforcement: A Commentary on the Anti-Counterfeiting Trade Agreement (ACTA)*, Cheltenham, UK: Edward Elgar Publishing.

Bodenhausen G.H.C. (1969). *Guide to the Application of the Paris Convention for the Protection of Industrial Property* (as revised at Stockholm in 1967). United International Bureaux for the Protection of Intellectual Property.

Bradford Scott C. and Robert Z. Lawrence (2004). *Has Globalization Gone Far Enough?: The Costs of Fragmented Markets*, Washington, D.C.: Peterson Institute.

Brownlie Ian (2008). *Principles of Public International Law*, Oxford University Press.

Carlarne Cinnamon Piñon (2010). *Climate Change Law and Policy: EU and US Approaches*, Oxford University Press.

Cassese Antonio (2001). *International Law*, Oxford University Press.

Chang Ha-Joon (2003). *Kicking Away the Ladder: Development Strategy in Historical Perspective*, London: Anthem Press.

(2008). *Bad Samaritans: The Guilty Secrets of Rich Nations and the Threat to Global Prosperity*, New York: Random House.

Cheng Bin (1953). *General Principles of Law as Applied by International Courts and Tribunals*, London: Stevens and Sons.

Correa Carlos M. (2000). *Intellectual Property Rights, the WTO and Developing Countries: The TRIPS Agreement and Policy Options*, London and New York: Zed Books, Third World Network.

(2007). *Trade Related Aspects of Intellectual Property Rights: A Commentary on the TRIPS Agreement*, Oxford Commentaries on International Law, Oxford University Press.

Cottier Thomas and Pierre Véron (2011). *Concise International and European IP Law: TRIPS, Paris Convention, European Enforcement and Transfer of Technology*, 2nd edn, New York: Kluwer Law International.

Davies Gillian (2002). *Copyright and the Public Interest*, 2nd edn, London: Sweet & Maxwell.

de Carvalho Nuno Pires (2010). *The TRIPS Regime of Patent Rights*, 3rd edn, New York: Kluwer Law International.

(2011). *The TRIPS Regime of Trademarks and Designs*, New York: Kluwer Law International.

Deere Carolyn (2009). *The Implementation Game: The TRIPS Agreement and the Global Politics of Intellectual Property Reform in Developing Countries*, Oxford University Press.

Dinwoodie Graeme B. and Rochelle C. Dreyfuss (2012). *A Neofederalist Vision of TRIPS: The Resilience of the International Intellectual Property Regime*, Oxford University Press.

Dörr Oliver and Kirsten Schmalenbach (2012). *Vienna Convention on the Law of Treaties: A Commentary*, Berlin and Heidelberg: Springer-Verlag.

Drahos Peter and John Braithwaite (2002). *Information Feudalism: Who Owns the Knowledge Economy?* Abingdon-on-Thames, UK: Earthscan Publications.

Dratler Jay (1991). *Intellectual Property Law: Commercial, Creative, and Industrial Property*, New York: Law Journal Press.

Dratler Jay and Stephen M. McJohn (2004). *Intellectual Property Law: Commercial, Creative, and Industrial Property*, Vol. I, New York: Law Journal Press.

(2006). *Intellectual Property Law: Commercial, Creative, and Industrial Property*, New York: Law Journal Press.

Dreyfuss Rochelle Cooper and Roberta Rosenthal Kwall (1996). *Intellectual Property: Trademark, Copyright, and Patent Law: Cases and Materials*, Eagan, MN: West Publishing Company.

Dutfield Graham (2000). *Intellectual Property Rights, Trade, and Biodiversity: Seeds and Plant Varieties*, Abingdon-on-Thames, UK: Earthscan Publications.

Engelen Frank (2004). *Interpretation of Tax Treaties under International Law*, IBFD Publications BV.

Fikentscher Wolfgang (1980). *The Draft International Code of Conduct on the Transfer of Technology: A Study in Third World Development*, Munich: Max Planck Institute for Foreign and International Patent, Copyright, and Competition Law,.

Foltea Marina (2012). *International Organisations in WTO Dispute Settlement: How Much Institutional Sensitivity?* Cambridge University Press.

French Duncan (2005). *International Law and Policy of Sustainable Development*, Manchester University Press.

Gardiner Richard K. (2008). *Treaty Interpretation*, Cambridge University Press.

Gervais Daniel (2012). *The TRIPS Agreement: Drafting History and Analysis*, 4th edn, London: Sweet & Maxwell.

Ghidini Gustavo (2010). *Innovation, Competition and Consumer Welfare in Intellectual Property Law*, Cheltenham, UK: Edward Elgar Publishing .

Gollin Micheal A. (2008). *Driving Innovation: Intellectual Property Strategies for a Dynamic World*, Cambridge University Press.

Harrison Jeffrey L. (2003). *Law and Economics in a Nutshell*, 3rd edn, Eagan, MN: West Group.

Haugen Hans Morten (2007). *The Right to Food and the TRIPS Agreement: With a Particular Emphasis on Developing Countries' Measures for Food Production and Distribution*, Leiden, Netherlands: Martinus Nijhoff Publishers.

Hestermeyer Holger (2007). *Human Rights and the WTO: The Case of Patents and Access to Medicines*, Oxford University Press.

Ho Cynthia M. (2011). *Access to Medicine in the Global Economy: International Agreements on Patents and Related Rights*, Oxford University Press.

Hoekman Bernard and Beata Smarzynska Javorcik (2006). *Global Integration and Technology Transfer*, World Bank, Basingstoke, UK: Palgrave Macmillan.

Honkonen Tuula (2009). *The Common but Differentiated Responsibility Principle in Multilateral Environmental Agreements: Regulatory and Policy Aspects*, New York: Kluwer Law International.

Howkins John (2002). *The Creative Economy: How People Make Money from Ideas*, London: Penguin Press.

Howse Robert (2007). *The WTO System: Law, Politics & Legitimacy*, London: Cameron May.

Jaffe Adam B. and Josh Lerner (2004). *Innovation and Its Discontents: How Our Broken Patent System Is Endangering Innovation and Progress, and What to Do about It*, Princeton University Press.

Joyner Daniel H. (2012). *Interpreting the Nuclear Non-proliferation Treaty*, Oxford University Press.

Khor Martin (2001). *Globalisation and the Crisis of Sustainable Development*, Penang, Malaysia: Third World Network.

Kim Linsu (1997). *Imitation to Innovation: The Dynamics of Korea's Technological Learning*, Cambridge, MA: Harvard Business Press.

Kim Linsu and Richard R. Nelson (2000). *Technology, Learning, and Innovation: Experiences of Newly Industrializing Economies*, Cambridge University Press.

Kingston William (2010). *Beyond Intellectual Property: Matching Information Protection to Innovation*, Cheltenham, UK: Edward Elgar Publishing.

Kinsella Stephan N. (2008). *Against Intellectual Property*, Auburn, AL: Ludwig von Mises Institute.

Kuanpoth Jakkrit (2010). *Patent Rights in Pharmaceuticals in Developing Countries: Major Challenges for the Future*, Cheltenham, UK: Edward Elgar Publishing.

Li Yuwen (1994). *Transfer of Technology for Deep Sea-bed Mining: The 1982 Law of the Sea Convention and Beyond*, Berlin, Germany: Kluwer Academic Publishers.

Linderfalk Ulf (2007). *On the Interpretation of Treaties: The Modern International Law as Expressed in the 1969 Vienna Convention on the Law of Treaties*, Houten: Springer Netherlands.

Luo Yan (2010). *Anti-dumping in the WTO, the EU and China: The Rise of Legalization in the Trade Regime and Its Consequences*, Vol. LXIX, New York: Kluwer Law International.

Maggiolino Mariateresa (2011). *Intellectual Property and Antitrust: A Comparative Economic Analysis of US and EU Law*, Cheltenham, UK: Edward Elgar Publishing.

Malbon Justin, Charles Lawson and Mark Davison (2014). *The WTO Agreement on Trade-Related Aspects of Intellectual Property Rights: A Commentary*, Cheltenham, UK: Edward Elgar Publishing.

Maskus Keith E. (2000). *Intellectual Property Rights in the Global Economy*, Washington, D.C.: Institute for International Economics.

Matsushita Mitsuo, Thomas J. Schoenbaum and Petros C. Mavroidis (2006). *The World Trade Organisation: Law, Practice, and Policy*, 2nd edn, Oxford University Press.

May Christopher (2007). *The World Intellectual Property Organisation: Resurgence and the Development Agenda*, London: Routledge.

McCarthy Thomas J. (1995). *McCarthy's Desk Encyclopaedia of Intellectual Property*, Washington, D.C.: Bureau of National Affairs.

McNair Arnold Duncan (1961). *The Law of Treaties*, Oxford: Clarendon Press.

Merrill Stephen A., Richard C. Levin and Mark B. Meyers (2004). *A Patent System for the 21st Century*, Washington, D.C.: National Academies Press.

Miller John C., Ruben M. Serrato, Jose Miguel Represas-Cardenas and Griffith A. Kundahl (2005). *The Handbook of Nanotechnology: Business, Policy and Intellectual Property Law*, Hoboken, NJ: John Wiley & Sons.

Monti Giorgio (2007). *EC Competition Law: Law in Context*, Cambridge University Press.

Moon Suerie and Wolfgang Hein (2013). *Informal Norms in Global Governance: Human Rights, Intellectual Property Rules and Access to Medicines*, Farnham, UK: Ashgate Publishing.

Muchlinski Peter (2007). *Multinational Enterprises and the Law*, 2nd edn, Oxford University Press.

Munro Joseph Edwin Crawford (1884). *The Patents, Designs, and Trade Marks Act, 1883*, Section 22, London: Stevens and Sons.

Nguyãên Tú Thanh (2010). *Competition Law, Technology Transfer and the TRIPS Agreement: Implications for Developing Countries*, Cheltenham, UK: Edward Elgar Publishing.

Ockwell David and Alexandra Mallett (2012). *Low-Carbon Technology Transfer: From Rhetoric to Reality*, London: Routledge.

OECD (1989). *Competition Policy and Intellectual Property Rights*, Paris: Organisation for Economic Co-operation and Development Publishing.

(1997). *Patents and Innovation in the International Context*, OCDE/GD (97) 210, Paris: Organisation for Economic Co-operation and Development Publishing.

O'Connell Donal (2011). *Harvesting External Innovation: Managing External Relationships and Intellectual Property*, London: Gower Publishing.

O'Keefe Roger and Christian J. Tams (2013). *The United Nations Convention on Jurisdictional Immunities of States and Their Property: A Commentary*, Oxford University Press.

O'Neill Aidan (2011). *EU Law for UK Lawyers*, Oxford, UK: Hart Publishing.

Orakhelashvili Alexander (2008). *The Interpretation of Acts and Rules in Public International Law*, Oxford University Press.

Papadopoulos Anestis S. (2010). *The International Dimension of EU Competition Law and Policy*, Cambridge University Press.

Park Jae Hun (2010). *Patents and Industry Standards*, Cheltenham, UK: Edward Elgar Publishing.

Patel Surendra J., Pedro Roffe and Abdulqawi A. Yusuf (2001). *International Technology Transfer: The Origins and Aftermath of the United Nations Negotiations on a Draft Code of Conduct*, New York: Kluwer Law International.

Pauwelyn Joost (2008). *Conflict of Norms in Public International Law: How WTO Law Relates to Other Rules of International Law*, Cambridge University Press.

Penrose Edith Tilton (1951). *The Economics of the International Patent System*, Johns Hopkins Press.

Pugatch Meir Perez (2006). *The Intellectual Property Debate: Perspectives from Law, Economics and Political Economy*, Cheltenham, UK: Edward Elgar Publishing.

Qureshi Asif H.(2012). *Interpreting WTO Agreements: Problems and Perspectives*, Cambridge University Press.

Radhakrishnan R. and S. Balasubramanian (2008). *Intellectual Property Rights: Text and Cases*, New Delhi: Anurag Jain for Excel Books.

Ramanathan Kavasseri, Keith Jacobs and Madhusudan Bandyopadhyay (2011). *Technology Transfer and Small and Medium Enterprises in Developing Countries*, New Delhi: Daya Publishing House.

Reinsdorf Marshall and Matthew J. Slaughter (2009). *International Trade in Services and Intangibles in the Era of Globalization*, University of Chicago Press.

Rimmer Matthew (2011). *Intellectual Property and Climate Change: Inventing Clean Technologies*, Cheltenham, UK: Edward Elgar Publishing.

Rodger Barry J. and Angus MacCulloch (2015). *Competition Law and Policy in the EU and UK*, London: Routledge.

Rodrigues Edson Beas (2012). *The General Exception Clauses of the TRIPS Agreement: Promoting Sustainable Development*, Vol. XVII, Cambridge University Press.

Ros Jaime (2013). *Rethinking Economic Development, Growth, and Institutions*, Oxford University Press.

Sampson Gary P. (2005). *The WTO and Sustainable Development*, Tokyo: UNU Press.

Sands Philippe and Jacqueline Peel (2012). *Principles of International Environmental Law*, Cambridge University Press.

Schmidt Hedvig (2009). *Competition Law, Innovation and Antitrust: An Analysis of Tying and Technological Integration*, Cheltenham, UK: Edward Elgar Publishing.

Schwarzenberger Georg (1965). *The Inductive Approach to International Law*, University of Michigan Library.

Sell Susan K. (1998). *Power and Ideas: North-South Politics of Intellectual Property and Antitrust*, State University of New York Press.

Senftleben Martin (2004). *Copyright, Limitations, and the Three-step Test: An Analysis of the Three-Step Test in International and EC Copyright Law*, New York: Kluwer Law International.

Sinclair Ian McTaggart (1984). *The Vienna Convention on the Law of Treaties*, Manchester University Press.

Stern Nicholas (2007). *The Economics of Climate Change – The Stern Review*, Cambridge University Press.

Stoll Peter-Tobias, Jan Busche and Katrin Arend (2009). *WTO: Trade-Related Aspects of Intellectual Property Rights*, Vol. VII, Leiden, Netherlands: Martinus Nijhoff Publishers.

Štrba Susan Isiko (2012). *International Copyright Law and Access to Education in Developing Countries: Exploring Multilateral Legal and Quasi-Legal Solutions*, Leiden, Netherlands: Martinus Nijhoff Publishers.

Taubman Antony (2011). *A Practical Guide to Working with TRIPS*, Oxford University Press.

Taubman Antony, Hannu Wager and Jayashree Watal (2012). *A Handbook on the WTO TRIPS Agreement*, Cambridge University Press.

Trebilcock Michael, Robert Howse and Antonia Eliason (2013). *The Regulation of International Trade*, 4th edn, London: Routledge.

UNCTAD (2010). *Intellectual Property in the World Trade Organisation: Turning It into Developing Countries' Real Property*, United Nations, New York and Geneva.

UNCTAD and ICTSD (2005). *Resource Book on TRIPS and Development*, Cambridge University Press.

UNDP (2001). *Human Development Report 2001: Making New Technologies Work for Human Development*, Oxford University Press.

(2003). *Making Global Trade Work for People*, Abingdon-on-Thames, UK: Earthscan Publications.

UNIDO (2008). *Public Goods for Economic Development*, Vienna: United Nations Industrial Development Organization.

Van Damme Isabelle (2009). *Treaty Interpretation by the WTO Appellate Body*, Oxford University Press.

van den Berg Hendrik and Joshua J. Lewer (2007). *International Trade and Economic Growth*, Armonk, NY: M.E. Sharpe.

van den Bossche Peter and Werner Zdouc (2013). *The Law and Policy of the World Trade Organisation*, 3rd edn, Cambridge University Press.

Villiger Mark Eugen (2009). *Commentary on the 1969 Vienna Convention on the Law of Treaties*, Leiden, Netherlands: Martinus Nijhoff Publishers.

Voigt Christina (2009). *Sustainable Development as a Principle of International Law: Resolving Conflicts between Climate Measures and WTO Law*, Leiden, Netherlands: Martinus Nijhoff Publishers.

Waincymer Jeff (2002). *WTO Litigation: Procedural Aspects of Formal Dispute Settlement*, London: Cameron May.

Wallerstein Mitchel B., Mary Ellen Mogee and Roberta A. Schoen (1993). *Global Dimensions of Intellectual Property Rights in Science and Technology*, Washington, D.C.: National Academy Press.

Watal Jayashree (2001). *Intellectual Property Rights in the WTO and Developing Countries*, New York: Kluwer Law International.

Weeramantry J. Romesh (2012). *Treaty Interpretation in Investment Arbitration*, Oxford University Press.

Weiler Todd (2013). *The Interpretation of International Investment Law: Equality, Discrimination and Minimum Standards of Treatment in Historical Context*, Leiden, Netherlands: Koninklijke Brill NV.

WIPO (1997). *Introduction to Intellectual Property: Theory and Practice*, New York: Kluwer Law International.

(2004). *WIPO Intellectual Property Handbook*, Publication No. 489(E), 2nd edn, Geneva: World Intellectual Property Organization. reprinted 2008.

(2007). *WIPO Patent Drafting Manual*, Publication No. 867(E), Geneva: World Intellectual Property Organization.

(2009). *WIPO Guide to Using Patent Information*, Geneva: World Intellectual Property Organization.

Witt Anne C. (2016). *The More Economic Approach to EU Antitrust Law*, Oxford and Portland, OR: Hart Publishing.

Wolfrum Rudiger and Nele Matz (2003). *Conflicts in International Environmental Law*, Vol. CLXIV, Berlin and Heidelberg: Springer-Verlag .

World Trade Organization (2008). *Understanding the WTO*, Geneva, Switzerland: World Trade Organisation.

(2012). *WTO Analytical Index: Guide to WTO Law and Practice*, 3rd edn, Vol. I, Cambridge University Press.

Xiong Ping (2012). *An International Law Perspective on the Protection of Human Rights in the TRIPS Agreement: An Interpretation of the TRIPS Agreement in Relation to the Right to Health*, Leiden, Netherlands: Martinus Nijhoff Publishers.

Yamane Hiroko (2011). *Interpreting TRIPS: Globalisation of Intellectual Property and Access to Medicines*, Oxford, UK: Hart Publishing.

Yamin Farhana and Joanna Depledge (2004). *The International Climate Change Regime: A Guide to Rules, Institutions and Procedures*, Cambridge University Press.

Yasseen Mustafa Kamil (1976). *L'interprétation des Traités d'après la Convention de Vienne sur le Droit des Traités*, Leiden, Netherlands: Martinus Nijhoff Publishers.

Zemer Lior (2007). *The Idea of Authorship in Copyright*, Farnham, UK: Ashgate Publishing.

Zimmermann Andreas (2011). *The 1951 Convention Relating to the Status of Refugees and Its 1967 Protocol: A Commentary*, Oxford University Press.

Zuniga P., D. Guellec, H. Dernis, M. Khan, T. Okazaki, and C Webb. (2009). *OECD Patent Statistics Manual*, Paris: Organisation for Economic Co-operation and Development.

BOOK CHAPTERS

Abbott Frederick M. (2004). WTO Dispute Settlement Practice Relating to the Agreement on Trade-Related Intellectual Property Rights, in Federico Ortino and Ernst-Ulrich Petersmann (eds.). *The WTO Dispute Settlement System 1995–2003*, New York: Kluwer Law International, pp. 421–53.

—— (2008). Intellectual Property Rights in World Trade, in Andrew T. Guzman and A. O. Sykes (eds.). *Research Handbook in International Economic Law*, Cheltenham, UK: Edward Elgar Publishing Limited, pp. 444–84.

Abi-Saab Georges (2010). The Appellate Body and Treaty Interpretation, in Malgosia Fitzmaurice, Olufemi Elias and Panos Merkouris (eds.). *Treaty Interpretation and the Vienna Convention on the Law of Treaties: 30 Years On*, Leiden, Netherlands: Martinus Nijhoff Publishers, pp. 99–109.

Alker Daniel and Franz Heidhues (2002). Farmers' Rights and Intellectual Property Rights – Reconciling Conflicting Concepts, in R.E. Evenson, V. Santaniello and V. Zilberman (eds.). *Economic and Social Issues in Agricultural Biotechnology*, Wallingford, UK: CABI Publishing, pp. 61–85.

Anderson Robert D. (2010). Competition Policy and Intellectual Property in the WTO: More Guidance Needed? in Josef Drexl (ed.). *Research Handbook on Intellectual Property and Competition Law*, Cheltenham, UK: Edward Elgar Publishing, pp. 451–73.

Asrani Rajesh (2015). Economic Implications of Intellectual Property Rights in Evolving Markets, in Mathew J. Manimala and Kishinchand Poornima Wasdani (eds.). *Entrepreneurial Ecosystem: Perspectives from Emerging Economies*, Delhi: Springer India, pp. 109–31.

Azmi, Ida Madieha bt Abdul GhaniS (2015). Scope and Duration of Compulsory Licensing: Lessons from National Experiences, in Reto M. Hilty and Kung-Chung Liu (eds.). *Compulsory Licensing: Practical Experiences and Ways Forward*, MPI Studies on Intellectual Property and Competition Law 22, Berlin and Heidelberg: Springer-Verlag, pp. 207–20.

Balasegaram Manica, Michelle Childs, and James Arkinstall (2014). The Fight for Global Access to Essential Health Commodities, in Garrett W. Brown, Gavin Yamey and Sarah Wamala (eds.). *The Handbook of Global Health Policy*, Hoboken, NJ: John Wiley & Sons, pp. 245–66.

Banasevic Nicholas and Per Hellstrom (2010). Windows into the World of Abuse of Dominance: An Analysis of the Commission's 2004 Microsoft Decision and the CFI's 2007 Judgment, in Luca Rubini (ed.). *Microsoft on Trial: Legal and Economic Analysis of a Transatlantic Antitrust Case*, Cheltenham, UK: Edward Elgar Publishing.

Barbosa Denis Borges (2010). Minimum Standards vs. Harmonization in the TRIPS Context: The Nature of Obligations under TRIPS and Modes of Implementation at the National Level in Monist and Dualist Systems, in Carlos M. Correa (ed.). *Research Handbook on the Protection of Intellectual Property under WTO Rules: Intellectual Property in the WTO*, Vol. I, Cheltenham, UK: Edward Elgar Publishing, pp. 52–109.

Chung Rae Kwon (1998). The Role of Government in the Transfer of Environmentally Sound Technology, in Tim Forsyth (ed.). *Positive Measures for Technology Transfer under the Climate Change Convention*, London: Royal Institute of International Affairs, pp. 47–61.

Correa Carlos M. (2003). Formulating Effective Pro-Development National Intellectual Property Policies, in Christophe Bellmann, Graham Dutfield and Ricardo Melendez-Ortiz (eds.). *Trading in Knowledge: Development Perspectives on TRIPS, Trade and Sustainability*, Abingdon-on-Thames, UK: Earthscan Publications, pp. 209–17.

(2005). Can the TRIPS Agreement Foster Technology Transfer to Developing Countries? in Keith E. Maskus and Jerome Reichman (eds.). *International Public Goods and Transfer of Technology under a Globalized Intellectual Property Regime*, Cambridge University Press, pp. 227–56.

(2007). The TRIPS Agreement and Developing Countries, in Arthur E. Appleton and Michael G. Plummer (eds.). *The World Trade Organization: Legal, Economic and Political Analysis*, New York: Springer Science + Business Media, pp. 420–55.

(2008). Patent Rights, in Carlos M. Correa and Abdulqawi Yusuf (eds.). *Intellectual Property and International Trade: The TRIPS Agreement*, New York: Kluwer Law International, pp. 227–57.

(2014). Intellectual Property and Competition – Room to Legislate under International Law, in Frederick Abbott et al. (eds.), *Using Competition Law to Promote Access to Health Technologies: A Guidebook for Low- and Middle-Income Countries*, New York: United Nations Development Programme, pp. 35–57.

Correa Carlos M. (2016). Intellectual Property Rights under the UNFCCC: Without Response to Developing Countries' Concerns, in Joshua D. Sarnoff (ed.), *Research Handbook on Intellectual Property and Climate Change*, Cheltenham, UK: Edward Elgar Publishing, pp. 74–91.

Cottier Thomas and Krista Nadakavukaren Schefer (2000). Good Faith and the Protection of Legitimate Expectations in the WTO, in Marco Bronckers and Reinhard Quick (eds.). *New Directions in International Economic Law: Essays in Honour of John H. Jackson*, New York: Kluwer Law International.

Dahrendorf Anke (2010). Global Proliferation of Bilateral and Regional Trade Agreements: A Threat for the World Trade Organisation and/or for Developing Countries? in Jana Hertwig and Sylvia Maus (eds.). *Global Risks: Constructing World Order Through Law, Politics and Economics*, Frankfurt, Germany: Peter Lang GmbH, pp. 39–66.

Dinwoodie Graeme B. and Rochelle Cooper Dreyfuss (2005). WTO Dispute Resolution and the Preservation of the Public Domain of Science under International Law, in Keith E. Maskus and Jerome Reichman (eds.). *International Public Goods and Transfer of Technology Under a Globalized Intellectual Property Regime*, Cambridge University Press, pp. 861–83.

Drexl Josef (2005). The Critical Role of Competition Law in Preserving Public Goods in Conflict with Intellectual Property Rights, in Keith E. Maskus and Jerome

Reichman (eds.). *International Public Goods and Transfer of Technology under a Globalized Intellectual Property Regime*, Cambridge University Press, pp. 707–25.

Fink Carsten (2005a). Comment: Competition Law as a Means of Containing Intellectual Property Rights, in Keith E. Maskus and Jerome Reichman (eds.). *International Public Goods and Transfer of Technology under a Globalized Intellectual Property Regime*, Cambridge University Press, pp. 770–3.

(2005b). Entering the Jungle of Intellectual Property Rights Exhaustion and Parallel Importation, in Carsten Fink and Keith E. Maskus (eds.). *Intellectual Property and Development: Lessons from Recent Economic Research*, World Bank and Oxford University Press, pp. 171–87.

(2013). Intellectual Property Rights: Economic Principles and Trade Rules, in Arvid Lukauskas, Robert M. Stern and Gianni Zanini (eds.). *Handbook of Trade Policy for Development*, Oxford University Press, pp. 740–67.

Fink Carsten and Carlos A. Primo Braga (2005). How Stronger Protection of Intellectual Property Rights Affects International Trade Flows, in Carsten Fink and Keith E. Maskus (eds.). *Intellectual Property and Development: Lessons from Recent Economic Research*, a copublication of the World Bank and Oxford University Press, pp. 19–40.

Fink Carsten and Patrick Reichenmiller (2006). Tightening TRIPS: Intellectual Property Provisions of US Free Trade Agreements, in Richard Newfarmer (ed.). *Trade, Doha, and Development: A Window into the Issues*, Washington, D.C.: World Bank, pp. 289–303.

Fisher William (2001). Theories of Intellectual Property, in Stephen R. Munzer (ed.). *New Essays in the Legal and Political Theory of Property*, Cambridge University Press, pp. 168–200.

Frankel Susy (2010). The Applicability of GATT Jurisprudence to the Interpretation of the TRIPS Agreement, in Carlos Correa (ed.). *Research Handbook on the Interpretation and Enforcement of Intellectual Property Under WTO Rules: Intellectual Property in the WTO*, Vol. II, pp. 3–23.

Galal Essam E. (2001). The Developing Countries' Quest for a Code, in J. Surendra Patel, Pedro Roffe and A. Abdulqawi Yusuf (eds.). *International Technology Transfer: The Origins and Aftermath of the United Nations Negotiations on a Draft Code of Conduct*, New York: Kluwer Law International, pp. 199–215.

Gallego Beatriz Conde (2010). Intellectual Property Rights and Competition Policy, in Carlos M. Correa (ed.). *Research Handbook on the Protection of Intellectual Property under WTO Rules: Intellectual Property in the WTO*, Vol. I, Cheltenham, UK: Edward Elgar Publishing, pp. 226–65.

Ganslandt Mattias and Keith E. Maskus (2008). Intellectual Property Rights, Parallel Imports and Strategic Behaviour, in Keith E. Maskus (ed.). *Intellectual Property, Growth and Trade*, Bingley, UK: Emerald Group Publishing, pp. 263–88.

Gervais Daniel J. (2007a). The TRIPS Agreement and the Changing Landscape of International Intellectual Property, in Paul Torremans, Hailing Shan and Johan Erauw (eds.). *Intellectual Property and TRIPS Compliance in China: Chinese and European Perspectives*, Cheltenham, UK: Edward Elgar Publishing, pp. 65–84.

Gervais Daniel J. (2007b). The TRIPS Agreement and the Doha Round: History and Impact on Economic Development, in Peter K. Yu (ed.). *Intellectual Property and Information Wealth: Issues and Practices in the Digital Age*, Vol. IV, pp. 23–72.

Grosse Ruse-Khan Henning (2011). Assessing the Need for a General Public Interest Exception in the TRIPS Agreement, in Annette Kur and Marianne Levin (eds.). *Intellectual Property Rights in a Fair World Trade System: Proposal for Reforms of TRIPS*, Cheltenham, UK: Edward Elgar Publishing, pp. 167–207.

Grotto Andrew J. (2004). Organizing for Influence: Developing Countries, Non-Traditional Intellectual Property Rights and the World Intellectual Property Organisation, in Armin Von Bogdandy, Armin Wolfrum and Christiane Philipp (eds.). *Max Planck Yearbook of United Nations Law*, 8(1). Leiden, Netherlands: Martinus Nijhoff Publishers, pp. 359–82.

Heinemann Andreas (1996). Antitrust Law of Intellectual Property in the TRIPS Agreement of the World Trade Organisation, in Friedrich-Karl Beier and Gerhard Schricker (eds.). *From GATT to TRIPS – The Agreement on Trade-Related Aspects of Intellectual Property Rights*, IIC Studies, Munich: Max Planck Institute for Foreign and International Patent, Copyright and Competition Law, pp. 239–47.

Howse Robert (2003). Comments on the Papers Presented by Ernst-Ulrich Petersmann and William J. Davey/Werner Zdouc, in Thomas Cottier, Petros Constantinos Mavroidis and Marion Panizzon (eds.). *Intellectual Property: Trade, Competition and Sustainable Development*, World Trade Forum Vol. III, Ann Arbor: University of Michigan Press, pp. 95–9.

Howse Robert L. and Makau Mutua (2001). Protecting Human Rights in a Global Economy Challenges for the World Trade Organization, in Hugo Stokke and Anne Tostensen (eds.). *Human Rights in Development Yearbook 1999/2000*, New York: Kluwer Law International.

Jager Melvin F. (2002). The Critical Role of Trade Secret Law in Protecting Intellectual Property Assets, in Robert Goldscheider (ed.). *Licensing Best Practices: The LESI Guide to Strategic Issues and Contemporary Realities*, Hoboken, NJ: John Wiley & Sons, pp. 127–38.

Janis Mark D. (2005). "Minimal" Standards for Patent-Related Antitrust Law under TRIPS, in Keith E. Maskus and Jerome Reichman (eds.). *International Public Goods and Transfer of Technology under a Globalized Intellectual Property Regime*, Cambridge University Press, pp. 774–92.

Kong Qingjiang (2011). China in the WTO: Enforcement of the TRIPS Agreement and the Doha Agenda, in Rohan Kariyawasam (ed.). *Chinese Intellectual Property and Technology Laws*, Cheltenham, UK: Edward Elgar Publishing, pp. 348–66.

Korean Trade Promotion Agency (2000). Case Study 4: The Republic of Korea and the Montreal Protocol, in Veena Jha and Ulrich Hoffmann (eds.). *Achieving Objectives of Multilateral Environmental Agreements: A Package of Trade Measures and Positive Measures*, UNCTAD/ITCD/TED/6, pp. 56–70.

Kur Annette (2011). Limitations and Exceptions under the Three-step-test – How Much Room to Walk the Middle Ground? in Annette Kur and Marianne Levin (eds.). *Intellectual Property Rights in a Fair World Trade System: Proposal for Reforms of TRIPS*, Cheltenham, UK: Edward Elgar Publishing, pp. 208–61.

Laperrouza Marc (2010). Trade, Technology Transfer and Institutional Catch-up, in Fabrice Lehmann and Jean-Pierre Lehmann (eds.). *Peace and Prosperity through World Trade*, Cambridge University Press, pp. 222–6.

Levin Marianne (2011). The Pendulum Keeps Swinging – Present Discussions on and around the TRIPS Agreement, in Annette Kur (ed.). *Intellectual Property Rights in a Fair World Trade System: Proposals for Reform of TRIPS*, Cheltenham, UK: Edward Elgar Publishing, pp. 3–60.

Lopez Andres (2009). Innovation and Appropriability, Empirical Evidence and Research Agenda, in *The Economics of Intellectual Property: Suggestions for Further Research in Developing Countries and Countries with Economies in Transition*, Geneva: World Intellectual Property Organization, pp. 1–32.

Lowe Vaughan (1999). Sustainable Development and Unsustainable Arguments, in Alan Boyle and David Freestone (eds.). *International Law and Sustainable Development: Past Achievements and Future Challenges*, Oxford University Press, pp. 19–38.

Machado-Filho Haroldo and Marcelo Khaled Poppe (2011). Transfer of Technology under the Climate Change Regime, in Ronaldo Seroa da Motta et al. (eds.). *Climate Change in Brazil: Economic, Social and Regulatory Aspects*, Brazil: Institute for Applied Economic Research, pp. 329–48.

Maskus Keith E. (2002). Benefiting from Intellectual Property Protection, in Bernard Hoekman, Aaditya Mattoo and Philip English (eds.). *Development, Trade and the WTO: A Handbook*, Washington, D.C.: World Bank, pp. 369–81.

Maskus Keith E. and Jerome Reichman (2005). The Globalization of Private Knowledge Goods and the Privatization of Global Public Goods, in Keith E. Maskus and Jerome Reichman (eds.). *International Public Goods and Transfer of Technology Under a Globalized Intellectual Property Regime*, Cambridge University Press, pp. 3–45.

McManis Charles R. and Jorge L. Contreras (2014). Compulsory Licensing of Intellectual Property: A Viable Policy Lever for Promoting Access to Critical Technologies, in Gustavo Ghidini, Rudolph J. R. Peritz and Marco Ricolfi (eds.). *TRIPS and Developing Countries: Towards a New IP World Order?* Cheltenham, UK: Edward Elgar Publishing, pp. 109–31.

Menell Peter S. (2000). Intellectual Property: General Theories, in Boudewijn Bouckaert and Gerrit De Geest (eds.). *Encyclopaedia of Law and Economics*, Cheltenham, UK: Edward Elgar Publishing, pp. 129–88.

Nelson Richard R. (1992). What Is "Commercial" and What Is "Public" About Technology, What Should Be? in Natham Rosenberg, Ralph Landau and David C. Mowery (eds.). *Technology and the Wealth of Nations*, Palo Alto, CA: Stanford University Press, pp. 57–71.

Nolte Georg (2013). Subsequent Agreements and Subsequent Practice of States Outside of Judicial or Quasi-judicial Proceedings, in Georg Nolte (ed.). *Treaties and Subsequent Practice*, Oxford University Press, pp. 307–86.

Nyman-Metcalf Katrin, Kumar Dutt Pawan and Archil Chochia (2014). The Freedom to Conduct Business and the Right to Property: The EU Technology Transfer Block Exemption Regulation and the Relationship between Intellectual Property and Competition Law, in Tanel Kerikmäe (ed.). *Protecting Human Rights in the EU: Controversies and Challenges of the Charter of Fundamental Rights*, Berlin, Heidelberg: Springer-Verlag, pp. 37–70.

Park Walter G. (2011). Intellectual Property Rights and Foreign Direct Investment: Lessons from Central America, in Humberto J. Lopez and Rashmi Shankar (eds.). *Getting the Most Out of Free Trade Agreements in Central America*, Washington, D.C.: International Bank for Reconstruction and Development/World Bank, pp. 275–308.

Petersmann Ernst-Ulrich (2003). From Negative to Positive Integration in the WTO: The TRIPS Agreement and the WTO Constitution, in Thomas Cottier and Petros C. Mavroidis (eds.). *Intellectual Property: Trade, Competition and Sustainable Development*, World Trade Forum Vol. 3, Ann Arbor: University of Michigan Press, pp. 21–52.

Pflüger Martin (2008). Paris Convention for the Protection of Industrial Property, in Thomas Cottier and Pierre Véron (eds.). *Concise International and European IP Law: TRIPS, Paris Convention, European Enforcement and Transfer of Technology*, New York: Kluwer Law International, pp. 175–269.

Rajamani Lavanya (2012). Developing Countries and Compliance in the Climate Regime, in Jutta Brunnée, Meinhard Doelle and Lavanya Rajamani (eds.). *Promoting Compliance in an Evolving Climate Regime*, Cambridge University Press, pp. 367–94.

Ramello Giovanni B. (2010). Intellectual Property, Social Justice and Economic Efficiency: Insights from Law and Economics, in Anne Flanagan and Maria L. Montagnani (eds.). *Intellectual Property Law: Economic and Social Justice Perspectives*, Cheltenham, UK: Edward Elgar Publishing, pp. 1–23.

Rao Niranjan C. (2009). TRIPS and Public Health, in Paramita Dasgupta (ed.). *The WTO at the Crossroads*, Cape Town: Concept Publishing Company, pp. 81–100.

Reichman Jerome H. (2014). Intellectual Property in the Twenty-First Century: Will the Developing Countries Lead or Follow? in Mario Cimoli, Giovanni Dosi, Keith E. Maskus, Ruth L. Okediji, Jerome H. Reichman and Joseph E. Stiglitz, (eds.). *Intellectual Property Rights: Legal and Economic Challenges for Development*, Oxford University Press, pp. 111–81.

Robbins Carlo A. (2009). Measuring Payments for the Supply and Use of Intellectual Property, in Marshall Reinsdorf and Matthew J. Slaughter (eds.). *International Trade in Services and Intangibles in the Era of Globalization*, University of Chicago Press, pp. 139–71.

Rodriguez Mendoza Miguel and Marie Wilke (2011). Revisiting the Single Undertaking: Towards a More Balanced Approach to WTO Negotiations, in Deere Birkbeck and Carolyn Birkbeck (eds.). *Making Global Trade Governance Work for Development: Perspectives and Priorities from Developing Countries*, Cambridge University Press, pp. 486–506.

Roffe Pedro (1998). Control of Anti-Competitive Practices in Contractual Licences under the TRIPS Agreement, in Carols M. Correa and Abdulqawi A. Yusuf (eds.). *Intellectual Property and International Trade: The TRIPS Agreement*, New York: Kluwer Law International, pp. 261–96.

(2005). Comment: Technology Transfer on the International Agenda, in Keith E. Maskus and Jerome Reichman (eds.). *International Public Goods and Transfer of Technology under a Globalized Intellectual Property Regime*, Cambridge University Press, pp. 257–64.

Roffe Pedro, Christoph Spennemann and Johanna Von Braun (2010). Intellectual Property Rights in Free Trade Agreements: Moving beyond TRIPS Minimum Standards, in Carlos Correa (ed.). *Research Handbook on the Protection of Intellectual Property under WTO Rules: Intellectual Property in the WTO*, Vol. I, Cheltenham, UK: Edward Elgar Publishing, pp. 266–316.

Sands Philippe (2003). International Courts and the Application of the Concept of "Sustainable Development", in John Hatchard and Amanda Perry-Kessaris (eds.).

Law and Development: Facing Complexity in the 21st Century, London: Cavendish Publishing, pp. 147–57.

Schovsbo Jens (2011). Fire and Water Make Steam – Redefining the Role of Competition Law, in Annette Kur and Marianne Levin (eds.). *Intellectual Property Rights in a Fair World Trade System: Proposal for Reforms of TRIPS*, Cheltenham, UK: Edward Elgar Publishing, pp. 308–58.

Shapiro Carl (2002). Navigating the Patent Thicket: Cross Licenses, Patent Pools, and Standard Setting, in Adam B. Jaffe, Josh Lerner, and Scott Stern (eds.). *Innovation Policy and the Economy*, Cambridge, MA: MIT Press, pp. 119–50.

Siplon Patricia (2013). The Troubled Path to HIV/AIDS Universal Treatment Access: Snatching Defeat from the Jaws of Victory? in Raymond A. Smith (ed.). *Global HIV/AIDS Politics, Policy, and Activism: Persistent Challenges and Emerging Issues*, Santa Barbara, CA: ABC-CLIO, LLC.

Straus Joseph (1996). Implications of the TRIPS Agreement in the Field of Patent Law, in Friedrich-Karl Beier and Gerhard Schricker (eds.). *From GATT to TRIPS: The Agreement on Trade-Related Aspects of Intellectual Property Rights*, Hoboken, NJ: John Wiley & Sons , pp. 160–215.

Thompson Dennis (2001). An Overview of the Draft Code, in Patel J. Surendra, Roffe Pedro and Yusuf A. Abdulqawi (eds.). *International Technology Transfer: The Origins and Aftermath of the United Nations Negotiations on a Draft Code of Conduct*, New York: Kluwer Law International, pp. 51–75.

Tian Yijun George (2012). Consumer Protection and IP Abuse Prevention under the WTO Framework, in Jeremy Malcolm (ed.). *Consumers in the Information Society: Access, Fairness and Representation*, Kuala Lumpur: Consumers International.

Ullrich Hanns (2005). Expansionist Intellectual Property Protection and Reductionist Competition Rules: A TRIPS Perspective, in Keith E. Maskus and Jerome Reichman (eds.). *International Public Goods and Transfer of Technology under a Globalized Intellectual Property Regime*, Cambridge University Press, pp. 726–57.

Villiger Mark E. (2011). The Rules on Interpretation: Misgivings, Misunderstandings, Miscarriage? The 'Crucible' Intended by the International Law Commission, in Enzo Cannizzaro (ed.). *The Law of Treaties beyond the Vienna Convention*, Oxford University Press, pp. 105–22.

Von Hase Andres Moncayo (2008). The Application and Interpretation of the Agreement on Trade-Related Aspects of Intellectual Property Rights, in Carlos M. Correa and Abdulqawi A. Yusuf (eds.). 2nd edn, *Intellectual Property and International Trade: The TRIPS Agreement*, New York: Kluwer Law International, pp. 83–124.

Watal Jayashree (2000). India: The Issue of Technology Transfer in the Context of the Montreal Protocol, in Veena Jha and Ulrich Hoffmann (eds.). *Achieving Objectives of Multilateral Environmental Agreements: A Package of Trade Measures and Positive Measures*, UNCTAD/ITCD/TED/6, pp. 45–55.

(2003). Parallel Imports and IPR-Based Dominant Positions: Where Do India's Interests Lie? in Thomas Cottier and Petros C. Mavroidis (eds.). *Intellectual Property: Trade, Competition and Sustainable Development*, University of Michigan Press, pp. 199–210.

Xu Shiying (2011). Intellectual Property Protection and Competition Law, in Rohan Kariyawasam (ed.). *Chinese Intellectual Property and Technology Laws*, Cheltenham, UK: Edward Elgar Publishing, pp. 323–47.

Yu Peter (2010). The Objectives and Principles of the TRIPS Agreement, in Carlos M. Correa (ed.). *Research Handbook on the Protection of Intellectual Property under WTO Rules: Intellectual Property in the WTO*, Vol. I, Cheltenham, UK: Edward Elgar Publishing, pp.146–91.

Yu Vicente Paolo B. (2010). The UN Climate Change Convention and Developing Countries: Towards Effective Implementation, in Julio Faundez and Tan Celine (eds.). *International Economic Law, Globalization and Developing Countries*, Cheltenham, UK: Edward Elgar Publishing, pp. 379–410.

Yusuf Abdulqawi A. (1989). Developing Countries and Trade-Related Aspects of Intellectual Property Rights, in UNCTAD (ed.). *Uruguay Round: Papers on Selected Issues*, UN Publication, UNCTAD/ITP/10.

(2001). Technology Transfer in the Global Environmental Agreements: A New Twist to the North-South Debate, in Surendra J. Patel, Pedro Roffe and Abdulqawi A. Yusuf (eds.). *International Technology Transfer: The Origins and Aftermath of the United Nations Negotiations on a Draft Code of Conduct*, New York: Kluwer Law International, pp. 313–20.

(2008). TRIPS: Background, Principles and General Provisions, in Carlos M. Correa and Abdulqawi A. Yusuf (eds.). *Intellectual Property and International Trade: The TRIPS Agreement*, 2nd edn, New York: Kluwer Law International, pp. 3–21.

Zhuang Wei (2013). Evolution of the Patent System in China, in Frederick M. Abbott, Carlos M. Correa and Peter Drahos (eds.). *Emerging Markets and the World Patent Order*, Cheltenham, UK: Edward Elgar Publishing, pp. 155–80.

ARTICLES

Abbott Frederick M. (2001). The TRIPS-Legality of Measures Taken to Address Public Health Crises: A Synopsis, *Widener Law Symposium Journal* 7, pp. 71–85.

(2002). The Doha Declaration on the TRIPS Agreement and Public Health: Lighting a Dark Corner at the WTO, *Journal of International Economic Law* 5(2), pp. 469–505.

(2004). Are the Competition Rules in the WTO TRIPS Agreement Adequate? *Journal of International Economic Law* 7(3), pp. 687–703.

(2005). Toward a New Era of Objective Assessment in the Field of TRIPS and Variable Geometry for the Preservation of Multilateralism, *Journal of International Economic Law* 8(1), pp. 77–100.

Adam Alexander (2009). Technology Transfer to Combat Climate Change: Opportunities and Obligations under TRIPS and Kyoto, *Journal of High Technology Law* 9 (1), pp. 1–20.

Anderson Robert D. (1998). The Interface between Competition Policy and Intellectual Property in the Context of the International Trading System, *Journal of International Economic Law*, pp. 655–78.

Anderson Robert D. and Hannu Wager (2006). Human Rights, Development and the WTO: The Case of Intellectual Property Rights and Competition Policy, *Journal of International Economic Law* 9(3), pp. 707–47.

Athreye Suma and John Cantwell (2007). Creating Competition? *Globalisation and the Emergence of New Technology Producers*, Research Policy 36, pp. 209–26.

Aution Erkko, Ari-Pekka Hameri and Olli Vuola (2004). A Framework of Industrial Knowledge Spillovers in Big-Science Centres, *Research Policy* 33, pp. 107–26.

Baird Sean (2013). Magic and Hope: Relaxing TRIPS-Plus Provisions to Promote Access to Affordable Pharmaceuticals, *Boston College Journal of Law & Social Justice* 33(1), pp. 107–45.

Barbosa Denis Borges, Margaret Chon and Andrés Moncayo Von Hase,(2007). Slouching towards Development in International Intellectual Property, *Michigan State Law Review*, pp. 71–141.

Barfield Claude E. and Mark A. Groombridge (1999). Parallel Trade in the Pharmaceutical Industry: Implications for Innovation, Consumer Welfare, and Health Policy, *Fordham Intellectual Property, Media & Entertainment Law Journal* 10, pp. 185–265.

Barral Virginie (2012). Sustainable Development in International Law: Nature and Operation of an Evolutive Legal Norm, *The European Journal of International Law* 23 (2), pp. 377–400.

Barrett Margreth (2000). United States' Doctrine of Exhaustion: Parallel Imports of Patented Goods, *Northern Kentucky Law Review* 27(5), pp. 911–84.

Barton John H. (2000). Reforming the Patent System, *Science* 287(5460), pp. 1933–4.

Bently Lionel (2011). Exclusions from Patentability and Exceptions to Patentees' Rights: Taking Exceptions Seriously, *Current Legal Problems*, pp. 1–33.

Berger Jonathan Michael (2002). Tripping over Patents, AIDS, Access to Treatment and The Manufacturing of Scarcity, *Connecticut Journal of International Law* 17, pp. 157–248.

Bettencourt Luis M. A., Jessika E. Trancik and Jasleen Kaur (2013). Determinants of the Pace of Global Innovation in Energy Technologies, *Plos One* 8(10), e67864.

Blalock Garrick and Francisco Veloso (2006). Imports, Productivity Growth, and Supply Chain Learning, Department of Engineering and Public Policy, Paper 127.

Bodansky Daniel (1993). The United Nations Framework Convention on Climate Change: A Commentary, *Yale Journal of International Law*, 18, pp. 451–558.

(2012). What's in a Concept? Global Public Goods, International Law and Legitimacy, *The European Journal of International Law*, 23(3), pp. 651–68.

Boldrin Michele and David Levine (2002). The Case against Intellectual Property, *The American Economic Review*, 92(2), pp. 209–12.

(2013). The Case against Patents, *Journal of Economic Perspectives*, 27(1), pp. 3–22.

Bolton Michele K. (1993). Imitation Versus Innovation: Lessons to be Learned from the Japanese, *Organisational Dynamics*, 21(3), pp. 30–45.

Borda Aldo Zammit (2013). A Formal Approach to Article 38(1)(d) of the ICJ Statute from the Perspective of the International Criminal Courts and Tribunals, *The European Journal of International Law*, 24(2), pp. 649–61.

Bozeman Barry (2000). Technology Transfer and Public Policy: A Review of Research and Theory, *Research Policy* 29, pp. 627–55.

Byers Michael (2002). Abuse of Rights, An Old Principle, A New Age, *McGill Law Journal*, 47, pp. 389–431.

Cameron Edwin (2004). Patents and Public Health: Principle, Politics and Paradox, *SCRIPT-ed*, 1(4), pp. 517–44.

Cann Wesley A. (2004). On the Relationship between Intellectual Property Rights and the Need of Less-Developed Countries for Access to Pharmaceuticals: Creating a

Legal Duty to Supply Under a Theory of Progressive Global Constitutionalism, *University of Pennsylvania Journal of International Economic Law*, 2(3), pp. 755–944.

Catanese Adrienne (1985). Paris Convention, Patent Protection, and Technology Transfer, *Boston University International Law Journal*, 3, pp. 209–27.

Champ Paul and Attaran Amir (2002). Patent Rights and Local Working under the WTO TRIPS Agreement: An Analysis of the U.S. – Brazil Patent Dispute, *The Yale Journal of International Law*, 27, pp. 365–93.

Chaudhuri Shubham, Pinelopi K. Goldberg and Panle Jia (2006). Estimating the Effects of Global Patent Protection in Pharmaceuticals: A Case Study of Quinolones in India, *American Economic Review*, 96(5), pp. 1477–1514.

Cheyne Ilona (2010). Intellectual Property and Climate Change from a Trade Perspective, *Nordic Environmental Law Journal*, 2, pp. 121–30.

Coe David T., Elhanan Helpman and Hoffmaister Alexander W. (1997). North-South R&D Spillovers, *The Economic Journal*, 107(440), pp. 134–49.

Consilvio Mark (2011). The Role of Patents in the International Framework of Clean Technology Transfer: A Discussion of Barriers and Solutions, *American University Intellectual Property Brief*, pp. 7–16.

Cordray Monique L. (1994). GATT v. WIPO, 76 J., *Journal of the Patent and Trademark Office Society*, pp. 121–44.

Correa Carlos M. (2001). Review of the TRIPS Agreement: Fostering the Transfer of Technology to Developing Countries, *TWN Trade & Development Series* 13, published by Third World Network, Penang.

(2003). Intellectual Property Rights and the Protection of Public Health in Developing Countries, *The World Bank Legal Review: Law and Justice for Development*, 1, pp. 161–205.

Cottier Thomas, Shaheeza Lalani and Michelangelo Temmerman (2014). Use It or Lose It: Assessing the Compatibility of the Paris Convention and TRIPS Agreement with Respect to Local Working Requirements, *Journal of International Economic Law*, pp. 1–35.

Davis Kevin E. (2005). Regulation of Technology Transfer to Developing Countries: The Relevance of Institutional Capacity, 27 *Law & Policy*, pp. 6–32.

de Werra Jacques (2010a). How to Protect Trade Secrets in High-Tech Sports? An Intellectual Property Analysis Based on the Experiences at the America's Cup and in the Formula One Championship, *European Intellectual Property Review*, 32 (4), pp. 155–64.

(2010b). What Color Is IP? in the Green Debate: IP Perspectives, *WIPO Magazine*, pp. 17–19.

Dechezleprêtre Antoine, Matthieu Glachant and Yann Ménière (2008). The Clean Development Mechanism and the International Diffusion of Technologies: An Empirical Study, *Energy Policy* 36(4), pp. 1273–83.

(2013). What Drives the International Transfer of Climate Change Mitigation Technologies? *Empirical Evidence from Patent Data*, *Environ Resource Econ*, 54, pp. 161–78.

Dechezleprêtre Antoine, Matthieu Glachant, Ivan Hascic, Nick Johnstone, and Yann Meniere (2011). Invention and Transfer of Climate Change-Mitigation Technologies: A Global Analysis, *Review of Environmental Economics and Policy* 5(1), pp. 109–30.

Derclaye Estelle (2008). Intellectual Property Rights and Global Warming, *Marquette Intellectual Property Law Review*, 12(2), pp. 264–97.

Doane Michael L. (1994). TRIPS and International Intellectual Property Protection in an Age of Advancing Technology, *American University International Law Review*, 9(2), pp. 465–97.

Drahos Peter (1995). Global Property Rights in Information: The Story of TRIPS at the GATT, *Prometheus*, 13(1), pp. 6–19.

(1999). Intellectual Property and Human Rights, *Intellectual Property Quarterly* 3, pp. 349–71.

(2002). Developing Countries and International Intellectual Property Standard-Setting, *The Journal of World Intellectual Property*, 5(5), pp. 765–89.

(2007). Four Lessons for Developing Countries from the Trade Negotiations over Access to Medicines, *Liverpool Law Review* 28, pp.11–39.

(2008). "Trust Me": Patent Offices in Developing Countries, *American Journal of Law and Medicine & Ethics*, pp. 151–74.

Drumbl Mark A. (2002). Poverty, Wealth, and Obligation in International Environmental Law, *Tulane Law Review*, 76(4), pp. 843–960.

Dufey Guillaume (2013). Patents and Standardisation: Competition Concerns in New Technology Markets, *Global Antitrust Review*, 6, pp. 7–48.

Eaton Jonathan and Samuel Kortum (1999). International Technology Diffusion: Theory and Measurement, *International Economic Review*, 40(3), pp. 537–70.

Ecos John, Sanjaya Lall and Mikyung Yuwen (1997). Transfer of Technology: An Update, *Asian-Pacific Economic Literature*, 11(1), pp. 56–66.

Ehlermann Claus-Dieter (2003). Reflections on the Appellate Body of the WTO, *Journal of International Economic Law* 6(3). pp. 695–708.

Eisenberg Rebecca S. (1989). Patents and the Progress of Science: Exclusive Rights and Experimental Use, *The University of Chicago Law Review*, 56(3), pp. 1017–86.

Encaoua David, Dominique Guellec, and Catalina Martinez (2006). Patent Systems for Encouraging Innovation: Lessons from Economic Analysis, *Research Policy* 35, pp. 1423–40.

Erlikhman Daniel (2003). Jazz Photo and the Doctrine of Patent Exhaustion: Implications to TRIPS and International Harmonization of Patent Protection, *Hastings Communications and Entertainment Law Journal*, 25 pp. 307–42.

Fair Robert (2009). Does Climate Change Justify Compulsory Licensing of Green Technology? *International Law & Management Review*, 6.

Falvey Rod, Neil Foster and David Greenaway (2009). Trade, Imitative Ability and Intellectual Property Rights, *Review of World Economics* 145, pp. 373–404.

Feldman Alexander M. (2009). Evolving Treaty Obligations: A Proposal for Analysing Subsequent Practice Derived from WTO Dispute Settlement, *International Law and Politics*, 41, pp. 655–706.

Fisher Larry R. (1967). The Misuse Doctrine and Post Expiration-Discriminatory-and Exorbitant Patent Royalties, *Indiana Law Journal*, Vol. 43(1), art. 6, pp. 106–29.

Fisher William (2001). Intellectual Property and Innovation: Theoretical, Empirical and Historical Perspectives, in Seminar on Intellectual Property and Innovation in the Knowledge-Based Economy, The Hague.

Frankel Susy (2006). WTO Application of "the Customary Rules of Interpretation of Public International Law" to Intellectual Property, *Virginia Journal of International Law*, 46, pp. 366–431.

(2009). Challenging TRIPS-Plus Agreements: The Potential Utility of Non-Violation Disputes, *Journal of International Economic Law* 12(4), pp. 1023–65.

Gaillard Jacques (2010). Measuring Research and Development in Developing Countries: Main Characteristics and Implications for the Frascati Manual, *Science, Technology & Society*, 15(1), pp. 77–111.

Gana Ruth L. (1996). Prospects for Developing Countries under the TRIPS Agreement, *Vanderbilt Journal of Transnational Law*, 29, pp. 735–75.

Gathii James Thuo (2002). The Legal Status of the Doha Declaration on TRIPS and Public Health under the Vienna Convention on the Law of the Treaties, *Harvard Journal of Law & Technology*, 15(2), pp. 292–317.

(2011). The Neoliberal Turn in Regional Trade Agreements, *Washington Law Review*, 86, pp. 421–74.

Geiger Christophe, Jonathan Griffiths and Reto M. Hilty (2008). Declaration on a Balanced Interpretation of the "Three-Step Test" in Copyright Law, *IIC*, 39, pp. 707–13.

Gervais Daniel J. (2005). Intellectual Property, Trade and Development: The State of Play, *Fordham Law Review*, 74 pp. 505–35.

(2006). The Changing Landscape of International Intellectual Property, *Journal of Intellectual Property Law and Practice*, 1(4), pp. 249–55.

Graham Lawrence D. and Richard O. Zerbe (1996). Economically Efficient Treatment of Computer Software: Reverse Engineering, Protection, and Disclosure, *Rutgers Computer & Technology Law Journal*, 22, pp. 61–142.

Graham Stuart J. H., Robert P. Merges, Pam Samuelson and Ted Sichelman (2010). High Technology Entrepreneurs and the Patent System: Result of the 2008 Berkeley Patent Survey, *Berkeley Technology Law Journal*, 24(4), pp. 1255–328.

Grosse Ruse-Khan Henning (2009). Time for a Paradigm Shift? *Exploring Maximum Standards in International Intellectual Property Protection, Trade, Law and Development*, 1, pp. 56–102.

(2011). The International Law Relation between TRIPS and Subsequent TRIPS-Plus Free Trade Agreements: Towards Safeguarding TRIPS Flexibilities? *Journal of Intellectual Property Law*, 18(2), pp. 325–65.

Haag Thomas A. (2002). TRIPS Since Doha: How Far Will the WTO Go toward Modifying the Terms for Compulsory Licensing? *Journal of the Patent and Trademark Office Society*, 84, pp. 945–81.

Haar Paul S. (1982). Revision of the Paris Convention: A Realignment of Private and Public Interests in the International Patent System, *Brooklyn Journal of International Law*, 8(1), pp. 77–108.

Hall Bronwyn H. and Christian Helmers (2010). The Role of Patent Protection in (Clean/Green) Technology Transfer, *Santa Clara High Technology Law Journal*, 26, pp. 487–532.

Halewood Michael (1997). Regulating Patent Holders: Local Working Requirements and Compulsory Licences at International Law, *Osgoode Hall Law Journal*, 35(2), art. 2.

Harris Donald P. (2006). Carrying a Good Joke Too Far: TRIPS and Treaties of Adhesion, *Journal of International Law*, 27(3).

Helfter Laurence R. (2004). Regime Shifting: The TRIPS Agreement and New Dynamics of International Intellectual Property Lawmaking, *The Yale Journal of International Law*, 29, pp. 1–83.

Heller Michael A. and Rebecca S. Eisenberg (1998). Can Patents Deter Innovation? The Anti-Commons in Biomedical Research, *Science*, 280, pp. 698–701.

Hesse Carla (2002). The Rise of Intellectual Property, 700 B.C.–A.D. 2000: An Idea in the Balance, *Daedalus*, pp. 26–45.

Hettinger Edwin C. (1989). Justifying Intellectual Property, *Philosophy & Public Affairs*, 18(1), pp. 13–52.

Ho Cynthia M. (2007). A New World Order for Addressing Patent Rights and Public Health, *Chicago – Kent Law Review*, 82, pp. 1469–1515.

(2009). Patent Breaking or Balancing?: Separating Strands of Fact from Fiction Under TRIPS, *North Carolina Journal of International Law and Commercial Regulation*, 34, pp. 371–469.

Ho Samuel P. S. (1997). Technology Transfer to China During the 1980s – How Effective? Some Evidence from Jiangsu, *Pacific Affairs* 70(1), pp. 85–106.

Hoekman Bernard M., Keith E. Maskus and Kamal Saggi (2005). Transfer of Technology to Developing Countries: Unilateral and Multilateral Policy Options, *World Development*, 33(10), pp. 1587–602.

Hoen Ellen't (2002). TRIPS, Pharmaceutical Patents, and Access to Essential Medicines: A Long Way From Seattle to Doha, *Chicago Journal of International Law*, 3 (1), pp. 27–46.

Howley Jessica (2009). The Gabčíkovo-Nagymaros Case: The Influence of the International Court of Justice on the Law of Sustainable Development, *Queensland Law Student Review*, 2(1), pp. 1–19.

Howse Robert (2000). The Canadian Generic Medicines Panel: A Dangerous Precedent in Dangerous Time, *The Journal of World Intellectual Property*, 3(4), pp. 493–507.

Javorcik Beata Smarzynska (2004). The Composition of Foreign Direct Investment and Protection of Intellectual Property Rights: Evidence from Transition Economies, *European Economic Review* 48, pp. 39–62.

Kampf Roger and Hannu Wager (2011). The Role of the TRIPS Agreement in the Global Health Policy, *Stanford Journal of Law, Science & Policy*, pp. 17–41.

Kastenmeier Robert W. and David Beier (1989). International Trade and Intellectual Property: Promise, Risks, and Reality, *Journal of Transnational Law | Vanderbilt University*, 22, pp. 285–307.

Keller Eric (2008). Time-Varying Compulsory License: Facilitating License Negotiation for Efficient Post-Verdict Patent Infringement, *Texas Intellectual Property Law Journal*, 16, pp. 427–51.

Kitch Edmund W. (1994). The Patent Policy of Developing Countries, *Pacific Basin Law Journal*, 13, pp. 166–78.

Kunz-Hallstein Hans Peter (1989). The United States Proposal for a GATT-Agreement on Intellectual Property and the Paris Convention for the Protection of Industrial Property, *Vanderbilt Journal of Transnational Law*, 22, pp. 265–84.

Kur Annette (2009). International Norm-Making in the Field of Intellectual Property: A Shift towards Maximum Rules? *The WIPO Journal*, 1, pp. 27–34.

Lane Eric (2010). Clean Tech Reality Check: Nine International Green Technology Transfer Deals Unhindered by Intellectual Property Rights, *Santa Clara Computer & High Technology Law Journal*, pp. 533–57.

Lanjouw Jean Olson and Ashoka Mody (1996). Innovation and the International Diffusion of Environmentally Responsive Technology, *Research Policy*, 25, pp. 549–71.

Lennard Michael (2002). Navigating by the Stars: Interpreting the WTO Agreements, *Journal of International Economic Law*, 5(1), pp. 17–89.

Levin Richard C., Alvin K. Klevorick, Richard R. Nelson, Sidney G. Winter (1987). Appropriating the Returns from Industrial Research and Development, *Brookings Papers on Economic Activity*, pp. 783–820.

Lewis Joanna I. (2007). Technology Acquisition and Innovation in the Developing World: Wind Turbine Development in China and India, *Studies in Comparative International Development*, 42, pp. 208–32.

Littleton Matthew (2009). The TRIPS Agreement and Transfer of Climate-Change-Related Technologies to Developing Countries, *Natural Resources Forum* 33, pp. 233–44.

Loughran Regina A. (1981). The United States Position on Revising the Paris Convention: Quid Pro Quo or Denunciation, *Fordham International Law Journal*, 5(2), pp. 411–39.

Luff David (1996). An Overview of International Law of Sustainable Development and a Confrontation between WTO Rules and Sustainable Development, *Revue Belge de Droit International*, 29(1), pp. 91–144.

Machlup Fritz and Edith Penrose (1950). The Patent Controversy in the Nineteenth Century, *The Journal of Economic History*, 10(1), pp. 1–29.

Mahajan Anthony J. (1999). Intellectual Property, Contracts, and Reverse Engineering After ProCD: A Proposed Compromise for Computer Software, *Fordham Law Review*, 67(6), pp. 3297–335.

Maitra Neel (2010). Access to Environmentally Sound Technology in Developing World: A Proposed Alternative to Compulsory Licensing, *Columbia Journal of Environmental Law*, 35, pp. 407–45.

Mansfield Edwin (1986). Patents and Innovation: An Empirical Study, *Management Science*, 32(2), pp. 173–81.

Mansfield Edwin, Mark Schwartz and Samuel Wagner (1981). Imitation Costs and Patents: An Empirical Study, *The Economic Journal*, 91(364), pp. 907–18.

Marceau Gabrielle (1999). A Call for Coherence in International Law: Praises for the Prohibition against "Clinical Isolation" in WTO Dispute Settlement, *Journal of World Trade*, 33(5), pp. 87–152.

(2001). Conflicts of Norms and Conflicts of Jurisdictions: The Relationship between the WTO Agreement and MEAs and Other Treaties, *Journal of World Trade*, 35 (6), pp. 1081–131.

(2002). WTO Dispute Settlement and Human Rights, *European Journal of International Law*, 13(4), pp. 753–814.

(2006). The WTO is NOT a Closed Box, *Proceedings of the Annual Meeting, American Society of International Law*, 100, pp. 29–31.

Marceau Gabrielle and Joel P. Trachtman (2014). A Map of the World Trade Organisation Law of Domestic Regulation of Goods: The Technical Barriers to Trade Agreement, the Sanitary and Phytosanitary Measures Agreement, and the General Agreement on Tariffs and Trade, *Journal of World Trade*, 48(2), pp. 351–432.

Marong Alhaji B. M. (2003). From Rio to Johannesburg: Reflections on the Role of International Legal Norms in Sustainable Development, *The Georgetown International Environmental Law Review*, 16, pp. 21–76.

Maskus Keith E. (1998). The Role of Intellectual Property Rights in Encouraging Foreign Direct Investment and Technology Transfer, *Duke Journal of Comparative and International Law*, 9, pp. 109–61.

    (2005). Using the International Trading System to Foster Technology Transfer for Economic Development, *Michigan State Law Review*, pp. 219–41.

Maskus Keith E. and Mohan Penubarti (1995). How Trade-Related Are Intellectual Property Rights? *Journal of International Economics*, 39, pp. 227–48.

McCulloch Rachel (1981). Technology Transfer to Developing Countries: Implications of International Regulation, *Annals of the American Academy of Political and Social Science* 458, pp. 110–22.

McLachlan Campbell (2005). The Principle of Systemic Integration and Article 31(3) (c) of the Vienna Convention, *International and Comparative Law Quarterly*, 54 (2) pp. 279–320.

Menescal Andrea Koury (2005). Changing WIPO's Ways? The 2004 Development Agenda in Historical Perspective, *The Journal of World Intellectual Property*, 8(6), pp. 761–96.

Mercurio Bryan (2005). The Impact of the Australia-United States Free Trade Agreement on the Provision of the Health Services in Australia, *Whittier Law Review*, 26, pp. 1051–100.

Mercurio Bryan and Mitali Tyagi (2010). Treaty Interpretation in WTO Dispute Settlement: The Outstanding Question of the Legality of Local Working Requirements, *Minnesota Journal of International Law*, 19(2), pp. 275–326.

Michaels Andrew C (2009). International Technology Transfer and TRIPS Article 66.2: Can Global Administrative Law Help Least-Developed Countries Get What They Bargained for? *Georgetown Journal of International Law*, 41, pp. 223–61.

Mitchell Andrew D. (2007). The Legal Basis for Using Principles in WTO Disputes, *Journal of International Economic Law*, 10(4), pp. 795–835.

Moon Suerie (2008). Does TRIPS Art. 66.2 Encourage Technology Transfer to LDCs?: An Analysis of Country Submissions to the TRIPS Council (1999–2007). UNCTAD-ICTSD Project on IPRs and Sustainable Development, Policy Brief No. 2.

    (2011). Meaningful Technology Transfer to the LDCs: A Proposal for a Monitoring Mechanism for TRIPS Article 66.2, UNCTAD-ICTSD Project on IPRs and Sustainable Development, Policy Brief No. 9.

Moore Adam D. (2003). Intellectual Property, Innovation, and Social Progress: The Case against Incentive Based Arguments, *Hamline Law Review*, 26(3), pp. 602–28.

Morin Jean-Frederic and Richard E. Gold (2010). Consensus-Seeking, Distrust and Rhetorical Entrapment: The WTO Decision on Access to Medicines, *European Journal of International Relations*, 16(4), pp. 563–87.

Nanda Nitya (2009). Diffusion of Climate-Friendly Technologies: Can Compulsory Licensing Help? *Journal of Intellectual Property Rights*, 14, pp. 241–46.

Ngassam Christopher (2004). Does the Presence or Lack of Intellectual Property Right Protection Affect International Trade Flows in Emerging Market Economies? An Exploratory Study, *Proceedings of the Academy for Studies in International Business*, 4(2), pp. 5–11.

Nguyãén Tú Thanh and Henrik Lidgard Hans (2008). The CFI Microsoft Judgment and TRIPS Competition Flexibilities, *International Trade Law Journal*, 16(3), pp. 41–51.

Nicholson Michael W. (2007). The Impact of Industry Characteristics and IPR Policy on Foreign Direct Investment, *Review of World Economics*, 143(1). pp. 27–54.

Noehrenberg Eric (2003). TRIPS, the Doha Declaration and Public Health, *The Journal of World Intellectual Property* 6, pp. 379–83.

Nunnenkamp Peter and Julius Spatz (2004). Intellectual Property Rights and Foreign Direct Investment: A Disaggregated Analysis, *Review of World Economics*, 140(3), pp. 393–414.

Odman Ayse N. (2000). Using TRIPS to Make the Innovation Process Work, *The Journal of World Intellectual Property* 3, pp. 343–71.

Oguamanam Chidi (2003). The Convention on Biological Diversity and Intellectual Property Rights: The Challenge of Indigenous Knowledge, *Southern Cross University Law Review*, 7, pp. 89–141.

Orellana Marcos A. (2009). Evolving WTO Law Concerning Health, Safety and Environmental Measures, *Trade, Law and Development*, 1, pp. 103–44.

Palmeter David and Petros Mavroidis (1998). The WTO Legal System: Sources of Law, *The American Journal of International Law*, 92, pp. 398–413.

Park Kichan, Murad Ali and Francoise Chevalier (2011). A Spiral Process Model of Technological Innovation in a Developing Country: The Case of Samsung, *African Journal of Business Management*, 5(13), pp. 5162–78.

Pauwelyn Joost (2010). The Dog That Barked But Didn't Bite: 15 Years of Intellectual Property Disputes at the WTO, *Journal of International Dispute Settlement*, 1(2), pp. 389–429.

Petersmann Ernst-Ulrich (2000). The WTO Constitution and Human Rights, *Journal of International Economic Law*, 3(1), pp. 19–25.

Popp David (2008). International Technology Transfer for Climate Policy, Centre for Policy Research, Paper 4.

Purcell Joseph M. (2014). The "Essential Facilities" Doctrine in the Sunlight: Stacking Patented Genetic Traits in Agriculture," *St. John's Law Review*, 85(3), pp. 1251–74.

Rai Rajnish Kumar (2008). Patentable Subject Matter Requirements: An Evaluation of Proposed Exclusions to India's Patent Law in Light of India's Obligations under the TRIPS Agreement and Options for India, *Chicago-Kent Journal of Intellectual Property*, 8, pp. 41–84.

Rai Rajnish Kumar and Sirnath Jagannathan (2012). Parallel Imports and Unparallel Laws: An Examination of the Exhaustion Doctrine through the Lens of Pharmaceutical Products, *Information and Communications Technology Law*, 21(1), pp. 53–89.

Rajamani Lavanya (2000). The Principle of Common but Differentiated Responsibility and the Balance of Commitments under the Climate Regime, *RECIEL*, 9(2), pp. 120–31.

Reddy G. B. and Harunrashid A. Kari (2013). Local Working of Patents-Law and Implementation in India, *Journal of Intellectual Property Rights*, 18, pp. 15–27.

Reichman Jerome H. (1995). Universal Minimum Standards of Intellectual Property Protection under the TRIPS Component of the WTO Agreement, *The International Lawyer*, 29(2), pp. 345–88.

(1996). From Free Riders to Fair Followers: Global Competition under the TRIPS Agreement, *N.Y.U Journal of International Law and Politics*, 29, pp. 11–93.

(1998). Securing Compliance with the TRIPS Agreement after US v. India, *Journal of International Economic Law*, pp. 585–601.

(2000). The TRIPS Agreement Comes of Age: Conflict or Cooperation with the Developing Countries? *Case Western Reserve Journal of International Law*, 32, pp. 441–70.

(2009a). Intellectual Property In the Twenty-First Century: Will the Developing Countries Lead or Follow? *Houston Law Review*, 46, pp. 1115–85.

(2009b). Compulsory Licensing of Patented Pharmaceutical Inventions: Evaluating the Options, *Journal of Law, Medicine & Ethics*, 37(2), pp. 247–63.

Reichman Jerome H. and David Lange (1998). Bargaining around the TRIPS Agreement: The Case for On-Going Public-Private Initiatives to Facilitate Worldwide Intellectual Property Transactions, *Duke Journal of Comparative & International Law*, 9, pp. 11–68.

Reichman Jerome H. and Ruth L. Okediji (2012). When Copyright Law and Science Collide: Empowering Digitally Integrated Research Methods on a Global Scale, *Minnesota Law Review*, 96, pp. 1362–480.

Reisman Michael W. (2009). Opinion with Respect to Selected International Legal Problems in LCIA Case No. 7941, United States of America v. Canada, London Court of International Arbitration (LCIA). LCIA Case No. 81010.

Ricolfi Marco (2006). Is There an Antitrust Antidote against IP Overprotection within TRIPS? *Marquette Intellectual Property Law Review*, 10(2), pp. 305–67.

Rodrigues Edson Beas Jr. and Murphy Bryan (2006). Brazil's Prior Consent Law: A Dialogue between Brazil and the United States Over Where the TRIPS Agreement Currently Sets the Balance between the Protection of Pharmaceutical Patents and Access to Medicines, *Albany Law Journal of Science and Technology*, 16, pp. 423–56.

Rosenne Shabtai (1982). The Election of Five Members of the International Court of Justice in 1981, *The American Journal of International Law*, 76(2), pp. 364–70.

Saha Subhasis (2009). Patent Law and TRIPS: Compulsory Licensing of Patents and Pharmaceuticals, *Journal of the Patent and Trademark Office Society*, 91, pp. 364–74.

Samuelson Pamela and Suzanne Scotchmer (2002). The Law and Economics of Reverse Engineering, *The Yale Law Journal*, 111, pp. 1575–663.

Sands Philippe (1994). The "Greening" of International Law: Emerging Principles and Rules, *Global Legal Studies Journal*, 1, pp. 293–323.

(1995). International Law in the Field of Sustainable Development, *British Yearbook of International Law*, 65(1), pp. 303–81.

Sell Susan K. (1989). Intellectual Property as a Trade Issue: From the Paris Convention to GATT, *Legal Studies Forum*, 13(4), pp. 407–22.

(2011). TRIPS Was Never Enough: Vertical Forum Shifting, FTAs, ACTA, and TPP, *Journal of Intellectual Property Law*, 18, pp. 447–78.

Sell Susan K. and Aseem Prakash (2004). Using Ideas Strategically: The Contest between Business and NGO Networks in Intellectual Property Rights, *International Studies Quarterly* 48, pp. 143–75.

Shabalala Dalindyebo (2009). An Introduction to this Issue: Climate Change and Technology Transfer, *Sustainable Development Law & Policy*, 9(3), Clean Technology and International Trade.

Shanker Daya (2002). The Vienna Convention on the Law of Treaties, the Dispute Settlement System of the WTO and the Doha Declaration on the TRIPS Agreement, *Journal of World Trade* 36(4), pp. 721–72.

Sharma Ruchi and K. K. Saxena (2012). Strengthening the Patent Regime: Benefits for Developing Countries – A Survey, *Journal of Intellectual Property Rights*, 17, pp. 122–32.

Shashikant Sangeeta (2009). No Patents on Climate-Friendly Technologies, Says South, *TWN Info Service on Intellectual Property Issues*, 12 June, available at www.twnside.org.sg/title2/intellectual_property/info.service/2009/twn.ipr.info.090 609.htm

Shavell Steven and Tanguy van Ypersele (2001). Rewards versus Intellectual Property Rights, *Journal of Law and Economics*, 44, pp. 525–47.

Smith Pamela J. (2001). How Do Foreign Patent Rights Affect U.S. Exports, Affiliate Sales, and Licenses? *Journal of International Economics*, 55, pp. 411–39.

Son Seungwoo (2002). Selective Refusals to Sell Patented Goods: The Relationship between Patent Rights and Antitrust Law, *Journal of Law, Technology & Policy*, 2002(1), pp. 109–91.

Sovacool Benjamin K. (2008). Placing a Glove on the Invisible Hand: How Intellectual Property Rights May Impede Innovation in Energy Research and Development (R&D), *Albany Law Journal of Science and Technology*, 18(2), pp. 381–440.

Stec Stephen and Gabriel E. Eckstein (1997). Of Solemn Oaths and Obligations: The Environmental Impact of the ICJ's Decision in the Case Concerning the Gabčíkovo-Nagymaros Project, *Yearbook of International Environmental Law*, 8, pp. 41–50.

Stewart Frances and Ejaz Ghani (1991). How Significant Are Externalities for Development? *World Development*, 19(6), pp. 569–94.

Stout Maria Victoria (2008). Crossing the TRIPS Non-discrimination Line: How CAFTA Pharmaceutical Patent Provisions Violate TRIPS Article 27.1, *Boston University Journal of Science and Technology Law*, 14, pp. 177–200.

Suwan-in Nattapong (2012). Compulsory Licensing, A Long Debate on TRIPS Agreement Interpretation: Discovering the Truth of Thailand's Imposition on Pharmaceutical Patents, *Asian Journal of WTO & International Health Law and Policy*, 7, pp. 225–61.

Sykes Alan O. (2002). TRIPS, Pharmaceuticals, Developing Countries, and the Doha "Solution", *Chicago Journal of International Law*, 3, pp. 47–68.

Taubman Antony (2008). Rethinking TRIPS: 'Adequate Remuneration' for Non-Voluntary Patent Licensing, *Journal of International Economic Law* 11(4), pp. 927–70.

Thomas Chantal (1999). Transfer of Technology in the Contemporary International Order, *Fordham International Law Journal*, 22, pp. 2096–111.

Timmermann Cristian and Henk van den Belt (2013). Intellectual Property and Global Health: From Corporate Social Responsibility to the Access to Knowledge Movement, *Liverpool Law Review*, 34(1), pp. 47–73.

Tully Danielle L. (2003). Prospects for Progress: The TRIPS Agreement and Developing Countries after the Doha Conference, *Boston College International & Comparative Law Review*, 26, pp. 129–43.

Ullrich Hanns (2004). Expansionist Intellectual Property Protection and Reductionist Competition Rules: A TRIPS Perspective, *Journal of International Economic Law*, pp. 401–30.

UNEP (2003). Phytotechnologies: A Technical Approach in Environmental Management, *IETC Freshwater Management Series*, 7, available at www.unep.or.jp/Ietc/Publications/Freshwater/FMS7/2.asp#Ia.

van Ark Bart, Mary O'Mahony and Marcel P. Timmer (2008). The Productivity Gap between Europe and the United States: Trends and Causes, *Journal of Economic Perspectives*, 22(1), pp. 25–44.

Verhoosel Gaetan (1998). Beyond the Unsustainable Rhetoric of Sustainable Development: Transferring Environmentally Sound Technologies, *The Georgetown International Environmental Law Review*, 11, pp. 49–76.

Weinreb Lloyd L. (1998). Copyright for Functional Expression, *Harvard Law Review*, 111(5), pp. 1149–254.

Yi Qian (2007). Do National Patent Laws Stimulate Domestic Innovation in a Global Patenting Environment? A Cross-Country Analysis of Pharmaceutical Patent Protection, 1978–2002, *The Review of Economics and Statistics* 89(3), pp. 436–53.

Yilmaz Kamil and Ashoka Mody (2002). Imports for Export Competitiveness, *World Bank Economic Review*, 16(1), pp. 23–48.

Young Margaret (2007). The WTO's Use of Relevant Rules of International Law: An Analysis of the Biotech Case, *The International and Comparative Law Quarterly*, 56(4), pp. 907–30.

Yu Peter K. (2009). The Objectives and Principles of the TRIPS Agreement, *Houston Law Review*, 46, pp. 979–1046.

Zaman Khorsed (2013). The TRIPS Patent Protection Provisions and Their Effects on Transferring Climate Change Technologies to LDCs and Poor Developing Countries: A Critical Appraisal, *Asian Journal of International Law*, 3, pp. 137–61.

Zeitler Helge Elisabeth (2005). "Good Faith" in the WTO Jurisprudence: Necessary Balancing Element or an Open Door to Judicial Activism, *Journal of International Economic Law* 8(3), pp. 721–58.

Zhou Yuanchun and Ji Zou (2009). The Intellectual Property Issues in International Development and Transfer of Climate-Friendly Technologies, [in Chinese], Paper presented in PACE Conference, 12–15 July.

Zhou Yuanchun, Ji Zou and Ke Wang (2010). How to Conquer the IPR Barriers in the Low Carbon Technologies? [in Chinese], *Environmental Protection*, 2, pp. 68–70.

Zhuang Wei (2011). Intellectual Property Rights and Transfer of Clean Energy Technologies, *International Journal of Public Law and Policy*, 1(4), pp. 384–401.

Zou Ji, Ke Wang, Sha Fu et al. (2009). *Proposal on Innovative Mechanism for Development and Transfer of Environmentally Sound Technologies*, Economic Science Press.

WORKING PAPERS OR POLICY BRIEFS

Abbot Frederick M. (2009). Innovation and Technology Transfer to Address Climate Change: Lessons from the Global Debate on Intellectual Property and Public Health, ICTSD's Programme on IPRs and Sustainable Development, Issue Paper No. 24, Geneva: ICTSD.

Athreye Suma and Yang Yong (2011). Disembodied Knowledge Flows in the World Economy, WIPO Economic Research Working Papers No. 3.

Ban Ki-moon (2008). Statement by United Nations Secretary-General Ban Ki-moon at the opening of the High-Level Segment of COP 14 in Poznan, available at http://unfccc.int/2860.php.

Barratt Amanda (2008). The Battelle for Policy Space: Strategic Advantages of a Human Rights Approach in International Intellectual Property Negotiations, unpublished PhD dissertation, University of Cape Town.

Barton John H. (2007a). New Trends in Technology Transfer: Implications for National and International Policy, Issue Paper No. 18, Geneva: ICTSD.

(2007b). Intellectual Property and Access to Clean Energy Technologies in Developing Countries: An Analysis of Solar Photovoltaic, Biofuel and Wind Technologies, Trade and Sustainable Energy Series Issue Paper No. 2, Geneva: ICTSD.

(2008). Mitigating Climate Change through Technology Transfer: Addressing the Needs of Developing Countries, Energy, Environment and Development Programme: Programme Paper 08/02, Chatham House.

Bollyky Thomas J. (2009). Intellectual Property Rights and Climate Change: Principles for Innovation and Access to Low-Carbon Technology, Centre for Global Development (CGD) Notes.

Brown Marilyn A., Jess Chandler, Melissa V. Lapsa and Benjamin K. Sovacool (2008). Carbon Lock-In: Barriers to Deploying Climate Change Mitigation Technologies, Oak Ridge National Laboratory managed by UT-Battelle, LLC for the U.S. Department of Energy, ORNL/TM-2007/124.

Baykal Yesim (2013). WIPO GREEN: the Sustainable Technology Marketplace, presented at the Conference on Climate Change in Africa: Advancing Knowledge, Technology, Policy and Practice, available at www.wipo.int/edocs/mdocs/africa/en/wipo_kenya_cic_jpo_inn_nbo_13/wipo_kenya_cic_jpo_inn_nbo_13_t_1.pdf

Cannady Cynthia (2009). Access to Climate Change Technology by Developing Countries: A Practical Strategy, ICTSD's Programme on IPRs and Sustainable Development, Issue Paper No. 25, Geneva: ICTSD.

Centre for International Environmental Law (2010). Technology Transfer in the UNFCCC and Other International Legal Regimes: The Challenges of Systemic Integration, Background Paper, International Council on Human Rights Policy.

Centre for International Environmental Law (CIEL) (2009). Frameworks and Options for Addressing Technology Cooperation in the UNFCCC: National and Multilateral Elements, Background Brief for the Workshop on: Operationalizing of

Technology Cooperation in the UNFCCC: Building Civil Society Viewpoints into Copenhagen, 11–15 May 2009.

CISDL(2002). The Principle of Common but Differentiated Responsibilities: Origins and Scope, A CISDL Legal Brief for the World Summit on Sustainable Development, available at http://cisdl.org/public/docs/news/brief_common.pdf.

Copenhagen Economics (2009). Are IPR a Barrier to the Transfer of Climate Change Technology? Report prepared by Copenhagen Economics A/S and The IPR Company ApS.

Correa Carlos M. (1999). Intellectual Property Rights and the Use of Compulsory Licenses: Options for Developing Countries, Geneva: South Centre Working Papers.

(2000). Integrating Public Health Concerns into Patent Legislation in Developing Countries, Geneva: South Centre Working Papers.

(2002). Implications of the Doha Declaration on the TRIPS Agreement and Public Health, Health Economics and Drugs EDM Series No. 12, published by WHO.

(2007). Intellectual Property and Competition Law: Exploring Some Issues of Relevance to Developing Countries, Geneva: ICTSD, ICTSD IPRs and Sustainable Development Programme Issue Paper No. 21.

(2009). The Push for Stronger Enforcement Rules: Implications for Developing Countries, The Global Debate on the Enforcement of Intellectual Property Rights and Developing Countries, Programme on IPRs and Sustainable Development, Issue Paper No. 22, Geneva: ICTSD, pp. 27–80.

(2011). Pharmaceutical Innovation, Incremental Patenting and Compulsory Licensing, Research Paper No. 41.

(2012). Mechanisms for International Cooperation in Research and Development: Lessons for the Context of Climate Change, Research Paper No. 43, Geneva: South Centre Working Papers.

(2013). Innovation and Technology Transfer of Environmentally Sound Technologies, presentation at the Centre for International Environmental Studies of the Graduate Institute of International and Development Studies, 9 October, Geneva.

Cottier Thomas, Shaheeza Lalani, and Michelangelo Temmerman (2013). Use It or Lose It? Assessing the Compatibility of the Paris Convention and TRIPS With Respect to Local Working Requirements, Working Paper No. 2012/11.

Dechezleprêtre Antoine (2013). Fast-Tracking Green Patent Applications: An Empirical Analysis, ICTSD Programme on Innovation, Technology and Intellectual Property, Issue Paper No. 37, Geneva: ICTSD.

Drahos Peter (2002). Developing Countries and International Intellectual Property Standard-Setting, Commission on Intellectual Property Rights, Study Paper 8.

Doranova Asel, Ionara Costa and Geert Duysters (2009). Knowledge Base Determinants of Technology Sourcing in the Clean Development Mechanism Projects, UNU-MERIT Working Paper Series No. 2009–015.

Dupasquier Chantal and Patrick N. Osakwe (2005). Foreign Direct Investment in Africa: Performance, Challenges and Responsibilities, African Trade Policy Centre, Work in Progress No. 21.

Dutfield Graham and Uma Suthersanen (2004). Harmonization or Differentiation in Intellectual Property Protection? Lessons from History, Occasional Paper 15, Geneva: QUNO.

Earth Negotiations Bulletin (2006). Summary of the Twelfth Conference of the Parties to the UN Framework Convention on Climate Change and Second Meeting of the Parties to the Kyoto Protocol: 6–17 November 2006.

(2007). Summary of the Thirteenth Conference of the Parties to the UN Framework Convention on Climate Change and Third Meeting of the Parties to the Kyoto Protocol: 3–15 December 2007.

Falvey Rod and Neil Foster (2006). The Role of Intellectual Property Rights in Technology Transfer and Economic Growth: Theory and Evidence, Vienna: UNIDO Working Papers.

Foray Dominique (2009). Technology Transfer in the TRIPS Age: The Need for New Types of Partnerships between the Least Developed and Most Advanced Economies, ICTSD programme on IPRs and Sustainable Development, Issue Paper No. 23, Geneva: ICTSD.

Garrison Christopher (2006). Exceptions to Patent Rights in Developing Countries, UNCTAD-ICTSD Project on IPRs and Sustainable Development, Issue Paper No. 17, Geneva: UNCTAD and ICTSD.

Gehl Sampath, Padmashree and Pedro Roffe (2012). Unpacking the International Technology Transfer Debate: Fifty Years and Beyond, ICTSD Programme on Innovation, Technology and Intellectual Property, working paper, Geneva: ICTSD.

Global Environment Facility (2010). Implementing the Poznan Strategic Program on Technology Transfer, Professional Graphics Printing Co.

Granstrand Ove (2003). Innovation and Intellectual Property, Background paper to the Concluding Roundtable Discussion on IPR at the DRUID Summer Conference 2003 on Creating, Sharing and Transferring Knowledge: The Role of Geography, Institutions and Organisations, Copenhagen 12–14 June.

Grosse Ruse-Khan Henning (2008). A Comparative Analysis of Policy Space in WTO Law, Research Paper Series No. 08–02, Munich: Max Planck Institute for Intellectual Property, Competition and Tax Law.

(2010). Sustainable Development in International Intellectual Property Law – New Approaches from EU Economic Partnership Agreements? ICTSD's Programme on IPRs and Sustainable Development, Issue Paper No. 29, Geneva: ICTSD.

Gueye Moustapha Kamal, Malena Sell and Janet Strachan (2009). Trade, Climate Change and Sustainable Development: Key Issues for Small States, Least Developed Countries and Vulnerable Economics, Commonwealth Secretariat, DOI: http://dx.doi.org/10.14217/9781848590007-en.

Harvey Ian (2008). Intellectual Property Rights: The Catalyst to Deliver Low Carbon Technologies, Briefing Paper: Breaking the Climate Deadlock, The Climate Group.

Hoekman Bernard M., Keith E. Maskus and Kamal Saggi (2004). Transfer of Technology to Developing Countries: Unilateral and Multilateral Policy Options, World Bank Policy Research Working Paper 3332.

Hutchison Cameron (2007). Does TRIPS Facilitate or Impede Climate Change Technology Transfer into Developing Countries, CISDL Legal Working Paper Series on Climate Change Law and Policy, CISDL.

ICTSD (2008). Climate Change, Technology Transfer and Intellectual Property Rights, paper prepared for the Trade and Climate Change Seminar, 18–20 June, Copenhagen, Denmark.

Iliev Ilian (2012). Role of Patents in Renewable Energy Technology Innovation, Presentation to IRENA Roundtable on Assessment of IPRs for Promoting Renewable Energy, 25 October, Cambridge Intellectual Property Ltd.

International Chamber of Commerce (2009). Climate Change and Intellectual Property, ICC Document No. 213/71 and No. 450/1050.

Johnson Daniel K. N. and Kristina M. Lybecker (2009). Innovating for an Uncertain Market: A Literature Review of the Constraints on Environmental Innovation, No. 2009–06. Colorado College Working Paper.

Johnson Daniel K. N. and Lybecker Kristina M. (2009). Challenges to Technology Transfer: A Literature Review of the Constraints on Environmental Technology Dissemination, Colorado College Working Paper 2009–07.

Khor Martin (2008). IPRs, Technology Transfer and Climate Change, Third World Network, available at www.un.org/esa/analysis/devplan/egm_climatechange/khor.pdf.

Kim Linsu (2003). Technology Transfer and Intellectual Property Rights: The Korean Experience, UNCTAD-ICTSD Project on IPRs and Sustainable Development, Issue Paper No. 2, Geneva: ICTSD and UNCTAD.

Lall Sanjaya (2003). Indicators of the Relative Importance of IPRs in Developing Countries, UNCTAD-ICTSD Project on IPRs and Sustainable Development, Issue Paper No. 3, Geneva: ICTSD and UNCTAD.

Lamy Pascal (2007). Globalization and the Environment in a Reformed UN: Charting a Sustainable Development Path, Speech at the 24th Session of the Governing Council/Global Ministerial Environmental Forum, Nairobi, 5 February 2007, available at www.wto.org/english/news_e/sppl_e/sppl54_e.htm.

Latif Ahmed Abdel (2012). Intellectual Property Rights and Green Technologies from Rio to Rio: An Impossible Dialogue? Policy Brief No. 14, Geneva: ICTSD.

Latif Ahmed Abdel, Keith E. Maskus, Ruth Okediji, Jerome Reichman and Pedro Roffe (2011). Overcoming the Impasse on Intellectual Property and Climate Change at the UNFCCC: A Way Forward, Policy Brief No.11.

Lemoine Francoise and Deniz Unal-kesenci (2003). Trade and Technology Transfers: A Comparative Study of Turkey, India and China, CEPII, Working Paper, No. 2003–16.

Lewis Joanna I. (2007). A Comparison of Wind Power Industry Development Strategies in Spain, India and China, prepared for the Centre for Resource Solutions Supported by the Energy Foundation, China Sustainable Energy Program, 19 July.

Littleton Matthew (2008). The TRIPS Agreement and Transfer of Climate-Change-Related Technologies to Developing Countries, DESA Working Paper No. 71, ST/ESA/2008/DWP/71.

Mansfield Edwin (1995). Intellectual Property Protection, Direct Investment and Technology Transfer: Germany, Japan and the United States, International Finance Corporation Discussion Paper No. 27, published by the World Bank and International Finance Corporation.

Maskus Keith E. (2004). Encouraging International Technology Transfer, ICTSD and UNCTAD Issue Paper No. 7, Geneva, Switzerland.

——— (2010). Differentiated Intellectual Property Regimes for Environmental and Climate Technologies, OECD Environment Working Papers, No. 17, at p. 7, OECD Publishing, doi: 10.1787/5kmfwjvc83vk-en.

Maskus Keith E. and Ruth L. Okediji (2010). Intellectual Property Rights and International Technology Transfer to Address Climate Change: Risks, Opportunities and Policy Options, ICTSD's Programme on IPRs and Sustainable Development, Issue Paper No. 32, Geneva: International Centre for Trade and Sustainable Development.

Max Planck Institute for Innovation and Competition (2014). Declaration on Patent Protection: Regulatory Sovereignty under TRIPS, available at www.ip.mpg.de/files/pdf2/Patent_Declaration1.pdf.

Misati Evans and Kiyoshi Adachi (2010). The Research and Experimentation Exceptions in Patent Law: Jurisdictional Variations and the WIPO Development Agenda, UNCTAD-ICTSD Project on IPRs and Sustainable Development, Policy Brief No. 7.

Moon Suerie (2011). Meaningful Technology Transfer to the LDCs: A Proposal for a Monitoring Mechanism for TRIPS Article 66.2, UNCTAD-ICTSD Project on IPRs and Sustainable Development, Policy Brief No. 9.

Moore Mike (2001). Countries Must Feel Secure That They Can Use TRIPS' Flexibility, 20 June, available at www.wto.org/english/news_e/news01_e/dg_trips_medicines_010620_e.htm.

Musungu Sisule F., Susan Villanueva and Roxana Blasetti (2004). Utilizing TRIPS Flexibilities for Public Health Protection through South – South Regional Frameworks, Geneva: South Centre.

Nanda Nitya and Nidhi Srivastava (2011). Facilitating Technology Transfer for Climate Change Mitigation and Adaptation, prepared for the 17th Conference of Parties to the United Nations Framework Convention on Climate Change, 28 November–9 December 2011, The Energy and Resources Institute.

OECD (1995). Technologies for Clearer Production and Products: Towards Technological Transformation for Sustainable Development, Paris: OECD.

Oliva Maria Julia (2009). Technologies for Climate Change and Intellectual Property: Issues for Small Developing Countries, Information Note No. 12.

Olivier et al. (2012). Trends in Global CO_2 Emissions: 2012 Report - Background Studies, PBL Netherlands Environmental Assessment Agency.

Panagariya Arvind (2000). The Millennium Round and Developing Countries: Negotiating Strategies and Areas of Benefits, G-24 Discussion Paper Series: Research Papers for the Intergovernmental Group of Twenty-Four on International Monetary Affairs, New York and Geneva: United Nations.

Park Walter G. and Douglas Lippoldt (2005). International Licensing and the Strengthening of Intellectual Property Rights in Developing Countries During the 1990s, OECD Economic Studies No. 40, 2005/1, pp. 7–48.

Pueyo Ana and Pedro Linares (2012). Renewable Technology Transfer to Developing Countries: One Size Does not Fit All, IDS Working Paper, Vol. 2012, No. 412, published by the Institute of Development Studies.

Reichman Jerome H. and Catherine Hasenzahl (2003). Non-voluntary Licensing of Patented Inventions: Historical Perspective, Legal Framework under TRIPS, and an Overview of the Practice in Canada and the United States of America, UNCTAD-ICTSD Project on IPRs and Sustainable Development, Issue Paper No. 5, Geneva: UNCTAD and ICTSD.

Reichman Jerome, K. Rai Arti, Richard G. Newell and Jonathan B. Wiener (2008). Intellectual Property and Alternatives: Strategies for Green Innovation, Energy, Environment and Development Programme Paper: 08/03, Chatham House, UK.

Saad Abughanm (2012). The Protection of Pharmaceutical Patents and Data under TRIPS and US – Jordan FTA: Exploring the Limits of Obligations and Flexibilities: A Study of the Impact on the Pharmaceutical Sector in Jordan, SJD thesis, University of Toronto.

Seaton Associates (2002). Knowledge Transfer, Discussion Paper prepared for the AQUADAPT workshop, Montpellier, France, 25–27 October.

Serafino David (2007). Survey of Patent Pools Demonstrates Variety of Purposes and Management Structures, KEI Research Note 2007.

Seres Stephen (2008). Analysis of Technology Transfer in CDM Projects, Prepared for the UNFCCC Registration and Issuance Unit CDM/SDM, http://cdm.unfccc .int/Reference/Reports/TTreport/TTrep08.pdf.

Shashikant Sangeeta (2009). Developing Countries Call for No Patents on Climate-Friendly Technologies, TWN Bonn News Update 15, Third World Network, 11 June 2009.

Singer Peter and Doris Schroeder (2009). Ethical Reasons for Intellectual Property Rights Reform, A Report (D 1.3) for INNOVA P2, CAPPE, University of Melbourne.

South Centre (2009). Accelerating Climate-Relevant Technology Innovation and Transfer to Developing Countries: Using TRIPS Flexibilities under the UNFCCC, SC/IAKP/AN/ENV/1, SC/GGDP/AN/ENV/8, August 2009, Geneva.

South Centre and CIEL (2008). The Technology Transfer Debate in the UNFCCC: Politics, Patents and Confusion, IP Quarterly Update, 4th Quarter.

Spennemann Christoph (2010). TRIPS Pre-Grant Flexibilities: Patentable Subject Matter, UNCTAD presentation, available at www.ictsd.org/downloads/2010/01/ patentability-criteria-rev.pdf.

Stilwell Matthews and Elisabeth Tuerk (2001). Towards a Full Review of the WTO's TRIPS Agreement under Article 71.1, Centre for International Environmental Law, available at www.ciel.org/Publications/Assessment_Trips_article711.pdf.

Syam Nirmalya (2010). Rush for Patents May Hinder Transfer of New Climate-Friendly Technologies, *South Bulletin*, 44, 8 March, pp. 11–12.

Taubman Antony and Jayashree Watal (2010). The WTO TRIPS Agreement – A Practical Overview for Climate Change Policymakers, Documentation used in technical cooperation activities of the WTO's Intellectual Property Division, available at www.wto.org/english/tratop_e/trips_e/ta_docs_e/8_3_overviewclimate change_e.pdf.

Teng Fei, Wenying Chen and Jiankun He (2008). Possible Development of a Technology Clean Development Mechanism in a Post-2012 Regime, prepared for the Harvard Project on International Climate Agreements, Discussion Paper 08–24.

The ICC Commission on Intellectual Property (2011). *Intellectual Property: Powerhouse for Innovation and Economic Growth*, Paris: International Chamber of Commerce.

Thomas John R. (2015). Tailoring the Patent System for Specific Industries, Congressional Research Service Report 7–5700.

UNCTAD (2003). Course on Dispute Settlement: International Centre for Settlement of Investment Disputes, Vol. 3, United Nations.

UNCTAD and ICTSD (2003). Intellectual Property Rights: Implications for Development, UNCTAD-ICTSD Project on IPRs and Sustainable Development, Policy Discussion Paper, Geneva: International Centre for Trade and Sustainable Development and United Nations Conference on Trade and Development.

UNDP (2011). Technological Cooperation and Climate Change: Issues and Perspectives, Working papers presented at the Ministry of Environment and Forests, Government of India-UNDP Consultation on Technology Cooperation for Addressing Climate Change, New Delhi: United Nations Development Program.

United Nations Conference on Sustainable Development (2012). Science and Technology for Sustainable Development, RIO 2012 Issue Briefs, No. 12.

Walker Simon (2001). The TRIPS Agreement, Sustainable Development and the Public Interest, Discussion Paper, IUCN, Gland.

Watson Jim, Gordon MacKerron, David Ockwell and Tao Wang (2007). Technology and Carbon Mitigation in Developing Countries: Are Cleaner Coal Technologies A Viable Option? Background Paper for Human Development Report 2007, UNDP.

Williams Heidi L. (2010). Intellectual Property Rights and Innovation: Evidence from the Human Genome, NBER Working Paper Series, Working Paper 16213, Cambridge, MA: National Bureau of Economic Research.

Wilson Tim (2008). Undermining Mitigation Technology: Compulsory Licensing, Patents and Tariffs, Melbourne: Institute of Public Affairs Backgrounder 21/1.

Wouters Jan, Dominic Coppens and Dylan Geraets (2011). The Influence of General Principles of Law, Working Paper No. 70, Leuven Centre for Global Governance Studies.

WTO (2012). Options for a Technology Facilitation Mechanism, Rio +20 – WTO Secretariat Contribution Regarding 'A Facilitation Mechanism That Promotes the Development, Transfer and Dissemination of Clean and Environmentally Sound Technologies', available at https://sustainabledevelopment.un.org/index .php?page=view&type=111&nr=1243&menu=35.

Yamane Hiroko (2014). Competition Analyses of Licensing Agreements: Considerations for Developing Countries under TRIPS, Discussion Paper, ICTSD Innovation, Technology and Intellectual Property, Geneva: ICTSD.

WEBSITE AND NEWS ARTICLES

Buxbaum A. Peter, Climate Change, Patent Pending, International Relations and Security Network (ISN ETH Zurich). 25 June 2009, available at www.isn.ethz .ch/DigitalLibrary/Articles/Detail//?ots591=4888CAA0-B3DB-1461-98B9-E20E7B9 C13D4&lng=en&id=102425.

Charges for the Use of Intellectual Property, payments (BoP, current US dollars). World Development Indicators, the World Bank, available at http://data.world bank.org/indicator/BM.GSR.ROYL.CD.

Chizuru Akoi, GEF Actions on Technology Transfer, www.thegef.org/gef/greenline/ Nov10/3.html.

Climate Change Centre and Network (2016). Countries Pledge Millions for Technology Transfer to Implement Paris Agreement, 16 November, available at www.ctc-n.org/news/countries-pledge-millions-technology-transfer-implement-paris-agreement

Correa Carlos M. (2012). Proliferation of Patents Hurts Public Interest, IDN-InDepth News Viewpoint, 26 July, available at www.indepthnews.info/index.php/global-issues/1065-proliferation-of-patents-hurts-public-interest.

European Commission (Directorate General Competition). Pharma Sector Inquiry-Main Issues Investigated, Human Rights in Patient Care, available at http://cop .health rights.org/files/5/f/5f178d13295196c057754618755566c4e.pdf.

GEF, What Is the GEF? available at www.thegef.org/gef/whatisgef.

Goldberg Keith, Clean Energy Boom Sets Stage for IP Wars, Law 360, New York, 30 October 2013, available at www.morganlewis.com/pubs/Law360_CleanEnergy PatentBoom_30oct13.pdf.

ICTSD (2012). UNFCCC Technology Executive Committee Seeks More 'Clarity' on IPRs, 22 November, Biores, Vol. 6, No. 4.

International Energy Agency, Prospect of Limiting the Global Increase in Temperature to 2°C Is Getting Bleaker, 30 May 2011, available at www.iea.org/journalists/latestinformation.asp.

Lane Eric, New Alliance's Big IDEA: Strong IP Is Essential for Green Innovation, Green Patent Blog, 17 May 2009, available at www.greenpatentblog.com/2009/05/17/new-alliances-big-idea-strong-ip-is-essential-for-green-innovation/.

Macguire Eoghan, 12 June 2012, Who's Funding the Green Energy Revolution? CNN, available at http://edition.cnn.com/2012/06/12/world/renewables-finance-unep.

Ministerial Conferences, WTO website, available at www.wto.org/english/thewto_e/minist_e/minist_e.htm.

OECD Patent Databases, Innovation in Science, Technology and Industry, OECD website, available at www.oecd.org/sti/inno/oecdpatentdatabases.htm.

Patents by Technology: Patents in Environment-related Technologies, OECD. Stat Extracts, available at http://stats.oecd.org/index.aspx?queryid=29068.

Raman Meena (2009). Wide North-South Divide Over IPRs and Climate Technologies, Bonn News Update No. 13, 9 June.

Ramanathan K. (2011). An Overview of Technology Transfer and Technology Transfer Models, 5 Apr 2011, available at www.businessasia.net/Pdf_Pages/Guidebook%20on%20Technology%20Transfer%20Mechanisms/An%20overview%20of%20TT%20and%20TT%20Models.pdf.

Rogers Simon and Lisa Evans (2011). World Carbon Dioxide Emissions Data by Country: China Speeds Ahead of the Rest, *The Guardian*, 31 January, available at www.guardian.co.uk/news/datablog/2011/jan/31/world-carbon-dioxide-emissions-country-data-co2.

Saez Catherine (2010). UN Climate Talks Find Make-Do Solution; IP Rights Dismissed, Intellectual Property Watch, 14 December.

(2013). Green Innovations, Owned by Developed Countries, Tied Up in Patents, Expert Says, Intellectual Property Watch, 14 October.

Schwartz Tessa and Tierney Sarah Niyogi (2009). Technology Transfer and Intellectual Property Issues Take Centre Stage in UNFCCC Negotiations, Cleantech Update.

Shashikant Sangeeta and Martin Khor (2010). Intellectual Property and Technology Transfer Issues in the Context of Climate Change, Jutaprint. Stanford Encyclopedia of Philosophy, 'Intellectual Property', available at http://plato.stanford.edu/entries/intellectual-property/

Telecommunications Services, WTO website, available at www.wto.org/english/tratop_e/serv_e/telecom_e/telecom_e.htm

Topal Claire (2014). The Globalization of China's Life Sciences Industry: Flashpoints in Sino-U.S. Trade Relations: An Interview with Ka Zeng, The National Bureau of Asian Research, available at www.nbr.org/research/activity.aspx?id=413.

U.S. Chamber of Commerce, Companies Launch Coalition to Defend IPR in Climate Change Talks, 22 May 2009, available at www.theglobalipcenter.com/companies-launch-coalition-defend-ipr-climate-change-talks/.

UNFCCC Secretariat, Governments Agree the Negotiating Text for the Paris Climate Agreement, Spirit of Lima Transforms into Spirit of Geneva En Route to December Climate Conference, Press Release, 13 February 2015.

UNFCCC website, available at http://unfccc.int.

Vadim Kotelnikov, Environmentally Sound Technologies (ESTs). Ten3, http://it4b.icsti.su/1000ventures_e/environment/est_main.html

Vidal John, Copenhagen Climate Summit in Disarray after "Danish Text?" Leak, The Guardian, 9 December 2009.

WIPO (2013). Refusals to License IP Rights – A Comparative Note on Possible Approaches, prepared by the Secretariat, available at www.wipo.int/export/sites/www/ipcompetition/en/studies/refusals_license_IPRs.pdf.

(2013). WIPO GREEN: New Online Marketplace Seeks Environmentally Sustainable Solutions for Climate Change, PR/2013/749, available at www.wipo.int/pressroom/en/articles/2013/article_0025.html.

Advice on Flexibilities under the TRIPS Agreement, available at www.wipo.int/ipdevelopment/en/legislative_assistance/advice_trips.html.

IPC Green Inventory, available at www.wipo.int/classifications/ipc/en/est/index.html.

Questionnaire on Exceptions and Limitations to Patent Rights: Tables and Links to the Replies Received from Member States and Regional Offices to the SCP, available at www.wipo.int/scp/en/exceptions/.

WIPO Treaties – General Information, available at www.wipo.int/treaties/en/general/.

WIPO's Contribution to Meeting the Challenges of Climate Change, available at www.wipo.int/about-wipo/en/climate_change_conf_09.html.

World Trade Organization, The Committee on Trade and Environment ("regular" CTE), available at www.wto.org/english/tratop_e/envir_e/wrk_committee_e.htm

Sustainable Development, available at www.wto.org/english/tratop_e/envir_e/sust_dev_e.htm

WTO, Glossary term, available at www.wto.org/english/thewto_e/glossary_e/parallel_imports_e.htm

(2005). Members OK amendment to make health flexibility permanent, Press/426, 6 December, available at www.wto.org/english/news_e/pres05_e/pr426_e.htm

(2007). Patents and Health: WTO Receives First Notification Under "Paragraph 6" System, TRIPS and Public Health, available at www.wto.org/english/news_e/news07_e/public_health_july07_e.htm

The Separate Declaration Explained, available at www.wto.org/english/tratop_e/trips_e/healthdeclexpln_e.htm

Under TRIPS, What Are Member Governments' Obligations on Pharmaceutical Patents? available at www.wto.org/english/tratop_e/trips_e/factsheet_pharm02_e.htm.

What Are Intellectual Property Rights? available at www.wto.org/english/tratop_e/trips_e/intel1_e.htm.

DICTIONARIES

American Heritage Dictionary of the English Language, 5th edn.

Dictionary.com. *Collins English Dictionary – Complete and Unabridged 10th Edition.* HarperCollins Publishers.

Dictionary.com. *Dictionary.com Unabridged.* Random House.

Shorter Oxford English Dictionary, 6th edn, vol. 2, Oxford University Press, 2007.

Index

Marrakesh Agreement (cont.)
  Article XVI:3, 192
  object and purpose, 193
  Preamble, 193–94, 226, 270
  US – Shrimp (1998), 193
Max Planck Declaration on Patents Protection,
  192, 235–36
Max Planck Institute for Innovation and
  Competition, 192
MEAs, 60, 78–79, 83, 108, 186
Measures to protect public health, 223
MFN, 65, 67, 112, 275–76
Minimum IPR protection standards, 344, 350,
  355
Minimum IPR standards, 98, 110
  'Berne-plus' or 'Paris-plus', 67
  Article 1.1 of TRIPS, 66
  commitments, 65–69
  concerns, 120
  controversy over the effect of, 119–21
  effects on technology transfer, 120
  enforcement of IPRs, 118–19
  implications, 69–74
  mandatory treaty obligation, 72
  patent protection, 111–14
  protection of trade secrets, 114–18
  regulatory "floor", 72
  reinforced the power of private parties,
    120
  the effect on innovation and technology
    transfer, 121
Minimum standards for IP protection and
  enforcement. *See* Minimum IPR
  standards
Ministerial Conference, 215–16, 218, 228
Ministerial Declaration, 179, 215, 226
  Doha Ministerial Declaration, 212
  Ministerial Declaration for climate change,
    232, 351
  Punta del Este Declaration, 62, 204
MNCs, 48, 52, 61, 134, 144, 153–54, 311, 325,
  349, 368
Monopoly, 63, 117, 128, 139, 146, 148, 154, 250,
  283, 339
Montreal Protocol, 79, 97, 149, 151
Mutually reinforcing, 163, 201
Mutually satisfactory solution, 239
Mutually supportive, 202

Napoleonic Code, 30
National development strategies, 233

National emergency, 224, 281, 283, 292, 302,
  353, 360
National emergency or other circumstances of
  extreme urgency, 302
National patent laws, 51, 247, 271, 279, 283–84
National security, 282
National treatment, 65, 67, 112, 233, 275–76
Necessity requirement
  Article XX of the GATT, 209
  Brazil – Retreaded Tyres (2007), 210
  Korea – Various Measures on Beef (2001),
    210
  weighing and balancing, 210
New Delhi Declaration of Principles of
  International Law Relating to
  Sustainable Development, 198
NGOs, 16, 239
No patents proposal, 100
Non-discrimination clause, 112, 237–39
  Article 27.1, 237
  availability of patents, 238
  bona fide exceptions, 245
  Canada – Pharmaceutical Patents (2000),
    243, 245
  certain product areas, 245
  differential treatment, 240
  differentiate, 243
  discrimination, 242
  enjoyment of patent rights, 238
  ESTs, 240
    differential treatment, 241
    field of technology, 241
    function of the technology, 241
  importation, 239
  imported and locally produced products,
    239
  local working requirements, 239
  non-discrimination as to the field of
    technology, 239–46
  patent-specific, 237
  place of invention, 238
  scope of application, 238
  structural effect, 244
  technological neutrality principle, 239
  unjustified differential treatment, 243
Non-discriminatory, 50, 65, 69, 195, 202, 275,
  287, 367
Non-patentability, 252
  contributes to protecting *ordre public* and
    morality, 253
  morality, 253

CPSIA information can be obtained
at www.ICGtesting.com
Printed in the USA
LVHW081746300719
625737LV00026BA/427/P